Exploring BeagleBone

Exploring BeagleBone

Tools and Techniques for Building with
Embedded Linux®

Derek Molloy

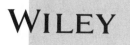

Exploring BeagleBone

Published by
John Wiley & Sons, Inc.
10475 Crosspoint Boulevard
Indianapolis, IN 46256
www.wiley.com

Copyright © 2015 by John Wiley & Sons, Inc., Indianapolis, Indiana
Published simultaneously in Canada

ISBN: 978-1-118-93512-5
ISBN: 978-1-118-93513-2 (ebk)
ISBN: 978-1-118-93521-7 (ebk)

Manufactured in the United States of America

10 9 8 7 6 5 4

For general information on our other products and services please contact our Customer Care Department within the United States at (877) 762-2974, outside the United States at (317) 572-3993 or fax (317) 572-4002.

Wiley publishes in a variety of print and electronic formats and by print-on-demand. Some material included with standard print versions of this book may not be included in e-books or in print-on-demand. If this book refers to media such as a CD or DVD that is not included in the version you purchased, you may download this material at http://booksupport.wiley.com. For more information about Wiley products, visit www.wiley.com.

Library of Congress Control Number: 2014951016

To Sally, Daragh, Eoghan, Aidan, and Sarah

(in order of age, not preference!)

About the Author

Dr. Derek Molloy is a senior lecturer in the School of Electronic Engineering, Faculty of Engineering and Computing, Dublin City University, Ireland. He lectures at undergraduate and postgraduate levels in object-oriented programming with embedded systems, digital and analog electronics, and 3D computer graphics. His research contributions are largely in the fields of computer and machine vision, 3D graphics and visualization, and e-Learning.

Derek produces a popular YouTube series on the BeagleBone platform and a wide variety of embedded Linux topics. His videos have introduced millions of people to the BeagleBone, embedded Linux, and digital electronics topics. In 2013, he launched a personal web/blog site, visited by thousands of people every day, which integrates his YouTube videos with support materials, source code, and user discussion.

Derek has received several awards for teaching and learning. He was the winner of the 2012 Irish Learning Technology Association (ILTA) national award for *Innovation in Teaching and Learning* for his learning-by-doing approach to undergraduate engineering education, which utilizes electronic kits and online video content. In 2012, he was also awarded the Dublin City University *President's Award for Excellence in Teaching and Learning*, as a result of fervent nominations from his students and peers.

You can learn more about Derek and his work at his personal website www.derekmolloy.ie.

About the Technical Editors

Jason Kridner is the Software Community Development Manager for Sitara ARM processors at Texas Instruments Incorporated (TI). During his over 20-year tenure with TI, he has become an active leader in TI's open source initiative and played an integral role in creating open-source development tools such as BeagleBoard, BeagleBoard-xM BeagleBone, and now BeagleBone Black, a credit-card-sized Linux computer platform based on TI's 1GHz Sitara AM335x ARM® Cortex-A8 processor that runs Android 4.0 and Ubuntu software. As a high-profile industry expert, Kridner has engaged audiences at a variety of industry and developer shows including Maker Faire, OSCON, CES, Design, Android Builders Summit, Linux Collaboration Summit, and the Embedded Linux Conference.

Robert Zhu is a principal development manager at Microsoft for the Windows Operating System Group. He is an expert in OS leading-edge development, research, and design in computer engineering such as kernel, device driver, and board support packages. Robert also gives training classes to OEMs on driver development and Windows OS research. Before working for Microsoft, he was with Digital Equipment Corporation (DEC), USA, as senior software engineer on the 64-bit DEC Alpha platform for workstation server optimization and performance tuning for Windows, and a software lead with Motorola Wireless Division, Canada. He obtained his master of computer science at the University of Washington; his master of computing and electrical engineering at Simon Fraser University (SFU), Canada; his bachelor of engineering at Tsinghua University; and did postgraduate work at SFU School of Engineering Science, Canada. Robert was a co-author on *Windows Phone 7 Programming for Android and iOS Developers*, as well as *Windows Phone Programming Essentials* and *Learn 2D Game Development with C#*.

Credits

Acquisitions Editor
Jim Minatel

Project Editor
Adaobi Obi Tulton

Technical Editors
Rob Zhu
Jason Kridner

Production Editor
Dassi Zeidel

Copy Editor
Luann Rouff

Manager of Content Development and Assembly
Mary Beth Wakefield

Marketing Director
David Mayhew

Marketing Manager
Carrie Sherrill

Professional Technology & Strategy Director
Barry Pruett

Business Manager
Amy Knies

Associate Publisher
Jim Minatel

Project Coordinator, Cover
Patrick Redmond

Proofreader
Amy J. Schneider

Indexer
John Sleeva

Cover Designer
Wiley

Cover Image
Courtesy of Derek Molloy

Acknowledgments

Thank you to everyone at Wiley Publishing for their outstanding work on this project: to Mary E. James, for encouraging me to take on this project, and for allowing me the latitude to develop a book that engages in deeper learning; to Jim Minatel for his expert support and help throughout the development of this book; to Adaobi Obi Tulton, the project editor, for keeping everything on track and for having the patience to deal with my many, many questions—I greatly appreciate her hard work, diligence, encouragement, and support; to Dassi Zeidel, the production editor, for her hard work in tying everything together to create such a polished final product; to Luann Rouff, the copy editor, for meticulously translating this book into readable U.S. English, and for adding all those Oxford commas! Thanks to the technical editors, Robert Zhu (Microsoft) and Jason Kridner (BeagleBoard.org Foundation), for their expert review and constructive feedback on the technical content in this book. Thanks also to Cathy Wicks (Texas Instruments) and Nuria Llin (Texas Instruments) for their advice and support in the development of this book.

Thank you also to the thousands of people who take the time to comment on my YouTube videos, blog, and website articles. I truly appreciate all of the feedback, advice, and comments—it has really helped in the development of the topics in this book.

The School of Electronic Engineering, Dublin City University, is a great place to work, largely because of its esprit de corps, and its commitment to rigorous, innovative, and accessible engineering education. Thanks to Patrick McNally, Head of School, and all of my colleagues in the school for supporting, encouraging, and even tolerating me in the development of this book. Thanks to (my brother) David Molloy for his expert software advice and support. Thanks, David, for keeping me grounded! Thanks to Jennifer Bruton for her meticulous and expert review of the circuits, software, and content in this book. Thanks, Jennifer, for listening! Thanks to Noel Murphy for his rigorous review of the hardware chapters—he clearly missed his calling as a technical copy editor! Thanks also to Martin Collier, Pascal Landais, Michele Pringle, Robert Sadleir, Ronan Scaife, and John Whelan for their expertise, support, and advice, which I sought on numerous occasions.

My biggest thank-you must, of course, go to my own family. This book was written over seven months, predominantly at night and on weekends. Thanks to my wife, Sally, and our children, Daragh, Eoghan, Aidan, and Sarah, for putting up with me while I was writing this book. Thank you, Mam, Dad, David, and Catriona for your lifelong inspiration, support, and encouragement. Finally, thank you to my extended family for graciously excusing my absence at family events for the past seven months—I have no excuses now!

Contents

Introduction

The BeagleBone is amazing! Given the proliferation of smartphones, the idea of holding in one hand a computer that is capable of performing two billion instructions per second is easy to take for granted—but the fact that you can modify the hardware and software of such a small yet powerful device and adapt it to suit your own needs and create your own inventions is nothing short of amazing. Even better, you can purchase it for as little as $45–$55.

The BeagleBone board on its own is too complex a device to be used by a general audience; it is the ability of the BeagleBone to run embedded Linux that makes the resulting platform accessible, adaptable, and powerful. Together, Linux and embedded systems enable ease of development for devices that can meet future challenges in smart buildings, the Internet of Things (IoT), robotics, smart energy, smart cities, human-computer interaction (HCI), cyber-physical systems, 3D printing, advanced vehicular systems, and many, many more applications.

The integration of high-level Linux software and low-level electronics represents a paradigm shift in embedded systems development. It is revolutionary that you can build a low-level electronics circuit and then install a Linux web server, using only a few short commands, so that the circuit can be controlled over the Internet. You can easily use the BeagleBone as a general-purpose Linux computer, but it is vastly more challenging and interesting to get underneath the hood and fully interface it to electronic circuits of your own design—and that is where this book comes in!

This book should have widespread appeal for inventors, makers, students, entrepreneurs, hackers, artists, dreamers—in short, anybody who wants to bring the power of embedded Linux to their products, inventions, creations, or projects and truly understand the BeagleBone in detail. This is not a recipe book—with few exceptions, everything demonstrated here is explained at a level that will enable you to design, build, and debug your own extensions of the concepts presented here. Nor is there any grand design project at the end of this book for which you must purchase a prescribed set of components and peripherals in order to achieve a very specific outcome. Rather, this book is about providing you with enough background knowledge and "under-the-hood" technical details to enable and motivate your own explorations.

I strongly believe in learning by doing, so I present low-cost, widely available hardware examples in order that you can follow along. Using these hands-on examples, I describe what each step means in detail, so that when you substitute your own hardware components, modules, and peripherals you will be able to adapt the content in this book to suit your needs. As for that grand project or invention—that is left up to you and your imagination!

When writing this book I had the following aims and objectives:

- To explain embedded Linux and its interaction with electronic circuits— taking you through the topics from mystery to mastery!

- To provide in-depth information and instruction on the Linux, electronics, and programming skills that are required to master a pretty wide and comprehensive variety of topics in this domain.

- To create a collection of practical "Hello World" hardware and software examples on each and every topic in the book, from low-level interfacing, general-purpose input/outputs (GPIOs), analog-to-digital converters (ADCs), buses, and UARTs, to high-level libraries such as OpenCV, Qt, and complex and powerful topics, such as real-time interfacing with the PRU-ICSS.

- To ensure that each circuit and segment of code is specifically designed to work on the BeagleBone. Every single circuit and code example in this book was built and tested on the BeagleBone.

- To use the "Hello World" examples to build a library of code that you can use and adapt for your own BeagleBone projects.

- To make all of the code available on GitHub in an easy-to-use form.

- To support this book with strong digital content, such as the videos on the DerekMolloyDCU YouTube channel, and a custom website www.exploringbeaglebone.com, which has been developed specifically to support this book.

- To ensure that by the end of this book you have everything you need to imagine, create, and build *advanced* BeagleBone projects.

Why the BeagleBone Black?

The BeagleBone Black is a powerful single-board computer (SBC), and while there are other SBCs available on the market such as the Raspberry PI and the Intel Galileo, the BeagleBone has one key differentiator—it was built to be interfaced to! For example, the BeagleBone's microprocessor even contains two additional on-chip microcontrollers that can be used for real-time interfacing—an area in which other Linux SBCs have significant difficulty.

Unlike most other SBCs, the BeagleBone is fully open source hardware. The BeagleBoard.org Foundation provides source schematics, hardware layout, a full bill of materials, and technical reference manuals, enabling you to modify the design of the BeagleBone platform and integrate it into your own product. In fact, you can even fork the hardware design on Upverter (www.upverter.com) under a Creative Commons Attribution-ShareAlike license (see tiny.cc/ebb002 for the full schematics). This is a very useful feature should you decide to take your newest invention to market!

How This Book Is Structured

There is no doubt that some of the topics in this book are quite complex—the BeagleBone is a complex device! However, everything that you need to master the device is present in the book within three major parts:

- Part I: BeagleBone Basics
- Part II: Interfacing, Controlling, and Communicating
- Part III: Advanced BeagleBone Systems

In the first part in the book, I introduce the hardware and software of the BeagleBone platform in Chapters 1 and 2, and subsequently provide three primer chapters:

- Chapter 3: Exploring Embedded Linux Systems
- Chapter 4: Interfacing Electronics
- Chapter 5: Practical BeagleBone Programming

If you are a Linux expert, electronics wizard, and/or software guru, then feel free to skip the primer chapters; however, for everyone else I have put in place a concise but detailed set of materials to ensure that you gain all the knowledge required to effectively and safely interface to the BeagleBone.

In the second part of the book, Chapters 6 to 9, I provide detailed information on interfacing to the BeagleBone GPIOs, analog inputs, buses (I^2C, SPI), UART devices, and USB peripherals. You'll learn how you can configure a cross-compilation environment so that you can build large-scale software applications for the BeagleBone. This part also describes how you can combine hardware and software in order to provide the BeagleBone with the ability to interact effectively with its physical environment.

The final part of the book, Chapters 10 to 13, describe how the BeagleBone can be used for advanced applications such as Internet of Things (IoT); rich user interfaces; images, video, and audio; and real-time interfacing. Along the way you will meet many technologies, including TCP/IP, ThingSpeak, Xively, PoE, Wi-Fi, Bluetooth, cron, Apache, PHP, e-mail, IFTTT, VNC, GTK+, Qt, XML, multi-threading, client/server programming, V4L2, video streaming, OpenCV, Boost, USB audio, Bluetooth A2DP, text-to-speech, and the PRU-ICSS.

Conventions Used in This Book

This book is filled with source code examples and snippets that you can use to build your own applications. Code and commands are shown as follows:

```
This is what source code looks like.
```

When presenting work performed in a Linux terminal it is often necessary to display both input and output in a single example. A bold type is used to distinguish the user input from the output—for example:

```
molloyd@beaglebone:~$ ping www.exploringbeaglebone.com
PING lb1.reg365.net (195.7.226.20) 56(84) bytes of data.
64 bytes from lb1.reg365.net (195.7.226.20): icmp_req=1 ttl=55 time=25.6 ms
64 bytes from lb1.reg365.net (195.7.226.20): icmp_req=2 ttl=55 time=25.6 ms
...
```

The $ prompt indicates that a regular Linux user is executing a command, and a # prompt indicates that a Linux superuser is executing a command. The ellipsis symbol "..." is used whenever code or output not vital to understanding a topic has been cut. Editing the output like this enables you to focus on only the most useful information. You are encouraged to repeat the steps in this book yourself, whereupon you will see the full output. In addition, the full source code for all examples is provided along with the book.

There are some additional styles in the text. For example:

- New terms and important words appear in *italics* when introduced.
- Keyboard strokes appear like this: Ctrl+C.
- All URLs in the book refer to HTTP addresses and appear like this: www.exploringbeaglebone.com.

- A URL shortening service is used to create aliases for long URLs that are presented in the book. These aliases have the form `tiny.cc/ebb102` (e.g., link two in Chapter 1). Should the link address change after this book is published, the alias will be updated.

There are several features used in this book to identify when content is of particular importance or when additional information is available:

WARNING   This type of feature contains important information that can help you avoid damaging your BeagleBone.

NOTE   This type of feature contains useful additional information, such as links to digital resources and useful tips, which can make it easier to understand the task at hand.

FEATURE TITLE

This type of feature goes into detail about the current topic or a related topic.

What You'll Need

Ideally you should have a BeagleBone Black before you begin reading this book so that you can follow along with the numerous examples in the text. Presently the board is manufactured by both CircuitCo and Embest—the boards from either manufacturer are compatible with the designs and operations in this book. You can purchase one of the boards in the U.S. from online stores such as Adafruit Industries, Digi-Key, Mouser, SparkFun, and Jameco Electronics. They are available internationally from stores such as Farnell, Radionics, Watterott, and Tigal.

A full list of recommended and optional accessories for the BeagleBone is provided in Chapter 1—if you do not yet have a BeagleBone, it would be worth reading that chapter before placing an order. In addition, each chapter contains a list of the electronics components and modules required if you wish to follow along with the text. The book website provides details about where these components can be acquired.

Errata

We have worked really hard to ensure that this book is error free; however, it is always possible that some were overlooked. A full list of errata is available on each chapter's web page at the companion website. If you find any errors in the text or in the source code examples, I would be grateful if you could please use the companion website to send them to me so that I can update the web page errata list and the source code examples in the code repository.

Digital Content and Source Code

The primary companion site for this book is www.exploringbeaglebone.com. It is maintained by the book's author and contains videos, source code examples, and links to further reading. Each chapter has its own individual web page. In the unlikely event that the website is unavailable, you can find the code at www.wiley.com/go/exploringbeaglebone.

I have provided all of the source code through GitHub, which allows you to download the code to your BeagleBone with one command. You can also easily view the code online at tiny.cc/ebb001. Downloading the source code to your BeagleBone is as straightforward as typing the following at the Linux shell prompt:

```
$ git clone https://github.com/derekmolloy/exploringBB.git
```

If you have never used Git before, don't worry—it is explained in detail in Chapter 3. Now, on with the adventures!

Exploring BeagleBone

Part

I

BeagleBone Basics

In This Part

The BeagleBone Hardware

In this chapter, you are introduced to the BeagleBone platform hardware. The chapter focuses on the BeagleBone Black and the various subsystems and physical inputs/outputs of the board. In addition, the chapter lists accessories that can be very helpful in developing your own BeagleBone-based projects. By the end of this chapter, you should have an appreciation of the power and complexity of this computing platform. You should also be aware of the first steps to take to protect your board from physical damage.

Introduction to the Platform

The BeagleBone is a compact, low-cost, open-source Linux computing platform that can be used to build complex applications that interface high-level software and low-level electronic circuits. It is an ideal platform for prototyping project and product designs that take advantage of the power and freedom of Linux, combined with direct access to input/output pins and buses, allowing you to interface with electronics components, modules, and USB devices. The characteristics of the BeagleBone platform are that it

- is powerful, as it contains a processor that can perform up to 2 billion instructions per second,
- is low-cost, available for as little as $45–$55,

- supports many standard interfaces for electronics devices,
- uses little power, running at between 1 W (idle) and 2.3 W (peak),
- is expandable through the use of daughterboards and USB devices,
- is supported by a huge community of innovators and enthusiasts, and
- is open-hardware and supports open-software tools and applications.

The BeagleBone runs the Linux operating system, which means that you can use many open-source software libraries and applications directly with it. Open-source software driver availability also enables you to interface devices such as USB cameras, keyboards and Wi-Fi adapters with your project, without having to source proprietary alternatives. Therefore, you have access to comprehensive libraries of code that have been built by a talented open-source community; however, it is important to remember that the code typically comes without any type of warranty or guarantee. If there are problems, then you have to rely on the good nature of the community to resolve them. Of course, you could also fix the problems yourself and make the solutions publicly available.

The BeagleBone platform is formed by the integration of a high-performance microprocessor on a printed circuit board (PCB) and an extensive software ecosystem. The physical PCB is not a complete product; rather it is a prototype reference design that you can use to build a complete product. It is an open-hardware platform, meaning that you can download and use the BeagleBone hardware schematics and layout directly within your own product design. In fact, despite the impressive capability of the BeagleBone platform, it does not fully expose all of the features and interfaces of the Texas Instruments Sitara AM335x microprocessor.

One impressive feature of the BeagleBone is that its functionality can be extended with daughterboards, called *capes*, that connect to the P8 and P9 headers (the two black 2×23 connector rows in Figure 1-1). You can design your

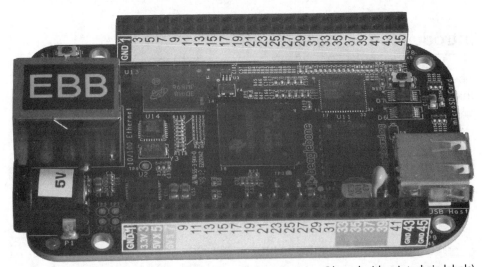

Figure 1-1: The BeagleBone Black computing platform (revision C board with printed pin labels)

own capes and attach them securely to your BeagleBone using these headers. In addition, many capes are available for purchase that can be used to expand the functionality of your BeagleBone platform. Some examples of these are described toward the end of this chapter.

The BeagleBone PCBs were designed by Gerald Coley, a co-founder of the BeagleBoard.org Foundation. However, the boards, and several of its capes, are manufactured by CircuitCo (www.circuitco.com). The PCB layout for the BeagleBone Black was also created by CircuitCo. Recently, Element14 (www.element14.com) has begun manufacturing a BeagleBoard.org-compliant version of the BeagleBone Black. Therefore, when you purchase a BeagleBone board, you are not purchasing it from BeagleBoard.org; rather, BeagleBoard.org is the focal point for a community of developers and users.

> **NOTE** CircuitCo has provided a short video of the BeagleBone Black manufacturing process at tiny.cc/ebb101—it highlights the complexity of the device and the work that goes into its manufacture.

Who Should Use the BeagleBone

Anybody who wishes to transform an engineering concept into a real interactive electronics product, project, prototype, or work of art should consider using the BeagleBone. That said, integrating high-level software and low-level electronics is not an easy task. However, the difficulty involved in an implementation depends on the level of sophistication that the project demands.

The BeagleBone community is working hard to ensure that the BeagleBone platform is accessible by everyone who is interested in integrating it into their projects, whether they are students, makers, artists, or hobbyists. Tools and software development environments, such as Jason Kridner's BoneScript library (Kridner is a co-founder of BeagleBoard.org and a technical editor of this book) and the Cloud9 integrated development environment (IDE), enable users to write and build code directly in a web browser that is capable of controlling electronics hardware. BoneScript is introduced in Chapter 2. Developments like Blockly (code.google.com/p/blockly) and Snap (snap.berkeley.edu) have the potential to be integrated with BoneScript to further improve accessibility for new users.

For more advanced users, with electronics or computing knowledge, the BeagleBone platform enables additional development and customization to meet specific project needs. Again, such customization is not trivial: You may be an electronics expert, but high-level software programming and/or the Linux operating system might cause you difficulty. Or, you may be a programming guru but you have never wired an LED! This book aims to cater to all types of users, providing each type of reader with enough Linux, electronics, and software exposure to ensure that you can be productive, regardless of your previous experience level.

When to Use the BeagleBone

The BeagleBone is perfectly placed for the integration of high-level software and low-level electronics in any type of project. Whether you are planning to build an automated home management system, robot, smart display, sensor network, vending machine, or Internet-connected work of interactive art, the BeagleBone has the processing power to do whatever you can imagine of an embedded device.

The major advantage of the BeagleBone over more traditional embedded systems, such as the Arduino, PIC, and AVR microcontrollers, is apparent when you leverage the Linux OS for your projects. For example, if you built a home automation system using the BeagleBone and you then decided that you wanted to make certain information available on the Internet, you could simply install the Apache web server. You could then use server-side scripting or your favorite programming language to interface with your home automation system in order to capture and share the information. Alternatively, your project might require secure remote shell access. In that case, you could install a secure shell (SSH) server, simply by using the Linux command `sudo apt-get install sshd` (these commands are covered in Chapter 2). This could potentially save you weeks of development work. In addition, you have the comfort of knowing that the same software is running securely on millions of machines around the world.

Linux also provides you with device driver support for many USB peripherals and adapters, making it possible for you to connect cameras, Wi-Fi adapters, and other low-cost consumer peripherals directly to your platform, without the need for complex and/or expensive software driver development.

When You Should Not Use the BeagleBone

The Linux OS was not designed for real-time or predictable processing. Its kernel is not preemptive, which means that once the processor begins executing kernel code it cannot be interrupted. This would be problematic if, for example, you wished to sample a sensor precisely every one millionth of a second. If the precise time arises to take a sample and the kernel is busy with a different task, then it cannot be interrupted. Therefore, in its default state, the BeagleBone is not an ideal platform for real-time systems applications. Real-time versions of Linux are available, but they are currently targeted at very experienced Linux developers. However, the BeagleBone does have an on-board solution that goes some way toward resolving this problem. Within the BeagleBone's AM335x, there are two on-board microcontrollers, called Programmable Real-time Units (PRUs), which can be programmed for real-time interfacing applications. This is an advanced topic that is described in Chapter 13.

There are low-cost dedicated solutions available for real-time sampling and control tasks (such as the TI Stellaris ARM platform) that may be more appropriate. It is also important to remember that you can interconnect such real-time microcontrollers to the BeagleBone via electrical buses (e.g., I²C, UART, CAN bus, and Ethernet) and have the BeagleBone act as the central processor for a distributed control system. This concept is described in Chapter 9 and Chapter 10.

The second application type that the BeagleBone platform will find difficult is that of playing high-definition video. The processing overhead of software decoding and playing encoded video streams is immense, and is beyond the capability of the BeagleBone at high-definition video resolutions. The Raspberry Pi (www .raspberrypi.org) board has this capability because its Broadcom BCM2835 processor[1] was designed for multimedia applications, and it has a hardware implementation of H.264/MPG-4 and MPG-2/VC-1 (via additional license) decoders and encoders. For applications such as running XMBC home media center (www.xbmc.org), you are better off purchasing a Raspberry Pi (Model B+), but for building advanced applications that interface to electronics, the BeagleBone is a clear choice.

BeagleBone Documentation

This book integrates my experiences in developing with the BeagleBone platform along with supporting background materials on embedded Linux, software development, and general electronics, to create an in-depth guide to building with this platform. However, it is simply not possible to cover everything in just one book, so I have avoided restating information that is listed in the key documents and websites described in this section. The first starting point for supporting documentation is always the following:

- **The BeagleBoard.org website:** This provides the main support for this platform, with software guides, community links, and downloads to support your development. An excellent "Getting Started" guide and blog is available at the website www.beagleboard.org.

A huge amount of documentation is available on the BeagleBone platform, but the most important documents are as follows:

- **BeagleBone Black System Reference Manual (SRM):** This is the core document that describes the BeagleBone Black hardware. Authored by Gerald Coley, it is a comprehensive document that is complex in parts, but it is important that you have a copy along with this book. It is a live document, approximately 125 pages, that is released with every new revision of the BeagleBone. It is available free from the BeagleBone "Getting Started" web page.

---

[1] See www.broadcom.com/products/BCM2835 for further details.

■ **Sitara AM335x Cortex-A8 Technical Reference Manual (TRM):** The key component of the BeagleBone is its Texas Instruments microprocessor, and this document contains anything you could possibly want to know about its internal workings. The AM335x is a complex device, and that is reflected in the length of the TRM—4,727 pages! If you need to understand something about the inner workings of the microprocessor or the device configuration on the BeagleBone, it is likely that the answer is contained in this document. I refer to tables in the TRM throughout this book so that hopefully you will become familiar with the language contained therein. This document is available free from `www.ti.com/product/am3358`.

Key websites are also available to support your learning on this platform, with combinations of tutorials, discussion forums, sample code libraries, Linux distributions, and project ideas to stimulate your creative side. Here is a selection of important websites:

■ **The website for this book:** `www.exploringbeaglebone.com`

■ **My personal blog site:** `www.derekmolloy.ie`

■ **The eLinux.org website:** `www.elinux.org`

■ **The eewiki:** `www.eewiki.net`

■ **Hipstercircuits.com:** `www.hipstercircuits.com`

■ **OZ9AEC:** `www.oz9aec.net`

Getting started with the BeagleBone platform software is described in Chapter 2. The remainder of this chapter discusses the BeagleBone PCB itself, explaining the functionality that is available, summarizing the SRM, and providing some examples of the types of peripherals and capes that you might like to connect to the BeagleBone.

The BeagleBone Hardware

At its heart, the BeagleBone Black uses the Texas Instruments Sitara AM335x Cortex A8 ARM microprocessor. While the BeagleBone Black is the focus of this book, multiple boards have been developed by BeagleBoard.org, including BeagleBoard, BeagleBoard XM, BeagleBone, BeagleBone Black, and the Arduino Tre (BeagleBoard and Arduino combined on a single board). The BeagleBone is discussed in detail in the next section, but here are some summary details on the different boards (in historical order):

■ **(2008) BeagleBoard ($125):** The original open-hardware ARM-based development board that had HD video support. It has a 720MHz ARM A8 processor but no on-board Ethernet.

- **(2010) BeagleBoard xM ($149):** Similar to BeagleBoard, except with a 1GHz ARM (AM37x) processor, 512MB memory, four USB ports, and Ethernet support. Despite the low cost of the new BeagleBone boards, the BeagleBoard xM is very popular for its C64+TMDSP core for digital signal processing (DSP) applications.

- **(2011) BeagleBone ($89):** Smaller footprint than the BeagleBoard. It has a 720MHz processor and 256MB memory, Ethernet support, and low-level/ output (e.g., analog to digital converters), but no on-board video support.

- **(2013) BeagleBone Black ($45–$55):** This board enhances the BeagleBone with a 1GHz processor, 512MB of DDR3 memory, Ethernet, eMMC storage, and HDMI video support.

The BeagleBone Black platform is the focus of this book, mainly due to its feature set and price point in comparison to the other offerings; however, most of the discussion in this book applies generally to all platforms.

BeagleBone Versions

As just mentioned, two versions of the BeagleBone are available: the older BeagleBone White (BBW), or just BeagleBone; and the newer BeagleBone Black (BBB). Both boards have a very small form factor, fitting neatly inside an Altoids mint tin, as shown in Figure 1-2(a). Traditionally, Altoids tins have been upcycled by engineers as a low-cost housing for electronics projects. Given the complexity of the BeagleBone boards, it is impressive that they fit inside the tin—it also helps to explain the rounded corners on the BeagleBone boards! Holes can be formed in the case to provide access to the board connectors, but of course it is necessary to electrically insulate the aluminum tin before using it to house your board.

(a)   (b)

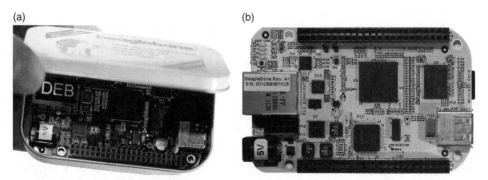

Figure 1-2: (a) The BeagleBone Black (BBB) in an Altoids tin box; (b) the BeagleBone White (BBW)

Table 1-1: The BeagleBone Black (BBB) vs. the BeagleBone White (BBW)

FEATURE	BEAGLEBONE BLACK (BBB)	BEAGLEBONE WHITE (BBW)
Price	About $45–$55	About $89
Processor	1GHz AM335x	720Mhz AM3359
Memory	512MB DDR3 (faster 1.6GB/s and lower power)	256MB DDR2
Storage	On-board 2GB eMMC (4GB eMMC on the Revision C board) and micro-SD card slot	Micro-SD card slot only
Video	On-board HDMI	No on-board HDMI. Optional cape available.
Debugging	JTAG header present but not populated	JTAG over USB available
Serial Connection	TTL header present but separate cable needed	Serial over USB
Input/Output Headers	Almost the same, but fewer GPIO pins might be available due to eMMC and HDMI functionality on the BBB	

To achieve such a small form factor, the components are densely placed on the BeagleBone, and a six-layer PCB is used to achieve interconnects. As an example, the AM335x (ZCZ) processors used on the BeagleBone platforms have a ball grid array of 324 pins, with a 0.80mm ball pitch.

Table 1-1 lists the main differences between the BBB boards and the BBW boards. The first obvious difference is the price. Despite the improvement in specification, the BBB is just over half the price of the BBW, and is very competitively priced with other embedded Linux boards, such as the Raspberry Pi (Model B+).

The manufacture cost of the BBB was reduced by removing certain functionality from the BBW, such as the USB serial connection, USB JTAG debug emulation, and a power expansion header. However, the step-up in functionality to include on-board eMMC storage, HDMI video output, twice the memory, and a faster processor for just over half the price means that the BBB represents particularly impressive value for the money. It is clear that the BBB has reached a price/performance sweet spot that has made it an exceptionally popular platform. The eLinux.org website maintains a record of board shipment numbers that currently indicates 13,000 boards are shipping per month from CircuitCo. Despite this fact, demand continues to outstrip supply, and recently new manufacturers have come on-stream to help with meeting this demand.

The BeagleBone Black Hardware

Figure 1-3 and Figure 1-4 detail the core systems of the BBB. The first set of callouts, 1 to 8, identify and describe the key systems on the BBB. The microprocessor on the BBB is a Texas Instruments Sitara AM335x Cortex A8 ARM

	Function	Physical	Details
①	Processor	AM335x	A powerful Texas Instruments Sitara 1 GHz ARM-A8 processor that is capable of 2 billion instructions per second.
		2 x PRUs	Programmable Real-time Units. Microcontrollers that allow for real-time interfacing. Discussed in Chapter 13.
		Graphics Engine	Processor has a 3D graphics engine (SGX530), which is capable of rendering 20 million polygons per second.
②	Graphics	HDMI Framer	The framer converts the LCD interface available on the AM335x processor into a HDMI signal (no HDCP).
③	Memory	512 MB DDR3	The amount of system memory affects performance and the type of applications that can be run.
④	Storage	eMMC (MMC1)	A 2/4 GB on-board embedded multi-media card (eMMC)—an SD card on a chip. The BBB can boot without an SD card.
⑤	Power Management	TPS65217C	Power management IC (PMIC). Sophisticated power management IC that has 4 LDO voltage regulators for the power rails. This IC is controlled via I²C.
⑥	Ethernet Processor	Ethernet PHY (10/100)	Can be immediately connected to a network (supports DHCP). The physical interface LAN8710A connects the physical RJ45 connector to the ARM microprocessor.
⑦	LEDs	7 x LEDs	Power LED (blue), 4 user LEDs (blue), and 2 LEDs on the RJ45 Ethernet socket (yellow = 100M link up, green = traffic).
⑧	Buttons	3 x Buttons	Power button for powering on/off. Reset button for resetting the board and boot switch button for choosing to boot from the eMMC or the SD card.
	Connectors		
⑨	Video Out	micro-HDMI (HDMI-D)	For connecting to monitors and televisions. Supports resolutions up to (1280x1024 at 60 Hz). It can run 1920x1080 but only at 24 Hz. Has HDMI CEC support.
		Audio Out (HDMI-D)	See the Optional Accessories section for details on how to break this out with a regular 3.5 mm audio jack.
⑩	Network	Ethernet (RJ45)	10/100 Ethernet via a RJ45 connector. No on-board Wi-Fi. See the section on Optional Accessories in this chapter.
⑪	DC Power	5 V DC Supply (5.5 mm)	For connecting 5 V mains PSUs to the BBB. See the Highly Recommended Accessories section in this chapter.
⑫	SD Card	card slot (MMC0) (micro-SD)	3.3 V micro-SD card slot. BBB can be booted from this slot, flashed from this slot, or used for additional storage when booting from the eMMC.
⑬	Serial Debug	6 Pin Connector (6 x 0.1")	(UART0) Used with a serial TTL3V3 cable to connect to the serial console of the BBB (this is not a JTAG connector— see the Highly Recommended Accessories section).
⑭	USB	1xUSB 2.0 Client (mini-USB)	(USB0) Connects to your desktop computer and can power the BBB directly and/or communicate to it.
⑮	USB	1xUSB 2.0 Host (USB-A)	(USB1) You can connect USB peripherals (e.g., Wi-Fi, keyboard, webcam) to the BBB with this USB connector. You can use a USB hub to add more than one USB device.
⑯⑰	P8 and P9 Expansion Headers	Two 2x23 pin 0.1" female headers	92 pins in two headers that are multiplexed to provide access to the features in Figure 1-5. Not all functionality is available at the same time. Can be used to connect capes.
⑱	Other Debug	JTAG	There is space for a JTAG connector on the bottom of the board. JTAG allows you to debug your board, but requires additional hardware and software.
⑲	Other Power	Battery Connectors	It is possible to solder pins and use these points to connect a battery supply. Read the SRM carefully!

Figure 1-3: Table of BBB subsystems and connectors

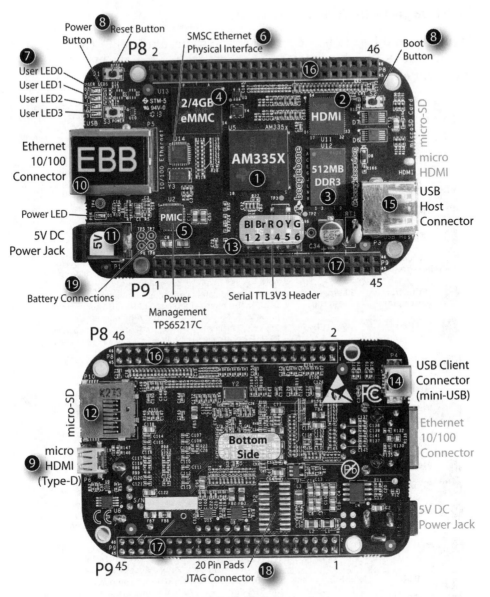

Figure 1-4: The BeagleBone Black (BBB) top and bottom views

Microprocessor.[2] It is a RISC (reduced instruction set computing) processor, so at 1,000MHz the processor executes 2,000 million instructions per second (MIPS). The processor runs at about 1W idle and 2.3W for heavy processing loads.

---

[2] Earlier BBB boards used an XAM3359AZCZ100 processor, but more recent boards (Rev B) use the AM3358BZCZ100. The feature set that is exposed to the BBB platform is the same, so the notation AM335x is used.

The next set of callouts, 9 to 19, identifies the various connectors on the BBB, their physical characteristics, and their function. For connector 18, the JTAG connector, there are 20 pre-tinned pads. You need to purchase a connector (such as Samtec FTR-110-03-G-D-06) for this and carefully solder it to the board. In addition, you need a JTAG interface and associated debug software. The BBW has on-board USB JTAG support.

If you would like these images for your own reference, Figures 1-3, 1-4, and 1-5 are available as a high-resolution PDF poster prints at the chapter web page: www.exploringbeaglebone.com/chapter1/.

Figure 1-5 details the various inputs and outputs that are available on the P8 and P9 headers. There are 92 pins in total on these headers (2×46); however, not all are available for general-purpose input/outputs (GPIOs). Several of the connections have a fixed configuration:

- Eight pins are connected to "digital" ground.

P8 and P9 Expansion Headers 16 17		There are 92 pins in two headers that are multiplexed. Not all of the functionality listed below is available simultaneously. Be very careful with current levels!
GPIO	65 x GPIOs	Maximum number of GPIOs is 65. All GPIOs are 3.3 V tolerant. Using buses and interfaces below reduces the number of available GPIOs.
Analog Output	8 x PWM	Pulse width modulated (PWM) outputs allow you to send a type of variable analog output (0 V to 3.3 V). PWM can be used to control servo motors. There are eight pins that can deliver this type of output.
Analog Inputs	7 x Analog Inputs	7 x 12-bit 1.8 V analog inputs that are always available on the headers. These can be used for reading sensor values, but be careful as they are only 1.8 V tolerant.
Power Supply	5 V, 3.3 V, 1.8 V	5 V and 3.3 V supplies and a 1.8 V reference supply (not a general supply!) for the analog inputs. Eight pins on the headers route to "regular" ground.
Timers	4 x Timers	Can be used to generate external clocks for interfacing to devices (Section 20 in the TRM).
Buses	2 x I²C	I²C is a digital bus that allows you to connect several modules to each of these two-wire buses at the same time. There are two public buses and one additional private bus.
	4 x UART	Used for serial communication between two devices. UART0 is the Serial Debug connector that is described in Figure 1-3.
	2 x CAN	CAN Bus is used for Controller Area Networks, often on industrial processes or vehicles to communicate between various networked systems. There is also a CAN cape available for the BeagleBone.
	2 x SPI	Serial peripheral interface provides a synchronous serial data link over short distances. It uses a master/slave configuration and requires four wires for communication on the BBB.
	GPMC	General-purpose memory controller is used to connect to external memory devices like FPGAs or ASICs. This fast bus will conflict with the eMMC on the board.
	2 x MMC	Interface buses that are used to connect the micro-SD card and the eMMC to the processor.
	LCD	Useful for LCD screens (e.g., LCD capes). This interface conflicts with the HDMI Framer (only one may be used simultaneously).
	2 x McASP	General-purpose audio serial port—multichannel audio serial port (McASP), connected to the HDMI framer.

Figure 1-5: Table of functionality available on the P8 and P9 headers

- Nine pins are required for the analog inputs (seven inputs, ground, and 1.8V reference voltage).

- Six pins are allocated to voltage supplies: 3.3V (up to 250mA), 5V system (up to 250mA) and 5V V_{DD} (up to 1A if powered via DC Jack—power can be supplied to the board via the VDD_5V pins).

- Two are allocated to one of the I²C buses.

- Two are allocated to the power and reset buttons.

The remaining 65 connectors are available to be multiplexed to many different functions, several of which are listed in Figure 1-5. The function of each of these input/output types is discussed in Chapter 6 and Chapter 8.

BeagleBone Accessories

The BBB board is packaged with a USB 2.0 cable (micro-USB plug to USB A plug), which is used to connect the BBB (via the USB Client Connector) to a desktop computer. It does *not* come with a micro-SD card, as the Linux installation is already present on the board's eMMC. It will boot to Linux directly out of the box. The BBW is packaged with a micro-SD card, as it has no on-board eMMC.

Highly Recommended Accessories

The following accessories are recommended for purchase along with your BBB board. If you are planning to carry out development work with the BBB, then you should probably have all of them.

Micro-SD Card (for Flashing the BBB)

A micro-SD card enables you to write new Linux images to your BBB. If you accidently damage the Linux file system during your experimentation with the BBB, the micro-SD card will enable you to restore your system. Ideally, you should have two dedicated SD cards, one for a boot image and one for a flasher image.

Purchase a micro-SD card of at least 4GB capacity. You may also require a micro-SD-to-SD adapter so that it can be used in your computer's card reader. Many micro-SD cards are bundled with the adapter, which is a cheaper option than purchasing them separately. The micro-SD card should be of Class 10 or greater, as the faster read/write speed will save you time in writing images in particular. A blank micro-SD card can also be used for additional file system storage (discussed in Chapter 3), so the greater the card capacity the better.

External 5V Power Supply (for Flashing and Peripherals)

You can power the BBB directly using the USB connection from your desktop/laptop computer to the USB client connector on the BBB. For getting started with the BBB, that is perfectly fine; however, once you begin to connect accessories such as Wi-Fi adapters, USB cameras, or on-board displays, it is possible that the power available over USB will not be sufficient for your configuration. Some early BBB boards would not flash a new system image correctly without being connected to an external 5V power supply.

You can purchase a 5V DC regulated switching power supply that plugs directly into a mains supply. It should have a minimum DC output current of 1A; however, you should aim for a 2A current supply (2A × 5V = 10W) if possible. The 5V barrel connector (5.5mm diameter) from the supply should be center positive. If you plan on running multiple BBBs simultaneously, then you will need to power them using external power supplies (barrel or USB), as connecting two BBBs to your PC simultaneously requires careful software configuration and can cause Internet connectivity instabilities under Windows.

Ethernet Cable (for Network Connection)

The BBB can use a special networking mode, called Internet-over-USB, to create a virtual network between the BBB and your desktop; however, if you are connecting the BBB to your home network, then don't forget to purchase a Cat5 network patch cable to connect your BBB to the network using its RJ-45 10/100 Ethernet connector. If you are planning to use more than one BBB simultaneously, you could invest in a low-cost four-port switch, which can be placed close to your desktop computer (see Chapter 2).

HDMI Cable (for Connection to Monitors/Televisions)

The BBB has a HDMI framer and can be easily connected to a monitor or television that has a HDMI or DVI connector. The BBB has a micro-HDMI socket (HDMI-D), so be careful to match that to your monitor/television type (usually HDMI-A or DVI-D). The cable you are likely to need is a "HDMI-Micro-D Plug to HDMI-A Male Plug." A 1.8m (6ft.) cable should cost no more than $10. Be very careful with your purchase—a HDMI-C (mini-HDMI) connector will *not* fit the BBB.

Alternatively, you can purchase a low-cost ($3) micro-HDMI (HDMI-D) plug to regular HDMI (HDMI-A) socket adapters or micro-HDMI (HDMI-D) plug to DVI-D socket adapter cables. These enable you to use regular-size HDMI-A or to connect to DVI-D devices, respectively (see Figure 1-6(a)).

(a)

(b)

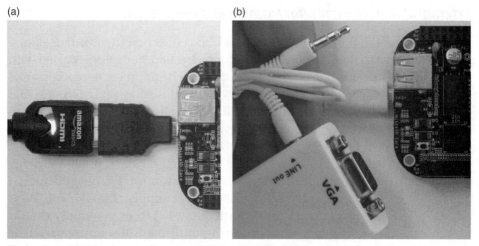

Figure 1-6: (a) BBB connected to micro-HDMI-to-HDMI adapter and then to a low-cost HDMI-A-to-DVI-D cable (b) A micro-HDMI-to-VGA adapter with audio line output

USB to Serial UART TTL 3.3V (for Finding Problems)

The USB-to-serial UART TTL serial cable is one accessory that is really useful when there are problems with the Linux distribution on your board. I find it invaluable when finding and fixing problems with my students' boards. It connects to the 6 pin J1 header, which is beside the P9 header on the BBB. The black side of the cable is connected to pin 1 (the white dot) and the green side is closest to the USB host connector (see Figure 1-7). Only three pins are used on the BBB: pin 1 ground (black), pin 4 receive (orange), and pin 5 transmit (yellow).

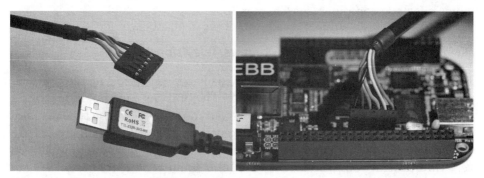

Figure 1-7: The USB-to-TTL 3.3V serial cable and its connection to the BBB (connection colors are black, brown, red, orange, yellow, and green)

Please ensure that you purchase the *3.3V level* version and ideally purchase a version with a six-way 0.1" female header pre-attached (it does sell with only bare wires, which I purchased by accident!). This cable contains a chipset and requires that you install drivers on your desktop computer, creating a new COM port. The FTDI TTL-232R-3V3 cable works very well and provides a very stable connection (about $20). See `tiny.cc/ebb102` for the datasheet and the "VCP" link to the software drivers for this adapter cable.

If you are planning to flash your own images to the BBB or if you have a board that is not booting, I recommend that you purchase one of these cables. The use of this cable is discussed in Chapter 2 and Chapter 3.

Optional Accessories

The following sections describe optional accessories that you may need, depending on the applications that you are developing (see Figure 1-8).

(a)   (b)   (c)

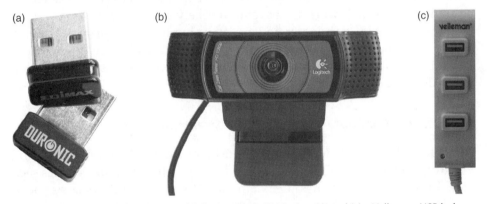

Figure 1-8: (a) USB Wi-Fi adapters; (b) the Logitech C920 camera; and (c) a Velleman USB hub (bus powered)

USB Hub (to Connect Several USB Devices to a USB Host)

If you are planning to connect more than one USB device to the BBB at the same time, then you will need a USB hub. USB hubs are either bus powered or externally powered. Externally powered hubs are more expensive; however, if you are powering several power-hungry adapters (Wi-Fi in particular), then you may need a powered hub. Ensure that you plug the USB hub into the BBB host connector *before* powering on the BBB. I have tried different brands of USB hub and they have all worked without difficulty.

Micro-HDMI to VGA adapters (for VGA Video and Sound)

Several low-cost micro-HDMI-to-VGA adapters are for sale (e.g., on Amazon or eBay) for converting the HDMI output to a VGA output. As well as providing for VGA video output, many of these connectors provide a separate 3.5mm audio line out, which can be used if you wish to play audio using your BBB, without requiring a television, high-end amplifier, or monitor (see Figure 1-6(b)). There are also USB audio adapters available that can provide high-quality playback and recording functionality. These adapters and their usage are described in Chapter 12.

Wi-Fi Adapters (for Wireless Networking)

Many different Wi-Fi adapters are available, such as those in Figure 1-8(a); however, not all adapters will work on the BBB. The Linux distribution and the chipset inside the adapter will determine the likelihood of success. You can find a list of adapters that are confirmed as working at `tiny.cc/ebb103`. However, please be aware that manufacturers can change chipsets within the same product and that buying an adapter from the list does not guarantee that it will work. You are more likely to succeed if you can confirm the chipset in the adapter you are planning to purchase, and evaluate that against the list. Wi-Fi configuration and applications are discussed in detail in Chapter 10, which tests a range of different low-cost adapters that are widely available.

USB Webcam (for Capturing Images and Streaming Video)

Attaching a USB webcam can be a low-cost method of integrating image and video capture into your BBB projects. In addition, utilizing Linux libraries such as Video 4 Linux and Open Source Computer Vision (OpenCV) enables you to build "seeing" applications.

In Chapter 12, different webcams are examined, but the text focuses on the use of the Logitech C920 webcam in particular for video streaming applications (see Figure 1-8(b)). It is a relatively pricey webcam (at about $70) but it is capable of streaming full HD video directly using the BBB, as it has H.264/MPG-4 hardware encoding built into the camera. This greatly reduces the workload for the BBB, allowing the processor to be available for other tasks. As with Wi-Fi adapters, it would be useful to confirm that a webcam works with the BBB before you purchase it for that specific purpose. I test several camera types in Chapter 12.

USB Keyboard and Mouse (for General-Purpose Computing)

It is possible to connect a USB keyboard and mouse separately to a USB hub or to use a 2.4GHz wireless keyboard and mouse combination. Very small wireless handheld combinations are available, such as the Rii 174 Mini, Rii i10, and eSynic mini, all of which include a handheld keyboard with integrated touchpad. A USB Bluetooth adapter is also useful for connecting peripherals to the BBB. A similar Bluetooth keyboard/touchpad is used in Chapter 11.

Capes

Capes are daughterboards that can be attached to the P8/P9 expansion headers on the BeagleBone. They are called capes (as in Superman's cape!) due to the shape of the boards as they wrap around the RJ-45 Ethernet connector. You can connect up to four capes at any one time, when they are compatible with each other.

Some capes use a significant number of pins. For example, you will look at the LCD4 cape in Chapter 11. It uses the P8 header pins 27 through 46 and some of the analog inputs for its buttons and resistive touch interface. If you are using the eMMC for booting the BBB, then very few pins remain for GPIO use. In addition, the LCD cape does not carry forward the pin headers. Figure 1-9 shows two views of this cape when connected to the BBB, running the standard BBB Debian Linux distribution.

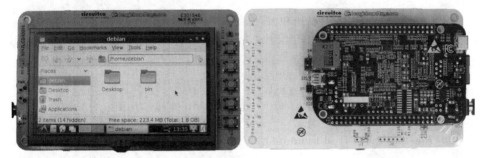

Figure 1-9: The LCD4 cape (top and bottom view)

More than 50 capes are currently available for the BeagleBone; a full list can be found at `www.beagleboard.org/cape`. Here is a selection of some example capes that you might find useful in your projects (see Figure 1-10):

- The LCD capes are available in different sizes: 7″ (800×480), 4″ (480×272), and 3″ (320×240), with the 4″ version captured in Figure 1-9. They have resistive touch screens, meaning you use a stylus (or fingernail) to interact with the screens. This is different than the capacitive touch screens on recent phones/tablets.

- The Adafruit Proto cape is a low-cost (~$10) bare cape, which you can use to transfer your breadboard design to a more solid platform. Several other breadboard and prototyping capes are available.

- The Replicape ($179) is an impressive open-source 3D printer cape that has five stepper motor drivers, including micro-stepping support. See `www.thing-printer.com` for more information.

- The Valent F(x) LOGi-Bone FPGA development board cape ($89) adds FPGA capabilities to the BBB with a Spartan 6 LX9. FPGAs provide programmable logic blocks that allow for very fast I/O operations, but does so with an increase in complexity. This cape also provides an Arduino header, enabling it to interface directly to shields that have been developed for the Arduino platform. This cape is discussed briefly at the beginning of Chapter 13.

- There are camera capes such as the 3.1MP Camera cape from www
.beagleboardtoys.com that provides an alternative to USB webcams; however, it cannot be used at the same time as the eMMC, so the BBB must be booted from the micro-SD card.

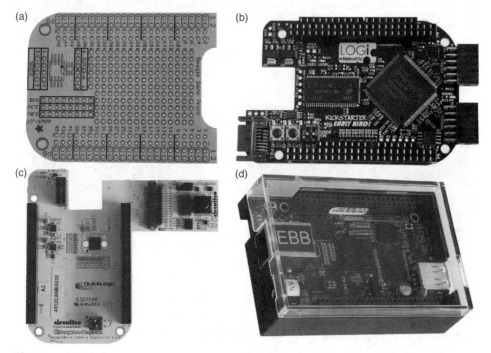

Figure 1-10: (a) The Proto cape; (b) Valent F(x) LOGi-Bone; (c) Camera cape; and (d) Adafruit BBB case

You have to be very careful about compatibility when interconnecting capes. There is a compatibility table covering the more common capes at tiny.cc/ ebb104. The preceding list is just a small selection. Many more capes are available and it is likely that additional capes will be developed over time.

How to Destroy Your BeagleBone!

The BBB and BBW are complex and delicate devices that are very easily damaged if you do not show due care. If you are moving up from boards like the Arduino to the BeagleBone platform, then you have to be especially careful when connecting circuits that you built for that platform to the BBB. Unlike the Arduino Uno, the microprocessor on the BBB cannot be replaced. If you damage the microprocessor, you will have to buy a new board!

Here are some things that you should *never* do:

- Do not shut the BBB down by pulling out the power jack/USB power. You should shut down the board correctly using a software shutdown (e.g., by pressing the power button once) or by holding the power button for about eight seconds for a "hard" power down. This enables the PMIC to shut down the board correctly. If you have to remove power by disconnecting the power supply, hold the reset button while doing so in order to lower system power usage.

- Do not place a powered BBB on metal surfaces (e.g., aluminum-finish computers) or on worktops with stray/cut-off wire segments, resistors, etc. If you short the pins on the P8/P9 headers you can easily destroy your board. You can buy a case from suppliers such as Adafruit (see Figure 1-10(d)). Alternatively, you can attach small rubber feet to the BBB.

- Do not connect circuits that source/sink other than very low currents from/to the P8/P9 headers. The maximum current that you can source from many of these header pins is 4-6mA and the maximum current you can sink is 8mA. The power rail and ground pins can source and sink larger currents. The Arduino allows currents of 40mA on each input/ output. This issue is covered in Chapter 4 and Chapter 6.

- The GPIO pins are 3.3V tolerant (the ADCs are 1.8V tolerant). Do not connect a circuit that is powered at 5V or you will destroy the board. This is discussed in Chapter 4, Chapter 6, and Chapter 8.

- Do not connect circuits that apply power to the P8/P9 pins while the BBB is not powered on. Make sure that all self-powered interfacing circuits are gated by the 3.3V supply line. This is covered in Chapter 6.

Here are two steps that you should *always* follow:

- Carefully check the pin numbers that you are using. There are 46 pins in each header, and it is very easy to plug into header connector 21 instead of 19. For connections in the middle of the headers, I always count twice—up from the left and down from the right. In addition, there is a very useful set of P8/P9 labels available at `tiny.cc/ebb105` that you can print at 100% scale and attach to your BBB, as illustrated in Figure 1-1.

- Read the SRM in detail before connecting complex circuits of your own design to the BBB.

If your BBB is dead and it *is* your fault, then I'm afraid that after you perform all of the checks at `www.beagleboard.org/support`, you will have to purchase a new board. If it *is not* your fault, then see the BBB SRM manual and www.beagleboard.org/support website to return a defective board for repair by requesting a return merchandise authorization (RMA) number.

Summary

After completing this chapter, you should be able to:

- Describe the capability of the BeagleBone and its suitability for different project types.
- Source the important documents that will assist you in working with the BBB platform.
- Describe the major hardware systems and subsystems on the BBB.
- Identify important accessories that you can buy to enhance the capability of your BBB.
- Have an appreciation of the power and complexity of the BBB as a physical computing platform.
- Be aware of the first steps to take in protecting your board from physical damage.

Support

The key sources of additional support documentation are listed earlier in this chapter. If you are having difficulty with the BeagleBone platform and the issues are not described in the documentation, then you should use these two resources:

- The BeagleBoard Google Group, which is available at groups .google.com/d/forum/beagleboard. Please read the frequently asked questions (FAQs) and search the current questions before posting a new question.
- There is a live chat available at www.beagleboard.org/chat or directly on the Beagle IRC channel (by joining #beagle on irc.freenode.net) using a free IRC client such as X-Chat for Linux, HexChat for Windows, or Colloquy for Mac OS X.

Please remember that the people in this group and IRC channel are community members who volunteer their time to respond to questions.

# CHAPTER 2

The BeagleBone Black Software

In this chapter, you are introduced to the Linux operating system and software tools that can be used with the BeagleBone. This chapter aims to ensure that you can connect to your BeagleBone and control it. By the end of this chapter you should be able to "blink" a system LED having followed a step-by-step guide that demonstrates how you can use Linux shell commands in a Linux terminal window. In this chapter, you are also introduced to a library of BeagleBone functions, called BoneScript, which can be used with Node.js and the Cloud9 integrated development environment to build code that flashes the same system LED.

Equipment Required for This Chapter:

- BeagleBone Black board
- Supplied USB cable (USB A male to mini-USB A male)
- Micro-SD card (4GB or greater; Class 10+) (optional)
- Network infrastructure and cabling (optional)

Further details on this chapter are available at www.exploringbeaglebone.com/chapter2/

Linux on the BeagleBone

A *Linux distribution* is a publicly available version of Linux that is packaged with a set of software programs and tools. There are many different Linux distributions, which are typically focused on different applications. For example, high-end server owners might install Red Hat Enterprise, Debian, or OpenSUSE; desktop users might install Ubuntu, Debian, Fedora, or Linux Mint. The list is endless, but at the core of all distributions is a common Linux kernel, which was conceived and created by Linus Torvalds in 1991.

In deciding on a Linux distribution to use for your embedded system platform, it would be sensible to choose one for which the following apply:

- The distribution is stable and well supported.
- There is a good package manager.
- The distribution is lean and suited to a low storage footprint.
- There is good community support for your particular device.
- There is device driver support for any peripherals you wish to attach.

Linux Distributions

There are many different distributions of Linux for embedded system platforms, including expensive proprietary versions for real-time programming. At their heart, they all use the mainline Linux kernel, but each distribution contains different tools and configurations that result in quite different user experiences. The main open-source distributions used by the community on the BBB board include Debian, Ångström, Ubuntu, and Arch Linux.

Debian (contraction of Debbie and Ian!) is a community-driven Linux distribution that has an emphasis on open-source development. There is no commercial organization involved in the development of Debian; in fact, there is a formal social contract (`tiny.cc/ebb201`) that states that Debian will remain entirely free (as in software freedom). The Debian distribution is used for many of the practical steps in this book and is recommended as the distribution of choice for the BBB, as it is currently distributed with new BBB boards. In addition, Debian is used throughout this book as the distribution for the Linux desktop computer, as it provides excellent support for cross-platform development through the Embedded Debian (*Emdebian*) project (see `www.debian.org`).

Ångström is a stable and lean Linux distribution that is widely used on embedded systems. The team of developers behind Ångström is experienced in customizing Linux distributions for embedded devices such as set-top boxes, mobile devices, and networking devices. Impressively, Ångström can scale down to devices with only megabytes of flash storage. Ångström makes extensive use of *BusyBox*, a multicall binary (a single executable that can do the job of many) used to create a compact version of command-line utilities that are found on

Linux systems. Many of my YouTube videos use Ångström, as it was the primary distribution for the BeagleBone for quite some time.

Ubuntu is very closely related to Debian; in fact, it is described on the Ubuntu website (www.ubuntu.com) as follows: "Debian is the rock upon which Ubuntu is built." Ubuntu is one of the most popular desktop Linux distributions, mainly because of its focus on making Linux more accessible to new users. It is easy to install and has excellent desktop driver support, and there are binary distributions available for the BBB.

Arch Linux is a lightweight and flexible Linux distribution that aims to "keep it simple," targeting competent Linux users in particular by giving them complete control and responsibility over the system configuration. There are pre-built versions of the Arch Linux distribution available for the BBB; however, compared to the other distributions, it currently has less support for new Linux users with the BBB platform (see www.archlinux.org).

NOTE Don't be too worried that you might damage the Linux file system when you are practicing with the BBB. In the worst case, you might have to write a new Linux image to the board. It takes about 20–45 minutes to write the image to the board. There is a guide to writing a new image to the BBB on this chapter's web page at www.exploringbeaglebone.com/chapter2/.

Communicating with the BBB

When you are ready to try out your BBB, the first thing you should do is connect it to your desktop computer using the supplied USB lead. After you apply power, the BBB will connect to the desktop in USB client mode. Once connected and discovered, your file manager, such as Windows Explorer, will display the contents of the BBB's FAT partition, as shown in Figure 2-1. The BeagleBoard.org team has put together a really excellent HTML guide on getting started with the BBB. You should double-click the START.htm file to display the guide, which is illustrated in Figure 2-1, within a web browser.

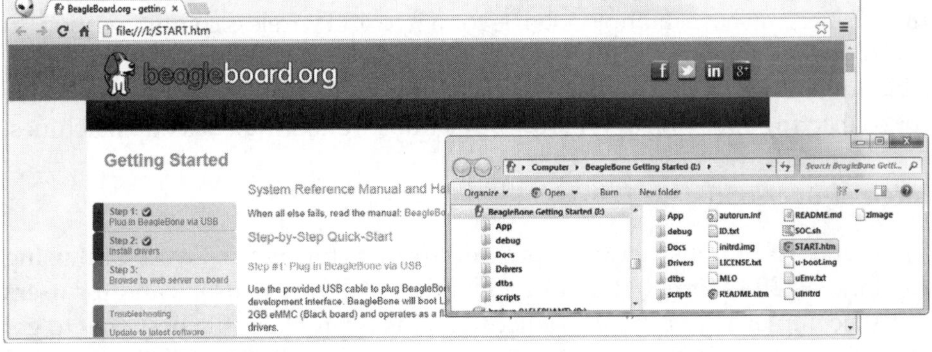

Figure 2-1: The BBB START.htm guide to setting up your BBB

> **WARNING** Be very careful that you do not delete the files that appear in the folder in Figure 2-1, such as `MLO`, `u-boot.img`, and `uEnv.txt`. These files are vital to your BBB booting correctly. In future releases of Linux for the BBB, it is likely that such files will move to the `/boot` directory on the Linux partition.

Installing Drivers

Follow the steps in the guide displayed in Figure 2-1, which mainly involve browsing to the `Drivers` folder and installing the correct version. Under Windows you may receive Windows driver certification warnings on multiple occasions. Continue with the process and *do not click Cancel*. Under Windows 8, you may have to restart the computer in a troubleshooting mode in order to disable "driver signature enforcement"—please see the chapter web page. Once this process is complete, several new devices are available on your desktop computer. For example, you will now have the following devices:

- Access to the FAT partition of the BBB (like a USB memory key).
- Serial access to the BBB using a new *Gadget Serial* driver.
- A *Linux USB Ethernet/RNDIS Gadget* (for Internet-over-USB). RNDIS stands for Remote Network Driver Interface Specification.

The Windows Device Manager displays these new devices. Similar steps for Linux and Macintosh desktop computers are available in the startup guide. These new devices can be used to connect to the BBB.

Network Connections

There are three main ways to connect to and communicate with the BBB over the network, each with its own advantages and disadvantages. The first way is to use *Internet-over-USB*, which creates a "private" virtual LAN using a single USB cable. The second way is to use *regular Ethernet*, and the third is to use an *Ethernet crossover cable*. Connecting to the BBB over a network can be a stumbling block for beginners. It is usually straightforward if you are working at home with control of your own network; however, complex networks, such as those in universities, can have multiple subnets for wired and wireless communication. In such complex networks, routing restrictions may make it difficult, if not impossible, to connect to the BBB over regular Ethernet. All three methods are suitable for connecting your BBB to Windows, Macintosh, and Linux desktop machines.

Internet-over-USB

The standard BBB distributions provide support for Internet-over-USB using the Linux USB Ethernet/RNDIS Gadget device. For new users, and for users within complex network infrastructures, this is probably the best way to get started with the BBB. For this setup you only need the BBB board, the supplied

USB cable, and access to a desktop computer, ideally with administrator access levels. Table 2-1 describes the advantages and disadvantages of Internet-over-USB for connecting to the BBB.

Table 2-1: Advantages and Disadvantages of BBB Internet-over-USB

ADVANTAGES	DISADVANTAGES
Provides a good stable network setup for beginners.	Without significant effort, you are limited to a single BBB per desktop.
When you do not have access to, or control of, network infrastructure hardware you can still connect the BBB to the Internet.	Network sharing configuration can be difficult, especially on Macintosh desktop computers. Additional configuration must also be performed on the BBB.
Power is supplied by your desktop machine over USB.	Your desktop machine must be running in order to transfer data to/from the Internet.

NOTE By default, with Internet-over-USB, the BBB has the fixed IP address 192.168.7.2 and the desktop machine has the fixed address 192.168.7.1.

For example, if you fully installed the BBB drivers under Windows, you should now have a new network connection (Start ➢ type `view Network Connections`). Figure 2-2 captures a typical Network Connections window under Windows. In this case, "Local Area Connection 9" is the Linux USB Ethernet/RNDIS Gadget. The desktop computer remains connected to your regular LAN, which provides access to the Internet, and to a new "private" LAN that contains only your desktop computer (192.168.7.1) and your BBB (192.168.7.2). You can open a web browser and connect to the BBB's web server by typing `192.168.7.2` in the address bar, as illustrated in Figure 2-2.

Figure 2-2: Windows Network Connections with Internet-over-USB connection LAN 9, and a web browser connection

At this point you can connect to the BBB's web server using a web browser, so you have a fully functional private network; however, you may also want the BBB to have full direct access to the Internet so that you can download files and update Linux software directly on the BBB. To do this, you need to share your main network adapter, so that traffic from the BBB can be routed through your desktop machine to the Internet. For example, under Windows use the following steps:

1. Choose your desktop/laptop network adapter that provides you with Internet access. Right-click it and choose Properties.

2. In the dialog that appears, as shown on the left-hand side of Figure 2-3, click the Sharing tab at the top and enable the option Allow other network users...

3. In the drop-down list, choose your BBB private LAN (e.g., referring back to Figure 2-2, this is "Local Area Connection 9"). Click OK.

4. Right-click the BBB private LAN (e.g., LAN 9) and select Properties.

5. Double-click Internet Protocol Version 4. In this dialog, select Obtain an IP address automatically and enable Obtain DNS server address automatically (see Figure 2-3 on the right-hand side).

6. Click OK and then OK again to save the configurations.

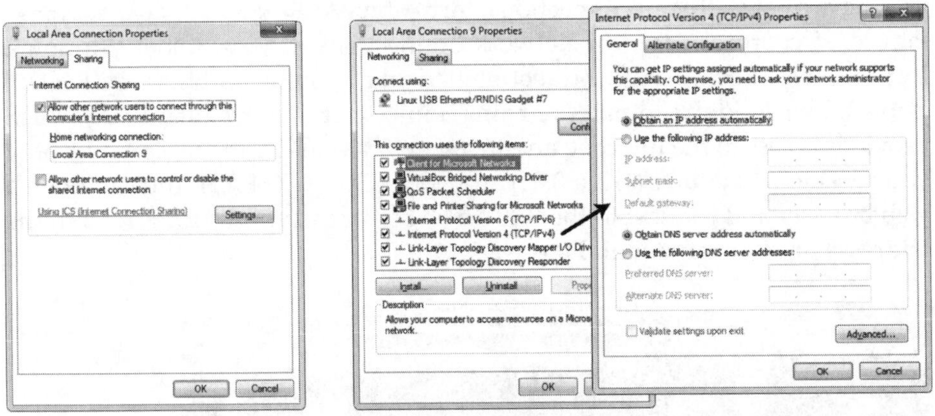

Figure 2-3: Configuring the Network Connection Sharing Properties under Windows

If all goes well, you will not have noticed any difference at this point and you should be able to reload the web page that is shown in Figure 2-2. The impact of the last two steps can only be appreciated when you open a terminal connection to the BBB. A link to a video guide for configuring network sharing for Mac OS X is available at `tiny.cc/ebb202`.

> **WARNING**   If you are planning to jump ahead, there is one more step to complete before your BBB will be able to "see" the Internet. This change, which has to be made directly on the BBB, is covered in the section titled "What Time Is It?"

NETWORK SHARING FOR LINUX DESKTOP USERS

The settings for a Linux desktop to enable network sharing are as follows:

1. With the Internet-over-USB device attached, type `ifconfig` or `ip addr` in a terminal, which results in a display of the attached network interfaces.

2. Find your main adapter (e.g., eth0) and Internet-over-USB adapter (e.g., eth1).

3. Use the iptables program to configure the Linux kernel firewall rules:
   ```
   molloyd@debian:~$ sudo iptables --table nat --append
   POSTROUTING --out-interface eth0 -j MASQUERADE
   molloyd@debian:~$ sudo iptables --append FORWARD --in-
   interface eth1 -j ACCEPT
   ```

4. Then, use the following command to turn on IP forwarding:
   ```
   molloyd@debian:~$ sudo sh -c "echo 1 > /proc/sys/net/ipv4/
   ip_forward"
   ```

Regular Ethernet

By "regular" Ethernet, I mean connecting the BBB to a network in the same way that you would connect your desktop computer using a wired connection. For the home user and power user, regular Ethernet is probably the best solution for networking and connecting to the BBB. Table 2-2 lists the advantages and disadvantages of using this type of connection. The main issue is the complexity of the network—if you understand your network configuration and have access to the router settings, then this is by far the best configuration. If your network router is distant from your desktop computer, you can use a small network switch, which can be purchased for as little as $10–$20. Alternatively, you could purchase a wireless access point with integrated multiport router, for $25–$35. This is useful for wireless BBB applications and also for extending the range of your wireless network.

Table 2-2: Regular BBB Ethernet Advantages and Disadvantages

ADVANTAGES	DISADVANTAGES
You have full control over IP address settings and dynamic/static IP settings.	You might need administrative control or knowledge of the network infrastructure.
You can connect and interconnect many BBBs to a single network (including wireless devices).	The BBB needs a source of power (which can be a mains-powered adapter).
The BBB can connect to the Internet without a desktop computer being powered on.	The setup is more complex for beginners if the network structure is complex.

The first challenge with this configuration is finding your BBB on the network. By default, the BBB is configured to request a *Dynamic Host Configuration*

Protocol (DHCP) IP address. In a home network environment this service is usually provided by a DHCP server that is running on the integrated Modem-Firewall-Router-LAN (or some similar configuration) that connects the home to an Internet Service Provider (ISP).

DHCP servers issue IP addresses dynamically from a pool of addresses for a fixed time interval, called the *lease time*, which is specified in your DHCP configuration. When this lease expires, your BBB is allocated a different IP address the next time it connects to your network. This can be frustrating, as you may have to search for your BBB on the network again. It is possible to set the IP address of your BBB to be *static*, so that it is fixed at the same address each time the board connects. Wireless connections and static IP connections are discussed in Chapter 10.

There are a few different ways to find your BBB's dynamic IP address:

- Use a web browser to access your home router (often address 192.168.1.1, 192.168.0.1, or 10.0.0.1). Log in and look under a menu such as "Status" for the "DHCP Table." You should see an entry that details the allocated IP address, the physical MAC address, and the lease time remaining for a device with host name "beaglebone," for example:

```
Leased Table
IP Address          MAC Address Client    Host Name    Register Information
192.168.1.116       c8:a0:30:c0:6b:48     beaglebone   Remains 23:59:51
```

- Use a port-scanning tool like *nmap* under Linux or the *Zenmap* GUI version that is available for Windows (see `tiny.cc/ebb203`). The command **nmap -T4 -F 192.168.1.*** will scan for devices on a subnet. You are searching for an entry that has three or four open ports (e.g., 22 for SSH, 80 for the BBB guide, 8080 for the Apache web server, and 3000 for the Cloud 9 IDE). It may also identify itself with Texas Instruments.

- You could use a Serial-over-USB connection to connect to the BBB and type **ifconfig** to find the IP address. The address is the "inet addr" associated with the `eth0` adapter. This is discussed shortly.

Once you have the IP address, you can test that it is valid by entering it in the address bar of your web browser—**192.168.1.116** in the example above. Your browser should display the page that is shown in Figure 2-2.

Ethernet Crossover Cable

An Ethernet crossover cable is a cable that has been modified to enable two Ethernet devices to be connected directly together, without the need for an Ethernet switch. It can be purchased as a cable or as a plug-in adapter. If you have an RJ-45 crimping tool, you could even make one by swapping the transmit pair (green, white/green) with the receive pair (orange, white/orange) on one end of a 10Base-T or 100Base-TX Ethernet cable (the Gigabit Ethernet cable is different). Many desktop machines have an automatic crossover detection function (Auto-MDIX) that enables a regular Ethernet cable to be used. Similar to the Internet-over-USB network configuration, this connection type can be used when you do not have access to network infrastructure and/or where the Internet-over-USB network configuration is not working correctly. Table 2-3 describes the advantages and disadvantages of this connection type.

Table 2-3: Crossover Cable Network Advantages and Disadvantages

ADVANTAGES	DISADVANTAGES
When you do not have access to network infrastructure hardware you can still connect to the BBB.	If your desktop machine has only one network adapter then you will lose access to the Internet. It is best used with a device that has multiple adapters.
BBB may have Internet access if the desktop has two network adapters.	BBB still needs a source of power (can be a mains-powered adapter).
Provides a reasonably stable network setup.	Requires a specialized Ethernet crossover cable or adapter, unless your desktop has Auto-MDIX.

Communicating with the BBB

Once you have networked the BBB, the next thing you might want to do is communicate with the BBB. You can connect to the BBB using either a serial connection over USB, USB-to-TTL, or a network connection, such as that just discussed. The network connection should be your main focus, as that type of connection provides your BBB with full Internet access. The serial connection is generally used as a fallback connection when problems arise with the network connection. As such, you may skip the next section, but the information is here as a reference for when problems arise.

> **NOTE** The default superuser account for Ångström, Debian, and Arch Linux has username `root` and no password (just press Enter). Ubuntu does not have a superuser login by default—log in as `ubuntu` with the password `temppwd`.

Serial Connection over USB

If you installed the device drivers for the BBB in the previous section, the *Gadget Serial device* will allow you to connect to the BBB directly using a terminal emulator program. Serial connections are particularly useful when the BBB is close to your desktop computer and connected via the USB cable. It is often a fallback communications method when something goes wrong with the network configuration or software services on the BBB.

To connect to the BBB via the serial connection, you need a terminal program. Several third-party applications are available for Windows, such as *RealTerm* (`tiny.cc/ebb204`) and *PuTTY* (`www.putty.org`). PuTTY is also used in the next section. Most distributions of desktop Linux include a terminal program (try Ctrl+Alt+T or use Alt+F2 and type `gnome-terminal` under Debian). A terminal emulator is included by default under Mac OS X (e.g., use `screen /dev/tty .usbmodemfa133 115200`).

To connect to the BBB over the USB serial connection you need to know some information:

- **Port number:** You can find this by opening the Windows Device Manager and searching under the Ports section. Figure 2-4 captures an example Device Manager, where the Gadget Serial device is listed as COM20. This will be different on different machines.

- **Speed of the connection:** By default you need to enter **115,200** baud to connect to the BBB.

- **Other information you may need for other terminal applications:** Data bits = 8; Stop bits = 1; Parity = none; and, Flow control = XON/XOFF.

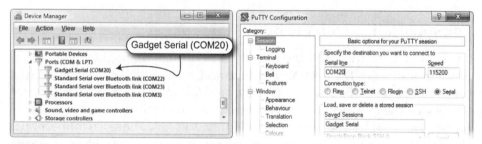

Figure 2-4: Windows Device Manager and opening a PuTTY serial connection to the BBB

Save the configuration with a session name so that it is available each time you wish to connect. After you click Open, it is important that you *press Enter when the window appears*. When connecting to Debian, you should see the following output:

```
Debian GNU/Linux 7 beaglebone ttyGS0
default username:password is [debian:temppwd]
The IP Address for usb0 is: 192.168.7.2
beaglebone login:
```

which allows you to log in with username `root`. There is no password by default (just press Enter).

On a Linux desktop computer you can install the `screen` program and connect to the serial-over-USB device with the commands:

```
molloyd@debian:~$ sudo apt-get install screen
molloyd@debian:~$ screen /dev/ttyUSB0/ 115200
```

Serial Connection with the USB-to-TTL 3.3V Cable

For this serial connection type you need the specialized cable that is described in Chapter 1. Find the COM port from Windows Device Manager that is associated with a device called "USB Serial Port." Plug in the cable to the 6-pin connector beside the P9 header (black lead to the white dot/J1). You can then open a serial connection using PuTTY (115,200 baud) and you will see the same BBB login prompt as above. However, when you reboot the board you will also see the full console output as the BBB boots, which begins with:

```
U-Boot 2013.10-00016-ga0e6bc6 (Feb 25 2014 - 10:27:54)
I2C:    ready
DRAM:   512 MiB . . .
```

This is the ultimate fallback connection, as it allows you to see what is happening during the boot process, which is described in the next chapter.

Connecting through Secure Shell (SSH)

Secure Shell (SSH) is a very useful network protocol for secure encrypted communication between network devices. You can use an SSH terminal client to connect to the SSH server that is running on port 22 of the BBB, which allows you to do the following:

- Log in remotely to the BBB and execute commands.
- Transfer files to and from the BBB using the *SSH File Transfer Protocol* (SFTP).
- Forward X11 connections, which allows you to perform virtual network computing (covered in Chapter 11).

By default, the BBB Linux distributions run an SSH server (*sshd* on Debian and *Dropbear* on Ångström) that is bound to port 22. There are a few advantages in having an SSH server available as the default method by which you log in remotely to the BBB. In particular, you can open port 22 of the BBB to the Internet using the port forwarding functionality of your router. Please ensure that you set a password on the root user account before doing this. You can then remotely log in to your BBB from anywhere in the world if you know the BBB's IP address. A service called *dynamic DNS* that is supported on most routers allows your router to register its latest address with an online service. The online service then maps a domain name of your choice to the latest IP address that your ISP has given you. The dynamic DNS service usually has an annual cost, for which it will provide you with an address of the form `dereksBBB.servicename.com`.

Secure Shell Connections using PuTTY

PuTTY (`www.putty.org`) was mentioned earlier as a way of connecting to the BBB using serial-over-USB. PuTTY is a free, open-source terminal emulator, serial console, and SSH client that you can also use to connect to the BBB over the network. PuTTY has a few very useful features:

- It supports serial and SSH connections.
- It installs an application called psftp that enables you to transfer files to and from the BBB over the network from your desktop computer.
- It supports SSH X11 forwarding, which is required in Chapter 11.

Figure 2-5 captures the PuTTY Configuration settings: Choose ssh as the connection type; enter the IP address for your BBB (`192.168.7.2` if you are using Internet-over-USB); accept Port `22` (the default); and then save the session with a useful name for future use. Click Open and log in using your username and password. You may get a security alert that warns about man-in-the-middle attacks, which may be a concern on insecure networks. Accept the fingerprint and continue. Mac OS X users can run the Terminal application with very similar settings (e.g., `ssh -X root@192.168.7.2`).

Figure 2-5: PuTTY SSH Configuration settings beside an open SSH terminal connection

You will see the basic commands that can be issued to the BBB later in this chapter, but first it is necessary to examine how you can transfer files to and from the BBB.

Chrome Apps: Secure Shell Client

The Chrome web browser has support for Chrome Apps—applications that behave like locally installed (or native) applications but are written in HTML5,

JavaScript, and CSS. Many of these applications use Google's Native Client (NaCl, or Salt!), which is a sandbox for running compiled C/C++ applications directly in the web browser, regardless of the OS. The benefit of NaCl is that applications can achieve near-native performance levels, as they can contain code that uses low-level instructions.

There is a very useful "terminal emulator and SSH client" Chrome App available. Open a new tab on the Chrome browser and click the Apps icon. Go to the Chrome Web Store and search the store for "Secure Shell." Once it is installed, it will appear as the Secure Shell App when you click the Apps icon again. When you start up the Secure Shell App, you will have to set the connection settings as in Figure 2-5, and the application will appear as in Figure 2-6.

Figure 2-6: The SSH Chrome App

Transferring Files Using PuTTY/psftp over SSH

The PuTTY installation also includes *file transfer protocol (ftp)* support that enables you to transfer files to and from the BBB over your network connection. You can start up the *psftp* (PuTTY secure file transfer protocol) application by typing **psftp** in the Windows Start command text field.

At the psftp> prompt you can connect to the BBB by typing **open root@192.168.7.2** (e.g., the BBB address for Internet-over-USB). Your desktop machine is now referred to as the local machine and the BBB is referred to as the remote machine. When you issue a command, you are typically issuing it on the remote machine. After connecting you are placed in the home directory of the user account that you used. Therefore, under the BBB Debian distribution, if you connect as root you are placed in the /root directory.

To transfer a single file c:\temp\test.txt from the local desktop computer to the BBB you can use the following steps:

```
psftp: no hostname specified; use "open host.name" to connect
psftp> open root@192.168.7.2
Using username "root". Debian GNU/Linux 7
Remote working directory is /root
psftp> lcd c:\temp
New local directory is c:\temp
```

```
psftp> mkdir test
mkdir /root/test: OK
psftp> put test.txt
local:test.txt => remote:/root/test.txt
psftp> dir test.*
Listing directory /root
-rw-r--r--    1 root      root           6 May 15 04:17 test.txt
```

Commands that are prefixed with an l refer to commands issued for the local machine, e.g., lcd (local change directory) or lpwd (local print working directory). To transfer a single file, the put command is issued, which transfers the file from the local machine to the remote machine. The get command can be used to transfer a file in reverse. To "put" or "get" multiple files you can use the mput or mget commands. Use help if you have forgotten a command.

If you are using a Linux client machine, you can use the command sftp instead of psftp. Almost everything else remains the same. The sftp client application is also installed on the BBB distribution by default, so you can reverse the order of communication, that is having the BBB act as the client and another machine as the server.

Here are some useful hints and tips with the psftp/sftp commands:

- mget -r * will perform a recursive get of a directory. This is very useful if you wish to transfer a folder that has several subfolders. The -r option can also be used on get, put, and mput commands.

- dir *.txt will apply a filter to display only the .txt files in the current directory.

- mv can be used to move a file/directory on the remote machine to a new location on the remote machine.

- reget can be used to resume a download that was interrupted. The partially downloaded file must exist on the local machine.

- The psftp command can be issued as a single line or a local script at the command prompt. You could create a file test.scr that contains a set of psftp commands to be issued. You can then execute psftp from the command prompt, passing the password using -pw and the script file using -b (or -be to continue on error, or -bc to display commands as they are run), as follows:

```
c:\temp>more test.scr
lcd c:\temp\down
cd /tmp/down
mget *
quit
c:\temp>psftp root@192.168.7.2 -pw mypassword -b test.scr
Using username "root".
Remote working directory is /home/root...
```

Controlling the BeagleBone

At this point you should be able to communicate with the BBB using an SSH client application, so this section investigates the commands that you can issue to interact with the BBB.

Basic Linux Commands

When you first connect to the BBB with SSH you are prompted to log in. You can log in with username `root`, which does not require a password:

```
login as: root
Debian GNU/Linux 7
BeagleBoard.org BeagleBone Debian Image 2014-10-08
Support/FAQ: http://elinux.org/Beagleboard:BeagleBoneBlack_Debian
root@beaglebone:~#
```

You are now connected to the BBB, and the Linux terminal is ready for your command. The # prompt means that you are logged in to a superuser account (discussed in Chapter 3). For a new Linux user this step can be quite daunting, as it is not clear what arsenal of commands is at your disposal. This section provides you with sufficient Linux skills to get by. It is written as a reference with examples, so that you can come back to it when you need help.

First Steps

The first thing you might do is determine which version of Linux you are running. This can be useful when you are asking a question on a forum:

```
root@beaglebone:~# uname -a
Linux beaglebone 3.8.13-bone67 #1 SMP Wed Sep 24 21:30:03 UTC 2014 armv7l
GNU/Linux
```

In this case, Linux 3.8.13 is being used, which was built for the ARMv.7 architecture on the date that is listed.

The Linux kernel version is described by numbers in the form $X.Y.Z$. The X number changes only very rarely (version 2.0 was released in 1996 and 3.0 in 2011). The Y value changes rarely, every two years or so (3.8 was released in February 2013 and 3.13 in January 2014). The Z value changes regularly.

Next, you could use the `passwd` command to set a superuser account password:

```
root@beaglebone:~# passwd
Enter new UNIX password:
Retype new UNIX password:
passwd: password updated successfully
```

Table 2-4 lists other useful first step commands.

Table 2-4: Useful First Commands in Linux

COMMAND	DESCRIPTION
`more /etc/issue`	Returns the Linux distribution you are using
`ps -p $$`	Returns the shell you are currently using (e.g., bash)
`whoami`	Returns who you are currently logged in as
`uptime`	Returns how long the system has been running
`top`	Lists all of the processes and programs executing. Press Ctrl+C to close the view

Basic File System Commands

This section describes the basic commands that you will need in order to move around on, and manipulate, a Linux file system. When using Debian and Ubuntu user accounts, you often must prefix the word `sudo` at the start of certain commands. That is because `sudo` is a program that allows users to run programs with the security privileges of the superuser. User accounts are discussed in the next chapter. For the moment, the basic file system commands that you need are listed in Table 2-5.

Table 2-5: Basic File System Commands

NAME	COMMAND	OPTIONS AND FURTHER INFORMATION	EXAMPLE(S)
List files	`ls`	`-a` shows all (including hidden files) `-l` displays long format `-R` gives a recursive listing `-r` gives a reverse listing `-t` sorts last modified `-S` sorts by file size `-h` gives human readable file sizes	`ls -al`
Current directory	`pwd`	Print the working directory `-P` prints the physical location	`pwd -P`
Change directory	`cd`	Change directory `cd` then Enter or `cd ~/` takes you to the home directory `cd /` takes you to the file system root `cd ..` takes you up a level	`cd /home/root` `cd /`
Make a directory	`mkdir`	Make a directory	`mkdir test`
Delete a file or directory	`rm`	Delete a file `-r` recursive delete (use for directories) `-d` remove empty directories	`rm bad.txt` `rm -r test`

NAME	COMMAND	OPTIONS AND FURTHER INFORMATION	EXAMPLE(S)
Copy a file or directory	cp	-r recursive copy -u copy only if the source is newer than the destination or the destination is missing -v verbose copy (i.e., show output)	cp a.txt b.txt cp -r test testa
Move a file or directory	mv	-i prompts before overwrite No -r for directory. Moving to the same directory performs a renaming.	mv a.txt c.txt mv test testb
Create an empty file	touch	Create an empty file or update the modification date of an existing file.	touch d.txt
View content of a file	more	View the contents of a file. Use the Space key for the next page.	more d.txt
Get the calendar	cal	Display a text-based calendar.	cal 01 2015

That covers the basics but there is so much more!—the next chapter describes file ownership, permissions, searching, I/O redirection, and more. The aim of this section is to get you up and running. Table 2-6 describes a few shortcuts that make life easier when working with most Linux shells.

Table 2-6: Some Time-Saving Terminal Keyboard Shortcuts

SHORTCUT	DESCRIPTION
Up arrow (repeat)	Gives you the last command you typed, and then the previous commands on repeated presses
Tab key	Auto-completes the file name, the directory name, or even the executable command name. For example, to change to the Linux /tmp directory you can type cd /t and then press Tab, which will auto-complete the command to cd /tmp/. If there are many options, press the Tab key again to see all of the options as a list
Ctrl+A	Brings you back to the start of the line you are typing
Ctrl+E	Brings you to the end of the line you are typing
Ctrl+U	Clears to the start of the line. Ctrl+E and then Ctrl+U clears the line
Ctrl+L	Clears the screen
Ctrl+C	Kills whatever process is currently running
Ctrl+Z	Puts the current process into the background. Typing **bg** then leaves it running in the background, and **fg** then brings it back to the foreground. This is discussed under Linux Processes in the next chapter

Here is an example that uses several of the commands in Table 2-5 to create a directory called test in which an empty text file hello.txt is created. The entire test directory is then copied to the /tmp directory, which is off the root directory:

```
root@beaglebone:~# cd ~/
root@beaglebone:~# pwd
/root
root@beaglebone:~# mkdir test
root@beaglebone:~# cd test
root@beaglebone:~/test# touch hello.txt
root@beaglebone:~/test# ls
hello.txt
root@beaglebone:~/test# cd ..
root@beaglebone:~# cp -r test /tmp
root@beaglebone:~# cd /tmp/test/
root@beaglebone:/tmp/test# ls
hello.txt
```

WARNING   Linux assumes that you know what you are doing! It will gladly allow you to do a recursive deletion of your root directory when you are logged in as root (I won't list the command). *Think before you type when logged in as root!*

NOTE   Sometimes it is possible to recover files that are lost through accidental deletion if you use the extundelete command immediately after the deletion. Read the command manual page carefully, then use steps, such as:

```
molloyd@beaglebone:~/ $ sudo apt-get install extundelete
molloyd@beaglebone:~/ $ mkdir ~/undelete
molloyd@beaglebone:~/ $ cd ~/undelete/
molloyd@beaglebone:~/undelete$ sudo extundelete --restore-all
--restore-directory . /dev/mmcblk0p2
```

Environment Variables

Environment variables are named values that describe the configuration of your Linux environment, such as the location of the executable files or your default editor. To get an idea of the environment variables that are set on the BBB, issue an env call, which provides you with a list of the environment variables on your account. Here, env is called on the Debian BBB image:

```
root@beaglebone:~# env
TERM=xterm
SHELL=/bin/bash
SSH_CLIENT=192.168.7.1 18533 22
```

```
SSH_TTY=/dev/pts/3
USER=root
PATH=/usr/local/sbin:/usr/local/bin:/usr/sbin:/usr/bin:/sbin:/bin . . .
```

You can view and modify environment variables according to the following example, which adds the /root directory to the PATH environment variable:

```
root@beaglebone:~# echo $PATH
/usr/local/sbin:/usr/local/bin:/usr/sbin:/usr/bin:/sbin:/bin
root@beaglebone:~# export PATH=$PATH:/root
root@beaglebone:~# echo $PATH
/usr/local/sbin:/usr/local/bin:/usr/sbin:/usr/bin:/sbin:/bin:/root
```

This change will be lost on reboot. Permanently setting environment variables requires modifications to your .profile file when using sh, ksh, or bash shells, and to your .login file when using csh or tcsh shells. To do this, you need to be able to perform file editing in a Linux terminal window.

Basic File Editing

A variety of editors are available, but perhaps one of the easiest to use for new users is also one of the most powerful—the *GNU nano editor*. You can start up the editor by typing **nano** followed by the name of an existing or new filename; for example, typing **nano hello.txt** will display the view captured in Figure 2-7 (after the text has been entered!). Typing **nano -c hello.txt** will also display line numbers, which is very useful when debugging program code. You can move freely around the file in the window using the arrow keys and edit or write text at the cursor location. You can see some of the nano shortcut keys listed on the bottom bar of the editor window, but there are many more, some of which are presented in Table 2-7.

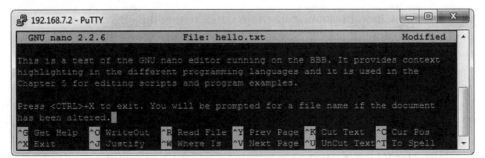

Figure 2-7: The GNU nano editor being used to edit an example file in a PuTTY Linux terminal window

Table 2-7: Nano Shortcut Keys—A Quick Reference

KEYS	COMMAND	KEYS	COMMAND
Ctrl+G	Help	Ctrl+Y	Previous page
Ctrl+C	Cancel	Ctrl+_ or Ctrl+/	Go to line number
Ctrl+X	Exit (prompts save)	Alt+/	Go to end of file
Ctrl+L	Enable long line wrapping	Ctrl+6	Start marking text (then move with arrows to highlight)
Ctrl+O	Save	Ctrl+K or Alt+6	Cut marked text
Arrows	Move around	Ctrl+U	Paste text
Ctrl+A	Go to start of line	Ctrl+R	Insert content of another file (prompts for location of file)
Ctrl+E	Go to end of line	Ctrl+W	Search for a string
Ctrl+Space	Next word	Alt+W	Find next
Alt+Space	Previous word	Ctrl+D	Delete character under cursor
Ctrl+V	Next page	Ctrl+K	Delete entire line

NOTE Ctrl+K appears to delete the entire line but it actually removes the line to a buffer, which can be pasted using Ctrl+U. This is a quick way of repeating multiple lines. Also, Mac users may have to set the meta key in the Terminal application to get the Alt functionality. Select Terminal ➤ Preferences ➤ Settings ➤ Keyboard, and choose Use option as meta key.

What Time Is It?

A simple question like this causes more difficulty than you can imagine. If you type `date` at the shell prompt, you may get the following:

```
root@beaglebone:~# date
Thu May 15 06:55:54 UTC 2014
```

which is many months out of date in this case, where the BBB connected to the desktop PC using an Internet-over-USB connection. However, it is likely that the date and time are correct if you are connected via "regular" Ethernet.

If it is wrong, why did the BBB team not set the clock time on your board? The answer is that they could not. Unlike a desktop PC, there is no battery backup on the BBB to ensure that the BIOS settings are retained—in fact, there is no BIOS! That topic will be examined in detail in the next chapter, but for the moment you need a way to set the time, and for that you can use the NTP (*Network Time Protocol*). The NTP is a networking protocol for synchronizing clocks between computers. If your BBB has the correct time, that is only because your BBB is obtaining it from your network.

One way to set the date and time is to find your closest NTP server pool by going to www.pool.ntp.org (the closest server to me is ie.pool.ntp.org for Ireland) and entering the following commands:

```
root@beaglebone:/etc/network# date
Thu May 15 07:28:21 UTC 2014
root@beaglebone:/etc/network# /usr/sbin/ntpdate -b -s -u ie.pool.ntp.org
root@beaglebone:/etc/network# date
Sun Oct 12 19:07:37 UTC 2014
```

The time is now correct, but that is only the case until you reboot. If this command failed (e.g., you received the message "Error resolving…"), then see the following feature on the "BeagleBone Internet-over-USB Settings."

BEAGLEBONE INTERNET-OVER-USB SETTINGS

If you are using Internet-over-USB, then the call to ntpdate likely failed, as you need to direct the IP traffic from your BBB through your desktop machine. You must first set up network connection sharing as detailed earlier in the "Internet-over-USB" section. Then, type the following in a BBB SSH terminal:

```
root@beaglebone:~# ping 8.8.8.8
connect: Network is unreachable
root@beaglebone:~# /sbin/route add default gw 192.168.7.1
root@beaglebone:~# ping 8.8.8.8
PING 8.8.8.8 (8.8.8.8) 56(84) bytes of data.
64 bytes from 8.8.8.8: icmp_req=2 ttl=51 time=13.0 ms ...
```

This change means that all traffic is being routed through your desktop computer to the Internet. If this step fails you should check your Internet-over-USB sharing settings (perhaps disable and re-enable sharing). You should now be able to resolve domain names too under Debian—for example:

```
root@beaglebone:~# ping www.google.com
PING www.google.com (74.125.138.106) 56(84) bytes of data.
64 bytes from www.google.com (74.125.138.106): icmp_req=2 ttl=51
time=13.0 ms ...
```

If the preceding step fails then you may need to update your nameserver as follows:

```
root@beaglebone:~# echo "nameserver 8.8.8.8" >> /etc/resolv.conf
```

This step should not be necessary if the resolv.conf file already contains nameserver entries. If you are still having problems, modify /etc/network/interfaces and add the following line to the file:

```
dns-nameservers 8.8.8.8
```

If you are still having difficulties, check whether your virus protection software is preventing ping calls and network connection sharing.

> All of the settings described above are lost on reboot. You can use nano to edit your .profile file (e.g., type nano ~/.profile) and add the following two lines to the end of your .profile file:
>
> ```
> /sbin/route add default gw 192.168.7.1
> /usr/sbin/ntpdate -b -s -u ie.pool.ntp.org
> ```
>
> This addition will slow down the login process. Alternatively, you can use a script such as the internetOverUSB script that is in the /chp02 directory of the GitHub repository. It must be executed using the sudo command. The latter approach is preferable if you are switching between "regular" Ethernet and Internet-over-USB.

After you set the time, you can set your time zone. Use the following command, which provides a text-based user interface that allows you to choose your location. The BBB is set for Irish Standard Time (IST) in this example:

```
root@beaglebone:~# dpkg-reconfigure tzdata
root@beaglebone:~# date
Mon Oct 13 00:16:47 IST 2014
```

Package Management

At the beginning of this chapter, a good package manager was listed as a key feature of a suitable Linux distribution. A *package manager* is a set of software tools that automate the process of installing, configuring, upgrading, and removing software packages from the Linux operating system. Different Linux distributions use different package managers: Ångström uses *OPKG*, Ubuntu and Debian use *APT* (Advanced Packaging Tool) over *DPKG* (Debian Package Management System), and Arch Linux uses *Pacman*. Each has its own usage syntax, but their operation is largely similar. For example, the first row in Table 2-8 lists the command for installing a package using different managers. The table also lists other package management commands that can be used.

Wavemon is a useful tool that you can use in configuring Wi-Fi connections (see Chapter 10). If you execute the command you will see that the package is not installed:

```
root@beaglebone:~# wavemon
-bash: wavemon: command not found
```

The platform-specific (Debian in this case) package manager can be used to install the package, once you determine the package name:

```
root@beaglebone:~# apt-cache search wavemon
wavemon - Wireless Device Monitoring Application
root@beaglebone:~# apt-get install wavemon
Reading package lists . . . Done . . .
Setting up wavemon (0.7.5-3) . . .
```

Table 2-8: Common Package Management Commands (Using Nano as an Example Package)

COMMAND	ÅNGSTRÖM	DEBIAN/UBUNTU
Install a package.	`opkg install nano`	`sudo apt-get install nano`
Update the package index.	`opkg update`	`sudo apt-get update`
Upgrade the packages on your system.*	`opkg upgrade`	`sudo apt-get upgrade`
Is nano installed?	`opkg list-installed |grep nano`	`dpkg-query -l |grep nano`
Is a package containing the string nano available?	`opkg list|grep nano`	`apt-cache search nano`
Get more information about a package.	`opkg info nano`	`apt-cache show nano` `apt-cache policy nano`
Get help.	`opkg`	`apt-get help`
Download a package to the current directory.	`opkg download nano`	`sudo apt-get download nano`
Remove a package.	`opkg remove nano`	`sudo apt-get remove nano`
Clean up old packages.	Nontrivial. Search for "opkg-clean script"	`sudo apt-get clean`

*It is not recommended that you do this. It can take quite some time to run (often several hours), and serious issues can arise if the BBB runs out of space during the upgrade.

The wavemon command now executes, but unfortunately it will not do anything until you configure a wireless adapter (see Chapter 10):

```
root@beaglebone:~# wavemon
wavemon: no supported wireless interfaces found
```

NOTE Sometimes package installations fail, perhaps because another required package is missing. There are *force options* available with the package commands to override checks. (e.g., `--force-yes` with the `apt-get` command). Try to avoid force options if possible, as having to use them is symptomatic of a different problem. Typing `sudo apt-get autoremove` can be very useful when packages fail to install.

Interacting with the BBB On-board LEDs

In this section you are going to examine how you can change the behavior of the BBB on-board user LEDs—the four blue LEDs in the top corner of the board. Each LED provides information about the BBB's state:

- USR0 flashes in a heartbeat sequence, indicating the BBB is alive.
- USR1 flashes during micro-SD card activity.

■ USR2 flashes depending on the level of CPU activity.

■ USR3 flashes during eMMC activity.

You can change the behavior of these LEDs to suit your own needs, but you will temporarily lose this useful activity information.

Sysfs is a virtual file system that is available under recent Linux kernels. It provides you with access to devices and drivers that would otherwise only be accessible within a restricted kernel space. This topic is discussed in detail in Chapter 6; however, at this point it would be useful to briefly explore the mechanics of how sysfs can be used to alter the behavior of the user LEDs.

Using your SSH client, you can connect to the BBB and browse to the directory /sys/class/leds. The output is as follows:

```
root@beaglebone:~# cd /sys/class/leds
root@beaglebone:/sys/class/leds# ls
beaglebone:green:usr0  beaglebone:green:usr2
beaglebone:green:usr1  beaglebone:green:usr3
```

NOTE Sysfs directory locations can vary somewhat under different versions of the Linux kernel. Please check the web page associated with this chapter if the preceding directory is not present on your Linux kernel.

You can see the four (green!) LED sysfs mappings—usr0, usr1, usr2, and usr3. You can change the directory to alter the properties of one of these LEDs—for example, usr3 (use the Tab key to reduce typing):

```
root@beaglebone:/sys/class/leds# cd beaglebone\:green\:usr3
root@beaglebone:/sys/class/leds/beaglebone:green:usr3# ls
brightness  device  max_brightness  power  subsystem  trigger  uevent
```

Here you see various different file entries that give you further information and access to settings. Please note that this section uses some commands that are explained in detail in the next chapter.

You can determine the current status of an LED by typing:

```
root@beaglebone:/sys/class/leds/beaglebone:green:usr3# cat trigger
none nand-disk mmc0 [mmc1] timer oneshot heartbeat backlight gpio cpu0 ...
```

where you can see that the USR3 LED is configured to show activity on the mmc1 device—the eMMC. You can turn this trigger off by typing:

```
root@beaglebone:/sys/class/leds/beaglebone:green:usr3# echo none > trigger
```

and you will see that the LED stops flashing completely. You can use more trigger to see the new state. Now that the LED trigger is off, you can turn the USR3 LED fully on or off using:

```
root@beaglebone:/sys/class/leds/beaglebone:green:usr3# echo 1 > brightness
root@beaglebone:/sys/class/leds/beaglebone:green:usr3# echo 0 > brightness
```

You can even set the LED to flash at a time interval of your choosing. If you watch carefully you will notice the dynamic nature of sysfs. If you perform an `ls` command at this point, the directory will appear as follows, but will shortly change:

```
root@beaglebone:/sys/class/leds/beaglebone:green:usr3# ls
brightness  device  max_brightness  power  subsystem  trigger  uevent
```

To make the LED flash you need to set the trigger to timer mode by typing `echo timer > trigger`. You will see the USR3 LED flash at a one-second interval. Notice that there are new `delay_on` and `delay_off` file entries in the `beaglebone:green:usr3` directory, as follows:

```
root@beaglebone:/sys/class/leds/beaglebone:green:usr3# echo timer > trigger
root@beaglebone:/sys/class/leds/beaglebone:green:usr3# ls
brightness  delay_on  max_brightness  subsystem  uevent
delay_off   device    power           trigger
```

The LED flash timer makes use of these new `delay_on` time and `delay_off` time file entries. You can find out more information about these values by using the concatenate (catenate) command, for example:

```
root@beaglebone:/sys/class/leds/beaglebone:green:usr3# cat delay_on
500
```

which reports the time delay in milliseconds. To make the USR3 LED flash at 10Hz (i.e., on for 50ms and off for 50ms) you can use:

```
root@beaglebone:/sys/class/leds/beaglebone:green:usr3# echo 50 > delay_on
root@beaglebone:/sys/class/leds/beaglebone:green:usr3# echo 50 > delay_off
```

Typing `echo mmc1 > trigger` returns the LED to its default state, which results in the `delay_on` and `delay_off` file entries disappearing.

Shutdown

WARNING   Physically disconnecting the power without allowing the kernel to unmount the eMMC or the SD card can cause corruption of your file system. The power management chip also needs to be informed of a shutdown.

One final issue to discuss in this section is the correct shutdown procedure for your BBB, as improper shutdown can potentially corrupt the ext4 file system and/or lead to increased boot times due to file system checks. Here are some important points on shutting down, rebooting, and starting the BBB:

■ Typing `shutdown -h now` shuts down the board correctly. You can delay this by five minutes by typing `shutdown -h +5`.

- Typing `reboot` will reset and reboot the board correctly.

- You can press the power button (see Figure 1-4) once to "soft" (as in software) shutdown the board correctly.

- Holding the power button for approximately eight seconds performs a hard system power down. This should be avoided unless the board is frozen and will not soft shutdown.

- Press the power button to start the board. Try to avoid physically disconnecting and reconnecting the power jack or USB lead.

If your project design is enclosed and you need an external soft power down, it is possible to wire an external button to a BBB GPIO input and write a shell script that runs on startup to poll the GPIO for an input. If that input occurs, then `/sbin/shutdown -h now` can be called directly.

Node.js, Cloud9, and BoneScript

The BBB Linux distribution comes complete with a set of technologies that you can use to quickly get started with developing software and hardware applications on the BBB. These are called Node.js, Cloud9, and BoneScript—*Node.js* is a programming language, *Cloud9* is a software development environment in which you can write Node.js code, and *BoneScript* is a library of code for Node.js that allows you to interact with BBB hardware.

Introduction to Node.js

Node.js is a platform for building network applications that uses the same JavaScript engine as the Google Chrome web browser. JavaScript is the programming language that is often used to create interactive interfaces within web pages. Simply put, Node.js is JavaScript on the server side. Its runtime environment and library of code enables you to run JavaScript code applications, without a browser, directly at the Linux shell prompt.

Node.js uses an event-driven, nonblocking input/output model. Event-driven programming is commonplace in user-interface programming. It essentially means that the program's flow of execution is driven by user actions or messages that are transferred from other threads or processes. Interestingly, the fact that it uses nonblocking I/O means that it is suitable for interfacing to the input/output pins on your BBB, safely sharing resources with other applications. As with all new languages, you should start with a "Hello World" example. Listing 2-1 sends the string "Hello World!" to the standard output, which is typically a Linux terminal.

LISTING 2-1: /chp02/HelloWorld.js

```
console.log("Hello World!");
```

Open an SSH connection to the BBB, create a directory to contain the
`HelloWorld.js` file, and then enter the code from Listing 2-1 using nano:

```
root@beaglebone:~# cd ~/
root@beaglebone:~# mkdir nodeTest
root@beaglebone:~# cd nodeTest
root@beaglebone:~/nodeTest# nano HelloWorld.js
```

To execute this code, type **node HelloWorld.js** in the directory containing
the JavaScript file. You should see the following output:

```
root@beaglebone:~/nodeTest# ls
HelloWorld.js
root@beaglebone:~/nodeTest# node HelloWorld.js
Hello World!
```

which should give you an idea of how you can write Node.js programs for the
BBB. The call to the `node` command works because the Node.js runtime environment is preinstalled on the BBB Linux image.

A more complex Node.js example is provided in Listing 2-2. It creates a web
server that runs on the BBB at port 5050 and serves a simple "Hello World"
message. Write the program code in the same `/nodeTest` directory:

LISTING 2-2: /chp02/SimpleWebServer.js

```
// A Simple Example Node.js Webserver Running on Port 5050
var http = require('http');  // require the http module
var server = http.createServer(
    function(req,res) {
        res.writeHead(200, {'Content-Type': 'text/plain'});
        res.end('Hello from the BeagleBone Black!\n');
    });
server.listen(5050);
console.log('BBB Web Server running at http://192.168.7.2:5050/');
```

The example code in Listing 2-2 begins by requiring the Node.js `http` module. It then calls the `http.createServer()` method, which returns an `http.
Server` object. The `server.listen()` method is called on the `http.Server`
object, where it causes the server to accept connections on a defined port
number (i.e., 5050). This method is asynchronous, meaning it does not have
to finish before the `console.log()` method is called on the next line. In fact,
unless you kill the process on the BBB, the `server.listen()` method will
listen forever. When a connection is made to port 5050, the server will call
the listening function, `function(req,res)`, to which is passed a copy of the
HTTP request and response references. In this case, the function responds
with a short plaintext message.

To execute this program you type `node SimpleWebServer.js` in the directory containing the source code file, and you should get the following:

```
root@beaglebone:~/nodeTest# ls
HelloWorld.js  SimpleWebServer.js
root@beaglebone:~/nodeTest# node SimpleWebServer.js
BBB Web Server running at http://192.168.7.2:5050/
```

where the output indicates that the server is running and listening on port 5050. You can then open a web browser and connect to this simple Node.js web server, where you will see the output as shown in Figure 2-8. You can use Ctrl+C to kill the web server in the SSH window.

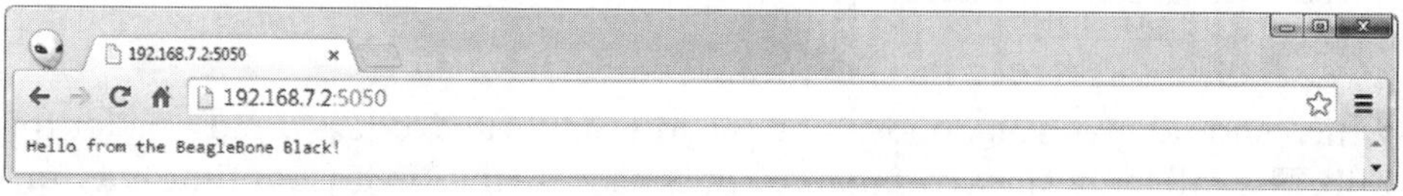

Figure 2-8: Connecting to the Node.js web server

Introduction to the Cloud9 IDE

Wouldn't it be great if there were a way to integrate the development of Node.js code with the execution environment? That is where the Cloud9 IDE is very useful. The Cloud9 integrated development environment (IDE) is an impressive web-based coding platform that supports many different programming languages, including JavaScript and Node.js. It enables you to write, run, and debug code directly within your web browser without installing any operating-system-specific tools or applications. If that is not impressive enough, the Cloud9 service has a low enough overhead to run directly on the BBB, and it comes preinstalled on the BBB Linux images.

To use the Cloud9 IDE, open Google Chrome or Firefox and connect to your BBB address on port 3000. For example, open `192.168.7.2:3000` using the address bar as shown in Figure 2-9. When you first open Cloud9 it provides an excellent introduction to the user interface and controls.

Rather than having to write the code on your desktop machine and transfer it to your BBB, the Cloud9 interface can save files directly on your BBB file system and can even execute them too. In Figure 2-9, a new .js file is created, which contains the code in Listing 2-2. *You must save the file using File ➤ Save.* You can click the Run button to execute the application. If the Debugger window appears, click Resume. You can click the hyperlink in the output console and the application output will be visible in the browser window that appears, as in Figure 2-9.

Remember that this `SimpleWebServer.js` program is running on the BBB itself. In fact, if you SSH into the BBB (or use the Cloud9 bash terminal window) and execute the following command (described in Chapter 3), you can see that the application process is running as follows:

```
root@beaglebone:~# ps aux|grep SimpleWebServer
root 4186 0.3 2.2 ... node .../var/lib/cloud9/EBB/SimpleWebServer.js
```

Clicking the Stop button in the Cloud9 IDE will kill this process.

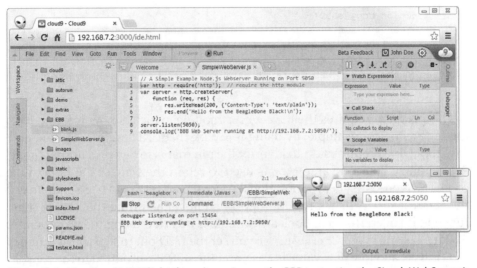

Figure 2-9: The Cloud9 IDE (light theme) running on the BBB, executing the SimpleWebServer.js example

NOTE The Cloud9 bash terminal window is a great alternative to PuTTY or the Chrome SSH App for opening a SSH session. The bash terminal is automatically logged in as root. Be careful of this fact if you are on an insecure network or are opening port 3000 on the BBB to the Internet.

Introduction to BoneScript

BoneScript is a library of BBB-specific functionality that has been written for Node.js by BeagleBoard.org co-founder Jason Kridner. The BoneScript library provides the type of input/output functionality that would be familiar to Arduino users, but with the advantage that it sits on top of the network capabilities of Node.js running on the BBB. There are detailed descriptions of BoneScript and its functionality at `tiny.cc/ebb205`.

You can use BoneScript to build a simple application to change the state of one of the system LEDs. The code in Listing 2-3 flashes the BBB on-board USR3 LED, once every second, by utilizing the BoneScript library.

LISTING 2-3: /chp02/BlinkLED3.js

```
var b = require('bonescript');  // using BoneScript
var LED3Pin = "USR3";           // USR3 is D5 on the BBB

b.pinMode(LED3Pin, b.OUTPUT);   // set up LED3Pin as an output
var isOn = false;               // isOn will be a Boolean flag
setInterval(toggleLED, 500);    // each half second call toggleLED()

function toggleLED(){
   isOn = !isOn;                       // invert the isOn state on each call
   if (isOn) b.digitalWrite(LED3Pin, 1);  // light the LED
   else b.digitalWrite(LED3Pin, 0);       // turn off the LED
   console.log('LED On is: ' + isOn);     // output the state
}
```

This program requires the `bonescript` module, which is now referred to in the code as `b`—for example, by using `b.someMethod()`. Therefore, `b.pinMode()` uses the string literal `"USR3"` to identify the pin that is to be set to output mode. A temporary Boolean value `isOn` is used to retain the state of the LED in the code. The Node.js asynchronous global function `setInterval()` is set up to call the `toggleLED()` callback function every 500ms. Each time the `toggleLED()` function is called the `isOn` Boolean variable is inverted using the NOT operator (i.e., `!true=false` and `!false=true`); you set the LED pin to high if the value of `isOn` is true, and low if its value is false; and the state is outputted to the console.

This program can be executed directly within the Cloud9 IDE. However, it is important to remember that you can still run programs that include the BoneScript library calls directly at the Linux console. Therefore, for example, if you transfer the `BlinkLED3.js` code to the BBB and execute it directly, it will also work perfectly, flashing the USR3 LED once per second:

```
root@beaglebone:~/nodeTest# node BlinkLED3.js
LED On is: true
LED On is: false . . .
```

BoneScript is very useful for the rapid prototyping of systems, particularly when those systems involve electronics that are to be connected to the Internet. However, it is not ideal for high-performance large-scale applications—alternative languages and approaches are described throughout this book for such applications.

Summary

After completing this chapter, you should be able to do the following:

▪ Communicate with the BBB from your desktop computer using network connections such as Internet-over-USB and regular Ethernet.

- Communicate with the BBB using fallback serial connections such as Serial-over-USB or by using a custom USB-to-TTL 3.3V cable.
- Interact with and control the BBB using simple Linux commands.
- Perform basic file editing using a Linux terminal.
- Manage Linux packages and set the system time.
- Use Linux sysfs to affect the state of BBB hardware.
- Safely shut down and reboot the BBB.
- Use Node.js, Cloud9, and BoneScript to write basic applications and code that interacts with BBB hardware.

Further Reading

There are many links to websites and documents provided throughout this chapter. The following additional links provide further information on the topics covered:

- The chapter web page includes a video on getting started with Internet-over-USB and burning a new image to the SD card: `www.exploringbeaglebone.com/chapter2/`
- Node.js API documentation: `nodejs.org/api/`
- BoneScript library guide: `tiny.cc/ebb205`

# CHAPTER 3

Exploring Embedded Linux Systems

This chapter exposes you to the core concepts, commands, and tools required to effectively manage embedded Linux systems. The first part of the chapter is descriptive—it explains the basics of embedded Linux and of the Linux boot process. After that, content on how to manage Linux systems is structured so that you can perform the steps yourself. You are strongly encouraged to open a terminal connection to your BeagleBone and follow along. Later in the chapter, the Git source code management system is described. It is an important topic, as the source code examples in this book are distributed via GitHub. Desktop virtualization is also described, as it is very useful for cross-platform development in later chapters. The chapter finishes by describing how you can download the source code examples for this book.

Equipment Required for This Chapter:

- BeagleBone Black with a terminal connection (see Chapter 2)

Further details on this chapter are available at: `www.exploringbeaglebone` `.com/chapter3/`

Embedded Linux Basics

First things first: There is no such thing as embedded Linux! There is no special version of the Linux kernel for embedded systems; it is just the mainline Linux kernel running on an embedded system. That said, the term *embedded Linux* has broad and common use; therefore, it will be used here rather than a more correct term, such as "Linux on an embedded system."

The word *embedded* in the term *embedded Linux* is used to convey the presence of an *embedded system*, a concept that can be loosely explained as some type of computing hardware with integrated software that was designed for a specific application. That contrasts somewhat with the personal computer (PC), which is a general-purpose device that is used for many applications, such as web browsing, word processing, and playing games. The line is blurring between embedded systems and general-purpose computing devices—the BBB can be both! However, here are some general characteristics of embedded systems:

- They tend to have specific and dedicated applications.
- Processing power, memory availability and storage capabilities are often limited.
- They are generally part of a larger system that may be linked to external sensors or actuators.
- They often have a role for which reliability is critical (e.g., controls in cars, airplanes, and medical equipment).
- In many cases they work in real time, where their outputs are directly related to current inputs (e.g., control systems).

Embedded systems are present everywhere in everyday life. Examples include vending machines, kitchen appliances, phones/smartphones, manufacturing/assembly lines, TVs, games consoles, cars (e.g., power steering, security, engine management, tire pressure, reversing sensors), network switches, routers, wireless access points, sound systems, medical monitoring equipment, printers, building access controls, parking meters, smart energy/water meters, watches, building tools, digital cameras, monitors, tablets, e-readers, anything robotic, smart card payment/access systems, and many, many more.

In recent years, there has been a huge proliferation of embedded Linux devices in everyday life, thanks in part to the rapid evolution of smartphone technology, which has helped drive down the unit price of ARM-based processors. ARM Holdings plc is a UK company that licenses the intellectual property of its processor design; it does not manufacture chips. ARM Holdings licenses its CPU model for a royalty of about 1–2% of the price of the processor, meaning that if Texas Instruments (TI) sells its AM3358 (the processor on the BBB) for $5, then they only have to pay a royalty fee of between five and ten cents on each processor sold. Despite what appears to be a low unit price, ARM Holdings earned $1.1 billion in 2013, as their partners shipped 10 billion ARM core chips in that period (ARM Holdings, 2014).

What Embedded Linux Offers

There are many embedded platform types, each with its own advantages and disadvantages. They range from low-cost embedded platforms, with volume prices of less than $1, such as the (8/16-bit) Atmel AVR, Microchip PIC, and TI Stellaris, to high-cost specialized platforms, such as TI 32-bit multicore DSPs that can cost up to $160. These platforms are typically programmed in C and/or assembly language, requiring that you have knowledge of the underlying systems architecture before you can develop useful applications. Embedded Linux offers an alternative to these platforms, in that significant knowledge of the underlying architecture is not required in order to start building applications. However, if you wish to interface to electronic modules or components, then that knowledge will be required. Here are some of the reasons why embedded Linux has seen such growth:

- Linux is an efficient and scalable OS, running on low-cost consumer-oriented devices to expensive large-scale servers. It has evolved over many years, from when computers were far less powerful than today, but it has retained many of the efficiencies.

- A huge number of open-source programs and tools have already been developed that can be readily deployed in an embedded application. If you need a web server for your embedded application, you can install the same one that you might use on a Linux server.

- There is excellent open-source support for many different peripherals and devices, from network adapters to displays.

- It is open-source and does not require a fee for its use.

- The kernel and application code is running worldwide on so many devices that bugs are infrequent and are detected very quickly.

One downside of embedded Linux is that it is not ideal for real-time applications due to the OS overhead. Therefore, for high-precision, fast-response applications, embedded Linux may not be the perfect solution. However, even in real-time applications, it is often used as the "central intelligence" and control interface for a network array of dedicated real-time sensors. In addition, there are developments underway in *real-time operating system* (RTOS) Linux that aim to use Linux in a preemptive way, interrupting the OS whenever required to maintain a real-time process. This is discussed in detail in Chapter 13.

Is Linux Open Source and Free?

Linux is released under the *GNU GPL* (General Public License), which grants users the freedom to use and modify its code in any way—so, "free" generally refers to "freedom," rather than "without cost." In fact, some of the most expensive Linux distributions are those for embedded architectures. There is a quick guide to the GPLv3 at www.gnu.org that lists the four freedoms that every user should have (Smith, 2013):

The freedom to use the software for any purpose;

The freedom to change the software to suit your needs;

The freedom to share the software with your friends and neighbors; and,

The freedom to share the changes you make.

Even if you are using a distribution that you downloaded "for free," it can cost you significant effort to tailor libraries and device drivers to suit the particular components and modules that you want to use in your product development.

Booting the BeagleBone

The first thing you should see when you boot a desktop computer is the *Unified Extensible Firmware Interface (UEFI)*, which provides legacy support for *BIOS* (Basic Input/Output System) services. The boot screen displays system information and invites you to press a key to alter these settings. UEFI tests the hardware components, such as the memory, and then loads the OS, typically from the SSD/hard drive. Therefore, when a desktop computer is powered on, the UEFI/BIOS performs the following steps:

- Takes control of the computer's processor
- Initializes and tests the hardware components
- Loads the OS off the SSD/hard drive

The UEFI/BIOS provides an abstraction layer for the OS to interact with the display and other input/output peripherals, such as the mouse/keyboard and storage devices. Its settings are stored in NAND flash and battery-backed memory—you can see a small coin battery on the PC motherboard that maintains the memory state and supports a real-time system clock.

The BeagleBone Bootloaders

Like most embedded Linux devices, the BBB does not have a BIOS or battery-backed memory; instead, it uses a combination of *bootloaders*. A bootloader is a very small (typically less than 128KB) program that loads the OS; however, the bootloader described here is a custom program that is tailored for each and every embedded Linux board, including the BBB.

Building a BBB-specific bootloader is an advanced topic that requires you to have a cross-compiler toolchain installed on your desktop computer. That topic is examined in Chapter 7; however, the key steps are as follows:

1. The primary Linux bootloader that is used on the BBB is called *Das U-Boot* (Universal Bootloader). The source code for *U-Boot* is downloaded (`git.denx.de/u-boot/`).

2. The source code for U-Boot is modified using patches that have been written specifically for the BBB (`tiny.cc/ebb301`).

3. The BBB-specific bootloader is then compiled to a binary file.

4. A `uEnv.txt` boot configuration text file is written that can be used to pass parameters to the Linux kernel (`tiny.cc/ebb302`)

These steps create three important files: `u-boot.img` (~360KB), `MLO` (~100KB), and `uEnv.txt` (<1KB). If these filenames seem familiar, it is because you saw them on the VFAT partition of your BBB the first time you plugged it in. Importantly, the `u-boot.img` and x-loader `MLO` files were built using a patched version of the standard U-Boot distribution that was built *with full knowledge of the hardware description of the BBB*. These `MLO`, `u-boot.img`, and `uEnv.txt` files are vital to your BBB booting. The `uEnv.txt` file sets the boot parameters for your BBB. By default, it contains information such as the console baud rate, cape options, HDMI options, etc.

> **WARNING**   The `uEnv.txt` file is visible on the file system that appears when Windows Autoplay runs. Do not edit `uEnv.txt` using Microsoft WordPad. This file requires Unix newline support. If you must edit `uEnv.txt` in Windows, install Notepad++ or a similar tool. Please be aware that changing `uEnv.txt` can prevent your board from booting, so edits should only be performed when you are sure that they are necessary.

The bootloaders perform the following critical functions, as illustrated in Figure 3-1, by linking the specific hardware of your board to the Linux OS:

- They initialize the controllers (memory, graphics, I/O).
- They prepare and allocate the system memory for the OS.
- They locate the OS and provide the facility for loading it.
- They load the OS and pass control to it.

Here is a typical boot sequence that was captured by using the *USB to 3V3 TTL serial cable* that is introduced in Chapter 1. The cable was attached to the BBB J1 Header (black side to the white dot) and the terminal was used to capture the boot sequence output:

```
U-Boot 2013.10-00016-g6adb529 (Feb 06 2014 - 14:54:24)
I2C:   ready
DRAM:  512 MiB
Net:   <ethaddr> not set. Validating first E-fuse MAC cpsw, usb_ether
Hit any key to stop autoboot:  0
gpio: pin 53 (gpio 53) value is 1
mmc0(part 0) is current device
```

```
mmc1(part 0) is current device
gpio: pin 54 (gpio 54) value is 1
SD/MMC found on device 1
reading uEnv.txt  ...
reading /dtbs/am335x-boneblack.dtb
24884 bytes read in 10 ms (2.4 MiB/s)
Kernel image @ 0x80300000 [ 0x000000 - 0x389fe8 ]
## Flattened Device Tree blob at 815f0000
   Booting using the fdt blob at 0x815f0000
   Using Device Tree in place at 815f0000, end 815f9133
Starting kernel ...
Uncompressing Linux... done, booting the kernel.
[    0.378480] omap2_mbox_probe: platform not supported
[    0.545287] tps65217-bl tps65217-bl: no platform data provided
[    0.608723] bone-capemgr bone_capemgr.9: slot #0: No cape found
...
Debian GNU/Linux 7 beaglebone ttyO0
default username:password is [debian:temppwd]
The IP Address for usb0 is: 192.168.7.2
beaglebone login:
```

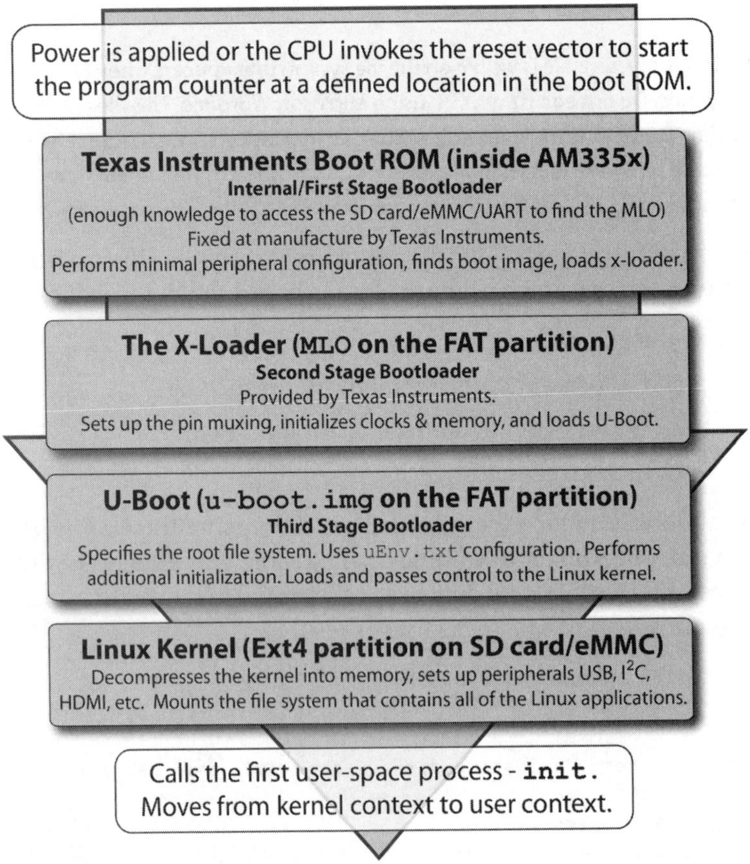

Power is applied or the CPU invokes the reset vector to start the program counter at a defined location in the boot ROM.

Texas Instruments Boot ROM (inside AM335x)
Internal/First Stage Bootloader
(enough knowledge to access the SD card/eMMC/UART to find the MLO)
Fixed at manufacture by Texas Instruments.
Performs minimal peripheral configuration, finds boot image, loads x-loader.

The X-Loader (MLO on the FAT partition)
Second Stage Bootloader
Provided by Texas Instruments.
Sets up the pin muxing, initializes clocks & memory, and loads U-Boot.

U-Boot (u-boot.img on the FAT partition)
Third Stage Bootloader
Specifies the root file system. Uses uEnv.txt configuration. Performs
additional initialization. Loads and passes control to the Linux kernel.

Linux Kernel (Ext4 partition on SD card/eMMC)
Decompresses the kernel into memory, sets up peripherals USB, I²C,
HDMI, etc. Mounts the file system that contains all of the Linux applications.

Calls the first user-space process - init.
Moves from kernel context to user context.

Figure 3-1: The full boot sequence on the BBB

You can see that the initial hardware state is set, but most messages will seem quite mysterious for the moment. There are some important points to note:

- After the SD card/eMMC is found, the uEnv.txt file is read.
- The uenvcmd from your uEnv.txt file is executed.
- The file /dtbs/am335x-boneblack.dtb is read in. This file contains the BBB's compiled device tree description, which is discussed shortly. After this description is read in, the flattened device tree blob is placed in memory at the address 0x815f0000.
- The kernel is decompressed and booted.
- The *Bone Cape Manager* is the management system for the pluggable BBB capes, which are described in Chapter 1.

READING MEMORY VALUES DIRECTLY (ADVANCED)

On some ARM devices you can configure the MAC address dynamically using uEnv.txt; however, page 4,708 of the *AM335x ARM Technical Reference Manual (TRM)* states that the "Device uses EFUSE registers mac_id0_lo and mac_id0_hi in the control module for the Ethernet MAC address of the device" (Texas Instruments, 2013). These values are stored in AM335x ROM and cannot be changed. The mac_id0_lo is at offset 630h from 0x44e10000 (see pg. 1,145) and mac_id0_hi is at offset 634h (see pg. 1,146). You can see these memory addresses using a small program called devmem2 that can be downloaded, built, and run as follows:

```
root@beaglebone:/# cd ~/
root@beaglebone:~# wget http://www.lartmaker.nl/lartware/port/devmem2.c
root@beaglebone:~# gcc devmem2.c -o devmem2
root@beaglebone:~# ./devmem2 0x44e10630
Value at address 0x44E10630 (0xb6fd1630): 0xBF1F
root@beaglebone:~# ./devmem2 0x44e10634
Value at address 0x44E10634 (0xb6fd8634): 0xAF30A0C8
root@beaglebone:~# ifconfig eth0
eth0      Link encap:Ethernet  HWaddr c8:a0:30:af:1f:bf
```

The IP address matches the memory values, but in reverse order. Your BBB needs to be connected to the Internet for these steps to work correctly.

Das U-Boot uses a board configuration file called a *device tree* (also called a *device tree binary*) containing the board-specific information that the kernel requires to boot the BBB. This file contains all the information needed to describe the memory size, clock speeds, on-board devices, and so on. This device tree binary or DTB (the binary) is created from a DTS (the source) file using the *Device Tree Compiler (dtc)*. This topic is described in detail in Chapter 6, when examining how to interface to the BBB's GPIOs.

The DTS has the same syntax as the following extract, which details the four user LED pins and one of the two I²C buses on the BBB:

```
am33xx_pinmux: pinmux@44e10800 {
    pinctrl-names = "default";
    pinctrl-0 = <&userled_pins>;

    userled_pins: pinmux_userled_pins {
        pinctrl-single,pins = <
            0x54 0x07        /* gpmc_a5.gpio1_21, OUTPUT | MODE7 */
            0x58 0x17        /* gpmc_a6.gpio1_22, OUTPUT_PULLUP | MODE7 */
            0x5c 0x07        /* gpmc_a7.gpio1_23, OUTPUT | MODE7 */
            0x60 0x17        /* gpmc_a8.gpio1_24, OUTPUT_PULLUP | MODE7 */
        >;
    };
    i2c0_pins: pinmux_i2c0_pins {
        pinctrl-single,pins = <
            0x188 0x70       /* i2c0_sda, SLEWCTRL_SLOW | INPUT_PULLUP */
            0x18c 0x70       /* i2c0_scl, SLEWCTRL_SLOW | INPUT_PULLUP */
        >;
    }; ...
};
```

The full description for the BBB device tree source for Linux 3.x.x is available with the source code distribution of this book in the Chapter 3 directory. You will see how to download this code at the end of the chapter. You can develop your own additions and modifications to the description using *device tree overlays (DTOs)*, which can be installed in the /lib/firmware directory of your BBB Linux distributions. This tree structure is discussed in detail in Chapter 6, when custom circuits are interfaced to the BBB.

Kernel Space and User Space

The Linux kernel runs in an area of system memory called the *kernel space*, and regular user applications run in an area of system memory called *user space*. There is a hard boundary between these two spaces, preventing user applications from accessing memory and resources that are required by the Linux kernel. This helps prevent the Linux kernel from crashing due to badly written user code, and also helps provide a degree of security.

The Linux kernel "owns" and has full access to all the physical memory and resources on the BBB. Therefore, you have to be careful that only the most stable and trusted code is permitted to run in kernel space. You can see the structure illustrated in Figure 3-2, where user applications use the *GNU C Library (glibc)* to make calls to the kernel's *system call interface*.

A *kernel module* is an object file that contains code, which can be loaded and unloaded from the kernel on demand. In many cases the kernel can even load

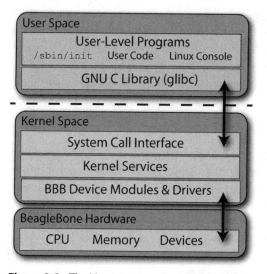

Figure 3-2: The Linux user space and kernel space

and unload modules while it is executing, without needing to reboot the BBB. For example, if you plug a USB Wi-Fi adapter into the BBB, it is possible for the kernel to use a *loadable kernel module* (*LKM*) to utilize the adapter when it boots up. You will first see how to interact with LKMs in Chapter 9, where Bluetooth on the BBB is discussed. Without this modular capability, the Linux kernel would be very large, as it would have to support every driver that would ever be needed on the BBB. You would also have to rebuild the kernel every time you wanted to add new hardware. The downside of LKMs is that driver files have to be maintained for each device.

The kernel services are then made available to the user space in a controlled way through the use of system calls. The kernel also prevents individual user-space applications from conflicting with each other.

As described in Figure 3-1, U-Boot passes control to the kernel after it has been decompressed into memory. The kernel then mounts the root file system (mmcroot and mmcrootfstype are defined in uEnv.txt) .The kernel's last step in the boot process is to call init (/sbin/init on the BBB), which is the first user-space process that is started, and the next topic to be discussed.

System V init (SysVinit)

Traditionally, the parent process that manages all systems and services for Linux is called *System V init* (and *systemd* under Debian). It is responsible for starting and stopping services (e.g., web server, SSH server) on the BBB, and it does so depending on the current state, or *runlevel*, which might be starting up, shutting down, and so on. The `init` process begins by reading the configuration file `/etc/inittab`, which defines details such as the default runlevel (Level 2 on the BBB) and what to do in single-user mode. *Single-user mode* is a stage during the boot process whereby exclusive access to all resources is required by the superuser account, for tasks such as checking the integrity of the file system using the `fsck` command. For example, single-user mode prevents other users from logging in and using the file system while it is being checked.

The *runlevel* defines the state of the BBB and controls which processes or services are started by the `init` system. For example, under Debian, which uses SystemV init, there are several runlevels, identified as 0–6 and S (see Table 3-1). When the `init` process begins, the runlevel starts at N (none). It then enters runlevel S to initialize the system in single-user mode, and finally enters one of the multi-user runlevels (2–5). On most distributions, runlevels 2 to 5 are identical copies, so that you can customize them for your needs. You can find the current runlevel by typing the following:

```
root@beaglebone:~# runlevel
N 5
root@beaglebone:~# who -r
         run-level 5  May 15 02:19
```

In this case, the BBB is currently running at runlevel 5. You can change the runlevel by typing `init` followed by the level number. For example, you can reboot your BBB by typing the following:

```
root@beaglebone:~# init 6
```

Table 3-1: Runlevels on the BBB Debian Distribution

LEVEL	DESCRIPTION	EXAMPLE USE
0	Halt the system	Shutdown scripts for all services
1	Single-user mode	For administrative functions such as checking the file system
2–5	Multi-user modes	Regular multi-user modes. Can be configured to have different meanings by the administrator account. All modes are the same by default on the BBB.
6	Reboot the system	Shutdown scripts for all services
S	Startup scripts	Single-user mode on boot. Do not change these links. Only for scripts such as keyboard setup that must run before root login.

If you go to the /etc directory you can see the rc directories that relate to the different runlevels:

```
root@beaglebone:/etc# ls -d rc*
rc.local    rc1.d/    rc3.d/    rc5.d/    rcS.d/
rc0.d/      rc2.d/    rc4.d/    rc6.d/    rcn-ee.conf
```

ls -d lists only directory entries (without listing their contents). The current runlevel is 5, so you can see what scripts are run at this level:

```
root@beaglebone:/etc# cd rc5.d
root@beaglebone:/etc/rc5.d# ls -al
...
lrwxrwxrwx 1 root root 17 Feb 18 22:56 S01rsyslog -> ../init.d/rsyslog
lrwxrwxrwx 1 root root 14 Feb 18 22:55 S01sudo -> ../init.d/sudo
lrwxrwxrwx 1 root root 17 Mar  1 14:21 S02apache2 -> ../init.d/apache2
```

The concept of symbolic links is discussed shortly, but for now just be aware that the entries in this directory are symbolic links to the related script in the /etc/init.d directory. The first letter S in the symbolic link name indicates that the linked service is to be started. If the first letter were K, it would indicate that the service should be stopped (killed). K scripts are always executed first (in numerical/alphabetical order), followed by the S scripts. Therefore, in the preceding listing, /init.d/sudo will be started before /init.d/apache2. It may be very important that one service starts before another, and this naming convention enables you to ensure that it does. You have seen that the /etc/rc5.d directory has symbolic links to the /etc/init.d directory. If you call ls in the init.d directory, you can see the scripts for many of the services on the BBB:

```
root@beaglebone:/etc/rc5.d# cd /etc/init.d
root@beaglebone:/etc/init.d# ls /etc/init.d
...
rsyslog              apache2              kmod
saned                avahi-daemon         lightdm ...
```

NOTE You can boot into single-user mode on the BBB by editing uEnv.txt and adding the word single at the end of the mmcargs line. This places the BBB in "rescue mode," which you might do for systems maintenance. Don't make such a change unless you are booting from the SD card or have access to a USB to 3V3 TTL cable, as you need to be able to reverse the change. Typing Ctrl+D at the console will return you to regular multi-user mode.

You can call the scripts in /etc/init.d manually. The Apache web server that is running on the Debian image of the BBB is used as an example. Note that it may be configured to run at port 8080, not the default port 80. Type **192.168.7.2:8080** into your browser address bar to load this website. You can find out the status of this service by typing the following:

```
root@beaglebone:~# service apache2 status
apache2.service - LSB: Start/stop apache2 web server
        Loaded: loaded (/etc/init.d/apache2)
        Active: active (running) since Wed, 19 Feb 2014 05:42:44 +0000;
       Process: 563 ExecStart=/etc/init.d/apache2 start (... SUCCESS)
        CGroup: name=systemd:/system/apache2.service
                    - 853 /usr/sbin/apache2 -k start
                    - 858 /usr/sbin/apache2 -k start
                    - 862 /usr/sbin/apache2 -k start
                    - 863 /usr/sbin/apache2 -k start
```

In this case, it is running as four processes, to handle simultaneous calls from multiple web browsers at the same time. You can manually control this service by typing (as root from any location) commands such as the following:

```
root@beaglebone:~# /etc/init.d/apache2 stop
[ ok ] Stopping apache2 (via systemctl): apache2.service.
root@beaglebone:~# /etc/init.d/apache2 start
[ ok ] Starting apache2 (via systemctl): apache2.service.
root@beaglebone:~# /etc/init.d/apache2 restart
[ ok ] Restarting apache2 (via systemctl): apache2.service.
```

Often, `reload` and `force-reload` service commands are also available in the scripts. If you type `more /etc/init.d/apache2`, you can view the source code for the `apache2` script. Approximately halfway through the script you will see code that looks like "`case $1 in start...`," which defines what happens when it is passed the word `start` from the user input. When the s symbolic link is created in the `rc2.d–rc5.d` directories, the `/etc/init.d/apache2` script will be called, just as if it were started manually. Similarly, when the κ symbolic link is created in the `rc0.d`, `rc1.d`, or `rc6.d` directories, a call will be made to the stop part of the script.

Finally, you can remove a script from starting on boot by using:

```
root@beaglebone:~# update-rc.d apache2 remove
update-rc.d: using dependency based boot sequencing
```

Or, conversely, add it according to its default settings:

```
root@beaglebone:~# update-rc.d apache2 defaults
update-rc.d: using dependency based boot sequencing
```

Over time, the init system is being replaced by the *systemd* system manage-ment daemon—a topic that is described in detail in Chapter 9. The next step is to look at the rest of the file system and the system administration commands that you need to fully interact with the BBB's Linux OS.

Managing Linux Systems

This section examines the Linux file system in more detail, building on the commands and tools that you read about in the last chapter, to ensure that you have full administrative control of the BBB. Please follow along with the steps in this discussion.

The Super User

On Linux systems, the system administrator account has the highest level of security access to all commands and files. Typically, this account is referred to as the *root account* or *superuser*. Under Debian and Ångström, this user account has the login name *root*. Therefore, when you logged in to your BBB for the first time using the `root` username in the last chapter, you were logged in as the superuser. The Ubuntu distribution encourages users not to log in as `root`—in fact, root login is not available by default; however, you can enable it by typing `sudo passwd root`.

It is recommended when performing general operations on a Linux system that you try to avoid being logged in as the superuser; however, it is important to also remember that when using the BBB, you are typically not running a server with thousands of user accounts! In many applications, a single root user account, with a non-default password, is likely sufficient. However, using a non-superuser account for your development work could protect you from yourself—for example, from accidentally deleting the file system.

Under many Linux distributions a special tool called *sudo* (*superuser do*) is used whenever you wish to perform system administration commands. The tool will prompt you for the administrator password and then authorize you to perform administrator operations for a short time period, also warning you that "with great power comes great responsibility." The next section discusses user accounts management, but if you create a new user account and wish to allow it to use the sudo tool, then the account name must be added to the *sudoers file*, `/etc/sudoers`, by using the *visudo* tool (type `visudo` while logged in as root). The BBB Debian distribution has the same sudo tool, but it allows root login by default. Sudo works very well; however, it can make the redirection of the output of a command more complex.

There is another command in Linux that allows you to run a shell with a substitute *u*ser: su. Typing `su -` (same as `su - root`) opens a new shell with full superuser access, and it can be used as follows (this may not make sense until you create user accounts, but it is here for reference):

```
molloyd@beaglebone:~$ whoami
molloyd
molloyd@beaglebone:~$ su -
```

```
root@beaglebone:/home/molloyd# whoami
root
root@beaglebone:/home/molloyd# exit
molloyd@beaglebone:~$ whoami
molloyd
```

To enable the `su` command under Ubuntu, you must enable root login as shown earlier in this section. To disable it again you can type `sudo passwd -l root`.

System Administration

The *Linux file system* is a hierarchy of directories that is used to organize files on a Linux system. This section examines the ownership of files, the use of symbolic links, and the concept of file system permissions.

The Linux File System

Linux uses data structures, called *inodes*, to represent file system objects such as files and directories. When a Linux *ext*ended file system (e.g., ext3/ext4) is created on a physical disk, an *inode table* is created. This table links to an inode data structure for each file and directory on that physical disk. The inode data structure for each file and directory stores information such as permission attributes; pointers to raw physical disk block locations; time stamps; and link counts. You can see this with an example by performing a listing `ls -ail` of the root directory, where `-i` causes `ls` to display the inode indexes. You will see the following for the `/tmp` directory entry:

```
root@beaglebone:/# cd /
root@beaglebone:/# ls -ail | grep tmp
63490 drwxrwxrwt   8 root root  4096 Feb 24 20:17 tmp
```

Therefore, 63490 is the `/tmp` directory's *inode index*. If you enter the `/tmp` directory by using `cd`, create a temporary file (`a.txt`), and perform `ls -ail`, you will see that the current (.) directory has the exact same inode index:

```
root@beaglebone:/# cd /tmp
root@beaglebone:/tmp# touch a.txt
root@beaglebone:/tmp# ls -ail
63490 drwxrwxrwt  5 root    root  4096 Feb 23 22:17 .
    2 drwxr-xr-x 22 root    root  4096 Feb 18 22:57 ..
73743 -rw-r--r--  1 root    root     0 Feb 23 20:15 a.txt
```

You can also see that the root directory (..) has the inode index of 2 and that a text file `a.txt` also has an inode index. You cannot `cd` directly to an inode index, as the inode index might not refer to a directory.

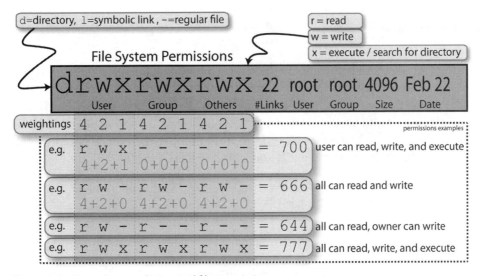

Figure 3-3: Linux directory listing and file permissions

Figure 3-3 illustrates several concepts in working with files under Linux. The first letter indicates the *file type*—for example, whether the listing is a (d) directory, (l) link, or (-) regular file. There are also some other obscure file types: (c) character special, (b) block special, (p) fifo, and (s) socket. Directories and regular files do not need further explanation, but links need special attention.

Linking to Files and Directories

There are two types of links in Linux: *soft links* and *hard links*. A soft link (or *symbolic link*) is a file that refers to the location of another file or directory. Hard links, conversely, link directly to the inode index, but they cannot be linked to a directory. You can create a link using `ln /path/to/file.txt linkname`. You create a symbolic link by adding `-s` to the call. To illustrate the usage, the following example creates a soft link and a hard link to a file `/tmp/test.txt`:

```
root@beaglebone:~# cd /tmp
root@beaglebone:/tmp# touch test.txt
root@beaglebone:/tmp# ln -s /tmp/test.txt softlink
root@beaglebone:/tmp# ln /tmp/test.txt hardlink
root@beaglebone:/tmp# ls -al
total 8
drwxrwxrwt  2 root root 4096 Feb 23 15:57 .
drwxr-xr-x 22 root root 4096 Feb 18 22:57 ..
```

```
-rw-r--r--  2 root root     0 Feb 23 15:57 hardlink
lrwxrwxrwx  1 root root    13 Feb 23 15:57 softlink -> /tmp/test.txt
-rw-r--r--  2 root root     0 Feb 23 15:57 test.txt
```

You can see there is a number 2 in front of the file test.txt (after the file permissions). This is the *number of hard links* that are associated with the file. This is a count value that was incremented by one when the hard link, called "hardlink," was created. If you were to delete the hard link (e.g., using **rm hardlink**) this counter would decrement back to 1. To illustrate the difference between soft links and hard links, some text is added to the test.txt file:

```
root@beaglebone:/tmp# echo "testing links" >> test.txt
root@beaglebone:/tmp# more hardlink
testing links
root@beaglebone:/tmp# more softlink
testing links
root@beaglebone:/tmp# mkdir subdirectory
root@beaglebone:/tmp# mv test.txt subdirectory/
root@beaglebone:/tmp# more hardlink
testing links
root@beaglebone:/tmp# more softlink
softlink: No such file or directory
```

You can see that when the test.txt file is moved to the subdirectory, the soft link breaks but the hard link still works perfectly. Therefore, symbolic links are not updated when the linked file is moved, but hard links always refer to the source, even if moved or removed. Just to illustrate the last point, the file test.txt can be removed using the following:

```
root@beaglebone:/tmp# rm subdirectory/test.txt
root@beaglebone:/tmp# more hardlink
testing links
```

Yet, it still exists! And it will not be deleted until you delete the hard link called "hardlink," decrementing the link count to 0. Therefore, if a file or directory has a hard link count of 0, and it is not being used by a process, it will be deleted. In effect, the filename itself, test.txt, was just a hard link. Please note that you cannot hard link across different file systems, as each file system will have its own inode index table that starts at 1. Therefore, inode 63490, which is the inode index of the /tmp directory, is likely describing something quite different on another file system. Type the command **man ln** to see a particularly useful guide on linking.

> **NOTE** You can type `history` to list all previous commands that you have typed. You can also use the keyboard combination Ctrl+R to get an interactive search of your history to find a recently used command. Pressing Enter will activate the command and pressing Tab will place it on your command line, so that it can be modified.

Users and Groups

Linux is a multi-user OS, which uses the following three distinct classes to manage access permissions:

- **User:** You can create different user accounts on your BBB. This is very useful if you wish to limit access to processes and areas of the file system. The `root` user account is the superuser of the BBB and has access to every file; so, for example, it may not be safe to run a public web server from this account if it supports local scripting.
- **Group:** User accounts may be flagged as belonging to one or more groups, whereby each group has different levels of access to different resources.
- **Others:** All users of the BBB.

You can create users at the Linux terminal. The full list of groups is available by typing **more /etc/group**. The following example demonstrates how you can create a new user account on the BBB and modify the properties of that account to suit your needs.

EXAMPLE: CREATING A NEW USER ACCOUNT ON THE BBB

This example demonstrates how you can create a user account and then retroactively change its properties, using the following steps:

1. The creation of a new user account called `molloyd` on the BBB
2. The retroactive addition of the account to the `users` group
3. The reset of the password for the new user account
4. Verification that the account is working correctly

Step 1: Create a user `molloyd` as follows:

```
root@beaglebone:~# adduser molloyd
Adding user 'molloyd' ...
Adding new group 'molloyd' (1001) ...
Adding new user 'molloyd' (1003) with group 'molloyd' ...
Creating home directory '/home/molloyd' ...
Copying files from '/etc/skel' ...
Enter new UNIX password:
Enter the new value, or press ENTER for the default
        Full Name []: Derek Molloy
Is the information correct? [Y/n] Y
Adding new user 'molloyd' to extra groups ...
```

Step 2: Retroactively add the user to another group as follows:

```
root@beaglebone:~# groupadd newgroup
root@beaglebone:~# adduser molloyd newgroup
Adding user 'molloyd' to group 'newgroup' ...
```

Step 3: To reset the password if required, use the following:

```
root@beaglebone:~# passwd molloyd
Enter new UNIX password:
Retype new UNIX password:
passwd: password updated successfully
```

You can force the password to expire on login by using `chage -d 0 molloyd`. The encrypted passwords are stored in the restricted file /etc/shadow, **not the public-readable** /etc/passwd **file.**

Step 4: You can test the account by typing `su molloyd` from the root account (you will not be prompted for a password going from `root` to `molloyd`, but you would the other way around), or you can log in with a new Linux terminal (using `pwd` to *print the working directory*):

```
login as: molloyd
molloyd@192.168.7.2's password:
molloyd@beaglebone:~$ pwd
/home/molloyd
molloyd@beaglebone:~$ touch test.txt
molloyd@beaglebone:~$ ls -l
-rw-r--r-- 1 molloyd users 0 Feb 23 18:37 test.txt
molloyd@beaglebone:~$ more /etc/group |grep newgroup
newgroup:x:1005:molloyd
```

You can see that the file has been created with the correct user and group id. To delete an account, type `userdel -r molloyd`, where `-r` deletes the home directory and any mail spool files.

You can change the user and group ownership of a file using the *change ownership* `chown` command. The *change group* `chgrp` command can change the group ownership of a file. Table 3-2 lists a few examples of the command structure for `chown` and `chgrp`.

Table 3-2: Commands for Working with Users, Groups, and Permissions

COMMAND	DESCRIPTION
`chown molloyd a.txt`	Change file owner.
`chown molloyd:users a.txt`	Change owner and group at the same time.
`chown -Rh molloyd /tmp/test`	Recursively change ownership of /tmp/test.
	-h affects symbolic links instead of referenced files.
`chgrp users a.txt`	Change group ownership of the file.
`chgrp -Rh users /tmp/test`	Recursively change with same -h as `chown`.

COMMAND	DESCRIPTION
`chmod 600 a.txt`	Change permissions (as in Figure 3-3) so user has read/write access to the file; group or others have no access.
`chmod ugo+rw a.txt`	Give users, group, and others read/write access to `a.txt`.
`chmod a-w a.txt`	Remove write access for all users using `a`, which describes *all* (the set of users, group, and others).
`chmod ugo=rw a.txt`	Set the permissions for all to be read/write.

`umask`
 	
`umask -S`
	List the default permissions settings. Using `-S` displays the umask in a more readable form.

`umask 022`
 	
`umask u=rwx,g=rx,o=rx`
	Change the default permissions on all newly created files and directories. The two `umask` commands here are equivalent. If you set this mask value and create a file or directory, it will be: `drwxr-xr-x` for the directory and `-rw-r--r--` for the file. You can set a user-specific `umask` in the account's `.login` file.

`chmod u+s myexe`	Set a special bit called the *setuid bit* (set user id on execute) and *setgid bit* (set group ID on execute), `s`, that allows a program to be executed as if by another logged-in user, but with the permissions of the file's owner or group. For example, you could use this to allow a particular program to execute as if the root user account executed it.
`chmod 6750 myexe`	Set the setuid bit in an absolute way. Both examples will give `myexe` the permissions `-rwsr-s---`, where both the setuid and setgid bits are set.
`chmod u=rwxs,g=rxs,o=myexe`	For security reasons, the setuid bit cannot be applied to shell scripts.
`stat /tmp/test.txt`	Provides very useful file system status information for a file or directory, such as its physical device and inode information; last access; and modify and change times.

The next example demonstrates how to change the ownership of a file. In order for the example to work using the sudo tool, the user `molloyd` must be present in the `sudoers` file, which is achieved by the root user executing the single-word command **visudo**. In the `sudoers` file, place an entry in the file, such as the following:

```
molloyd ALL=(ALL) ALL
```

EXAMPLE: CHANGING THE OWNERSHIP AND GROUP OF A FILE

Use superuser access to change a file `test.txt` in the `/tmp` directory that is owned by the user `molloyd` with the group `users`, to have owner `root` and group `root`:

```
molloyd@beaglebone:~$ cd /tmp
molloyd@beaglebone:/tmp$ ls -l
total 0
-rw-r--r-- 1 molloyd users 0 Feb 24 23:48 test.txt
molloyd@beaglebone:/tmp$ sudo chgrp root test.txt
[sudo] password for molloyd:
molloyd@beaglebone:/tmp$ sudo chown root test.txt
molloyd@beaglebone:/tmp$ ls -l
total 0
-rw-r--r-- 1 root root 0 Feb 24 23:48 test.txt
```

File System Permissions

The *file system permissions* state what levels of access each of these categories have to a file or directory. The *change mode* command `chmod` allows a user to change the access permissions for file system objects. You can specify the permissions in a relative way, e.g., **chmod a+w test.txt**, would give all users write access to a file `test.txt` but leave all other permissions the same. You can also apply the permissions in an absolute way, e.g., **chmod a=r test.txt**, which would set all users to only have read access to the file `test.txt`. Table 3-2 also lists some example commands for working with users, groups, and permissions. The next example demonstrates how to modify the file system permissions of a file using the `chmod` command.

EXAMPLE: USING CHMOD IN DIFFERENT FORMS

Change a file "test2.txt" in the `/tmp` directory so that users and group members have read and write access, but others only have read access. Do this task in three different ways.

```
molloyd@beaglebone:/tmp$ touch test2.txt
molloyd@beaglebone:/tmp$ ls -l
-rw-r--r-- 1 molloyd users 0 Feb 25 00:07 test2.txt
molloyd@beaglebone:/tmp$ chmod g+w test2.txt
molloyd@beaglebone:/tmp$ ls -l
-rw-rw-r-- 1 molloyd users 0 Feb 25 00:07 test2.txt
molloyd@beaglebone:/tmp$ chmod 664 test2.txt
molloyd@beaglebone:/tmp$ ls -l
-rw-rw-r-- 1 molloyd users 0 Feb 25 00:07 test2.txt
molloyd@beaglebone:/tmp$ chmod u=rw,g=rw,o=r test2.txt
molloyd@beaglebone:/tmp$ ls -l
-rw-rw-r-- 1 molloyd users 0 Feb 25 00:07 test2.txt
```

All three calls to `chmod` above have the exact same outcome.

Here is an example of the last entry in Table 3-2, the stat command:

```
root@beaglebone:/tmp# stat test.txt
  File: 'test.txt'
  Size: 0            Blocks: 0        IO Block: 4096    regular empty file
Device: b302h/45826d    Inode: 72000        Links: 2
Access: (0644/-rw-r--r--) Uid: (    0/    root)  Gid: (    0/    root)
Access: 2014-02-23 16:57:18.590773186 +0000
Modify: 2014-02-23 16:57:18.590773186 +0000
Change: 2014-02-23 16:57:47.520773190 +0000
 Birth: -
```

Just to finish the discussion of Figure 3-3: The example in the figure has 22 hard links to the file. For a directory this represents the number of subdirectories, the parent directory (..), and itself (.). The entry is owned by root and it is in the root group. The next entry of 4096 is the size required to store the metadata about files contained in that directory (the minimum size is one sector, typically 4,096 bytes). ls -lh lists with (h) human-readable file sizes.

One final point: if you perform a directory listing ls -l in the root directory you will see a t bit on the /tmp directory. This is called the *sticky bit*, meaning that write permission is not sufficient to delete files. Therefore, in the /tmp directory any user can create files, but no user can delete another user's files:

```
molloyd@beaglebone:~$ cd /
molloyd@beaglebone:/$ ls -ld tmp
drwxrwxrwt   5 root root   4096 Feb 23 21:17 tmp
```

Exploring the File System

Exploring the Linux file system can be daunting for new Linux users. If you go to the top-level directory using cd / on the BBB and type ls, you will get the top-level directory structure, of the following form:

```
root@beaglebone:/# ls
bin    dev  home  lost+found  mnt  proc  run   selinux  sys  usr
boot   etc  lib   media       opt  root  sbin  srv      tmp  var
```

What does it all mean? Well, each of these directories has a role, and if you understand the roles, then you can start to get an idea of where to search for configuration files or the binary files that you need. Table 3-3 briefly describes the content of each top-level Linux subdirectory.

Commands for File Systems

Commands for working with files and directories on file systems are described in the previous section, but there are also commands for working with the file system itself. The first commands you should examine are df (remember as *d*isk

Table 3-3: The Linux Top-Level Directory

DIRECTORY	DESCRIPTION
bin	Contains the binary executables used by all of the users and is present in the PATH environment variable by default. Another directory, /usr/bin, contains executables that are not core to booting or repairing the system
boot	Contains the device tree binaries for the BBB
dev	Contains the device nodes (linked to device drivers)
etc	Configuration files for the local system
home	The user home directories (/home/root can be the root user home)
lib	Contains the standard system libraries
lost+found	After running fsck (file system check and repair) unlinked files will appear here. The mklost+found command will recreate the lost+found directory if it is deleted
media	Used for mounting removable media, such as a micro-SD cards
mnt	Typically used for mounting temporary file systems
opt	A good place for installing third-party (non-core Linux) "optional" software packages
proc	This is a virtual file representation of processes running on the BBB (for example, if you go into /proc and type **cat iomem** you can see the memory mapping addresses)
root	The home directory of root account under the Debian distribution. This is /home/root on other distributions
run	Provides information about the running system since the last boot
sbin	Contains executables for root user (superuser) system management
selinux	Under Debian, relates to the security-enhanced Linux control system
srv	Stores data related to ftp, web servers, rsync, etc.
sys	A directory containing a virtual file system that describes the system sysfs. This is discussed in detail in Chapter 6
tmp	Temporary files location. See the note on the t bit in the last section
usr	Contains application programs for all of the users and many subdirectories such as /usr/include (C/C++ header files), /usr/lib (C/C++ library files), /usr/src (Linux kernel source), /usr/bin (user executables), /usr/local (similar to /usr but for local users), and /usr/share (shared files and media between users)
var	Contains variable files such as system logs

free) and `mount`. The `df` command provides you with an overview of the file systems on the BBB. If you add the `-T` option, it also lists the file system types:

```
root@beaglebone:/# df -T
Filesystem       Type      1K-blocks      Used Available Use% Mounted on
rootfs           rootfs     1715936   1435760    174960  90% /
udev             devtmpfs     10240         0     10240   0% /dev
tmpfs            tmpfs       101052      1492     99560   2% /run
/dev/disk/by-u   ext4       1715936   1435760    174960  90% /
tmpfs            tmpfs       252620         0    252620   0% /dev/shm
tmpfs            tmpfs       252620         0    252620   0% /sys/fs/cgroup
tmpfs            tmpfs         5120         0      5120   0% /run/lock
tmpfs            tmpfs       102400         0    102400   0% /run/user
/dev/mmcblk0p1   vfat         98094     87464     10630  90% /boot/uboot
```

The `df` command is very useful for determining if you are running short on disk space; you can see that the root file system `rootfs` is 90% used in this case, with 175MB available for additional installations. The `rootfs` is listed a second time as `/dev/disk/by-uuid. . .`, showing that it is an ext4 extended file system that supports large disk sizes. Also listed are several temporary file system (`tmpfs`) entries that actually refer to virtual file systems, which are mapped to the BBB's DDR3 memory. The `/sys/fs` entry is discussed in detail in Chapter 6. In addition, the last entry in the list is `/dev/mmcblk0p1` and it has a 98MB VFAT file system partition of the BBB's eMMC. This is the VFAT file system that appears when you plug your BBB into the USB port of your desktop computer. You can see that this file system `/dev/mmcblk0p1` is *mounted* on (attached to) `/boot/uboot`. You can `cd /boot/uboot` to list the contents, which you will recognize from Chapter 2 when the BBB was attached to the desktop computer.

> **NOTE**   If you are running out of space on the BBB, check the system logs: `/var/log`. You can clear a log by typing `cat /dev/null > /var/log/messages` (check `kern.log` and `syslog` too), as it will empty the file without deleting it or resetting the permissions. If your logs are filling up, it is symptomatic of a system problem.

```
root@beaglebone:/# cd /boot/uboot/
root@beaglebone:/boot/uboot# ls
App              LICENSE.txt SOC.sh       dtbs         scripts    uInitrd
BASIC_START.ht   MLO         START.htm    dtbs_bak     u-boot.img uInitrd_bak
Docs             README.htm  autorun.inf  initrd.bak   uEnv.txt   zImage
Drivers          README.md   debug        initrd.img   uImage     zImage_bak
```

The list block devices command `lsblk` provides you with a concise list of the block devices, such as eMMC and SD cards (if any), in a tree-like structure. As shown in the following output, you can see that `mmcblk1` (the eMMC) has been partitioned into two partitions: `p1`, which is attached to `/boot/uboot`, and `p2`, which is attached to the root of the file system `/`. `mmcblk1boot0` and `1` are the eMMC boot partitions that are required for MLO and U-Boot to do their jobs.

```
root@beaglebone:~# lsblk
NAME            MAJ:MIN RM    SIZE RO TYPE MOUNTPOINT
mmcblk1boot0 179:16    0     1M  1 disk
mmcblk1boot1 179:24    0     1M  1 disk
mmcblk1          179:8     0   1.8G  0 disk
|-mmcblk1p1  179:9     0    96M  0 part /boot/uboot
'-mmcblk1p2  179:10    0   1.7G  0 part /
```

The `mount` command provides you with further information about the file system. Typing `mount -l` gives you detailed file system information (`-l` with labels) such as the following:

```
root@beaglebone:/# mount -l
sysfs on /sys type sysfs (rw,nosuid,nodev,noexec,relatime)
proc on /proc type proc (rw,nosuid,nodev,noexec,relatime)
...
/dev/mmcblk0p1 on /boot/uboot type vfat (rw,relatime,fmask=0022,
dmask=0022,codepage=437,iocharset=iso8859-1,shortname=mixed,
errors=remount-ro) [boot]
```

Table 3-4 describes some file system commands that you can use to manage your file system.

The micro-SD slot on the BBB can be used as an additional storage device. This is useful if you are capturing video data and not enough storage space exists on the eMMC. The following two examples describe how the eMMC can be rescued from an accidental corruption of the `uEnv.txt` file by booting Linux from the SD card, and how a SD card can be used on the BBB for additional file storage.

Table 3-4: Useful Commands for File Systems

COMMAND	DESCRIPTION

`du -h /opt`
`du -hs /opt/*`
 	
`du -hc *.jpg`
	Disk usage—find out how much space a directory tree uses. Options: (`-h`) human readable form; (`-s`) summary; (`-c`) total. The last command finds the total size of the jpg format files in the current directory.

`df -h`	Display system disk space in (`-h`) human-readable form.
`lsblk`	List block devices.

`dd if=test.img`
`of=/dev/mmcblkX`
 	
`dd if=/dev/mmcblkX`
`of=test.img`
	dd converts and copies a file, where `if` is the input file and `of` is the output file. You can use this command under Linux to write an image to the SD card. This is typically used under desktop Linux with the form
	
	`sudo dd if=./BBB*.img of=/dev/sdX`
	
	where `/dev/sdX` is the SD card reader/writer.

`cat /proc/partitions`	List all registered partitions.

COMMAND	DESCRIPTION
`mkfs /dev/mmcblkXpX`	Make a Linux file system. See also `mkfs.ext4`, `mkfs.vfat`.
`fdisk -l`	Note that `fdisk` can be used to manage disks, create partitions, delete partitions, etc. `fdisk -l` displays all existing partitions.
`badblocks /dev/mmcblkX`	Check for bad blocks on the SD card. SD cards have wear-levelling controller circuitry. If you get errors, get a new card—don't record them using `fsck`. Run this with root permissions and be aware it takes some time to run.
`mount /media/store`	This will mount a partition if it is listed in `/etc/fstab`.
`umount /media/store`	Unmount a partition. You will be informed if a file is open on this partition.

EXAMPLE: FIXING UENV.TXT PROBLEMS ON THE EMMC

As discussed, the `uEnv.txt` file plays a very important role in the boot process. One consequence of making edits to this file, which is necessary in later chapters, is that an editing mistake (or a purposeful disabling of the eMMC) can prevent your BBB from booting. If you see the prompt (`initramfs`) on your USB-3.3V-TTL serial connection, then it is likely that your `uEnv.txt` file could not be parsed correctly.

To edit this file after your board fails to boot from the eMMC, use an SD card boot image and hold the boot button on power up until the user LEDs light. Importantly, do *not* boot the BBB using a flasher image, as it will overwrite the current data on your eMMC. If you do not have a boot image, download one from BeagleBoard.org. Carefully label your boot and flasher image SD cards, as mixing them up could result in a loss of data.

After booting with the SD card boot image, the following steps will give you access to edit the `uEnv.txt` file that is on the eMMC:

```
debian@arm:~$ cd /mnt
debian@arm:/mnt$ sudo mkdir vfat
debian@arm:/mnt$ sudo mount /dev/mmcblk1p1 /mnt/vfat
debian@arm:/mnt$ cd /mnt/vfat
debian@arm:/mnt/vfat$ ls
App          Docs      ID.txt       MLO          scripts     u-boot.img
autorun.inf  Drivers   initrd.img   README.htm   SOC.sh      uEnv.txt
debug        dtbs      LICENSE.txt  README.md    START.htm   uInitrd
debian@arm:/mnt/vfat$ sudo nano uEnv.txt
debian@arm:/mnt/vfat$ sudo shutdown -h now
```

Finally, remove the SD card and boot as normal from the eMMC.

It is likely that the VFAT partition structure will be removed from future versions of the BBB distribution—check the chapter web page for updates.

EXAMPLE: MOUNT AN SD CARD AS ADDITIONAL STORAGE ON THE BBB

In this example the following steps are performed:

1. Mounting an SD card that is in the BBB SD card slot for additional removable file storage

2. Formatting the file system to be a Linux ext4 file system

3. Mounting the SD card as `/media/store`

4. Checking how much storage is available on the card

Note that these instructions vary according to the Linux distribution being used and could change or become invalid depending on updates to the BBB. Check the chapter web page if you are having difficulties.

Step 1: In this example, the card is a 16GB card taken straight from the package and placed in the BBB's micro-SD card slot (while the BBB is running). You can see it by typing the following:

```
root@beaglebone:/# mount -l
...
/dev/mmcblk1p1 on /media/6462-3062 type vfat rw,nosuid,nodev,relatime
,uid=1000,gid=1002,fmask=0022,dmask=0077,codepage=437,...
```

It has been automatically mounted at `/media/6462-3062` with type `vfat`. Use the following to check if there is any data on the card:

```
root@beaglebone:/# cd /media/9016-4EF8/
root@beaglebone:/media/6462-3062# ls -l
total 0
```

There are no files on the card.

Step 2: Next you should format it as an ext4 file system for use on the BBB. Be very careful that you choose the correct device (e.g., mmcblk1p1 in this example). In addition, if there is data on your SD card, then it will be lost as a result of the following operations.

```
root@beaglebone:/media/9016-4EF8# cd /
root@beaglebone:/# umount /dev/mmcblk1p1
root@beaglebone:/# mkfs.ext4 /dev/mmcblk1p1
mke2fs 1.42.5 (29-Jul-2012)
OS type: Linux
Block size=4096 (log=2)
...
Writing superblocks and filesystem accounting information: done
```

Step 3: Next, you need to create a mount point for the card, `/media/store`, and mount the card at that point using the `mount` command (`-t` indicates the file type; if it is omitted, `mount` will try to auto-detect the file system type), passing the mount point and the device name. You can then confirm that it is there. The steps are as follows:

```
root@beaglebone:/# cd /
root@beaglebone:/# mkdir /media/store
root@beaglebone:/# mount -t ext4 /dev/mmcblk1p1 /media/store
root@beaglebone:/# cd /media/store
root@beaglebone:/media/store# ls
lost+found
root@beaglebone:/media/store# mount -l
/dev/mmcblk1p1 on /media/store type ext4 (rw,relatime,data=ordered)
```

Step 4: To check how much capacity is available, type df -k, which results in:

```
root@beaglebone:/media/store# df -k
/dev/mmcblk1p1   15178708    37984   14363024    1% /media/store
root@beaglebone:/media/store# touch test.txt
root@beaglebone:/media/store# ls
lost+found   test.txt
```

In this case, the 16GB micro-SD card now has 1% of its capacity used. The rest is now available for use.

There is a further step on the chapter web page that details how you can ensure that the SD card is mounted automatically when the BBB is booted.

find and whereis

The find command is very useful for searching a directory structure for a particular file. It is incredibly comprehensive; type **man find** for a full list of commands. For example, use the following to find the C++ header file iostream somewhere on the BBB file system (this may take a few seconds):

```
root@beaglebone:/# cd /
root@beaglebone:/# find -name iostream*
./usr/include/c++/4.6/iostream
```

Using -iname instead of -name ignores upper/lowercase letters in the search name. For example, the following command finds files with the extension .gz that were modified in the last 24 hours:

```
root@beaglebone:/# find -ctime 1 -iname *.gz
./usr/share/man/man5/wavemonrc.5.gz ...
```

The whereis command is different in that it can be used to search for a binary, source code, and manual page for a program:

```
root@beaglebone:~# whereis find
find: /usr/bin/find /usr/bin/X11/find /usr/share/man/man1/find.1.gz
```

In this case, the binary command is in /usr/bin (X11 is a symbolic link to the current directory .) and the man page is in /usr/share/man/man1 (stored in gzip form to save space).

more or less

The more command has been used several times already, and you have likely gleaned its use. It allows you to view a large file or output stream, one page at a time. Therefore, to view a long file you can type **more filename**. For example, there is a log file /var/log/dmesg that contains all the kernel output messages. You can view this file line by line by typing **more /var/log/dmesg**. However, if you want to keep the display concise, use **-5** to set the page length to be five rows:

```
root@beaglebone:~# more -5 /var/log/dmesg
[    0.000000] Booting Linux on physical CPU 0x0
[    0.000000] Initializing cgroup subsys cpuset
[    0.000000] Initializing cgroup subsys cpu
[    0.000000] Initializing cgroup subsys cpuacct
[    0.000000] Linux version 3.13.4-bone5 (root@imx6q-sabrelite-1gb-0)
--More--(1%)
```

You can page through the content using the space bar and use the q key to quit. There is an even more powerful command called less that you can access by typing:

```
root@beaglebone:~# less /var/log/dmesg
```

It gives you a fully interactive view using the keyboard; you can use the arrow keys to move up and down through the text. There are too many options to list; however, for example, you can page down using the space bar, search for a string by typing / (e.g., type **/usb** to find messages related to USB devices) and then press the n key to go to the next match and the N key to go to the previous match. That only touches on the capability of the less command.

Linux Commands

When you are working at the Linux terminal and you type commands such as **date**, the output of these commands is sent to the standard output. As a result, the output is displayed in your terminal window.

Standard Input and Output Redirection (>, >>, and <)

It is possible to *redirect* the output to a file using *redirection symbols* > and >>. You used the latter symbol earlier to add text to temporary files. The > symbol can be used to send the output to a new file. For example:

```
root@beaglebone:~# cd /tmp
root@beaglebone:/tmp# date > a.txt
```

```
root@beaglebone:/tmp# more a.txt
Wed Feb 26 15:41:12 UTC 2014
root@beaglebone:/tmp# date > a.txt
root@beaglebone:/tmp# more a.txt
Wed Feb 26 15:41:25 UTC 2014
```

The >> symbol indicates that you wish to append to the file. The following example illustrates the use of >> with the new file a.txt:

```
root@beaglebone:/tmp# date >> a.txt
root@beaglebone:/tmp# more a.txt
Wed Feb 26 15:41:25 UTC 2014
Wed Feb 26 15:43:26 UTC 2014
```

Standard input using the < symbol works in much the same way. The -e enables parsing of escape characters, such as the return (\n) characters:

```
root@beaglebone:/tmp# echo -e "dog\ncat\nfish\nbird" > animals.txt
root@beaglebone:/tmp# sort < animals.txt
bird
cat
dog
fish
```

You can combine input and output redirection operations. Using the same animals.txt file, you can perform operations such as:

```
root@beaglebone:/tmp# sort < animals.txt > sorted.txt
root@beaglebone:/tmp# more sorted.txt
bird
cat
dog
fish
```

Pipes (| and tee)

Simply put, *pipes* (|) allow you to connect Linux commands together. Just as you redirected the output to a file, you can redirect the output of one command into the input of another command. For examples, to list the root directory (from anywhere on the system) and send (or "pipe") the output into the sort command, where it is listed in reverse (-r) order, use the following:

```
root@beaglebone:/# ls / | sort -r
var
usr
...
boot
bin
```

You can find out which user installations in the /opt directory are occupying the most disk space: du gives you the disk used. Passing the argument -d1 means only list the sizes of 1 level below the current directory level, and -h means list the values in human-readable form. You can pipe this output into the sort filter command to do a numeric sort in reverse order (largest at the top). Therefore, the command looks like:

```
root@beaglebone:/# cd /opt
root@beaglebone:/opt# du -d1 -h | sort -nr
74M     .
58M     ./cloud9
15M     ./source
1.1M    ./scripts
```

There is one more useful tool, tee, which allows you to both redirect an output to a file and pass it on to the next command in the pipe (e.g., store and view). Using the previous example, if you wanted to send the unsorted output of du to a file but display a sorted output, you could enter the following:

```
root@beaglebone:/opt# du -d1 -h | tee /tmp/unsorted.txt | sort -nr
74M     .
58M     ./cloud9
15M     ./source
1.1M    ./scripts
root@beaglebone:/opt# more /tmp/unsorted.txt
15M     ./source
1.1M    ./scripts
58M     ./cloud9
74M     .
```

You can also use tee to write the output to several files at the same time, as shown in this example:

```
root@beaglebone:/opt# du -d1 -h | tee /tmp/1.txt /tmp/2.txt /tmp/3.txt
```

Filter Commands (from sort to xargs)

There are filtering commands, each of which provides a useful function:

- sort: This command has several options, including (-r) sorts in reverse; (-f) ignores case; (-d) uses dictionary sorting, ignoring punctuation; (-n) numeric sort; (-b) ignores blank space; (-i) ignores control characters; (-u) displays duplicate lines only once; and (-m) merges multiple inputs into a single output.
- wc (word count): This can be used to calculate the number of words, lines, or characters in a stream. For example:

```
root@beaglebone:/tmp# wc < animals.txt
   4   4  18
```

This has returned that there are 4 lines, 4 words, and 18 characters. You can select the values independently by using (-1) for line count; (-w) for word count; (-m) for character count; and (-c) for the byte count (which would also be 18 in this case).

▪ head: Displays the first lines of the input. This is useful if you have a very long file or stream of information and you want to examine only the first few lines. By default it will display the first 10 lines. You can specify the number of lines using the -n option. For example, to get the first five lines of output of the dmesg command (display message or driver message), which displays the message buffer of the kernel, you can use the following:

```
root@beaglebone:/tmp# dmesg | head -n5
[    0.000000] Booting Linux on physical CPU 0x0
[    0.000000] Initializing cgroup subsys cpuset
[    0.000000] Initializing cgroup subsys cpu
[    0.000000] Initializing cgroup subsys cpuacct
[    0.000000] Linux version 3.13.4-bone5(root@imx6q-sabrelite-1gb-0)
```

▪ tail: This is just like head except that it displays the last lines of a file or stream. Using it in combination with dmesg provides useful output, as shown here:

```
root@beaglebone:/tmp# dmesg | tail -n2
[   36.123251] libphy: 4a101000.mdio:00 - Link is Up - 100/Full
[   36.123421] IPv6:ADDRCONF(NETDEV_CHANGE): eth0:link becomes ready
```

▪ grep: A very powerful filter command that can parse lines using text and regular expressions. You can use this command to filter output with options, including (-i) ignore case; (-m 5) stop after five matches; (-q) silent, will exit with return status 0 if any matches are found; (-e) specify a pattern; (-c) print a count of matches; (-o) print only the matching text; and (-1) list the filename of the file containing the match. For example, the following examines the dmesg output for the first three occurrences of the string "usb," using -i to ignore case:

```
root@beaglebone:/tmp# dmesg |grep -i -m3 usb
[    1.948582] usbcore: registered new interface driver usbfs
[    1.948637] usbcore: registered new interface driver hub
[    1.948795] usbcore: registered new device driver usb
```

You can combine pipes together. For example, you get the exact same output by using head and displaying only the first three lines of the grep output:

```
root@beaglebone:/tmp# dmesg |grep -i usb |head -n3
[    1.948582] usbcore: registered new interface driver usbfs
[    1.948637] usbcore: registered new interface driver hub
[    1.948795] usbcore: registered new device driver usb
```

■ `xargs`: This is a very powerful filter command that enables you to construct an argument list that you use to call another command or tool. In the following example, a text file `args.txt` that contains three strings is used to create three new files. The output of `cat` is piped to `xargs`, where it passes the three strings as arguments to the `touch` command, creating three new files `a.txt`, `b.txt`, and `c.txt`:

```
molloyd@beaglebone:~$ echo "a.txt b.txt c.txt" > args.txt
molloyd@beaglebone:~$ cat args.txt | xargs touch
molloyd@beaglebone:~$ ls
a.txt  args.txt  b.txt  c.txt
```

Other useful filter commands include `awk` (to program any type of filter), `fmt` (to format text), `uniq` (to find unique lines), and `sed` (to manipulate a stream). These commands are beyond the scope of this text—for example, `awk` is a full programming language! Table 3-5 describes a few useful piped commands to give you some ideas of how you can use them.

Table 3-5: Pipe Examples for the BBB

COMMAND	DESCRIPTION
`du	sort -nr`	`du` returns the amount of disk used, and in this example it will list the disk used by subdirectories off the current directory, sorting them according to how much they store, with the largest at the top.
`ls -lt	head`	Display the newest files in the current directory.
`cat urls.txt	xargs wget`	Download the files, listed by URLs in a text file `urls.txt`.

echo and cat

The `echo` command simply `echoes` a string, output of a command, or a value to the standard output. Here are a few examples:

```
root@beaglebone:/tmp# echo 'hello'
hello
root@beaglebone:/tmp# echo "Today's date is $(date)"
Today's date is Wed Feb 26 15:16:47 UTC 2014
root@beaglebone:/tmp# echo $PATH
/usr/local/sbin:/usr/local/bin:/usr/sbin:/usr/bin:/sbin:/bin
```

In the first case, a simple string is echoed. In the second case, the " " are present as a command is issued within the echo call, and in the final case the PATH environment variable is echoed. The echo command also enables you to see the exit status of a command using `$?`. For example:

```
root@beaglebone:~# ls /tmp
test.txt
```

```
root@beaglebone:~# echo $?
0
root@beaglebone:~# ls /madeupdirectory
ls: cannot access /madeupdirectory: No such file or directory
root@beaglebone:~# echo $?
2
```

The exit status for date is 0 for a successful call and 2 for a directory that does not exist. This can be very useful when you are writing scripts and your own C/C++ programs that return a value from the main() function.

The cat command (con*cat*enation) enables you to join two files together at the command line. The following example uses echo to create two files a.txt and b.txt; cat concatenates the files to create a new file c.txt. You need to use -e if you want to enable the interpretation of escape characters in the string that is passed to echo. For example, "\n" adds a new line to your output.

```
root@beaglebone:/tmp# cd /tmp
root@beaglebone:/tmp# echo "hello" >> a.txt
root@beaglebone:/tmp# echo -e "to\nthe\nworld" >> b.txt
root@beaglebone:/tmp# cat a.txt b.txt >> c.txt
root@beaglebone:/tmp# more c.txt
hello
to
the
world
```

diff

The diff command enables you to easily find the differences between two files. It provides a very basic output:

```
molloyd@beaglebone:~$ echo -e "dog\nfish\nbird" > list1.txt
molloyd@beaglebone:~$ echo -e "dog\nshark\nbird" > list2.txt
molloyd@beaglebone:~$ diff list1.txt list2.txt
2c2
< fish
---
> shark
```

The value 2c2 in the output indicates that line 2 in the first file *c*hanged to line 2 in the second file, and the change is that "fish" changed to "shark." The char-acter *a* would mean appended, and *d* would mean deleted. For a side-by-side comparison, you can use

```
molloyd@beaglebone:~$ diff -y -W80 list1.txt list2.txt
dog                              dog
fish                           | shark
bird                             bird
```

where -y enables the side-by-side view, and -W80 sets the width of the display to 80 characters.

If you are looking for a more intuitive (but challenging) difference between two files, you can use the vimdiff command, which shows a side-by-side comparison of the files using the vim (Vi IMproved) text editor (type **vimdiff list1 .txt list2.txt** and use the VI key sequence: **Escape : q !** twice to quit, or **Escape : w q** to save the changes and quit). Vim requires a lot of practice to be used as a general editor.

tar

The tar command is an archiving utility that enables you to combine files and directories into a single file (like an uncompressed zip file). This file can then be compressed to save space. To archive and compress a directory of files, use

```
molloyd@beaglebone:~$ tar cvfz newArchiveName.tar.gz /tmp
```

where (c) means new archive, (v) means verbosely list files, (z) means compress with gzip, and (f) means archive name follows. You might also see .tar.gz represented as .tgz. See Table 3-6 for more examples.

Table 3-6: Useful tar Commands

COMMAND	DESCRIPTION
tar cvfz name.tar.gz	Compress with gzip form.
tar cvfj name.tar.bz2	Compress with bzip2 compression (typically a longer delay, but smaller, file).
tar xvf name.tar.gz	Decompress gzip file (x indicates extract). It will auto-detect compression type (e.g., gzip, bz2).
tar xvf name.tar /dir/ filename	Extract a single file from an archive. Works for a single directory too. Use z and j as required.
tar rvf name.tar filename	Add another file to the archive.
tar cfz name-$(date +%d%m%y). tar.gz /dir/filename	Create an archive with the current day's date. Very useful for scripts and cron job backups. Note: There must be a space between date and +%d%m%y.

md5sum

The md5sum command enables you to check the hash code, in order to verify that the files have not been corrupted maliciously or accidentally in transit. In the following example, the wavemon tool is downloaded as a .deb package, but not installed. The md5sum command can be used to generate the md5 checksum:

```
root@beaglebone:~# apt-get download wavemon
Get:1 Downloading wavemon 0.7.5-3 [52.1 kB]
Fetched 52.1 kB in 0s (66.7 kB/s)
root@beaglebone:~# ls
wavemon_0.7.5-3_armhf.deb
root@beaglebone:~# md5sum wavemon_0.7.5-3_armhf.deb
f70117682d2b148b11514337a622eb4c  wavemon_0.7.5-3_armhf.deb
```

You can now check this checksum against the official checksum to ensure you have a valid file that has not been tampered with. Unfortunately, it can be difficult to find the checksums for individual packages online. If it was installed (as you did in Chapter 2), the checksum for wavemon is in /var/lib/dpkg/info/ wavemon.md5sums. You can install a utility under Debian called *debsums* to check the integrity of the file and its constituent parts:

```
root@beaglebone:~# debsums wavemon_0.7.5-3_armhf.deb
/usr/bin/wavemon                                              OK
/usr/share/doc/wavemon/changelog.Debian.gz                    OK
```

If you are building your own packages that you wish to distribute, it would be useful to also distribute a checksum file.

Linux Processes

A process is an instance of a program that is running on the OS. You need to be able to manage the processes that are running on your BBB, understand foreground and background processes, and kill a process that becomes locked.

Controlling Linux Processes

The ps command lists the processes that are currently running on the BBB. Typing **ps** shows that the BBB in the following example is running two processes, the bash shell with process ID (PID) 2200 and the ps command itself, which is running with PID 13507. The ps PID is different every time you run it:

```
root@beaglebone:~# ps
PID    TTY          TIME CMD
2200   pts/0    00:00:02 bash
13507  pts/0    00:00:00 ps
```

To see every process that is running on the system, use **ps ax**. In the next example, it is filtered to look for the string "apache" to discover information about the apache server process that is running on the BBB:

```
root@beaglebone:/opt# ps ax|grep apache
869    ?         Ss     0:08 /usr/sbin/apache2 -k start
```

```
875    ?         S       0:00 /usr/sbin/apache2 -k start
879    ?         Sl      0:00 /usr/sbin/apache2 -k start
880    ?         Sl      0:00 /usr/sbin/apache2 -k start
13579 pts/0      S+      0:00 grep apache
```

Interestingly, `apache2` appears four times, meaning there are four different processes running for the web server, allowing it to handle multiple simultaneous connections.

Foreground and Background Processes

Linux is a multitasking OS that allows you to run processes in the *background* while using a program that is running in the *foreground*. This concept is similar to the behavior of a windowing system (e.g., Windows, Mac OS X)—for example, the desktop clock will continue to update the time while you use a web browser.

The same is true of applications that run in a terminal window. To demonstrate that, here is a small segment of C code to display "Hello World!" every five seconds in a Linux terminal. Exactly how this works is covered in Chapter 5, but for the moment you can enter the code verbatim into a file called `HelloWorldSleep.c` using the nano file editor.

```
molloyd@beaglebone:~$ cd ~/
molloyd@beaglebone:~$ more HelloWorldSleep.c
#include<unistd.h>
#include<stdio.h>

int  main(){
   int x = 0;
   do{
        printf("Hello World!\n");
        sleep(5);
   }while(x++<100);
}
```

After saving the file as `HelloWorldSleep.c`, it can be compiled by typing the following (-o specifies the executable file name):

```
molloyd@beaglebone:~$ gcc HelloWorldSleep.c -o HelloWorldSleep
molloyd@beaglebone:~$ ls -l
total 12
-rwxr-xr-x 1 molloyd users 5191 Feb 26 23:48 HelloWorldSleep
-rw-r--r-- 1 molloyd users  147 Feb 26 23:48 HelloWorldSleep.c
```

If this works correctly you will now have the source file and the executable program called `HelloWorldSleep` (note that the executable x flag is set). It can be run by typing the following:

```
molloyd@beaglebone:~$ ./HelloWorldSleep
Hello World!
Hello World!
```

It will continue to output "Hello World!" every five seconds. This application can be killed using Ctrl+C. However, if you would like to run this in the background, there are two ways to do that.

The first way is that, instead of using Ctrl+C to kill the process, use Ctrl+Z, and then at the prompt use the bg (background) command:

```
molloyd@beaglebone:~$ ./HelloWorldSleep
Hello World!
Hello World!
^Z
[1]+  Stopped                 ./HelloWorldSleep
molloyd@beaglebone:~$ bg
[1]+ ./HelloWorldSleep &
molloyd@beaglebone:~$ Hello World!
Hello World!
Hello World!
```

You can see that when you type Ctrl+Z, the ^z appears in the output. When **bg** is entered, the program is placed in the background and continues to execute. In fact, you can continue to use the terminal but it will be frustrating, as every five seconds "Hello World!" will appear. You can bring this process back into the foreground using the fg command:

```
molloyd@beaglebone:~$ fg
./HelloWorldSleep
Hello World!
^C
molloyd@beaglebone:~$
```

The application is killed when Ctrl+C is typed (appears as ^c above).

The second way to place this application in the background is to execute the application with an & symbol after the application name:

```
molloyd@beaglebone:~$ ./HelloWorldSleep &
[1] 14442
molloyd@beaglebone:~$ Hello World!
Hello World!
```

It has been placed in the background with PID 14442 in this case. To stop the process, you can use ps to find the PID:

```
molloyd@beaglebone:~$ ps aux|grep Hello
molloyd 14442 0.0 0.0 1176 308 pts/1  S  Feb26 0:00 ./HelloWorldSleep
molloyd 14478 0.0 0.1 1604 564 pts/1  S+ 00:01 0:00 grep Hello
```

This process can be killed by using the kill command:

```
molloyd@beaglebone:~$ kill 14442
[1]+  Terminated              ./HelloWorldSleep
```

You can confirm that a process is dead by using ps again. If a process doesn't die, you can use a -9 argument, which ensures death (e.g., kill -9 14442). A separate command, pkill, will kill a process based on its name, so in this case you can kill the process as follows:

```
root@beaglebone:~# pkill HelloWorldSleep
```

One more command worth mentioning is watch, which executes a command at a regular interval and shows the outcome full-screen on the terminal. For example, if you want to watch the kernel message log, you could use the following:

```
root@beaglebone:~# watch dmesg
```

You can specify the time interval between each execution using -n followed by the number of seconds. A good way to understand watch is to execute it as follows:

```
root@beaglebone:~# watch ps a
Every 1.0s: ps a        Sat Mar  1 23:11:16 2014
  PID TTY        STAT    TIME COMMAND
 1234 pts/0      Ss      0:00 -bash
 5908 pts/0      S+      0:00 watch -n 1 ps a
 5913 pts/0      S+      0:00 watch -n 1 ps a
 5914 pts/0      S+      0:00 sh -c ps a
 5915 pts/0      R+      0:00 ps a
```

You will see the PID of ps, sh, and watch changing every one (1) second, making it clear that watch is actually executing the command (ps) by passing it to a new shell using sh -c. The reason why watch appears twice in the list is that it spawns itself temporarily at the exact moment that it executes ps a.

The BusyBox Multi-call Binary

As discussed in Chapter 2, *BusyBox* is a multi-call binary that reduces overhead by combining many commands inside a single busybox command. You can type busybox to see the available utilities. It is used in varying degrees on Ångström and Debian. If you look in the directory /usr/bin and type ls -al|grep busybox you will may see symbolic links like these:

```
lrwxrwxrwx 1 root   root   17 Mar 18  2013 time -> ../../bin/busybox
lrwxrwxrwx 1 root   root   17 Mar 18  2013 traceroute -> ../../bin/busybox
lrwxrwxrwx 1 root   root   17 Mar 18  2013 unzip -> ../../bin/busybox
lrwxrwxrwx 1 root   root   17 Mar 18  2013 wget -> ../../bin/busybox
lrwxrwxrwx 1 root   root   17 Mar 18  2013 xargs -> ../../bin/busybox
```

All these utilities link back to the BusyBox executable. Therefore, when you type time, the system calls BusyBox with the argument argv[0]="/bin/usr/

time" (arguments are examined in the next chapter), allowing the multi-call binary to perform the correct task.

Other Linux Topics

At this point of the book you have covered the core commands for working with Linux on the BBB; however, there is much more to cover on the topic of Linux. For example: How do you configure a Wi-Fi adapter? How do you use `cron` to schedule jobs with the BBB? These topics and many others are detailed as you work through the remaining chapters. For example, Wi-Fi adapters and cron jobs are covered in Chapter 10, in the context of the Internet of Things.

Git

Simply put, *Git* is a system that enables you to track changes to the content of a software project as it develops over time. Git was designed by Linus Torvalds and is used today for mainline Linux kernel development. The word *git* is U.K. slang for "a stupid, worthless person, or a despicable, unpleasant man." According to the Git FAQ on kernel.org (Git FAQ, 2013), Linus is quoted as saying, "I'm an egotistical bastard, and I name all my projects after myself. First 'Linux', now 'Git.'" Despite the name, Git is an incredibly useful system to understand, for two main reasons: You can use Git when developing your own software, and you can gain an appreciation of how to work with Linux kernel source distributions.

Git is a *distributed version control system* (DVCS) for source control management. A version control system (VCS) tracks and manages changes to documents of any type. Typically, documents that have been changed are marked with revision numbers and time stamps. It is possible to compare revisions and even revert to older versions of the documents. There are two types of VCSs:

- **Centralized:** These systems, such as Apache Subversion (SVN), work on the basis that there is a single "master" copy of the project. The workflow is quite straightforward: You pull down changes from a central server, make your own changes, and then commit them back to the master copy.

- **Distributed:** Using these systems, such as Git and Selenic Mercurial, you do not pull down changes; rather you *clone* the entire *repository*, including its entire history. The clone of the repository is just as complete as the master copy and can even become the master copy if required. Thankfully, by today's standards, text documents and programming source code do not occupy much disk space. Importantly, the DVCS model does not prevent you from having a central master repository that everybody uses—have a look at `git.kernel.org`.

The main advantages of a DVCS over a CVCS are that you can very quickly commit and test changes locally, on your own system, without ever having to push them to a master copy; however, changes can be pushed when they reach an appropriate level of quality. The only significant disadvantage is the amount of disk space required to store the project and its entire history, which grows over time.

Git is a DVCS that is focused on programming source control and management. It enables you to create parallel developments that do not affect the original. You can even revert to an older version of one of the source code files, or an older version of the entire project. This is particularly useful in large-scale programming projects for which you may go down a development pathway with the project that is ultimately unsuccessful. The facility for parallel development is also very important if you have several people working on the same project.

The project, with its associated files and history, is called a *repository*, and a different version of the project is called a *snapshot*. Git is written in C, and while it originated from the need for version control tools in the development of Linux kernel code, it is used by many other open-source developments such as Eclipse and Android.

The easiest way to understand Git is to go through the steps of actually using it. Therefore, the next section is structured as a step-by-step guide. Git is installed on all standard distributions for the BBB, so you should be able to follow the steps, directly at the terminal. *GitHub* is used in this book as the remote repository for providing the source code examples. Except for pushing the source code to the server, you can do everything in this guide without requiring an account. GitHub provides free public repository accounts, but charges a fee for private repositories, such as those that would be required for retaining intellectual property rights.

> **NOTE** If you are planning to write a large software project and do not wish to make it publicly available on www.github.com or pay a subscription fee, you can install your own rich user-interface Git server, such as www.gitlab.org or www.getgitorious.com.

Getting Started with Git

In this guide I create a repository called "test" on GitHub. Initially, it contains only a README.md file with a short description of the test project.

As shown in Figure 3-4, nearly every operation is a local operation. A *checksum* is performed on every file in Git before it is stored. This ensures that Git will be aware if a modification is made outside Git itself, including file system corruption. Git uses 40-character hash codes for the checksums. This helps Git to keep track of changes between the local repository and remote repository, which enables the range of local operations.

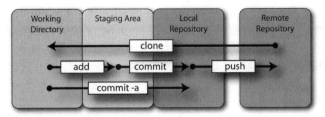

Figure 3-4: The basic Git workflow

Cloning a Repository (git clone)

Cloning a repository means making a copy of all the files in the repository on your local file system, as well as the history of changes to that project. You do this operation only once. To clone the repository, issue the command `git clone` followed by the fully formed repository name:

```
$ cd ~/
$ git clone https://github.com/derekmolloy/test.git
Cloning into 'test'...
remote: Counting objects: 3, done.
remote: Compressing objects: 100% (2/2), done.
remote: Total 3 (delta 0), reused 0 (delta 0)
Unpacking objects: 100% (3/3), done.
```

You now have a full copy of the "test" repository. Your repository is just as complete as the version on the GitHub server and if you were to deploy it over a network, file system, other Git server, or even on a different GitHub account, it could assume the role as the main version of this repository. While there is no need for a central server, it is usually the case, as it enables multiple users to check in source to a known master repository. The repository is created in the test directory and it currently contains the following:

```
~/test$ ls -al
total 24
drwxr-xr-x 3 root root 4096 Feb 22 01:08 .
drwx------ 3 root root 4096 Feb 22 01:02 ..
drwxr-xr-x 8 root root 4096 Feb 22 01:17 .git
-rw-r--r-- 1 root root   61 Feb 21 23:42 README.md
```

You can see the README.md file that was created and you can also see a hidden subdirectory .git, which contains the following files and directories:

```
~/test/.git$ ls
COMMIT_EDITMSG HEAD       branches description index logs     packed-refs
FETCH_HEAD     ORIG_HEAD config    hooks           info  objects refs
```

The hidden .git folder is in the project's root directory and it contains all of the information about the repository, such as commit messages, logs, and the data objects. The "Further Reading" section at the end of this chapter directs you to an excellent book on Git, which is freely available online. Thankfully, in the following discussion you will not have to make changes in the .git directory structure, as you have Git commands to do that for you.

Getting the Status (git status)

Now that the repository exists, the next step is to add a new text file to the *working directory*, where it will be it in an *untracked* state. When you call the command git status, you can see a message stating that "untracked files" are present:

```
~/test$ echo "Just some Text" > newfile.txt
~/test$ git status
# On branch master
# Untracked files:
#   (use "git add <file>..." to include in what will be committed)
#       newfile.txt
nothing added to commit but untracked files present ...
```

The next step is to add these untracked files to the *staging area*. However, if you did not want to add a set of files, you could also create a .gitignore file to ignore those files. For example, this could be useful if you are building C/C++ projects and you decide that you do not want to add intermediate .o files. Here is an example of creating a .gitignore file in order to ignore C/C++ .o files:

```
~/test$ echo "*.o" > .gitignore
~/test$ more .gitignore
*.o
~/test$ touch testobj.o
~/test$ git status
# On branch master
# Untracked files:
#   (use "git add <file>..." to include in what will be committed)
#       .gitignore
#       newfile.txt
nothing added to commit but untracked files present ...
```

In this case, two files are untracked, but there is no mention of the testobj.o file, as it is being correctly ignored.

Adding to the Staging Area (git add)

The files in the working directory can now be added to the *staging area* by typing **git add .**, which will add all the files in the working directory. However, for clarity, each file is being added explicitly here:

```
~/test$ git add .gitignore
~/test$ git add newfile.txt
```

The two files have been added from the working directory to the staging area. The status of the repository can then be displayed using:

```
~/test$ git status
# On branch master
# Changes to be committed:
#   (use "git reset HEAD <file>..." to unstage)
#
#       new file:   .gitignore
#       new file:   newfile.txt
```

To delete/remove a file from the staging area you can use `git rm somefile.ext`.

Committing to the Local Repository (git commit)

Once you have added the files to the staging area, you can then "commit" the changes from the staging area to the local git repository. First, you may wish to add your name and e-mail address variables, to make it clear who is committing the changes to the repository:

```
~/test$ git config -global user.name "Derek Molloy"
~/test$ git config -global user.email derek@mailaccount.com
```

These values are set against your Linux user account, so they will remain when you next log in. You can see them if you type `more ~/.gitconfig`. The changes can be permanently committed to the local git repository using the `git commit` command:

```
~/test$ git commit -m "Testing the Repository"
[master 46207db] Testing the Repository
2 files changed, 2 insertions(+)
create mode 100644 .gitignore
create mode 100644 newfile.txt
```

The changes will be flagged with the username, and a message is also required. If you wish to detail the message inline, you can use `-m "the message"` to set the commit message.

NOTE The shortcut `git commit -a` will commit modified files directly to the staging area, without requiring a call to `add`. It does not add new files.

Pushing to the Remote Repository (git push)

To perform this step you must have your own GitHub account. The `git push` command pushes any code updates to the remote repository. You must be registered to make changes to the remote repository for the changes to be applied.

It can be called as follows (replace the user details and repository name with your own account details):

```
~/test$ git push
Username for 'https://github.com': derekmolloy
Password for 'https://derekmolloy@github.com':
Counting objects: 7, done.
Compressing objects: 100% (4/4), done.
Writing objects: 100% (6/6), 666 bytes, done.
Total 6 (delta 0), reused 0 (delta 0)
To https://github.com/derekmolloy/test.git
   22df5ee..46207db  master -> master
```

Once the code has been pushed to the remote repository, you can pull changes back to a local repository on any machine by issuing a `git pull` command from within the local repository working directory:

```
~/test$ git pull
Already up-to-date.
```

In this case everything is already up-to-date.

Advanced Git

Git supports the concept of branching, which allows you to work on multiple different versions of the set of files within your project. For example, if you wanted to develop a new feature in your project (Version 2) but maintain the code in the current version (Version 1), you could create a new branch (Version 2). New features and changes that are made to Version 2 will not affect the code in Version 1. You can then easily switch between branches.

Creating a Branch (git branch)

Suppose, for example, you wanted to create a new branch called "mybranch"; you can do so using the command `git branch mybranch` and then you can switch to that branch using `git checkout mybranch` as shown here:

```
~/test$ git branch mybranch
~/test$ git checkout mybranch
Switched to branch 'mybranch'
```

Now, to demonstrate how this works, suppose a temporary file is added to the repository called `testmybranch.txt`. This could be a new code file for your project. You can see that the status of the branch makes it clear that there is an untracked file in the working directory:

```
~/test$ touch testmybranch.txt
~/test$ ls
```

```
README.md  newfile.txt  testmybranch.txt  testobj.obj
~/test$ git status
# On branch mybranch
# Untracked files:
#   (use "git add <file>..." to include in what will be committed)
#        testmybranch.txt
nothing added to commit but untracked files present ...
```

You can then add this new file to the staging area of the branch using the same commands as before:

```
~/test$ git add .
~/test$ git status
# On branch mybranch
# Changes to be committed:
#   (use "git reset HEAD <file>..." to unstage)
#        new file:   testmybranch.txt
```

You can commit this change to the mybranch branch of the local repository. This change will affect the mybranch branch but have no impact on the master branch:

```
~/test$ git commit -m "Test commit to mybranch"
[mybranch 02eb0fb] Test commit to mybranch
 0 files changed
 create mode 100644 testmybranch.txt
~/test$ git status
# On branch mybranch
nothing to commit (working directory clean)
~/test$ ls
README.md  newfile.txt  testmybranch.txt  testobj.obj
```

You can see from the preceding output that the file testmybranch.txt is committed to the local repository and you can see the file in the directory.

If you now switch from the branch mybranch back to the master branch using the call git checkout master, you will see that something interesting happens when you request the directory listing:

```
~/test$ git checkout master
Switched to branch 'master'
~/test$ ls
README.md  newfile.txt  testobj.obj
```

Yes, the file testmybranch.txt has disappeared from the directory. It still exists, but it is in a blob form inside the .git/objects directory. If you switch back to the branch and list the directory, you will see the following:

```
~/test$ git checkout mybranch
Switched to branch 'mybranch'
```

```
~/test$ ls
README.md   newfile.txt   testmybranch.txt   testobj.obj
```

The file now reappears. Therefore, you can see just how well integrated the branching system is. At this point, you can go back to the master branch and make changes to the original code without the changes in the `mybranch` branch having any impact on the master code. Even if you change the code in the same file, it has no effect on the original code in the master branch.

Merging the Branch (git merge)

What if you want to apply the changes that you made in the `mybranch` branch to the master project? You can do this by using `git merge`:

```
~/test$ git checkout master
Switched to branch 'master'
~/test$ git merge mybranch
Updating 46207db..02eb0fb
Fast-forward
 0 files changed
 create mode 100644 testmybranch.txt
~/test$ git status
# On branch master
# Your branch is ahead of 'origin/master' by 1 commit.
nothing to commit (working directory clean)
~/test$ ls
README.md   newfile.txt   testmybranch.txt   testobj.obj
```

Now the `testmybranch.txt` file is in the master branch and any changes that were made to other documents in the master have been applied. The local repository is now one commit ahead of the remote repository and you could use a `git push` to update the remote repository.

Deleting a Branch (git branch -d)

If you wish to delete a branch, you can do so using the `git branch -d mybranch` command:

```
~/test$ git branch -d mybranch
Deleted branch mybranch (was 02eb0fb).
~/test$ ls
README.md   newfile.txt   testmybranch.txt   testobj.obj
```

You can see that the file `testmybranch.txt` is still present in the master project, and it should be, as the branch was merged with the master project. If the branch was deleted before the merge was performed, then the file would have been lost.

Conclusions on Git

Table 3-7 provides a summary of the main Git commands. At this point you have seen the core use of Git, and hopefully you have been encouraged to use Git in your own project development. If you are developing code directly on the BBB, Git can be very useful, as you can easily push your developments to a remote repository. That can be useful in backing up your code and redeploying the code to multiple BBBs. At the end of this chapter, instructions are provided for downloading the source code for this book using Git. Later in the book, you will see how you can integrate Git with the Eclipse development environment for general software management tasks.

Table 3-7: Summary of the Main Git Commands

OPERATION	DESCRIPTION	OPERATION	DESCRIPTION
git clone	Clone from the remote repository.	git rm	Delete a file or directory from the staging area.
git init	Create a wholly new repository.	git mv	Move or rename a file or folder in the staging area.
git pull	Merge changes from a master repository.	git log	Display a log of commits. The project history.
git fetch	Find what has changed in a master repository without merging.	git tag	You can give a commit a name, e.g., version 2.
git status	Show the status of the project.	git merge [name]	Merge the branch.
git add	Add a new file or edit an existing file.	git show	Get details about the current or other commit.
git diff	Show the differences that are to be committed.	git branch [name]	Create a new branch. Use -d to delete.
git commit	Commit to the repository.	git checkout [name]	Switch to a different branch.
git push	Push changes from the local repository to a remote repository.		

Desktop Virtualization

Desktop *virtualization* enables a single desktop computer to run multiple OS instances simultaneously. It uses technology called *hypervisors*, which consist of hardware, firmware, and software elements, to create and run software-emulated machines, which are termed *virtual machines (VMs)*. If you wish to run multiple OS instances on a single computer, VMs provide an alternative to creating a multi-boot configuration.

In virtualization, there are usually two or more distinct OS instances. The *host* OS is the one that was first installed on the physical machine. The hypervisor software is then used to create a *guest* OS within a virtual machine. Figure 3-5 captures a host Windows desktop computer running a guest Debian 64-bit Linux VM within a window.

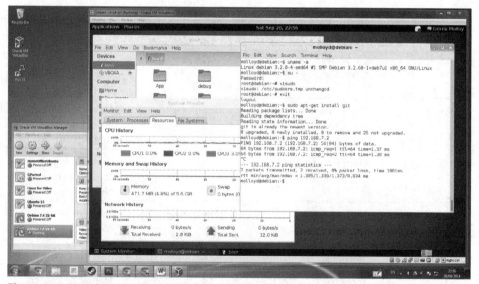

Figure 3-5: VirtualBox running Debian as a guest OS on a Windows host machine

Many virtualization products are available, but most have significant costs and proprietary licenses and are limited in the type of guest and host OSs that they support. Two of the most popular Linux desktop virtualization products are *VMware Player* and *VirtualBox*. VMware Player (www.vmware.com/products/player/) is provided by VMware and is available free of charge for personal use. VirtualBox (www.virtualbox.org) was created by Innotek, which was acquired by Oracle, and is available under a GNU GLPv2 license (some features are available free under a proprietary license).

Both products use *hosted hypervisors* (Type-2) for virtualization, meaning that they run within a regular OS, allowing you to use both machines at the same time. VirtualBox is available to run on Windows, Mac OS X, and Linux machines, and it can be used to host guest OSs such as Linux, Windows, and Mac OS X. Currently, VMware Player is not available for Mac OS X host installations; instead, you must purchase a product called VMware Fusion.

Both products are powerful and it is difficult to distinguish between them; however, VirtualBox is released under a GPL and it supports a feature called *snapshots*, which can be very useful. A user interface makes it possible to take a snapshot of the guest OS that can be saved for later use. For example, you could take a snapshot before you make a significant configuration change to your guest OS, enabling you to roll back to that configuration should problems arise. The snapshot stores the VM settings, changes in the contents of the virtual disks, and the memory state of the machine at that point in time. Therefore, when a snapshot is restored, the VM continues running at the exact same point as when the snapshot was taken.

All Linux packages and software in this book are built using a Debian 64-bit desktop distribution that is installed within a VirtualBox VM. If you install the VirtualBox "Guest Additions" you are able to copy-and-paste text between your guest and host OSs, share directories, and even resize the VirtualBox guest OS window dynamically. The chapter web page provides advice on installing a Linux guest OS under a Windows host OS.

Code for This Book

Now that you have your Desktop Linux installation up and running under VirtualBox, or you are running a regular Linux desktop installation, you can download all of the source code, scripts, and documentation discussed in this book by opening a Linux console/terminal and typing the following:

```
~$ sudo apt-get install git
Reading package lists... Done
~$ git clone https://github.com/derekmolloy/exploringBB.git
Cloning into ...
```

Under the Debian desktop distribution you need to add yourself to the sudoers file before you can install Git. Type the following: **su** - then **visudo** and add the line molloyd ALL=(ALL:ALL) ALL underneath the %sudo line. If you wish to download the code from within Windows or Mac OS X, a graphical user interface is available from windows.github.com and mac.github.com that can be used for working with GitHub repositories.

NOTE If you have your own GitHub account, you can use its web interface to *fork* this repository to your own account or you can *watch* the repository for updates and changes. A GitHub account without private repositories is currently free of charge. In addition, students and academics can apply for a free Micro account, which provides for five private repositories for two years.

Summary

After completing this chapter, you should be able to:

- Describe the basic concept of an embedded Linux system.
- Describe how an embedded Linux device, such as the BeagleBone, boots the Linux OS.
- Describe important Linux concepts, such as kernel space, user space, and system initialization.
- Perform system administration tasks on the BBB.
- Use the BBB file system effectively.
- Use a range of Linux commands for file and process management.
- Manage your own software development projects using Git.
- Install a Linux distribution on your desktop computer host OS using desktop virtualization tools, such as VirtualBox.
- Download the source code for this book using Git.

Further Reading

This chapter has provided a whirlwind introduction to embedded Linux, Linux administration, Git, and virtualization. The following excellent texts can help you close any gaps:

- Christopher Hallinan's *Embedded Linux Primer: A Practical Real-World Approach, Second Edition* (Upper Saddle River, NJ: Prentice Hall, 2011)
- The Debian Policy Manual: `tiny.cc/ebb303`
- To learn more about Git, start with a call to `man gittutorial` and then if you need detailed information, see Scott Chacon's excellent reference *Pro Git*, at `www.git-scm.com/book`; also available in paperback (New York: Apress Media, 2009).

# CHAPTER 4

Interfacing Electronics

This chapter introduces you to the type of practical electronics that you need in order to work effectively and correctly with the BeagleBone platform. One chapter cannot be a substitute for full textbooks on digital and analog electronics; however, there are concepts with which you must be comfortable before connecting electronics to the interface headers on the BeagleBone, as incorrect configurations can easily destroy the board.

Equipment Required for This Chapter:

- Components for this chapter (if following along): The full list is provided at the end of this chapter.
- Digilent Analog Discovery *or* access to a digital multimeter, signal generator, and oscilloscope.

Recommended Equipment

When developing electronics circuits for the BBB platform, it is useful to have the following tools so that you can analyze a circuit before you connect it to the BBB inputs/outputs, in order to reduce the chance of damaging your board. In particular, it would be useful if you had access to a digital multimeter and a mixed-signal oscilloscope.

> **NOTE**   All of the following tools are listed to provide you with options to consider. Please do your own homework and seek independent advice before choosing any such product. In addition, none of the products listed in this book are the result of any type of product placement agreement or request. All prices are approximate and indicative only.

Digital Multimeter

A *digital multimeter* (*DMM*) is an invaluable tool when working with BBB circuits for measuring voltage, current, and resistance/continuity. You possibly already have one, but if not you should try to purchase one with the following features:

- **Auto power off:** It is easy to waste batteries.
- **Auto range:** It is vital that you can select different measurement ranges. Mid-price meters often have automatic range selection functionality that can reduce the time required to take measurements.
- **Continuity testing:** This should provide an audible beep unless there is a break in the conductor (or excessive resistance).
- **True RMS readings:** Most low-cost meters use averaging to calculate AC(~) current/voltage. True RMS meters process the readings using a *true root mean square* (RMS) calculation, which makes it possible to account for distortions in waveforms when taking readings. This is useful for analyzing phase controlled equipment, solid-state devices, motorized devices, etc.
- **Other useful options:** Not strictly necessary but helpful are backlit displays; a measurement hold; large digit displays; a greater number of significant digits; PC connectivity (ideally opto-isolated); temperature probe; and diode testing.
- **Case:** Look for a good-quality rubberized plastic case.

Generally, most of the preceding features are available on mid-price DMMs with a good level of accuracy (1% or better), high input impedances (>10MΩ), and good measurement ranges. High-end multimeters mainly offer faster measurement speed and greater levels of measurement accuracy; some may also offer features such as measuring capacitance, frequency, temperature using an infra-red sensor, humidity, and transistor gain. Some of the best-known brands are Fluke, Tenma, Agilent, Extech, and Klein Tools.

Oscilloscopes

Standard DMMs provide you with a versatile tool that enables you to measure average voltage, current, and resistance. *Oscilloscopes* typically only measure voltage, but they enable you to see how the voltage changes with respect to time.

You can typically view two or more voltage waveforms simultaneously that are captured within a certain bandwidth and number of analog samples (memory). The *bandwidth* defines the range of signal frequencies that an oscilloscope can measure accurately (typically to the 3dB point, i.e., the frequency at which a sine wave amplitude is ~30% lower than its true amplitude). To achieve accurate results, the number of analog samples needs to be a multiple of the bandwidth (you will see why later in this chapter when the Nyquist rate is discussed); and for modern oscilloscopes, this value is typically 4–5 times the bandwidth, so a 25MHz oscilloscope should have 100 million samples per second or greater. The bandwidth and number of analog samples have the greatest influence on the cost of an oscilloscope.

Several low-cost two-channel oscilloscopes are available, such as those by Owen PDS5022S 25MHz (~$200), feature-rich Siglent SDS1022DL 25MHz (~$325), Rigol DS1052 50MHz (~$325), and Owen SDS6062 60MHz (~$349). Prices rise considerably as the bandwidth increases, to around $1,500 for a 300MHz scope. Agilent digital storage (DSOX) and mixed-signal (MSOX) series scopes would be considered to be mid/high range and cost $3,000 (100MHz) to $16,000 (1GHz). Mixed-signal scopes also provide you with digital bus analysis tools. Remember that mid-range scopes also require good quality "fast" 10× probes, which attach to your circuit.

The Digilent Analog Discovery with Waveforms (see Figure 4-1) is used to test all of the circuits in this chapter. The Analog Discovery is a USB oscilloscope, waveform generator, digital pattern generator, and logic analyzer for the Windows environment. It is priced at $99 for U.S. students and is generally available for $219. If you are starting out, or refreshing your electronics skills, then it is a really great piece of equipment for the price.

NOTE I made a video on the use of this device that is available at the chapter web page: www.exploringbeaglebone.com/chapter4. It demonstrates three different measurement applications of the Analog Discovery: analog analysis of a rectifier diode; using the digital pattern generator and logic analyzer to investigate the behavior of a JK flip-flop; and using the logic analyzer and its I²C interpreter to connect to the BeagleBone I²C bus and analyze how it behaves.

The Analog Discovery is the tool used to generate all of the oscilloscope plots that are presented in this book, as all examples have been implemented using real circuits. The scope is limited to two channels at 5MHz per channel and 50 million samples per second, for both the waveform generator and the differential oscilloscope. As such, it is mainly focused on students and learners; however, it can also be useful in deciding upon "must-have" features for your next, more expensive, equipment.

There are alternative mixed-signal USB scopes, such as PicoScopes, which range from $160 to $10,000 (www.picotech.com), and the BitScope DSO, from

$150 to $1,000 (www.bitscope.com), which has Linux support. However, based on the feature set that is currently available on USB oscilloscopes, it may be the case that a bench scope with a USB logic analyzer (to provide mixed-mode functionality, such as the Saleae logic analyzer—www.saleae.com) provides the best "bang for your buck."

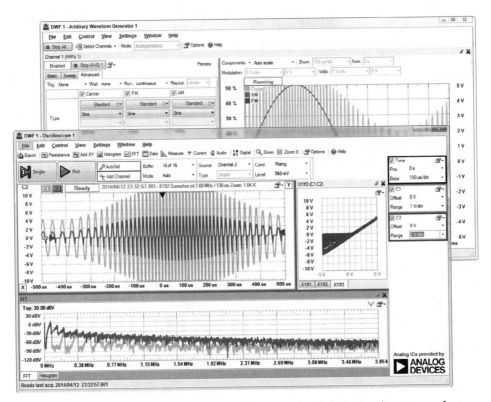

Figure 4-1: The Waveforms application generating a signal and displaying the response from the physical circuit

Basic Circuit Principles

Electronic circuits contain arrangements of components that can be described as being either passive or active. *Active components*, such as transistors, are those that can adaptively control the flow of current, whereas *passive components* cannot (e.g., resistors, capacitors, diodes). The challenge in building circuits is designing a suitable arrangement of appropriate components. Fortunately, there are *circuit analysis* equations to help you with this challenge.

Voltage, Current, Resistance, and Ohm's Law

The most important equation that you need to understand is Ohm's Law. It is simply stated as follows:

$$V = I \times R$$

where:

- *Voltage* (V), measured in *volts*, is the difference in *potential* energy that forces electrical current to flow in the circuit. A water analogy is very useful when thinking of voltage; many houses have a buffer tank of water in the attic that is connected to the taps in the house. Water flows when a tap is turned on, due to the height of the tank and the force of gravity. If the tap were at the same height as the top of the tank of water, then no water would flow, as there would be no potential energy. Voltage behaves in much the same way; when a voltage on one side of a component, such as a resistor, is greater than on the other side, then electrical current can flow across the component.

- *Current* (I), measured in *amps*, is the flow of electrical charge. To continue the water analogy, current would be the flow of water from the tank (with a high potential) to the tap (with a lower potential). Remember that the tap still has potential and water will flow out of the drain of the sink, unless it is at ground level (GND). To put the level of current in context, when we build circuits to interface with the BBB's GPIOs, they usually source or sink only about 5mA, where a milliamp is one thousandth of an amp.

- *Resistance* (R), measured in *ohms* (Ω), discourages the flow of charge. A resistor is a component that reduces the flow of current through the dissipation of power. It does this in a linear fashion, where the power dissipated in *watts* (W), is given by $P = V \times I$ or, alternatively by integrating Ohm's law: $P = I^2 R = V^2/R$. The power is dissipated in the form of heat, and all resistors have a *maximum dissipated power rating*. Common metal film or carbon resistors typically dissipate 0.125W to 1W, and the price increases dramatically if this value has to exceed 3W. To finish with the water analogy, resistance is the friction between the water and the pipe, which results in a heating effect and a reduction in the flow of water. This resistance can be increased by increasing the surface area over which the water has to pass, while maintaining the pipe's cross-sectional area (e.g., placing small pipes within the main pipe).

For example, if you had to buy a resistor that limits the flow of current to 100mA when using a 5V supply, as illustrated in Figure 4-2(a), which resistor should you buy? The voltage dropped across the resistor, V_R, must be 5V, as it is the only component in the circuit. Because $V_R = I_R \times R$, it follows that the resistor should have the value $R = V_R/I_R = 5V/100mA = 50\Omega$, and the power dissipated by this resistor can be calculated using any of the general equations $P = VI = I^2R = V^2/R$ as 0.5W.

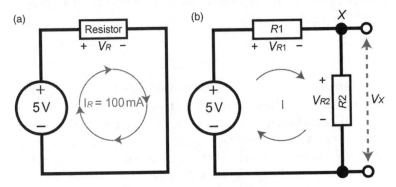

Figure 4-2: (a) Ohm's law circuit example (b) Voltage divider example

Buying one through-hole, fixed-value 50Ω metal-film resistor with a 1% tolerance (accuracy) costs about $0.10 for a 0.33W resistor and $0.45 for a 1W power rating. You should be careful with the power rating of the resistors you use in your circuits, as underspecified resistors can blow. A 30W resistor will cost $2.50 and can get extremely hot—not all resistors are created equally!

WARNING   Why would it be bad practice to connect a voltage supply's positive terminal to the negative terminal without a resistor? This is called a *short circuit* and it is the quickest way to damage a sensitive device like the BBB. Connection (hook-up) wire by its nature is a very good conductor, and it has a very small resistance. A 100m (328 ft) roll of 0.6mm (0.023") hook-up wire has a total resistance of about 5Ω; therefore, connecting a 6" length of connection wire between a BBB 3.3V supply and its GND terminal would in theory draw 433A (*I* = V/R = 3.3V/0.0076Ω). In practice this will not happen, but it would likely damage your BBB! Also, remember that LEDs do not include a fixed internal resistance and so behave somewhat like a short circuit when forward-biased. That topic is described later in this chapter.

Voltage Division

If the circuit in Figure 4-2(a) is modified to add another resistor *in series* as illustrated in Figure 4-2(b), what will be the impact on the circuit?

■ Since one resistor is after the other (they're in series), the total resistance that the current must pass through to circulate in the circuit is the sum of the two values: $R_T = R1 + R2$.

■ The supply voltage must drop across the two resistors, so you can say that $V_{supply} = V_{R1} + V_{R2}$. The voltage that drops across each resistor is inversely proportional to the resistor's value. This circuit is called a *voltage divider*.

Suppose you want to calculate on paper the voltage value at point X in Figure 4-2(b) if $R1 = 25\Omega$ and $R2 = 75\Omega$. The total resistance in the circuit is $R_T = 25+75 = 100\Omega$, and the total voltage drop across the resistors must be 5V; therefore, by using Ohm's law, the current flowing in the circuit is $I = V/R = 5V/100\Omega = 50\text{mA}$. If the resistance of $R1$ is 25Ω, then the voltage drop across $V_{R1} = I \times R1 = 0.05\text{A} \times 25\Omega = 1.25\text{V}$ and the voltage drop across $V_{R2} = I \times R1 = 0.05\text{A} \times 75\Omega = 3.75\text{V}$. You can see that the sum of these voltages is 5V, thus obeying *Kirchoff's voltage law*, which states that the sum of the voltage drops in a series circuit equals the total voltage applied.

To answer the question fully: In this circuit, 1.25V is dropped across $R1$ and 3.75V is dropped across $R2$, so what is the voltage at X? To know that, you have to measure X with respect to some other point! If you measured X with respect to the negative terminal of the supply, then the voltage drop is V_X in Figure 4-2(b) and it is the same as the voltage drop across $R2$, so it is 3.75V. However, it would be equally as valid to ask the question "What is the voltage at X with respect to the positive terminal of the supply?" In that case, it would be the negative of the voltage drop across $R1$ (as X is at 3.75V with respect to the negative terminal and the positive terminal is at +5V with respect to the negative terminal); therefore, the voltage at X with respect to the positive terminal of the supply is –1.25V.

To calculate the value of V_X in Figure 4-2(b), the *voltage divider rule* can be generalized to the following:

$$V_X = V \times \frac{R2}{R1+R2}$$

You can use this rule to determine a voltage V_X, but unfortunately this configuration is quite limited in practice, because it is very likely that the circuit to which you connect this voltage supply, V_X, will itself have a resistance (or load). This will alter the characteristic of your voltage divider circuit, changing the voltage V_X. However, most circuits that follow voltage dividers are usually input circuits that have very high input impedances, and therefore the impact on V_X will be minimal.

Figure 4-3(a) captures a *variable resistor*, or *potentiometer (pot)*, and an associated circuit where it is used as a standalone voltage divider. The resistance between pins 1 and 3 is a fixed value, $10\text{k}\Omega$ in the case of the blue multi-turn pot; however, the resistance between pins 3 and the wiper pin (pin 2) varies between 0Ω and $10\text{k}\Omega$. Therefore, if the resistance between pins 2 and 3 is $2\text{k}\Omega$, then the resistance between pins 1 and 2 will be $10\text{k}\Omega - 2\text{k}\Omega = 8\text{k}\Omega$. In such a case, the output voltage, V_{out}, will be 1V and it can be varied between 0V and 5V by turning the small screw on the pot, using a trim tool or screwdriver.

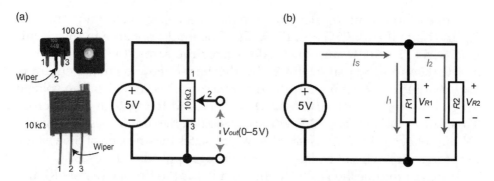

Figure 4-3: (a) Potentiometers and using a variable voltage supply (b) Current divider example

Current Division

If the circuit is modified as in Figure 4-3(b) to place the two resistors in parallel, then you now have a *current divider* circuit. Current will follow the path of least resistance, so if $R1 = 100\Omega$ and $R2 = 200\Omega$, then a greater proportion of the current will travel through $R1$. So, what is this proportion? In this case the voltage drop across $R1$ and $R2$ is 5V in both cases. Therefore, the current I_1 will be $I = V/R = 5V/100\Omega = 50\text{mA}$ and the current I_2 will be $I = 5V/200\Omega = 25\text{mA}$. Therefore, twice as much current travels through the 100Ω resistor as the 200Ω resistor. Clearly, current favors the path of least resistance.

Kirchoff's current law states that the sum of currents entering a junction equals the sum of currents exiting that junction. This means that $I_S = I_1 + I_2 = 25\text{mA} + 50\text{mA} = 75\text{mA}$. The *current divider rule* can be stated generally as follows:

$$I_1 = I \times \left(\frac{R2}{R1+R2} \right), \quad \text{and} \quad I_2 = I \times \left(\frac{R1}{R1+R2} \right)$$

However, this requires that you know the value of the current I (I_S in this case) that is entering the junction. To calculate I_S directly, you need to calculate the equivalent resistance (R_T) of the two parallel resistors, which is given as follows:

$$\frac{1}{R_T} = \frac{1}{R_1} + \frac{1}{R_2}, \quad \text{or} \quad R_T = \frac{R_1 \times R_2}{R_1 + R_2},$$

This is 66.66Ω in Figure 4-3(b); therefore $I_S = V/R = 5V/66.66\Omega = 75\text{mA}$, which is consistent with the initial calculations.

The power delivered by the supply: $P = VI = 5V \times 0.075A = 0.375W$. This should be equal to the sum of the power dissipated by $R1 = V^2/R = 5^2/100 = 0.25\,W$ and $R2 = V^2/R = 5^2/200 = 0.125W$, giving $0.375W$ total, confirming that the law of conservation of energy applies!

Implementing Circuits on a Breadboard

The breadboard is a great platform for prototyping circuits and it works perfectly with the BBB. Figure 4-4 illustrates a breadboard, describing how you can use the two horizontal power rails for 3.3V and 5V power. Remember to bridge the two ground rails on the board.

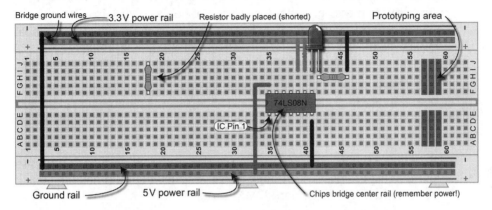

Figure 4-4: The breadboard with a 7408 IC (quad two-input AND gates)

A good-quality breadboard like that in Figure 4-4 (830 tie points) will cost about $6 to $10. Giant breadboards (3,220 tie points) are available for about $20. Here are some tips for using breadboards:

- Whenever possible, place pin 1 of your ICs on the bottom left so that you can easily debug your circuits. Always line up the pins carefully with the breadboard holes before applying pressure and "clicking" it home. Also, ICs need power!

- Leaving a wire disconnected is *not* the same as connecting it to GND (discussed later in this chapter).

- Use a flat-head screwdriver to slowly lever ICs out of the breadboard from both sides to avoid bending the IC's legs.

- Be careful not to bridge resistors and other components by placing two of the pins in the same vertical rail. Also, trim resistor leads before placing them in the board, as long resistor leads can accidentally touch and cause circuit debugging headaches.

- Momentary push buttons typically have four legs that are connected in two pairs; make sure that you orient them correctly (use a DMM continuity test).

- Staples make great bridge connections!

- Some boards have a break in the power rails—bridge this where necessary.

- Breadboards typically have 0.1" spacing (lead pitch) between the tie points, which is 2.54mm metric. Try to buy all components and connectors with that spacing. For ICs, choose the DIP package (the IC code ends with an N); for other components, choose the "through-hole" form.

■ Use the color of the hook-up wire to mean something—e.g., use red for 5V and black for GND; it can really help when debugging circuits. Solid-core 22AWG wire serves as perfect hook-up wire and is available with many different insulator colors. Pre-formed jumper wire is available, but long wires lead to messy circuits. A selection of hook-up wire in different colors and a good-quality wire-stripping tool enables the neatest and most stable breadboard layouts.

Digital Multimeters (DMMs) and Breadboards

Measuring voltage, current and resistance is fairly straightforward once you take a few rules into account (with reference to Figure 4-5):

■ **DC voltage (DCV):** is measured in parallel with (i.e., across) the component that experiences the voltage drop. The meter should have the black probe in the COM (common) DMM input.

■ **DC current (DCA):** is measured in series, so you will have to "break" the connection in your circuit and wire the DMM as if it were a component in series with the conductor in the circuit in which you are measuring current. Use the black probe lead in COM and the red lead in the μAmA input (or equivalent). Do not use the 10A unfused input.

■ **Resistance:** cannot usually be measured in-circuit, as other resistors or components will act as parallel/series loads in your measurement. Isolate the component and place your DMM red probe in the VΩ input and set the meter to measure Ω. The *continuity test* can be reasonably effectively used in-circuit, provided that it is de-energized.

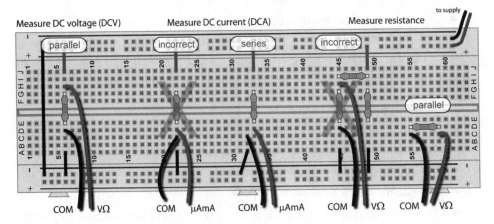

Figure 4-5: Measuring voltage, current, and resistance

If your DMM is refusing to function, you may have blown the internal fuse. Disconnect the DMM probes and open the meter to find the small glass fuse. If you have a second meter you can perform a continuity test to determine whether it has blown. Replace it with a like value (or PTC)—not a mains fuse!

WARNING   Measuring current directly across a voltage supply (even a 9V battery) with no load is the quickest way to blow the DMM fuse, as most are rated at about 200mA. Check that you have the probe in VΩ before measuring voltage.

Example Circuit: Voltage Regulation

Now that you have read the principles, a more complex circuit is discussed in this section, and then the components are examined in detail in the following sections. Do not build the circuit in this section; it is intended as an example to introduce the concept of interconnected components.

A *voltage regulator* is a complex but easy-to-use device that accepts a varied input voltage and outputs a constant voltage almost regardless of the attached load, at a lower level than the input voltage. The voltage regulator maintains the output voltage within a certain tolerance, preventing voltage variations from damaging downstream electronics devices.

The BBB has a very advanced Power Management IC (PMIC) that can supply different voltage levels to different devices at different output pins. For example, there is a 5V output, a 3.3V output, and a 1.8V reference for the analog-to-digital converters. You can use the 5V and 3.3V supplies on the BBB to drive your circuits, but only within certain current supply limits. The BBB can supply up to 1A on the VDD_5V pins on the P9 header (pins 5 and 6) if the BBB is connected to a DC power supply via the 5V jack, and 250mA on the DC_3.3V pins (pins 3 and 4).

If you wish to draw larger currents for applications like driving motors then you may need to use voltage regulators like that in Figure 4-6. You can build this directly on a breadboard or you can purchase a "breadboard power supply stick 5V/3.3V" from SparkFun (www.sparkfun.com) for about $15.

As shown in Figure 4-6, the pin on the left of the regulator is the voltage supply input. When delivering a current of 500mA, the KA7805/LM7805 voltage regulator will accept an input voltage range of 8V–20V, and will output a voltage (on the right) in the range of 4.8V–5.2V. The middle pin should be connected to the ground rail. The aluminum plate at the back of the voltage regulator is there to dissipate heat. The hole enables you to bolt on a heat sink, allowing for greater output currents, of up to 1A.

The minimum input voltage required is about 8V in order to drive the KA7805/LM7805 voltage regulator. If your supply voltage is lower than that, then you could use a low-dropout (LDO) voltage regulator, which can require a supply as low as 6V to operate a 5V regulator. The implementation circuit in Figure 4-6 has the following additional components that enable it to deliver a clean and steady 5V, 1A supply:

- The diode ensures that if the supply is erroneously connected with the wrong polarity (e.g., 9V and GND are accidentally swapped), then the circuit is protected from damage. Diodes like the 1N4001 (1A supply) are very low cost, but the downside is that there will be a small forward voltage drop (about 1V@1Amp) across the diode in advance of the regulator.

- The switch can be used to power the circuit on or off. A slider switch enables the circuit to remain continuously powered.

- The *Positive Temperature Coefficient* (PTC) resettable fuse is very useful for preventing damage from overcurrent faults, such as accidental short circuits or component failure. The PTC enables a *holding current* to pass with only a small resistance (about 0.25Ω); but once a greater *tripping current* is exceeded, the resistance increases rapidly, behaving like a circuit breaker. When the power is removed, the PTC will cool (for a few seconds) and it regains its pre-tripped characteristics. In this circuit a 60R110 or equivalent Polyfuse would be appropriate, as it has a holding current of 1.1A and a trip current of 2.2A, at a maximum voltage of 60V DC.

- The 0.33µF capacitor is on the supply side of the regulator and the 0.1µF capacitor is on the output side of the regulator. These are the values recommended in the datasheet to remove noise (*ripple rejection*) from the supply. Capacitors are discussed shortly.

- The LED and appropriate current-limiting resistor provide an indicator light that makes it clear when the supply is powered. LEDs are also discussed shortly.

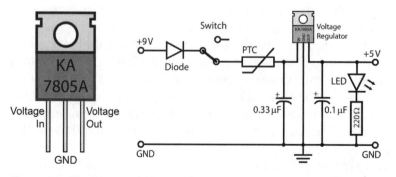
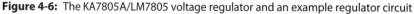

Figure 4-6: The KA7805A/LM7805 voltage regulator and an example regulator circuit

> **NOTE** There are two main notations to represent current flow: The first is *electron current flow* and it is the flow of negative charge. The second is *conventional flow* notation and it is precisely the opposite—it is the flow of positive charge and it is consistent with all semiconductor symbols. This book uses the conventional flow notation to describe current flow direction.

Discrete Components

The previous example circuit used a number of discrete components to build a standalone power supply circuit. In this section, the types of components that compose the power supply circuit are discussed in more detail. These components can be applied to many different circuit designs, and it is important to discuss them now, as many of them are used in designing circuits that interface to the BBB input/outputs in Chapter 6.

Diodes

Simply put, a *diode* is a discrete *semiconductor* component that allows current to pass in one direction but not the other. As the name suggests, a "semi" conductor is neither a conductor nor an insulator. Silicon is a semiconductive material, but it becomes much more interesting when it is *doped* with an impurity, such as phosphorus. Such a negative (n-type) doping results in a weakly bound electron in the valence band. It can also be positively doped (p-type) to have a hole in the valence band, using impurities such as boron. When you join a small block of p-type and n-type doped silicon together, you get a *pn-junction*—a diode! The free electrons in the valence band of the n-type silicon flow to the p-type silicon, creating a *depletion layer* and a potential barrier that must be overcome before current can flow.

When a diode is *forward-biased* it allows current to flow through it; when it is reverse-biased, no current can flow. A diode is forward-biased when the voltage on the anode (+*ve*) terminal is greater than the voltage on the cathode (−*ve*) terminal; however, the biasing must also exceed the depletion layer potential barrier (*knee voltage*) before current can flow, which is typically between 0.5V and 0.7V for a silicon diode. If the diode is *reverse-biased* by applying a greater voltage on the anode than the cathode, then almost no current can flow (maybe 1nA or so). However, if the reverse-biased voltage is increasingly raised, then eventually the diode will break down and allow current to flow in the reverse direction. If the current is low then this will not damage the diode—in fact, a special diode called a *Zener diode* is designed to operate in this breakdown region, and it can be configured to behave just like a voltage regulator.

The 1N4001 is a low-cost silicon diode that can be used in a simple circuit, as illustrated in Figure 4-7 to demonstrate the use and behavior of diodes. The

1N4001 has a peak reverse breakdown voltage of 50V. In this circuit, a sine wave is applied that alternates from +5V to –5V, using the waveform generator of the Analog Discovery. When the V_{in} voltage is positive and exceeds the knee voltage, then current will flow and there will be a voltage drop across the load resistor V_{load}, which is slightly less than V_{in}. There is a small voltage drop across the diode V_d and you can see from the oscilloscope measurements that this is 0.67V, which is within the expected range for a silicon diode.

The diode is used in the circuit in Figure 4-6 as a reverse polarity protector. It should be clear from the plot in Figure 4-7 why it is effective, as when V_{in} is negative, the V_{load} is zero. This is because current cannot flow through the diode when it is reverse-biased. If the voltage exceeded the breakdown voltage for the diode then current would flow; but since that is 50V for the 1N4001, it will not occur in this case. Note that the bottom right-hand corner of Figure 4-7 shows an XY-plot of output voltage (*y*-axis) versus input voltage (*x*-axis). You can see that for negative input voltage the output voltage is 0, but once the knee voltage is reached (0.67V), the output voltage increases linearly with the input voltage. This circuit is called a *half-wave rectifier*. It is possible to connect four diodes together in a bridge formation to create a full-wave rectifier.

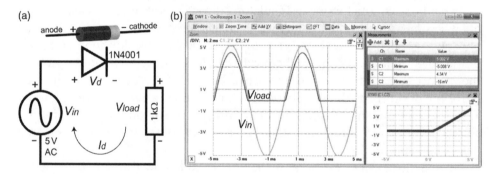

Figure 4-7: Circuit and behavior of a 1N4001 diode with a 5V AC supply and a 1kΩ load resistor

Light-Emitting Diodes (LEDs)

A *light-emitting diode (LED)* is a semiconductor-based light source that is often used as a state indication light in all types of devices. Today, high-powered LEDs are being used in car lights, in back lights for televisions, and even in place of filament lights for general-purpose lighting (e.g., home lighting, traffic lights, etc.) mainly due to their longevity and extremely high efficiency in converting electrical power to light output. LEDs provide very useful status and debug information about your circuit, often used to indicate whether a state is true or false.

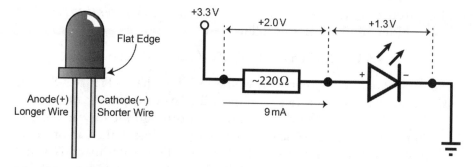

Figure 4-8: LED example and a circuit to drive an LED with appropriate forward current and voltage levels

Like diodes, LEDs are *polarized*. The symbol for an LED is illustrated in Figure 4-8. To cause an LED to light, the diode needs to be forward biased by connecting the *anode* (+) to a more positive source than the *cathode* (–). For example, the anode could be connected to +3.3V and the cathode to GND; however, also remember that the same effect would be achieved by connecting the anode to 0V and the cathode to –3.3V.

Figure 4-8 illustrates an LED that has one leg longer than the other. The longer leg is the anode (+) and the shorter leg is the cathode (–). The plastic LED surround also has a flat edge, which indicates the cathode (–) leg of the LED. This flat edge is particularly useful when the LED is in-circuit and the legs have been trimmed.

LEDs have certain operating requirements, defined by a *forward voltage* and a *forward current*. Every LED is different, and you need to reference the datasheet of the LED to determine these values. An LED does not have a significant resistance, so if you were to connect the LED directly across your BBB's 3.3V supply, the LED would act like a short circuit, and you would drive a very large current through the LED, damaging it—but more important, damaging your BBB! Therefore, to operate an LED within its limits you need a series resistor, called a *current-limiting resistor*. Choose this value carefully to maximize the light output of the LED and to protect the circuit.

WARNING   Do not connect LEDs directly to the GPIOs on the BeagleBone's P8/ P9 headers without using current-limiting resistors and/or transistor switching, as you will likely damage your board. The maximum current that the BBB can source from a GPIO pin is about 4–6mA.

Referring to Figure 4-8, if you are supplying the LED from the BBB's 3.3V supply and you wish to have a forward voltage drop of 1.3V across the LED, you need the difference of 2V to drop across the current-limiting resistor. The LED specifications require you to limit the current to 9mA, so you need to calculate a current-limiting resistor value as follows:

$$\text{As } V = IR, \text{ then } R = V/I = 2\text{V}/0.009\text{A} = 222\Omega$$

Therefore, a circuit to light an LED would look like that in Figure 4-8. Here a 220Ω resistor is placed in series with the LED. The combination of the 3.3V supply and the resistor drives a current of 9mA through the forward-biased LED; as with this current the resistor has a 2V drop across it, then accordingly the LED has a forward voltage drop of 1.3V across it. Please note that this would be fine if you were connecting to the BBB's DC_3.3V output, but it is *not* fine for use with the BBB's GPIOs, as the maximum current that the BBB can source from a GPIO pin is about 4–6mA. You will see a solution for this shortly, and again in Chapter 6.

It is also worth mentioning that you should not dim LEDs by reducing the voltage across the LED. An LED should be thought of as a current-controlled device, where driving a current through the LED causes the forward voltage drop. Therefore, trying to control an LED with a variable voltage will not work as you might expect. To dim an LED you can use a *pulse width modulated* (PWM) signal, essentially rapidly switching the LED on and off. For example, if a rapid PWM signal is applied to the LED that is off for half of the time and on for half of the time, then the LED will appear to be only emitting about half of its regular operating condition light level. Our eyes don't see the individual changes if they are fast enough—they average over the light and dark interval to see a constant, but dimmer illumination.

Figure 4-9 illustrates a PWM square wave signal at different duty cycles. The *duty cycle* is the percentage of time that the signal is high versus the time that the signal is low. In this example, a high is represented by a voltage of 3.3V and a low by a voltage of 0V. A duty cycle of 0% means that the signal is constantly low, and a duty cycle of 100% means that the signal is constantly high.

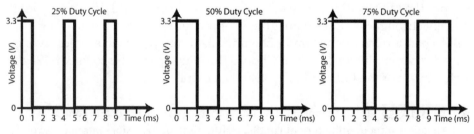

Figure 4-9: Duty cycles of pulse width modulation (PWM) signals

PWM can be used to control the light level of LEDs, but it can also be used to control the speed of DC motors, the position of servo motors, and many more applications. You will see such an example in Chapter 6 when the built-in PWM functionality of the BBB is used.

The *period* (*T*) of a repeating signal (a *periodic signal*) is the time it takes to complete a full cycle. In the example in Figure 4-9, the period of the signal in all three cases is 4ms. The *frequency* (*f*) of a periodic signal describes how often a signal goes through a full cycle in a given time period. Therefore, for a signal with a period of 4ms, it will cycle 250 times per second (1/0.004), which is 250 hertz (Hz). We can state that f (Hz) = $1/T$ (s) or T (s) = $1/f$ (Hz). Some high-end DMMs measure frequency, but generally you use an oscilloscope to measure frequency. PWM signals need to switch at a frequency to suit the device to be controlled; typically, the frequency is in the kHz range for motor control.

Smoothing and Decoupling Capacitors

A *capacitor* is a passive electrical component that can be used to store electrical energy between two insulated plates when there is a voltage difference between them. The energy is stored in an electric field between the two plates, with positive charge building on one plate and negative charge building on the other plate. When the voltage difference is removed or reduced, then the capacitor discharges its energy to a connected electrical circuit.

For example, if you modified the diode circuit in Figure 4-7 to add a 10μF *smoothing capacitor* in parallel with the load resistor, the output voltage would appear as shown in Figure 4-10. When the diode is forward biased there is a potential across the terminals of the capacitor and it quickly charges (while a current also flows through the load resistor in parallel). When the diode is reverse biased, there is no external supply generating a potential across the capacitor/resistor combination, so the potential across the terminals of the capacitor (because of its charge) causes a current to flow through the load resistor, and the capacitor starts to discharge. The impact of this change is that there is now a more stable voltage across the load resistor that varies between 2.758V and 4.222V (the *ripple voltage* is 1.464V), rather than between 0V and 4.34V.

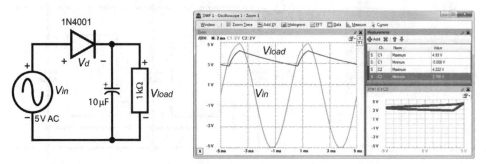

Figure 4-10: Circuit and behavior of a 1N4001 diode with a 5V AC supply, 1kΩ load, and parallel 10μF capacitor

Capacitors use a *dielectric material*, such as ceramic, glass, paper, or plastic, to insulate the two charged plates. Two very common capacitor types are ceramic and electrolytic capacitors. *Ceramic capacitors* are small and low cost and degrade over time. *Electrolytic capacitors* can store much larger amounts of energy, but also degrade over time. Glass, mica, and tantalum capacitors tend to be more reliable, but are considerably more expensive.

Figure 4-11 illustrates a 100nF (0.1µF) ceramic capacitor and a 47µF electrolytic capacitor. Note that the *electrolytic capacitor* is *polarized*, with the negative lead marked on the capacitor surface with a band; like the LED, the negative lead is shorter than the positive lead. The numbering for capacitors is reasonably straightforward; unfortunately, on ceramic capacitors it can be very small and hard to read:

- The first number is the first digit of the capacitor value.

- The second number is the second digit of the capacitor value.

- The third number is the number of zeroes, where the capacitor value is in pF (picofarads).

- Additional letters can be ignored for the moment, but represent the tolerance and voltage rating of the capacitor.

Therefore, for example:

- 10$\underline{4}$ = 100$\underline{000}$pF = 100nF = 0.1µF

- 10$\underline{2}$ = 1,$\underline{000}$pF = 1nF

- 47$\underline{2}$ = 4,$\underline{700}$pF = 4.7nF

The voltage regulator circuit presented earlier (refer to Figure 4-6) used two capacitors to smooth out the ripples in the supply by charging and discharging in opposition to those ripples. Capacitors can also be used for a related function known as decoupling.

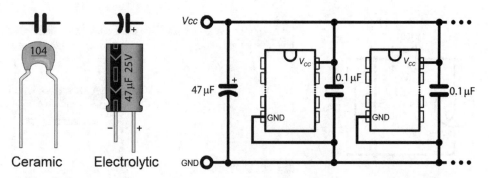

Figure 4-11: Ceramic (nonpolarized) and electrolytic (polarized) capacitors and an example decoupling circuit

Coupling is often an undesirable relationship that occurs between two parts of a circuit due to the sharing of power supply connections. This relationship means that if there is a sudden high power demand by one part of the circuit, then the supply voltage will drop slightly, affecting the supply voltages of other parts of the circuit. ICs impart a variable load on the power supply lines—in fact, a load that can change very quickly, causing a high-frequency voltage variation on the supply lines to other ICs. As the number of ICs in the circuit increases, the problem will be compounded.

Small capacitors, known as *decoupling capacitors*, can act as a store of energy that removes the noise signals that may be present on your supply lines as a result of these IC load variations. An example circuit is illustrated in Figure 4-11, where the larger 47µF capacitor filters out lower-frequency variations and the 0.1µF capacitors filter out higher-frequency noise. Ideally the leads on the 0.1µF capacitors should be as short as possible to avoid producing undesirable effects (relating to inductance) that will limit it from filtering the highest-level frequencies. Even the surface-mounted capacitors used on the BBB to decouple the ball grid array (BGA) pins on the AM335x produce a small inductance of about 1–2nH. As a result, one 0.1µF capacitor is recommended for every two power balls, and the traces (board tracks) have to be as "short as humanly possible" (Texas Instruments, 2011).[1] See `tiny.cc/ebb401` for a full guide.

Transistors

Transistors are one of the core ingredients of the BBB's microprocessor, and indeed almost every other electronic system. Simply put, their function can be to amplify a signal or to turn a signal on or off, whichever is required. The BBB GPIOs can only handle very small currents, so we need transistors to help us when interfacing them to electronic circuits that require larger currents to operate.

Bipolar junction transistors (BJTs), usually just called *transistors*, are formed by adding another doped layer to a pn-junction diode to form either a p-n-p or an n-p-n transistor. There are other types of transistors, such as field effect transistors (FETs), that is discussed shortly. The name *bipolar* comes from the fact that the current is carried by both electrons and holes. They have three terminals, with the third terminal connected to the middle layer in the sandwich, which is very narrow, as illustrated in Figure 4-12.

Figure 4-12 presents quite an amount of information about transistors, including the naming of the terminals as the *base* (B), *collector* (C), and *emitter* (E). Despite there being two main types of BJT transistor (NPN and PNP), the NPN transistor is the most commonly used. In fact, the transistor examples in this chapter all use a single BC547 NPN transistor.

The BC547 is a 45V, 100mA general-purpose transistor that is commonly available, is low cost, and is provided in a leaded TO-92 package. The identification of the legs in the BC547 is provided in Figure 4-12, but please be aware that this order is not consistent with all transistors—always check the datasheet! The maximum V_{CE} (aka V_{CEO}) is 45V and the maximum collector current (I_C) is 100mA for the BC547. It has a typical DC current gain (h_{FE}) of between 180 and 520, depending on the group used (e.g., A, B, C). Those characteristics are explained in the next sections.

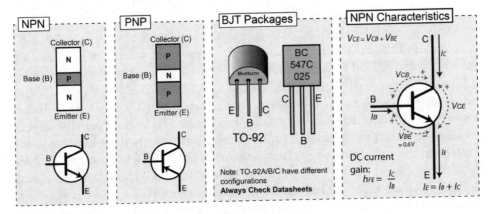

Figure 4-12: Bipolar junction transistors (BJTs)

Transistors as Switches

NOTE   For the remainder of this book, FETs rather than BJTs are used in the BBB circuits for switching loads. If you become overwhelmed by the detail in this section, skip ahead to FETs.

Let's examine the characteristics for the NPN transistor as illustrated in Figure 4-12 (on the rightmost diagram). If the base-emitter junction is forward biased and a small current is entering the base (I_B), then the behavior of a transistor is such that a proportional but much larger current ($I_C = h_{FE} \times I_B$) will be allowed to flow into the collector terminal, as h_{FE} will be a value of 180 to 520 for a transistor such as the BC547. Because I_B is much smaller than I_C, you can also assume that I_E is approximately equal to I_C.

Figure 4-13 illustrates the example of a BJT being used as a switch. In part (a) the voltage levels have been chosen to match those available on the BBB. The resistor on the base is chosen to have a value of 2.2kΩ, so that the base current will be small ($I = V/R = (3.3V - 0.7V)/2200Ω$ which is about 1.2mA). The resistor on the collector is small, so the collector current will be reasonably large ($I = V/R = (5V - {\sim}0.2V)/100Ω = 48mA$).

Figure 4-13(b) illustrates what happens when an input voltage of 3.3V is applied to the base terminal. The small base current causes the transistor to behave like a closed switch (with a very low resistance) between the collector and the emitter. This means that the voltage drop across the collector-emitter will be almost zero and all of the voltage is dropped across the 100Ω *load resistor*, causing a current to flow directly to ground through the emitter. The transistor is *saturated* because it cannot pass any further current. Because there is almost no voltage drop across the collector-emitter, the output voltage, V_{out}, will be almost 0V.

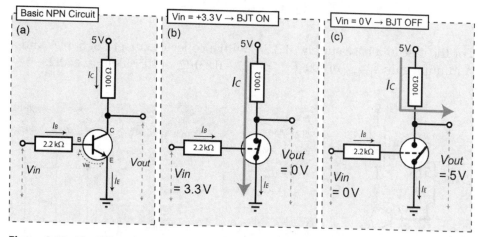

Figure 4-13: The BJT as a switch

Figure 4-13(c) illustrates what happens when the input voltage V_{in} = 0V is applied to the base terminal and there is no base current. The transistor behaves like an open switch (very large resistance). No current can flow through the collector-emitter junction, as this current is always a multiple of the base current and the base current is zero; therefore, almost all of the voltage is dropped across the collector-emitter. In this case the output, V_{out}, can be up to +5V (though as implied by the illustrated flow of I_C through the output terminal, the exact value of V_{out} depends on the size of I_C, as any current flowing through the 100Ω resistor will cause a voltage drop across it).

Therefore, the switch behaves somewhat like an *inverter*. If the input voltage is 0V, then the output voltage is +5V, and if the input voltage is +3.3V, then the output voltage will be 0V. You can see the actual measured values of this circuit in Figure 4-14, when the input voltage of 3.3V is applied to the base terminal. In this case the Analog Discovery Waveform Generator is used to output a 1kHz square wave, with an amplitude of 1.65V and an offset of +1.65V (forming a 0V to 3.3V square wave signal), so it appears like a 3.3V source turning on and then off, 1,000 times per second. All of the measurements in this figure were captured with the input at 3.3V. The base-emitter junction is forward biased, and just like the diode before, this will have a forward voltage of about 0.7V. The actual voltage drop across the base-emitter is 0.83V, so the voltage drop across the base resistor will be 2.440V. The actual base current is 1.1mA ($I = V/R = 2.44V/2,185\Omega$). This current turns on the transistor, placing the transistor in saturation, so the voltage drop across the collector-emitter is very small (measured at 0.2V). Therefore, the collector current is 49.8mA ($I = V/R = (4.93V - 0.2V)/96\Omega$ approx.). To choose an appropriate base resistor to place the BJT deep in saturation, use the following practical formula:

$$R_{Base} = \frac{(V_B - V_{BE(sat)})}{(2 \times (I_C \div h_{FE(min)}))}$$

For the case of a base supply of 3.3V, with a collector current of 50mA and a minimum gain $h_{FE(min)}$ of 100, $R_{Base} = (3.27 - 0.83)/(2 \times (0.05/100)) = 2,440\Omega$.

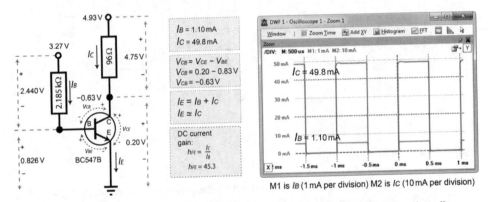

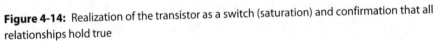

M1 is I_B (1 mA per division) M2 is I_C (10 mA per division)

Figure 4-14: Realization of the transistor as a switch (saturation) and confirmation that all relationships hold true

> **NOTE**   You can use the Analog Discovery's differential input feature to "measure" current by placing the probes on either side of a resistor (to measure the voltage across it), and then creating a custom math channel that divides the waveform by the resistor's known resistance value. You then set the units to amps in the channel settings.

You can find all of these values in the transistor's datasheet. $V_{BE(SAT)}$ is typically provided on a plot of V_{BE} versus I_C at room temperature, where we require I_C to be 50mA. The value of $V_{BE(SAT)}$ is between 0.6V and 0.95V for the BC547, depending on the collector current and the room temperature. The resistor value is further divided by two to ensure that the transistor is placed deep in the saturation region (maximizing I_C). Therefore, in this case a 2.2kΩ resistor is used, as it is the closest generally available nominal value.

Why should you care about this with the BBB? Well, because the BBB can only source or sink very small currents from its GPIO pins, you can connect the BBB GPIO pin to the base of a transistor so that a very small current entering the base of the transistor can switch on a much larger current, with a much greater voltage range. Remember that in the example in Figure 4-14, a current of 1.1mA is able to switch on a large current of 49.8mA (45 times larger, but still lower than the 100mA limit of the BC547). Using this transistor arrangement with the BBB will allow a 5mA current at 3.3V from a BBB GPIO to safely drive a 100mA current at up to 45V by choosing suitable resistor values.

One constraint in using transistors to drive a circuit is that they have a maximum switching frequency. If you increase the frequency of the input signal to the circuit in Figure 4-15 to 500kHz, then the output is distorted, though it is still switching from low to high. However, increasing this to 1MHz means that the controlled circuit never switches off.

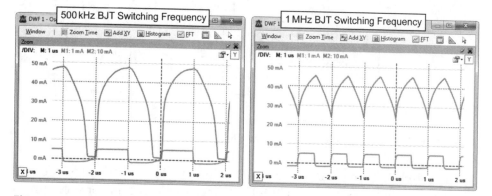

Figure 4-15: Frequency response of the BJT circuit (frequency is 500kHz and 1MHz)

Field Effect Transistors (FETs) as Switches

A simpler alternative to using BJTs as switches is to use *field effect transistors* (FETs). FETs are different from BJTs in that the flow of current in the load circuit is controlled by the voltage, rather than the current, on the controlling input. Therefore, it is said that FETs are voltage-controlled devices and BJTs are current-controlled devices. The controlling input for a FET is called the *gate* (G) and the controlled current flows between the *drain* (D) and the *source* (S).

Figure 4-16 illustrates how you can use an n-channel FET as a switch. Unlike the BJT, the resistor on the controlling circuit (1MΩ) is connected from the input to GND, meaning that a very small current ($I = V/R$) will flow to GND, but the voltage at the gate will be the same as the V_{in} voltage. A huge advantage of FETs is that almost no current flows into the gate control input. However, the voltage on the gate is what turns on and off the controlled current, I_d, which flows from the drain to the source in this example.

When the input voltage is high (3.3V), the drain-source current will flow ($I_D = 50$mA), so the voltage at the output terminal will be 0.17V, but when the input voltage is low (0V), no drain-source current will flow. Just like the BJT, if you were to measure the voltage at the drain terminal, the output voltage (V_{out}) would be high when the input voltage is low, and the output voltage would be low when the input voltage is high, though again the actual value of the "high" output voltage depends on the current drawn by the succeeding circuit.

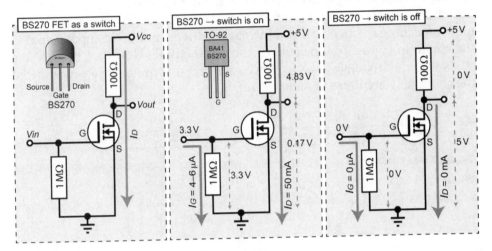

Figure 4-16: Field effect transistor (FET) as a switch

The Fairchild Semiconductor BS270 N-Channel Enhancement Mode FET is a low-cost device (~$0.10) in a TO-92 package that is capable of supplying a continuous drain current (I_D) of up to 400mA at a drain-source voltage of up to 60V. The current is considerably higher than the BJT circuit and it can do so at a threshold voltage (V_{GS}) of as low as 2.1V. This makes it ideal for use with the BBB, as the GPIO voltages are in range and the current required to switch on the FET is about 3µA–6µA depending on the gate resistor chosen. One other feature of using a FET as a switch is that it can cope with much higher switching frequencies, as shown in Figure 4-17. Remember that in Figure 4-15 the BJT switching waveform is very distorted at 1MHz. It should be clear from Figure4-17 that the FET circuit is capable of dealing with much higher switching frequencies than the BJT circuit.

The BS270 also has a high-current diode that is used to protect the gate from the type of reverse inductive voltage surges that could arise if the FET were driving a DC motor.

Optocouplers/Opto-isolators

Optocouplers (or *opto-isolators*) are small, low-cost digital switching devices that are used to isolate two electrical circuits from each other. This can be important for your BBB circuits if you have a concern that a design problem with a connected circuit could possibly source or sink a large current from/to your BBB. They are available in low-cost (~$0.15) four-pin DIP packages.

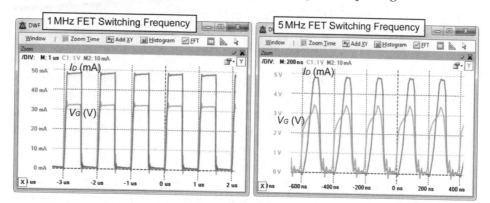

Figure 4-17: Frequency response of the FET circuit as the switching frequency is set at 1MHz and 5MHz

An optocoupler uses an LED emitter that is placed close to a photodetector transistor, separated by an insulating film within a silicone dome. When a current (I_f) flows through the LED emitter legs, the light that falls on the photodetector transistor from the LED allows a separate current (I_c) to flow through the collector-emitter legs of the photo detector transistor (see Figure 4-18). When the LED emitter is off, no light falls on the photo detector transistor, and there will be almost no collector emitter current (I_c). There is no electrical connection between one side of the package and the other, as the signal is transmitted only by light, providing electrical isolation for up to 5,300V_{RMS} for an optocoupler such as the SFH617A. You can even use PWM with optocouplers, as it is a binary on/off signal.

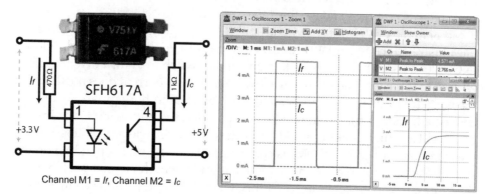

Figure 4-18: Optocoupler (617A) circuit with the captured input and output characteristics

Figure 4-18 illustrates an example optocoupler circuit and the resulting oscilloscope traces for the resistor and voltage values chosen. These values were chosen to be consistent with those that you might use with the BBB. The resistor value of 470Ω was chosen to allow the 3.3V output to drive a forward current I_f of about 4.5mA through the LED emitter. From the datasheet (Vishay Semiconductors, 2013),[2] this results in a forward voltage of about 1.15V across the diode); $R = V/I = (3.3V - 1.15V)/0.0045mA = 478Ω$. Therefore, the circuit was built using the closest nominal value of 470Ω.

The oscilloscope is displaying current by using the differential inputs of the Analog Discovery to measure the voltage across the known resistor values, and using two mathematical channels to divide by the resistance values. In Figure 4-18 you can see that I_f is 4.571mA and that I_c is 2.766mA. The proportionality of the difference is the current transfer ratio (CTR) and it varies according to the level of I_f and the operating temperature. Therefore, the current transfer at 4.571mA is 60.5% ($100 \times I_c/I_f$), which is consistent with the datasheet. The rise time and fall time are also consistent with the values in the datasheet of $t_r = 4.6\mu s$ and $t_f = 15\mu s$. These values limit the switching frequency. Also, if it is important to your circuit that you achieve a high CTR, there are optocouplers with built-in Darlington transistor configurations that result in CTRs of up to 2,000% (e.g., the 6N138 or HCPL2730). Finally, there are high-linearity analog optocouplers available (e.g., the HCNR200 from Avago) that can be used to optically isolate analog signals.

Switches and Buttons

Other components with which you are likely to need to work are switches and buttons. They come in many different forms: toggle, push button, selector, proximity, joystick, reed, pressure, temperature, etc. However, they all work under the same binary principles of either interrupting the flow of current (open) or enabling the flow of current (closed). Figure 4-19 illustrates several different common switch types and outlines their general connectivity.

Momentary push button switches (SPST, single pole, single throw) like the one illustrated in Figure 4-19 are either normally open (NO) or normally closed (NC). NO means that you have to activate the switch to allow current to flow, whereas NC means that when you activate the button, current does not flow. For the particular push button illustrated, both pins 1 and both pins 2 are always connected, and for the duration of time you press the button, all four pins are connected together. Looking at slider switches (SPDT—single pole, double throw), the common connection (COM) is connected to either 1 or 2 depending on the slider position. In the case of microswitches and the high-current push button, the COM pin is connected to NC if the switch is pressed, and is connected to NO if the switch is depressed. Finally, the rocker switch illustrated often has an LED that lights when the switch is closed, connecting the power (VCC) leg to the circuit (CCT) leg.

All of these switch types suffer from mechanical switch bounce, which can be extremely problematic when interfacing to microcontrollers like the BBB. Switches are mechanical devices and when they are pressed, the force of contact causes the switch to repeatedly bounce from the contact on impact. It only bounces for a small duration (typically milliseconds), but the duration is sufficient for the switch to apply a sequence of inputs to a microprocessor.

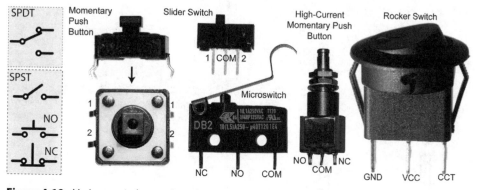

Figure 4-19: Various switches and configurations

Figure 4-20(a) illustrates the problem in action using the rising/falling-edge trigger condition of the Analog Discovery Oscilloscope. A momentary push button is placed in a simple series circuit with a 10kΩ resistor and the voltage is measured across the resistor. When the switch hits the contact, the output is suddenly high, but the switch then bounces back from the contact and the voltage falls down again. After about 2–3ms (or longer) it has almost fully settled. Unfortunately, this small bounce can lead to false inputs to a digital circuit. For example, if the threshold were 3V, this may be read in as 101010101.

There are a number of ways to deal with switch bounce in microprocessor interfacing:

- A low-pass filter can be added in the form of a resistor-capacitor circuit as illustrated in Figure 4-20(c) using a 1μF capacitor. Unfortunately this leads to delay in the input. If you examine the time base, it takes about 2ms before the input reaches 1V. Also, bounce conditions can delay this further. These values are chosen using the *RC time constant* $\tau = R \times C$, so $\tau\,(s) = 1,000\Omega \times 10^{-6}\,F = 1ms$, which is the time taken to charge a capacitor to ~63.2% or discharge it to ~36.8%. This value is marked on Figure 4-20(b).

- Software may be written so that after a rising edge occurs, it delays a few milliseconds and then reads the "real" state.

- For slider switches (SPDT), an SR-latch can be used.

- For momentary push button switches (SPSTs), a Schmitt trigger (74HC14N), which is discussed in the next section, can be used with an RC low-pass filter as in Figure 4-20(c).

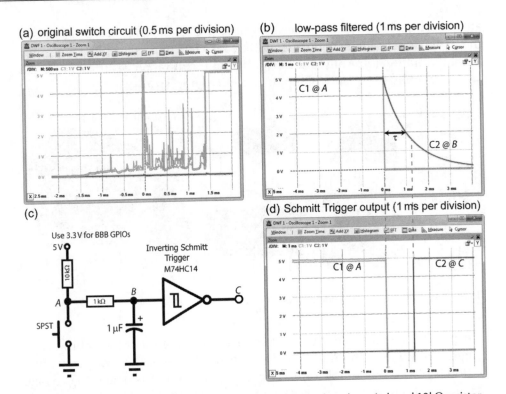

Figure 4-20: (a) Switch bouncing with no components other than the switch and 10kΩ resistor (b) Low-pass filtered output at point *B* (c) A Schmitt trigger circuit (d) Output of the Schmitt trigger circuit at point *C*, versus the input at point *A*

NOTE There are videos on debouncing SPDT and SPST switches on the web page associated with this chapter: www.exploringbeaglebone.com/chapter4.

Hysteresis

Hysteresis is designed into electronic circuits to avoid rapid switching, which would wear out circuits. A *Schmitt trigger* exhibits hysteresis, which means that its output is dependent on the present input and the history of previous inputs. This can be explained with an example of an oven baking a cake at 350degrees Fahrenheit:

▪ **Without hysteresis:** The element would heat the oven to 350°F. Once 350°F is achieved the element would switch off. It would cool below 350°F and the element would switch on again. Rapid switching!

▪ **With hysteresis:** The circuit would be designed to heat the oven to 360°F and at that point the element would switch off. The oven would cool, but it is not designed to switch back on until it reaches 340°F. The switching would not be rapid, protecting the oven, but there would be a greater variation in the baking temperature.

With an oven that is designed to have hysteresis, is the element *on* or *off* at 350°F? That depends on the history of inputs—it is *on* if the oven is heating; it is *off* if the oven is cooling.

The *Schmitt trigger* in Figure 4-20(c) exhibits the same type of behavior. The V_{T+} for the M74HC14 Schmitt trigger is 2.9V and the V_{T-} is 0.93V when running at a 5V input, which means that a rising input voltage has to reach 2.9V before the output changes high, and a falling input voltage has to drop to 0.93V before the output changes low. Any bounce in the signal within this range is simply ignored. The low-pass filter reduces the possibility of high-frequency bounces. The response is presented in Figure 4-20(d). Note that the time base is 1ms per division, illustrating how "clean" the output signal is. The configuration uses a pull-up resistor, the need for which is discussed shortly.

Logic Gates

Boolean algebra functions have only two possible outcomes, either *true* or *false*, which makes them ideal for developing a framework to describe electronic circuits that are either *on* or *off* (*high* or *low*). Logic gates perform these Boolean algebra functions and operations, forming the basis of the functionality inside modern microprocessors, such as the AM335x in the BBB. Boolean values are not the same as *binary* numbers—binary numbers are a base 2 representation of whole and fractional numbers, whereas Boolean refers to a data type that has only two possible values, either true or false.

It is often the case that you will need to interface to different types of logic gates and systems using the BBB's GPIOs in order to perform an operation such as gating an input or sending data to a shift register. Logic gates fall into two main categories:

- **Combinational logic:** The current output is dependent on the current inputs only (e.g., AND, OR, decoders, multiplexers, etc.).

- **Sequential logic:** The current output is dependent on the current inputs and previous inputs. They can be said to have different *states,* and what happens with a given input depends on what state they are in (e.g., latches, flip-flops, memory, counters, etc.).

BINARY NUMBERS

Simply put, *binary* numbers are a system for representing numbers (whole or fractional) within a device whereby the *only* symbols available are 1s and 0s. That is a strong *only*, as when you are implementing binary circuits, you don't have a minus sign or a decimal point (binary point to be precise). Like decimal numbers, you use a place-weighted system to represent numbers of the form:

$$1001_2 = (1 \times 2^3) + (0 \times 2^2) + (0 \times 2^1) + (1 \times 2^0) = 8 + 0 + 0 + 1 = 9_{10}$$

If you only have four bits to represent your numbers, then you can only represent $2^4 = 16$ possible decimal numbers in the range 0–15. You can add and subtract numbers, just as you can in decimal, but you tend to add the negative value of the RHS of the operation, instead of building subtraction circuits. Therefore, to perform 9 – 5, you would typically perform 9 + (–5).To represent negative numbers, the *2's complement form* is used. Essentially, this involves inverting the symbols in the binary representation of the number and adding 1, so –5 would be +5 (0101), inverted to (1010) + 1 = 1011_2. Importantly, you need to know that this number is in 2's complement form, otherwise it could be mistaken for 11_{10}. Therefore, to perform 9 – 5 on a four-bit computer, perform 9 + –5 = 1001 + (1011) = 10100. The four-bit computer ignores the fifth bit (otherwise it would be a five-bit computer!), so the answer is 0100, which is 4_{10}. See the video at the chapter web page: www.exploringbeaglebone/chapter4.

To multiply by 2 you simply shift the binary digits left (inserting a zero on the rightmost position), e.g., $4_{10} = 0100_2$. Shift all the digits left, bringing in a 0 on the RHS, giving $1000_2 = 8_{10}$. Divide by 2 by shifting to the right.

Finally, understanding binary makes the following infamous joke funny: "There are 10 types of people, those who understand binary and those who don't!"—well, almost funny!

Combinational logic circuits will provide the same output for the same set of inputs, regardless of the order in which the inputs are applied. Figure 4-21 illustrates the core combinational logic gates with their logic symbols, truth tables, and IC numbers. The truth table provides the output that you will get from the gate on applying the listed inputs.

NOTE   You can find a video on wiring an AND gate at the web page associated with this chapter: www.exploringbeaglebone.com/chapter4.

ICs have a number that describes their manufacturer, function, logic family, and package type. For example, the MM74HC08N in Figure 4-22(a) has a manufacturer code of MM (Fairchild Semiconductor), is a 7408 (quad two-input AND gates), is of the HC (CMOS) logic family, and is in an N (plastic dual in-line) package.

ICs are available in different package types. Figure 4-22(a) shows to scale a PDIP (plastic dual in-line package) and a small outline package TSSOP (thin shrink small outline package). There are many types: surface mount, flat package, small outline package, chip-scale package, and ball grid array (BGA). You have to be careful when ordering ICs that you have the capability to use them. DIP/PDIP ICs have perfect forms for prototyping on breadboards as they have a 0.1" leg spacing. There are adapter boards available for converting small outline packages to 0.1" leg spacing. Unfortunately, BGA ICs, such as the AM335x, require sophisticated equipment for soldering.

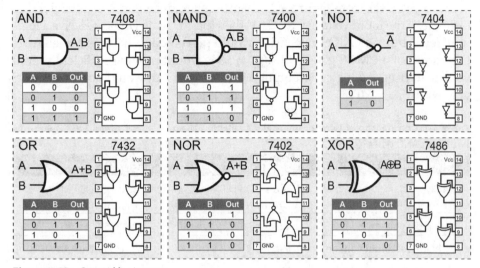

Figure 4-21: General logic gates

The family of currently available ICs is usually transistor-transistor logic (TTL) (with Low-power Schottky (LS)) or some form of complementary metal-oxide-semiconductor (CMOS). Table 4-1 compares these two families of 7408 ICs using their respective datasheets. The *propagation delay* is the longest delay between an input changing value and the output changing value for all possible inputs to a logic gate. This delay limits the logic gate's speed of operation.

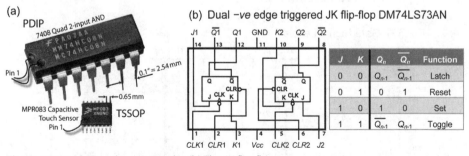

Figure 4-22: (a) IC package examples (b) The JK flip-flop

Figure 4-23 illustrates the acceptable input and output voltage levels for both TTL and CMOS logic gates when $V_{DD} = 5V$. The *noise margin* is the absolute difference between the output voltage levels and the input voltage levels. This noise margin ensures that if the output of one logic gate is connected to the input of a second logic gate, that noise will not affect the input state. The CMOS logic family input logic levels are dependent on the supply voltage, V_{DD}, where the high-level threshold is $0.7 \times V_{DD}$, and the low-level threshold is $0.3 \times V_{DD}$. It should be clear from Figure 4-23 that there are differences in behavior. For example, if the input voltage were 2.5V, then the TTL gate would perceive a logic high level, but the CMOS gate (@5V) would perceive an undefined level. Also, the output of a CMOS gate, with $V_{DD} = 3.3V$, would provide sufficient output voltage to trigger a logic high input on a TTL gate, but would not on a CMOS gate with $V_{DD} = 5.0V$.

Table 4-1: Comparison of Two Commercially Available TTL and CMOS ICs for a 7408 Quadruple Two-input AND gates IC

CHARACTERISTIC	SN74LS08N	SN74HC08N
Family	Texas TTL PDIP Low-power Schottky (LS)	Texas CMOS PDIP High-speed CMOS (HC)
V_{CC} supply voltage	4.5V to 5.5V (5V typical)	2V to 6V
V_{IH} high-level input voltage	Min 2V	V_{CC}@5V Min = 3.5V
V_{IL} low-level input voltage	Max 0.8V	V_{CC}@5V Max = 1.5V
Time propagation delay (T_{PD})	Typical 12ns(LH) 17.5ns(HL)	Typical 8ns
Power (@5V)	5mW max	0.1mW max

HC can support a wide range of voltage levels, including the BBB 3.3V input/outputs. The GND label is commonly used to indicate the ground supply voltage, where V_{EE} is often used for BJT-based devices and V_{SS} for FET-based devices. Traditionally, V_{CC} was used as the label for the positive supply voltage on BJT-based devices and V_{DD} for FET-based devices; however, it is now very common to see V_{CC} being used for both.

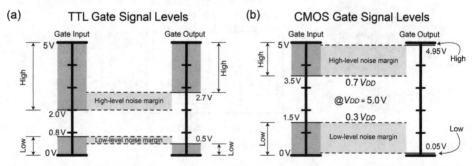

Figure 4-23: Gate signal levels on the input and output of logic gates (a) TTL (b) CMOS at 5V

Figure 4-22(b) illustrates a sequential logic circuit, called a JK flip-flop. JK flip-flops are core building blocks in circuits such as counters. These differ from combinational logic circuits in that the current state is dependent on the current inputs and the previous state. You can see from the truth table that if $J = 0$ and $K = 0$ for the input, then the value of the output Q_n will be the output value that it was at the previous time step (it behaves like a one-bit memory). A time step is defined by the clock input (CLK), which is a square wave synchronizing signal. The same type of timing signal is present on the BBB—it is the clock frequency, and the clock goes through up to 1,000,000,000 square wave cycles per second!

NOTE The web page associated with this chapter has a video that explains JK flip-flops in detail, and a video on building a 555 timer circuit, which can be used as a low-frequency clock signal for testing logic circuits.

Floating Inputs

One very common mistake when working with digital logic circuits is to leave unused logic gate inputs "floating," or disconnected. The family of the chip has a large impact on the outcome of this mistake. With the TTL logic families these inputs will "float" high and can be reasonably expected to be seen as logic-high inputs. With TTL ICs it is good practice to "tie" (i.e., connect) the inputs to ground or the supply voltage, so that there is absolutely no doubt about the logic level being asserted on the input at all times.

With CMOS circuits the inputs are very sensitive to the high voltages that can result from static electricity and electrical noise and should also never be left floating. Figure 4-24 gives the likely output of an AND gate that is wired as shown in the figure. The correct outcome is displayed in the "Required (A.B)" column.

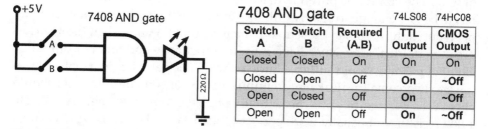

7408 AND gate   74LS08   74HC08

Switch A	Switch B	Required (A.B)	TTL Output	CMOS Output
Closed	Closed	On	On	On
Closed	Open	Off	On	~Off
Open	Closed	Off	On	~Off
Open	Open	Off	On	~Off

Figure 4-24: An AND gate with the inputs accidentally left floating when the switches are open

Unused CMOS inputs that are left floating (between V_{DD} and GND) can gradually charge up due to leakage current, and depending on the IC design could provide false inputs, or waste power by causing a DC current to flow (from V_{DD} to GND). To solve this problem you can use pull-up or pull-down resistors, depending on the desired input state (these are ordinary resistors with suitable values—it's their role that is "pull up" or "pull down"), which are described in the next section.

Pull-Up and Pull-Down Resistors

To avoid floating inputs, you can use pull-up or pull-down resistors as illustrated in Figure 4-25. Pull-down resistors are used if you want to guarantee that the inputs to the gate are low when the switches are open, and pull-up resistors are used if you want to guarantee that the inputs are high when the switches are open.

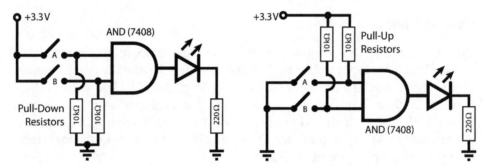

Figure 4-25: Pull-down and pull-up resistors, used to ensure that the switches do not create floating inputs

The resistors are important, because when the switch is closed, the switch would form a short circuit to ground if they were omitted and replaced by lengths of wire. The size of the pull-down/up resistors is also important—their value has to be low enough to solidly pull the input low/high when the switches are open but high enough to prevent too much current flowing when the switches are closed. Ideal logic gates have infinite impedance and any resistor value (short of infinite) would suffice. However, real logic gates leak current and you have to overcome this leakage. To minimize power consumption, you should choose the maximum value that actually pulls the input low/high. A 3.3kΩ to 10kΩ resistor will usually work perfectly, but 3.3V will drive 1mA to 0.33mA through them respectively and dissipate 3.3mW to 1mW of power respectively when the switch is closed. For power-sensitive applications you could test larger resistors of 50kΩ or greater.

The BBB has weak internal pull-up and pull-down resistors that can be used for this purpose. This is discussed in Chapter 6. One other issue is that inputs will have some stray capacitance to ground. Adding a resistor to the input creates an RC low-pass filter on the input signal that can delay input signals. That is not important for manually pressed buttons, as the delay will be on the order of 0.1µs for the preceding example, but it could affect the speed of digital communication bus lines.

Open-Collector and Open-Drain Outputs

To this point in the chapter, all of the ICs have a regular output, where it is driven very close to GND or the supply voltage of the IC (V_{CC}). If you are connecting to another IC or component that uses the same voltage level, then that should be fine. However, if the first IC had a supply voltage of 3.3V and you needed to drive the output into an IC that had a supply voltage of 5V, then you may need to perform *level shifting*.

Many ICs are available in a form with *open-collector outputs*, which are particularly useful for interfacing between different logic families and for level shifting. This is because the output is not at a specific voltage level, but rather attached to the base input of an NPN transistor that is inside the IC. The output of the IC is the "open" collector of the transistor, and the emitter of the transistor is tied to the IC's GND. It is possible to use a FET (74HC03) instead of a BJT (74LS01) inside the IC, and while the concept is the same it is called an *open-drain output*. Figure 4-26 illustrates this concept and provides an example circuit using a 74HC03 (quad, two-input NAND gates with open-drain outputs) to drive a 5V circuit. The advantage of the open-drain configuration is that CMOS ICs support the 3.3V level available on the BBB's GPIOs. Essentially, the drain resistor that is used in Figure 4-16 is placed outside the IC package, as illustrated in Figure 4-26, it has a value of 10kΩ in this case.

Interestingly, a NAND gate with one input tied high (or the two inputs tied together) behaves like a NOT gate. In fact, NAND or NOR gates, each on their own, can replicate the functionality of any of the logic gates, and for that reason they are called *universal gates*.

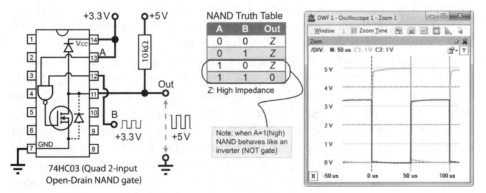

Figure 4-26: Open-drain level-shifting example

Open-collector outputs are often used to connect multiple devices to a bus. You will see this in Chapter 8 when the BBB's I²C bus is described. When you examine the truth table in the datasheet of an IC, such as the 74HC03, you will see the letter Z used to represent the output (as in Figure 4-26). This means that it is a high-impedance output and the external pull-up resistor can pull the output to the high state.

Interconnecting Gates

To create useful circuits, logic gates are interconnected to other logic gates and components. It is important to understand that there are limits to the interconnect capabilities of gates.

The first limit is the ability of the logic gate to source or sink current. When the output of a gate is logic high, it acts as a *current source*, providing current for connected logic gates or the LED shown in Figure 4-25. If the output of the gate is logic low, then the gate acts as a *current sink*, whereby current flows into the output. Figure 4-27(a) demonstrates this by placing a current-limiting resistor and an LED between V_{CC} and the output of the logic gate, with the LED cathode connected to the logic gate output. When the output of the gate is high, there is no potential difference and the LED will be off; but when the output is low, a potential difference is created and current will flow through the LED and be sinked by the output of the logic gate. According to the datasheet of the 74HC08, it has an output current limit (I_O) of ±25mA, meaning that it can source or sink 25mA. Exceeding these values will damage the IC.

It is often necessary to connect the output of a single (driving) gate to the input of several other gates. Each of the connected gates will draw a current, thus limiting the total number of connected gates. The *fan-out* is the number of gates that are connected to the output of the driving gate. As illustrated in Figure 4-27(b), for TTL the maximum fan-out depends on the output (I_O) and input current (I_I) requirement values when the state is low (= $I_{OL(max)}/I_{IL(max)}$) and the state is high (= $I_{OH(max)}/I_{IH(max)}$). Choose the lower value, which is commonly 10 or greater. The *fan-in* of an IC is the number of inputs that it has. For the 7408 they are two-input AND gates, so they have a fan-in of 2.

CMOS gate inputs have extremely large resistance and draw almost no current, allowing for large fan-out capability (>50); however, each input adds a small capacitance ($C_L \approx 3-10pF$) that must be charged and discharged by the output of the previous stage. The greater the fan-out, the greater the capacitive load on the driving gate, which lengthens the propagation delay. For example, the 74HC08 has a propagation delay (t_{pd}) of about 11ns and an input capacitance (C_I) of 3.5pF (assuming for this example that this leads to $t_{pd} = RC = 3.5ns$ per connection). If one 78HC08 were driving 10 other similar gates, and each added 3.5ns of delay, then the propagation delay would increase to $11+(10\times3.5)=46$ns of delay, reducing the maximum operating frequency from 91 MHz to 22 MHz.

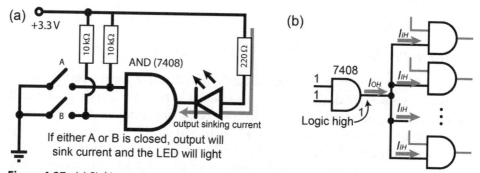

Figure 4-27: (a) Sinking current on the output (b) TTL fan-out example

Analog-to-Digital Conversion

The BBB has seven analog-to-digital converter (ADC) inputs that can be used to take an analog signal and create a digital representation of this signal. This enables us to connect many different types of sensors, such as distance sensors, temperature sensors, light-level sensors, and so on. However, you have to be careful with these inputs, as they should not source or sink current, because the analog outputs of the sensors are likely to be very sensitive to any additional load in parallel with the output. To solve this problem you need to first look at how operational amplifiers function.

Analog signals are continuous signals that represent the measurement of some physical phenomenon. For example, a microphone is an analog device, generally known as transducer, that can be used to convert sound waves into an electrical signal that, for example, varies between –5V and +5V depending on the amplitude of the sound wave. Analog signals use a continuous range of values to represent information, but if you wish to process that signal using your BBB, then you need a discrete digital representation of the signal. This is one that is sampled at discrete instants in time, and subsequently quantized to discrete values of voltage, or current—for example audio signals will vary over time, so to sample a transducer signal in order to digitally capture human speech (e.g., speech recognition), you need be cognizant of two factors:

- **Sampling rate:** Defines how often you are going to sample the signal. Clearly, if you create a discrete digital sample by sampling the voltage every one second, the speech will be indecipherable.

- **Sampling resolution:** Defines the number of digital representations that you have to represent the voltage at the point in time when the signal is sampled. Clearly, if you had only one bit, you could only capture if the signal were closer to +5 or –5V, and again the speech signal would be indecipherable.

Sampling Rate

To represent a continuous signal perfectly in a discrete form would require an infinite amount of digital data. Fortunately (!), there are limits to how well human hearing performs and therefore we can place limits on the amount of data to be discretized. For example, 44.1kHz and 48kHz are common digital audio sampling rates for encoding MP3 files, which means that if you use the former, you will have to store 44,100 samples of your transducer voltage every second. The sample rate is generally determined by the need to preserve a certain frequency content of the signal. For example, humans (particularly children) can hear audio signals at frequencies from about 20Hz up to about 20kHz. *Nyquist's sampling theorem* states that the sampling frequency must be at least twice the highest frequency component present in the signal. Therefore, if you wish to sample audio signals, you need to use a sampling rate of at least twice 20kHz, which is 40kHz, which helps explain the magnitude of the sampling rates used in encoding MP3 audio files (typically 44,100 samples per second—i.e. 44.1kS/s).

Quantization

The BBB has seven 12-bit ADC inputs that work in the range of 0–1.8V, which means that there are $2^{12} = 4,096$ possible discrete representations (numbers) for this sampling resolution. If the voltage is exactly 0V, we can use the decimal number 0 to represent it. If the voltage is exactly 1.8V, we can use the number 4,095 to represent it. So, what voltage does the decimal number 1 represent? It is $(1 \times 1.8)/4096 = 0.000439453125\,V$. Therefore, each decimal number between 0 and 4,095 (4,096 values) represents a step of about 0.44mV.

The preceding audio sampling example also illustrates one of the challenges you face with the BBB. If the sensor outputs a voltage of –5 to +5V, or more commonly 0V to +5V, you need to alter that range to be between 0 and 1.8V to be compatible with the ADC. In Chapter 6, you'll look at how you can solve this problem. A second and more complex problem is that we must not source or sink current from/to the BBB's ADC circuitry, and to solve that we need to introduce a powerful concept that predates the digital computer, called the operational amplifier.

Operational Amplifiers

Earlier in this chapter, the BJT transistor is described. Operational amplifiers (op-amps) are composed from many BJTs or FETs within the one IC (e.g., the LM741). They can be used to create several very useful circuits, one of which you will need in Chapter 6 in order to safely and correctly read values from the BBB's analog-to-digital converters.

Ideal Operational Amplifiers

Figure 4-28(a) illustrates an ideal op-amp, placed in a very basic circuit with no feedback (aka open-loop). The op-amp has two inputs: a *non-inverting input* (+) and an *inverting input* (–), and it produces an output that is proportional to the difference between them, i.e., $V_{out} = G(V_1 - V_2)$, where V_1 and V_2 are the voltage levels on these two inputs, respectively. Some of the characteristics of an *ideal* op-amp include the following:

- An infinite open-loop gain, G
- An infinite input impedance
- A zero output impedance

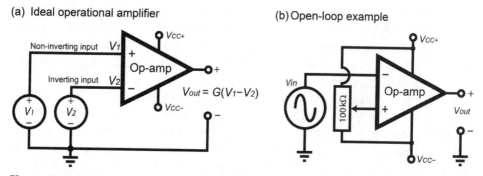

Figure 4-28: (a) The ideal op-amp (b) An open-loop comparator example

No real-world op-amp has an infinite open-loop gain, but voltage gains of 200,000 to 30,000,000 are commonplace. Such a gain can be treated as infinite, which means in theory that even a very small difference between the inputs would lead to a completely impractical output. For example, a difference of 1V between V_1 and V_2 would lead to a voltage output of at least 200,000V! If that were really the case, I would now be issuing health warnings on the use of the BBB! The output voltage is of course limited by the supply voltage (V_{CC+} and V_{CC-} in Figure 4-28(a)). Therefore, if you supply V_{CC+} = +5V and V_{CC-} = 0V

(GND) to an op-amp using the BBB, the maximum real-world output would be in the range of 0V to 5V approximately, depending on the exact op-amp used. Likewise, a real-world op-amp does not have infinite input impedance, but it is in the range of 250kΩ to 2MΩ. The term *impedance* is used instead of *resistance*, as the input may be an AC rather than just a DC supply. Likewise, a zero output impedance is not possible, but it will likely be <100Ω.

The LM358 Dual Operational Amplifier is used for the following circuit configurations (www.ti.com/product/lm358). It is an eight-pin IC in a PDIP package that contains two op-amps that have a typical open-loop differential voltage gain of 100dB, which is 100,000 in voltage gain (*voltage gain in dB = 20 × log (V_{out}/V_{in})*). One advantage of this IC is that it has a wide supply range, in the range of 3V to 32V, meaning that you can use the BBB's 3.3V or 5V power rails. The LM358 can typically source up to 30mA or sink up to 20mA on the output. See Figure 4-28(b).

The behavior of an open-loop op-amp is best explained with an example, which is illustrated in Figure 4-28(b). Please note that in this case the input is connected to the inverting input of the op-amp (–*ve*), rather than the non-inverting input (+*ve*), which means that V_{out} will be positive when V_{in} is lower than the reference voltage. The circuit was built using the LM358, with a supply of $V_{CC}+ = 5V$ and $V_{CC-} = 0V$ (GND). A 100kΩ potentiometer was used to allow the voltage on the +*ve* input to be varied. This is the voltage that we are effectively comparing the input voltage with, so this circuit is called a *comparator*. When the voltage on the –*ve* input is greater than the +*ve* input, by even a very small amount, the output will quickly saturate in the negative direction to 0V. When the voltage on the –*ve* input is less than the voltage on the +*ve* input, then the output V_{out} will immediately saturate in the +*ve* direction to the maximum allowable by this configuration with the value of V_{CC} applied.

The actual output of this circuit can be seen in Figure 4-29(a). In this view, the potentiometer is adjusted to give a voltage on the V+ input of 1.116V. When V– is lower than this value, the output V_{out} is saturated to the maximum positive value; in this case it is 3.816V (LM358 positive saturation voltage). When V– is greater than 1.116V, then the output V_{out} saturates to the lowest value, which is almost zero (–2 mV). Note the inversion that is taking place.

If everything remains exactly the same but the potentiometer is adjusted to give a different value for V+, in this case 0.645V, the output will be as shown in Figure 4-29(b), where the duty cycle of the output V_{out} will be different. This comparator circuit could also be used to detect low voltage conditions—for example, lighting a warning LED if a battery's voltage output fell below a certain value. The circuit example used in 4-27(b) could be used to generate a PWM signal with a controllable duty cycle, according to the controlling voltage V+.

The very large open-loop gain means that op-amps are generally used with feedback, which is directed to the negative or positive op-amp input. This feedback opens up an enormous range of other applications for the op-amp.

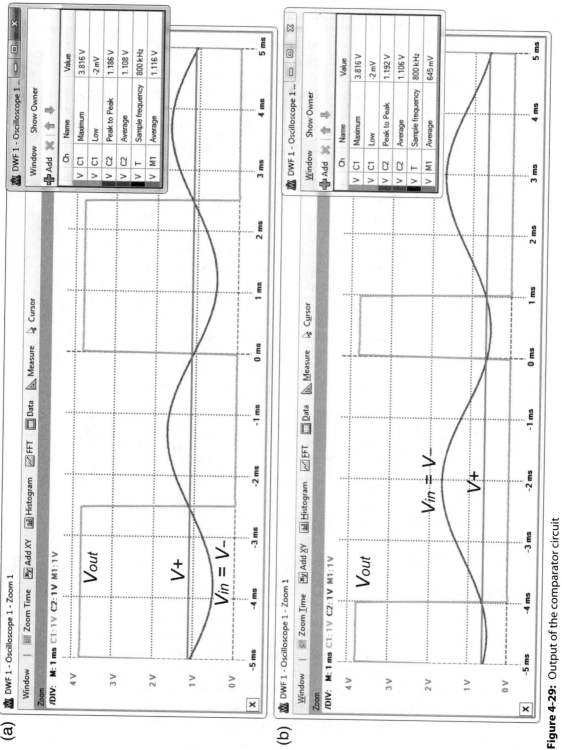

Figure 4-29: Output of the comparator circuit

Negative Feedback and Voltage Follower

Negative feedback is formed when you connect the output of an op-amp (V_{out}) back to the inverting input ($V-$). When you apply a voltage (V_{in}) to the non-inverting input ($V+$) and increase it slowly, as V_{in} increases, then so would the difference between $V+$ and $V-$; however, the output voltage also increases according to $G(V_1 - V_2)$ and this feeds back into the $V-$ input, causing the output voltage V_{out} to be reduced. Essentially, the op-amp attempts to keep the voltage on the inverting ($V-$) input the same as the non-inverting ($V+$) input by adjusting the output. The impact of this action is that the value of V_{out} is stabilized to be the same as the V_{in} voltage on $V+$; the higher the gain of the op-amp, the closer this difference will be to zero.

That action on its own is not very useful to us, except for the fact that the current required to set the voltage on the input is very small, and the op-amp can control much larger currents on the output side. Because the negative feedback keeps the output voltage the same as the input voltage, the configuration as a whole has a gain of 1. This configuration is known as a *voltage follower*, or *unity-gain buffer*, and is illustrated in Figure 4-30. This configuration is very important, as it is used in Chapter 6 to protect the ADC circuitry in the BBB, and it is also used to ensure that the ADC reference voltage is not modified by connecting it to a circuit.

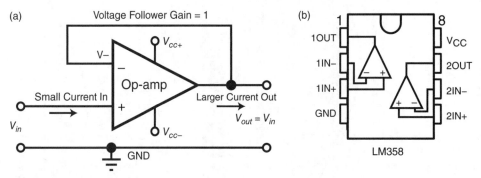

Figure 4-30: The voltage follower op-amp circuit

Positive Feedback

Negative feedback is the most common type of feedback used with op-amps due to its stabilizing impact. An op-amp in a positive feedback configuration is one in which the output is returned to the positive non-inverting input of the op-amp. In such a case the feedback signal supports the input signal. For example, positive feedback can be used to add hysteresis to the open-loop op-amp comparator circuit, by connecting V_{out} to $V+$ through a positive feedback resistor. This can be used to reduce the comparator's response to noise on the input signal.

Concluding Advice

There is a lot of material covered in this chapter. So to finish, here is some general advice for working with electrical components and the BBB:

- Never leave inputs floating. Use pull-up/pull-down resistors on all switches. Check if unused IC pins need to be tied high/low.
- Ensure that all of the GNDs in your circuit are connected.
- Remember to power your chips with the correct voltage level.
- Don't assume that a new diode, FET, BJT, or logic gate has the same pin layout as the previous component that you used.
- Just like programming, build a simple circuit first, test it, and then add the next layer of complexity. Never assume something works!
- Don't leave wire joints and croc clip connections hanging where they could touch off each other—the same for resistors on breadboards.
- Use a flat-head screwdriver to remove ICs from breadboards, as it is very easy to bend the IC legs beyond repair.
- CMOS ICs are statically sensitive, so touching them with your fingers may damage them, due to the buildup of static electricity on your body. Touch the back of a computer or some grounding metal object before you touch the ICs.
- Don't assume that components have exact or consistent values—in particular, transistor gains and resistor ranges.

Summary

After completing this chapter, you should be able to do the following:

- Describe the basic principles of electrical circuit operation, build circuits on breadboards, and measure voltage and current values
- Use discrete components such as diodes, LEDs, transistors, and capacitors in your own circuit designs
- Use transistors and FETs as switches to control higher current and voltage signals than would be possible by using the BBB outputs on their own
- Interconnect and interface to logic gates, being particularly aware of the issues that arise with "floating" inputs
- Describe the principles of analog-to-digital conversion and design basic operational-amplifier circuits
- Combine all of these skills to build the type of circuits that are important for safely interfacing to the BBB GPIOs and ADCs

Further Reading

Documents and links for further reading have been listed throughout this chapter, but there are some further reference documents:

- T. R. Kuphaldt, "Lessons in Electric Circuits," a free series of textbooks on the subjects of electricity and electronics: `www.ibiblio.org/kuphaldt/electricCircuits/`.
- All About Circuits: `www.allaboutcircuits.com` provides excellent applied examples of many types of electronic circuits.
- The Electronics Club: `www.electronicsclub.info` provides electronics projects for beginners and for reference.
- Neil Storey, *Electronics: A Systems Approach*, 5th ed., New York: Pearson, 2013.

Here is a full list of the components that are used in this chapter:

- Breadboard
- Diodes: 1N4001, general-purpose LED
- Transistors: NPN: BC547, FET: BS270
- Voltage regulator: KA7805/LM7805
- PTC: 60R110
- Button and Switch: General purpose SPST and SPDT
- ICs: 74HC73N, 74HC03N, 74LS08N, 74HC08N, 74HC14, LM358N
- Resistors: 1MΩ, 2.2kΩ, 2×10kΩ, 50kΩ, 100Ω, 50Ω, 1kΩ, 470Ω, 220Ω, 100kΩ POT.
- Capacitors: 10μF, 1μF, 0.33μF, 0.1μF.
- Opto-isolator: SFH617A

Notes

1. Texas Instruments. (December 10, 2011). General hardware design/BGA PCB design/BGA decoupling. Retrieved April 10, 2014, from Texas Instruments Wiki `tiny.cc/ebb402`.

2. Vishay Semiconductors. (January 14, 2013). SFH617A Datasheet. Retrieved April 13, 2014, from Vishay Semiconductors `tiny.cc/ebb403`.

# CHAPTER 5

Practical BeagleBone Programming

This chapter describes several different programming options for the BeagleBone, including scripted and compiled languages. An LED flashing example is provided in all of the languages so that you can investigate each language's structure and syntax. The advantages and disadvantages of each language are discussed along with example uses. The chapter then focuses on the C/C++ programming languages, describing the principles of these languages, and why object-oriented programming (OOP) is appropriate and necessary for the development of scalable embedded systems applications. Finally, the chapter details how you can interface directly to the Linux kernel using the GNU C Library. A single chapter can only touch the surface of programming languages, but this one is focused on programming the BeagleBone. I have made my module notes about OOP available at `ee402.eeng.dcu.ie` to support this chapter.

Equipment Required for This Chapter:

- BeagleBone Black with console connection (see Chapter 2)
- Desktop Linux Installation (e.g., Debian in a VM—see Chapter 3)

Introduction

As discussed in Chapter 3, embedded Linux is essentially "Linux on an embedded system." If your favorite programming language is available under Linux, then it is also likely to be available for the BBB. So, is your favorite language suitable for programming the BBB? That depends on what you intend to do with the board. Are you interfacing to electronics devices/modules? Do you plan to write rich user interfaces? Are you planning to write a device driver for Linux? Is performance very important, or are you developing an early pre-prototype? Each of the answers to these questions will impact your decision regarding which language you should use. In this chapter, you are introduced to several different languages, and the advantages and disadvantages of each category of language are outlined. As you read through the chapter, try to avoid focusing on a favorite language, but instead use the correct language for the job at hand.

How does programming on embedded systems compare to programming on desktop computers? Here are some points to consider:

- You should always write the clearest and cleanest code that is as maintainable as possible, just as you would on a desktop PC.

- Don't optimize your code until you are certain that it is complete.

- You typically have to be more aware of how you are consuming resources than when programming on the desktop computer. The size of data types matters, and passing data correctly really matters. You have to be concerned with memory availability, file system size, and data communication availability/bandwidth.

- You often have to learn about the underlying hardware platform. How does it handle the connected hardware? What data buses are available? How do you interface with the operating system and low-level libraries? Are there any real-time constraints?

For the upcoming discussion, it is assumed that you are planning to do some type of physical computing—that is, interfacing to the different input or outputs on the BBB. Therefore, the example that is used to describe the structure and syntax of the different languages is a simple interfacing example. Before looking at the languages themselves, we will begin with a brief performance evaluation of different languages running on the BBB, in order to put the following discussions in context.

Performance of Different Languages

Which language is the fastest on the BBB? Well, that is an incredibly emotive and difficult question to answer. Different languages perform better on different benchmarks and different tasks. In addition, a program written in a particular language can be optimized for that language to the point that it is barely recognizable as the original code. Nor is speed of execution always an important factor; you may be more concerned with memory usage, the portability of the code, or the ability to quickly apply changes.

However, if you are planning to develop high-speed or real-time number-crunching applications, then performance may be a key factor in your choice of programming language. In addition, if you are setting out to learn a new language, and you may possibly be developing algorithmically rich programs in the future, then it may be useful to keep performance in mind.

A simple test has been put in place on the BBB to determine the performance of the languages discussed in this chapter. The test uses the *n*-body benchmark (gravitational interaction of planets in the solar system) code from `benchmarksgame.alioth.debian.org`. The code uses the exact same algorithm for all languages and the BBB is running in the exact same state in all cases. The test uses 5 million iterations of the algorithm to ensure that the script used for timing does not have to be highly accurate. All of the programs gave the same correct result, indicating that they all ran correctly and to completion. The test is available in the book's Git repository in the directory `chp05/performance/`. Note that you must have installed Java on the BBB in order to run all of the tests. That is discussed later in this chapter. Use the following call to execute the test:

```
/chp05/performance$ ./run
Running the Tests:
The C/C++ Code Example
-0.169075164   -0.169083134
It took 33 seconds to run the C/C++ test ...
Finished Running the Benchmarks
```

The results of the tests are displayed in Table 5-1. In the first column you can see the results for the BBB, running at its top processor frequency of 1 GHz. For this number-crunching application, C++ performs the task in the shortest time, taking 33 seconds to complete. This time has been weighted as one unit. Therefore, Java takes 1.18 times longer to complete the same task, Node.js (for BoneScript) 2.36 times longer, Perl 27.8 times longer, and Python 32.2 times longer. The processing durations are provided in parentheses. As you move across the columns you can see that this performance is relatively consistent, even as the processor frequency is adjusted (discussed in the next section) or a desktop i7 64-bit processor is used.

Table 5-1: Numerical Computation Time for 5,000,000 Iterations of the *n*-Body Algorithm on a BBB Debian Hard-float Image

VALUE	BBB@1GHZ	BBB@800MHZ	BBB@300MHZ	DEBIAN 64-BIT I7 PC
C++	1.00× (33s)	1.00× (42s)	1.00× (114s)	1.00× (0.821s)
C++11	1.15× (38s)	1.16× (48s)	1.16× (132s)	0.91× (0.746s)
Java	1.18× (39s)	1.16× (49s)	1.19× (134s)	1.24× (1.023s)
Node.js	2.36× (78s)	2.21× (93s)	2.19× (248s)	5.78× (4.523s)
Perl	27.8× (917s)	27.9× (1170s)	28.7× (3244s)	75.64× (62.1s)
Python	32.2× (1063s)	30.8× (1294s)	31.7× (3586s)	83.92× (68.9s)

All of the programs use between 98% and 99% of the CPU while they are executing. In addition, the C++ program used ~0.1% of memory, the Java and Node.js programs used ~2.3% of memory, and the Python application used ~0.8% of memory while executing. The relative performance of Java and Node.js is impressive given that code is compiled dynamically ("just-in-time"), which is discussed later in this chapter. Any dynamic compilation latency is included in the timings, as the test script includes the following Bash script code to calculate the execution duration of each program:

```
Duration="5000000"
echo -e "\nThe C/C++ Code Example"
T="$(date +%s%N)"
./n-body $Duration
T="$(($(date +%s%N)-T))"
T=$((T/1000000))
echo "It took ${T} milliseconds to run the C/C++ test"
```

The C++11 code is the version of the C++ programming language that was approved in mid-2011 (needs gcc 4.7+). This is discussed again in Chapter 7. The program contains optimizations that are specific to this release of C++ and interestingly, while this version performs better on the desktop computer, it underperforms on the BBB. The Java program uses the +AgressiveOpts flag to enable performance optimization, and it was used because it did not involve modifying the source code.

The results for Python are particularly poor due to the algorithmic nature of the problem. However, the benchmarks at (debian.org, 2013),[1] indicate that the range will be 9 to 100 times slower than the optimized C++ code for general processing to algorithm-rich code, respectively. If you are very comfortable with Python and you would like to improve upon its performance, then you can investigate *Cython*, which is a Python compiler that automatically removes the dynamic typing capability and enables you to generate C code directly from your Python code. On the Debian image you can enter apt-get install cython and apt-get install python-dev.

The final column provides the results for the same code running on a desktop computer virtual machine (a 64-bit Ubuntu 3.11.0 kernel in a VirtualBox VM, allocated one thread on one core of an Intel i7@3.5 GHz processor and 10 GB of RAM, with no processing cap). You can see that the relative performance of the applications is broadly in line, but also note that the C++ program runs 40 times faster on the single i7 thread than it does on the BBB at 1 GHz. Hopefully that will help you frame your expectations with respect to the type of numerical processing that is possible on a standard BBB, particularly when investigating computationally expensive applications like signal processing and computer vision.

As previously discussed, this is only one numerically-oriented benchmark test, but it is somewhat indicative of the type of performance you should expect from each language. There have been many studies on the performance of languages; however, a recent and well-specified analysis by Hundt (2011) has found that in terms of performance, "C++ wins out by a large margin. However, it also required the most extensive tuning efforts, many of which were done at a level of sophistication that would not be available to the average programmer" (Hundt, 2011).[2]

Setting the BBB CPU Frequency

In the previous section, the clock frequency of the BBB was adjusted dynamically at run time. The BBB has various *governors* that can be used to profile the performance/power usage ratio. For example, if you were building a battery-powered BBB application that has low processing requirements, you could reduce the clock frequency to conserve power. You can find out information about the current state of the BBB by typing the following:

```
root@beaglebone:~# cpufreq-info
... available frequency steps: 300 MHz, 600 MHz, 800 MHz, 1000 MHz
    governors: conservative, ondemand, userspace, powersave, performance
    current CPU frequency is 1000 MHz (asserted by call to hardware).
    cpufreq stats: 300 MHz:95.04%, 600 MHz:0.15%, 800 MHz:0.05%,
        1000 MHz:4.76%  (159)
```

You can see that different governors are available, with the profile names conservative, ondemand, userspace, powersave, and performance. To enable one of these governors type the following:

```
root@beaglebone:~# cpufreq-set -g performance
root@beaglebone:~# cpufreq-info
    current policy: frequency should be within 300 MHz and 1000 MHz.
            The governor "performance" may decide which speed to use
root@beaglebone:~# cpufreq-set -f 800MHz
root@beaglebone:~# cpufreq-info
  current CPU frequency is 800 MHz (asserted by call to hardware)
```

These commands need to be executed with root privileges. If these tools are not installed on your BBB, you can install the cpufrequtils package. The default governor is ondemand, which will dynamically switch CPU frequencies if the BBB reaches 95% of CPU load.

Scripting Languages

A scripting language is a computer programming language that is used to specify script files, which are *interpreted* directly by a run-time environment to perform tasks. Many scripting languages are available, such as Bash, Perl, and

Python, and these can be used to automate the execution of tasks on the BBB, such as system administration, interaction, and even interfacing to electronic components.

Scripting Language Options

Which scripting language should you choose for the BBB? There are many strong opinions and it is a difficult topic, as Linux users tend to have a favorite scripting language; however, you should choose the scripting language with features that suit the task at hand. For example:

- **Bash scripting:** Is a great choice for short scripts that do not require advanced programming structures. Bash scripts are used extensively in this book for small, well-defined tasks, such as the timing code in the previous section. You can use the Linux commands discussed in Chapter 3 in your Bash scripts.

- **Perl:** Is a great choice for scripts that parse text documents or process streams of data. It enables you to write straightforward scripts and even supports the object-oriented programming (OOP) paradigm, which is discussed later in this chapter.

- **Python:** Is great for scripts that need more complex structure and are likely to be built upon or modified in the future. Python supports the OOP paradigm and dynamic typing, which is discussed shortly.

These three scripting languages are available pre-configured on the BBB standard Debian image. It would be very useful to have some knowledge of all of these scripting languages, as you may find third-party tools or libraries that make your current project very straightforward. This section provides a brief overview of each of these languages, including a concise segment of code that performs the same function in each language. It finishes with a discussion about the advantages and disadvantages of scripting languages in general.

NOTE All of the code that follows in this chapter is available in the associated GitHub repository in the `chp05` directory. If you have not done so already, use the command `git clone https://github.com/derekmolloy/exploringBB.git` in a Linux terminal window to clone this repository.

In Chapter 2 an approach is described for changing the state of the on-board LEDs using Linux shell commands. It is possible to turn an LED on or off, and even make it flash. For example, you can use:

```
root@beaglebone:/sys/class/leds/beaglebone:green:usr3# echo none > trigger
root@beaglebone:/sys/class/leds/beaglebone:green:usr3# echo 1 > brightness
root@beaglebone:/sys/class/leds/beaglebone:green:usr3# echo 0 > brightness
```

to turn a user LED on and off. This section examines how it is possible to do the same tasks but in a structured programmatic form.

Bash

Bash scripts are a great choice for short scripts that do not require advanced programming structures, and that is exactly the application to be developed here. The first program leverages the Linux console commands such as echo and cat to create the concise script in Listing 5-1 that enables you to choose, using command-line arguments, whether you wish to turn USR3 LED on or off, or place it in a flashing mode. For example, using this script by calling `./bashLED on` would turn the USR3 LED on. It also provides you with the trigger status information:

LISTING 5-1: chp05/bashLED/bashLED

```
#!/bin/bash
LED3_PATH=/sys/class/leds/beaglebone:green:usr3

function removeTrigger
{
  echo "none" >> "$LED3_PATH/trigger"
}

echo "Starting the LED Bash Script"
if [ $# != 1 ]; then
  echo "There is an incorrect number of arguments. Usage is:"
  echo -e " bashLED Command \n  where command is one of "
  echo -e "   on, off, flash or status  \n e.g. bashLED on "
  exit 2
fi
echo "The LED Command that was passed is: $1"
if [ "$1" == "on" ]; then
  echo "Turning the LED on"
  removeTrigger
  echo "1" >> "$LED3_PATH/brightness"
elif [ "$1" == "off" ]; then
  echo "Turning the LED off"
  removeTrigger
  echo "0" >> "$LED3_PATH/brightness"
elif [ "$1" == "flash" ]; then
  echo "Flashing the LED"
  removeTrigger
  echo "timer" >> "$LED3_PATH/trigger"
  echo "50" >> "$LED3_PATH/delay_on"
  echo "50" >> "$LED3_PATH/delay_off"
```

continues

LISTING 5-1: *(continued)*

```
elif [ "$1" == "status" ]; then
  cat "$LED3_PATH/trigger";
fi
echo "End of the LED Bash Script"
```

The script is available in the directory /chp05/bashLED. If you entered the script manually using the nano editor, then the file needs to have the executable flag set before it can be executed (the Git repository retains executable flags). Therefore, to allow all users to execute this script, use the following:

```
/chp05/bashLED$ chmod ugo+x bashLED
```

What is happening within this script? First, all of these command scripts begin with a *sha-bang* #! followed by the name and location of the interpreter to be used, so #!/bin/bash in this case. The file is just a regular text file, but the sha-bang is a *magic-number* code to inform the OS that the file is an executable. Next, the script defines the path to the LED for which you wish to change state using the variable LED3_PATH. This allows the default value to be easily altered if you wish to use a different user LED or path.

The script contains a function called removeTrigger, mainly to demonstrate how functions are structured within Bash scripting. This function is called later in the script. Each if is terminated by a fi. The ; after the if statement terminates that statement and allows the statement then to be placed on the same line. The elif keyword means else if, which allows you to have multiple comparisons within the one if block. The newline character \n terminates statements.

> **NOTE** If you happen to be writing scripts under Windows, do not use Windows Notepad/WordPad to enter a Bash script. It will place a carriage return and line feed at the end of each line, which will mean that you get an error message like "bad interpreter" on the first line of your scripts when they are executed under Linux. If necessary, you can install and use Notepad++ under Windows.

The first if statement confirms that the number of arguments passed to the script ($#) is not equal to 1. Remember that the correct way to call this script is of the form ./bashLED on. Therefore, on will be the first user argument that is passed ($1) and there will be one argument in total. If there are no arguments, then the correct usage will be displayed and the script will exit with the return code 2. This value is consistent with Linux system commands, where an exit value of 2 indicates incorrect usage. Success is indicated by a return value of 0, so any other non-zero return value generally indicates the failure of a script.

If the argument that was passed is on then the code displays a message; calls the removeTrigger function; and writes the string "1" to the brightness file in the LED3 /sys directory. The remaining functions modify the USR3 LED values in the same way as described in Chapter 2. You can execute the script as follows:

```
/chp05/bashLED$ ./bashLED
There are no arguments. Usage is:
 bashLED Command, where command is one of
    on, off, flash or status e.g., bashLED on
/chp05/bashLED$ ./bashLED status
The LED Command that was passed is: status
[none] rc-feedback mmc0 mmc1 timer oneshot heartbeat backlight gpio cpu0
/chp05/bashLED$ sudo ./bashLED on
The LED Command that was passed is: on
Turning the LED on
/chp05/bashLED$ sudo ./bashLED flash
/chp05/bashLED$ sudo ./bashLED off
```

Notice that the script was prefixed by sudo when it was called. This is required, as the script was executed by the molloyd user account. The LED sysfs directory is owned by the root account and regular users do not have write access to change the state. For security reasons, you cannot use the setuid bit on a script to set it to execute as root. If users had write access to this script and its setuid bit was set as root, then they could inject any command that they wished into the script and would have *de facto* superuser access to the system.

A short script restoreDefaultLEDs is available in the repository chp05 directory. It returns the BBB LEDs back to their default states. For a comprehensive online guide to Bash scripting, please see Mendel Cooper's "Advanced Bash-Scripting Guide": www.tldp.org/LDP/abs/html/.

Perl

Perl is a feature-rich scripting language that provides you with access to a huge library of reusable modules and portability to other OSs (including Windows). Perl is best known for its text processing and regular expressions modules. In the late 1990s it was a very popular language for server-side scripting for the dynamic generation of web pages. Later it was superseded by technologies such as Java servlets, Java Server Pages (JSP), and PHP. The language has evolved since its birth in the 1980s and now includes support for the OOP paradigm. Perl 5 (v14+) is installed by default on the BBB Debian Linux image. Listing 5-2 provides a segment of a Perl example that has the same structure as the Bash script, so it is not necessary to discuss it in detail. Apart from the syntax, very little has actually changed in the translation to Perl.

LISTING 5-2: chp05/perlLED/perlLED.pl (segment)

```perl
#!/usr/bin/perl
$LED3_PATH = "/sys/class/leds/beaglebone:green:usr3";
$command = $ARGV[0];

# Perl Write to LED3 function, the filename  $_[0] is the first argument
#    and the value to write is the second argument $_[1]
sub writeLED3{
  open(FILE, ">" . $LED3_PATH . $_[0] )
     or die "Could not open the file, $!";
  print FILE $_[1] ;
  close(FILE);
}
sub removeTrigger{
  writeLED3 ( "/trigger", "none");
}

print "Starting the LED Perl Script\n";
# 0 means that there is exactly one argument
if ( $#ARGV != 0 ){
  print "There are an incorrect number of arguments. Usage is:\n";
  print " bashLED Command, where command is one of\n";
  print "   on, off, flash or status e.g. bashLED on\n";
  exit 2;
}
print "The LED Command that was passed is: " . $command . "\n";
if ( $command eq "on" ){
  print "Turning the LED on\n";
  removeTrigger();
  writeLED3 ("/brightness", "1");
}
...   //full listing available in chp05/perlLED/perlLED.pl
```

A few small points are worth noting in the code: The "<" or ">" sign on the filename indicates whether the file is being opened for read or write access, respectively; the arguments are passed as $ARGV[0...n] and the number of arguments is available as the value $#ARGV; a file open, followed by a read or write, and a file close are necessary to write the values to /sys; and the arguments are passed to the subroutine writeLED3 and these are received as the values $_[0] and $_[1], which is not the most beautiful programming syntax, but it works perfectly well. To execute this code, simply type sudo ./perlLED.pl on, as the sha-bang identifies the Perl interpreter. You could also execute it by typing perl perlLED.pl status.

For a good resource about getting started with installing and using Perl 5, see the guide "Learning Perl" at learn.perl.org.

Python

Python is a dynamic and strongly typed OOP language that was designed to be easy to learn and understand. *Dynamic typing* means that you do not have to associate a type (e.g., integer, character, string) with a variable; rather, the value of the variable "remembers" its own type. Therefore, if you were to create a variable x=5, the variable x would behave as an integer; but if you subsequently assign it using x="test", it would then behave like a string. *Statically typed* languages such as C/C++ or Java would not allow the re-definition of a variable in this way (within the same scope). *Strongly typed* means that the conversion of a variable from one type to another requires an explicit conversion. The advantages of object-oriented programming structures are discussed later in this chapter. Python is installed by default on the Debian BBB image. The Python example to flash the LED is provided in Listing 5-3.

LISTING 5-3: chp05/pythonLED/pythonLED.py

```python
#!/usr/bin/python
import sys
LED3_PATH = "/sys/class/leds/beaglebone:green:usr3"

def writeLED ( filename, value, path=LED3_PATH ):
   "This function writes the passed value to the file in the path"
   fo = open( path + filename,"w")
   fo.write(value)
   fo.close()
   return

def removeTrigger():
   writeLED (filename="/trigger", value="none")
   return

print "Starting the LED Python Script"
if len(sys.argv)!=2:
   print "There are an incorrect number of arguments"
   print " usage is:  pythonLED.py command"
   print " where command is one of on, off, flash or status."
   sys.exit(2)
if sys.argv[1]=="on":
   print "Turning the LED on"
   removeTrigger()
   writeLED (filename="/brightness", value="1")
elif sys.argv[1]=="off":
   print "Turning the LED off"
   removeTrigger()
   writeLED (filename="/brightness", value="0")
elif sys.argv[1]=="flash":
   print "Flashing the LED"
   writeLED (filename="/trigger", value="timer")
   writeLED (filename="/delay_on", value="50")
   writeLED (filename="/delay_off", value="50")
```

continues

LISTING 5-3: *(continued)*

```
elif sys.argv[1]=="status":
   print "Getting the LED trigger status"
   fo = open( LED3_PATH + "/trigger", "r")
   print fo.read()
   fo.close()
else:
   print "Invalid Command!"
print "End of Python Script"
```

The formatting of this code is important—in fact, Python enforces the layout of your code by making indentation a structural element. For example, after the line "if len(sys.argv)!=2:" the next few lines are "tabbed" in. If you did not tab in one of the lines—for example, the sys.exit(2) line—then it would not be part of the conditional if statement and the code would always exit at this point in the program. To execute this example, in the pythonLED directory enter the following:

```
/chp05/pythonLED$ sudo ./pythonLED.py flash
Flashing the LED
/chp05/pythonLED$ ./pythonLED.py status
Getting the LED trigger status
none rc-feedback mmc0 mmc1 [timer] oneshot heartbeat backlight gpio cpu0
```

Python is very popular on the BBB, and most of the other books currently available on the BBB use Python as the core programming language. A list of books is provided at the end of this chapter. Compared to Perl, the syntax is very straightforward and there is not too much to explain about the preceding code, having explained the Bash and Perl versions.

To conclude this discussion of scripting, there are several strong choices for applications on the BBB. Table 5-2 lists some of the key advantages and disadvantages of command scripting on the BBB, when considered in the context of the compiled languages which are discussed shortly.

Table 5-2: Advantages and Disadvantages of Command Scripting on the BBB

ADVANTAGES	DISADVANTAGES
Perfect for automating Linux system administration tasks that require calls to Linux commands.	Performance is poor for complex numerical or algorithmic tasks.
Easy to modify and adapt to changes. Source code is always present and complex toolchains (see Chapter 7) are not required in order to make modifications. Generally, nano is the only tool that you need.	Generally, relatively poor/slow programming support for data structures, graphical user interfaces, sockets, threads, etc.

ADVANTAGES	DISADVANTAGES
Generally, straightforward programming syntax and structure that is reasonably easy to learn when compared to languages like C++ and Java.	Generally, poor support for complex applications involving multiple, user-developed modules or components (Python and Perl do support OOP).
Generally, quick turnaround in coding solutions by occasional programmers.	Code is in the open. Direct access to view your code can be an intellectual property or a security concern.
	Lack of development tools (e.g., refactoring).

JavaScript and Java

With the interpreted languages just discussed, the source code text file is "executed" by the user passing it to a run-time interpreter, which then translates or executes each line of code. JavaScript and Java have different life cycles and are quite distinct languages.

JavaScript and Node.js on the BBB

As discussed in Chapter 2, in the section "Node.js, Cloud9, and BoneScript," Node.js is JavaScript that is run on the server side. JavaScript is an interpreted language by design; however, thanks to the V8 engine that was developed by Google for their Chrome web browser, Node.js actually compiles JavaScript into native machine instructions as it is loaded by the engine. This is called *just-in-time* (JIT) compilation or *dynamic translation*. As demonstrated at the beginning of this chapter, Node.js's performance for the numerical computation tasks is very impressive for an interpreted language.

Listing 5-4 shows the same LED code example written using JavaScript and executed by calling the nodejs executable:

LISTING 5-4: chp05/nodejsLED/nodejsLED.js

```
// Ignore the first two arguments (nodejs and the program name)
var myArgs = process.argv.slice(2);
var LED3_PATH = "/sys/class/leds/beaglebone:green:usr3"

function writeLED( filename, value, path ){
  var fs = require('fs');
  try {
  // The next call must be syncronous, otherwise the timer will not work
    fs.writeFileSync(path+filename, value);
  }
  catch (err) {
```

continues

LISTING 5-4: *(continued)*

```
        console.log("The Write Failed to the File: " + path+filename);
    }
}
function removeTrigger(){
    writeLED("/trigger", "none", LED3_PATH);
}

console.log("Starting the LED Node.js Program");
if (myArgs[0]==null){
    console.log("There is an incorrect number of arguments.");
    console.log("  Usage is: nodejs nodejsLED.js command");
    console.log("  where command is one of: on, off, flash or status.");
    process.exit(2);   //exits with the error code 2 (incorrect usage)
}
switch (myArgs[0]) {
    case 'on':
        console.log("Turning the LED On");
        removeTrigger();
        writeLED("/brightness", "1", LED3_PATH);
        break;
    case 'off':
        console.log("Turning the LED Off");
        removeTrigger();
        writeLED("/brightness", "0", LED3_PATH);
        break;
    case 'flash':
        console.log("Making the LED Flash");
        writeLED("/trigger", "timer", LED3_PATH);
        writeLED("/delay_on", "50", LED3_PATH);
        writeLED("/delay_off", "50", LED3_PATH);
        break;
    case 'status':
        console.log("Getting the LED Status");
        fs = require('fs');
        fs.readFile(LED3_PATH+"/trigger", 'utf8', function (err, data) {
            if (err) { return console.log(err); }
            console.log(data);
        });
        break;
    default:
        console.log("Invalid Command");
}
console.log("End of Node.js script");
```

The code is available in the /chp05/nodejsLED/ directory and it can be executed by typing **nodejs nodejsLED.js [option]**. The code has been structured in the same way as the previous examples and there are not too many syntactical differences; however, there is one major difference between Node.js and other languages: *functions are called asynchronously*. Up to this point, all of the languages discussed followed a sequential-execution mode. Therefore, when a function is called, the *program counter* (also known as the *instruction pointer*) enters that function and does not reemerge until the function is complete. Consider, for example, code like this:

```
functionA();
functionB();
```

The `functionA()` is called and `functionB()` will not be called until `functionA()` is fully complete. This is *not* the case in Node.js! In Node.js, `functionA()` is called first and then Node.js continues executing the subsequent code, including entering `functionB()`, while the code in `functionA()` is still being executed. This presents a serious difficulty for the current application, with this segment of code in particular:

```
case 'flash':
    console.log("Making the LED Flash");
    writeLED("/trigger", "timer", LED3_PATH);
    writeLED("/delay_on", "50", LED3_PATH);
    writeLED("/delay_off", "50", LED3_PATH);
    break;
```

The first call to `writeLED()` sets up the `sysfs` file system (as described in Chapter 2) to now contain new `delay_on` and `delay_off` file entries. However, due to the asynchronous nature of the calls, the first `writeLED()` call has not finished setting up the file system before the next two `writeLED()` calls are performed. This means that the `delay_on` and `delay_off` file system entries are not found, and the code to write to them fails. You should test this by changing the call near the top of the program from `fs.writeFileSync(...)` to `fs.writeFile(...)`.

To combat this issue you can *synchronize* (prevent threads from being interrupted) the block of code where the three `writeLED()` functions are called, ensuring that the functions are called sequentially. Alternatively, as shown in this code example, you can use a special version of the Node.js `writeFile()` function called `writeFileSync()` to ensure that the first function call to modify the file system blocks the other `writeFileSync()` calls from taking place.

Node.js allows asynchronous calls because they help ensure that your code is "lively." For example, if you performed a database query, your code may be able to do something else useful while awaiting the result. When the result is available, a *callback function* is executed in order to process the received data. This asynchronous structure is perfect for Internet-attached applications, where posts and requests are being made of websites and web services, and it is not clear when a response will be received (if at all). Node.js has an *event loop* that manages all the asynchronous calls, creating threads for each call as required, and ensuring that the callback functions are executed when an asynchronous call completes its assigned tasks.

Java on the BBB

Up to this point in the chapter, *interpreted languages* are examined, meaning the source code file (a text file) is executed using an interpreter or dynamic translator at run time. Importantly, the code exists in source code form, right up to the point when it is executed using the interpreter.

With traditional *compiled languages*, the source code (a text file) is translated directly into machine code for a particular platform using a set of tools, which we will call a *compiler* for the moment. The translation happens when the code is being developed; once compiled, the code can be executed without needing any additional run-time tools.

Java is a hybrid language: You write your Java code in a source file, e.g., example.java, which is a regular text file. The Java compiler (javac) compiles and translates this source code into machine code instructions (called *bytecodes*) for a Java *virtual machine* (VM). Regular compiled code is not portable between hardware architectures, but bytecode files (.class files) can be executed on any platform that has an implementation of the Java VM. Originally, the Java VM interpreted the bytecode files at run time; however, more recently, dynamic translation is employed by the VM to convert the bytecodes into native machine instructions at run time.

The key advantage of this life cycle is that the compiled bytecode is portable between platforms; and because it is compiled to a generic machine instruction code, the dynamic translation to "real" machine code is very efficient. The downside of this structure when compared to compiled languages is that the VM adds overhead to the execution of the final executable.

Presently, there is no version of the Java Development Kit for embedded Linux, which prevents you from compiling code directly on the BBB. In addition, the Java Runtime Environment (JRE), which provides the Java virtual machine (JVM), is not installed on the BBB by default.

> **NOTE** Large installations such as the JRE might cause you to run out of space on your BBB. You can find the biggest packages that are installed on your distribution using the command dpkg-query -Wf '${Installed-Size}\ t${Package}\n' | sort -n. You can then remove large unused packages using apt-get remove.

There is a full guide to installing the JRE on the BBB and the JDK on a desktop Linux machine at the chapter web page. Listing 5-5 provides a source code example that is also available in the GitHub repository in byte-code form.

LISTING 5-5: chp05/javaLED/LEDExample.java (Segment)

```java
package exploringBB;
import java.io.*;

public class LEDExample {
  private static String LED3 = "/sys/class/leds/beaglebone:green:usr3";

  private static void writeLED(String fname, String value, String path){
     try{
        BufferedWriter bw = new BufferedWriter(new FileWriter(path+fname));
        bw.write(value);
        bw.close();
     }
     catch(IOException e){
        System.err.println("Failed to access Sysfs: " + fname);
     }
}

private static void removeTrigger(){
    writeLED("/trigger", "none", LED3);
}

public static void main(String[] args) {
    System.out.println("Starting the LED Java Application");
    if(args.length!=1) {
       System.out.println("Incorrect number of arguments."); ...
       System.exit(2);
    }
    if(args[0].equalsIgnoreCase("On")||args[0].equalsIgnoreCase("Off")){
       System.out.println("Turning the LED " + args[0]);
       removeTrigger();
       writeLED("/brightness",args[0].equalsIgnoreCase("On")?"1":"0",LED3);
    }
    ...  // full code available in the repository directory
 }
}
```

Early versions of Java suffered from poor computational performance; how-ever, more recent versions take advantage of dynamic translation at run time (just-in-time, or JIT, compilation) and, as demonstrated at the start of this chapter, the performance was less than 20% slower (including dynamic translation) than that of the natively compiled C++ code, with only a minor additional memory overhead. Table 5-3 lists some of the advantages and disadvantages of using Java for development on the BBB.

Table 5-3: Advantages and Disadvantages of Java on the BBB

ADVANTAGES	DISADVANTAGES
Code is portable. Code compiled on the PC can be executed on the BBB or another embedded Linux platform.	You cannot currently build your Java applications directly on the BBB.
There is a vast and extensive library of code available that can be fully integrated in your project.	Executing as root is slightly difficult due to required environment variables.
Full OOP support.	It's not suitable for scripting.
Can be used for user-interface application development on the BBB when it is attached to a display.	Computational performance is very respectable, but slower than optimized C/C++ programs. Slightly heavier on memory.
Strong support for multi-threading.	Strictly typed and no unsigned integer types.
Has automatic memory allocation and de-allocation using a garbage collector, removing memory leak concerns.	Royalty payment required if deployed to a platform that "involves or controls hardware" (Oracle, 2014).[3]
	Sandboxed applications do not have access to system memory, registers or system calls (except through /proc) or JNI (Java Native Interface).

To execute a Java application under Debian/Ubuntu, where it needs access to the /sys directory, you need the application to run with root access. Unfortunately, because you need to pass the bytecode (.class) file to the Java VM, you have to call sudo and create a temporary shell of the form **sudo sh -c 'java myClass'**. However, because you set the environment variables for PATH and JAVA_HOME within the user account, these will not be present in the root account. For example:

```
/chp05/javaLED$ export TEST=test
/chp05/javaLED$ sudo sh -c 'echo $TEST'
/chp05/javaLED$ sudo -E sh -c 'echo $TEST'
test
```

NOTE Instead of logging out and logging in again to apply profile settings, you can use the source command, which evaluates a file as a Tcl (Tool Command Language) script to reload your .profile settings. Type source ~/.profile.

In the first case, there was no output, as the TEST environment variable is not passed to the root shell; however, the addition of -E means that the variable is passed. Unfortunately, this will not work for PATH, because to prevent Trojan horse application attacks, the root PATH is set in the /etc/sudoers file. Therefore, to execute your Java application, you have to modify the sudoers configuration file using **sudo visudo** and add the following modifications:

- Change secure_path to include /usr/java/jre/bin/.

- Add the line Defaults env_keep += "JAVA_HOME".

The application can eventually be executed using the following:

```
/chp05/javaLED$ sudo sh -c 'java exploringBB.LEDExample On'
/chp05/javaLED$ sudo sh -c 'java exploringBB.LEDExample Off'
```

C and C++ on the BeagleBone

C++ was developed by Bjarne Stroustrup at Bell Labs (now AT&T Labs) during 1983–1985. It is based on the C language (named in 1972) that was developed at AT&T for UNIX systems in the early 1970s (1969–1973) by Dennis Ritchie. As well as adding an *object-oriented* (OO) framework (originally called "C with Classes"), C++ also improves the C language by adding features such as better type checking. It quickly gained widespread usage, which was largely due to its similarity to the C programming language syntax, and the fact that it allowed existing C code to be used when possible. C++ is not a pure OO language but rather a hybrid, having the organizational structure of OO languages but retaining the efficiencies of C, such as typed variables and pointers.

Unlike Java, C++ is not "owned" by a single company. In 1998 the ISO (International Organization for Standardization) committee adopted a worldwide uniform language specification that aimed to remove inconsistencies between the various C++ compilers (Stroustrup, 1998).[4] This standardization continues today with C++11 approved by the ISO in 2011 (gcc 4.7+ supports the flag -std=c++11) and more new features appearing in compilers today with the approval of C++14 in August 2014.

Why am I covering C and C++ in more detail than other languages in this book?

- First, I believe that if you can understand the workings of C and C++, then you can understand the workings of any language. In fact, most compilers (Java native methods, Java virtual machine, JavaScript) and interpreters (Bash, Perl, Python) are written in C.

- At the beginning of this chapter, a significant performance advantage of C/C++ over other languages was described (yes, it was demonstrated using only one random test!). It is also important to remember that the same code running on the BBB at 1 GHz was 40 times slower than the same code running on only one thread (two available on each core) of one core (four available) of an Intel i7 3.5 GHz processor. Resources on the BBB are not so plentiful that they can be wasted with inefficiencies.

- If you are to build upon the content of this book and develop your own device drivers, or contribute to Linux kernel development, you need to understand C and/or C++. Later in this chapter, code is provided that demonstrates how you can communicate directly with Linux kernel space using the GNU C Library (glibc).

- Many of the application examples in this book such as streaming network data and image processing use C++ and a comprehensive library of C++ code called Qt.

Table 5-4 lists some advantages and disadvantages of using C/C++ on the BBB. The next section reviews some of the fundamentals of C and C++ programming, in order to ensure that you have the skills necessary for the remaining chapters in this book. It is not possible to cover every aspect of C and C++ programming in just one chapter of one book. The Further Reading section at the end of this chapter directs you to recommended texts.

Table 5-4: Advantages and Disadvantages of C/C++ on the BBB

ADVANTAGES	DISADVANTAGES
You can build code directly on the BBB or you can cross-compile code. The C/C++ languages are ISO standards, not owned by a single vendor.	Compiled code is not portable. Code compiled for your x86 desktop will not run on the BBB ARM processor.
C++ has full support for procedural programming, OOP, and support for generics through the use of STL (Standard Template Library).	Many consider the languages to be complex to master. There is a tendency to need to know everything before you can do anything.
It gives the best computational performance, especially if optimized; however, optimization can be difficult and can reduce the portability of your code.	The use of pointers and the low-level control available makes code prone to memory leaks. With careful coding these can be avoided and can lead to efficiencies over dynamic memory management schemes.
Can be used for user-interface application development on the BBB using third-party libraries. Libraries such as Qt and Boost provide extensive additional libraries for components, networking, etc.	By default, C and C++ do not support graphical user interfaces, network sockets, etc. Third-party libraries are required.
Offers low-level access to glibc for integrating with the Linux system. Programs can be `setuid` to root.	Not suitable for scripting (there is a C shell, csh, that does have syntax like C). Not ideal for web development either.
The Linux kernel is written in C and having knowledge of C/C++ can help if you ever have to write device drivers or contribute to Linux kernel development.	C++ attempts to span from low-level to high-level programming tasks, but it can be difficult to write very scalable enterprise or web applications.

The next section provides a revision of the core principles that have been applied to examples on the BBB. It is intended to serve as an overview and a set of reference examples that you can come back to again and again. It also focuses on topics that cause my students difficulties, pointing out common mistakes. Also, please remember that course notes for my OOP module are publicly available at ee402.eeng.dcu.ie along with further support materials.

C and C++ Language Overview

The following examples can be edited using the nano editor and compiled on the BBB directly using the *gcc* and *g++* compilers, which are installed by default. The code is in the directory chp05/overview.

The first example you should always write in any new language is "Hello World." Listing 5-6 and 5-7 provide C and C++ code respectively, for the purpose of a direct comparison of the two languages.

LISTING 5-6: chp05/overview/helloworld.c

```
#include <stdio.h>
int main(int argc, char *argv[]){
    printf("Hello World!\n");
    return 0;
}
```

LISTING 5-7: chp05/overview/helloworld.cpp

```
#include<iostream>
int main(int argc, char *argv[]){
    std::cout << "Hello World!" << std::endl;
    return 0;
}
```

The #include call is a pre-processor directive that effectively loads the contents of the stdio.h file (/usr/include/stdio.h) in the C case, and the iostream header (/usr/include/c++/4.X/iostream) file in the C++ case, and copies and pastes the code in at this exact point in your source code file. These header files contain the function prototypes, enabling the compiler to link to and understand the format of functions such as printf() in stdio.h and streams like cout in iostream. The actual implementation of these functions is in shared library dependencies. The angular brackets (< >) around the include filename means that it is a standard, rather than a user-defined include (which would use double quotes).

The main() function is the starting point of your application code. There can only be one function called main() in your application. The int in front of `main()` indicates that the program will return a number back to the shell prompt. As stated before, it is good to use `0` for successful completion, `2` for invalid usage, and any other set of numbers to indicate failure conditions. This value is returned to the shell prompt using the line `return 0` in this case. The `main()` function will return `0` by default. Remember that you can use `echo $?` at the shell prompt to see the last value that was returned.

The *parameters* of the `main()` function are `int argc` and `char *argv[]`. As you saw in the scripting examples, the shell can pass *arguments* to your application, providing the number of arguments (`argc`) and an array of strings (`*argv[]`). In C/C++ the first argument passed is `argv[0]` and it contains the name and full path used to execute the application.

The C code line `printf("Hello World!\n");` allows you to write to the Linux shell, with the `\n` representing a new line. The `printf()` function provides you with additional formatting instructions for outputting numbers, strings, etc. Note that every statement is terminated by a semicolon.

The C++ code line `std::cout << "Hello World!" << std::endl;` outputs a string just like the `printf()` function. In this case `cout` represents the output stream; and the function used is actually the `<<`, which is called the *output stream operator*. The syntax is discussed later, but `std::cout` means the output stream in the namespace `std`. The `endl` (end line) representation is the same as `\n`. This may seem more verbose, but you will see why it is useful later in the discussion on C++ classes. These programs can be compiled and executed directly on the BBB by typing the following:

```
/chp05/overview$ gcc helloworld.c -o helloworldc
/chp05/overview$ ./helloworldc
Hello World!
/chp05/overview$ g++ helloworld.cpp -o helloworldcpp
/chp05/overview$ ./helloworldcpp
Hello World!
```

The sizes of the C and C++ executables are different to account for the different header files, output functions, and exact compilers that are used:

```
/chp05/overview$ ls -l helloworldc*
-rwxr-xr-x 1 molloyd users 5053 Mar 14 12:23 helloworldc
-rwxr-xr-x 1 molloyd users 6559 Mar 14 12:24 helloworldcpp
```

Compiling and Linking

You just saw how to build a C or C++ application, but there are a few intermediate steps that are not obvious in the preceding example, as the intermediate stage outputs are not retained by default. Figure 5-1 illustrates the full build process from preprocessing right through to linking.

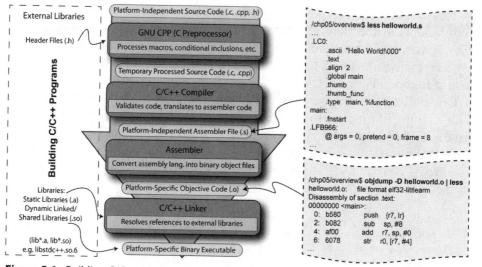

Figure 5-1: Building C/C++ applications on the BBB

You can perform the steps in Figure 5-1 yourself. Here is an example of the actual steps that were performed using the `Helloworld.cpp` code example. The steps can be performed explicitly as follows, so that you can view the output at each stage:

```
/chp05/overview$ ls
helloworld.cpp
/chp05/overview$ g++ -E helloworld.cpp > processed.cpp
/chp05/overview$ ls
helloworld.cpp  processed.cpp
/chp05/overview$ g++ -S processed.cpp -o helloworld.s
/chp05/overview$ ls
helloworld.cpp  helloworld.s  processed.cpp
/chp05/overview$ g++ -c helloworld.s
/chp05/overview$ ls
helloworld.cpp  helloworld.o  helloworld.s  processed.cpp
/chp05/overview$ g++ helloworld.o -o helloworld
/chp05/overview$ ls
helloworld  helloworld.cpp  helloworld.o  helloworld.s  processed.cpp
/chp05/overview$ ./helloworld
Hello World!
```

You can see the text format output after preprocessing by typing `less processed.cpp`, where you will see the necessary header files pasted in at the top of your code. At the very bottom of the file you will find your code. This file is passed to the C/C++ compiler, which validates the code and generates platform-independent assembler code (`.s`). You can view this code by typing `less helloworld.s`, as illustrated in Figure 5-1.

This .s text file is then passed to the assembler, which converts the platform-independent instructions into binary instructions for the BBB platform (the .o file). You can see the assembly language code that was generated if you use the objdump (object file dump) tool on the BBB by typing objdump -D helloworld.o, as illustrated in Figure 5-1.

Object files contain generalized binary assembly code that does not yet provide enough information to be executed on the BBB. However, after linking the final executable code, helloworld contains the target-specific assembly language code that has been combined with the libraries, statically and dynamically as required—you can use the objdump tool again on the executable, which results in the following output:

```
/chp05/overview$ objdump -D helloworld | less
helloworldcpp:     file format elf32-littlearm
Disassembly of section .interp:
00008134 <.interp>:
    8134:    62696c2f     rsbvs   r6, r9, #12032   ; 0x2f00
    8138:    2d646c2f     stclcs  12, cr6, [r4, #-188]! ; 0xffffff44
    813c:    756e696c     strbvc  r6, [lr, #-2412]!     ; 0x96c
 ...
```

The meaning of these instructions is another book in and of itself (see infocenter.arm.com for reference documentation), but for example in this case the mnemonic rsbvs refers to a type of reverse subtraction on the two of the ARM processor's 16, 32-bit registers (labeled r0–r15). Finally, just so you are aware, it is possible to disassemble executable code, in order that the source code can be reverse engineered. For example:

```
/chp05/overview$ objdump -S --disassemble helloworld > test.dump
/chp05/overview$ less test.dump
```

Writing the Shortest C/C++ Program

Is the HelloWorld example the shortest program that can be written in C or C++? No, Listing 5-8 is the shortest valid C and C++ program.

LISTING 5-8: chp05/overview/short.c

```
main(){}
```

This is a fully functional C and C++ program that compiles with no errors and works perfectly, albeit with no output. Therefore, in building a C/C++ program, there is no need for libraries; there is no need to specify a return type for main(), as it defaults to int; the main() function returns 0 by default in C++ and a random number in C (see echo $? call below); and an empty function is a valid function. This program will compile as a C or C++ program as follows:

```
/chp05/overview$ gcc short.c -o shortc
/chp05/overview$ g++ short.c -o shortcpp
/chp05/overview$ ls -l short*
-rw-r--r-- 1 molloyd users    9 Mar 14 12:34 short.c
-rwxr-xr-x 1 molloyd users 4912 Mar 14 12:40 shortc
-rwxr-xr-x 1 molloyd users 5040 Mar 14 12:40 shortcpp
/chp05/overview$ ./shortc
/chp05/overview$ echo $?
97
/chp05/overview$ ./shortcpp
/chp05/overview$ echo $?
0
```

This is one of the greatest weaknesses of C and C++. There is an assumption that you know everything about the way the language works before you write anything. In fact, aspects of the preceding example might be used by a programmer to demonstrate how clever they are, but they are actually demonstrating poor practice in making their code unreadable by less "expert" programmers. For example, if you rewrite the C++ code in short.cpp to include comments and explicit statements, to create short2.cpp, and then compile both using the -O3 optimization flag, the output will be as follows:

```
/chp05/overview$ more short.cpp
main(){}
/chp05/overview$ more short2.cpp
// A really useless program, but a program nevertheless
int main(int argc, char **argv){
    return 0;
}
/chp05/overview$ g++ -O3 short.cpp -o short1
/chp05/overview$ g++ -O3 short2.cpp -o short2
/chp05/overview$ ls -l short*
-rw-r--r-- 1 molloyd users    9 Mar 14 13:20 short.cpp
-rwxr-xr-x 1 molloyd users 5030 Mar 14 13:28 short1
-rwxr-xr-x 1 molloyd users 5031 Mar 14 13:28 short2
-rw-r--r-- 1 molloyd users  107 Mar 14 12:59 short2.cpp
```

Note that the difference in the executable size is only one byte! Adding the comment, the explicit return statement, the explicit return type, and explicit arguments has had no impact on the size of the final binary application. The binary executable is one byte longer because the source filename is one byte longer (i.e., short2.cpp rather than short.cpp). However, the benefit is that the actual functionality of the code is much more readily understood by a novice programmer.

You can build with the flag -static to statically link the libraries, rather than the default form of linking dynamically with shared libraries. This means that the compiler and linker effectively place all the library routines required by your code directly within the program executable:

```
/chp05/overview$ g++ -O3 short.cpp -static -o shortst
/chp05/overview$ ls -l shortst
-rwxr-xr-x 1 molloyd users 455914 Mar 14 12:46 shortst
```

It is clear that the program executable size has grown significantly. One advantage of this form is that the program can be executed by ARM systems on which the C++ standard libraries are not installed.

With dynamic linking, it is useful to note that you can discover which shared library dependencies your compiled code is using, by calling ldd:

```
/chp05/overview$ ldd short1
    libstdc++.so.6 => /usr/lib/arm-linux-gnueabihf/libstdc++.so.6 (0xb...)
    libm.so.6 => /lib/arm-linux-gnueabihf/libm.so.6 (0xb6ea4000)
    libgcc_s.so.1 => /lib/arm-linux-gnueabihf/libgcc_s.so.1 (0xb6e80000)
    libc.so.6 => /lib/arm-linux-gnueabihf/libc.so.6 (0xb6d9b000)
    /lib/ld-linux-armhf.so.3 (0xb6fc9000)
```

You can see that the g++ compiler (and glibc) on the Debian image for the BBB has been patched to support the generation of hard floating-point (HardFP) instructions by default. This allows for faster code execution with floating-point numbers than if it used the soft floating-point ABI (application binary interface) to emulate floating-point support in software (SoftFP ABI).

Variables and Operators in C/C++

A variable is a data item stored in a block of memory that has been reserved for it. The type of the variable defines the amount of memory reserved and how it should behave (see Figure 5-2). This figure describes the output of the code example sizeofvariables.c in Listing 5-9.

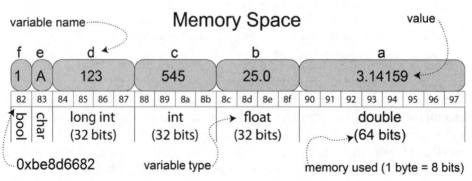

Figure 5-2: Memory allocation for variables running on the 32-bit BBB

Listing 5-9 details various variables available in C/C++. When you create a *local variable* c below, it is allocated a box/block of memory on the *stack* (predetermined reserved fast memory) depending on its type. In this case, c is an int value; therefore, four bytes (32 bits) of memory is allocated to store the value. Assume that variables in C/C++ are initialized with random values; therefore, in this case c = 545; replaces that initial random value by placing the number 545 in the box. It does not matter if you store the number 0 or 2,147,483,647 in this box: it will still occupy 32 bits of memory! Please note that there is no guarantee regarding the ordering of local variable memory—it was fortuitously linear in this particular example.

LISTING 5-9: chp05/overview/sizeofvariables.c

```
#include<stdio.h>
#include<stdbool.h>   //required for the C bool typedef

int main(){
    double a = 3.14159;
    float b = 25.0;
    int c = 545;      //Note: variables are not = 0 by default!
    long int d = 123;
    char e = 'A';
    bool f = true;  // no need for definition in C++
    printf("a val %.4f & size %d bytes (@addr %p).\n", a, sizeof(a),&a);
    printf("b val %4.2f & size %d bytes (@addr %p).\n", b, sizeof(b),&b);
    printf("c val %d (oct %o, hex %x) & " \
           "size %d bytes (@addr %p).\n", c, c, c, sizeof(c), &c);
    printf("d val %d & size %d bytes (@addr %p).\n", d, sizeof(d), &d);
    printf("e val %c & size %d bytes (@addr %p).\n", e, sizeof(e), &e);
    printf("f val %5d & size %d bytes (@addr %p).\n", f, sizeof(f), &f);
}
```

The function sizeof(c) returns the size of the type of the variable in bytes. In this example, it will return 4 for the size of the int type. The &c call can be read as the *"address of"* c. This provides the address of the first byte that stores the variable c, in this case returning 0xbe8d6688. The %.4f on the first line means display the floating-point number to four decimal places. Executing this program on the BBB gives the following:

```
/chp05/overview$ ./sizeofvariables
a val 3.1416 & size 8 bytes (@addr 0xbe8d6690).
b val 25.00 & size 4 bytes (@addr 0xbe8d668c).
c val 545 (oct 1041, hex 221) & size 4 bytes (@addr 0xbe8d6688).
d val 123 & size 4 bytes (@addr 0xbe8d6684).
e val A & size 1 bytes (@addr 0xbe8d6683).
f val     1 and size 1 bytes (@addr 0xbe8d6682).
```

The BBB has a 32-bit microcontroller, so you are using four bytes to represent the `int` type. The smallest unit of memory that you can allocate is one byte, so, yes, you are representing a Boolean value with one byte, which could actually store eight unique Boolean values. You can operate directly on variables using operators. The program `operators.c` in Listing 5-10 contains some points that often cause difficulty in C/C++:

LISTING 5-10: chp05/overview/operators.c

```c
#include<stdio.h>

int main(){
    int a=1, b=2, c, d, e, g;
    float f=9.9999;
    c = ++a;
    printf("The value of c=%d and a=%d.\n", c, a);
    d = b++;
    printf("The value of d=%d and b=%d.\n", d, b);
    e = (int) f;
    printf("The value of f=%.2f and e=%d.\n", f, e);
    g = 'A';
    printf("The value of g=%d and g=%c.\n", g, g);
    return 0;
}
```

This will give the following output:

```
/chp05/overview$ ./operators
The value of c=2 and a=2.
The value of d=2 and b=3.
The value of f=10.00 and e=9.
The value of g=65 and g=A.
```

On the line `c=++a;` the value of `a` is pre-incremented before the equals assignment to `c` on the left-hand side. Therefore, `a` was increased to `2` before assigning the value to `c`, so this line is equivalent to two lines: `a=a+1; c=a;`. However, on the line `d=b++;` the value of `b` is post-incremented and is equivalent to two lines: `d=b; b=b+1;` The value of `d` is assigned the value of `b`, which is `2`, before the value of `b` is incremented to `3`.

On the line `e=(int)f;` a C-style cast is being used to convert a floating-point number into an integer value. Effectively, when programmers use a cast they are notifying the compiler that they are aware that there will be a loss of precision in the conversion of a floating-point number to an `int`. The fractional part will be truncated, so `9.9999` will be converted to `e=9`, as the `.9999` is removed by the truncation. One other point to note is that the `printf("%.2f",f)` will display the floating-point variable to two decimal places, in contrast, rounding the value.

On the line `g='A'`, g is assigned the ASCII equivalent value of capital A, which is 65. The `printf("%d %c", g, g);` will display either the `int` value of g if `%d` is used, or the ASCII character value of g if `%c` is used.

A *const* keyword can be used to prevent a variable from being changed. There is also a *volatile* keyword that is useful for notifying the compiler that a particular variable might be changed outside its control, and that the compiler should not apply any type of optimization to that value. This notification is useful on the BBB if the variable in question is shared with another process or physical input/output.

It is possible to define your own type in C/C++ using the *typedef* keyword. For example, if you did not want to include the header file `stdbool.h` in the `sizeofvariables.c` previous example, it would be possible to define it in this way instead:

```
typedef char bool;
#define true 1
#define false 0
```

Probably the most common and most misunderstood mistake in C/C++ programming is present in the following code segment:

```
if (x=y){
    // perform a body statement z
}
```

When will the body statement z be performed? The answer is whenever y is not equal to 0 (the current value of x is irrelevant!). The mistake is placing a single = (assignment) instead of == (comparison) in the `if` statement. The assignment operator returns the value on the RHS, which will be automatically converted to `true` if y is not equal to 0. If y is equal to zero, then a `false` value will be returned. Java does not allow this error, as there is no implicit conversion between 0 and `false` and 1 and `true`.

Pointers in C/C++

A pointer is a special type of variable that stores the address of another variable in memory—we say that the pointer is "pointing at" that variable. Listing 5-11 is a code example that demonstrates how you can create a pointer p and make it point at the variable y:

LISTING 5-11: chp05/overview/pointers.c

```
#include<stdio.h>

int main(){
    int y = 1000;
```

continues

LISTING 5-11: *(continued)*

```
int *p;
p = &y;
printf("The variable has value %d and the address %p.\n", y, &y);
printf("The pointer stores %p and points at value %d.\n", p, *p);
printf("The pointer has address %p and size %d.\n", &p, sizeof(p));
return 0;
}
```

When this code is compiled and executed, it will give the following output:

```
/chp05/overview$ ./pointers
The variable has value 1000 and the address 0xbede26bc.
The pointer stores 0xbede26bc and points at value 1000.
The pointer has address 0xbede26b8 and size 4.
```

So, what is happening in this example? Figure 5-3 illustrates the memory locations and the steps involved. In Step 1, the variable y is created and assigned the initial value of 1000. A pointer p is then created with the dereference type of int. In essence, this means that the pointer p is being established to point at int values. In Step 2, the statement p = &y; means "let p equal the address of y," which sets the value of p to be the 32-bit address 0xbede26bc. We now say that p is pointing at y. These two steps could have been combined using the call int *p = &y; (i.e., create a pointer p of dereference type int and assign it to the address of y).

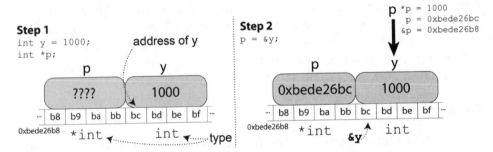

Figure 5-3: Example of pointers in C/C++ on the BBB (with 32-bit addresses)

Why does a pointer need a dereference type? For one example, if a pointer needs to move to the next element in an array, then it needs to know whether it should move by four bytes, eight bytes, etc. Also, in C++ you need to be able to know how to deal with the data at the pointer based on its type. Listing 5-12 is an example of working with pointers and arrays.

LISTING 5-12: chp05/overview/pointerarray.c

```c
#include<stdio.h>

int main(){
    int x[5] = { 100, 200, 300, 400, 500 };
    int *p = &x[0], i;

    for(i=0; i<5; i++){
        (*(p++))++;
    }
    for(i=0; i<5; i++).{
        printf("The value of x[%d] is %d\n", i, x[i]);
    }
    return 0;
}
```

This will give the output as follows:

```
/chp05/overview$ ./pointerarray
The value of x[0] is 101
The value of x[1] is 201
The value of x[2] is 301
The value of x[3] is 401
The value of x[4] is 501
```

In this example, the pointer p is of dereference type int and it is set to point at the first element in an array of five int values using the statement int *p = &x[0];. The line of code to focus on here is (*(p++))++; (this is why pointers have a bad name!). Please note that the () are very important, as they set the order of operations. In this case the inner (p++) makes the pointer point at the next element in the array; however, because it is a post-increment, the increment happens after the end of this line. Therefore, this entire line could be written as :(*p)++; p++;. The (*p)++ means increment the value stored at the address, changing 100 to 101 on the first iteration of the for loop. Pointer notation can be complex, but remember that the dereference type is needed because in this case the p++ call needs to know to move four bytes forward in memory. If p were of dereference type double (i.e., double *p;), then the pointer would move by eight bytes when p++; is called.

Part of the difficulty of using pointers in C/C++ is understanding the order of operations in C/C++, called the *precedence* of the operations. For example, if you write the statement

```c
int x = 1 + 2 * 3;
```

what will the value of x be? In this case it will be 7, because in C/C++ the multiplication operator has a higher level of precedence than the addition operator. The same issue occurs if you believe that you are incrementing the value at x by the statement *x++, as the ++ operator will be applied before the dereference operator, incrementing the pointer and uselessly dereferencing x.

There are approximately 58 operators in C++, with 18 different major precedence levels. Even if you know the precedence table, you should still make it clear for other users what you intend in a statement by using round brackets (()), which have the highest precedence level after the scope resolution (::), increment (++), and decrement (--) operators. Therefore, you should always write the following:

```
int x = 1 + (2 * 3);
```

Finally, on the topic of C pointers, there is also a *void* pointer* that can be declared as void *p;, which effectively states that the pointer p does not have a dereference type and it will have to be assigned at a later stage (see /chp05/overview/void.c) using the following syntax:

```
int a = 5;
void *p = &a;
printf("p points at address %p and value %d\n", p, *((int *)p));
```

When executed, this code will give an output like the following:

```
The pointer p points at address 0xbea546c8 and value 5
```

Therefore, it is possible to cast a pointer from one deference type to another and the *void pointer* can potentially be used to store a pointer of any dereference type. In Chapter 6 void pointers are used to develop an enhanced GPIO interface.

C-Style Strings

The C language has no built-in string type but rather uses an array of the character type, terminated by the null character (\0), to represent a string. There is a standard C library for strings that can be used as shown in Listing 5-13:

LISTING 5-13: chp05/overview/cstrings.c

```
#include<stdio.h>
#include<string.h>
#include<stdlib.h>

int main(){
   char a[20] = "hello ";
   char b[] = {'w','o','r','l','d','!','\0'};  // the \0 is important

   a[0]='H';                    // set the first character to be H
   char *c = strcat(a,b);       // join/concatenate a and b
   printf("The string c is: %s\n", c);
   printf("The length of c is: %d\n", strlen(c));  // call string length
```

```
// find and replace the w with a W
char *p = strchr(c,'w');  // returns pointer to first 'w' char
*p = 'W';
printf("The string c is now: %s\n", c);

if (strcmp("cat", "dog")<=0){      // ==0 would be equal
   printf("cat comes before dog (lexiographically)\n");
}
//insert "to the" into middle of "Hello World!" string - very messy!
char *d = " to the";
char *cd = malloc(strlen(c) + strlen(d));
memcpy(cd, c, 5);
memcpy(cd+5, d, strlen(d));
memcpy(cd+5+strlen(d), c+5, 6);
printf("The cd string is: %s\n", cd);

//tokenize cd string using spaces
p = strtok(cd," ");
while(p!=NULL){
   printf("Token:%s\n", p);
   p = strtok(NULL, " ");
}
return 0;
}
```

The code is explained by the comments within the example. When executed, this code will give the following output:

```
/chp05/overview$ ./cstrings
The string c is: Hello world!
The length of c is: 12
The string c is now: Hello World!
cat comes before dog (lexiographically)
The cd string is: Hello to the World
Token:Hello
Token:to
Token:the
Token:World
```

LED Flashing Application in C

Now that you have covered enough C programming to get by, you can look at how to write the LED flashing application in C. In Listing 5-14 the same structure as the other examples has been retained:

LISTING 5-14: chp05/makeLED/makeLED.c

```
#include<stdio.h>
#include<stdlib.h>
#include<string.h>
```

continues

LISTING 5-14: *(continued)*

```
#define LED3_PATH "/sys/class/leds/beaglebone:green:usr3"

void writeLED(char filename[], char value[]);  //function prototypes
void removeTrigger();

int main(int argc, char* argv[]){
   if(argc!=2){
        printf("Usage is makeLEDC and one of:\n");
        printf("   on, off, flash or status\n");
        printf(" e.g. makeLED flash\n");
        return 2;
   }
   printf("Starting the makeLED program\n");
   printf("The current LED Path is: " LED3_PATH "\n");

   // select whether command is on, off, flash or status
   if(strcmp(argv[1],"on")==0){
        printf("Turning the LED on\n");
        removeTrigger();
        writeLED("/brightness", "1");
   }
   else if (strcmp(argv[1],"off")==0){
        printf("Turning the LED off\n");
        removeTrigger();
        writeLED("/brightness", "0");
   }
   else if (strcmp(argv[1],"flash")==0){
        printf("Flashing the LED\n");
        writeLED("/trigger", "timer");
        writeLED("/delay_on", "50");
        writeLED("/delay_off", "50");
   }
   else if (strcmp(argv[1],"status")==0){
      FILE* fp;   // see writeLED function below for description
      char  fullFileName[100];
      char line[80];
      sprintf(fullFileName, LED3_PATH "/trigger");
      fp = fopen(fullFileName, "rt"); //reading text this time
      while (fgets(line, 80, fp) != NULL){
         printf("%s", line);
      }
      fclose(fp);
   }
   else{
        printf("Invalid command!\n");
   }
   printf("Finished the makeLED Program\n");
   return 0;
}
void writeLED(char filename[], char value[]){
   FILE* fp;   // create a file pointer fp
```

```
    char  fullFileName[100];   // to store the path and filename
    sprintf(fullFileName, LED3_PATH "%s", filename); // write path/name
    fp = fopen(fullFileName, "w+"); // open file for writing
    fprintf(fp, "%s", value);   // send the value to the file
    fclose(fp);   // close the file using the file pointer
}

void removeTrigger(){
    writeLED("/trigger", "none");
}
```

The only topic that you have not seen before is the use of files in C, but the worked example should provide you with the information you need in the writeLED() function. The FILE pointer fp points to a description of the file that identifies the stream, the read/write position, and its state. The file is opened using the fopen() function that is defined in stdio.h, which returns a FILE pointer. In this case it is being opened for write/update (w+). The alternatives would be as follows: read (r), write (w), append (a), read/update (r+), and append/update (a+). If you are working with binary files you would append a b to the state—e.g., "w+b" would open a new binary file for update (write and read). Also, "t" can be used to explicitly state that the file is in text format.

For a full reference of C functions available in the standard libraries, see www.cplusplus.com/reference/.

The C of C++

As discussed previously, the C++ language was built on the C language, adding support for OOP classes; however, a few other differences are immediately apparent when you start working with general C++ programming. Initially, the biggest change that you will notice is the use of input/output streams and the general use of strings.

First Example and Strings in C++

Listing 5-15 shows is the string example, rewritten to use the C++ string library:

LISTING 5-15: chp05/overview/cppstrings.cpp

```
#include<iostream>
#include<sstream>      // to tokenize the string
//#include<cstring>    // how to include a c header if needed
using namespace std;
int main(){
    string a = "hello ";
    char temp[] = {'w','o','r','l','d','!','\0'};   //the \0 is important!
```
continues

LISTING 5-15: *(continued)*

```
    string b(temp);

    a[0]='H';
    string c = a + b;
    cout << "The string c is: " << c << endl;
    cout << "The length of c is: " << c.length() << endl;

    int loc = c.find_first_of('w');
    c.replace(loc,1,1,'W');
    cout << "The string c is now: " << c << endl;

    if (string("cat")< string("dog")){
        cout << "cat comes before dog (lexiographically)\n";
    }
    c.insert(5," to the");
    cout << "The c string is now: " << c << endl;

    // tokenize string using spaces - could use Boost.Tokenizer
    // or C++11 to improve syntax. Using stringstream this time.
    stringstream ss;
    ss << c;  // put the c string on the stringstream
    string token;
    while(getline(ss, token, ' ')){
        cout << "Token: " << token << endl;
    }
    return 0;
}
```

Build this code by typing `g++ cppstrings.cpp -o cppstrings`. When executed, this code gives the same output as the `cstrings.c` example. Some aspects are more straightforward in C++ but there are some points worth mentioning.

The code uses the `iostream` and `sstream` header files, which are C++ headers. If you wish to use a C header file, you need to prepend the name with a "c"; therefore, to use the C `string.h` header file you would use `#include<cstring>`. There is a concept called *namespaces* in C++ that enables a programmer to limit a function or class to a particular scope. In C++ all the standard library functions and classes are limited to the *standard namespace*. You can explicitly identify that you wish to use a class from the `std` namespace by using `std::string`. However, that is quite verbose. The alternative is to use the statement `using namespace std;`, which brings the entire namespace into your code. Do *not* do this in one of your C++ header files, as it will pollute the namespace for anyone who uses your header file.

The code uses `cout`, which is the standard output stream, and the output stream operator (`<<`) to display strings. There is an equivalent standard input stream (`cin`) and the input stream operator (`>>`). The output stream operator "looks to" its right and identifies the type of the data. It will display the data depending on its type, so there is no need for `%s`, `%d`, `%p`, and so on, as you would use in the `printf()` function. The `endl` stream manipulation function inserts a newline character and flushes the stream.

The string objects are manipulated in this example using + to append two strings, and < or == to compare two strings. These operators are essentially functions like `append()` and `strcmp()`. In C++ you can define what these operators do for your own data types (operator overloading).

Passing by Value, Pointer, and Reference

As you have seen with the code samples, functions enable us to write a section of code that can be called several times, from different locations in our code. There are three key ways of passing a value to a function:

- **Pass by value:** This will create a new variable (`val` in the following code example) and will store a copy of the value of the source variable (`a`) in this new variable. Any changes to the variable `val` will not have any impact on the source variable `a`. Pass by value can be used if you want to prevent the original data from being modified; however, a copy of the data has to be made, and if you are passing a large array of data, such as an image, then copying will have a memory and computational cost. An alternative to pass by value is to *pass by constant reference*. In the following example, `a` is also passed as the second argument to the function by constant reference and is received as the value `cr`. The value `cr` can be read in the function, but it cannot be modified.

- **Pass by pointer:** You can pass a pointer to the source data. Any modifications to the value at the pointer (`ptr`) will affect the source data. The call to the function must pass an address (`&b`—address of `b`).

- **Pass by reference:** In C++ you can pass a value by reference. The function determines whether an argument is to be passed by value or passed by reference, through the use of the ampersand symbol. In the following example, `&ref` indicates that the value `c` is to be passed by reference. Any modifications to `ref` in the function will affect the value of `c`.

Here is a function with all four examples (`passing.cpp`):

```
int afunction(int val, const int &cr, int *ptr, int &ref){
    val+=cr;
// cr+=val; // not allowed because it is constant
    *ptr+=10;
    ref+=10;
    return val;
}

int main(){
    int a=100, b=200, c=300;
    int ret;
    ret = afunction(a, a, &b, c);
```

```
cout << "The value of a = " << a << endl;
cout << "The value of b = " << b << endl;
cout << "The value of c = " << c << endl;
cout << "The return value is = " << ret << endl;
return 0;
}
```

When executed, this code will result in the following output:

```
/chp05/overview$ ./passing
The value of a = 100
The value of b = 210
The value of c = 310
The return value is = 200
```

If you wish to pass a value to a function that is to be modified by that function in C++, then you can pass it by pointer or by reference; however, unless you are passing a value that could be NULL, or you need to re-assign the pointer in the function (e.g., iterate over an array), then always use pass by reference. Now you are ready to write the LED code in C++!

Flashing the LEDs Using C++ (non-OO)

The C++ LED flashing code is available in makeLED.cpp in the /chp05/makeLED/ directory. As most of the code is very similar to the C example, it is not repeated here. However, it is worth displaying the following segment, which is used to open the file using the fstream file stream class. The output stream operator (<<) in this case sends the string to fstream:

```
void writeLED(string filename, string value){
    fstream fs;
    string path(LED3_PATH);
    fs.open((path + filename).c_str(), fstream::out);
    fs << value;
    fs.close();
}
```

The c_str() method returns a C++ string as a C string. Once again, this code can be executed with root privileges.

Writing Your Own Multi-Call Binary

In Chapter 3, you saw how multi-call binaries can be used in Linux to build a single application that does the job of many. BusyBox was listed as an example of one of these binaries. There is an example in the chp05/ makeLEDmulti directory called makeLEDmulti.cpp that uses the very first command-line argument to switch the functionality of the application based on the command name that was called. The code has been modified to add a small function:

```
bool endsWith(string const &in, string const &comp){
    return (0==in.compare(in.length()-comp.length(),comp.length(),comp));
}
```

This function checks to see if the `in` string *ends with* the contents of the `comp` string. This is important, because the application could be called using `./flashled` or `./chp05/makeLEDmulti/flashled`, depending on its location. The switching comparison then looks like the following:

```
if(endsWith(cmd,"onled")){
    cout << "Turning the LED on" << endl;
    removeTrigger();
    writeLED("/brightness", "1");
}
```

If you list the files in the directory after calling `./build` you will see the following files and symbolic links:

```
/chp05/makeLEDmulti$ ls -l
-rwxr-xr-x 1 molloyd users    542 Mar  8 02:37 build
lrwxrwxrwx 1 molloyd users     12 Mar  8 02:44 flashled -> makeLEDmulti
lrwxrwxrwx 1 molloyd users     12 Mar  8 02:44 ledstatus -> makeLEDmulti
-rwxr-xr-x 1 molloyd users  11888 Mar  8 02:44 makeLEDmulti
-rw-r--r-- 1 molloyd users   2477 Mar  8 02:43 makeLEDmulti.cpp
lrwxrwxrwx 1 molloyd users     12 Mar  8 02:44 offled -> makeLEDmulti
lrwxrwxrwx 1 molloyd users     12 Mar  8 02:44 onled -> makeLEDmulti
```

Each one of these symbolic links looks like an individual command, even though they link back to the same executable `makeLEDmulti`. The `makeLEDmulti` parses `argv[0]` to determine which symbolic link was used. You can see the impact of that here, where the symbolic links are called:

```
/chp05/makeLEDmulti$ sudo ./onled
The current LED Path is: /sys/class/leds/beaglebone:green:usr3
Turning the LED on
/chp05/makeLEDmulti$ ./ledstatus
The current LED Path is: /sys/class/leds/beaglebone:green:usr3
Current trigger details:
[none] rc-feedback mmc0 mmc1 timer oneshot heartbeat ...
```

C++ with Classes

Object-oriented programming is a programming approach (or paradigm) that enables organizing software as a collection of objects, which consist of both data and behavior. In contrast to the functional programming examples you have seen to this point, you don't ask the question "what does it do?" first, but rather, "what is it?" In theory, this means that your code is written to allow for future changes to the functionality, without having to redesign the structure of your code. In addition, it should also mean that you can decompose your code into modules that can be reused by you and others in future projects.

Overview of Object-Oriented Programming

The following sections discuss a few key ideas that you have to understand before you can write object-oriented code.

Classes and Objects

Think about the concept of a television: You do not have to remove the case to use it, as there are controls on the front and on the remote; you can still understand the television, even if it is connected to a games console; it is complete when you purchase it, with well-defined external requirements, such as power supply and signal inputs; and your television should not crash! In many ways that description captures the properties that should be present in a class.

A *class* is a description. It should describe a well-defined interface to your code; represent a clear concept; be complete and well documented; and be robust, with built-in error checking. Class descriptions are built using two building blocks:

- **States (or data):** The state values of the class.
- **Methods (or behavior):** How the class interacts with its data. Method names usually include an action verb (e.g., setX()).

For example, here is pseudo-code (i.e., not real C++ code) for an illustrative Television class:

```
class Television{
    int channelNumber;
    bool on;
    powerOn() { on = true; }
    powerOff(){ on = false;}
    changeChannel(int x) { channelNumber = x; }
};
```

Therefore, the example Television class has two states and three methods. The benefit of this structure is that you have tightly bound the states and methods together within a class structure. The powerOn() method means nothing outside this class. In fact, you can write a powerOn() method in many different classes without worrying about naming collisions.

An *object* is the realization of the class description—an instance of a class. To continue the analogy, the Television class is the blueprint that describes how you would build a television, and a `Television` object is the physical realization of those plans into a physical television. In pseudo-code this realization might look like this:

```
void main(){
    Television dereksTV();
    Television johnsTV();
    dereksTV.powerOn();
    dereksTV.changeChannel(52);
    johnsTV.powerOn();
    johnsTV.changeChannel(1);
}
```

Therefore, `dereksTV` and `johnsTV` are objects of the `Television` class. Each has its own independent state, so changing the channel on `dereksTV` has no impact on `johnsTV`. To call a method, it must be prefixed by the object name on which it is to be called (e.g., `johnsTV.powerOn()`); calling the `changeChannel()` method on `johnsTV` objects does not have any impact on the `dereksTV` object.

In this book, a class name generally begins with a capital letter, e.g., `Television`, and an object generally begins with a lowercase letter, e.g., `dereksTV`. This is consistent with the notation used in many languages, such as Java. Unfortunately, the C++ standard library classes (e.g., `string`, `sstream`) do not follow this naming convention.

Encapsulation

Encapsulation is used to hide the mechanics of an object. In the physical television analogy, encapsulation is provided by the box that protects the inner electronic systems. However, you still have the remote control that will have a direct impact on the way the inner workings function.

In OOP, you can decide what workings are to be hidden (e.g., TV electronics) using an *access specifier* keyword called *private*, and what is to be part of the *interface* (TV remote control) using the access specifier keyword *public*. It is good practice to always set the states of your class to be private, so that you can control how they are modified by public interface methods of your own design. For example, the pseudo-code might become the following:

```
class Television{
    private:
        int channelNumber;
        bool on;
        remodulate_tuner();
    public:
        powerOn() { on = true; }
        powerOff(){ on = false;}
        changeChannel(int x) {
            channelNumber = x;
            remodulate_tuner();
        }
};
```

Now the `Television` class has private state data (`on`, `channelNumber`) that is affected only by the public interface methods (`powerOn()`, `powerOff()`, `changeChannel()`) and a private implementation method `remodulate_tuner()` that cannot be called from outside the class.

There are a number of advantages of this approach: First, users of this class (another programmer) need not understand the inner workings of the `Television` class; they just need to understand the public interface. Second, the author of the `Television` class can modify and/or perfect the inner workings of the class without affecting other programmers' code.

Inheritance

Inheritance is a feature of OOP that enables building class descriptions from other class descriptions. Humans do this all the time; for, example, if you were asked, "What is a duck?" you might respond with, "It's a bird that swims, and it has a bill instead of a beak." This description is reasonably accurate, but it assumes that the concept of a bird is also understood. Importantly, the description states that the duck has the *additional behavior* of swimming, but also that it has the *replacement behavior* of having a bill instead of a beak. You could loosely code this with pseudo-code as follows:

```
class Bird{
   public:
      void fly();
      void describe() { cout << "Has a beak and can fly"; }
};

class Duck: public Bird{    // Duck IS-A Bird
      Bill bill;
   public:
      void swim();
      void describe() { cout << "Has a bill and can fly and swim"; }
};
```

In this case, you can create an object of the Duck class:

```
int main(){
   Duck d;         //creates the Duck instance object d
   d.swim();       //specific to the Duck class
   d.fly();        //inherited from the parent Bird class
   d.describe();   //describe() is inheritated and over-ridden in Duck
                   //so, "Has a bill and can fly and swim" would appear

}
```

The example here illustrates why inheritance is so important. You can build code by inheriting from, and adding to, a class description (e.g., `swim()`), or inheriting from a parent class and replacing a behavior (e.g., `describe()`) to provide a more specific implementation—this is called *overriding* a method, which is a type of *polymorphism* (multiple forms). Another form of polymorphism is called overloading, which means multiple methods can have the same name, in the same class, disambiguated by the compiler by having different parameter types.

You can check that you have an inheritance relationship by the *IS-A* test; for example, a "duck is a bird" is valid, but a "bird is a duck" would be invalid because not all birds are ducks. This contrasts to the *IS-A-PART-OF* relationship; for example, a "bill is a part of a duck." An IS-A-PART-OF relationship indicates that the bill is a member/state of the class. Using this simple check can be very useful when the class relationships become complex.

You can also use pointers with objects of a class; for example, to dynamically allocate memory for two Duck objects, you can use:

```
int main(){
    Duck *a = new Duck();
    Bird *b = new Duck(); //a pointer of the parent can point to a child object
    b->describe();        //will actually describe a duck (if virtual)
    //b->swim();          //not allowed! Bird does not 'know' swim()
}
```

Interestingly, the Bird pointer b is permitted to point at a Duck object. As the Duck class is a child of a Bird class, all of the methods that the Bird pointer can call are "known" by the Duck object. Therefore the describe() method can be called. The arrow notation (b->describe()) is simply a neater way of writing (*b).describe(). In this case the Bird pointer b has the *static type* Bird and the *dynamic type* Duck.

One last point is that an additional access specifier called *protected* can be used through inheritance. If you wish to create a method or state in the parent class that you want to be available to the child class but you do not want to make public, then use the protected access specifier.

NOTE   Remember that I have notes available at ee402.eeng.dcu.ie on these topics. In particular, Chapter 3 and 4 describe this topic in much greater detail, including material on abstract classes, destructors, multiple inheritance, friend functions, the standard template library (STL), etc.

Object-Oriented LED Flashing Code

These OOP concepts can now be applied a real C++ application on the BBB, by restructuring the functionally oriented C++ code into a class called LED, which contains states and methods. One difference with the code that is presented in Listing 5-16 is that it allows you to control the four user LEDs using the same OO code. Therefore, using the LED class, four different LED instance objects are created, each controlling one of the BBB's four physical user LEDs.

LISTING 5-16: chp05/makeLEDOOP/makeLEDs.cpp

```cpp
#include<iostream>
#include<fstream>
#include<string>
#include<sstream>
using namespace std;

#define LED_PATH "/sys/class/leds/beaglebone:green:usr"

class LED{
   private:
      string path;
      int number;
      virtual void writeLED(string filename, string value);
      virtual void removeTrigger();
   public:
      LED(int number);
      virtual void turnOn();
      virtual void turnOff();
      virtual void flash(string delayms);
      virtual void outputState();
      virtual ~LED();
};

LED::LED(int number){
   this->number = number;    // set number state to be the number passed
   // next part is easier with C++11 (see Chp.7) using to_string(number)
   ostringstream s;          // using a stream to contruct the path
   s << LED_PATH << number;  // append LED number to LED_PATH
   path = string(s.str());   // convert back from stream to string
}

void LED::writeLED(string filename, string value){
   ofstream fs;
   fs.open((path + filename).c_str());
   fs << value;
   fs.close();
}

void LED::removeTrigger(){
   writeLED("/trigger", "none");
}

void LED::turnOn(){
   cout << "Turning LED" << number << " on." << endl;
   removeTrigger();
   writeLED("/brightness", "1");
}

void LED::turnOff(){
   cout << "Turning LED" << number << " off." << endl;
```

```
        removeTrigger();
        writeLED("/brightness", "0");
    }

    void LED::flash(string delayms = "50"){
        cout << "Making LED" << number << " flash." << endl;
        writeLED("/trigger", "timer");
        writeLED("/delay_on", delayms);
        writeLED("/delay_off", delayms);
    }

    void LED::outputState(){
        ifstream fs;
        fs.open( (path + "/trigger").c_str());
        string line;
        while(getline(fs,line)) cout << line << endl;
        fs.close();
    }

    LED::~LED(){    // A destructor - called when the object is destroyed
        cout << "destroying the LED with path: " << path << endl;
    }

    int main(int argc, char* argv[]){
        if(argc!=2){
            cout << "Usage is makeLEDs <command>" << endl;
            cout << "  command is one of: on, off, flash or status" << endl;
            cout << " e.g. makeLEDs flash" << endl;
        }
        cout << "Starting the makeLEDs program" << endl;
        string cmd(argv[1]);

        // Create four LED objects and put them in an array
        LED leds[4] = { LED(0), LED(1), LED(2), LED(3) };

        // Do the same operation on all four LEDs - easily changed!
        for(int i=0; i<=3; i++){
            if(cmd=="on")leds[i].turnOn();
            else if(cmd=="off")leds[i].turnOff();
            else if(cmd=="flash")leds[i].flash("100"); //default is "50"
            else if(cmd=="status")leds[i].outputState();
            else{ cout << "Invalid command!" << endl; }
        }
        cout << "Finished the makeLEDs program" << endl;
        return 0;
    }
```

This code can be built and executed by typing the following:

```
/chp05/makeLEDOOP$ ./build
/chp05/makeLEDOOP$ ./makeLEDs status
/chp05/makeLEDOOP$ sudo ./makeLEDs flash
/chp05/makeLEDOOP$ sudo ./makeLEDs off
```

There is a script in the directory /chp05 to return the LEDs to their standard state, called restoreDefaultLEDs:

```
/chp05$ sudo ./restoreDefaultLEDs
```

This code is structured as a single class LED with private states for the path and the number, and private implementation methods writeLED() and removeTrigger(). These states and helper methods are not accessible outside the class. The public interface methods are turnOn(), turnOff(), flash(), and outputState(). There are two more public methods:

- The first is a *constructor*, which enables you to initialize the state of the object. It is called by LED led(0) to create the object led of the LED class with number 0. This is very similar to the way that you assign initial values to an int, e.g., int x = 5;. A constructor must have the exact same name as the class name (LED in this case) and it cannot return anything, not even void.

- The last is a *destructor* (~LED()). Like a constructor, it must have the exact same name as the class name and is prefixed by the tilde (~) character. This method is called automatically when the object is being destroyed. You can see this happening when you run the code sample.

The keyword *virtual* is also new. You can think of this keyword as "allowing overriding to take place when an object is dynamically bound." It should always be there (except for the constructor), unless you know that there will definitely be no child class. Removing the virtual keyword will result in a slight improvement in the performance of your code.

The syntax void LED::turnOn(){...} is simply used to state that the turnOn() method is the one associated with the LED class. It is possible to have many classes in the one .cpp file, and it would be possible for two classes to have a turnOn() method; therefore, the explicit association allows you to inform the compiler of the correct relationship. I have written this code in a single file, as it is the first example. However, you will see in later examples that it is better practice to break your code into *header* files (.h) and *implementation* files (.cpp).

Hopefully the layout of the C++ version of the LED flashing code is clear at this point. The advantage of this OOP version is that you now have a structure that can be built upon when you wish to provide additional functionality to interact with the system LEDs. In a later chapter you will see how you can build similar structures to wrap electronic modules such as accelerometers and temperature sensors, and how to use the encapsulation property of OOP to hide some of the more complex calculations from programmers that interface to the code.

/Proc—Process Information File System

In Chapter 3, the Linux directory structure is discussed and one of the directories discussed is the /proc directory—the process information virtual file system. It provides you with information about the run-time state of the kernel and it enables you to send control information to the kernel. In effect, it provides you with a file-based interface from user space to kernel space. There is a Linux kernel guide to the /proc file system at tiny.cc/ebb501. For example, if you type

```
/proc# cat cpuinfo
processor       : 0
model name      : ARMv7 Processor rev 2 (v7l) ...
```

it provides you with information on the CPU. Try some of the following: cat uptime, cat interrupts, cat version in the same directory. The example, chp05/proc/readUptime.cpp, provides an example program to read the system uptime and calculate the percentage of system idle time.

A program that is executed with superuser privileges can read or write to files in /proc. However, you have to be careful with the consistency of files in the /proc directory. The Linux kernel provides for *atomic* operations—instructions that execute without interruption. Certain "files" within /proc (such as /proc/uptime) are totally atomic and cannot be interrupted while they are being read; however, other files such as /proc/net/tcp are only atomic within each row of the file, meaning that the file will change as it is being read, and therefore simply reading the file may not provide a consistent snapshot.

GLIBC and Syscall

The Linux GNU C Library, *glibc*, provides an extensive set of wrapper functions for system calls. It includes functionality for handling files, signals, mathematics, processes, users, and much, much more. See tiny.cc/ebb502 for a full description of the GNU C Library. If there is an equivalent glibc function it is much more straightforward to call this function than to parse the /proc entries. Here is a simple C example that uses glibc:

```
/chp05/proc$ more whologgedin.c
#include<unistd.h>
#include<stdio.h>
int main(){
   printf("The user logged in is %s\n", getlogin());
   return 0;
}
/chp05/proc$ gcc whologgedin.c -o who
/chp05/proc$ ./who
The user logged in is molloyd
```

There are many, many glibc functions, but one function in particular deserves some attention, and that is the *syscall* function, as it performs a general system call using the arguments that you pass to the function. The first argument is a system call number, all of which are defined in /sys/syscall.h. You can open this file (/usr/include/arm-linux-gnueabihf/sys/syscall.h) and search for the numbers or you can use syscalls.kernelgrok.com to search for numbers on your Linux kernel architecture. As illustrated in Listing 5-17, the syscall function can pass one or more arguments depending on the type of syscall function.

LISTING 5-17: chp05/syscall/syscall.cpp

```
#include<gnu/libc-version.h>
#include<sys/syscall.h>
#include<sys/types.h>
#include<iostream>
#include<signal.h>
using namespace std;

int main(){
   cout << "The GNU libc version is " << gnu_get_libc_version() << endl;

   // process id tid is thread identifier - see: sys/syscall.h
   pid_t tid;                  //pid_t is of type integer
   tid = syscall(SYS_gettid);   // make system call to get process id
   cout << "The Current PID is: " << tid << endl;
   //can also get by calling getpid() function from signal.h
   cout << "The Current PID is: " << getpid() << endl;

   // Can get current UserID by using:
   int uid = syscall(SYS_getuid);
   cout << "It is being run by user with ID: " << uid << endl;
      // or getting the value from syscalls.kernelgrok.com
   uid = syscall(0xc7);
   cout << "It is being run by user with ID: " << uid << endl;
   return 0;
}
```

When executed, this code will result in the output

```
/chp05/syscall$ ./syscall
The GNU libc version is 2.13
The Current PID is: 3625
The Current PID is: 3625
It is being run by user with ID: 1001
It is being run by user with ID: 1001
```

You can find out which user account is 1001 as follows:

```
/chp05/syscall$ cat /etc/passwd|grep "1001"
molloyd:x:1001:100::/home/molloyd:/bin/bash
```

Therefore, you can use C/C++ to make calls directly to Linux to using the syscall function. You can call functions like chmod (see /chp05/syscall/callchmod .cpp) by passing the required properties as second and third arguments:

```
int ret = syscall(SYS_chmod, "test.txt", 0777);
```

Use syscalls.kernelgrok.com and search for chmod. You will see the eax is 0x0f (i.e., SYS_chmod defined in syscall.h), const char __user *filename is "test.txt", and mode_t mode is 0777, which sets the text file to be executable (-rwxrwxrwx)—not a great idea!

Summary

After completing this chapter, you should be able to:

- Describe the multitude of issues that would impact on your choice of programming languages to use in building applications for the BBB.
- Write basic scripting language program code on the BBB that interfaces to the on-board LEDs.
- Compare and contrast scripting, hybrid, and compiled programming languages, and their application to the BBB.
- Write C code examples that interface to the BBB's on-board LEDs.
- Wrap C code in C++ classes to provide greater program structure.
- Write advanced C/C++ code that is capable of interfacing to Linux operating system commands.

Further Reading

Most of the sections in this chapter contain links to the relevant websites for further reading and reference materials. Here is a list of some books on programming that are relevant to the materials in this chapter:

- *Bad to the Bone: Crafting Electronics Systems with BeagleBone and BeagleBone Black*, Steven Barrett and Jason Kridner (Morgan & Claypool, 2013).

- *Getting Started with BeagleBone: Linux-Powered Electronic Projects with Python and JavaScript*, Matt Richardson (MakerMedia, 2013).

- *Programming the BeagleBone Black: Getting Started with JavaScript and BoneScript*, Simon Monk (McGraw-Hill/TAB Electronics, 2014).

Notes

1. debian.org. (Dec. 1, 2013). The Computer Lanugage Benchmarks Game. Retrieved Mar. 7, 2014, from Debian.org: `http://benchmarksgame.alioth.debian.org/`.

2. Hundt, R. (2011). Loop Recognition in C++/Java/Go/Scala. Proceedings of Scala Days 2011. Mountain View, CA: `http://www.scala-lang.org/`.

3. Oracle. (Mar. 10, 2014). Java SE Embedded FAQ. Retrieved Mar. 10, 2014, from Oracle. Com: `http://www.oracle.com/technetwork/java/embedded/resources/se-embeddocs/index.html`.

4. Stroustrup, B. (Oct. 14, 1998). International standard for the C++ programming language published. Retrieved Mar. 18, 2014, from `www.stroustrup.com`: `http://www.stroustrup.com/iso_pressrelease2.html`.

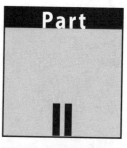

Part

II

Interfacing, Controlling, and Communicating

Interfacing to the BeagleBone Input/Outputs

This chapter integrates the Linux, programming, and electronics groundwork from earlier chapters to show you how to build circuits and write programs that interface to the BeagleBone's single-wire inputs and outputs. In this chapter, you will see practical examples that explain how to use a general-purpose input/output (GPIO) to output a binary signal to switch on an LED, or to read in a binary input from a push button. Also included are the steps required to read in an analog input and to send out a pulse-width modulated (PWM) output. Interfacing to GPIOs is a reasonably complex topic due to a recent change incorporated into the Linux kernel. However, the BBB has cape management features, and code is made available throughout this chapter that you can use to make interfacing reasonably straightforward.

Equipment Required for This Chapter:

- BeagleBone Black
- Component set from Chapter 4 and a generic light-dependent resistor

Further details on this chapter are available at www.exploringbeaglebone .com/chapter6/.

General-Purpose Input/Outputs

At this point in the book, you have seen how to administrate a Linux system, write high-level programming code, and build basic, but realistic, electronic interfacing circuits. It is now time to bring those different concepts together so that you can build software applications that run on Linux in order to control, or take input from, electronics circuits of your own design.

Introduction to GPIO Interfacing

It is possible to interface electronic circuits and modules to the BBB in several different ways. For example:

- **Using the GPIOs on the BBB's P8/P9 headers:** This provides you with versatility in terms of the type of circuits that you can connect and is the subject of this chapter.

- **Using the buses (e.g., I²C, SPI), or UARTs on the P8/P9 headers:** Bus connections enable communications to complex modules such as sensors and displays. This topic is discussed in Chapter 8.

- **Connecting USB modules (e.g., keyboards, Wi-Fi):** If Linux drivers are available, many different electronic device types can be connected to the BBB. Examples are provided in later chapters.

- **Communicating through Ethernet/Wi-Fi/Bluetooth to electronics modules:** It is possible to build network-attached sensors that communicate to the BBB using network connections. Chapter 9 first introduces, and Chapter 10 then focuses on, this topic.

The next step in working with the BBB is to connect it to circuits using the GPIOs and analog inputs of the P8 and P9 expansion headers (as illustrated in Figure 1-4 in Chapter 1). The background material of earlier chapters is very important, as this is a surprisingly complex topic that will take some time to get used to, particularly the content on device tree overlays and pin multiplexing. However, code and example circuits are provided throughout this chapter that you can use to help you build your own circuits.

Figure 6-1 provides you with a first view of the functionality of the inputs and outputs on the BBB's P8 and P9 headers. Many of these pins are *multiplexed*, meaning they have many more functions than what is displayed in the figure. The name listed typically describes the default operation of the pin.

This chapter discusses how you can interface to the BBB's P8/P9 header pins in the following different ways:

- **Digital output:** How you can use a GPIO to turn an electrical circuit on or off. The example uses an LED, but the principles hold true for any circuit type; for example, you could even use a relay to turn on/off high-powered devices. A circuit is provided to ensure that you do not draw too much current from a GPIO. A C++ class is developed to make software interfacing straightforward and efficient.

- **Digital input:** How you can read in a digital output from an electrical circuit into a software application running under Linux. Circuits are provided to ensure that this is performed safely for the BBB. At the end of the chapter, more advanced digital input that allows for very efficient detection of an input state change is also discussed.

- **Analog input:** How you can read in an analog output from an electrical circuit in the range of 0 V to 1.8 V using one of the BBB's seven on-board analog-to-digital converters (ADCs). A circuit is provided to ensure that you do not draw current from the reference supply, which would mean that its voltage value could no longer be guaranteed.

- **Analog output:** How you can use PWM to output a proportional signal that can be used as an analog voltage level or as a control signal for certain types of devices, such as servo motors.

P9

Name				Name
GND	P9_01	O O	P9_02	GND
DC_3.3V	P9_03	O O	P9_04	DC_3.3V
VDD_5V	P9_05	O O	P9_06	VDD_5V
SYS_5V	P9_07	O O	P9_08	SYS_5V
PWR_BUT	P9_09	O O	P9_10	SYS_RESETn
UART4_RXD	P9_11	O O	P9_12	GPIO1_28
UART4_TXD	P9_13	O O	P9_14	EHRPWM1A
GPIO1_16	P9_15	O O	P9_16	EHRPWM1B
I2C1_SCL	P9_17	O O	P9_18	I2C1_SDA
I2C2_SCL	P9_19	O O	P9_20	I2C2_SDA
UART2_TXD	P9_21	O O	P9_22	UART2_RXD
GPIO1_17	P9_23	O O	P9_24	UART1_TXD
GPIO3_21	P9_25	O O	P9_26	UART1_RXD
GPIO3_19	P9_27	O O	P9_28	SPI1_CS0
SPI1_D0	P9_29	O O	P9_30	SPI1_D1
SPI1_SCLK	P9_31	O O	P9_32	VADC
AIN4	P9_33	O O	P9_34	AGND
AIN6	P9_35	O O	P9_36	AIN5
AIN2	P9_37	O O	P9_38	AIN3
AIN0	P9_39	O O	P9_40	AIN1
GPIO3_20	P9_41	O O	P9_42	GPIO0_7
GND	P9_43	O O	P9_44	GND
GND	P9_45	O O	P9_46	GND

USB

P8

Name				Name
GND	P8_01	O O	P8_02	GND
GPIO1_6	P8_03	O O	P8_04	GPIO1_7
GPIO1_2	P8_05	O O	P8_06	GPIO1_3
TIMER4	P8_07	O O	P8_08	TIMER7
TIMER5	P8_09	O O	P8_10	TIMER6
GPIO1_13	P8_11	O O	P8_12	GPIO1_12
EHRPWM2B	P8_13	O O	P8_14	GPIO0_26
GPIO1_15	P8_15	O O	P8_16	GPIO1_14
GPIO0_27	P8_17	O O	P8_18	GPIO2_1
EHRPWM2A	P8_19	O O	P8_20	GPIO1_31
GPIO1_30	P8_21	O O	P8_22	GPIO1_5
GPIO1_4	P8_23	O O	P8_24	GPIO1_1
GPIO1_0	P8_25	O O	P8_26	GPIO1_29
GPIO2_22	P8_27	O O	P8_28	GPIO2_24
GPIO2_23	P8_29	O O	P8_30	GPIO2_25
UART5_CTSN	P8_31	O O	P8_32	UART5_RTSN
UART4_RTSN	P8_33	O O	P8_34	UART3_RTSN
UART4_CTSN	P8_35	O O	P8_36	UART3_CTSN
UART5_TXD	P8_37	O O	P8_38	UART5_RXD
GPIO2_12	P8_39	O O	P8_40	GPIO2_13
GPIO2_10	P8_41	O O	P8_42	GPIO2_11
GPIO2_8	P8_43	O O	P8_44	GPIO2_9
GPIO2_6	P8_45	O O	P8_46	GPIO2_7

Figure 6-1: The BBB P8/P9 headers with pin names, which describe each pin's default functionality

This chapter assumes that you have read Chapter 4—in particular, switching circuits using FETs and the use of pull-up/down resistors.

WARNING   Please be especially careful when working with the P8/P9 headers, as incorrect connections can, and will, destroy your board. Please test all new circuits to ensure that their voltage *and* current levels are within range before connecting them to the headers. Also, please follow the advice on interfacing circuits using FETs, optocouplers, and op-amps, as described in this chapter.

GPIO Digital Output

The example output configuration illustrated in Figure 6-2 uses a GPIO connected to a FET in order to switch a circuit. As described in Chapter 4, when a voltage is applied to the gate input of a FET, it will close the virtual drain-source "switch," enabling current to flow from the 5 V supply through the 220 Ω current-limiting resistor, to GND through a lighting LED. The advantage of this type of circuit is that it can be applied to many on/off digital output applications, as the BS270 FET data sheet indicates that it can drive a constant current of up to 400 mA (and a pulsed current of up to 2 A) across the drain-source at up to 60 V. However, the maximum current is limited in this circuit by the FET (see the note), and, because the SYS_5V pin (P9_07) can supply a maximum of 250 mA. As an alternative, the VDD_5V (P9_05 and P9_06) can supply up to 1 A, but it is only active if a power supply is plugged into the 5 V DC jack.

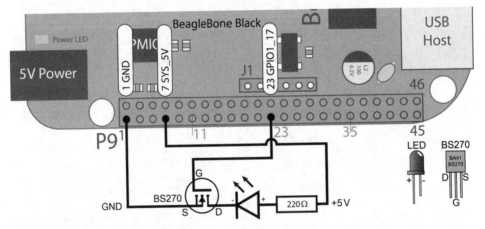

Figure 6-2: A FET-driven LED circuit

BBB GPIOs are 3.3 V tolerant and you can only source 4–6 mA and sink about 8 mA to each pin. In the example, it is safe to use the 5 V supply to drive the LED, as the drain-source circuit of the FET is never connected to the gate input. You will also notice that, unlike the example in Chapter 4, there is no resistor on the gate of the FET. It is not necessary in this particular case, because an *internal* pull-down resistor is enabled within the BBB, by default, on this pin. This is discussed shortly.

> **NOTE** The BS270 can switch a maximum drain current of approximately 130 mA at a gate voltage of 3.3 V. The high input impedance of the gate means that you can use two BS270s in parallel to double the maximum current to approximately 260 mA at the same gate voltage. The BS270 can also be used as a gate driver for Power FETs, which can switch much higher currents.

Once the circuit is built and attached to the BBB, you can boot the board and control the LED using a Linux terminal. For the moment, you will have to perform these operations as the root user. At the end of this chapter, a solution is discussed to remove that restriction.

As described in Figure 6-1, the P9 header pin 23(P9_23) is GPIO1_17. This means that it is GPIO 17 of 32 (0–31) on the second GPIO chip of four (0–3). As there are 32 GPIOs on each GPIO chip, the internal GPIO number corresponding to pin GPIO1_17 is calculated as follows: $(1 \times 32) + 17 = 49$. The total range will be 0 (GPIO0_0) to 127 (GPIO3_31), but as previously discussed, not all AM335x GPIOs are available on the headers. GPIOs on the P8 header can also be used, but to keep the figures concise the P9 header GPIOs are chosen. To enable GPIO 49, use the following commands at the Linux shell prompt:

```
root@beaglebone:~# cd /sys/class/gpio
root@beaglebone:/sys/class/gpio# ls
export gpiochip0 gpiochip32 gpiochip64 gpiochip96 unexport
root@beaglebone:/sys/class/gpio# echo 49 > export
root@beaglebone:/sys/class/gpio# ls
export gpio49 gpiochip0 gpiochip32 gpiochip64 gpiochip96 unexport
```

You can see that a new sysfs directory has appeared, and it can be used to change the properties of the GPIO as follows:

```
root@beaglebone:/sys/class/gpio# cd gpio49
root@beaglebone:/sys/class/gpio/gpio49# ls -l
total 0
-rw-r--r-- 1 root root 4096 May  4 19:43 active_low
-rw-r--r-- 1 root root 4096 May  4 19:43 direction
-rw-r--r-- 1 root root 4096 May  4 19:43 edge
drwxr-xr-x 2 root root    0 May  4 19:43 power
lrwxrwxrwx 1 root root    0 May  4 19:43 subsystem -> ...
-rw-r--r-- 1 root root 4096 May  4 19:43 uevent
-rw-r--r-- 1 root root 4096 May  4 19:43 value
root@beaglebone:/sys/class/gpio/gpio49# cat direction
in
root@beaglebone:/sys/class/gpio/gpio49# echo out > direction
root@beaglebone:/sys/class/gpio/gpio49# cat direction
out
```

The GPIO is now set up as an output and the value can be changed, which results in the LED being turned on and off:

```
root@beaglebone:/sys/class/gpio/gpio49# echo 1 > value
root@beaglebone:/sys/class/gpio/gpio49# echo 0 > value
```

If you wished at this point, you could remove the GPIO as follows:

```
root@beaglebone:/sys/class/gpio# echo 49 > unexport
```

To test the performance of this approach, a short script to flash the LED as quickly as possible, using a bash shell script, follows. This does not result in a visible "blink," as the LED is flashing faster than can be visibly observed; however, it can be visualized using an oscilloscope.

```
~/exploringbb/chp06/flash_script$ sudo su -s /bin/bash
/home/molloyd/exploringbb/chp06/flash_script# more flash.sh
#!/bin/bash
echo 49 > /sys/class/gpio/export
echo "out" > /sys/class/gpio/gpio49/direction
COUNTER=0
while [ $COUNTER -lt 100000 ]; do
    echo 0 > /sys/class/gpio/gpio49/value
    echo 1 > /sys/class/gpio/gpio49/value
    let COUNTER=COUNTER+1
done
echo 49 > /sys/class/gpio/unexport
/home/molloyd/exploringbb/chp06/flash_script# ./flash.sh
```

NOTE When using `sudo su` on the BBB, you can use `sudo su -s /bin/bash` to specify the specific shell that you would like, in order to have functionality such as file completion using the Tab key.

You can see from the oscilloscope trace in Figure 6-3 that the output is cycling every 0.45 ms approximately (although not all cycles are the same length), equating to a frequency of just over 2.2 kHz, which is not very high for an embedded controller. In addition, the `top` command (executed in another Linux terminal window) indicates that the CPU load for this script is 98.1%. You can also see that the current driving the LED is 12 mA, which is large enough to damage the BBB if this current were directly sourced from, or sinked to, the BBB GPIO itself.

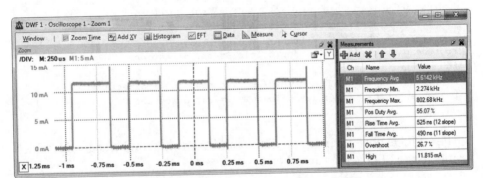

Figure 6-3: Scope output measuring the current through the LED for the flash.sh script

A C++ class is presented later in this chapter that can be used to control a GPIO and it achieves higher switching frequencies, but with similar CPU loads.

If you require a high-frequency periodic switching signal, then PWM, which is discussed later in this chapter, can be used. PWM can achieve frequencies of 1 MHz or higher, without a significant CPU load. If you require a nonperiodic output at a high frequency, then you will have to investigate the Programmable Real-Time Units (PRUs) in Chapter 13. However, many applications require the activation of a switched circuit at low frequencies (e.g., controlling motors, smart home control, etc.), and in such cases this configuration is perfectly valid.

GPIO Digital Input

The next application is to use a GPIO as a *digital input*, which will enable software written on the BBB to read the state of a push button or any other logic high/low input. This task is first performed using a Linux terminal and then it is performed using C/C++ code. The LED circuit can be left connected when building this circuit.

The circuit shown in Figure 6-4 uses a normally-open push button (SPST) that is connected to the BBB pin 27 on the P9 header, which is GPIO3_19.

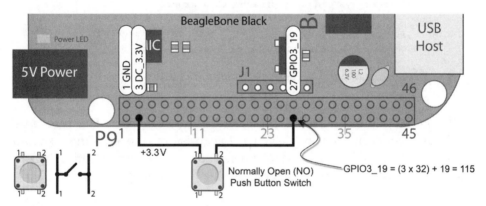

Figure 6-4: A GPIO button input example

You will notice that, having discussed the need for pull-up or pull-down resistors on push button switches in Chapter 4, none are present in this circuit. This is not accidental, as pin 27 on the P9 header is connected by default to GND using an internal pull-down resistor. This is discussed shortly. Use the following steps to read the state of the button (i.e., either 0 or 1) using a Linux terminal:

```
root@beaglebone:/sys/class/gpio# echo 115 > export
root@beaglebone:/sys/class/gpio# cd gpio115
root@beaglebone:/sys/class/gpio/gpio115# ls -l
total 0
-rw-r--r-- 1 root root 4096 May  4 21:47 active_low
-rw-r--r-- 1 root root 4096 May  4 21:47 direction
```

```
-rw-r--r-- 1 root root 4096 May  4 21:47 edge
drwxr-xr-x 2 root root    0 May  4 21:47 power
lrwxrwxrwx 1 root root    0 May  4 21:47 subsystem -> ...
-rw-r--r-- 1 root root 4096 May  4 21:47 uevent
-rw-r--r-- 1 root root 4096 May  4 21:47 value
root@beaglebone:/sys/class/gpio/gpio115# echo in > direction
root@beaglebone:/sys/class/gpio/gpio115# cat value
0
root@beaglebone:/sys/class/gpio/gpio115# cat value
1
root@beaglebone:/sys/class/gpio/gpio115# cat value
0
```

Therefore, the value is 1 when the button is pressed and 0 when it is released. Each time you type cat value, you are *polling* the input to check the value. The downside of this approach is that you will not identify a change in the value of the input unless you constantly poll the value state.

Interestingly, if you connect nothing to P9_12, which is GPIO1_28 = GPIO 60, and enter the same sequence of commands, you will get a different output:

```
root@beaglebone:/sys/class/gpio# echo 60 > export
root@beaglebone:/sys/class/gpio# cd gpio60
root@beaglebone:/sys/class/gpio/gpio60# echo in > direction
root@beaglebone:/sys/class/gpio/gpio60# cat direction
in
root@beaglebone:/sys/class/gpio/gpio60# cat value
1
```

With nothing connected to this input, it registers a value of 1. That is because this input is connected via an internal *pull-up* resistor to the 3.3 V line. It should be clear at this stage that you need to understand the GPIO configuration, including these internal resistors, in order to use the GPIO pins properly.

GPIO Configuration

The importance of pull-up and pull-down resistors is discussed in some detail in Chapter 4. They ensure that open switches do not allow a GPIO input to float. Such external resistors are typically "strong" pull-up/down resistors in that they "strongly" tie the input to a high/low value using relatively low resistance values (e.g., 5–10 kΩ).

Internal Pull-up and Pull-down Resistors

The BBB has "weak" *internal pull-up* and *internal pull-down* resistors that can be configured by setting internal registers in the AM335x using the Linux device tree, which is discussed in the next section.

You can physically check whether an internal pull-up or pull-down resistor is enabled on a pin by connecting a 100 kΩ resistor between the pin and GND (as shown in Figure 6-5(a), where the shaded area represents functionality that is internal to the AM335x), and then between the pin and the 3.3 V supply (as shown in Figure 6-5(b)). If you connect a 100 kΩ resistor (the one I used had an actual value of 98.6 kΩ) to P8_12 and measure the voltage across it, you will see that the voltage drop is 0 V when the resistor is connected to GND, and I measured 2.739 V (not 3.3 V) when it was connected to the 3.3 V rail. This indicates that there is an internal pull-down resistor enabled, and the combination of these resistors is behaving like a voltage divider circuit. You can even estimate the value of the internal pull-down resistor as in Figure 6-5(b).

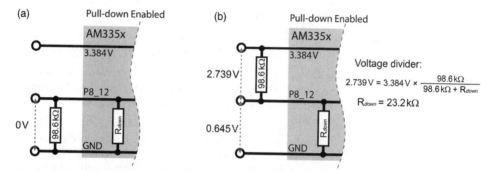

Figure 6-5: Internal pull-down resistor example, with an external resistor connected (a) from the pin to GND, and (b) from the pin to the 3.3 V supply

Clearly P8_12, which is GPIO1_12, has an internal pull-down resistor enabled, but if you perform the same test on P8_26, which is GPIO1_29, you will get a completely different response. When you connect the resistor as shown in Figure 6-5(a) you will get a voltage drop of ~2.624 V across the 100 kΩ resistor, and almost 0 V (~0.162 V) when you connect it as in Figure 6-5(b). That is because P8_26 has an internal pull-up resistor enabled. Performing the same calculations gives an internal pull-up resistor value of about 28.6 kΩ.

You need to factor these resistor values into the behavior of your input/output circuits and you need to be able to alter the internal resistor configuration in certain circumstances. For the next section, remember that the physical measurements indicate that P8_12 has a pull-down resistor, and P8_26 has a pull-up resistor, both enabled by default.

GPIO Pin Configuration Settings

As well as configuring pins to have either a pull-up or a pull-down resistor configuration, there are also seven different modes for each pin. This is called the *multiplexer mode* (*mmode*) for the pin and it is set using a three-digit binary number, as described in the first row of Table 6-1. This table is based on information provided in the *AM335x TRM* (GPIOs conf_<module>_<pin> - Table 9-60 of the TRM). Using these bit settings, you can construct a seven-bit value that can be used to configure the exact behavior of a GPIO pin within Linux using device tree overlays, which is discussed shortly.

Table 6-1: GPIO Pin User-Configuration Settings

BIT	AM335x FIELD	DESCRIPTION
0,1,2	mmode	The multiplexer mode: Using the three least-significant bits you can select a mode between 0 and 7, e.g., 000=0, 111=7. This enables each pin to have up to eight different modes.
3	puden	Enable internal pull-up/pull-down resistor: Enable=0, Disable=1.
4	putypesel	Select internal pull-up or pull-down form: Pull-down=0, Pull-up=1.
5	rxactive	*Input Active*: Receiver disabled=0, Input enabled=1. If this bit is set high, the pin will be an input; otherwise, it will be an output.
6	slewctrl	*Slew Control*: Fast=0, Slow=1. *Slew rate* provides control over the rise/fall time of an output. You would only set this value to slow if you were using long interconnects, such as on I²C buses.

NOTE There is a video on the use of these settings on the web page associated with this chapter at www.exploringbeaglebone.com/chapter6/ and at tiny.cc/ ebb601 that you can refer to while reading this chapter.

The mmode is discussed shortly, but when working with GPIOs the mmode will be 7, and therefore the most common hexadecimal values that are used to configure a GPIO's settings are as follows (bit 6 is the most significant bit (MSB) and is on the LHS):

- 0x27 (0100111) Fast, **Input**, Pull-Down, Enabled and Mux Mode 7
- 0x37 (0110111) Fast, Input, **Pull-Up**, Enabled, Mux Mode 7
- 0x07 (0000111) Fast, Output, Pull-down, **Enabled**, Mux Mode 7
- 0x17 (0010111) Fast, Output, Pull-up, Enabled, **Mux Mode 7**

These configuration values are very useful, as they enable you to set the pins into the exact operational mode that you require. The tables shown in Figures 6-6 and 6-7 provide the most important information required when interfacing the BBB. They have been generated using the *BBB SRM*, the *AM335x*

Pin	$PINS	ADDR Offset from	GPIO	Name	Mode7	Mode6	Mode5	Mode4	Mode3	Mode2	Mode1	Mode0	CPU	Notes
P8_01				DGND										Ground
P8_02		44e10800		DGND										Ground
P8_03	6	0x818/018	38	GPIO1_6	gpio1[6]						mmc1_dat6	gpmc_ad6	R9	Allocated emmc2
P8_04	7	0x81c/01c	39	GPIO1_7	gpio1[7]						mmc1_dat7	gpmc_ad7	T9	Allocated emmc2
P8_05	2	0x808/008	34	GPIO1_2	gpio1[2]						mmc1_dat2	gpmc_ad2	R8	Allocated emmc2
P8_06	3	0x80c/00c	35	GPIO1_3	gpio1[3]						mmc1_dat3	gpmc_ad3	T8	Allocated emmc2
P8_07	36	0x890/090	66	TIMER4	gpio2[2]					timer4		gpmc_advn_ale	R7	
P8_08	37	0x894/094	67	TIMER7	gpio2[3]					timer7		gpmc_oen_ren	T7	
P8_09	39	0x89c/09c	69	TIMER5	gpio2[5]					timer5		gpmc_be0n_cle	T6	
P8_10	38	0x898/098	68	TIMER6	gpio2[4]					timer6		gpmc_wen	U6	
P8_11	13	0x834/034	45	GPIO1_13	gpio1[13]	pr1_pru0_pru_r30_15		eQEP2B_in	mmc2_dat1	mmc1_dat5	lcd_data18	gpmc_ad13	R12	
P8_12	12	0x830/030	44	GPIO1_12	gpio1[12]	pr1_pru0_pru_r30_14		eQEP2A_in	mmc2_dat0	mmc1_dat4	lcd_data19	gpmc_ad12	T12	
P8_13	9	0x824/024	23	EHRPWM2B	gpio0[23]			ehrpwm2B	mmc2_dat5	mmc1_dat1	lcd_data22	gpmc_ad9	T10	
P8_14	10	0x828/028	26	GPIO0_26	gpio0[26]			ehrpwm2_tripzone_in	mmc2_dat6	mmc1_dat2	lcd_data21	gpmc_ad10	T11	
P8_15	15	0x83c/03c	47	GPIO1_15	gpio1[15]	pr1_pru0_pru_r31_15		eQEP2_strobe	mmc2_dat3	mmc1_dat7	lcd_data16	gpmc_ad15	U13	
P8_16	14	0x838/038	46	GPIO1_14	gpio1[14]	pr1_pru0_pru_r31_14		eQEP2_index	mmc2_dat2	mmc1_dat6	lcd_data17	gpmc_ad14	V13	
P8_17	11	0x82c/02c	27	GPIO0_27	gpio0[27]			ehrpwm0_synco	mmc2_dat7	mmc1_dat3	lcd_data20	gpmc_ad11	U12	
P8_18	35	0x88c/08c	65	GPIO2_1	gpio2[1]	mcasp0_fsr			mmc2_clk	gpmc_wait1	lcd_memory_clk	gpmc_clk_mux0	V12	
P8_19	8	0x820/020	22	EHRPWM2A	gpio0[22]			ehrpwm2A	mmc2_dat4		lcd_data23	gpmc_ad8	U10	
P8_20	33	0x884/084	63	GPIO1_31	gpio1[31]	pr1_pru1_pru_r31_13	pr1_pru1_pru_r30_13			mmc1_cmd	gpmc_be1n	gpmc_csn2	V9	Allocated emmc2
P8_21	32	0x880/080	62	GPIO1_30	gpio1[30]	pr1_pru1_pru_r31_12	pr1_pru1_pru_r30_12			mmc1_clk	gpmc_clk	gpmc_csn1	U9	Allocated emmc2
P8_22	5	0x814/014	37	GPIO1_5	gpio1[5]	pr1_pru1_pru_r31_8	pr1_pru1_pru_r30_8				mmc1_dat5	gpmc_ad5	V8	Allocated emmc2
P8_23	4	0x810/010	36	GPIO1_4	gpio1[4]	pr1_pru1_pru_r31_9	pr1_pru1_pru_r30_9				mmc1_dat4	gpmc_ad4	U8	Allocated emmc2
P8_24	1	0x804/004	33	GPIO1_1	gpio1[1]	pr1_pru1_pru_r31_11	pr1_pru1_pru_r30_11				mmc1_dat1	gpmc_ad1	V7	Allocated emmc2
P8_25	0	0x800/000	32	GPIO1_0	gpio1[0]	pr1_pru1_pru_r31_10	pr1_pru1_pru_r30_10				mmc1_dat0	gpmc_ad0	U7	Allocated emmc2
P8_26	31	0x87c/07c	61	GPIO1_29	gpio1[29]							gpmc_csn0	V6	
P8_27	56	0x8e0/0e0	86	GPIO2_22	gpio2[22]						gpmc_a8	lcd_vsync	U5	Allocated HDMI
P8_28	58	0x8e8/0e8	88	GPIO2_24	gpio2[24]						gpmc_a10	lcd_pclk	V5	Allocated HDMI
P8_29	57	0x8e4/0e4	87	GPIO2_23	gpio2[23]						gpmc_a9	lcd_hsync	R5	Allocated HDMI
P8_30	59	0x8ec/0ec	89	GPIO2_25	gpio2[25]						gpmc_a11	lcd_ac_bias_en	R6	Allocated HDMI
P8_31	54	0x8d8/0d8	10	UART5_CTSN	gpio0[10]	uart5_ctsn			mcasp0_axr1	eQEP1_index	gpmc_a18	lcd_data14	V4	Allocated HDMI
P8_32	55	0x8dc/0dc	11	UART5_RTSN	gpio0[11]	uart5_rtsn			mcasp0_ahclkx	eQEP1_strobe	gpmc_a19	lcd_data15	T5	Allocated HDMI
P8_33	53	0x8d4/0d4	9	UART4_RTSN	gpio0[9]	uart4_rtsn			mcasp0_fsr	eQEP1B_in	gpmc_a17	lcd_data13	V3	Allocated HDMI
P8_34	51	0x8cc/0cc	81	UART3_RTSN	gpio2[17]	uart3_rtsn			mcasp0_ahclkr	ehrpwm1B	gpmc_a15	lcd_data11	U4	Allocated HDMI
P8_35	52	0x8d0/0d0	8	UART4_CTSN	gpio0[8]	uart4_ctsn			mcasp0_aclkr	eQEP1A_in	gpmc_a16	lcd_data12	V2	Allocated HDMI
P8_36	50	0x8c8/0c8	80	UART3_CTSN	gpio2[16]	uart3_ctsn			mcasp0_axr0	ehrpwm1A	gpmc_a14	lcd_data10	U3	Allocated HDMI
P8_37	48	0x8c0/0c0	78	UART5_TXD	gpio2[14]	uart5_txd			mcasp0_aclkx	ehrpwm1_tripzone_in	gpmc_a12	lcd_data8	U1	Allocated HDMI
P8_38	49	0x8c4/0c4	79	UART5_RXD	gpio2[15]	uart5_rxd			mcasp0_fsx	ehrpwm0_synco	gpmc_a13	lcd_data9	U2	Allocated HDMI
P8_39	46	0x8b8/0b8	76	GPIO2_12	gpio2[12]	pr1_pru1_pru_r31_6	pr1_pru1_pru_r30_6				gpmc_a6	lcd_data6	T3	Allocated HDMI
P8_40	47	0x8bc/0bc	77	GPIO2_13	gpio2[13]	pr1_pru1_pru_r31_7	pr1_pru1_pru_r30_7	pr1_edio_data_out7			gpmc_a7	lcd_data7	T4	Allocated HDMI
P8_41	44	0x8b0/0b0	74	GPIO2_10	gpio2[10]	pr1_pru1_pru_r31_4	pr1_pru1_pru_r30_4				gpmc_a4	lcd_data4	T1	Allocated HDMI
P8_42	45	0x8b4/0b4	75	GPIO2_11	gpio2[11]	pr1_pru1_pru_r31_5	pr1_pru1_pru_r30_5				gpmc_a5	lcd_data5	T2	Allocated HDMI
P8_43	42	0x8a8/0a8	72	GPIO2_8	gpio2[8]	pr1_pru1_pru_r31_2	pr1_pru1_pru_r30_2				gpmc_a2	lcd_data2	R3	Allocated HDMI
P8_44	43	0x8ac/0ac	73	GPIO2_9	gpio2[9]	pr1_pru1_pru_r31_3	pr1_pru1_pru_r30_3				gpmc_a3	lcd_data3	R4	Allocated HDMI
P8_45	40	0x8a0/0a0	70	GPIO2_6	gpio2[6]	pr1_pru1_pru_r31_0	pr1_pru1_pru_r30_0				gpmc_a0	lcd_data0	R1	Allocated HDMI
P8_46	41	0x8a4/0a4	71	GPIO2_7	gpio2[7]	pr1_pru1_pru_r31_1	pr1_pru1_pru_r30_1				gpmc_a1	lcd_data1	R2	Allocated HDMI
P9 Header	ADDR +	cat $PINS	GPIO NO.	Name	Mode 7	Mode 6	Mode 5	Mode 4	Mode 3	Mode 2	Mode 1	Mode 0	CPU	

Figure 6-6: The BBB P8 header pins

Pin	SPINS	ADDR	GPIO	Name	Mode7	Mode6	Mode5	Mode4	Mode3	Mode2	Mode1	Mode0	CPU	Notes
P9_01		44e10000		GND										Ground
P9_02		Offset from:		GND										Ground
P9_03		44e10800		DC_3.3V										250mA Max Current
P9_04				DC_3.3V										250mA Max Current
P9_05				VDD_5V										1A Max Current
P9_06				VDD_5V										1A Max Current
P9_07				SYS_5V										250mA Max Current
P9_08				SYS_5V										250mA Max Current
P9_09				PWR_BUT										5V Level (pulled up PMIC)
P9_10				SYS_RESETn								RESET_OUT	A10	All GPIOs to 4-6mA output
P9_11	28	0x870/070	30	UART4_RXD	gpio0[30]	uart4_rxd_mux2		mmc1_sdcd	rmii2_crs_dv	gpmc_csn4	mii2_crs	gpmc_wait0	T17	and approx. 8mA on input.
P9_12	30	0x878/078	60	GPIO1_28	gpio1[28]	mcasp0_aclkr_mux3		gpmc_dir	mmc2_dat3	gpmc_csn6	mii2_col	gpmc_be1n	U18	
P9_13	29	0x874/074	31	UART4_TXD	gpio0[31]	uart4_txd_mux2		mmc2_adcd	mmc2_rxerr	gpmc_csn5	mii2_rxerr	gpmc_wpn	U17	
P9_14	18	0x848/048	50	EHRPWM1A	gpio1[18]	ehrpwm1A_mux1		gpmc_a18	mmc2_dat1	rgmii2_td3	mii2_txd3	gpmc_a2	U14	
P9_15	16	0x840/040	48	GPIO1_16	gpio1[16]	ehrpwm1_tripzone_input		gpmc_a16	mii2_txen	rgmii2_txtl	mii2_txen	gpmc_a0	R13	
P9_16	19	0x84c/04c	51	EHRPWM1B	gpio1[19]	ehrpwm1B_mux1		gpmc_a19	mmc2_dat2	rgmii2_td2	mii2_txd2	gpmc_a3	T14	
P9_17	87	0x95c/15c	5	I2C1_SCL	gpio0[5]			prt_uart0_txd		I2C1_SCL	mmc2_sdwp	spi0_cs0	A16	
P9_18	86	0x958/158	4	I2C1_SDA	gpio0[4]			prt_uart0_rxd	ehrpwm0_synco	I2C1_SDA		spi0_d1	B17	
P9_19	95	0x97c/17c	13	I2C2_SCL	gpio0[13]		prt_uart0_rts_n	spi1_cs1	ehrpwm0_tripzone	I2C2_SCL	timer5	uart1_rtsn	D17	Allocated I2C2
P9_20	94	0x978/178	12	I2C2_SDA	gpio0[12]		prt_uart0_cts_n	spi1_cs0	I2C2_SDA	I2C2_SDA	timer6	uart1_ctsn	D18	Allocated I2C2
P9_21	85	0x954/154	3	UART2_TXD	gpio0[3]	EMU3_mux1		prt_uart0_txd_n	ehrpwm0B	I2C2_SCL	uart2_txd	spi0_d0	B17	
P9_22	84	0x950/150	2	UART2_RXD	gpio0[2]	EMU2_mux1		prt_uart0_cts_n_o	ehrpwm0A	I2C2_SDA	uart2_rxd	spi0_sclk	A17	
P9_23	17	0x844/044	49	GPIO1_17	gpio0[17]	ehrpwm0_synco		gpmc_a17	mmc2_dat0	rgmii2_rxdv	uart2_rxd	gpmc_a1	V14	
P9_24	97	0x984/184	15	UART1_TXD	gpio0[15]	prt_pru0_pru_r31_16			I2C1_SCL	dcan1_rx	mmc2_sdwp	uart1_txd	D15	
P9_25	107	0x9ac/1ac	117	GPIO3_21	gpio3[21]	prt_pru0_pru_r31_7		EMU4_mux2	mcasp1_axr1	mcasp0_axr3	eQEP0_strobe	mcasp0_ahclkx	A14	Allocated mcasp0_pins
P9_26	96	0x980/180	14	UART1_RXD	gpio0[14]	prt_pru1_pru_r31_16			I2C1_SDA	dcan1_tx	mmc1_sdwp	uart1_rxd	D16	
P9_27	105	0x9a4/1a4	115	GPIO3_19	gpio3[19]	prt_pru0_pru_r30_5		EMU2_mux2	mcasp1_fsx	mcasp0_axr3	ehrpwm0_synci	mcasp0_fsr	C13	Allocated mcasp0_pins
P9_28	103	0x99c/19c	113	SPI1_CS0	gpio3[17]	prt_pru0_pru_r30_3		eCAP2_in_PWM2_out	spi1_cs0	mcasp0_axr2	ehrpwm0_synci	mcasp0_ahclkr	C12	Allocated mcasp0_pins
P9_29	101	0x994/194	111	SPI1_D0	gpio3[15]	prt_pru0_pru_r30_1		mmc1_sdcd_mux1	spi1_d0		ehrpwm0B	mcasp0_fsx	B13	Allocated mcasp0_pins
P9_30	102	0x998/198	112	SPI1_D1	gpio3[16]	prt_pru0_pru_r30_2		mmc2_sdcd_mux1	spi1_d1		ehrpwm0_tripzone	mcasp0_axr0	D12	Allocated mcasp0_pins
P9_31	100	0x990/190	110	SPI1_SCLK	gpio3[14]	prt_pru0_pru_r30_0		mmc0_sdcd_mux1	spi1_sclk		ehrpwm0A	mcasp0_aclkx	A13	Allocated mcasp0_pins
P9_32				VADC										1.8V ADC Volt. Ref.
P9_33				AIN4									C8	1.8V input
P9_34				AGND										Ground for ADC
P9_35				AIN6									A8	1.8V input
P9_36				AIN5									B8	1.8V input
P9_37				AIN2									B7	1.8V input
P9_38				AIN3									A7	1.8V input
P9_39				AIN0									B6	1.8V input
P9_40				AIN1									C7	1.8V input
P9_41A	109	0x9b4/1b4	20	CLKOUT2	gpio0[20]	EMU3_mux0	prt_pru0_pru_r31_16	timer7_mux1	clkout2	tclkin		xdma_event_intr1	D14	Both to P21 of P11
P9_41B		0x9a8/1a8	116	GPIO3_20	gpio3[20]	prt_pru0_pru_r31_6		emu3	Mcasp1_axr0		eQEP0_index		D13	Both to P21 of P11
P9_42A		0x964/164	7	GPIO0_7	gpio0[7]	xdma_event_intr2	mmc0_sdwp	spi1_sclk	prt_ecap0_ecap_capin_apwm_o	spi1_cs1	uart3_txd	eCAP1_in_PWM0_out	eCAP0A_in	C18	Both to P22 of P11
P9_42B	89	0x9a0/1a0	114	GPIO3_18	gpio3[18]	prt_pru0_pru_r31_4		Mcasp0_aclkx	spi1_sclk	eQEP0A_in	Mcasp0_axr2	Mcasp0_aclkr	B12	Allocated mcasp0_pins
P9_43				GND										- See Pg.50 of the SRM
P9_44				GND										Ground
P9_45				GND										Ground
P9_46				GND										Ground
	cat		(Mode 7)	GND	Mode 7									Ground
P9	SPINS	ADDR +	GPIO NO.	Name	Mode 7						Mode 1	Mode 0	CPU	Notes

Figure 6-7: The BBB P9 header pins

TRM, and information that can be gleaned from the BBB Linux distribution. The figures illustrate the mmode options that are available on each of the BBB's P8 and P9 headers. They are available in PDF form in the GitHub repository (chp06/P8P9headers) so that they can be displayed on your computer in color, and printed as required.

Quite a large amount of information is presented in these two tables, and subsequent chapters in the book will frequently refer back to them. For the moment, note a few points that are particularly important:

- Any pin that is highlighted in the $PINS column is already allocated and should not be used unless you disable the functionality that it is allocated to (e.g., the HDMI output or the eMMC). See the Notes column for further details.

- Mode7 is the GPIO mmode.

- As discussed, the GPIO number is calculated by taking the GPIO chip number, multiplying it by 32, and then adding the offset. For example, GPIO1_12 = (1 × 32) + 12 = GPIO 44.

- Very importantly, the $PINS number is *not* the GPIO number. This $PINS number in the table is a BBB software reference for each of the pins and these values are provided in the second column of the table.

- Highlighted items in the Mode6 and Mode5 columns relate to PRU functionality, discussed in Chapter 13.

The BBB P8 header pins P8_12 and P8_26 can be used as an illustration of the information in these tables. These are the pins that were physically tested as described earlier. If you examine Figure 6-6, you will see under P8_12 and P8_26 the following values:

```
Head    $PINS   ADDR/OFFSET   GPIO      Name      Mode7
P8_12    12      0x830/030     44      GPIO1_12  gpio1[12] ...
P8_26    31      0x87c/07c     61      GPIO1_29  gpio1[29] ...
```

The fact that the name of the pin is the same as its Mode7 value means that Mode7 is most likely enabled by default. You can test this in Linux as follows:

```
molloyd@beaglebone:~$ sudo su -s /bin/bash
root@beaglebone:/home/molloyd# cd /sys/kernel/debug/pinctrl/
root@beaglebone:/sys/kernel/debug/pinctrl# ls
44e10800.pinmux  pinctrl-devices  pinctrl-handles  pinctrl-maps
root@beaglebone:/sys/kernel/debug/pinctrl# cd 44e10800.pinmux/
root@beaglebone:/sys/kernel/debug/pinctrl/44e10800.pinmux# ls
gpio-ranges  pinconf-pins  pinmux-functions  pins
inconf-groups  pingroups  pinmux-pins
root@beaglebone:/sys/kernel/debug/pinctrl/44e10800.pinmux# more pins
registered pins: 142
...
```

```
pin 12 (44e10830) 00000027 pinctrl-single
...
pin 31 (44e1087c) 00000037 pinctrl-single
...
```

The pin number is the $PINS value of the pin in question. Therefore, you can see that P8_12 ($PINS value 12) is in mode 0x27, which is an input in Mode7 (gpio1[12]) with a pull-down resistor enabled. Similarly, P8_26 is $PINS value 31, which is in mode 0x37. This is an input in Mode7 (gpio1[29]), with a pull-up resistor enabled. Viewing the pins file confirms the test readings that were taken earlier on the 100 kΩ resistor using the DMM.

There is more information available in this directory about which pins are allocated. For example, use the following to check if the pins are allocated:

```
/sys/kernel/debug/pinctrl/44e10800.pinmux# cat pinmux-pins
Pinmux settings per pin
Format: pin (name): mux_owner gpio_owner hog?
pin 0 (44e10800): mmc.11 (GPIO UNCLAIMED) function pinmux_emmc2_pins
group pinmux_emmc2_pins
...
pin 12 (44e10830): (MUX UNCLAIMED) (GPIO UNCLAIMED)
...
pin 31 (44e1087c): (MUX UNCLAIMED) (GPIO UNCLAIMED)
```

You can see that pin 0 is allocated to the eMMC, but the pins on the P8 header that were tested using the DMM are not being claimed and are available for use.

You can actually query the value at the memory address itself using C code that accesses /dev/mem directly. Because P8_12 ($PINS12) is mapped at the memory address 44e10830 (see the ADDR column in Figure 6-6, or the preceding pinmux-pins file), you can use the following steps to install Jan-Derk Bakker's devmem2 program:

```
~$ wget http://www.lartmaker.nl/lartware/port/devmem2.c
--2014-05-05 11:22:54--  http://www.lartmaker.nl/lartware/port/devmem2.c
...
2014-05-05 11:22:54 (14.7 MB/s) - 'devmem2.c' saved [3551/3551]
~$ gcc devmem2.c -o devmem2
~$ sudo ./devmem2 0x44e10830
/dev/mem opened.
Memory mapped at address 0xb6f5f000.
Value at address 0x44E10830 (0xb6f5f830): 0x27
```

The value 0x27 is expected for $PINS12. You can investigate the source code of devmem2 to see how it can be integrated into your projects.

C++ Control of GPIOs

A C++ class has been written for this book that wraps the GPIO functionality on the BBB in order to make it easier to use. Here is a segment of the class description that lists its basic I/O functionality. The more advanced functionality that has been removed from this code fragment is discussed at the end of this chapter. The implementation of this functionality is similar to the code that was written previously for the BBB LEDs. The full code listing is in `/library/gpio/GPIO.h` and `GPIO.cpp`. Listing 6-1 provides a partial listing of the `GPIO` class source code.

The C++ code is separated into header (`.h`) and implementation (`.cpp`) files, and the process of building applications in this form is called *separate compilation*. Separate compilation makes building large projects more efficient, but it can be difficult to manage all the files. The next chapter introduces the Eclipse integrated development environment (IDE) for cross-compilation, in order to make this process seamless.

LISTING 6-1: /library/gpio/GPIO.h (partial listing)

```
// GPIO Class written by Derek Molloy (www.derekmolloy.ie)
#include<string>
#include<fstream>
using std::string;
using std::ofstream;
#define GPIO_PATH "/sys/class/gpio/"

namespace exploringBB {   //All code is within a namespace

// Enumerations are used to restrict the options
enum GPIO_DIRECTION{ INPUT, OUTPUT };
enum GPIO_VALUE{ LOW=0, HIGH=1 };
enum GPIO_EDGE{ NONE, RISING, FALLING, BOTH };

class GPIO {
private:
   int number, debounceTime;
   string name, path;
public:
   GPIO(int number);        //constructor will export the pin
   virtual int getNumber() { return number; }

   // General Input and Output Settings
   virtual int setDirection(GPIO_DIRECTION);
   virtual GPIO_DIRECTION getDirection();
   virtual int setValue(GPIO_VALUE);
   virtual int toggleOutput();
   virtual GPIO_VALUE getValue();
   virtual int setActiveLow(bool isLow=true);  //low=1, high=0
   virtual int setActiveHigh(); //default
   //software debounce input (ms) - default 0
   virtual void setDebounceTime(int time){this->debounceTime = time;}
```

continues

LISTING 6-1: *(continued)*

```cpp
   // Advanced OUTPUT: Faster write using a stream (~20x)
   virtual int streamOpen();
   virtual int streamWrite(GPIO_VALUE);
   virtual int streamClose();

   ...  // Advanced INPUT: presented at the end of this chapter
   virtual ~GPIO();  //destructor will unexport the pin

private: // Hidden functionality
   int write(string path, string filename, string value);
   int write(string path, string filename, int value);
   string read(string path, string filename);
   int exportGPIO();
   int unexportGPIO();
   ofstream stream;
   ...
};/* End of GPIO class */
} /* namespace exploringBB */
```

You can extend this class through inheritance in order to add the functionality that you require, and you can integrate it into your projects without restrictions on its use. Use of this class is demonstrated in the following short code example that interacts with the LED and button circuits described earlier in this chapter:

```cpp
~/exploringbb/chp06/GPIO$ more simple.cpp
#include<iostream>
#include<unistd.h> // required for usleep - microsecond sleep
#include"GPIO.h"   // using user-include syntax
using namespace exploringBB;  // bring in everything from this namespace
using namespace std;          // bring in standard namespace

int main(){
   GPIO outGPIO(49), inGPIO(115);   //P9_23 and P9_27 respectively

   // Basic Output - Flash the LED 10 times, once per second
   outGPIO.setDirection(OUTPUT);
   for (int i=0; i<10; i++){
      outGPIO.setValue(HIGH);   // LED on
      usleep(500000);           // sleep 0.5 seconds
      outGPIO.setValue(LOW);    // LED off
      usleep(500000);
   }

   // Basic Input example
   inGPIO.setDirection(INPUT);   // is the button pressed?
   cout << "The value of the input is: "<< inGPIO.getValue() << endl;
```

```
    // Fast write to the GPIO 1 million times
    outGPIO.streamOpen();
    for (int i=0; i<1000000; i++){
       outGPIO.streamWrite(HIGH); // no sleep. As fast as possible.
       outGPIO.streamWrite(LOW);
    }
    outGPIO.streamClose();            // close the stream and exit
    return 0;
}
~/exploringbb/chp06/GPIO$ g++ simple.cpp GPIO.cpp -o simple -pthread
~/exploringbb/chp06/GPIO$ sudo ./simple
The value of the input is: 0
```

In the preceding build instruction, you need to pass both .cpp files to the compiler, as due to separate compilation the source code is split over multiple files. The -pthread flag is required for class functionality that is described later in this chapter.

This code example flashes the LED 10 times, reads the state of the button, and then flashes the LED one million times (in about eight seconds).

To test the performance of this structure, Figure 6-8 captures the signal output of the LED flashing in (a) when the setValue() method is used with no sleep call, and in (b) when the streamWrite() method is used. In (a) it is flashing at about 5.5 kHz and in (b) it is flashing at about 125 kHz. Unfortunately, the C++ application had to run at 98% of CPU usage to generate these outputs, which is not really practical on a multi-user, multi-process OS such as Linux, and it is certainly not very efficient.

PWM is discussed later in this chapter, illustrating how to switch a GPIO using a regular periodic signal, at a fixed frequency, with negligible CPU load. For fast GPIO switching using a nonperiodic signal, the PRU-ICSS (see Chapter 13) would likely be required. An unsafe technique that uses direct access to system memory is also possible, and although it is definitely not recommended, it is explained next because of its value in learning about what is going on "under the hood."

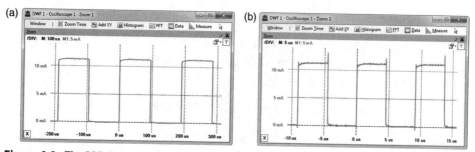

Figure 6-8: The BBB C++ class flashing the LED

MEMORY-BASED GPIO SWITCHING (ADVANCED)

If the preceding code is not switching fast enough for your applications, mechanisms are available for making a GPIO circuit switch at much higher frequencies, using the information from Chapter 25 in the *AM335x TRM*. However, by doing this you are effectively bypassing the Linux OS, which means that if two processes try to access the same GPIO registers at the same time, then a resource conflict could occur. *These operations are unsafe and could lock up your Linux kernel*. However, a reboot will put everything back in order. Therefore, while it is not recommended for general programming under Linux, an example provides useful insight into how the GPIOs function at the register level and how you can use some of the detail in the *AM335x TRM*.

At the beginning of this section, the devmem2 application is used to read the pin mux settings. You can use the same program to also set values in the AM335x registers. Section 25.4.1 in Chapter 25 of the *AM335x TRM* provides you with the addresses for the bank of GPIOs (from its Table 25-5):

13C **GPIO_DATAOUT: Used to read the GPIO state**
190 **GPIO_CLEARDATAOUT: Used to set a GPIO low**
194 **GPIO_SETDATAOUT: Used to set a GPIO high**

These values are offset from the base GPIO bank address. Because GPIO1_17 is on the GPIO1 bank, you need the base address, which is available in the Memory Map table (Table 2-3) of the TRM and has the value 0x4804C000. **For reference, GPIO0 is** 0x44E07000, **GPIO2 is** 0x481AC000, **and GPIO3 is** 0x481AE000. **Therefore, you can turn off the LED on P9_23 (GPIO1_17) using the call**

```
molloyd@beaglebone:~$ sudo ./devmem2 0x4804c190 w 0x00020000
/dev/mem opened.
Memory mapped at address 0xb6f41000.
Value at address 0x4804C190 (0xb6f41190): 0x820000
Written 0x820000; readback 0x0
```

where the value you are writing to the GPIO_CLEARDATAOUT offset (190) from the base of address of GPIO1 (0x4804C000) is the 17th bit—i.e., 100000000000000000$_2$ converted to hexadecimal = 0x00020000. This will turn the LED off. To turn it on, use the GPIO_SETDATAOUT (194) offset:

```
molloyd@beaglebone:~$ sudo ./devmem2 0x4804c194 w 0x00020000
/dev/mem opened.
Memory mapped at address 0xb6f26000.
Value at address 0x4804C194 (0xb6f26194): 0x800000
Written 0x820000; readback 0x820000
```

To read the current state, you can use the GPIO_DATAOUT offset (13C):

```
molloyd@beaglebone:~$ sudo ./devmem2 0x4804c13c
/dev/mem opened.
```

```
Memory mapped at address 0xb6fcd000.
Value at address 0x4804C13C (0xb6fcd13c): 0x820000
```

where 0x8200000 = 100000100000000000000000$_2$. Therefore, the 17th bit from the right (GPIO1_17) and the 23rd bit from the right (GPIO1_23, which is the USR2 LED) are both on. Remember that you downloaded the source code for `devmem2.c` and it can be modified, should you wish to perform this type of high-speed, but unsafe, GPIO switching. This topic is examined again in Chapter 13, when the PRU-ICSS is discussed.

The Linux Device Tree

The first introduction to the Linux boot process is in Chapter 3, where it is made clear that Linux running on an embedded device, such as the BBB, does not have a BIOS. Rather, in order to boot and configure the device, it uses files on the SD card or eMMC that describe the machine's hardware. Every type of embedded Linux device has its own unique set of files to describe its platform hardware.

When the BeagleBone was running older Linux kernels, the specific modifications required to those Linux kernels were applied to the Linux source code directly by using a file called `board-am335xevm.c`. Older Linux kernels (before 3.7) also provided an easy-to-use OMAP MUX to handle configuration of the BeagleBone's pins. The popularity of ARM-based microprocessers led to a proliferation of Linux kernel customizations. As a result, Linus Torvalds was unhappy with the amount of code that was being added directly to mainline Linux to describe each and every feature, for each and every ARM device being manufactured (the `board-am335xevm.c` has over 4,000 lines of code). Therefore, new ARM boards using the latest Linux kernels use *flattened device tree* (FDT) models instead, a technology which has been used by PowerPC developers for many years (Kridner, 2013).[1]

NOTE There is a video on this topic available at the chapter web page, `www.exploringbeaglebone.com/chapter6`, and `tiny.cc/ebb601`, which gives an overview of the Linux device tree on the BBB.

The Flattened Device Tree (FDT)

The *FDT* is simply a data structure that describes the hardware on the board. In the GitHub repository directory that follows, the device tree for the BBB Linux 3.8.13 kernel is made available so that you can review it:

```
~/exploringbb/chp06/deviceTree/DTSource3.8.13$ ls
am335x-bone-common.dtsi   am335x-boneblack.dts   skeleton.dtsi
am335x-bone.dts           am33xx.dtsi            tps65217.dtsi
```

In particular, examine the beginning of the file, am335x-bone-common.dtsi, as shown in Listing 6-2.

LISTING 6-2: chp06/deviceTree/DTSource3.8.13/am335x-bone-common.dtsi

```
/* Copyright (C) 2012 Texas Instruments Incorporated ... */

/include/ "am33xx.dtsi"
/ {
    model = "TI AM335x BeagleBone";
    compatible = "ti,am335x-bone", "ti,am33xx";


    cpus {
        cpu@0 {
            cpu0-supply = <&dcdc2_reg>;
        };
    };
    memory {
        device_type = "memory";
        reg = <0x80000000 0x10000000>; /* 256 MB */
    };


    am33xx_pinmux: pinmux@44e10800 {
        pinctrl-names = "default";
            pinctrl-0 = <&userled_pins>;
                userled_pins: pinmux_userled_pins {
                    pinctrl-single,pins = <
                        0x54 0x7   /* gpmc_a5.gpio1_21, OUTPUT | MODE7 */
                        0x58 0x17  /* gpmc_a6.gpio1_22, OUTPUT_PULLUP | MODE7 */
                        0x5c 0x7   /* gpmc_a7.gpio1_23, OUTPUT | MODE7 */
                        0x60 0x17  /* gpmc_a8.gpio1_24, OUTPUT_PULLUP | MODE7 */
                    >;
                };
                i2c0_pins: pinmux_i2c0_pins {
                    pinctrl-single,pins = <
                        0x188 0x70 /* i2c0_sda, SLEWCTRL_SLOW | INPUT_PULLUP | MODE0 */
                        0x18c 0x70 /* i2c0_scl, SLEWCTRL_SLOW | INPUT_PULLUP | MODE0 */
                    >;
                };
    ...
```

This file describes the CPU, memory, the USR LEDs, and the I2C0 bus. There is a full description about what each field in the FDT means at devicetree.org/ Device_Tree_Usage. Some of the values should look familiar; for example, the pinmux offset is listed as 44e10800, just as in the tables in Figures 6-6 and 6-7. You can see that the first USR LED0 is attached to GPIO1_21 at the offset 0x54 from 44e10800, as described in the same tables. Also, the pin mode is 0x07 (Fast, Output, Pull-down, Enabled, Mode 7).

This file is compiled into a binary form using a *device tree compiler* (DTC) and is placed on the Linux boot image at /boot/uboot/dtbs, as shown by the following:

```
root@beaglebone:/boot/uboot/dtbs# ls am*
am335x-boneblack.dtb   am335x-evm.dtb      am335x-tester.dtb
am335x-bone.dtb        am335x-evmsk.dtb
```

These files are used as part of the boot process. To modify the hardware that is enabled on your BBB, you could modify these DTS files, compile them using the compiler, deploy them to the boot directory, and then reboot your board. However, that would be quite onerous.

Device Tree Overlays (DTOs)

Unfortunately, the FDT is not suitable for the runtime configuration (i.e., after Linux has booted) of inputs and outputs, which in the absence of an alternative would make dynamically adding capes or adding virtual overlays to the BBB extremely problematic. Fortunately, Pantelis Antoniou (Antoniou Consulting) developed a solution for this problem using *device tree overlays* (*DTOs*) and a *cape manager* (as described at www.elinux.org/Capemgr). The best way to explain DTOs is to write one and deploy it to your BBB. For more information on the Linux device tree, see the guide at www.elinux.org/Device_Tree and Jason Kridner's guide at tiny.cc/ebb605.

Writing an Overlay

If you examine Figure 6-7, which describes the P9 header, you will see that P9_11 and P9_13 are allocated to the receiver and transmitter pins of UART4, respectively. For this example, it is assumed that you have decided to reallocate these pins to GPIO0_30 and GPIO0_31, which are Mode7 in both cases. A DTO is written as shown in Listing 6-3.

LISTING 6-3: /chp06/overlay/EBB-GPIO-Example.dts

```
/* OUTPUT  GPIO(mode7) 0x07 pulldown, 0x17 pullup, 0x?f no pullup/down */
/* INPUT   GPIO(mode7) 0x27 pulldown, 0x37 pullup, 0x?f no pullup/down */

/dts-v1/;
/plugin/;

/{
    compatible = "ti,beaglebone", "ti,beaglebone-black";
    part-number = "EBB-GPIO-Example";
    version = "00A0";
```

continues

LISTING 6-3: *(continued)*

```
fragment@0 {
    target = <&am33xx_pinmux>;

    __overlay__ {
        ebb_example: EBB_GPIO_Example {
            pinctrl-single,pins = <
                0x070 0x07  // P9_11 $28 GPIO0_30=30 Output Mode7 pulldown
                0x074 0x37  // P9_13 $29 GPIO0_31=31 Input Mode7 pullup
            >;
        };
    };
};
fragment@1 {
    target = <&ocp>;
    __overlay__ {
        gpio_helper {
            compatible = "gpio-of-helper";
            status = "okay";
            pinctrl-names = "default";
            pinctrl-0 = <&ebb_example>;
        };
    };
};
};
```

Compiling and Deploying an Overlay

On the BBB, compile the device tree source (.dts) file into a device tree blob object (.dtbo) using the device tree compiler (dtc) with the following syntax (use 00A0 as the revision number):

```
$ dtc -O dtb -o EBB-GPIO-Example-00A0.dtbo -b 0 -@ EBB-GPIO-Example.dts
```

There is a build script (build) in the overlay directory that contains this command syntax. To deploy the overlay, copy the output binary (.dtbo) file to the /lib/firmware directory on the BBB:

```
$ sudo cp EBB-GPIO-Example-00A0.dtbo /lib/firmware
```

The BBB Cape Manager

As discussed in Chapter 1, capes are expansion boards that can be plugged into the BBB. Each cape has an associated .dtbo file. Ideally, when you plug a cape into the BBB, the appropriate .dtbo file should be loaded in order to configure the P8/P9 header pins that interface to the cape. The cape manager is designed to allow capes to be loaded dynamically at run time, without the requirement to recompile the Linux kernel. The cape manager is implemented entirely in the Linux kernel, but it loads .dtbo files from the /lib/firmware directory at run time.

Loading a Device Tree Overlay

The first step that you should perform in order to use the cape manager is to set up two environment variables (please check that the paths are valid on your BBB, as they are subject to change):

```
~$ export SLOTS=/sys/devices/bone_capemgr.9/slots
~$ export PINS=/sys/kernel/debug/pinctrl/44e10800.pinmux/pins
```

Because you are likely to do this very often, you should add these two lines to your .profile file, in the home directory on the BBB. Using the call **nano ~/.profile**, add the following lines at the end of the file:

```
export SLOTS=/sys/devices/bone_capemgr.9/slots
export PINS=/sys/kernel/debug/pinctrl/44e10800.pinmux/pins
```

Then use the source command to set these environment variables. They will be automatically set when you boot. You can then check the cape manager's slots to see which capes are loaded and which pins are allocated, as follows:

```
molloyd@beaglebone:~$ source ~/.profile
molloyd@beaglebone:~$ cat $SLOTS
 0: 54:PF---
 1: 55:PF---
 2: 56:PF---
 3: 57:PF---
 4: ff:P-O-L Bone-LT-eMMC-2G,00A0,Texas Instrument,BB-BONE-EMMC-2G
 5: ff:P-O-L Bone-Black-HDMI,00A0,Texas Instrument,BB-BONELT-HDMI
molloyd@beaglebone:~$ sudo cat $PINS
registered pins: 142
pin 0 (44e10800) 00000031 pinctrl-single
...
pin 141 (44e10a34) 00000020 pinctrl-single
```

Slots 0–3 are reserved for physically attached capes, while device tree overlays (virtual capes) will receive higher slot allocations. You can get further details about the occupied slots using the files in the cape's sysfs directory—for example:

```
molloyd@beaglebone:$ cd /sys/devices/bone_capemgr.9/
molloyd@beaglebone:/sys/devices/bone_capemgr.9$ ls
baseboard  modalias  slot-4  slot-7  slots      uevent
driver     power     slot-5  slot-8  subsystem
```

The slot numbers will differ depending on the real and virtual capes attached to the BBB. Use the following to find out further details about the overlay at slot 7:

```
molloyd@beaglebone:/sys/devices/bone_capemgr.9$ cd slot-7/
molloyd@beaglebone:/sys/devices/bone_capemgr.9/slot-7$ ls
board-name              header         part-number    sys-5v        version
dc-supplied             manufacturer   pin-usage      vdd-3v3exp
eeprom-format-revision  number-of-pins serial-number  vdd-5v
```

As discussed in Chapter 3, environment variables do not transfer to the root user session. To fix this permanently for SLOTS and PINS, log in as root and type **visudo**. Under the line containing env_reset, set sudo to retain the SLOTS and PINS environment variables on a **su** call:

```
Defaults        env_reset
Defaults        env_keep += "SLOTS"
Defaults        env_keep += "PINS"
```

Save the changes, and use the following (do *not* use **sudo su -**) and you will see that the variables have been transferred to the root user session. Then, load the new overlay, BBB-GPIO-Example, as follows:

```
molloyd@beaglebone:/lib/firmware$ sudo su
root@beaglebone:/lib/firmware# echo EBB-GPIO-Example > $SLOTS
root@beaglebone:/lib/firmware# cat $SLOTS
 0: 54:PF---
 1: 55:PF---
 2: 56:PF---
 3: 57:PF---
 4: ff:P-O-L Bone-LT-eMMC-2G,00A0,Texas Instrument,BB-BONE-EMMC-2G
 5: ff:P-O-L Bone-Black-HDMI,00A0,Texas Instrument,BB-BONELT-HDMI
 6: ff:P-O-L Override Board Name,00A0,Override Manuf,EBB-GPIO-Example
```

The overlay has been loaded in slot number 6. You can test that the overlay has been loaded correctly by viewing the slots and/or by typing **dmesg|more** to see the log as the virtual cape was being attached to the slot—for example, by using **dmesg|grep EBB** in this case.

Finally, to test that the overlay is working correctly (remembering that P9_11 is $PINS 28 and P9_13 is $PINS29) you can perform the following:

```
root@beaglebone:/lib/firmware# cat $PINS |more
registered pins: 142
pin 0 (44e10800) 00000031 pinctrl-single
...
pin 28 (44e10870) 00000007 pinctrl-single
pin 29 (44e10874) 00000037 pinctrl-single
```

The pins are set up exactly as requested in the device tree overlay file in Listing 6-3, with P9_11 set to mode 0x07 and P9_13 set to mode 0x37.

Removing an Overlay

You can remove an overlay from a slot by passing the minus sign, followed by the slot number, to the cape manager, as follows:

```
root@beaglebone:/lib/firmware# echo -6 > $SLOTS
root@beaglebone:/lib/firmware# cat $SLOTS
 0: 54:PF---
 1: 55:PF---
 2: 56:PF---
 3: 57:PF---
 4: ff:P-O-L Bone-LT-eMMC-2G,00A0,Texas Instrument,BB-BONE-EMMC-2G
 5: ff:P-O-L Bone-Black-HDMI,00A0,Texas Instrument,BB-BONELT-HDMI
```

This procedure works for most slots, but at the time of writing, this can lock up the Linux terminal for certain capes, requiring a reboot of the BBB. The HDMI and eMMC overlays occupy many of the P8/P9 header pins and the overlays must be removed in order to access the alternative pins. Disabling the HDMI cape or eMMC is not so straightforward, as you must modify the uEnv.txt file, using Notepad++ (the ordinary Notepad will not work correctly) or a similar application, or directly on the BBB as follows:

```
molloyd@beaglebone:/media$ sudo mkdir /mnt/vfat
molloyd@beaglebone:/media$ sudo mount /dev/mmcblk0p1 /mnt/vfat
molloyd@beaglebone:/media$ cd /mnt/vfat/
molloyd@beaglebone:/mnt/vfat$ sudo nano uEnv.txt
```

Uncomment the following line, but be careful not to uncomment the similar HDMI/eMMC line, or your BBB will not boot from the eMMC:

```
##Disable HDMI
optargs=capemgr.disable_partno=BB-BONELT-HDMI,BB-BONELT-HDMIN
```

Unmount the file system and reboot:

```
molloyd@beaglebone:/mnt/vfat$ cd ..
molloyd@beaglebone:/mnt$ sudo umount /mnt/vfat
molloyd@beaglebone:/mnt$ sudo reboot
molloyd@beaglebone:~$ cat $SLOTS
...
 4: ff:P-O-L Bone-LT-eMMC-2G,00A0,Texas Instrument,BB-BONE-EMMC-2G
 5: ff:P-O--- Bone-Black-HDMI,00A0,Texas Instrument,BB-BONELT-HDMI
 6: ff:P-O--- Bone-Black-HDMIN,00A0,Texas Instrument,BB-BONELT-HDMIN
```

The letter "L" means that the cape is enabled, so if it is absent then the cape is disabled. If you need to disable the eMMC in order to use the header pins that it occupies, be aware that the BBB must be booted from an SD card. If you introduce an error into your uEnv.txt file, then the BBB may not boot. See the note near the middle of Chapter 3 on how to fix such a problem.

There are many overlays on the BBB in the `/lib/firmware` directory. For example, there are overlays to enable the I²C and SPI buses that are needed in Chapter 8:

```
root@beaglebone:/lib/firmware# ls BB-SPI*
BB-SPIDEV0-00A0.dtbo   BB-SPIDEV1-00A0.dtbo   BB-SPIDEV1A1-00A0.dtbo
```

Loading an Overlay on Boot

If you wish to load an overlay every time the board boots, modify the `uEnv.txt` file as just discussed, and add a new `optargs` line:

```
##Disable HDMI
#optargs=capemgr.disable_partno=BB-BONELT-HDMI,BB-BONELT-HDMIN
optargs=capemgr.enable_partno=BB-SPIDEV0
```

After reboot you will see that there is a new virtual cape in the next free slot:

```
molloyd@beaglebone:~$ cat $SLOTS
 ..
 4: ff:P-O-L Bone-LT-eMMC-2G,00A0,Texas Instrument,BB-BONE-EMMC-2G
 5: ff:P-O-L Bone-Black-HDMI,00A0,Texas Instrument,BB-BONELT-HDMI
 7: ff:P-O-L Override Board Name,00A0,Override Manuf,BB-SPIDEV0
```

You may have to disable the SPI overlay to follow the steps in the next section; otherwise, the terminal may crash and the BBB may need to be rebooted.

NOTE The cape manager is currently work in progress and is subject to change. At the time of writing, it is not possible to load your own custom overlay on boot without rebuilding the Linux kernel. This problem and the issues with terminal lock-up on removal of capes should be corrected over time. In fact, it is likely that more user-friendly interfaces will be developed to configure pin settings.

Analog Inputs and Outputs

In Chapter 4, the concept of analog-to-digital conversion (ADC) is introduced and an operational amplifier voltage-follower circuit is described that can be used to safely read analog inputs. The next section describes how you can interface such a circuit to the BBB and use Linux `sysfs` to read values into your software applications.

Analog Inputs

The AM335x has a 12-bit successive approximation register (SAR) ADC that is capable of 200,000 samples per second. The input to the SAR is internally selected using an 8:1 analog switch, and the BBB makes seven of these switched inputs available on the P9 header as ADC inputs. Among other things, the analog inputs can be configured to be used as a four-wire, five-wire, or eight-wire resistive touch screen controller (TSC), and this application is used in Chapter 11. In the present section, the ADC inputs are used as simple one-wire ADC inputs. By default, these inputs are not enabled on the BBB, so the first step is to enable them.

Enabling the Analog Inputs

The analog inputs can be enabled with the use of the cape manager to load a DTO, as follows:

```
molloyd@beaglebone:~$ cd /sys/bus/iio
/sys/bus/iio$ ls
devices  drivers  drivers_autoprobe  drivers_probe  uevent
/sys/bus/iio$ cd devices/
/sys/bus/iio/devices$ ls
iio_sysfs_trigger
/sys/bus/iio/devices$ sudo sh -c "echo BB-ADC > $SLOTS"
/sys/bus/iio/devices$ cat $SLOTS
...
 4: ff:P-O-L Bone-LT-eMMC-2G,00A0,Texas Instrument,BB-BONE-EMMC-2G
 5: ff:P-O-L Bone-Black-HDMI,00A0,Texas Instrument,BB-BONELT-HDMI
 7: ff:P-O-L Override Board Name,00A0,Override Manuf,BB-ADC
```

Once you attach the BB-ADC overlay to the slot, you will see that there is now a new entry in the devices directory, in which you will find file entries that allow you to read the raw ADC values directly:

```
/sys/bus/iio/devices$ ls
iio:device0  iio_sysfs_trigger
molloyd@beaglebone:/sys/bus/iio/devices$ cd iio:device0
molloyd@beaglebone:/sys/bus/iio/devices/iio:device0$ ls
buffer           in_voltage2_raw  in_voltage6_raw  scan_elements
dev              in_voltage3_raw  in_voltage7_raw  subsystem
in_voltage0_raw  in_voltage4_raw  name             trigger
in_voltage1_raw  in_voltage5_raw  power            uevent
```

If you read the analog input (AIN0), using cat in_voltage0_raw, when nothing is connected, the result will be an integer value between 0 and 4,095. The BBB has 12-bit ADCs (2^{12} = 4,096), meaning a value between 0 and $2^{12} - 1$ (0 to 4,095) will be returned. You can test this by using the following:

```
/sys/bus/iio/devices/iio:device0$ cat in_voltage0_raw
3831
/sys/bus/iio/devices/iio:device0$ cat in_voltage0_raw
3847
```

Next, a simple light-level meter application is built to demonstrate how you can attach sensor circuits to the BBB that can be used for sampling and data-logging applications.

Input Application—A Simple Light Meter

To choose a suitable pairing resistor value R for a *typical light-dependent resistor* (LDR) voltage divider circuit, a good rule of thumb is to use the equation $R = \sqrt{R_{MIN} \times R_{MAX}}$, where R_{MIN} is the measured resistance of the LDR when it is covered (e.g., with your finger) and R_{MAX} is the measured resistance of the LDR when a light source (e.g., phone torch app) is close to its surface. In this example, the resistance of the LDR was $6\,k\Omega$ when covered and $100\,\Omega$ when the light source was close. The preceding formula thus gives a value for R of $775\,\Omega$, so the combination of a $470\,\Omega$ and a $330\,\Omega$ resistor in series provides a suitable value for the potential divider. You could wire the circuit as shown in Figure 6-9, but it is not a recommended configuration.

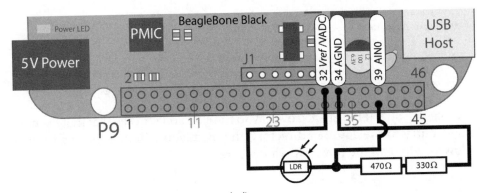

Figure 6-9: ADC LDR circuit (not recommended)

NOTE If you are following this chapter by building the circuits, do not disassemble the LED and button circuits, as they are required later in this chapter.

The problem with the circuit in Figure 6-9 is that it will draw a current from the *Vref*/VADC(P9_32) pin and act as a variable load. The resistance between *Vref* and AGND varies from $900\,\Omega$ in the brightest case to $6.8\,k\Omega$ in the darkest case. In the brightest case, because *Vref* = 1.8 V, this means that the current being sourced from *Vref*, $I = 1.8\,V/900\,\Omega = 2\,mA$. If you were to wire seven separate circuits like this one, you could end up sourcing up to 14 mA from *Vref*, which could damage the BBB. The AM335x analog front end (AFE) switches between inputs, but the supply voltage will remain powered for all seven circuits. Even if the current is not large enough to damage the BBB, drawing current from

Vref will affect the voltage level of the reference voltage itself, which defeats the purpose of having a reference voltage.

To avoid drawing any significant current from the BBB 1.8 V *Vref*, an op-amp voltage-follower circuit can be used. This op-amp configuration is discussed in Chapter 4. The implementation described in Figure 6-10 uses a LM358P (dual op-amp) IC, where V_{CC} is connected to the SYS_5V rail (DC_3.3V could also have been used) and the positive input (2IN+) to the second op-amp is the BBB 1.8 V analog reference voltage *Vref*/VADC(P9_32).

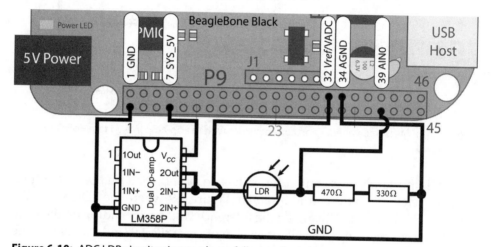

Figure 6-10: ADC LDR circuit using a voltage-follower circuit (recommended)

The raw voltage levels can be read from the ADC using `sysfs`. For the following sample values, the first reading was taken at regular room light levels, the second reading was taken with the LDR surface covered, and the third reading was taken with a light source very close to the sensor:

```
/sys/bus/iio/devices/iio:device0# cat in_voltage0_raw
959
/sys/bus/iio/devices/iio:device0# cat in_voltage0_raw
304
/sys/bus/iio/devices/iio:device0# cat in_voltage0_raw
3651
```

The circuit provides a good range of decimal input values, due to the resistor calculation at the start of this section. The current required for input offset and input biasing is typically 2 nA and 20 nA, respectively, for the LM358, meaning that it will not draw any significant current from the BBB *Vref* pin (P9_32). The actual measured voltage and current values for this circuit are displayed in Figure 6-11, where the "light level" as read from `in_voltage0_raw` was the value

3,466. It should be clear from this figure that there is almost no current being sourced from or sinked to the analog *Vref, AGND,* or *AIN0* pins, even though the current flowing through the LDR was about 2 mA (as the light level in the room was bright and the LDR resistance was low).

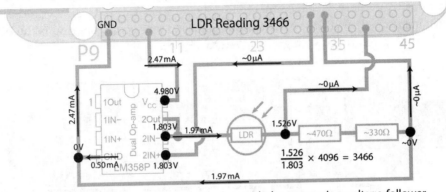

Figure 6-11: Measured voltages and current values with the op-amp in a voltage-follower configuration

Very importantly, this configuration has no *loading effect* on the *Vref* output. This is in contrast to the configuration in Figure 6-9, where the LDR and resistors load the *Vref* output, skewing the reference voltage depending on the load, which varies according to the light level. Note that the 1.97 mA current on the bottom GND rail was the current returning to the grounding point (it behaves exactly like the return connection from the resistor in Figure 4-2(a)).

Here is a simple C++ application that reads in the LDR value. It is structured so that it reads a single value from any of the AIN pins, by passing the pin number (0–6) to the readAnalog() function:

```
~/exploringbb/chp06/ADC# more readLDR.cpp
#include<iostream>
#include<fstream>
#include<string>
#include<sstream>
using namespace std;

#define LDR_PATH "/sys/bus/iio/devices/iio:device0/in_voltage"

int readAnalog(int number){    // returns the input as an int
    stringstream ss;
    ss << LDR_PATH << number << "_raw";
    fstream fs;
    fs.open(ss.str().c_str(), fstream::in);
    fs >> number;
    fs.close();
    return number;
}
```

```
int main(int argc, char* argv[]){
   cout << "Starting the readLDR program" << endl;
   int value = readAnalog(0);
   cout << "The LDR value was " << value << " out of 4095." << endl;
   return 0;
}
~/exploringbb/chp06/ADC# g++ readLDR.cpp -o readLDR
~/exploringbb/chp06/ADC# ./readLDR
Starting the readLDR program
The LDR value was 463 out of 4095.
```

This code works perfectly for reading a sensor occasionally, but it is not very good for reading a sensor many times per second.

Analog Outputs (PWM)

The next functionality to be examined is the use of the BBB's pulse-width modulation (PWM) outputs to provide low-frequency digital-to-analog conversion (DAC), or for the generation of control signals for motors and certain types of servos. There are eight PWM outputs, three eHRPWM modules (two outputs each), and two eCAP modules. These outputs are described in Figures 6-6 and 6-7, where you can see that the six eHRPWM outputs are each available on two separate pins (e.g., output 2B is available on P8_13 and P8_46). Like the ADC functionality, the PWM pins are enabled using overlays, which are available in the /lib/firmware directory:

```
/lib/firmware$ ls bone_pwm*
bone_pwm_P8_13-00A0.dtbo bone_pwm_P8_46-00A0.dtbo
bone_pwm_P9_28-00A0.dtbo bone_pwm_P8_19-00A0.dtbo
bone_pwm_P9_14-00A0.dtbo bone_pwm_P9_29-00A0.dtbo
bone_pwm_P8_34-00A0.dtbo bone_pwm_P9_16-00A0.dtbo
bone_pwm_P9_31-00A0.dtbo bone_pwm_P8_36-00A0.dtbo
bone_pwm_P9_21-00A0.dtbo bone_pwm_P9_42-00A0.dtbo
bone_pwm_P8_45-00A0.dtbo bone_pwm_P9_22-00A0.dtbo
```

To enable P9_22 as a PWM output, you have to pass two separate overlays to the cape manager (you may have to remove the BB-ADC overlay):

```
/lib/firmware$ sudo sh -c "echo bone_pwm_P9_22 > $SLOTS"
/lib/firmware$ sudo sh -c "echo am33xx_pwm > $SLOTS"
/lib/firmware$ cat $SLOTS
...
 4: ff:P-O-L Bone-LT-eMMC-2G,00A0,Texas Instrument,BB-BONE-EMMC-2G
 5: ff:P-O-L Bone-Black-HDMI,00A0,Texas Instrument,BB-BONELT-HDMI
 7: ff:P-O-L Override Board Name,00A0,Override Manuf,bone_pwm_P9_22
 8: ff:P-O-L Override Board Name,00A0,Override Manuf,am33xx_pwm
```

The HDMI cape is blocking several of the PWM outputs. For example, if you try to load the P8_34 overlay and HDMI is enabled you will see the following:

```
/lib/firmware$ sudo sh -c "echo bone_pwm_P8_34 > $SLOTS"
bash: echo: write error: File exists
```

If you follow the steps for disabling HDMI provided earlier in the chapter, you can then load the PWM overlay and it should function without error.

To access the properties of the PWM output, change to the following directory and you will see the available options:

```
molloyd@beaglebone:~$ cd /sys/devices/ocp.3/pwm_test_P9_22.15/
molloyd@beaglebone:/sys/devices/ocp.3/pwm_test_P9_22.15$ ls -l
total 0
lrwxrwxrwx 1 root root    0 May  7 12:41 driver -> ...
-rw------- 1 root root 4096 May  7 12:41 duty
-r--r--r-- 1 root root 4096 May  7 12:41 modalias
-rw------- 1 root root 4096 May  7 12:41 period
-rw------- 1 root root 4096 May  7 12:41 polarity
drwxr-xr-x 2 root root    0 May  7 12:41 power
-rw------- 1 root root 4096 May  7 12:41 run
lrwxrwxrwx 1 root root    0 May  7 12:27 subsystem -> ...
-rw-r--r-- 1 root root 4096 May  7 12:27 uevent
```

To set up a PWM signal, the period is supplied in nanoseconds. Therefore, to output a PWM signal that has a period of 10 µs and a 50% duty cycle, you set the time period and not the duty cycle percentage:

```
/sys/devices/ocp.3/pwm_test_P9_22.15$ sudo su
/sys/devices/ocp.3/pwm_test_P9_22.15# echo 5000 > duty
/sys/devices/ocp.3/pwm_test_P9_22.15# echo 10000 > period
/sys/devices/ocp.3/pwm_test_P9_22.15# echo 1 > run
```

If you connect a DMM between the P9_22 pin and GND, the voltage measured with a 5,000 duty period should be 1.657 V when the duty period is set as 5,000 and the period is set at 10,000 (that is, the output is 3.314 V for half of each cycle and 0 V for the other half, and the DMM averages this to 1.657 V). Changing the duty cycle period results in the following DMM measurements by default: $0 \rightarrow 3.314$ V, $2500 \rightarrow 2.485$ V, $7500 \rightarrow 0.828$ V, and $10,000 \rightarrow 0.6$ mV. This relationship can be inverted (i.e., $10,000 \rightarrow 3.314$ V) by changing the polarity using `echo 0 > polarity`. Setting these values provides you with DAC capability that can be combined with an optocoupler or transistor to limit the current drawn from the GPIO pin.

The duty cycle has to be lower than the period, so set it first if you are decreasing the period; otherwise, you will get an error "Invalid argument." Figures 6-12 and 6-13 display the output of the BBB when PWM signals of 100 kHz and 1 MHz, respectively, are specified.

An unwanted oscillation of the voltage signal, known as *ringing,* is clearly visible in Figure 6-12(b) in the step response at 1 MHz. However, many applications for which PWM is used require comparatively low frequencies, so this is not a problem. For example, to control a typical servo motor, periods of tens of milliseconds are required (i.e., less than 100 Hz).

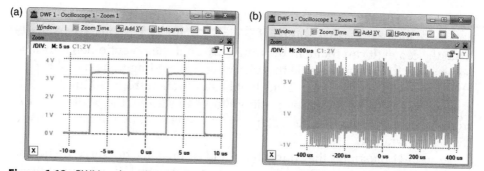

Figure 6-12: PWM cycle with period 10,000 ns (100 kHz) and duty cycle of 50%

A C++ class called PWM is provided in the GitHub repository for setting up a PWM signal or outputting an analog voltage. The code requires that a suitable DTO is applied, and the PWM pin name is passed to the constructor of the PWM class. For example, use the following to perform the previous steps (see chp06/API/gpio/PWM.h):

```
PWM pwm("pwm_test_P9_22.15");    //create the PWM object
pwm.setPeriod(10000);            //set the period in ns
pwm.setDutyCycle(50.0f);         //can use percentage or time in ns
pwm.setPolarity(PWM::ACTIVE_LOW);    //ACTIVE_LOW or ACTIVE_HIGH
pwm.run();                       //start the output
```

Or, to output an analog voltage on P9_22:

```
PWM pwm("pwm_test_P9_22.15");    //create the PWM object
pwm.calibrateAnalogMax(3.318);   //defaults to 3.3V
pwm.analogWrite(1.25);           //DMM will give ~1.25V on P9_22
```

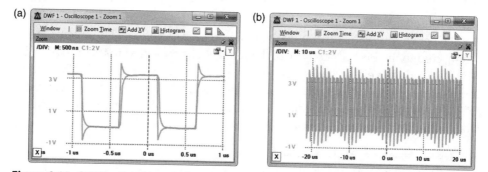

Figure 6-13: PWM cycle with period 1,000 ns (1 MHz) and duty cycle of 50%

Output Application—Controlling a Servo Motor

Servo motors consist of a DC motor that is attached to a potentiometer and a control circuit. The position of the motor shaft can be controlled by sending a PWM signal to the controller.

The Hitec HS-422 is a low-cost (less than $10), good quality, and widely available servo motor that can be supplied using a 5 V supply. It is rated to rotate ±45° from the center. It can rotate in the range ±90°, but the potentiometer does not behave in a linear way outside the ±45° range. According to its datasheet, the HS-422 expects a pulse every 20 ms that has a duration from 1100 μs (to set the position to –45° from the center position) to 1900 μs (to set the position to +45° from the center position). The center position can be set by passing a pulse of 1500 μs in duration.

Figure 6-14 illustrates the connections and timings for the servo motor that enables it to rotate from –90° using a pulse of 570 μs to +90° using a pulse of 2350 μs. These values and the center point of 1460 μs were manually calibrated, and will vary for each individual servo motor.

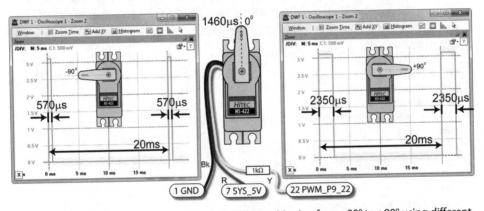

Figure 6-14: Controlling a servo motor using PWM, positioning from –90° to +90° using different pulse widths

The servo motor has three leads: black, red, and yellow. The black lead is connected to the BBB GND (P9_01); the red lead is connected to the BBB SYS_5V (P9_07); and the yellow lead is connected via a 1 kΩ resistor to the PWM output (ehrpwm0A) on the BBB (P9_22). The 1 kΩ resistor limits the current sourced from P9_22 to about 0.01 mA. To manually control a servo motor using sysfs, perform the following steps (as the root user):

```
~# echo bone_pwm_P9_22 > $SLOTS
~# echo am33xx_pwm > $SLOTS
/lib/firmware# cd /sys/devices/ocp.3/pwm_test_P9_22.15/
/sys/devices/ocp.3/pwm_test_P9_22.15# ls
driver  duty  modalias  period  polarity  power  run  subsystem  uevent
```

The polarity value should be set to 0 for servo motors, so that the duty value represents the duration of a high pulse. If the polarity value is 1, then the signal is inverted and the duty value would effectively specify the duration of a low pulse, with the signal being high for the remainder of the period. The period is set to 20 ms and the output is enabled:

```
/sys/devices/ocp.3/pwm_test_P9_22.15# echo 0 > polarity
/sys/devices/ocp.3/pwm_test_P9_22.15# echo 20000000 > period
/sys/devices/ocp.3/pwm_test_P9_22.15# echo 1 > run
```

The arm can be rotated to –90°, followed by 0°, and then +90°, with the last step turning off the output, removing the holding torque, and reducing the power consumption of the motor:

```
/sys/devices/ocp.3/pwm_test_P9_22.15# echo 570000 > duty
/sys/devices/ocp.3/pwm_test_P9_22.15# echo 1460000 > duty
/sys/devices/ocp.3/pwm_test_P9_22.15# echo 2350000 > duty
/sys/devices/ocp.3/pwm_test_P9_22.15# echo 0 > run
```

Advanced GPIO Topics

One serious problem with the GPIO digital input application described earlier is that it requires the sysfs file to be repeatedly polled in order to determine whether a change in its state has occurred. This is processor intensive, or prone to long latency if the frequency of the checks is reduced. This section examines how this problem can be addressed using two different techniques. The first technique involves a significant enhancement of the GPIO C++ class, and the second uses the Linux GPIO-KEYS driver.

More C++ Programming

To understand the first technique, it is necessary to examine some additional programming concepts in C/C++ that are to be used, and which can be applied generally to enhance your BBB applications. Callback function, POSIX threads, and use of Linux system polling can be used to create a highly efficient GPIO poll that has negligible CPU overhead and fast response times (i.e., less than 0.5 ms). The GPIO class that is written for this chapter is enhanced to support this functionality so an overview of these programming techniques is all that you require.

Callback Functions

Chapter 2 describes the use of callback functions as they are used in Node.js with asynchronous function calls. Essentially, a *callback function* (or *listener function*) is a function that is executed when some type of event occurs. This is vital for asynchronous function calls like those in JavaScript, but it is also useful in C++ applications. For example, in the enhanced GPIO class, this structure is used so that a function can be executed when a physical button is pressed.

Callback functions are typically implemented in C++ using function pointers. *Function pointers* are pointers that store the address of a function. It is possible to pass these pointers to other functions, which can dereference the function pointer and call the function that is passed. This is demonstrated with the code example in Listing 6-4.

LISTING 6-4: /chp06/callback/callback.cpp

```
typedef int (*CallbackType)(int);

// some function that receives a callback function
int doSomething(CallbackType callback){
   return callback(10);  //execute callback function, pass 10
}

// the callback function that receives an int value
int callbackFunction(int var){
   cout << "I am the Callback Function! var=" << var << endl;
   return 2*var;
}

int main() {
   cout << "Hello BeagleBone" << endl;
   // pass the address of the callbackFunction() to doSomething()
   int y = doSomething(&callbackFunction);
   cout << "Value of y is: " << y << endl;
}
```

Creating a type using `typedef` simply makes it easier to change the type at a later stage and cleans up the syntax somewhat. The address of the `call-backFunction()` is passed as a pointer to the `doSomething()` function. When executed, the output of this code is as follows:

```
Hello BeagleBone
I am the Callback Function! var=10
Value of y is: 20
```

This programming structure is quite common in (and underneath) user-interface programming, where functions can be called when a user interacts with display user-interface components such as buttons and menus. It makes sense to apply the same structure to physical push buttons and switches.

POSIX Threads

POSIX threads (Pthreads) is a set of C functions, types, and constants that provides everything you need in order to implement threading within your C/C++ applications on the BBB. Adding *threading* to your code allows parts of your code to execute apparently concurrently (the BBB has a single core processor), with each thread receiving a "slice" of processing time.

To use Pthreads in your application you need to include the `pthread.h` header file and use the `-pthread` flag when compiling and linking the code using gcc/g++.[1] All the Pthread functions are prefixed with `pthread_`. Listing 6-5 is an example of using Pthreads on the BBB to create two parallel counters (the comments describe the structure of the code):

LISTING 6-5: /chp06/pthreads/pthreads.cpp

```cpp
#include <iostream>
#include <pthread.h>
#include <unistd.h>
using namespace std;


// Thread function that will execute when the thread is created
//  it passes and receives data by void pointers (See Chapter 5)
void *threadFunction(void *value){
   int *x = (int *)value; // cast the data passed to an int pointer
   while(*x<5){            // while the value of x is less than 5
      usleep(1000);        // sleep for 1ms - encourage main thread
      (*x)++;              // increment the value of x by 1
   }
   return x;               // return the pointer x (as a void*)
}


int main() {              // the main thread
   int x=0, y=0;
   pthread_t thread;      // this is our handle to the pthread
   // create thread, pass reference, addr of the function and data
   if(pthread_create(&thread, NULL, &threadFunction, &x)){
      cout << "Failed to create the thread" << endl;
      return 1;
   }
   // at this point the thread was created successfully
   while(y<5){                    // loop and increment y, displaying values
      cout << "The value of x=" << x << " and y=" << y++ << endl;
      usleep(1000);               // encourage the pthread to run
   }
   void* result;                  // OPTIONAL: receive data back from pthread
```

continues

LISTING 6-5: *(continued)*

```
pthread_join(thread, &result);    // allow the pthread to complete
int *z = (int *) result;          // cast from void* to int* to get z
cout << "Final: x=" << x << ", y=" << y << " and z=" << *z << endl;
return 0;
}
```

Building and executing as follows will result in the following output:

```
~/exploringbb/chp06/pthreads$ g++ -pthread pthreads.cpp -o pthreads
~/exploringbb/chp06/pthreads$ ./pthreads
The value of x=0 and y=0
The value of x=0 and y=1
The value of x=1 and y=2
The value of x=2 and y=3
The value of x=3 and y=4
Final: x=5, y=5 and z=5
```

Run it again, and you may get a different output!

```
The value of x=0 and y=0
The value of x=1 and y=1
The value of x=1 and y=2
The value of x=2 and y=3
The value of x=3 and y=4
Final: x=5, y=5 and z=5
```

The code may result in a slightly different result each time. The `usleep()` calls have been introduced to encourage the thread manager to switch to the main thread at that point. While the order of the output may change, the final results will always be consistent due to the `pthread_join()` function call, which blocks execution at this point until the thread has run to completion.

Linux poll (sys/poll.h)

At the beginning of this chapter, code is presented that can be used to detect the state of a button by checking the state of the `value` file. This is a very processor-intensive operation and not really practical. If you listed the contents of the `/sys/class/gpio` directory you may have also noticed a file entry called `edge` that up to now has had no relevance:

```
molloyd@beaglebone:/sys/class/gpio$ sudo sh -c "echo 115 > export"
molloyd@beaglebone:/sys/class/gpio$ cd gpio115
molloyd@beaglebone:/sys/class/gpio/gpio115$ ls
active_low  direction  edge  power  subsystem  uevent  value
```

You can use a system function called `poll()` from the `sys/poll.h` header file, which has the syntax

```
int poll(struct pollfd *ufds, unsigned int nfds, int timeout);
```

where the first argument specifies a pointer to an array of `pollfd` structures, each of which identifies a file entry to be monitored and the type of event to be monitored (e.g., `EPOLLIN` to read operations, `EPOLLET` edge triggered, and `EPOLLPRI` for urgent data). The next argument, `nfds`, identifies how many elements are in the first argument array. The final argument identifies a timeout in milliseconds. If this value is `-1`, then the kernel will wait forever for the activity identified in the array. This code has been added to the following enhanced GPIO class in the `waitForEdge()` methods.

Enhanced GPIO Class

The programming concepts just discussed are complex and may be difficult to understand if it is your first time seeing them; however, these techniques have been used to enhance the GPIO class so that it is faster and more efficient than before. The code in Listing 6-6 integrates the earlier GPIO functionality and the programming concepts that have been just introduced. The public interface methods are also provided.

LISTING 6-6: /chp06/GPIO/GPIO.h

```
#define GPIO_PATH "/sys/class/gpio/"
namespace exploringBB {

typedef int (*CallbackType)(int);
enum GPIO_DIRECTION{ INPUT, OUTPUT };
enum GPIO_VALUE{ LOW=0, HIGH=1 };
enum GPIO_EDGE{ NONE, RISING, FALLING, BOTH };

class GPIO {
private:
   int number, debounceTime;
   string name, path;
public:
   GPIO(int number); //constructor will export the pin
   virtual int getNumber() { return number; }

   // General Input and Output Settings
   virtual int setDirection(GPIO_DIRECTION);
```

continues

LISTING 6-6: *(continued)*

```
virtual GPIO_DIRECTION getDirection();
virtual int setValue(GPIO_VALUE);
virtual int toggleOutput();
virtual GPIO_VALUE getValue();
virtual int setActiveLow(bool isLow=true);   //low=1, high=0
virtual int setActiveHigh(); //default
//software debounce input (ms) - default 0
virtual void setDebounceTime(int time) { this->debounceTime = time; }


// Advanced OUTPUT: Faster write by keeping the stream alive (~20X)
virtual int streamOpen();
virtual int streamWrite(GPIO_VALUE);
virtual int streamClose();


virtual int toggleOutput(int time); //threaded invert output every X ms.
virtual int toggleOutput(int numberOfTimes, int time);
virtual void changeToggleTime(int time) { this->togglePeriod = time; }
virtual void toggleCancel() { this->threadRunning = false; }


// Advanced INPUT: Detect input edges; threaded and non-threaded
virtual int setEdgeType(GPIO_EDGE);
virtual GPIO_EDGE getEdgeType();
virtual int waitForEdge(); // waits until button is pressed
virtual int waitForEdge(CallbackType callback); // threaded with callback
virtual void waitForEdgeCancel() { this->threadRunning = false; }


virtual ~GPIO();   //destructor will unexport the pin
...
} /* namespace exploringBB */
```

The tests to evaluate the performance of the class are provided as examples of how to use this class. The test circuit is the combination of the button circuit in Figure 6-4 and the LED circuit in Figure 6-2. Therefore, the button is attached to P9_27 (GPIO 115) and the LED is attached to P9_23 (GPIO 49). In these tests, the LED will light when the button is pressed.

Listing 6-7 tests the performance of a synchronous poll that forces the program to wait for the button to be pressed before proceeding.

LISTING 6-7: /chp06/GPIO/tests/test_syspoll.cpp

```
#include<iostream>
#include"GPIO.h"
using namespace exploringBB;
using namespace std;
```

```
int main(){
   if(getuid()!=0){
      cout << "You must run this program as root. Exiting." << endl;
      return -1;
   }
   GPIO outGPIO(49), inGPIO(115);
   inGPIO.setDirection(INPUT);       // button is an input
   outGPIO.setDirection(OUTPUT);     // LED is an output
   inGPIO.setEdgeType(RISING);       // wait for rising edge
   outGPIO.streamOpen();             // fast write, ready file
   outGPIO.streamWrite(LOW);         // turn the LED off
   cout << "Press the button:" << endl;
   inGPIO.waitForEdge();             // will wait here forever
   outGPIO.streamWrite(HIGH);        // button pressed, light LED
   outGPIO.streamClose();            // close the output stream
   return 0;
}
```

The response time of this code is captured in Figure 6-15(a). This code runs with a ~0% CPU load, as the polling is handled efficiently by the Linux kernel. Using an oscilloscope, the electrical response time is measured between the first rising edge of the button press and the LED turning on. This program responds in 0.327 ms, which is well within physical debounce filter times. Using the class's debounce filter will not affect this performance, only the delay between repeated button presses. The downside of this code is that the program cannot perform other operations while awaiting the button press.

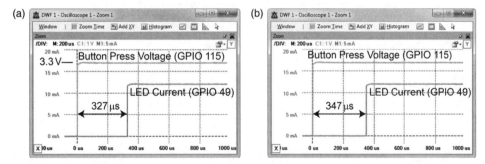

Figure 6-15: Time delay in lighting an LED in response to a button press at ~0% CPU usage (a) using sys/poll.h (b) integrating callback functions and Pthreads

The second example, in Listing 6-8, tests the performance of an asynchronous call to the `waitForEdge()` method, which accepts a function pointer and uses Pthreads to free up the program to perform other operations. In this example the main thread sleeps, but it could be performing other tasks.

LISTING 6-8: /chp06/GPIO/tests/test_callback.cpp

```cpp
#include<iostream>
#include<unistd.h>                 // for usleep
#include"GPIO.h"
using namespace exploringBB;
using namespace std;

GPIO *outGPIO, *inGPIO;            // global pointers

int activateLED(int var){          // the callback function
   outGPIO->streamWrite(HIGH);     // turn on the LED
   cout << "Button Pressed" << endl;
   return 0;
}

int main(){
   if(getuid()!=0){
      cout << "You must run this program as root. Exiting." << endl;
      return -1;
   }
   inGPIO = new GPIO(115);         // button
   outGPIO = new GPIO(49);         // LED
   inGPIO->setDirection(INPUT);    // button is an input
   outGPIO->setDirection(OUTPUT);  // LED is an output
   outGPIO->streamOpen();          // fast write to LED
   outGPIO->streamWrite(LOW);      // turn the LED off
   inGPIO->setEdgeType(RISING);    // wait for rising edge
   cout << "You have 10 seconds to press the button:" << endl;
   inGPIO->waitForEdge(&activateLED); // pass the function
   cout << "Listening, but also doing something else..." << endl;
   usleep(10000000);               // allow 10 seconds
   outGPIO->streamWrite(LOW);      // then turn the LED off
   outGPIO->streamClose();         // shutdown
   return 0;
}
```

The significant change in this code is that when the setEdgeType() method is called, a new thread is created within the method and it immediately returns control so that the main thread can continue to perform operations. The main thread simply sleeps for 10 seconds in this case before turning off the LED. If the button is pressed, the activateLED() function will be called. Whether the button is pressed or not, the LED will be turned off and the program will exit after the sleep has finished.

The response time of this code is captured in Figure 6-15(b) and it is only marginally slower than the previous code (by 20 µs), which is the cost of the callback function and the Pthreads code. Again, this code has no significant load on the CPU. The full implementation code is available in the GPIO.cpp file, and it can be edited to suit your needs. A more advanced version would use *functors* (function objects) and the C++ Standard Template Library (STL) to remove the requirement for global variables for the callback code.

GPIO-KEYS

An alternative to the enhanced GPIO code just presented is to use a GPIO-KEYS overlay, which results in a new Linux device that acts like a keyboard. The device can be interrogated for key events, but it requires a custom overlay. The example in Listing 6-9 builds a single button keyboard, using P9_15 (GPIO48), but it can be extended to have many keys. Please note that this code has been written using the LCD7 Cape DTO as a reference. The overlays for the various capes provide excellent examples of the DTO syntax to be used. Use the following command to download a comprehensive set of cape sources:

```
$ git clone https://github.com/jadonk/cape-firmware.git
```

LISTING 6-9: /chp06/BONE-KEYS/BB-BONE-KEYS-00A0.dts

```
/dts-v1/;
/plugin/;
/{
    compatible = "ti,beaglebone", "ti,beaglebone-black";
    part-number = "BB-BONE-KEYS";
    version = "00A0";

    fragment@0 {
        target = <&am33xx_pinmux>;
        __overlay__ {
            pushbutton_pins: pinmux_pushbutton_pins{
                pinctrl-single,pins = <
                    0x040 0x37 // P9_15 pull-up mode 7 GPIO1_16
                >;
            };
        };
    };

    fragment@1 {
        target = <&ocp>;
        __overlay__ {
            /* avoid warnings */
            #address-cells = <1>;
            #size-cells = <1>;

            gpio_keys {
                compatible = "gpio-keys";
                pinctrl-names = "default";
```

continues

LISTING 6-9: *(continued)*

```
            pinctrl-0 = <&pushbutton_pins>;
            #address-cells = <1>;
            #size-cells = <0>;

            button_P9_15 {
                debounce_interval = <50>;
                linux,code = <28>;
                label = "button9_15";
                gpios = <&gpio2 16 0x1>;
                gpio-key,wakeup;
                autorepeat;
            };
        };
    };
};
};
```

This overlay can be compiled and deployed using the same process as the custom overlay presented earlier in the chapter:

```
$ dtc -O dtb -o BB-BONE-KEYS-00A0.dtbo -b o -@ BB-BONE-KEYS-00A0.dts
$ ls
BB-BONE-KEYS-00A0.dtbo  BB-BONE-KEYS-00A0.dts  build
$ sudo cp BB-BONE-KEYS-00A0.dtbo /lib/firmware
$ sudo sh -c "echo BB-BONE-KEYS > $SLOTS"
$ cat $SLOTS
...
9: ff:P-O-L Override Board Name,00A0,Override Manuf,BB-BONE-KEYS
```

As before, `dmesg` can be used to check for any issues that might arise. A new device added to the BBB, `event1`, can be catenated to display its output when the button is pressed; however, the output will not be in a human-readable form:

```
$ cd /dev/input
/dev/input$ ls
by-path  event0  event1  mice
molloyd@beaglebone:/dev/input$ sudo cat event1
3eS
    3eS
      3eSB
```

It is necessary to write code to correctly interrogate this device. Listing 6-10 uses the `linux/input.h` header file and the input documentation at www.kernel .org to build an example for the BBB that can parse the events that occur when the virtual keyboard button is pressed.

LISTING 6-10: /chp06/BONE-KEYS/bone_keys.cpp

```cpp
/** BB-BONE-GPIO Test code to test the GPIO-KEYS interface.
* Written by Derek Molloy (www.derekmolloy.ie) for the book
* Exploring BeagleBone. This code is based on the work in:
*      www.kernel.org/doc/Documentation/input/input.txt */


#include<iostream>
#include<fcntl.h>
#include<stdio.h>
#include<stdlib.h>
#include<linux/input.h>
using namespace std;

#define KEY_PRESS 1
#define KEY_RELEASE 0

int main(){
    int fd, count=0;
    struct input_event event[64];
    if(getuid()!=0){
        cout << "You must run this program as root. Exiting." << endl;
        return -1;
    }
    cout << "Starting BB-BONE-GPIO Test (press 10 times to end):" << endl;
    if ((fd = open("/dev/input/event1", O_RDONLY)) < 0){
        perror("Failed to open event1 input device. Exiting.");
        return -1;
    }
    while(count < 20){  // Press and Release are one loop each
        int numbytes = (int)read(fd, event, sizeof(event));
        if (numbytes < (int)sizeof(struct input_event)){
            perror("The input read was invalid. Exiting.");
            return -1;
        }
        for (int i=0; i < numbytes/sizeof(struct input_event); i++){
            int type = event[i].type;
            int val  = event[i].value;
            int code = event[i].code;
            if (type == EV_KEY) {
                if (val == KEY_PRESS){
                    cout << "Press  : Code "<< code <<" Value "<< val<< endl;
                }
                if (val == KEY_RELEASE){
                    cout << "Release: Code "<< code <<" Value "<< val<< endl;
                }
            }
        }
    }
```

continues

LISTING 6-10: *(continued)*

```
        count++;
    }
    close(fd);
    return 0;
}
```

As illustrated in Figure 6-16(a), a push button is connected to the P9_15 (GPIO 49), and because the mode is set to be `0x37` in the overlay, the input on P9_15 is normally high when the button is not pressed, and low when the button is pressed. The code in Listing 6-10 can be tested as follows:

```
~/exploringbb/chp06/BONE-KEYS$ g++ bone_keys.cpp -o bone_keys
~/exploringbb/chp06/BONE-KEYS$ ./bone_keys
You must run this program as root. Exiting.
~/exploringbb/chp06/BONE-KEYS$ sudo ./bone_keys
Starting BB-BONE-GPIO Test (press 10 times to end):
Press  : Code 28 Value 1
Release: Code 28 Value 0 ...
```

The value 28 is the Linux key code for the Enter key. A test version of this code, available in `/chp06/GPIO/tests/test_gpiokeys.cpp`, triggers an LED to light when an event is received.

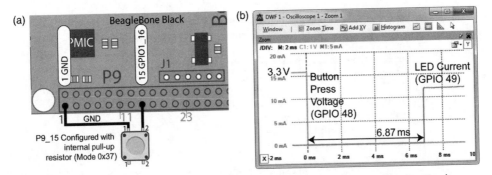

Figure 6-16: (a) Push button configured with an internal pull-up resistor making it active low, and (b) the time response of the Bone Keys C++ example

The performance of this approach is captured in Figure 6-16(b) and, while its response is slower than the enhanced `GPIO` class, it is still well within debounce tolerances. The main advantage of this approach is that you could direct the Linux `event1` device to third-party applications without recoding them to use the custom `GPIO` class.

Using GPIOs without Using sudo

Throughout this chapter, all programs that interface to the GPIOs are executed using sudo. This can be frustrating, but the alternative of running applications as the superuser is dangerous, in that a coding mistake could damage the file system. It would be very useful to set up the GPIOs so that they are owned by a particular user or group, while still protecting the file system.

To address this issue, you can use an advanced feature of Linux called *udev rules* that enables you to customize the behavior of the *udevd* service, which runs on the BBB Debian distribution. This service gives you some userspace control over devices on the BBB, such as renaming devices, changing permissions and executing a script when a device is attached. The first step is to find out information about the /sys/class/gpio directory:

```
~$ udevadm info ---path=/sys/class/gpio ---attribute-walk
...
   looking at device '/class/gpio':
     KERNEL=="gpio"
     SUBSYSTEM=="subsystem"
     DRIVER==""
```

The rules are contained in the /etc/udev/rules.d directory. A new rule can be added as a file using these values, where the file begins with a priority number. The following creates a new rule with the lowest priority, so that it does not interfere with other device rules:

```
molloyd@beaglebone:~$ cd /etc/udev/rules.d
molloyd@beaglebone:/etc/udev/rules.d$ ls
50-spi.rules  70-persistent-net.rules
molloyd@beaglebone:/etc/udev/rules.d$ sudo nano 99-gpio.rules
molloyd@beaglebone:/etc/udev/rules.d$ more 99-gpio.rules
KERNEL=="gpio*", SUBSYSTEM=="gpio", ACTION=="add", PROGRAM="/bin/sh -c
'chown -R molloyd:users /sys/class/gpio'"
KERNEL=="gpio*", SUBSYSTEM=="gpio", ACTION=="add", PROGRAM="/bin/sh -c
'chown -R molloyd:users /sys/devices/virtual/gpio'"
```

Essentially, the rule executes a single line script to change the owner of a GPIO device to be molloyd when it is added. This rules file is in the Git repository in the /chp06/udev/ directory. Edit it to suit your user and group requirements, and test that it works as follows:

```
/etc/udev/rules.d$ sudo udevadm test ---action=add /class/gpio
run_command: calling: test
adm_test: version 175
...
udev_device_new_from_syspath: device 0x371a8 has devpath '/class/gpio'
udev_device_new_from_syspath: device 0x38748 has devpath '/class/gpio'
...
```

```
ACTION=add
DEVPATH=/class/gpio
SUBSYSTEM=subsystem
UDEV_LOG=6
USEC_INITIALIZED=14466366151
```

If you list the /sys/class/gpio directory, the owner will have changed and, in this case, the user molloyd can export a GPIO pin:

```
molloyd@beaglebone:/etc/udev/rules.d$ cd /sys/class/gpio
molloyd@beaglebone:/sys/class/gpio$ ls
export  gpiochip0  gpiochip32  gpiochip64  gpiochip96  unexport
molloyd@beaglebone:/sys/class/gpio$ echo 60 > export
molloyd@beaglebone:/sys/class/gpio$ ls -l
total 0
--w------- 1 molloyd users 4096 May  9 00:41 export
lrwxrwxrwx 1 molloyd users    0 May  9 00:41 gpio60 -> ...
lrwxrwxrwx 1 molloyd users    0 May  9 00:26 gpiochip0 -> ...
lrwxrwxrwx 1 molloyd users    0 May  9 00:26 gpiochip32 -> ...
lrwxrwxrwx 1 molloyd users    0 May  9 00:26 gpiochip64 -> ...
lrwxrwxrwx 1 molloyd users    0 May  9 00:26 gpiochip96 -> ...
--w------- 1 molloyd users 4096 May  9 00:40 unexport
```

For a comprehensive guide on writing udev rules, see tiny.cc/ebb604.

Summary

After completing this chapter, you should be able to do the following:

- Use a BBB GPIO to output a binary signal to a digital circuit, or read in a binary input from a digital circuit.
- Write shell scripts and C++ code in order to control a BBB GPIO.
- Describe the use of internal pull-up and pull-down resistors.
- Write a Linux device tree overlay that can configure the BBB's P8 and P9 header pins to suit your application needs.
- Use a BBB PWM pin to output an analog voltage or as a control signal for motors and certain types of servos.
- Use a BBB analog input to read in a value from an analog circuit, using an op-amp to protect the BBB from damage and/or invalid measurement.
- Write C++ code, which utilizes advanced functionality, to efficiently read in a digital input using a custom GPIO class.
- Use a GPIO-KEYS device tree overlay to create a Linux virtual keyboard device using GPIO inputs.
- Use an advanced Linux configuration that allows for user-level control of the sysfs GPIO entries.

Further Reading

There are many links to websites and documents provided throughout this chapter. The following additional links provide further information on the topics covered:

- www.exploringbeaglebone.com/chapter6/: All links and videos in the chapter are provided at this site.

- www.exploringbeaglebone.com/API/: Provides the documentation for the GPIO, PWM, ServoMotor, and Analog classes described in this chapter.

Note

1. Kridner, J. (June 2013). Validation-Scripts/Test-Capemgr. Retrieved May 5, 2014, from Jadonk GitHub Repository: https://github.com/jadonk/validation-scripts/tree/master/test-capemgr.

# CHAPTER 7

Cross-Compilation and the Eclipse IDE

To this point in the book, all of the code is built and executed directly on the BeagleBone. However, for larger projects this can be impractical, as you may need to manage many source files within a single project. In addition, compilation times can be slow on the BBB for building large projects. This chapter first describes how you can use your desktop computer to develop applications that can be deployed directly to the BBB. The Eclipse integrated development environment (IDE) is then introduced, which allows for advanced development capabilities, such as remote debugging. The chapter finishes by outlining how you can build a custom Linux kernel.

Equipment Required for This Chapter:

- A desktop computer running Linux (ideally Debian) or Debian running in a virtual machine
- BeagleBone Black for deployment and debugging

Further details on this chapter are available at `www.exploringbeaglebone.com/chapter7/`.

Setting Up a Cross-Compilation Toolchain

This section describes how you can establish a fully featured cross-compilation environment for building code for the BBB using your desktop computer.

A typical C/C++ compiler that is executed on a desktop computer (e.g., Intel x86) will build executable machine code for that platform only. Therefore, a *cross-compiler* is required, as it is capable of creating executable code for the BBB ARM platform directly from your desktop computer, even though it has a different hardware architecture.

Linux is generally used on the desktop computer for this task, as cross-compiling code that is written on Windows/Mac devices to run on an ARM device is an incredibly challenging process, particularly when integrating third-party libraries. Therefore, if you are using a Windows/Mac OS X environment, you can use the VirtualBox configuration that is described in Chapter 3. In fact, a VirtualBox Debian 64-bit VM is used for all of the examples in this chapter.

The environment and configuration for cross-platform development is an ever-evolving process. While all of the steps in this chapter work at the time of publication, it is entirely possible that some steps in this chapter will change as updates are performed on the Linux kernel, to the toolchain, and to the Eclipse development environment. Please visit the web page associated with this chapter to check for updates: www.exploringbeaglebone.com/chapter7/. The primary aim of this chapter is to ensure that you grasp the concepts behind cross-compilation and that you see practical examples of the various tools in use.

If you wish to cross-compile Linux applications, the first step is to install a *Linux toolchain*. A *toolchain* is suitably named, as it is a set of software development tools and libraries (such as gcc, gdb, glibc) that are chained together to enable you to build executable code on one operating system on one type of machine, such as a 64-bit Linux OS on an Intel x86 machine, but execute them on a different operating system and/or a different architecture, such as a 32-bit Linux OS on an ARM device.

I have previously created a full video on integrating a soft float cross-compilation toolchain with Ångström under Ubuntu; while there have been changes (including problems with access to the Ångström distribution website), the instructions in the video are largely valid (see tiny.cc/ebb701). It is not possible to cover absolutely everything in just one book, so here I focus on a toolchain for hard floats under Debian. Please use the following discussion, combined with the YouTube video that is available on the chapter web page to complete the installation of either toolchain.

A Toolchain for Debian

To begin, you can discover detailed information about your Linux version by typing the following commands individually or together using &&:

```
molloyd@beaglebone:~$ uname -a && cat /etc/os-release && cat /proc/version
Linux beaglebone 3.8.13-bone50 #1 SMP Tue May 13 2014 armv7l GNU/Linux
PRETTY_NAME="Debian GNU/Linux 7 (wheezy)"
NAME="Debian GNU/Linux" . . .
```

In this example, a Debian 7.x image is used on the desktop machine. The steps in this description are based on the work at `tiny.cc/ebb702`. A Debian 64-bit "Wheezy" VirtualBox VM is used on the desktop machine, so required tools need to be installed using the following steps (on the desktop machine):

1. Change to a root shell:

```
molloyd@debian:~$ sudo sh -
```

2. Go to the `/etc/apt` directory and add any necessary repositories to your `sources.list` file:

```
root@debian:~# cd /etc/apt
root@debian:/etc/apt# nano sources.list
```

3. Check the repositories that are needed for your distribution. In this case, the following entries need to be added to the bottom of the `sources.list` file:

```
#Emdebian entries
deb http://www.emdebian.org/debian unstable main
deb http://ftp.us.debian.org/debian unstable main contrib non-free
```

4. Save the file and return to the shell and install `emdebian-archive-keyring`, which provides Debian key signatures for release files, in order to make it easier to use the Debian installer:

```
root@debian:~# apt-get install emdebian-archive-keyring
root@debian:~# apt-get update
```

NOTE Using *hard floats* means that when you are working with floating-point numbers on the BBB you are using the on-chip floating-point unit (FPU). Using *soft floats* means that the floating-point arithmetic is performed in software. Therefore, hard float operations are much faster than soft float operations. Because the AM335x implements hard-float operations, you should always choose the hard float option when available.

Use `apt-get update` to download the latest package lists from the repositories and update the local lists to contain information on the latest versions of packages and their dependencies. Use `apt-cache` to search for the latest ARM compiler. The BBB with its Debian distribution supports hard floats (hf), so use hard-float tools if they are available:

```
root@debian:~# apt-cache search gnueabihf
binutils-arm-linux-gnueabihf - GNU binary utilities, arm-linux-gnueabihf...
g++-4.7-arm-linux-gnueabihf - GNU C++ compiler
gcc-4.7-arm-linux-gnueabihf - GNU C compiler
gcc-4.7-arm-linux-gnueabihf-base - GCC, the GNU Compiler Collection...
```

You can see from this list that the latest g++ compiler number available that supports hard floats, at the time of writing, is g++-4.7-arm-linux-gnueabihf. Install the latest version available to you and any dependencies, which should be automatically identified. You may have already installed some of these dependencies in earlier steps (e.g., adding Guest Additions to the Debian VM), but here is the list that was required for this installation:

```
~# apt-get install build-essential libc6-armhf-cross libc6-dev-armhf-cross
~# apt-get install binutils-arm-linux-gnueabihf linux-libc-dev-armhf-cross
~# apt-get install libstdc++6-armhf-cross
~# apt-get install gcc-4.7-arm-linux-gnueabihf g++-4.7-arm-linux-gnueabihf
```

Please note that hard floats are being used here. If you wished to use soft floats for a different platform, then you would replace *armhf* with *armel* and *gnueabihf* with *gnueabi* in the preceding list. If you are having problems with dependencies, type sudo apt-get autoremove and try an older version of the gcc and g++ compilers.

If all goes well, you should be able to execute the cross-compiler at this point; however, you may have multiple versions installed, or you may wish to install multiple versions in the future. If you change directory to /usr/bin and perform ls arm* you might see something like the following:

```
root@debian:/usr/bin# ls arm*
arm-linux-gnueabihf-g++-4.7      arm-linux-gnueabi-readelf
arm-linux-gnueabihf-gcc-4.6      arm-linux-gnueabi-strings
arm-linux-gnueabihf-gcc-4.7      arm-linux-gnueabi-strip...
```

For convenience, you can create generic symbolic links to the version of the compilers that you wish to use. In this case symbolic links are created to the gXX-4.7 compilers. This generic symbolic link is used when the Eclipse build settings are configured in the next section:

```
.../usr/bin# ln -s arm-linux-gnueabihf-gcc-4.7 arm-linux-gnueabihf-gcc
.../usr/bin# ln -s arm-linux-gnueabihf-g++-4.7 arm-linux-gnueabihf-g++
```

You can test that these symbolic links work, from any location (as /usr/bin is in the PATH by default), by using the following:

```
molloyd@debian:~$ arm-linux-gnueabihf-g++ -v
gcc version 4.7.2 (Debian 4.7.2-5)...
```

Testing the Toolchain

At this point, you can build a test application to check that everything is working before you begin configuring Eclipse. You should write a small C++ program, build it on your desktop machine, and then deploy it to the BBB. For example, enter the following on the desktop machine:

```
molloyd@debian:~$ nano testARM.cpp
molloyd@debian:~$ more testARM.cpp
#include<iostream>
int main(){
    std::cout << "Testing Toolchain" << std::endl;
    return 0;
}
molloyd@debian:~$ arm-linux-gnueabihf-g++ testARM.cpp -o testARM
molloyd@debian:~$ ./testARM
bash: ./testARM: cannot execute binary file
```

At this point, the binary executable will not execute on your desktop machine, as it contains ARM hard float instructions. However, please note that if you install QEMU (in the Installing a Change Root section of this chapter), then the program will execute. Next, transfer the binary executable to the BBB:

```
molloyd@debian:~$ sftp molloyd@192.168.7.2
BeagleBoard.org BeagleBone Debian Image 2014-05-14
Connected to 192.168.7.2.
sftp> put testARM
Uploading testARM to /root/testARM...
sftp> exit
```

Finally, SSH to the BBB to confirm that the new binary works correctly:

```
molloyd@debian:~$ ssh root@192.168.7.2
BeagleBoard.org BeagleBone Debian Image 2014-05-14...
molloyd@beaglebone:~$ ./testARM
Testing Toolchain
```

Success! If you see this output, then you are able to build a binary on the desktop machine that can be executed directly on the BBB. The next section is an advanced topic and is required if you wish to use third-party libraries with your cross-compilation environment. If you wish, you can skip this section for the moment and go directly to the Cross-Compilation Using Eclipse section.

Cross-Compilation with Third-Party Libraries (Multiarch)

This section is not necessary in order to cross-compile C/C++ applications; however, it is likely that you will need to add third-party libraries in the future for tasks such as image and numerical processing. Traditionally, this has been a very difficult topic, but thanks to very recent releases in Debian and Ubuntu, this problem has become much more manageable.

For the purpose of this discussion, you should have your cross-compiler in place and you should currently be able to cross-compile applications that use the standard C/C++ libraries. However, what if you wish to build a C/C++ application that uses a third-party library? If you install the library on your x86 desktop machine, then that library code will contain native x86 instructions. If you wish to use the third-party library and deploy it to your BBB, then you need to use a library that contains ARM machine code instructions.

Traditionally, we have used tools like xapt, which converts Debian packages to a cross-platform version on-the-fly (e.g., xapt -a armhf -m libopencv-dev). However, recent releases of Debian (Wheezy+) now support *multiarch*—multi-architecture package installs.

Here is an example of how you can use a multiarch-capable package installer to install a BBB armhf library on a desktop machine. You can determine the current architecture (on the x86 64-bit desktop machine) using:

```
molloyd@debian:~$ dpkg --print-architecture
amd64
molloyd@debian:~$ dpkg --version
Debian 'dpkg' package management program version 1.16.15 (amd64).
```

The version of dpkg has to be greater than 1.16.2 for multiarch support. You can add the armhf target architecture for the BBB Debian image using:

```
molloyd@debian:~$ sudo dpkg --add-architecture armhf
molloyd@debian:~$ dpkg --print-foreign-architectures
armhf
```

Install a sample third-party library package after performing an update (note the armhf after the package name):

```
molloyd@debian:~$ sudo apt-get update
molloyd@debian:~$ sudo apt-get install libicu-dev:armhf
Reading package lists... Done
Building dependency tree       ...
Setting up libicu-dev:armhf (52.1-6)...
```

These third-party libraries for utilizing Unicode are installed in the /usr/lib/arm-linux-gnueabihf directory. This keeps them separate from the x86 libraries that are stored in the /usr/lib directory, as otherwise you would likely overwrite your current x86 libraries with the armhf libraries:

```
molloyd@debian:/usr/lib/arm-linux-gnueabihf$ ls libicu*
libicudata.a     libicuio.so.52.1     libicutest.so.52...
```

And you are done! You can now configure your C++ build environment to use the libraries in the `/usr/lib/arm-linux-gnueabihf` directory. This procedure works well and it is reasonably straightforward; however, it is new to Linux, and interdependency problems currently arise. See `wiki.debian.org/Multiarch/HOWTO` for more information on multiarch packages. An alternative to multiarch package installations is to mirror the entire Linux root of your ARM target platform, and to do this you can use a change root.

Installing a Change Root

A *change root* allows you to change the apparent Linux root directory to another directory on your system. Why would you do this? The most common reason is that you might like to try a new Linux kernel, use new tools, or install a new library on your Linux installation; and you would like to test it first in case it brings down the entire system. A change root enables you to replicate your Linux installation in a subdirectory (e.g., have a subdirectory of the root directory called "newroot" that has `/etc`, `/bin`, `/home`, `/usr`, etc.) that has a full Linux distribution. You can then install your new libraries and tools in this new (possibly temporary) root directory.

You can instruct your Linux system to change the root temporarily to this new root directory. Once started, you enter *chroot jail* and do not have access to any files outside the new root directory. You can test all of the new features of your new Linux installation, and when you are finished you can type **exit** to return to your "real" root, leaving the chroot jail.

This structure is useful for the BBB because this new root directory does not have to have the same flavor of Linux or even the same architecture as your main desktop Linux installation. You can install an armhf version of Linux in the new change root directory and then use a tool called *QEMU* (Quick *Emu*lator) to emulate that the Linux OS is running on an ARM platform. Working through an example should help make this concept clear.

Installing an armhf Change Root

The *debootstrap* (Debian bootstrap) tool enables you to install a Debian base system into a subdirectory of your current desktop Debian system. You can do this using the following instructions, where you choose the architecture as `armhf`, the initial package, the distribution name (`wheezy` in this case), the installation directory (`/BBBchroot` in this case), and the source for install files (`ftp.us.debian.org`). Type the following (noting that the third command is all typed on one line and there are no spaces beside the commas):

```
molloyd@debian:~$ sudo mkdir /BBBchroot
molloyd@debian:~$ sudo apt-get install debootstrap
```

```
molloyd@debian:~$ sudo debootstrap --foreign --verbose --arch=armhf
--include=aptitude,iputils-ping,module-init-tools,ifupdown,iproute,
nano,wget,udev wheezy /BBBchroot http://ftp.us.debian.org/debian
I: Retrieving Release...
```

You now have a root file system for ARM hard floats just off the main root directory of your desktop machine (/BBBchroot in this case). You can view the files in this directory and even try to execute commands, but they will fail because they contain ARM machine instructions:

```
molloyd@debian:~$ cd /BBBchroot/
molloyd@debian:/BBBchroot$ ls
bin   debootstrap  etc   lib  proc  run   selinux  tmp  var
boot  dev          home  mnt  root  sbin  sys      usr
molloyd@debian:/BBBchroot$ cd bin
molloyd@debian:/BBBchroot/bin$ ls
...     findmnt   mkdir    rbash      sync    which    ...
molloyd@debian:/BBBchroot/bin$ ./mkdir
bash: ./mkdir: cannot execute binary file
```

Emulating the armhf Architecture

To emulate the armhf architecture, you can install a package called QEMU that enables you to emulate the ARM microprocessor on your x86 machine. This is called *user-mode emulation*. QEMU can also perform full *computer-mode emulation*, just like VirtualBox. You can install the QEMU user-mode emulation package by typing the following:

```
molloyd@debian:~$ sudo apt-get install qemu-user-static
```

Next, place the statically compiled emulator within the change root directory. Once you perform the chroot command, you do not have access to any of the files outside the new root directory, including dynamic libraries (remember that you will be in chroot jail). The steps are as follows:

```
molloyd@debian:~$ cd /usr/bin
molloyd@debian:/usr/bin$ sudo cp qemu-arm-static /BBBchroot/usr/bin
```

Now you can change root to the /BBBchroot directory:

```
molloyd@debian:~$ sudo chroot /BBBchroot/
```

You should see the following shell prompt, which results from the fact that there is no passwd file. You need to complete the installation of the packages that are specified in the earlier call to the debootstrap command and set a password for the root account:

```
I have no name!@debian:/# uname -a
Linux debian 3.2.0-4 #1 SMP Debian 3.2.60-1+deb7u3 armv7l GNU/Linux
```

```
I have no name!@debian:/# cd /debootstrap
I have no name!@debian:/debootstrap# ./debootstrap --second-stage
I have no name!@debian:/debootstrap# passwd
I have no name!@debian:/debootstrap# exit
```

When you call the `chroot` command again you should now have a "root" prompt and the packages are now installed, for example:

```
molloyd@debian:~$ sudo chroot /BBBchroot/
root@debian:~# ping 8.8.8.8
PING 8.8.8.8 (8.8.8.8) 56(84) bytes of data....
```

You can now build code on the chroot and deploy it to the BBB, but to do this you need to install the `build-essential` package on your chroot, even though you have already installed it on your main root. First you must identify the package sources as follows:

```
root@debian:~# nano /etc/apt/sources.list
root@debian:~# more /etc/apt/sources.list
deb http://ftp.us.debian.org/debian wheezy main
deb-src http://ftp.us.debian.org/debian wheezy main
root@debian:~# apt-get update
root@debian:~# apt-get install build-essential
```

Then you can write a simple C++ example, which can be executed on the chroot using QEMU and remotely deployed to the BBB:

```
root@debian:~# more test.cpp
#include<iostream>
int main(){
    std::cout<<"Hello World running on armhf\n";
}
root@debian:~# g++ test.cpp -o testARM
root@debian:~# ./testARM
Hello World running on armhf
```

Despite this message, it has not yet been sent to the BBB. It is being emulated on the desktop machine using QEMU. Transfer this binary file to the BBB to test that it works there too. To do this, you can install the `openssh-client` package on your change root. Of course, you could exit the change root and transfer it directly, but this step provides you with the facility to transfer the file directly from within the change root from now on:

```
root@debian:~# apt-get install openssh-client
root@debian:~# sftp molloyd@192.168.7.2
molloyd@192.168.7.2's password:...
sftp> put testARM
Uploading testARM to /home/molloyd/testARM
sftp> exit
```

Then connect to the BBB and test the code on the BBB:

```
root@debian:~# ssh molloyd@192.168.7.2
molloyd@beaglebone:~$ ./testARM
Hello World running on armhf
```

As you can see, the executable also worked on the BBB; therefore it is clear that the change root compilation process is working correctly. Applications can be built on the desktop machine with the ARM hard float instruction set and ARM-specific libraries can be installed on the chroot by simply using the `apt-get` command. You are now emulating ARMv71 on your desktop Linux installation (yes, in a VirtualBox instance under Windows!). You can use this environment to cross-build code for your BBB, using the power of your desktop machine. Remember that you can type **exit** to return to your regular root at any stage.

Cross-Compilation Using Eclipse

Eclipse is an integrated development environment (IDE) that enables you to manage your code and integrate cross-compilation tools, debuggers, and other plug-ins to create a sophisticated development platform. It can even be extended to provide full remote debugging support for applications that are physically running on your BBB. This is a powerful feature that enables you to debug software applications that are interfacing with the real hardware in your projects, but view the debug values within your desktop Eclipse environment.

Eclipse is written in Java and was initially focused on Java software development. However, Eclipse has excellent support for C/C++ development using the C/C++ Development Tooling (CDT) extension.

Installing Eclipse on Desktop Linux

Using a web browser on your Linux desktop or Linux desktop VM running under Windows (see Chapter 3), download Eclipse from `www.eclipse.org`. There is a version that has CDT (C/C++ Development Tooling) integration (e.g., Eclipse IDE for C/C++ Developers), which you should install. The version of Eclipse that is used in this guide is Luna.

After you have downloaded Eclipse, decide if you wish to install it for all users or just for the main user, by extracting the archive in a suitable location (such as the user home directory in the following example). Chromium will download the file to the user `~/Downloads` directory by default. Therefore, use the following steps to install eclipse in the user account, and execute it directly (in the background using &):

```
~/Downloads$ mv eclipse* ~/
~/Downloads$ cd ~/
```

```
~$ tar -xvf eclipse-cpp-luna-SR1-linux-gtk-x86_64.tar.gz
~$ cd eclipse
~/eclipse$ ./eclipse &
```

At this point you can create C++ applications on the desktop machine that are deployed to the desktop machine using Eclipse. However, since the target platform is the BBB, Eclipse must be configured for cross-compilation.

NOTE You may need to install a new Java runtime environment (JRE) for Eclipse to execute (depending on the specific release) on your desktop PC. If that is the case, go to www.oracle.com and search for JRE. You will find an installer (e.g., JRE 8u20), which can be downloaded and installed using steps such as:

```
molloyd@debian:~/Downloads$ tar zxvf jre-8u20-linux-x64.tar.gz
molloyd@debian:~/Downloads$ sudo mkdir /usr/java
molloyd@debian:~/Downloads$ sudo mv jre1.8.0_20/ /usr/java
molloyd@debian:~/Downloads$ sudo update-alternatives --install "/usr/
bin/java" "java" "/usr/java/jre1.8.0_20/bin/java" 1
molloyd@debian:~/Downloads$ sudo update-alternatives --set java
 /usr/java/jre1.8.0_20/bin/java
molloyd@debian:~/Downloads$ java -version
java version "1.8.0_20"...
```

Configuring Eclipse for Cross-Compilation

When Eclipse starts you should see a brief guide that describes C/C++ development. Close it when you are ready and then test that the environment works by creating a new project using File ≻ New ≻ C++ project. As illustrated in Figure 7-1(a), set the project name to "BBBTest," pick the project type "Hello World C++ Project," and the Toolchain to be "Cross GCC." Then click Finish. Repeatedly click Next until you see the "Cross GCC Command," as illustrated in Figure 7-1(b). Enter arm-linux-gnueabihf- for the cross-compiler prefix and set the path to /usr/bin. Finally, click Finish.

The Eclipse IDE is now configured for cross-compilation using the cross-compilation toolchain that was set up at the beginning of this chapter. You can choose Project ≻ Build All and then run on the desktop machine by clicking the green arrow or (Run ≻ Run). In Figure 7-2 this results in the message !!!Hello World!!! appearing in the Console window. This only appears on the desktop computer if you have installed QEMU, as the executable contains ARM machine code, which is clear from the binary name "BBBTest - [arm/le]" that is highlighted on the top left of Figure 7-2.

The preceding steps provide a quick way of configuring the cross-compilation settings within Luna. Older versions of Eclipse (e.g., Kepler) require you to configure the cross-compiler using the project settings. That option is still available within Eclipse Luna—select the project that was just created, and then go to Project ≻ Properties (If the option is grayed out, it likely means that the project is not selected). Go to C/C++ Build ≻ Settings and under the Tool Settings tab you should see the Cross Settings as illustrated in Figure 7-3. Effectively, these settings mean that the `arm-linux-gnueabihf-g++` command (a symbolic link that is described at the beginning of this chapter) is used to compile the project code.

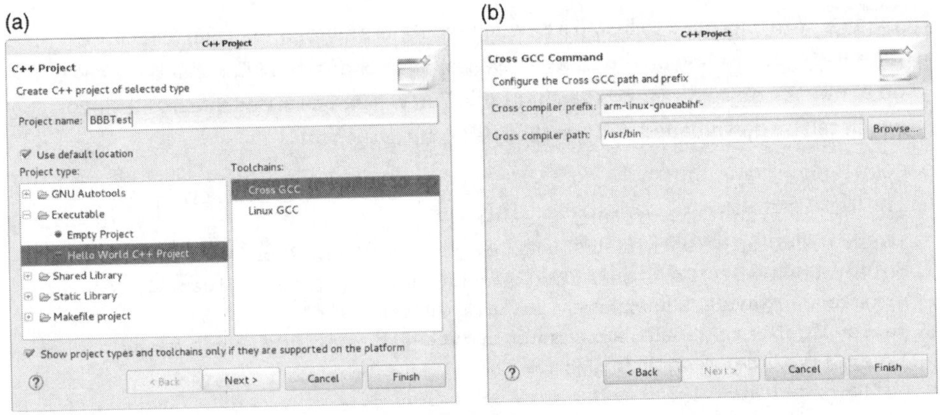

Figure 7-1: Creating a new C++ project in Eclipse: (a) the project settings, and (b) the cross-compiler prefix

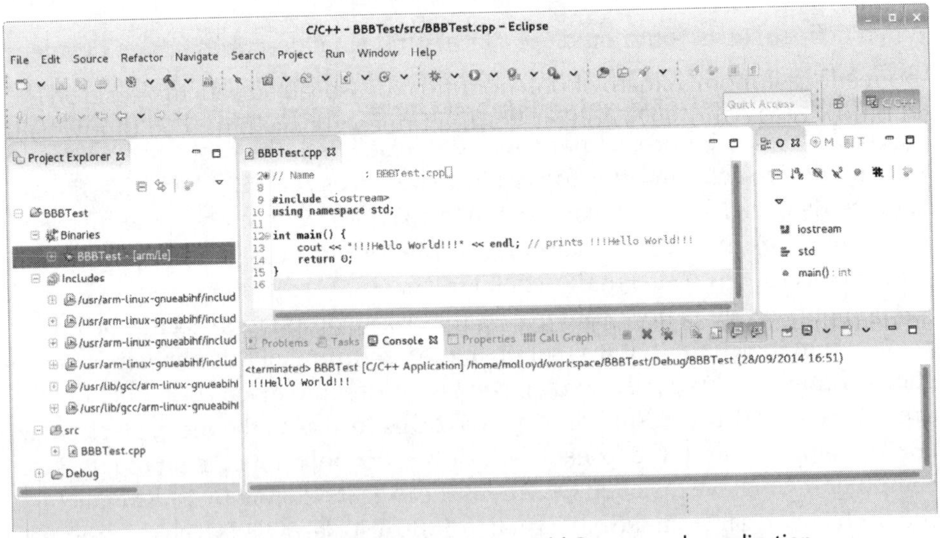

Figure 7-2: The Eclipse IDE cross-compiling a Hello World C++ example application

While it may not be necessary to set the C/C++ includes and library settings explicitly, it may be necessary at a later stage, particularly when using third-party libraries. To do this, go to Project ≻ Properties ≻ C/C++

General ➤ Paths and Symbols, and set the following (according to your version of gcc and g++):

- Includes (tab) ➤ GNU C (Include directories) ➤ Add ➤ File System ➤ File System ➤/usr/arm-linux-gnueabihf/include and click Add
- Includes (tab) ➤ GNU C++ (Include directories) ➤ Add ➤ File System ➤ File System ➤/usr/arm-linux-gnueabihf/include/c++/4.7.2 or your current version.
- Library Paths (not Libraries) ➤ Add ➤ File System ➤ File System ➤/usr/arm-linux-gnueabihf/lib
- Click OK to apply the configuration.

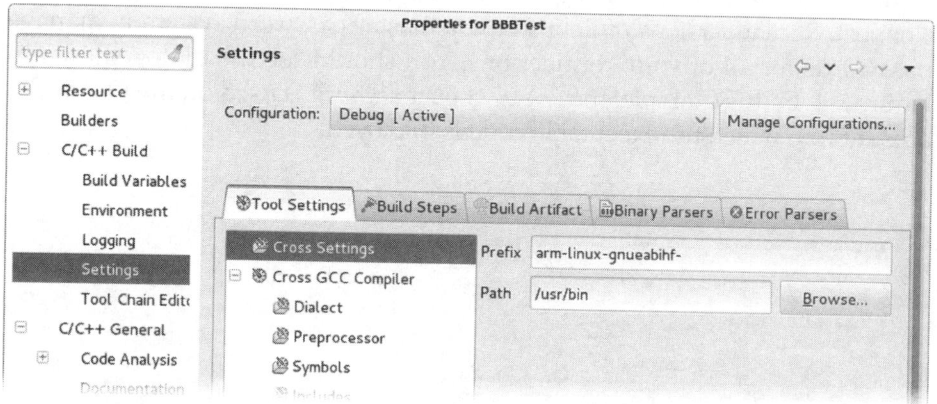

Figure 7-3: Eclipse Luna settings for cross-compilation

Now you should be able to deploy the binary application directly to the BBB, as it contains ARM machine code instructions. You can transfer the binary application to the BBB using sftp, but it would be better in the longer term if you had a direct link to the BBB from within Eclipse—for this you can use the Remote System Explorer plug-in.

Remote System Explorer

The Remote System Explorer (RSE) plug-in enables you to establish a direct connection between your Eclipse environment and the BBB, over a network connection, by using the SSH server on your BBB. You can install the RSE within Eclipse using Help ➤ Install New Software. Choose "Luna..." in the Work with: section and then select General Purpose Tools ➤ Remote System Explorer User Actions. Click Next, follow the steps, then restart Eclipse.

You should now have RSE functionality within Eclipse. Go to Window ➤ Show View ➤ Other ➤ Remote Systems ➤ Remote Systems. In the Remote

Systems frame that appears, click the icon for Define a Connection to a Remote System, and in the New Connection dialog, select the following:

- Choose Linux Type ➤ Next.
- Host Name: Enter your BBB IP address—e.g., 192.168.7.2
- Connection Name: Change it to "BeagleBone Black" ➤ Next
- [Files] Configuration ➤ ssh.files ➤ Next
- [Processes] Configuration ➤ processes.shell.linux ➤ Next
- [Shells] Configuration ➤ ssh.shells ➤ Next
- [Ssh Terminals] (no change) ➤ Finish

You can then right-click BeagleBone Black in the bottom frame and choose Connect. Recent versions of Eclipse use a master password system to manage passwords for all of your connections. You should see the dialog shown in Figure 7-4. In this example, the molloyd user account is used on the BBB as the account into which the executable code is deployed.

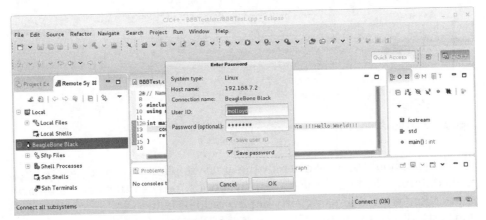

Figure 7-4: Connecting to the BBB for the first time

Once you are connected to the BBB you can go to the Project Explorer window, right-click the executable that you just built (BBBTest [arm/le]) and choose Copy. Then go to a directory on the Remote Explorer, such as tmp (see Figure 7-5). Right-click it and choose Paste. The file is now on the BBB and can be executed from the built-in Terminals window, as captured in Figure 7-5, once you have changed the permissions for the file to be executable.

One way to automate the process of copying the files from the desktop computer to the BBB is by using the secure copy command scp (described in detail in Chapter 11). You can set up your desktop computer so that it does not need to use a password to ssh to the BBB by using the following steps on the desktop computer (when prompted you should leave the passphrase blank):

```
molloyd@debian:~$ ssh-keygen
molloyd@debian:~$ ssh-copy-id molloyd@192.168.7.2
molloyd@debian:~$ ssh-add
molloyd@debian:~$ ssh molloyd@192.168.7.2
```

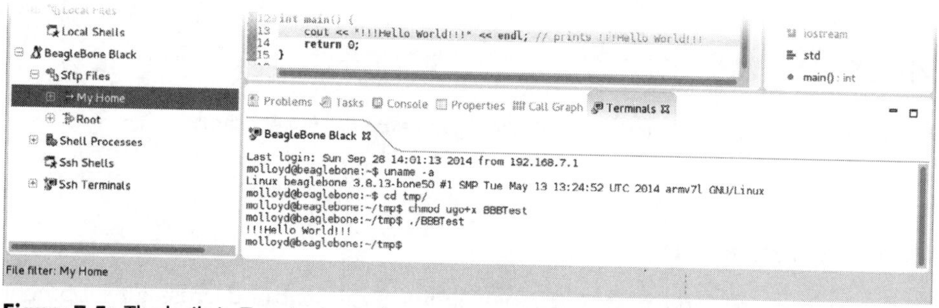

Figure 7-5: The built-in Terminals window, connected to the BBB and executing the cross-compiled BBBTest C++ application

You should now be able to ssh to the BBB without requiring a password. You can then configure Eclipse to deploy the executable automatically by setting the Command to be scp BBBTest molloyd@192.168.7.2:/home/molloyd/tmp/ under Project ➢ Properties ➢ C/C++ Build ➢ Settings ➢ Build Steps ➢ Post-build steps.

Integrating GitHub into Eclipse

There is a very useful plug-in that can be installed into Eclipse that allows for full GitHub integration, enabling you to link to your own GitHub repositories or to get easy access to the example code and resources for this book. To install it, open Help ➢ Install New Software and choose "Luna…" in the Work with: section. Then, under the tree item Collaboration, choose "Eclipse GitHub integration with task focused interface."

Once this plug-in is installed, you can open Window ➢ Show View ➢ Other ➢ Git, and there are several options, such as Git Interactive Rebase, Git Reflog, Git Repositories, Git Staging, and Git Tree Compare. If you choose Git Repositories, you then get a dialog with the option to "Clone a Git repository" ➢ GitHub, and you can search for "exploringBB." You should find the repository "derekmolloy/ ExploringBB." If not, you can add the repository directly using the full URL: https:// github.com/DerekMolloy/ExploringBB.git. You will then have full access to the source code in this book directly from within the Eclipse IDE, as captured in Figure 7-6. Because there are so many projects in this repository, the easiest way to use this code repository is to copy the files that you need into a new project.

Figure 7-6: Eclipse GitHub integration, displaying the exploringBB repository

Remote Debugging

Remote debugging is the next step in developing a full-featured, cross-development platform configuration. As you are likely planning to interact with hardware modules that are physically connected to the BBB, it would be ideal if you could debug your code live on the BBB. Remote debugging with Eclipse enables you to control the execution steps and even view debug messages and memory values directly from within Eclipse on your desktop machine.

For this example you can use the makeLED.cpp example that you cloned from the Git repository. Select the makeLED.cpp file in the editor (refer to Figure 7-6), and use File ≻ Save As to add this file to the current project (~/workspace/BBBTest in this case). Comment out the main() function in the HelloWorld example, as you cannot have two main() functions in a single C/C++ project.

On the BBB you need the debug server gdbserver to run in order for the Eclipse installation to connect to the debugger. This tool is installed by default on the Debian BBB image, but you can install or update it using the following command:

```
molloyd@beaglebone:~$ sudo apt-get install gdbserver
```

The gdbserver executes on the BBB when it is called by the Eclipse IDE on the desktop machine using RSE. On the Linux desktop machine you need to install the GNU multi-architecture debugger, as follows:

```
molloyd@debian:~/$ sudo apt-get install gdb-multiarch
```

Then on the desktop machine, create a file called .gdbinit in the project folder using nano and add the line set architecture arm:

```
molloyd@debian:~/workspace/BBBTest$ more .gdbinit
set architecture arm
```

Eclipse needs to be configured to use the multiarch debugger. Go to Run ➢ Debug Configurations ➢ Debugger, and delete any current debug configurations. Select C/C++ Remote Applications on the left-hand side and right-click it to create a new configuration. In this example it is called "BBBTest Debug" as captured in Figure 7-7.

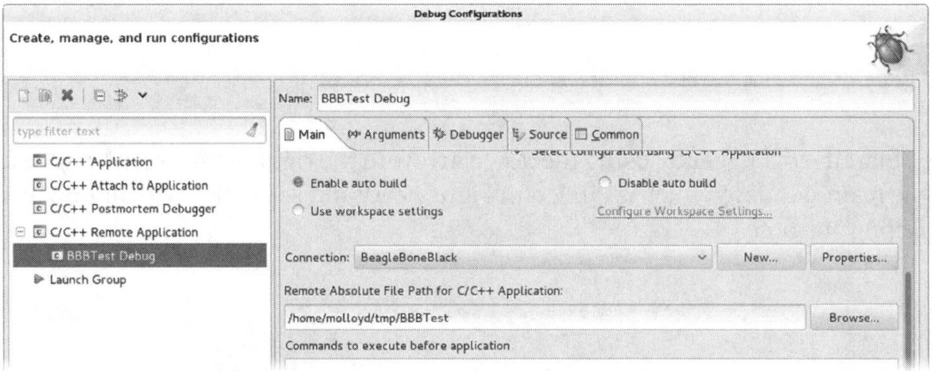

Figure 7-7: Setting the debug configuration

Change the debugger command from `gdb` to `gdb-multiarch`, as illustrated in Figure 7-8. You also need to attach the `.gdbinit` file that was just created. Click the Browse button to the right of "GDB command File" and locate your workspace directory. You may have to right-click the File Explorer window and choose Show hidden files to find the file `.gdbinit`. That configuration file can be used to set many more configuration options. For example, it can be used to configure the remote server and choose different breakpoints.

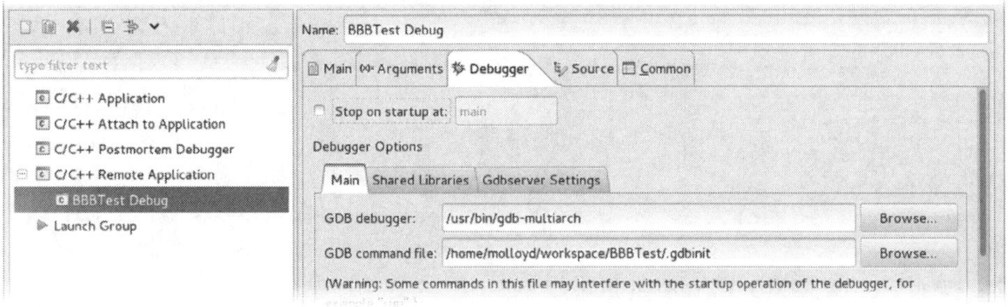

Figure 7-8: Setting up gdb-multiarch

Any program arguments can be added to the Arguments tab in Figure 7-8. In this example the string "flash" is used. The argument is passed to the application that is executing on the BBB when the `gdbserver` command executes.

Finally, under the Gdbserver Settings tab (see Figure 7-9), set the executable path and an arbitrary port number for the `gdbserver` command. This allows the desktop computer to remotely invoke the `gdbserver` command on the BBB and to connect to it over TCP using its port number.

Figure 7-9: Setting the BBB gdbserver port

Start the debugger by using the down arrow to the right of the green "bug" on the main window, which is circled in Figure 7-10, and select the "DebugBBBTest Debug" option.

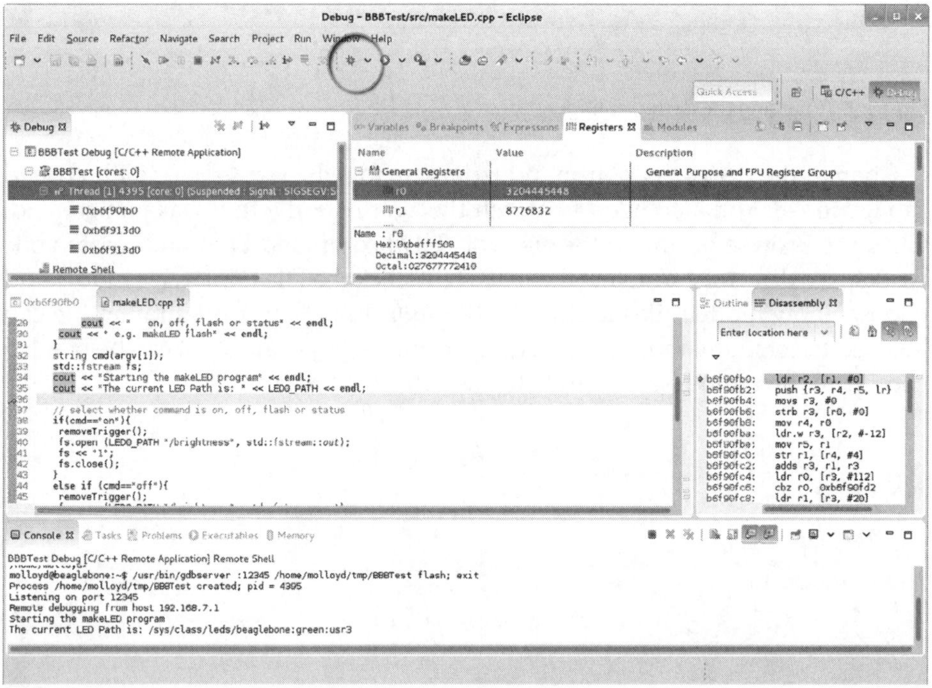

Figure 7-10: The Debug Perspective view

Figure 7-10 is a screen capture of the Debug Perspective view in action. You can see that the program is currently halted at a breakpoint on line 36 of the program code. The output at this point is visible in the Console window at the bottom. This type of debug view can be invaluable when developing complex applications, especially when the BBB is connected to electronic circuits and modules. At this point you can use the Step Over button to step through each line of your code, watching the variable values, while seeing how the program interacts with physically connected circuits.

Automatic Documentation (Doxygen)

As your BBB projects grow in capability and complexity, it will become especially important that your code is self-documenting. If you follow good programming practice when naming variables and methods, as discussed in Chapter 5, then you will not have to document every single line of code. Rather, you should write inline documentation comments, using automatic documentation tools like Doxygen or Javadoc, for every class, method, and state. This will enable other programmers to have an immediate understanding of what your code does and how it is structured.

Javadoc is an automatic documentation generator that generates HTML code directly from Java source code. Likewise, *Doxygen* is a tool that can be used for generating documentation from annotated C++ source files in HTML, LaTeX, and other formats. Doxygen can also generate documentation for the other programming languages that were discussed in Chapter 5, but the following discussion focuses on how it can be used for C++ documentation and how it can be integrated with the Eclipse IDE. An example output, which documents the C++ GPIO class from Chapter 6, is displayed in Figure 7-11.

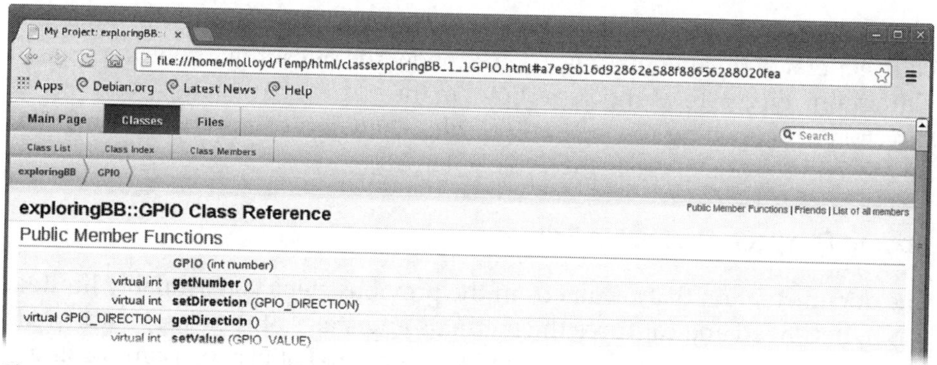

Figure 7-11: Example Doxygen HTML output

First, you need to install Doxygen on the Linux desktop machine using the following command:

```
molloyd@debian:~/eclipse$ sudo apt-get install doxygen
```

Depending on your desktop installation, it may download many additional dependencies (as much as 1GB of files). Once installed, you can immediately begin generating documentation for your project. For example, copy the GPIO.h and GPIO.cpp files from the Git repository in the chp06/GPIO/ directory into a temporary directory such as ~/Temp and then build the documentation as follows:

```
molloyd@debian:~/Temp$ ls
GPIO.cpp  GPIO.h
molloyd@debian:~/Temp$ doxygen -g
Configuration file 'Doxyfile' created...
molloyd@debian:~/Temp$ ls
Doxyfile  GPIO.cpp  GPIO.h
molloyd@debian:~/Temp$ doxygen -w html header.html footer.html
stylesheet.css
molloyd@debian:~/Temp$ ls
Doxyfile  footer.html  GPIO.cpp  GPIO.h  header.html  stylesheet.css
```

This automatically generates HTML files that you can customize for your project, adding headers, footers, and style sheets to suit your needs. Next, call the doxygen command on the Doxyfile configuration:

```
molloyd@debian:~/Temp$ doxygen Doxyfile
Searching for include files...
Searching for example files....
molloyd@debian:~/Temp$ ls
Doxyfile     GPIO.cpp  header.html  latex
footer.html  GPIO.h    html         stylesheet.css
```

You can see that there are html and latex folders containing the automatically generated documentation. You can view the output by browsing (e.g., in Chromium, type file:// and press Enter in the address bar) to the ~/Temp/html/ directory and opening the index.html file. There is a comprehensive manual on the features of Doxygen at www.doxygen.org.

Adding Doxygen Support in Eclipse

The documentation that results from the previous steps is reasonably limited. It is hyperlinked and captures the methods and states of the class, but there is no deeper description. By integrating Doxygen into Eclipse, you can configure and execute the Doxygen tools directly, and you can also provide inline commentary that is integrated into your generated documentation output. The first step is to enable Doxygen in the editor.

In Eclipse, go to Window ➤ Preferences ➤ C/C++ ➤ Editor. In the window at the bottom, under "Workspace default" select Doxygen. Apply the settings, and then in the editor type /** followed by the Return key above any method, and the IDE will automatically generate a comment as follows:

```
/**
 * @param number
 */
GPIO::GPIO(int number) {
```

You can then add a description of what the method does, as shown in the following example:

```
/**
 * Constructor for the General Purpose Input/Output (GPIO) class. It
 * will export the GPIO automatically.
 * @param number The GPIO number for the BBB pin
 */
GPIO::GPIO(int number) {
```

To complete the installation, you can install the *Eclox plug-in* for Eclipse by going to Help ➤ Install New Software and, using the steps outlined earlier, add a new site http://download.gna.org/eclox/update/ and then select and install the Eclox plug-in. After restarting Eclipse, select File ➤ New ➤ Other ➤ Other ➤ Doxyfile to add a Doxygen configuration file (*Doxyfile*) to your src/ directory.

There is now a new file in your project with a Doxyfile .doxyfile extension that you will be able to configure as shown in Figure 7-12. You can also see a blue @ sign in the top bar of Eclipse. Click this button to build the Doxyfile in order to generate the documentation for your project. You can then browse to the Documentation directory and open the html/index.html file directly within Eclipse.

Figure 7-12: Doxygen Eclox plug-in running within Eclipse

At this point you have everything you need to cross-compile applications for your BBB. The next part of this chapter outlines how you can cross-compile the Linux kernel itself and deploy a custom Linux distribution.

Building Debian for the BBB

The BBB contains a full Linux distribution when it is shipped; however, advanced users may wish to replace this image with a lean image and/or they may wish to install a Linux kernel that supports specific functionality (e.g., real-time kernel support). The tools that are described in this chapter can be used to build a Linux kernel for your BBB using a desktop Linux installation. The steps involved in this process are constantly undergoing change, so they have been presented on the chapter web page at www.exploringbeaglebone.com/chapter7 and a summary of the steps is presented in this section.

Robert C. Nelson is an applications engineer at Digi-Key Corporation, a large electronic component distributor in North America. He is a self-professed kernel hacker and he has been instrumental in developing the Debian Linux image for the BBB and many other embedded Linux devices. He has provided a comprehensive set of scripts for building Linux for the BBB. Robert has developed a script to enable you to build the Debian image directly on your desktop computer. The scripts and a full guide to their usage are available at: tiny.cc/ebb703.

Here is a summary of the steps involved in building and writing a new Linux image to the BBB:

1. **Build Das U-Boot**: Download the source code for the bootloader from git.denx.de and apply the latest u-boot patches for the AM335x processor. Build the bootloader using the cross-compilation toolchain that is described at the beginning of this chapter. After the build process you will have an x-loader MLO file and the u-boot file that allow you to boot your custom Linux kernel.

2. **Build the Linux kernel**: Clone the source code for the Linux kernel using a script from the "RobertCNelson" GitHub account. Start the build process by calling the ./build_kernel.sh script. This will prompt you to install any missing dependencies. After the build process begins you will be invited to customize the kernel settings using the Kernel Configuration tool, which is illustrated in Figure 7-13. The build process will complete after several hours and will result in a compressed kernel image (in the deploy directory).

3. **Download a root file system**: At this point you only have a Linux kernel and not a Linux distribution—there are no commands or utilities (e.g., those in the /bin directory). A minimal file system can be downloaded from: tiny.cc/ebb704.

4. **Prepare an SD card**: An SD card must be formatted and a boot and root partition added. The kernel image, MLO file, u-boot file, and a uEnv.txt file are placed on the boot partition. The minimal file system should be extracted to the root partition.

5. **Configure the Linux image startup settings**: You can edit the configuration files on the Linux file system before you boot the BBB for the first time with the new Linux image. For example, you can configure the file system (using /etc/fstab) and configure the network settings (using /etc/network/interfaces).

6. **Boot the BBB**: The BBB can then be booted using the new image on the SD card. Remember to hold the BBB's boot button. Finally, you can use Robert's eMMC flasher script to write this new image to the BBB's eMMC.

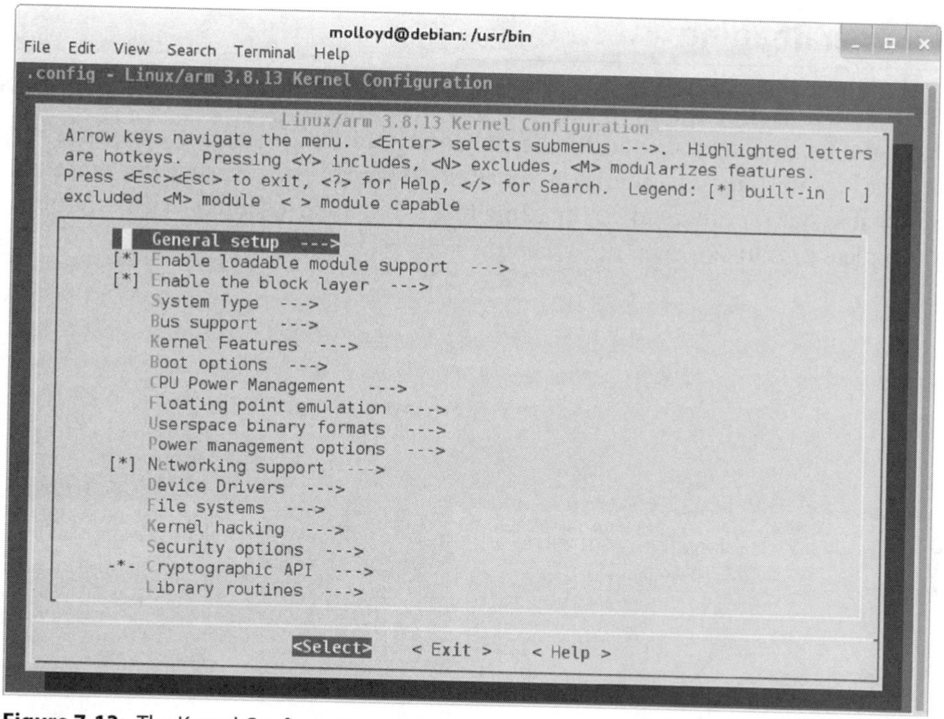

Figure 7-13: The Kernel Configuration tool

Summary

After completing this chapter, you should be able to:

- Install a cross-compilation toolchain on desktop Linux that can be used to build applications for the BBB using your desktop PC.

- Use a multiarch package manager to install multi-architecture third party libraries that may be required for cross-compilation.

- Set up a change root on a Linux desktop computer that can be used to maintain an ARM Linux distribution.

- Emulate the ARM architecture on the desktop PC using QEMU.

- Install and configure the Eclipse integrated development environment (IDE) for cross-compilation to build BBB applications.

- Configure Eclipse for remote deployment of applications, remote debugging, GitHub integration, and automated documentation.

- Describe the steps involved in building a custom Linux distribution and use external resources on the chapter web page to build a custom kernel.

Further Reading

The steps in this chapter are prone to changes in terms of the Linux distribution, the Eclipse version, and the kernel configuration. If you are experiencing difficulties with this configuration or wish to contribute information that will make it easier for others to do the same tasks that are presented in this chapter, then please go to www.exploringbeaglebone/chapter7/.

CHAPTER 8

Interfacing to the BeagleBone Buses

This chapter describes bus communication in detail, explaining and comparing the different bus types that are available on the BeagleBone. It describes how you can configure them for use, and how you can communicate with and control I²C, SPI, and UART devices, using both Linux tools and custom-developed C and C++ code. Practical examples are provided that use a low-cost accelerometer, a serial shift register, and the Arduino microcontroller. After reading this chapter, you should have the skills necessary to interface the BeagleBone to almost all of its available bus types.

Equipment Required for This Chapter:

- BeagleBone Black (BBB)
- ADXL345 accelerometer on a breakout board
- 74HC595 shift register, LEDs, and resistors
- 3.3V Arduino microcontroller or 5V Arduino microcontroller and logic-level translator

Further details on this equipment and chapter are available at www .exploringbeaglebone.com/chapter8/.

Introduction to Bus Communication

In Chapter 6, the use of GPIOs and analog I/O is discussed in detail, which makes it clear how you can connect the BBB to standalone components. This chapter examines more complex communications that can be performed using the bus interfaces that are available on the BBB. *Bus communication* is a mechanism that enables data to be transferred between the high-level components of an embedded platform, using standardized communications protocols. The two most commonly used embedded systems buses are available on the BBB, and they are the subject of this chapter: *Inter-Integrated Circuit (I^2C)* and *Serial Peripheral Interface (SPI)*. In addition, *Universal Asynchronous Receiver/Transmitter (UART)* devices are discussed. These are computer hardware devices that can be configured and used to send and receive serial data. When combined with appropriate driver interfaces, UARTs can implement standard serial communications protocols, such as RS-232, RS-422, or RS-485.

Understanding the behavior and use of bus communications protocols and devices enables the possibility of building advanced BBB electronics systems. There are a huge number of complex sensors, actuators, input devices, I/O expanders, and other microcontrollers that conform to these communications protocols, and the BBB is capable of communicating with them all.

The topics discussed in this chapter are all demonstrated using practical examples of devices that were chosen based on their wide availability and low cost. However, the focus of this chapter is imparting an understanding of the techniques employed in using the BBB's buses, rather than just describing the specific bus devices used. To this end, the chapter provides generic communications code that you can use in order to apply the principles described to any device of your choosing.

I^2C

Inter-Integrated Circuit (IIC or I^2C) is a straightforward two-wire bus that was designed by Philips in the 1980s to interface microprocessors or microcontrollers to low-speed peripheral devices. A *master* device, such as the BBB, controls the bus, and many addressable *slave* devices can be attached to the same two wires. It has remained popular over the years, mainly due to its relative simplicity and breadth of adoption. It is currently used in smartphones, most microcontrollers, and even environmental management applications in large-scale server farms. Here are some general features of the I^2C bus:

- Only two signal lines are required for communication, the *Serial Data (SDA)* line for the bidirectional transmission of data, and the *Serial Clock (SCL)* line, which is used to synchronize the data transfer. Because the bus uses this synchronizing clock signal, the data transfer is said to be *synchronous*. The transmission is said to be *bidirectional* because the same SDA wire can be used for sending and receiving data.

- Each device on the bus can act as a master or a slave. The *master device* is the one that initiates communication and the *slave device* is the one that responds. Designated slave devices cannot initiate communication with the master device.

- Each slave device attached to the bus is pre-assigned a unique address, which is in either 7-bit or 10-bit form. In the following example, 7-bit addressing is used, i.e., 0x00 to 0x80 ($2^7 = 128_{10} = 0x80$).

- It has true *multi-master bus facilities*, including collision detection and arbitration if two or more master devices activate at once.

- On-chip noise filtering is built in as standard.

I²C Hardware

Figure 8-1(a) illustrates the interconnection of multiple slave devices to the I²C bus. All output connections to the SDA and SCL lines are in open-drain configuration (discussed in Chapter 4), whereby all devices share a common ground connection. This means that devices with different logic families can be intermixed on the bus, and that a large number of devices can be added to a single bus. In theory, up to 128 devices could be attached to a single bus, but doing so would greatly increase the capacitance of the interconnecting lines. The bus is designed to work over short distances, as long bus lines are prone to electrical interference and *capacitance effects* (e.g., a pair of 22 AWG shielded wire has a capacitance of about 15pF/ft).

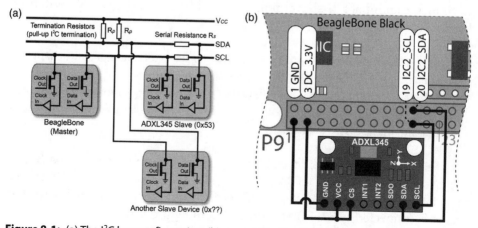

Figure 8-1: (a) The I²C bus configuration; (b) connecting the ADXL345 to the I2C2 bus on the BBB

Transmission line capacitance has a huge impact on data transmission rates. In Chapter 4 (see Figure 4-10), when a 10μF capacitor is connected in parallel with a resistive load and an AC voltage supply is applied, the capacitor had a very clear smoothing effect on the voltage across the load. This smoothing effect is unwelcome in the transmission of digital data—for example, if a random binary signal (0V–3.3V) switches at a high frequency, then severe smoothing could result in a constant 1.65V signal, which carries no binary information at all. Typically, the longer the bus length and the more I²C devices that are attached to it, then the slower the speed of data transmission. There are I²C repeaters available that act as current amplifiers to help solve the problems associated with long lines.

The BBB supports bus frequencies of up to 400kHz. NXP (formerly a division of Philips) has newer I²C Fast-mode Plus (FM+) devices that can communicate at up to 1MHz,[1] but this capability is not available on the BBB.

The I²C bus requires pull-up resistors (R_P) on both the SDA and SCL lines, as illustrated in Figure 8-1(a). These are called *termination resistors* and they usually have a value of between 1kΩ and 10kΩ. Their role is to pull the SDA and SCL lines up to V_{CC} when no I²C device is pulling them down to GND. This pull-up configuration enables multiple master devices to take control of the bus, and for the slave device to "stretch" the clock signal (i.e., hold SCL low). *Clock stretching* can be used by the slave device to slow down data transfer until it has finished processing and is ready to transmit. These resistors are often already present on the breakout board that is associated with an I²C device. This can be a useful feature, but it may cause difficulty if you wish to use several breakout boards on the same bus.

The *serial resistors* (R_S) shown in Figure 8-1(a) usually have low values (e.g., 250Ω), and can help protect against overcurrent conditions. The I²C devices are attached to the SDA and SCL lines using Schmitt trigger inputs (see Chapter 4) to reduce the impact of signal noise by building in a degree of switching hysteresis.

> **NOTE** There is a video on the use of I²C with a BMA180 accelerometer at the chapter web page: www.exploringbeaglebone.com/chapter8.
>
> In the video, an application is built using the Qt development environment to capture and graphically display the output of the accelerometer on a desktop computer. That type of application is discussed in Chapter 11.

In the I²C demonstration application discussed in this chapter, the BBB is the master device and the ADXL345 is the slave device. The ADXL345 is on a breakout board that already has 4.7kΩ termination resistors on the board. The sensor is connected to the BBB as illustrated in Figure 8-1(b).

The I²C slave address is determined by the slave device itself. For example, the ADXL345 breakout board has the address 0x53, which is determined at manufacture. Many devices, including the ADXL345, have selection inputs that allow you to alter this value within a defined range. However, the breakout board to which the device is attached needs to support this change of address facility. In the following example, you could not connect two ADXL345 breakout board devices to the same bus, as their addresses would conflict. However, there are I²C multiplexers available that would enable you to overcome this problem.

Further documentation on the I²C bus is available from NXP directly at `tiny.cc/ebb802`.

> **WARNING**   The I²C bus on the BBB is 3.3V tolerant; consequently, you will need logic-level translation circuitry if you wish to connect 5V powered I²C devices to it. That topic is discussed at the end of this chapter.

The ADXL345 Accelerometer

The Analog Devices ADXL345 is a small, low-cost *accelerometer* that can measure angular position with respect to the direction of Earth's gravitational force. For example, a single-axis accelerometer at rest on the surface of Earth, with the sensitive axis parallel to Earth's gravity, will measure an acceleration of 1*g* (9.81 m/s²) straight upward. While accelerometers provide absolute orientation measurement, they suffer from high-frequency noise, so they are often paired with gyroscopes for accurate measurement of change in orientation (e.g., in game controllers). However, accelerometers have excellent characteristics for applications in which low-frequency absolute rotation is to be measured. For simplicity, an accelerometer is used on its own in the following discussions, because the main aim is to impart an understanding of the I²C bus.

The ADXL345 can be set to measure values with a fixed 10-bit resolution, or using a 13-bit resolution at up to ±16*g*. It can be interfaced to the BBB using the I²C or SPI bus, which makes it an ideal sensor to use in this chapter as an example device. Even if you do not have this particular sensor, the following discussion is fully representative of the steps required to connect any type of I²C sensor to the BBB. The chapter web page identifies suppliers from whom you can purchase this particular sensor.

The data sheet for the ADXL345 is an important document that should be read along with this chapter. It is linked from the chapter web page or at `www.analog.com/ADXL345` (or `tiny.cc/ebb801`).

The physical connection to the ADXL345 is illustrated in Figure 8-1(b). When the CS input is tied high, the ADXL345 is placed in I²C mode. The breakout board contains the resistors that are required for the I²C bus to work correctly. The ADXL345's ALT Address pin is fixed to GND on the breakout board, placing the device at I²C address 0x53.

The I2C0 and I2C2 buses are present by default in the Debian BBB image and, perhaps erroneously, they map to the Linux device names `i2c-0` and `i2c-1`, respectively. You can enable the second public I²C bus (see Table 8-1), `i2c-2` (I2C1) using the following command:

```
molloyd@beaglebone:/dev$ sudo sh -c "echo BB-I2C1 > $SLOTS"
molloyd@beaglebone:/dev$ ls i2*
i2c-0  i2c-1  i2c-2
```

Table 8-1: I²C Buses on the BBB Debian Image

H/W BUS	S/W DEVICE	SDA PIN	SCL PIN	DESCRIPTION
I2C0	/dev/i2c-0	N/A	N/A	Internal bus for HDMI control.
I2C1	/dev/i2c-2	P9_18	P9_17	General I²C bus. Disabled by default.
I2C2	/dev/i2c-1	P9_20	P9_19	General I²C bus. Enabled by default.

Using Linux I2C-Tools

Linux provides a set of tools, called *i2c-tools*, for interfacing to I²C bus devices; it includes a bus probing tool, a chip dumper, and register-level access helpers. These tools are already installed on the BBB Debian image, but they can be updated or installed on different images using the following:

```
molloyd@beaglebone:~$ sudo apt-get install i2c-tools
i2c-tools is already the newest version.
```

i2cdetect

The first step is to detect that the device is present on the bus. When the second public I²C bus is enabled, and the clock line (SCL) or data line (SDA) are not connected to any device, the `i2cdetect` command will display the following output:

```
molloyd@beaglebone:~$ i2cdetect -l
i2c-0  i2c     OMAP I2C adapter      I2C adapter
i2c-1  i2c     OMAP I2C adapter      I2C adapter
i2c-2  i2c     OMAP I2C adapter      I2C adapter
```

The /dev/i2c-1 bus can then be probed for connected devices:

```
molloyd@beaglebone:~$ i2cdetect -y -r 1
     0  1  2  3  4  5  6  7  8  9  a  b  c  d  e  f
00:       -- -- -- -- -- -- -- -- -- -- -- -- -- --
10: -- -- -- -- -- -- -- -- -- -- -- -- -- -- -- --
20: -- -- -- -- -- -- -- -- -- -- -- -- -- -- -- --
30: -- -- -- -- -- -- -- -- -- -- -- -- -- -- -- --
40: -- -- -- -- -- -- -- -- -- -- -- -- -- -- -- --
50: -- -- -- -- UU UU UU UU -- -- -- -- -- -- -- --
60: -- -- -- -- -- -- -- -- -- -- -- -- -- -- -- --
70: -- -- -- -- -- -- -- --
```

where the addresses 0x03 to 0x77 are displayed by default. Using -a will display the full range 0x00 to 0x7F. When -- is displayed, the address was probed but no device responded. When UU is displayed, probing was skipped, as the address is already in use by a driver. You can identify which driver by using the following (0x54 in this example):

```
molloyd@beaglebone:/sys/bus/i2c/devices/1-0054$ cat modalias
i2c:24c256
```

When the ADXL sensor is physically connected to the I²C bus (I2C2) as shown in Figure 8-1(b), the I2C2 bus can be probed again using the same command:

```
molloyd@beaglebone:~$ i2cdetect -y -r 1
     0  1  2  3  4  5  6  7  8  9  a  b  c  d  e  f
...
50: -- -- -- 53 UU UU UU UU -- -- -- -- -- -- -- --
...
```

and if the device is functioning and correctly wired, it will appear at its predefined address, which is 0x53 for this breakout board implementation.

Running i2cdetect on the internal I2C0 bus will highlight that there is already a device at 0x34, which relates to the *consumer electronics control (CEC)* interface on the HDMI framer for the BBB. Address 0x70 is also used by the HDMI framer.

```
molloyd@beaglebone:~$ i2cdetect -y -r 0
     0  1  2  3  4  5  6  7  8  9  a  b  c  d  e  f
...
30: -- -- -- -- 34 -- -- -- -- -- -- -- -- -- -- --
...
```

i2cdump

The i2cdump command can be used to read in the values of the registers of the device attached to an I²C bus and display them in a hexadecimal block form. You should not use this command without consulting the datasheet for the slave device, as in certain modes the i2cdump command will write to the device. The ADXL345 can be safely probed, and its output should be given by

```
molloyd@beaglebone:~$ i2cdump -y 1 0x53
No size specified (using byte-data access)
     0  1  2  3  4  5  6  7  8  9  a  b  c  d  e  f    0123456789abcdef
00: e5 00 00 00 00 00 00 00 00 00 00 00 00 00 00 4a    ?..............J
10: 00 00 10 00 00 00 00 00 00 00 00 00 00 00 00 00    ..?.............
20: 00 00 00 00 00 00 00 00 00 00 00 00 0a 00 00 00    ............?...
30: 02 00 00 00 00 00 00 00 00 00 00 00 00 00 00 00    ?...............
```

where many of the registers are empty because the device is in power-saving mode by default. However, you can see that the first value at address 0x00 is 0xe5, and this value corresponds to the DEVID entry in Table 8-2—successful communication has been verified!

As previously stated, the datasheet for the ADXL345 from Analog Devices is available at www.analog.com/ADXL345. It is a comprehensive and well-written datasheet that details every feature of the device. In fact, the real challenge in working with new bus devices is in decoding the datasheet and the intricacies of the device's behavior. The ADXL345 has 30 public registers and Table 8-2 lists those that are accessed in this chapter. Other registers enable you to set power save inactivity periods, orientation offsets, and interrupt settings for free-fall, tap, and double-tap detection.

The x, y, and z-axis acceleration values are stored using a 10-bit or 13-bit resolution; therefore, two bytes are required for each reading, as the data is in 16-bit two's complement form (see Chapter 4). To sample at 13 bits, the ADXL345 must be set to the ±16g range. Figure 8-2 (from the ADXL345 datasheet) describes the signal sequences required to read and write to the device.

For example, to write a single byte to a device register, the master/slave access pattern in the first row is used as follows:

1. The master sends a *start bit* (i.e. it pulls SDA low, while SCL is high).

2. While the clock toggles, the seven-bit slave address is transmitted one bit at a time.

3. A read bit (1) or write bit (0) is sent, depending on whether the master wants to read or write to/from a slave register.

4. The slave then responds with an *acknowledge bit* (ACK = 0).

5. In write mode, the master sends a byte of data one bit at a time, after which the slave sends back an ACK bit. To write to a register, the register address is sent, followed by the data value to be written.

6. Finally, to conclude communication, the master sends a *stop bit* (i.e., it allows SDA to float high, while SCL is high).

Table 8-2: Subset of the Registers in the ADXL345 Register Map

ADDR	NAME	TYPE	DESCRIPTION
0x00	DEVID	R	The device ID: This should be 11100101_2, which is $E5_{16}$. Most devices have a fixed ID at the address 0x00, which is a useful check on a successful connection.
0x2D	POWER_CTL	R/W	Power-saving features control: Six bits that specify the sleep mode, measurement mode, etc. (see page 25 of the datasheet, register 0x2D). For example, 00001000_2 places the device in measurement mode with no sleep functionality enabled.
0x31	DATA_FORMAT	R/W	Data format control: Seven bits that set the self-test, SPI mode, interrupt inversion, zero bit, resolution, justify bit, and *g* range settings (two bits); e.g., 00000100_2 would set the range to ±2 *g* in 10-bit mode, with left-justified (MSB) mode (see page 26 of the datasheet, register 0x31).
0x32	DATAX0	R	X-Axis Data 0: One byte containing the least significant byte of the X-axis acceleration data.
0x33	DATAX1	R	X-Axis Data 1: Most significant byte
0x34	DATAY0	R	Y-Axis Data 0: Least significant byte
0x35	DATAY1	R	Y-Axis Data 1: Most significant byte
0x36	DATAZ0	R	Z-Axis Data 0: Least significant byte
0x37	DATAZ1	R	Z-Axis Data 1: Most significant byte

From Table 19 in the Analog Devices ADXL345 datasheet. There are 30 publicly accessible registers in total.

These handshaking sequences will shortly be confirmed by reading and writing from/to the device and by physically analyzing the I²C bus communication.

i2cget

The i2cget command can be used to read the value of a register in order to test the device, or as an input for Linux shell scripts. For example, to read the DEVID of the attached device, which should be 0xE5 in this case, use the following:

```
molloyd@beaglebone:~$ i2cget -y 1 0x53 0x00
0xe5
```

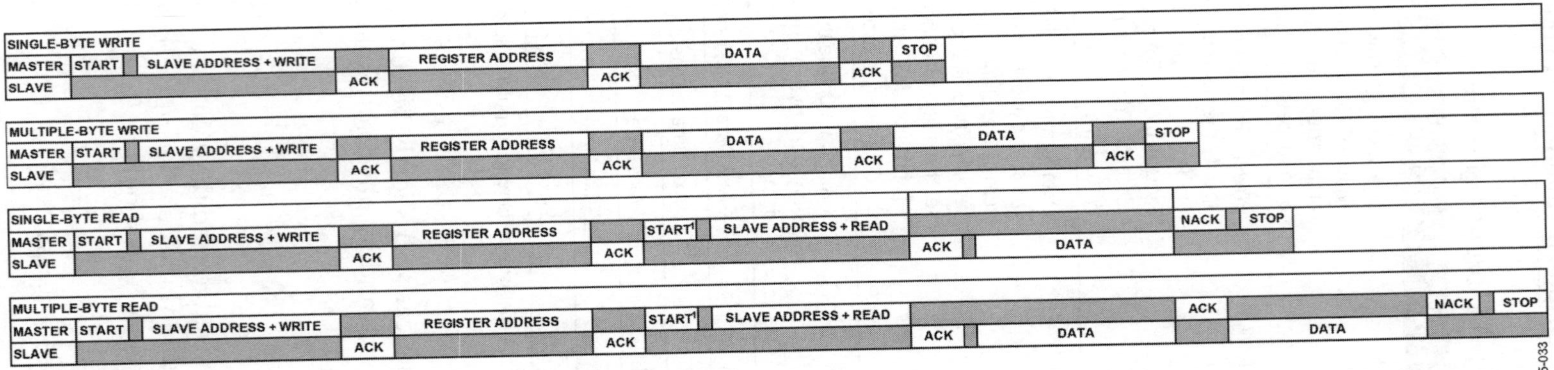

NOTES
1. THIS START IS EITHER A RESTART OR A STOP FOLLOWED BY A START.
2. THE SHADED AREAS REPRESENT WHEN THE DEVICE IS LISTENING.

Figure 41. I²C Device Addressing

Figure 8-2: Timings required for single/multiple read/write operations on the ADXL345 device

Image courtesy of Analog Devices, Inc.

The Analog Discovery digital logic analyzer functionality can be used to physically analyze the I²C bus in order to view the interaction of SDA and SCL signals as data is written to and read from the I²C bus. The logic analyzer functionality has interpreters for I²C buses, SPI buses, and UART devices, which can display the hexadecimal equivalents of the serial data carried on the bus. Figure 8-3 captures the signal transitions of the i2cget command used in the preceding example. Here, you can see that the clock is running at I²C *standard data transfer mode* (100kHz). This accelerometer also supports *fast data transfer mode* (400kHz). The timing signals displayed in Figure 8-3 confirm those on the third row of Figure 8-2 for a single byte read. The top row in Figure 8-3 (I2C2) details the interpretation of the SDA and SCL signals that are displayed on the second and third rows.

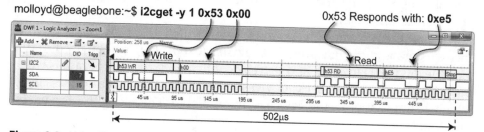

Figure 8-3: Using i2cget to read the DEVID register value

i2cset

The i2cset command can be used to set a register. This is required, for example, to take the ADXL345 out of power-saving mode, by writing 0x08 to the POWER_CTL register, which is at 0x2D. The value is written and then confirmed as follows:

```
molloyd@beaglebone:~$ i2cset -y 1 0x53 0x2D 0x08
molloyd@beaglebone:~$ i2cget -y 1 0x53 0x2D
0x08
```

If the i2cdump command is then used, the registers 0x32 through 0x37 (as identified in Table 8-2) will display the acceleration values, which change as the sensor is physically rotated and the i2cdump command is repeatedly called:

```
molloyd@beaglebone:~$ i2cdump -y 1 0x53
No size specified (using byte-data access)
     0  1  2  3  4  5  6  7  8  9  a  b  c  d  e  f    0123456789abcdef
00: e5 00 00 00 00 00 00 00 00 00 00 00 00 00 00 4a    ?..............J
10: 82 00 30 00 00 01 fc 1d 00 00 00 22 00 00 00 00    ?.0..???..."....
20: 00 00 00 00 00 00 00 00 00 00 00 00 0a 08 00 00    ............??..
30: 83 01 06 00 f1 ff 75 00 00 00 00 00 00 00 00 00    ???.?.u.........
```

The next step is to write program code that can interpret the values contained in these registers. First, C code to do this is presented, and then a C++ class is written that introduces a more structured programming approach.

I²C Communication in C

The ADXL345 digital accelerometer measures acceleration in three axes using analog sensors, which are internally sampled and filtered according to the settings that are placed in its registers. The acceleration values are then available for you to read from these registers. Therefore, the sensor performs timing-critical signal processing that would otherwise have to be performed by the BBB. However, further numerical processing is still required in converting the 16-bit two's complement values stored in its registers into values that describe angular pitch and roll. As such, C/C++ is a good choice for this type of numerical processing.

The first C programming example, in Listing 8-1, simply reads in all of the registers and displays the first register (0x00). This can be used to display the device ID (DEVID), and thereby confirm that the C program is working correctly. Many other I²C devices have device IDs at the address 0x00, which do not change as the device is manipulated. Therefore, this is a useful first test.

LISTING 8-1: exploringbb/chp08/i2c/test/testADXL345.c

```c
#include<stdio.h>
#include<fcntl.h>
#include<sys/ioctl.h>
#include<linux/i2c.h>
#include<linux/i2c-dev.h>

// Small macro to display value in hexadecimal with 2 places
#define DEVID      0x00
#define BUFFER_SIZE 40

int main(){
   int file;
   printf("Starting the ADXL345 test application\n");
   if((file=open("/dev/i2c-1", O_RDWR)) < 0){
      perror("failed to open the bus\n");
      return 1;
   }
   if(ioctl(file, I2C_SLAVE, 0x53) < 0){
      perror("Failed to connect to the sensor\n");
      return 1;
   }
   char writeBuffer[1] = {0x00};
   if(write(file, writeBuffer, 1)!=1){
      perror("Failed to reset the read address\n");
```

```
      return 1;
   }
   char readBuffer[BUFFER_SIZE];
   if(read(file, readBuffer, BUFFER_SIZE)!=BUFFER_SIZE){
      perror("Failed to read in the buffer\n");
      return 1;
   }
   printf("The Device ID is: 0x%02x\n", readBuffer[DEVID]);
   close(file);
   return 0;
}
```

The code can then be executed as follows:

```
molloyd@beaglebone:~/exploringbb/chp08/test/i2c$ ./build
Building the ADXL345 example applications
molloyd@beaglebone:~/exploringbb/chp08/test/i2c$ ./testADXL345
Starting the ADXL345 test application
The Device ID is: 0xe5
```

This program outputs that the device ID value is 0xE5, which confirms that the ADXL345 is attached at the address 0x53 and therefore that the code is working correctly.

To display all the registers and to process the accelerometer values, a new program (chp08/i2c/test/ADXL345.cpp) is written that breaks the calls into functions, such as the readRegisters() function:

```
// Read the entire 40 registers into the buffer (10 reserved)
int readRegisters(int file){
   // Writing a 0x00 to the device sets the address back to
   //   0x00 for the coming block read
   writeRegister(file, 0x00, 0x00);
   if(read(file, dataBuffer, BUFFER_SIZE)!=BUFFER_SIZE){
      cout << "Failed to read in the full buffer." << endl;
      return 1;
   }
   if(dataBuffer[DEVID]!=0xE5){
      cout << "Problem detected! Device ID is wrong" << endl;
      return 1;
   }
   return 0;
}
```

This code writes the address 0x00 to the device, causing it to send back the full 0x40 registers (BUFFER_SIZE). In order to process the two raw 8-bit acceleration registers, code to combine two bytes into a single 16-bit value is written as follows:

```
// short is 16-bits on the BBB
short combineValues(unsigned char upper, unsigned char lower){
```

```
    //shift the most significant byte left by 8 bits and OR with the
    // least significant byte
    `return ((short)upper<<8)|(short)lower;
}
```

The types of the data are vital in this function, as the register data is returned in two's complement form. If an `int` type (of size 32-bits, `int32_t`) were used instead of `short` 16-bit integral data (`int16_t`), then the sign bit would be dislocated. This function shifts the upper byte left (multiply) by eight places (equivalent to a multiplication by $2^8 = 256$) and ORs the result with the lower byte, which replaces the lower byte with eight zeroes that are introduced by the shift). This results in a 16-bit signed value (`int16_t`) that has been created from two separate 8-bit values (`uint8_t`). When executed, the `ADXL345.cpp` application will give the following output, with the program updating the acceleration data on the same console line:

```
molloyd@beaglebone:~/exploringbb/chp08/i2c/test$ ./ADXL345
Starting the ADXL345 sensor application
The Device ID is: e5
The POWER_CTL mode is: 08
The DATA_FORMAT is: 00
X=13 Y=-35 Z=232 sample=17
```

Additional code is required to convert these values into a pitch and roll form. This is added to the C++ class in the next section. For your information, the logic analyzer indicates that it takes 4.19ms to read in the full set of 40 registers at a bus speed of 100kHz.

Wrapping I²C Devices with C++ Classes

Object-oriented programming is described in Chapter 5 as a suitable framework for developing code for embedded systems. As a programmer, one of your key aims should be to avoid writing the same code twice. You could repeatedly copy-and-paste code from project to project, but if you subsequently discover an error, it will have to be corrected in several locations. A danger arises when you forget to change the copied code in one or more locations.

A specific C++ class can be written to wrap the functionality of the ADXL345 accelerometer; because it is likely that you will need to write code to control several different types of I²C device, it would be useful if the general I²C code could be extracted and placed in a parent class. To this end, a class has been written for this chapter called `I2CDevice` that captures the general functionality you would associate with an I²C bus device. You can extend this code to control any type of I²C device. It can be found in the `I2CDevice.cpp` and `I2CDevice.h` files in the `chp08/i2c/cpp/` directory. Later in this chapter the code is further restructured and placed in the `/library/bus` GitHub directory. The class has the structure as described in Listing 8-2.

LISTING 8-2: /exploringbb/chp08/i2c/cpp/I2CDevice.h

```
class I2CDevice {
private:
    unsigned int bus, device;
    int file;
public:
    I2CDevice(unsigned int bus, unsigned int device);
    virtual int open();
    virtual int write(unsigned char value);
    virtual unsigned char readRegister(unsigned int registerAddress);
    virtual unsigned char* readRegisters(unsigned int number,
                                         unsigned int fromAddress=0);
    virtual int writeRegister(unsigned int registerAddress, unsigned char value);
    virtual void debugDumpRegisters(unsigned int number);
    virtual void close();
    virtual ~I2CDevice();
};
```

The implementation code is available in the `chp08/i2c/cpp/` directory. This class can be extended to control any type of I²C device, and in this case it is used as the parent of a specific device implementation class called `ADXL345`. Therefore, you can say that `ADXL345` IS-A `I2CDevice`. This inheritance relationship means that any methods available in the `I2CDevice` class are now available in the `ADXL345` class in Listing 8-3 (e.g., `readRegister()`).

LISTING 8-3: /exploringbb/chp08/i2c/cpp/ADXL345.h

```
class ADXL345:protected I2CDevice{
    // protected inheritance means that the public I2C methods are no
    //   longer publicly accessible by an object of the ADXL345 class
public:
    enum RANGE {          // enumerations are used to limit the options
        PLUSMINUS_2_G = 0,
        PLUSMINUS_4_G = 1,
        PLUSMINUS_8_G = 2,
        PLUSMINUS_16_G = 3
    };
    enum RESOLUTION {
        NORMAL = 0,
        HIGH = 1
    };

private:
    unsigned int I2CBus, I2CAddress;
    unsigned char *registers;
```

continues

LISTING 8-3: *(continued)*

```
    ADXL345::RANGE range;
    ADXL345::RESOLUTION resolution;
    // raw 2's complement values
    short accelerationX, accelerationY, accelerationZ;
    float pitch, roll;    // in degrees
    short combineRegisters(unsigned char msb, unsigned char lsb);
    void calculatePitchAndRoll();
    virtual int updateRegisters();
public:
    ADXL345(unsigned int I2CBus, unsigned int I2CAddress=0x53);
    virtual int readSensorState();
    virtual void setRange(ADXL345::RANGE range);
    virtual ADXL345::RANGE getRange() { return this->range; }
    virtual void setResolution(ADXL345::RESOLUTION resolution);
    virtual ADXL345::RESOLUTION getResolution() { return this->resolution; }
    virtual short getAccelerationX() { return accelerationX; }
    virtual short getAccelerationY() { return accelerationY; }
    virtual short getAccelerationZ() { return accelerationZ; }
    virtual float getPitch() { return pitch; }
    virtual float getRoll() { return roll; }
    // Debugging method to display and update the pitch/roll on the one line
    virtual void displayPitchAndRoll(int iterations = 600);
    virtual ~ADXL345();
};
```

The enumeration structures are used to constrain the range and resolution selections to contain only valid options. A short example (`application.cpp`) can be used to test this structure, as follows:

```
int main(){
    ADXL345 sensor(1,0x53);    // sensor is on bus 1 at the address 0x53
    sensor.setResolution(ADXL345::NORMAL);    // using 10-bit resolution
    sensor.setRange(ADXL345::PLUSMINUS_4_G); // range is +/-4g
    sensor.displayPitchAndRoll();    // put the sensor in display mode
    return 0;
}
```

This code can be built and executed as follows, where the pitch and roll are angular values that each vary between ±90°:

```
/chp08/i2c/cpp$ g++ application.cpp I2CDevice.cpp ADXL345.cpp -o ADXL345
/chp08/i2c/cpp$ ./ADXL345
Pitch:5.71592 Roll:-31.5256
```

You can use this general structure to build wrapper classes for any type of I²C sensor, and it will work perfectly well. However, later in this chapter an additional software design issue must be addressed, meaning that the structure presented here for the ADXL345 class requires further modification.

SPI

The *Serial Peripheral Interface (SPI)* bus is a fast, full-duplex synchronous serial data link that enables devices such as the BBB to communicate with other devices over short distances. Therefore, like I²C, the SPI bus is synchronous, but unlike the I²C bus the SPI bus is *full-duplex*. This means that it can transmit and receive data at the same time, by using separate lines for both sending data and receiving data.

In this section the SPI bus is introduced, and two separate applications are developed. The first uses the SPI bus to drive an LED bar graph display using the ubiquitous 74HC595 eight-bit shift register. The second application interfaces to the ADXL345 accelerometer again, this time using its SPI bus instead of the I²C bus used previously.

SPI Hardware

SPI communication takes place between a single master device and one or more slave devices. Figure 8-4(a) illustrates a single slave example, where four signal lines are connected between the master and slave devices. To communicate with the slave device, the following steps take place:

1. The *SPI master* defines the clock frequency at which to synchronize the data communication channels.

2. The SPI master pulls the *chip select* (CS) line low, which activates the client device—it is therefore said to be active low. This line is also known as *slave select* (SS).

3. After a short delay, the SPI master issues clock cycles, sending data out on the *master out-slave in* (MOSI) line and receiving data on the *master in-slave out* (MISO) line. The *SPI slave* device reads data from the MOSI line and transmits data on the MISO line. One bit is sent and one bit is received on each clock cycle. The data is usually sent in one-byte (eight-bit) chunks.

4. When complete, the SPI master stops sending a clock signal and then pulls the CS line high, deactivating the SPI slave device.

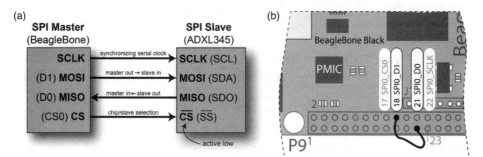

Figure 8-4: (a) Using SPI to connect to one slave; (b) testing SPI using a Linux configuration

Unlike I²C, the SPI bus does not require pull-up resistors on the communication lines, so connections are very straightforward. A summary comparison of I²C versus SPI is provided in Table 8-3.

Table 8-3: Comparison of I²C versus SPI on the BBB

	I²C	SPI
Connectivity	Two wires, to which up to 128 addressable devices can be attached.	Typically four wires, and requires additional logic for more than one slave device.
Data rate	I²C fast mode is 400 kHz. Uses half-duplex communication.	Faster performance, typically over 10 MHz. Full duplex (except three-wire variant).
Hardware	Pull-up resistors required.	No pull-up resistors required.
BBB support	Fully supported with two external buses (plus one internal).	Fully supported with two buses. Only one slave selection pin on each bus.
Features	Can have multiple masters. Slaves have addresses, acknowledge transfer, and can control the flow of data.	Simple and fast, but only one master device, no addressing, and no slave control of data flow.
Application	Intermittently accessed devices, e.g., real-time clock, EEPROMs.	For devices that provide data streams, e.g., ADCs.

The SPI bus operates using one of four different modes, which is chosen according to the specification defined in the SPI slave device's datasheet. Data is synchronized using the clock signal, and one of the *SPI communication modes* described in Table 8-4 is set to describe how the synchronization is performed. The *clock polarity* defines whether the clock is low or high when it is idle (i.e., when CS is high). The *clock phase* defines whether the data on the MOSI and MISO lines is captured on the rising edge or falling edge of the clock signal. When a clock's polarity is 1, the clock signal is equivalent to an inverted version of the same signal with a polarity of 0. Therefore, a rising edge on one form of clock signal polarity is the equivalent of a falling edge on the other. You need to examine the datasheet for the slave device in order to determine the SPI mode.

The SPI protocol does not define a maximum data rate, flow control, or communication acknowledgment. Therefore, implementations vary from device to device, so it is very important to study the datasheet of each type of SPI slave device. There are some three-wire SPI variants that use a single bidirectional MISO/MOSI line instead of two individual lines. For example, the ADXL345 sensor supports I²C, and both *four-wire* and *three-wire SPI* communication.

Table 8-4: SPI Communication Modes

MODE	CLOCK POLARITY (CPOL)	CLOCK PHASE (CPHA)
0	**0** (low at idle)	**0** (data captured on the rising edge of the clock signal)
1	**0** (low at idle)	**1** (data captured on the falling edge of the clock signal)
2	**1** (high at idle)	**0** (data captured on the falling edge of the clock signal)
3	**1** (high at idle)	**1** (data captured on the rising edge of the clock signal)

WARNING   Do not connect a 5V-powered SPI slave device to the MISO input on the BBB. Logic-level translation is discussed at the end of this chapter.

SPI on the BBB

The P9 header layout in Figure 6-7 of Chapter 6 identifies that the SPI0 and SPI1 buses are accessible from this header. SPI1 clashes with the mcasp0_pins, so to use SPI1 you have to disable HDMI. As illustrated in Figure 8-4(b), the pins for SPI0 are as follows:

- **Chip Select:** P9_17 spi0_cs0 (Mode 0) $PINS 87 Offset 0x15C.
- **MOSI:** P9_18 spi0_d1 (Mode 0) $PINS 86 Offset 0x158.
- **MISO:** P9_21 spi0_d0 (Mode 0) $PINS 85 Offset 0x154.
- **Clock:** P9_22 spi0_sclk (Mode 0) $PINS 84 Offset 0x150.

The SPI0 and SPI1 buses are disabled by default, so to enable them you use device tree overlays, as described in Chapter 6. The BB-SPIDEV0-00A0.dts file defines how this overlay is configured, with internal pull-up resistors enabled and inputs/outputs defined as shown in the partial listing in Listing 8-4. The full listing is linked from the web page associated with this chapter.

LISTING 8-4: BB-SPIDEV0-OOAO.dts (partial)

```
/* Copyright (C) 2013 CircuitCo */
...
fragment@0 {
    target = <&am33xx_pinmux>;
    __overlay__ {
        /* default state has all gpios released and mode set to uart1 */
        bb_spi0_pins: pinmux_bb_spi0_pins {
            pinctrl-single,pins = <
```

continues

LISTING 8-4: *(continued)*

```
            0x150 0x30    /* spi0_sclk.spi0_sclk,  INPUT_PULLUP  | MODE0 */
            0x154 0x30    /* spi0_d0.spi0_d0,      INPUT_PULLUP  | MODE0 */
            0x158 0x10    /* spi0_d1.spi0_d1,      OUTPUT_PULLUP | MODE0 */
            0x15c 0x10    /* spi0_cs0.spi0_cs0,    OUTPUT_PULLUP | MODE0 */
        >;
    };
  };
};
fragment@1 {
    target = <&spi0>;   /* spi0 is numbered correctly */
    __overlay__ {
        #address-cells = <1>;
        #size-cells = <0>;
        status = "okay";
        pinctrl-names = "default";
        pinctrl-0 = <&bb_spi0_pins>;
        channel@0 {
            #address-cells = <1>;
            #size-cells = <0>;
            compatible = "spidev";
            reg = <0>;
            spi-max-frequency = <16000000>;
            spi-cpha;
        };
        channel@1 { ...
        };
    };
};
```

Enabling the First SPI Bus (SPI0)

To enable the SPI buses, the requisite overlay must be loaded, using the same syntax discussed in Chapter 6:

```
molloyd@beaglebone:/lib/firmware$ ls *SPI*
ADAFRUIT-SPI0-00A0.dtbo   BB-SPIDEV0-00A0.dtbo   BB-SPIDEV1A1-00A0.dtbo
ADAFRUIT-SPI1-00A0.dtbo   BB-SPIDEV1-00A0.dtbo
molloyd@beaglebone:/lib/firmware$ sudo sh -c "echo BB-SPIDEV0 > $SLOTS"
molloyd@beaglebone:/lib/firmware$ cat $SLOTS
...
 4: ff:P-O-L Bone-LT-eMMC-2G,00A0,Texas Instrument,BB-BONE-EMMC-2G
 5: ff:P-O-L Bone-Black-HDMI,00A0,Texas Instrument,BB-BONELT-HDMI
 7: ff:P-O-L Override Board Name,00A0,Override Manuf,BB-SPIDEV0
```

If the overlay is loaded correctly into a slot, then there will now be two new devices in /dev as follows, where spidev1.0 means chip select 0 on bus 1:

```
molloyd@beaglebone:/lib/firmware$ cd /dev
```

```
molloyd@beaglebone:/dev$ ls sp*
spidev1.0  spidev1.1
```

Testing the SPI Bus

To test the SPI bus you can use a program called `spidev_test.c` that is available from `www.kernel.org`. However, the latest version at the time of writing has added support for dual and quad data-wire SPI transfers, which are not supported on the BBB. An older version of this code has been placed in `/chp08/spi/spidev_test/` and can be built using the following:

```
~/exploringbb/chp08/spi/spidev_test$ gcc spidev_test.c -o spidev_test
```

Because the pins have been enabled in pull-up mode, the output displayed by the `spidev_test` program should be 0xFF when nothing is connected to the bus and the test program is executed:

```
~/exploringbb/chp08/spi/spidev_test$ ./spidev_test
spi mode: 0
bits per word: 8
max speed: 500000 Hz (500 KHz)
FF FF FF FF FF FF
FF FF FF FF FF FF
FF FF FF FF FF FF
FF FF FF FF FF FF
FF FF FF FF FF FF
FF FF FF FF FF FF
FF FF
```

Connect the spi0_d1 (P9_18) and spi0_d0 (P9_21) header input/outputs together so that the BBB MOSI is connected to the BBB MISO, as in Figure 8-4(b). When the test program is executed again, the output should be as follows:

```
~/exploringbb/chp08/spi/spidev_test$ ./spidev_test
spi mode: 0
bits per word: 8
max speed: 500000 Hz (500 KHz)
FF FF FF FF FF FF
40 00 00 00 00 95
FF FF FF FF FF FF
FF FF FF FF FF FF
FF FF FF FF FF FF
DE AD BE EF BA AD
F0 0D
```

This is the exact block of data that is defined in the `tx[]` array inside the `spidev_test.c` code. Therefore, in this case, the block of data has been successfully transmitted from P9_18 (MOSI) and received by P9_21 (MISO). This program can be executed on the second SPI bus as follows:

```
~/exploringbb/chp08/spi/spidev_test$ ./spidev_test -D /dev/spidev2.0
```

A First SPI Application (74HC595)

The first application to test the SPI bus is illustrated in Figure 8-5. It uses a 74HC595, which is an eight-bit shift register with latched outputs that can be supplied at 3.3V logic levels. The 74HC595 can typically be used at frequencies of 20MHz or greater, depending on the supply voltage V_{CC}. The circuit in Figure 8-5 uses an LED bar graph and a resistor network in order to minimize the number of connections, but an equivalent circuit with individual LEDs and resistors is just as functionally valid.

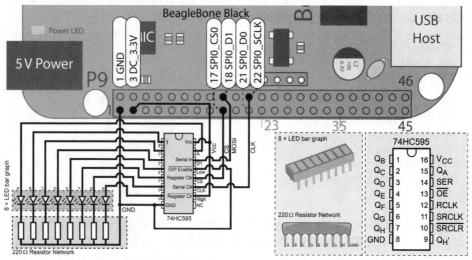

Figure 8-5: The 74HC595 SPI example

NOTE For a video on serial-to-parallel conversion that explains the concept of output latching by comparing the 74HC164 to the 74HC595, see the chapter web page: www.exploringbeaglebone.com/chapter8.

Wiring the 74HC595 Circuit

The 74HC595 is connected to the BBB using three of the four SPI lines, as a MISO response from the 74HC595 is not required (you could connect the MISO line to $Q_{H'}$ as a further test). The connections are as follows:

- P9_22 SPI0_SCLK is connected to the Serial Clock input (pin 11) of the 74HC595. This line is used to synchronize the transfer of SPI data on the MOSI line.

■ P9_18 SPI0_D1 is the MOSI line and is used to transfer the data from the BBB to the 74HC595 Serial Input (pin 14). This will send one byte (eight bits) at a time, which is the full capacity of the 74HC595.

P9_17 SPI0_CS0 is the slave select line. This line is important, as it is used to latch the data to the output of the 74HC595 when its state transitions from low to high. As such, it is connected to the Register Clock input (pin 12) of the 74HC595. The LEDs on the bar graph will light according to the bytes that are transferred. For example, sending 0xAA should light every second LED on the bar graph if the setup is working correctly, as 0xAA = 10101010_2. This circuit is useful for controlling eight outputs using a single serial data line and it can be extended further by daisy chaining 74HC595 ICs together. This is particularly useful for driving arrays of seven-segment displays, and is discussed in the next chapter.

Once the overlay is loaded, you can write directly to the device as follows to light *most* of the LEDs (-n suppresses the newline character, -e enables escape character interpretation, and \x escapes the subsequent value as hexadecimal):

```
molloyd@beaglebone:/dev$ echo -ne "\xFF" > /dev/spidev1.0
```

The following will turn *most* of the LEDs off:

```
molloyd@beaglebone:/dev$ echo -ne "\x00" > /dev/spidev1.0
```

However, this may not work exactly as expected, as the current SPI communication mode does not align by default with the operation of the 74HC595, as wired in Figure 8-5. As a test, it is useful to confirm that there is some level of response from the circuit. The transfer mode issue is corrected within the following code example.

SPI Communication Using C

A C program can be written to control the LED bar graph. Basic open() and close() operations on the /dev/spidevX.Y devices work, but if you need to alter the low-level SPI transfer parameters, then a more sophisticated interface is required.

The following program uses the Linux user space SPI API, which supports reading and writing to SPI slave devices. It is accessed using Linux ioctl() requests, which support SPI through the sys/ioctl.h and linux/spi/spidev.h header files. A full guide on the use of this API is available at www.kernel.org/doc/Documentation/spi/.

The program in Listing 8-5 will cycle the LEDs in the bar graph from 00000000 to 11111111 and output the count to a Linux terminal. The transfer() function is the most important part of the code example.

LISTING 8-5: /exploringbb/chp08/spi/spi595Example/spi595.c

```c
/** SPI C Transfer Example, Written by Derek Molloy (www.derekmolloy.ie)
 *     for the book Exploring BeagleBone. Based on the spidev_test.c code
 *     example at www.kernel.org */

#include<stdio.h>
#include<fcntl.h>
#include<unistd.h>
#include<sys/ioctl.h>
#include<stdint.h>
#include<linux/spi/spidev.h>

#define SPI_PATH "/dev/spidev1.0"

int transfer(int fd, unsigned char send[], unsigned char receive[], int length){
   struct spi_ioc_transfer transfer;          // the transfer structure
   transfer.tx_buf = (unsigned long) send;     // the buffer for sending data
   transfer.rx_buf = (unsigned long) receive;  // the buffer for receiving data
   transfer.len = length;                       // the length of buffer
   transfer.speed_hz = 1000000;                 // the speed in Hz
   transfer.bits_per_word = 8;                  // bits per word
   transfer.delay_usecs = 0;                    // delay in us
   // send the SPI message (all of the above fields, inc. buffers)
   int status = ioctl(fd, SPI_IOC_MESSAGE(1), &transfer);
   if (status < 0) {
      perror("SPI: SPI_IOC_MESSAGE Failed");
      return -1;
   }
   return status;
}

int main(){
   unsigned int fd, i=0;                // file handle and loop counter
   unsigned char value, null=0x00;      // sending only a single char
   uint8_t bits = 8, mode = 3;          // 8-bits per word, SPI mode 3
   uint32_t speed = 1000000;            // Speed is 1 MHz

   // The following calls set up the SPI bus properties
   if ((fd = open(SPI_PATH, O_RDWR))<0){
      perror("SPI Error: Can't open device.");
      return -1;
   }
   if (ioctl(fd, SPI_IOC_WR_MODE, &mode)==-1){
      perror("SPI: Can't set SPI mode.");
      return -1;
   }
   if (ioctl(fd, SPI_IOC_RD_MODE, &mode)==-1){
      perror("SPI: Can't get SPI mode.");
      return -1;
   }
   if (ioctl(fd, SPI_IOC_WR_BITS_PER_WORD, &bits)==-1){
      perror("SPI: Can't set bits per word.");
      return -1;
```

```
   }
   if (ioctl(fd, SPI_IOC_RD_BITS_PER_WORD, &bits)==-1){
      perror("SPI: Can't get bits per word.");
      return -1;
   }
   if (ioctl(fd, SPI_IOC_WR_MAX_SPEED_HZ, &speed)==-1){
      perror("SPI: Can't set max speed HZ");
      return -1;
   }
   if (ioctl(fd, SPI_IOC_RD_MAX_SPEED_HZ, &speed)==-1){
      perror("SPI: Can't get max speed HZ.");
      return -1;
   }
   // Check that the properties have been set
   printf("SPI Mode is: %d\n", mode);
   printf("SPI Bits is: %d\n", bits);
   printf("SPI Speed is: %d\n", speed);
   printf("Counting through all of the LEDs:\n");

   // Loop from 0 to 255 and light the LED bar as a binary counter
   for (i=0; i<255; i++)
   {
      // This function can send and receive data, but just sending here
      if (transfer(fd, (unsigned char*) &i, &null, 1)==-1){
         perror("Failed to update the display");
         return -1;
      }
      printf("%4d\r", i);    // print the number on the same line
      fflush(stdout);        // need to flush the output, as no \n
      usleep(100000);        // sleep for 100ms each loop
   }
   close(fd);                // close the file
   return 0;
}
```

The `main()` function sets the SPI control parameters. These are `ioctl()` requests that allow you to override the device's current settings for parameters such as the following, where xx is both RD (read) and RW (write):

- SPI_IOC_xx_MODE: The SPI transfer mode (0–3)

- SPI_IOC_xx_BITS_PER_WORD: Number of bits in each word

- SPI_IOC_xx_LSB_FIRST: 0 is MSB first, 1 is LSB first

- SPI_IOC_xx_MAX_SPEED_HZ: Maximum transfer rate in Hz

The current Linux implementation provides for synchronous transfers only. When executed, this code will result in the following output, where the count value continually increases on the one line of the terminal window:

```
molloyd@beaglebone:~/exploringbb/chp08/spi/spi595Example$ ./spi595
SPI Mode is: 3
SPI Bits is: 8
```

```
SPI Speed is: 1000000
Counting through all of the LEDs:
 163
```

At the same time, this code is sending signals to the 74HC595 as captured using the SPI interpreter of the Analog Discovery in Figure 8-6, when the count is at $163_{10} = 0xA3$. At this point in time, the CS line is pulled low, while a clock (SCLK) that is "high at idle" is toggled by the SPI master after a short delay. The data is then sent on the SDIO line, MSB first, to the 74HC595, and it is transferred on the rising edge of the clock signal. This confirms that the SPI transfer is taking place in mode 3, as described in Table 8-4.

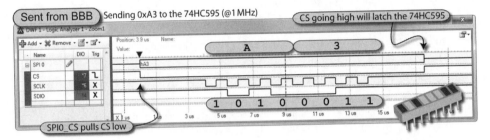

Figure 8-6: The 74HC595 SPI signal and output

The total transfer takes less than 18μs. If the channel were held open, it would be capable of transferring a maximum of 91kB/s (727kb/s) at 1MHz, if there were no delay between each byte transfer.

Bidirectional SPI Communication in C++

The 74HC595 example sent data from the BBB to the 74HC595, and as such is a unidirectional communication example. It is possible to use the Q_H, serial output (pin 9) of the 74HC595 as a test example of bidirectional data transfer, because when eight bits of data are shifted into the 74HC595, the previous eight bits are shifted out through this output pin. The pin could then be connected to the MISO input on the BBB. However, a more generally applicable example of bidirectional communication that involves register addressing can be demonstrated with the ADXL345 sensor.

As discussed previously, the AXL345 has both an I²C and an SPI communications interface. This makes it a useful device with which to examine bidirectional SPI communication here, as the register structure has already been discussed in detail. In addition, its use brings up some interesting software design challenges. The second SPI bus is used in the following example, so that it can be tested and so that the previous circuit can be temporarily preserved.

> **NOTE**   For reference, the main guide for writing user space code for bidirectional
> SPI communication under Linux is available at www.kernel.org/doc/
> Documentation/spi/spidev.

The Second SPI Bus (SPI1)

The second SPI Bus, SPI1, can be enabled, but not if the HDMI interface is in use.
The HDMI overlay can be disabled using the steps described in Chapter 6 (see
"Removing an Overlay"). When the second overlay is loaded, the slots should
be populated as follows:

```
molloyd@beaglebone:~$ sudo sh -c "echo BB-SPIDEV1 > $SLOTS"
molloyd@beaglebone:~$ cat $SLOTS
...
 4: ff:P-O-L Bone-LT-eMMC-2G,00A0,Texas Instrument,BB-BONE-EMMC-2G
 5: ff:P-O-- Bone-Black-HDMI,00A0,Texas Instrument,BB-BONELT-HDMI
 6: ff:P-O-- Bone-Black-HDMIN,00A0,Texas Instrument,BB-BONELT-HDMIN
 7: ff:P-O-L Override Board Name,00A0,Override Manuf,BB-SPIDEV1
```

Once loaded, the SPI bus has the following configuration:

- **Chip Select:** P9_28 spi1_cs0 (Mode 3) $PINS 103 Offset 0x19C
- **MOSI:** P9_30 spi1_d1 (Mode 3) $PINS 102 Offset 0x198
- **MISO:** P9_29 spi1_d0 (Mode 3) $PINS 101 Offset 0x194
- **Clock:** P9_31 spi1_sclk (Mode 3) $PINS 100 Offset 0x190

Depending on the number of SPI overlays that you have loaded, the SPI1 device
will appear as either spidev1.0 and spidev1.1 or spidev2.0 and spidev2.1.
With both SPI buses enabled, you should see the following:

```
molloyd@beaglebone:/dev$ ls spi*
spidev1.0  spidev1.1  spidev2.0  spidev2.1
```

The ADXL345 SPI Interface

SPI is not a formal standard with a standards body controlling its implementation, and therefore it is vital that you study the datasheet for the device that you
wish to attach to the BBB. In particular, the SPI communication timing diagram
should be studied in detail. This is presented for the ADXL345 in Figure 8-7.

Note the following very important points, which can be observed directly
from the datasheet:

- To write to an address, the first bit on the SDI line must be low. To read
  from an address the first bit on the SDI line must be high.
- The second bit is called MB. From further analysis of the datasheet, this bit
  enables multiple byte reading/writing of the registers (i.e., send the first

address and data will be continuously read from that register forward). This leaves six bits in the first byte for the address ($2^6 = 64_{10} = 40_{16}$), which is sufficient to cover the available registers.

- As shown in the figure, the SCLK line is high at rest and data is transferred on the rising edge of the clock signal. Therefore, the ADXL345 device must be used in communications mode 3 (refer to Table 8-4).

- When writing (top figure), the address (with a leading 0) is written to SDI, followed by the byte value to be written to the address.

- When reading (bottom figure), the address (with a leading 1) is written to SDI. A second byte is written to SDI and will be ignored. While the second (ignored) byte is being written to SDI, the response will be returned on SDO detailing the value stored at the register address.

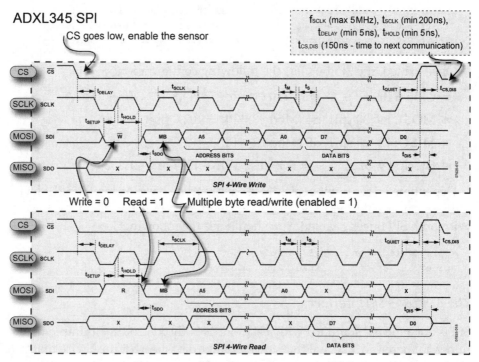

Figure 8-7: The ADXL345 SPI communication timing chart (from the ADXL345 datasheet)

Underlying image is courtesy of Analog Devices, Inc.

Connecting the ADXL345 to the BBB

The ADXL345 breakout board can be connected to the SPI1 bus as illustrated in Figure 8-8, where MOSI on the BBB is connected to SDI and MISO is connected to SDO. The clock lines and the slave select lines are also interconnected.

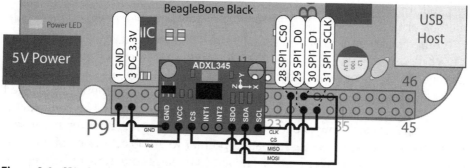

Figure 8-8: SPI1 Connection to the ADXL345

Wrapping SPI Devices with C++ Classes

A C++ class has also been written in order to wrap the software interface to the SPI bus, using the OOP techniques that are described in Chapter 5. Before discussing it, there is an interesting OOP design problem that needs to be solved. In theory, if your OOP structure is designed properly then you should never need to write the same code twice. This is desirable because copying and pasting code will result in twice the amount of code, which will need to be debugged and maintained. Earlier in this chapter a structure is presented whereby the class ADXL345 is a child of the I2CDevice class. That is a reasonable design given the information available at that point. However, because the ADXL345 also has an SPI interface, it is necessary now to update the software structure. One possible solution is illustrated in Figure 8-9(a), which is presented in a pseudo-UML form.

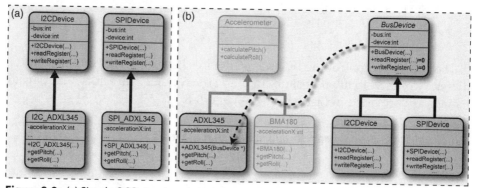

Figure 8-9: (a) Simple OOP structure (not recommended); (b) more appropriate OOP design

Unfortunately, this structure involves copying and pasting code, as the same code will have to be written in both the I2C_ADXL345 and the SPI_ADXL345 classes. As this code is implemented in C++, you could use some form of multiple inheritance, but you would have to build in function pointer switches, or explicitly indicate whether you are using the `I2CDevice::readRegister()` method or the `SPIDevice::readRegister()` method.

A different structure is presented in Figure 8-9(b). In this design, a new abstract class called `BusDevice` is created that describes, but does not implement, the methods that are common to both I²C and SPI devices (e.g., `readRegister()` or `writeRegister()`). The actual implementation of these methods is provided in the `I2CDevice` and `SPIDevice` child classes, respectively. The constructor of the `ADXL345` class now expects an object of `BusDevice`. However, because it is an abstract class, you actually pass a pointer to an object of one of its child classes (`I2CDevice` or `SPIDevice`). The `ADXL345` class code now only needs to be written in one location.

One additional advantage of this structure is that if you were writing code for different accelerometer types (e.g., the Bosch BMA180), then you could create a new general class (e.g., `Accelerometer`) that would contain functionality that is common to all accelerometer types, such as the numerical calculation of pitch and roll values.

This approach may seem overly complex, but the actual usage is very straightforward. For example, if you assume that two ADXL345 sensors are attached to the BBB, one to the SPI bus and the second to the I2C bus, you can use the exact same `ADXL345` class to create two objects in the following way:

```
int main() {
    SPIDevice spi(1,0);
    ADXL345 acc1(&spi);
    acc1.displayPitchAndRoll(100);

    I2CDevice i2c(1,0x53);
    ADXL345 acc2(&i2c);
    acc2.displayPitchAndRoll(100);
}
```

The classes for controlling I²C and SPI devices have been added to the library directory of the GitHub repository in the `/library/bus/` directory, and partial listings are provided in Listings 8-6, 8-7, and 8-8.

LISTING 8-6:   /library/bus/BusDevice.h (partial)

```
class BusDevice {
protected:
    unsigned int bus;
    unsigned int device;
    int file;
public:
    BusDevice(unsigned int bus, unsigned int device);
    virtual int open()=0;
    virtual unsigned char readRegister(unsigned int registerAddress)=0;
```

```
    virtual unsigned char* readRegisters(unsigned int number,
                                unsigned int fromAddress=0)=0;
    virtual int write(unsigned char value)=0;
    virtual int writeRegister(unsigned int registerAddress,
                            unsigned char value)=0;
    virtual void debugDumpRegisters(unsigned int number = 0xff)=0;
    virtual void close()=0;
    virtual ~BusDevice();
};
```

LISTING 8-7: /library/bus/SPIDevice.h (partial)

```
class SPIDevice:public BusDevice {
public:
    /// The SPI Mode
    enum SPIMODE{
        MODE0 = 0,    //!< Low at idle, capture on rising clock edge
        MODE1 = 1,    //!< Low at idle, capture on falling clock edge
        MODE2 = 2,    //!< High at idle, capture on falling clock edge
        MODE3 = 3     //!< High at idle, capture on rising clock edge
    };
private:
    std::string filename;
public:
    SPIDevice(unsigned int bus, unsigned int device);
    virtual int open();
    virtual unsigned char readRegister(unsigned int registerAddress);
    virtual unsigned char* readRegisters(unsigned int number,
                                    unsigned int fromAddress=0);
    virtual int writeRegister(unsigned int registerAddress, unsigned char value);
    virtual void debugDumpRegisters(unsigned int number = 0xff);
    virtual int write(unsigned char value);
    virtual int setSpeed(uint32_t speed);
    virtual int setMode(SPIDevice::SPIMODE mode);
    virtual int setBitsPerWord(uint8_t bits);
    virtual void close();
    virtual ~SPIDevice();
private:
    virtual int transfer(unsigned char read[], unsigned char write[], int length);
    SPIMODE mode;
    uint8_t bits;
    uint32_t speed;
    uint16_t delay;
};
```

LISTING 8-8: /library/sensor/ADXL345.h (partial)

```
class ADXL345{

public:
    /// An enumeration to define the gravity range of the sensor
```

continues

LISTING 8-8: *(continued)*

```
    enum RANGE {
        PLUSMINUS_2_G = 0,//!< plus/minus 2g
        PLUSMINUS_4_G = 1,//!< plus/minus 4g
        PLUSMINUS_8_G = 2,//!< plus/minus 8g
        PLUSMINUS_16_G = 3 //!< plus/minus 16g
    };
    /// The resolution of the sensor. High is only available in +/- 16g range.
    enum RESOLUTION {
        NORMAL = 0,//!< NORMAL 10-bit resolution
        HIGH = 1   //!< HIGH 13-bit resolution
    };
private:
    BusDevice *device;
    unsigned char *registers;
    ADXL345::RANGE range;
    ADXL345::RESOLUTION resolution;
    short accelerationX, accelerationY, accelerationZ;
    float pitch, roll; // in degrees
    short combineRegisters(unsigned char msb, unsigned char lsb);
    void calculatePitchAndRoll();
    virtual int updateRegisters();
public:
    ADXL345(BusDevice *busDevice);
    virtual int readSensorState();
    virtual void setRange(ADXL345::RANGE range);
    virtual ADXL345::RANGE getRange() { return this->range; }
    virtual void setResolution(ADXL345::RESOLUTION resolution);
    virtual ADXL345::RESOLUTION getResolution() { return this->resolution; }
    virtual short getAccelerationX() { return accelerationX; }
    virtual short getAccelerationY() { return accelerationY; }
    virtual short getAccelerationZ() { return accelerationZ; }
    virtual float getPitch() { return pitch; }
    virtual float getRoll() { return roll; }
    virtual void displayPitchAndRoll(int iterations = 600);
    virtual ~ADXL345();
};
```

The SPI class in Listing 8-7 can also be used in a standalone form. For example, to read and write from the ADXL345 device without using a specific accelerometer child class, the following code structure can be used:

```
int main() {
    SPIDevice spi(1,0);                    // chip select 0 on bus 1
    spi.setSpeed(1000000);                 // set the speed to 1 MHz
    cout << "The device ID is: " << (int) spi.readRegister(0x00) << endl;
    spi.setMode(SPIDevice::MODE3);         // set the mode to Mode3
    spi.writeRegister(0x2D, 0x08);         // POWER_CTL for the ADXL345
    spi.debugDumpRegisters(0x40);          // Dump the 64 registers from 0x00
}
```

This will give the following output when built and executed (0xE5 = 229_{10}):

```
molloyd@beaglebone:~$ ./SPITest
The device ID is: 229
SPI Mode: 3
Bits per word: 8
Max speed: 1000000
Dumping Registers for Debug Purposes:
e5 00 00 00 00 00 00 00 00 00 00 00 00 00 00 4a
82 00 30 00 00 01 ff 3a 00 00 00 6c 00 00 00 00
00 00 00 00 00 00 00 00 00 00 00 00 0a 08 00 00
02 00 05 00 fd ff e9 00 00 00 00 00 00 00 00 00
```

Once again, a logic analyzer is very useful for debugging problems that can occur with SPI bus communication. For example, Figure 8-10 captures a read operation at address 0x00. You may notice that the value that was sent was 0x80 and not 0x00. This is because (as detailed in Figure 8-7), the leading bit must be a 1 to read and a 0 to write from/to an address. Sending 0x00 is a write request to address 0x00 (which is not possible), and sending 0x80 (i.e., *1*0000000 + 00*000000*) is a request to read the value at address 0x00. The second bit is 0 in both cases, thus disabling multiple-byte read functionality.

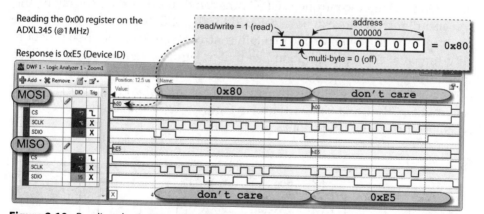

Figure 8-10: Reading the 0x00 register on the ADXL345 using SPI

Three-Wire SPI Communication

The ADXL345 supports *three-wire SPI* (*half duplex*). In this mode the data is read and transmitted on the same SDIO line. To enable this mode on the ADXL345, the value 0x40 must be written to the 0x31 (DATA_FORMAT) register and a 10kΩ resistor should be placed between SD0 and V_{CC} on the ADXL345. Figure 8-11 illustrates the communication that should take place.

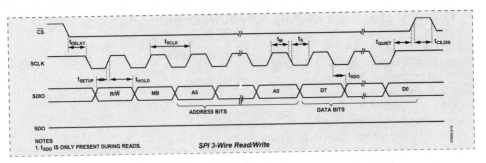

Figure 8-11: ADXL345 three-wire SPI communication

Image courtesy of Analog Devices, Inc.

There is a draft project in place in the `chp08/spi/spiADXL345/3-wire` directory that contains a device tree overlay, which sets the `spi-3wire` property on the SPI bus fragment. Unfortunately, at the time of writing, there is no support for this mode in the current BBB Linux distribution.

Multiple SPI Slave Devices on the BBB

One of the advantages of the SPI bus is that it can be shared with *multiple slave devices*, provided that only one slave device is active when communication takes place. On most microcontrollers, GPIO pins can be used as slave selection pins, and a similar structure can be developed for the BBB. If you wish to allow the Linux SPI interface library code to retain control of the slave selection functionality, then a wiring configuration like that in Figure 8-12 could be used. This configuration uses OR gates and an inverter to ensure that only one CS input is pulled low at a single time. In Figure 8-12(a), the ADXL345 slave device is active when CS = 0 and GPIO = 0, and in Figure 8-12(b), the second slave device is active when CS = 0 and GPIO = 1.

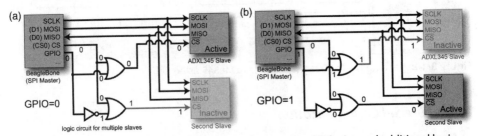

Figure 8-12: BBB control of more than one slave device using GPIO pins and additional logic

Depending on the particular slave devices being used, the GPIO output combined with a single inverter may be sufficient, as you could "permanently" pull the $\overline{CS}$ line low on the slave device, ignoring the CS output of the master.

However, this would not work for the 74HC595 example, as the BBB's CS line is used to latch the data to the output LEDs.

For more than two slave devices, a 3-to-8 line decoder, such as the 74HC138, would be a good solution. It has inverted outputs, which means that only one of its eight outputs is low at a single point in time. This device could be controlled using three of the BBB's GPIOs and it could enable one of eight slave devices ($2^3 = 8$). There are also 4-to-16 line decoders with inverting outputs, such as the 74HC4515, which would enable you to control 16 slave devices with only four GPIOs ($2^4 = 16$). For both of these devices, the BBB CS output could be connected to their $\bar{E}$ enable input(s).

UART

A *universal asynchronous receiver/transmitter (UART)* is a microprocessor peripheral device used for the serial transfer of data, one bit at a time, between two electronic devices. UARTs were originally standalone ICs, but now are often integrated with the host microprocessor/microcontroller. A UART is not, strictly speaking, a bus, but its capacity to implement serial data communications overlaps with similar capacities of the I²C and SPI buses described earlier. A UART is described as *asynchronous* because the sender does not have to send a clock signal to the recipient in order to synchronize the transmission, rather a communication structure is agreed upon that uses start and stop bits to synchronize the transmission of data. Because no clock is required, the data is typically sent using only two signal lines. Just like a regular telephone line, the *transmit data connection (TXD)* from one end is connected to the *receive data connection (RXD)* on the other end of the connection, and vice versa.

Traditionally, UARTs have been used with level converters/line drivers to implement interfaces such as RS-232 or RS-485, but for short-distance communications, it is possible to use the original logic level for the UART outputs and inputs to enable two UARTs to communicate with each other. Note that this is a perfectly possible but nonstandardized use of UARTS.

The number of symbols per second is known as the *baud rate* or modulation rate. With certain encoding schemes a symbol could be used to represent two bits (i.e., four states, for example, by using quadrature phase-shift keying (QPSK)). Then the *bit rate* would be twice the baud rate. However, for a simple bi-level UART connection, the baud rate is the same as the bit rate.

The transmitter and receiver agree upon a bit rate before communication begins. The *byte rate* is somewhat lower than 1/8 of the bit rate, as there are overhead bits associated with the serial transmission of data. Transmission begins when the transmitter sends a *start bit* (logic low), as shown in Figure 8-13. On the receiver's end, the falling edge of the start bit is detected and then after 1.5 bit periods, the first bit value is sampled. Every subsequent bit is sampled after 1.0 bit periods, until the agreed upon number of bits is transferred (typically seven or eight). The *parity bit* is optional (though both devices must be configured to either use it or not); if used, it can identify whether a transmission error has occurred. It would be high or low, depending on whether odd or even *parity checking* is employed. Finally, one *stop bit* is sent (or optionally two stop bits), which is always a logic high value. The examples that follow in this section all use a standard *8N1* form, which means that eight bits are sent in each frame, with no parity bits and one stop bit.

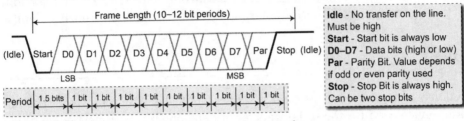

Figure 8-13: UART transmission format for a one-byte transfer

> **WARNING** Again, it is important that you do not connect a 5V UART device to the UART RXD input of the BBB or you will damage the BBB. A solution to this problem is provided at the end of the chapter.

UARTs on the BBB

The BBB has four UARTs that are accessible via its P8 and P9 headers at the pin locations listed in Table 8-5.

Table 8-5: BBB UART Header Pins (mux mode in brackets)

	UART1	UART2	UART3	UART4	UART5
TXD	P9_24 (0)	P9_21 (1)	Not exposed	P9_13 (6)	P8_37 (4)
RXD	P9_26 (0)	P9_22 (1)	Not exposed	P9_11 (6)	P8_38 (4)

For the following example, the BBB's UART4 is used. As detailed in Table 8-5, the pins for UART4 are as follows:

- **P9_13 UART4_TXD:** Output that transmits data to a receiver
- **P9_11 UART4_RXD:** Input that receives data from a transmitter

The first test is to connect these two pins together as in Figure 8-14(a), so that the BBB UART4 is literally "talking to itself." Once the wiring is complete, the UART4 overlay is loaded in order to enable the UART, as otherwise there will be no accessible terminal device present:

```
molloyd@beaglebone:/lib/firmware$ ls *UART*
ADAFRUIT-UART1-00A0.dtbo   BB-UART1-00A0.dtbo   BB-UART4-RTSCTS-00A0.dtbo
```

```
ADAFRUIT-UART2-00A0.dtbo   BB-UART2-00A0.dtbo   BB-UART5-00A0.dtbo
ADAFRUIT-UART4-00A0.dtbo   BB-UART2-RTSCTS-00A0.dtbo
ADAFRUIT-UART5-00A0.dtbo   BB-UART4-00A0.dtbo
molloyd@beaglebone:/lib/firmware$ sudo su -c "echo BB-UART4 > $SLOTS"
molloyd@beaglebone:/lib/firmware$ cat $SLOTS
...
 8: ff:P-O-L Override Board Name,00A0,Override Manuf,BB-UART4
```

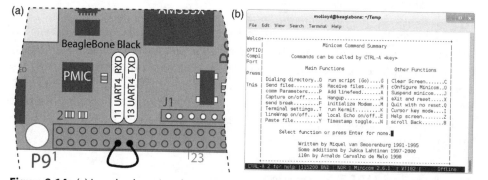

Figure 8-14: (a) Loopback testing the UART; (b) configuring the minicom program settings

When the overlay is loaded, the contents of the /dev directory now includes a new entry for tty04 (letter O, not zero). This is the "teletype" (terminal) device, which is a software interface that enables you to send and receive data on the UART. First, check the available terminal devices:

```
molloyd@beaglebone:/lib/firmware$ cd /dev
molloyd@beaglebone:/dev$ ls ttyO*
ttyO0   ttyO4
```

> **NOTE** The first human-computer interface was the teletypewriter, also known as the teletype or TTY, an electromechanical typewriter that can be used to send and receive messages. This terminology is still in use today!

To test the device, you can use the agetty (*alternative getty*) command or the minicom terminal emulator, both of which enable you to send and receive data on the tty04 device. The minicom program enables you to dynamically change the serial settings while it is executing (e.g., number of bits in a frame, number of stop bits, parity settings) by typing Ctrl+A followed by Z. Install and execute minicom using the following commands:

```
molloyd@beaglebone:~$ sudo apt-get install minicom
...
molloyd@beaglebone:~$ minicom -b 9200 -o -D /dev/ttyO4

Welcome to minicom 2.6.1
OPTIONS: I18n
```

```
Compiled on Feb 11 2012, 18:45:56.
Port /dev/tty04
Press CTRL-A Z for help on special keys
```

At this point you should type Ctrl+A followed by Z and then E to turn on local Echo. Now when you press a key, you should see the following impact when you type:

```
tteesstt iinngg 112233
```

Whichever key you press is transmitted from the TXD output, and is also echoed on the console. When the character is received on the RXD input, it is then displayed on the console. Therefore, if you can see the characters appearing twice for the keys that you are pressing, then the simple UART test is working correctly. You can verify this by briefly disconnecting one end of the TXD-RXD loopback wire, whereupon the key presses will only appear once.

The Arduino UART Example

The *Arduino* (www.arduino.cc) is a popular, low-cost, and powerful microcontroller that can be a very useful companion controller for the BBB. The Arduino platform was designed as an introductory platform for embedded systems. It is programmed using the Arduino programming language, in the Arduino development environment, which are both designed to be as user-friendly as possible. An in-depth study of the Arduino is beyond the scope of this book, but it is a very suitable platform with which to test the UART functionality of the BBB. It can also be used to develop a first framework for BBB applications that distribute workload to other embedded systems while still maintaining high-level control.

> **NOTE** There are some videos on getting started with the Arduino on the web page associated with this chapter: www.exploringbeaglebone.com/chapter8.
>
> In addition, there is a comprehensive book on the Arduino available in this Wiley miniseries, called *Exploring Arduino*, by Jeremy Blum. Please see www.exploringarduino.com for more details.

The Arduino is available in many different forms. However, an open-hardware 3.3V Arduino Pro Mini is chosen for this task for three reasons:

- The voltage levels are consistent with the BBB, which simplifies communication, as no logic-level translation circuitry is required.

- It is a low-cost, open-hardware device (less than $10) that is only 1.3"× 0.7" (33mm × 18mm) in size.

- There is no USB input on the board (reducing size and cost), but it can be programmed using the same USB-to-Serial UART TTL 3.3V cable discussed in Chapter 1.

Figure 8-15 illustrates the programming environment for the Arduino, and the program that is displayed can be used to test that the UART connection to the Arduino is working correctly. The code is available in the GitHub repository in /chp08/uart/arduino/BBBSerialEcho.ino. The Arduino platform uses the Arduino's RXD and TXD pins to program the Arduino microcontroller, so a lot of spurious data is transmitted on these lines while it is being programmed.

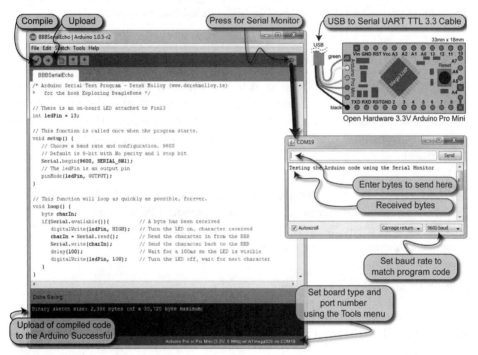

Figure 8-15: The Arduino platform

The setup() function is called once when the program is started. It configures the serial port to use 9,600 baud with the 8N1 format. It also sets up an on-board LED to be an output, in order to visually indicate interaction.

NOTE It is very important that you choose the correct Arduino board in the Tools menu, especially when using the Pro Mini board. If the incorrect board is chosen, the code may compile and upload correctly to the board, but the serial communication channel may appear corrupt.

The loop() function will repeat as fast as it possibly can. In this case, it waits until serial data is available on the RXD pin. When it is, the LED is turned on, and a character is read in from the RXD pin. The character is then written to the TXD pin. The program sleeps for 100ms to ensure that the LED flash is visible, before it is turned off again. The program then loops in preparation for the next character to be received on the RXD pin.

The Serial Monitor window can be opened in the Arduino development environment by pressing the button in the top right-hand corner. Choose the baud rate that corresponds to that in the program code. When a string is entered in the text field and the Send button is pressed, the string is sent to the Arduino and the response should display in the text area.

Once you are certain that the Arduino program is working correctly, it is an ideal platform with which to test the BBB UART functionality.

BeagleBone to Arduino Serial Communication

The Arduino Pro Mini 3.3V is used to test the UART communication capability of the BBB, first by using the `minicom` program and then by writing a C program to echo information to/from the Arduino. In the next section this is further developed to create a serial client/server command control framework.

> **WARNING**   The Arduino Pro is used because it is a 3.3V version of the Arduino and can be connected directly to the BBB. Do *not* connect a 5V Arduino to the BBB using the UART connection or you will damage your BBB. If you have to connect a 5V device, a solution is presented at the end of this chapter.

Echoing the Minicom Program

The Arduino code from the last section has been modified slightly to increase the baud rate and remove the LED flash function, as shown in Listing 8-9.

LISTING 8-9: /exploringbb/chp08/uart/uartEchoC/BBBSerialEcho.ino

```
// This function is called once when the program starts.
void setup() {
   // Choose a baud rate and configuration. 115200
   // Default is 8-bit with No parity and 1 stop bit
   Serial.begin(115200, SERIAL_8N1);
}
// This function will loop as quickly as possible, forever.
void loop() {
   byte charIn;
   if(Serial.available()){          // A byte has been received
      charIn = Serial.read();       // Read the character in from the BBB
```

```
        Serial.write(charIn);          // Send the character back to the BBB
    }
}
```

This program should be uploaded to the Arduino, where it will then execute, awaiting communication on its RXD pin. The next step is to connect the Arduino as illustrated in Figure 8-16, ensuring that the TXD pin on the BBB is connected to the RXD pin on the Arduino and that the RXD pin on the BBB is connected to the TXD pin on the Arduino.

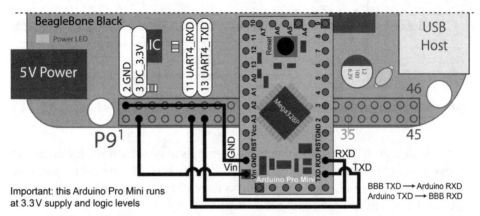

Figure 8-16: UART communication between the BBB and the Arduino Pro Mini 3.3V

When you are modifying the Arduino source code and uploading it to the Arduino, you should disconnect the UART connection to the BBB each time, before connecting the USB-to-Serial UART TTL 3.3V cable. Otherwise, the process of programming the Arduino will likely fail.

Once the Arduino is attached to the BBB, the next step is to open the `minicom` program and test the connection. The baud rate is set at 115,200 in the Arduino code, so the same setting must be passed to the `minicom` command. If the connection is displaying incorrect data, then reduce the baud rate to a lower rate, such as 57,600, 38,400, 19,200, or 9,600:

```
molloyd@beaglebone:~$ minicom -b 115200 -o -D /dev/ttyO4
Welcome to minicom 2.6.1
OPTIONS: I18n
Compiled on Feb 11 2012, 18:45:56.
Port /dev/ttyO4
Press CTRL-A Z for help on special keys

This string is being sent character by character to the Arduino
```

The Analog Discovery has an interpreter that can be used for analyzing serial data communication. The logic analyzer can be connected in parallel to the TXD and RXD lines in order to analyze the transfer of data from the BBB to the Arduino. An example of the resulting signals is displayed in Figure 8-17 when only the letter "A" is being transmitted. The start and stop bits can be observed, along with the eight-bit data as it is sent, LSB first, from the BBB to the Arduino, at a sample bit-period of 8.7 μs.

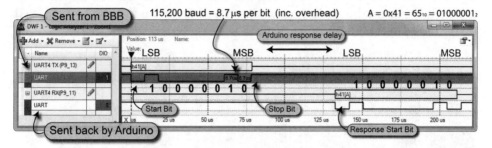

Figure 8-17: Analysis of the UART communication between the BBB and the Arduino Pro Mini 3.3 V

At a baud rate of 115,200, the effective byte rate will be somewhat lower, due to the overhead of transmitting start, stop, and parity bits. The Arduino response delay is the time it takes for the Arduino to read the character from its RXD input and transmit it back to its TXD output.

UART Echo Example in C

The next step is to write C code on the BBB that can communicate with the Arduino program. The Arduino code has been adapted slightly to reduce the baud rate to 9,600 in order ensure that signaling noise does not affect the data transfer, effectively isolating problems to the program code. All code is available in the /chp08/uart/uartEchoC GitHub repository directory.

The C program available in Listing 8-10 sends a string to the Arduino and reads the responding echo. It uses the Linux *termios* library, which provides a general terminal interface that can control asynchronous communication ports.

LISTING 8-10: exploringbb/chp08/uart/uartEchoC/BBBEcho.c

```
#include<stdio.h>
#include<fcntl.h>
#include<unistd.h>
#include<termios.h>    // using the termios.h library

int main(){
    int file, count;
```

```
if ((file = open("/dev/tty04", O_RDWR | O_NOCTTY | O_NDELAY))<0){
    perror("UART: Failed to open the file.\n");
    return -1;
}
struct termios options;          // the termios structure is vital
tcgetattr(file, &options);       // sets the parameters associated with file

// Set up the communications options:
//    9600 baud, 8-bit, enable receiver, no modem control lines
options.c_cflag = B9600 | CS8 | CREAD | CLOCAL;
options.c_iflag = IGNPAR | ICRNL;    // ignore partity errors, CR -> newline
tcflush(file, TCIFLUSH);             // discard file information not transmitted
tcsetattr(file, TCSANOW, &options); // changes occur immmediately
unsigned char transmit[18] = "Hello BeagleBone!";  // the string to send
if ((count = write(file, &transmit,18))<0){        // send the string
    perror("Failed to write to the output\n");
    return -1;
}
usleep(100000);                       // give the Arduino a chance to respond

unsigned char receive[100];      // declare a buffer for receiving data
if ((count = read(file, (void*)receive, 100))<0){   // receive the data
    perror("Failed to read from the input\n");
    return -1;
}
if (count==0) printf("There was no data available to read!\n");
else {
    printf("The following was read in [%d]: %s\n",count,receive);
}
close(file);
return 0;
}
```

This code uses the `termios` structure, setting flags to define the type of communication that should take place. The `termios` structure has the following members:

- `tcflag_t c_iflag`: Sets the input modes
- `tcflag_t c_oflag`: Sets the output modes
- `cflag_t c_cflag`: Sets the control modes
- `tcflag_t c_lflag`: Sets the local modes
- `cc_t c_cc[NCCS]`: For special characters

A full description of the `termios` functionality and flag settings is available by typing **man termios** at the BBB console. The code in this section can be modified to create the following very useful BBB application.

UART Command Control of an Arduino

One method of overcoming the real-time limitations of the BBB discussed in Chapter 1 is to outsource some of its workload to other embedded controllers, such as those provided by the Arduino, PIC, and Stellaris platforms. These embedded microcontrollers share common communication interfaces with the BBB that could be used for this task, including SPI, I²C, and the use of GPIO *bit-banging* (manual serial communication using a GPIO by toggling its state in a user-defined way). However, using a UART connection is probably the most straightforward, and it has the additional advantage that there can be some degree of physical distance between the two controllers. Table 8-6 lists some advantages and disadvantages of using a UART in comparison to using I²C or SPI.

Table 8-6: Advantages and Disadvantages of UART Communication

ADVANTAGES	DISADVANTAGES
Simple, single-wire transmission and single-wire reception of data with error checking.	The typical maximum data rate is low compared to SPI (typically 460.8kb/sec).
Easy interface for interconnecting embedded devices and desktop computers, etc., especially when that communication is external to the device and/or over a significant distance—some tens of feet. I²C and SPI are not suited for external/distance communication.	Because it is asynchronous, the clock on both devices must be accurate, particularly at higher baud rates. You should investigate CAN bus for high-speed external asynchronous data transfer.
Can be directly interfaced to popular RS-232 physical interfaces, enabling long-distance communication (15 meters or greater). The longer the cable, the lower the speed. RS-422/485 allows for 100-meter runs at greater than 1Mb/s.	UART settings need to be known in advance of the transfer, such as the baud rate, data size and parity checking type.

The Arduino code in Listing 8-9 has been adapted as shown in Listing 8-11. The code is designed to expect two string commands, either "on" or "off." If the program receives the "on" command on its RXD input, it will light the on-board LED and respond on its TXD output with the response "LED On." Similarly for the "off" command, it will turn the LED off and send the response "LED off." If the command string is not recognized, it will simply echo the command string back to the sender. This program will continue to run on the Arduino forever.

LISTING 8-11: /exploringbb/chp08/uart/uartC/ BBBSerialCommand.ino

```
/* Arduino Serial Command Program - Derek Molloy (www.derekmolloy.ie)
*   for the book Exploring BeagleBone */
// There is an on-board LED attached to Pin 13
int ledPin=13;

void setup() {
   // Baud of 57600 works fine over short distances (twist cables)
   Serial.begin(57600, SERIAL_8N1);
   // The ledPin is and output pin
   pinMode(ledPin, OUTPUT);
}

// This function will loop forever.
void loop() {
   String command, inChar;
   if (Serial.available()>0){     // A byte has been received
      command = Serial.readStringUntil('\0'); // String terminated by /0
      if(command=="on"){          // Turn on the on-board LED
         digitalWrite(ledPin, HIGH);
         Serial.print("LED On");
      }
      else if (command=="off") {  // Turn off the on-board LED
         digitalWrite(ledPin, LOW);
         Serial.print("LED Off");
      }
      else {                      // Otherwise return string passed
         Serial.print(command);
      }
   }
}
```

The C program that is presented in Listing 8-12 sends the command-line argument, which is passed to the executable program over the UART connection to the Arduino at run time. It follows the same syntax as the echo example in the previous section, with the exception that the baud rate has been increased to 57,600 in both the C and Arduino program code.

LISTING 8-12: /exploringbb/chp08/uart/uartC/ uart.c

```
/* Simple send and receive C example for communicating with the
* Arduino echo program using UART4. Written by Derek Molloy
* (www.derekmolloy.ie) for the book Exploring BeagleBone. */

#include<stdio.h>
#include<fcntl.h>
```

continues

LISTING 8-12: *(continued)*

```c
#include<unistd.h>
#include<termios.h>
#include<string.h>

int main(int argc, char *argv[]){
   int file, count;
   if(argc!=2){
      printf("Invalid number of arguments, exiting!\n");
      return -2;
   }
   if ((file = open("/dev/ttyO4", O_RDWR | O_NOCTTY | O_NDELAY))<0){
      perror("UART: Failed to open the file.\n");
      return -1;
   }
   struct termios options;
   tcgetattr(file, &options);
   options.c_cflag = B57600 | CS8 | CREAD | CLOCAL;
   options.c_iflag = IGNPAR | ICRNL;
   tcflush(file, TCIFLUSH);
   tcsetattr(file, TCSANOW, &options);
   // send the string plus the null character
   if ((count = write(file, argv[1], strlen(argv[1])+1))<0){
      perror("Failed to write to the output\n");
      return -1;
   }
   usleep(100000);
   unsigned char receive[100];
   if ((count = read(file, (void*)receive, 100))<0){
      perror("Failed to read from the input\n");
      return -1;
   }
   if (count==0) printf("There was no data available to read!\n");
   else {
      receive[count]=0;  //There is no null character sent by the Arduino
      printf("The following was read in [%d]: %s\n",count,receive);
   }
   close(file);
   return 0;
}
```

When the code is executed, it will give the following output, with the LED on the Arduino turning on and off as expected:

```
molloyd@beaglebone:~/exploringbb/chp08/uart/uartC$ ./uart on
The following was read in [6]: LED On
molloyd@beaglebone:~/exploringbb/chp08/uart/uartC$ ./uart off
The following was read in [7]: LED Off
molloyd@beaglebone:~/exploringbb/chp08/uart/uartC$ ./uart HelloArduino
The following was read in [12]: HelloArduino
```

The transfer of data can be observed in Figure 8-18. The response time of the Arduino is less than the time taken to transfer the command and respond at 57,600 baud.

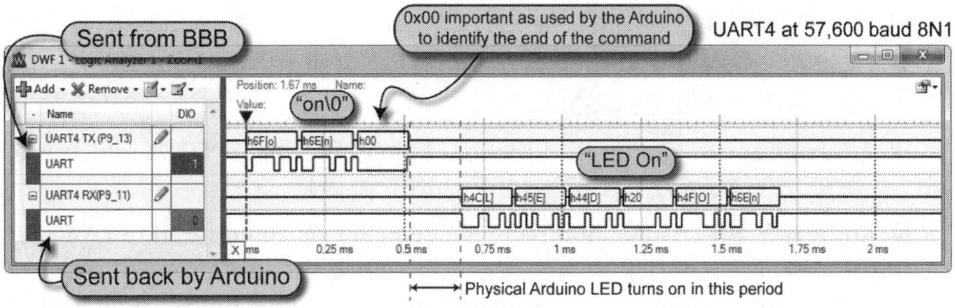

Figure 8-18: Sending the command "On\0" to the Arduino and receiving the response string "LED On"

The performance of the code could be improved by defining a list of single-byte commands and responses, in order to minimize data transfer time. In addition, it is worth mentioning that the multi-call binary example discussed in Chapter 5 could be adapted to create single-word Linux commands on the BBB that would execute directly on the Arduino.

This framework could be used to create a simple distributed embedded controller platform. An alternative would be to use the CAN bus controllers that are available on-board the BBB and through third-party capes. In Chapter 10, a network-socket based framework is also introduced. It is a very powerful framework for interconnecting high-level embedded computing platforms through the use of their networking interfaces.

Logic-Level Translation

As noted throughout this chapter, it is important that you are cognizant of the voltage levels used in communicating with the BBB. If you connect a device that uses 5V logic levels, then when the device is sending a high state to the BBB, it will apply a voltage of 5V to the BBB's input pins. This would likely permanently damage the BBB. Many embedded systems have overvoltage-tolerant inputs, but the BBB does not. Therefore, *logic-level translation* circuitry is required if you wish to connect the buses to 5V or 1.8V logic-level circuits.

For *unidirectional data buses*, like four-wire SPI, logic-level translation can be achieved using a combination of diodes (using their ~0.6V forward-voltage drop characteristic) combined with resistors, or transistors. However, *bidirectional data buses* like the I²C bus are more complex because the level must be translated in both directions on a single line. This requires circuits that use devices such as

N-channel MOSFETs (e.g., the BSS138). They are available in surface-mounted packages and, unfortunately, there are very few through-hole alternatives. Fortunately, this is a common problem and there are straightforward unidirectional and bidirectional breakout board solutions available from several suppliers, including the following:

- Sparkfun Logic Level Converter Bi-directional (BOB-12009), which uses the BSS138 MOSFET (~$3)

- Adafruit Four-channel Bi-directional Level Shifter (ID:757), which uses the BSS138 MOSFET (1.8V to 10V shifting)(~$4)

- Adafruit Eight-channel Bi-directional Logic-level Converter (ID:395), which uses the TI TXB0108 voltage-level translator that auto senses direction (1.2 to 3.6V or 1.65 to 5.5V translation), but it does not work well with I²C due to the pull-up resistors required (~$8). However, it can switch at frequencies greater than 10MHz.

- Watterott Four-channel Level Shifter (20110451), which uses the BSS138 MOSFET (~$3)

Some of these products are displayed in Figure 8-19. With the exception of the Adafruit eight-channel converter, they all use BSS138 MOSFETs. A small test was performed to check the switching frequency of these devices, as displayed in Figure 8-20, and it is clear from the oscilloscope traces that there are data-switching performance limitations when using these devices.

Figure 8-19: Adafruit four-channel, Adafruit eight-channel, and Watterott four-channel logic-level translators

The logic-level translation boards solve the problem that is mentioned several times during this chapter, as a traditional 5V Arduino can now be connected to the BBB for UART communication using the circuit that is illustrated in Figure 8-21. The BBB 3.3V supply, TXD, and RXD pins are connected to the *Lv*, *1*, and *2* connections, respectively, on the logic-level translator board. On the other side of the logic-level translator, the Arduino 5V supply, RXD, and TXD pins are connected to the *Hv*, *1*, and *2* connection pins, respectively. The grounds of the BBB and Arduino are also tied together.

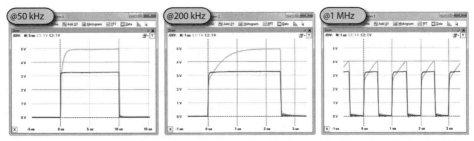

Figure 8-20: Switching BSS138-based translators from 3.3V to 5V logic levels at 50kHz, 200kHz, and 1MHz

The application that is used to provide UART command control of the Arduino now works with this 5V Arduino. For further information on logic-level shifting techniques in I²C-bus design, see the application notes from NXP (AN97055), which is linked on the chapter web page and also available at `tiny.cc/ebb806`.

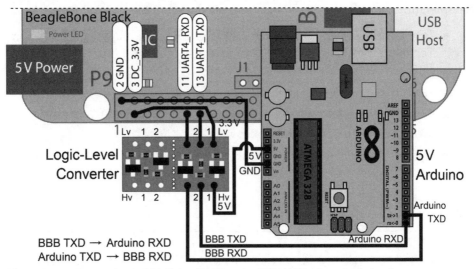

Figure 8-21: Connecting a 5V Arduino UART to the BBB UART using a logic-level converter

Summary

After completing this chapter, you should be able to do the following:

- Describe the most commonly used buses or interfaces that are available on the BBB, and choose the correct bus to use for your application.
- Configure the BBB to enable I²C, SPI, and UART capabilities.
- Attach circuits to the BBB that interface to its I²C bus, and use the Linux I2C-Tools to communicate with those circuits.
- Build circuits that interface to the SPI bus using shift registers, and write C code that controls low-level SPI communication.
- Write C code that interfaces to, and C++ code that "wraps" the functionality of devices attached to the I²C and SPI buses.
- Communicate between UART devices using both Linux tools and custom C code.
- Build a basic distributed system that uses UART connections to the Arduino microcontroller to "outsource" workload.
- Add logic-level translation circuitry to your circuits in order to communicate between devices with different logic-level voltages.

Further Reading

Documents and links for further reading have been listed throughout this chapter, but here are some further reference documents:

- *The I²C Manual*, Jean-Marc Irazabal and Steve Blozis, Philips Semiconductors, TecForum at DesignCon 2003 in San Jose, CA, on January 27, 2003, at `tiny.cc/ebb805`.
- *The Linux I²C Subsystem*, at `i2c.wiki.kernel.org`.
- *Serial Programming Guide for POSIX Operating Systems*, 5th ed., Michael R. Sweet, 1994-99, at `tiny.cc/ebb803`.
- *Serial Programming HOWTO*, Gary Frerking, Revision 1.01, at `tiny.cc/ebb804`.

Note

1. In 2012 NXP released Ultra Fast-Mode (UfM) I²C, which offers a 5MHz mode. However, it is quite different from other I²C modes as it is unidirectional and there is only a single master. It is currently not widely adopted.

# CHAPTER 9

Interacting with the Physical Environment

In this chapter you can learn how to build on your knowledge of GPIO and bus interfacing. In particular, you can combine hardware and software in order to provide the BBB with the ability to interact with its physical environment in the following three ways: First, by controlling actuators such as motors, the BBB can affect its environment, which is very important for applications such as robotics and home automation. Second, the BBB can gather information about its physical environment by communicating with sensors. Third, by interfacing to display modules, the BBB can present information. This chapter explains how each of these interactions can be performed. Physical interaction hardware and software provides you with the capability to build advanced projects; for example, to build a robotic platform that can sense and interact with its environment. The chapter ends by presenting a framework that enables you to remotely control the BBB using a wired serial connection or a wireless Bluetooth connection to a desktop computer or mobile device.

Equipment Required for This Chapter:

- BeagleBone Black, DMM, and oscilloscope
- DC motor and H-bridge interface board
- Stepper motor and EasyDriver interface board
- Op-amps (LM358, MCP6002/4), Diodes, Resistors, 5V Relay
- Sharp infrared distance sensor

- 74HC595 serial shift registers
- Seven-segment display modules
- LCD character display module
- ADXL335 analog three-axis accelerometer
- Bluetooth adapter (e.g., Kinivo BTD-400 Bluetooth 4.0 USB)

Further details on this chapter are available at `www.exploringbeaglebone.com/chapter9/`.

Interfacing to Actuators

Electric motors can be controlled by the BBB in order to make physical devices move or operate. They convert electrical energy into mechanical energy that can be used by devices to act upon their surroundings. A device that converts energy into motion is generally referred to as an *actuator*. Interfacing the BBB to actuators provides a myriad of application possibilities, including robotic control, home automation (watering plants, controlling blinds), camera control, unmanned aerial vehicles (UAVs), 3D printer control, and many more.

Electric motors typically provide rotary motion around a fixed axis, which can be used to drive wheels, pumps, belts, electric valves, tracks, turrets, robotic arms, and so on. In contrast to this, *linear actuators* create movement in a straight line, which can be very useful for position control in computer numerical control (CNC) machines and 3D printers. In some cases they convert rotary motion into linear motion using a screw shaft that translates a threaded nut along its length as it rotates. In other cases, a solenoid moves a shaft linearly through the magnetic effects of an electric current.

Three main types of motors are commonly used with the BBB: servo motors, DC motors, and stepper motors. A summary comparison of these motor types is provided in Table 9-1. Interfacing to servo motors (also known as *precision actuators*) through the use of PWM outputs is discussed in Chapter 6, so this section focuses on interfacing to DC motors and stepper motors.

High-current inductive loads are challenging to interface with the BBB—they invariably require more current than the BBB can supply, and they generate voltage spikes that can be extremely harmful to the interfacing circuitry. The applications discussed in this section often require a secondary power supply, which could be an external battery pack in the case of a mobile platform or a high-current supply for powerful motors. The BBB needs to be isolated from these supplies; as a result, generic motor controller boards are described here for interfacing to DC motors and stepper motors. Circuitry is also carefully designed for interfacing to relay devices.

Table 9-1: Summary Comparison of Common Motor Types

	SERVO MOTOR	DC MOTOR	STEPPER MOTOR
Typical application	When high torque, accurate rotation is required	When fast, continuous rotation is required	When slow and accurate rotation is required
Control hardware	Position is controlled through PWM. No controller required. May require PWM tuning.	Speed is controlled through PWM. Additional circuitry required to manage power requirements.	Typically requires a controller to energize stepper coils. The BBB can perform this role, but an external controller is preferable and safer.
Control type	Closed-loop, using a built-in controller	Typically closed-loop using feedback from optical encoders	Typically open-loop, as movement is precise and steps can be counted
Features	Known absolute position. Typically, limited angle of rotation.	Can drive very large loads. Often geared to provide very high torque.	Full torque at standstill. Can rotate a large load at very low speeds. Tendency to vibrate.
Example applications	Steering controllers, camera control, and small robotic arms	Mobile robot movement, fans, water pumps, and electric cars	CNC machines, 3D printers, scanners, linear actuators, and camera lenses

DC Motors

DC motors are used in many applications, from toys to advanced robotics. They are ideal motors to use when continuous rotation is required, such as in the wheels of an electric vehicle. Typically, they have only two electrical terminals to which a voltage is applied. The speed of rotation and the direction of rotation can be controlled by varying this voltage. The tendency of a force to rotate an object about its axis is called *torque*, and for a DC motor, torque is generally proportional to the current applied.

DC motors, such as the one in Figure 9-1(a), often require more current than the BBB can supply; therefore, you might be tempted to drive them from the

BBB by simply using a transistor or FET. Unfortunately, this will not work well, due to a phenomenon known as *inductive kickback*, which results in a large voltage spike that is caused by the inertia of current flowing through an inductor (i.e. the motor's coil windings) being suddenly switched off. Even for modest motor power supplies, this large voltage could exceed 1 kV for a very short period of time. The FETs discussed in Chapter 4 cannot have a drain-source voltage of greater than 60 V and will therefore be damaged by such large voltages. Figure 9-1(b) illustrates a simple solution to this problem: placing a *kickback diode* (aka *flyback diode*) across the terminals of the DC motor.

(a)   (b)

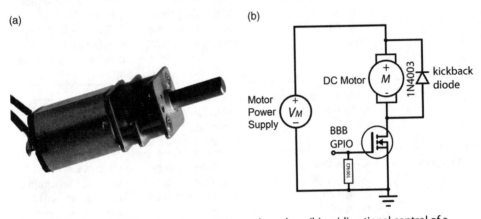

Figure 9-1: (a) A small DC motor with an integrated gearbox; (b) unidirectional control of a DC motor

The kickback diode is reverse-biased during regular operation of the motor and will therefore have no impact. However, the diode is forward-biased by a kickback voltage spike. Therefore, the voltage spike is limited to the motor power supply voltage (plus the forward voltage drop of the diode, ~0.7 V). A resistor or Zener diode can be placed in series with the kickback diode to further improve the level of protection.

An alternative to this configuration is to place a Zener diode across the drain-source terminals of the FET (or collector-emitter of a transistor). The Zener diode limits the voltage across the drain-source terminals to that of its reverse breakdown voltage. The downside of this alternative configuration is that the ground supply has to sink a large current spike, which could lead to the type of noise in the circuit that is discussed in Chapter 4. With either of these types of protection in place, it is possible to use a BBB PWM output to control the speed of the DC motor. With a PWM duty cycle of 50%, the motor will rotate at half the speed that it would if directly connected to the motor supply voltage.

The previous approach provides for the unidirectional control of a DC motor. For *bidirectional control*, a circuit configuration called an *H-bridge* can be used, which has a circuit layout in the shape of the letter H, as illustrated in Figure 9-2. Notice that it has Zener diodes to protect the four FETs. To drive the motor in a forward (assumed to be clockwise) direction, the top-left and bottom-right FETs can be switched on. This causes a current to flow from the positive to the negative terminal of the DC motor. When the opposing pair of FETs is switched on, current flows from the negative terminal to the positive terminal of the motor and the motor reverses (turns counterclockwise). The motor does not rotate if two opposing FETs are switched off (open circuit).

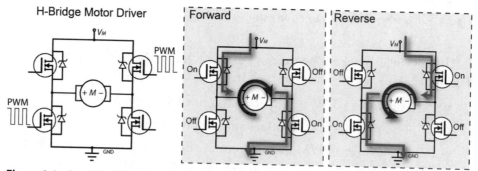

Figure 9-2: Simplified H-bridge description

Four of the BBB PWM header pins could be connected to the H-bridge circuit, but particular care would have to be taken to ensure that the two FETs on the left-hand side or the right-hand side of the circuit are not turned on at the same time, as this would result in a large current (*shoot-through current*)—the motor supply would effectively be shorted (V_M to GND). As high-current capable power supplies are often used for the motor power supply, this is very dangerous, as it could even cause a power supply or a battery to explode! An easier and safer approach is to use an H-bridge driver that has already been packaged in an IC, such as the SN754410, a quadruple high-current half-H driver, which can drive 1A at 4.5V to 36V per driver (see `tiny.cc/ebb901`).

A BBB DC Motor Driver Circuit

There are many more recently introduced drivers that can drive even larger currents using smaller package sizes than the SN754410. In this example, a DRV8835 dual low-voltage motor driver carrier on a breakout board from `www.pololu.com` is used, as illustrated in Figure 9-3. The DRV8835 itself is only 2mm × 3mm in dimension and can drive 1.5A (max) per H-bridge at a motor supply voltage up to 11 V. It can be driven with logic levels of 2V to 7V, which enables it to be used with the BBB.

Figure 9-3: Driving a DC motor using an example H-Bridge driver breakout board

The DRV8835 breakout board can be connected to the BBB as illustrated in Figure 9-3. This circuit uses four pins from the BBB:

- P9_3 provides a 3.3V supply for the control logic circuitry.
- P9_45 provides a GND for the logic supply circuitry.
- P9_42 provides a PWM output from the BBB that can be used to control the rotation speed of the motor, as it is connected to the A_{ENABLE} input on the DRV8835.
- P9_41 provides a GPIO output that can be used to set whether the motor is rotating clockwise or counterclockwise, as it is connected to the A_{PHASE} input.

The motor power supply voltage is set according to the specification of the DC motor that is chosen. By tying the *Mode* pin high, the DRV8835 is placed in PHASE/ENABLE mode, which means that one input is used for direction and the other is used for determining the rotation speed.

WARNING The DRV8835 IC can get hot enough to burn, even while operating within its normal operating parameters. This is a common characteristic of motor driver ICs—so be careful! Heat sinks can be added to dissipate heat, and they have the added advantage of extending the constant run time, as thermal protection circuitry will shut motor driver ICs down to prevent them from overheating when driving large loads.

Controlling a DC Motor Using sysfs

With a circuit wired as shown in Figure 9-3, the DC motor can be controlled using sysfs. In this example, P9_41 (GPIO3_20 = 116) is connected to the

A_{PHASE} input. Therefore, this pin can be enabled, and the motor's direction of rotation can be controlled using the following (with the HDMI overlay disabled):

```
molloyd@beaglebone:/sys/class/gpio/$ echo 116 > export
molloyd@beaglebone:/sys/class/gpio/$ cd gpio116
molloyd@beaglebone:/sys/class/gpio/gpio116$ ls
active_low  direction  edge  power  subsystem  uevent  value
molloyd@beaglebone:/sys/class/gpio/gpio116$ echo out > direction
molloyd@beaglebone:/sys/class/gpio/gpio116$ echo 1 > value
molloyd@beaglebone:/sys/class/gpio/gpio116$ echo 0 > value
```

The speed of the motor can be controlled using a BBB PWM output. The overlays can be loaded, and the motor can be controlled using the PWM overlay that is associated with P9_42, as follows:

```
molloyd@beaglebone:~$ sudo sh -c "echo am33xx_pwm > $SLOTS"
molloyd@beaglebone:~$ sudo sh -c "echo bone_pwm_P9_42 > $SLOTS"
molloyd@beaglebone:~$ cat $SLOTS
7: ff:P-O-L Override Board Name,00A0,Override Manuf,bone_pwm_P9_42
10: ff:P-O-L Override Board Name,00A0,Override Manuf,am33xx_pwm
molloyd@beaglebone:~$ sudo su -
root@beaglebone:~# cd /sys/devices/ocp.3/pwm_test_P9_42.12/
root@beaglebone:/sys/devices/ocp.3/pwm_test_P9_42.12# ls
driver  duty  modalias  period  polarity  power run subsystem uevent
root@beaglebone:/sys/devices/ocp.3/pwm_test_P9_42.12# echo 0 > run
root@beaglebone:/sys/devices/ocp.3/pwm_test_P9_42.12# echo 0 > polarity
root@beaglebone:/sys/devices/ocp.3/pwm_test_P9_42.12# echo 4000 > period
root@beaglebone:/sys/devices/ocp.3/pwm_test_P9_42.12# echo 1000 > duty
root@beaglebone:/sys/devices/ocp.3/pwm_test_P9_42.12# echo 2000 > duty
root@beaglebone:/sys/devices/ocp.3/pwm_test_P9_42.12# echo 4000 > duty
root@beaglebone:/sys/devices/ocp.3/pwm_test_P9_42.12# echo 0 > run
```

Here, the PWM frequency is set to 250kHz and the duty cycle is adjusted from 25% to 50%, and then to 100%, changing the rotation speed of the motor accordingly. As with servo motors, DC motors should be controlled with the PWM polarity set to 0, so that the duty period represents the time when the pulse is high, rather than low. The direction of rotation can be adjusted at any stage using the gpio116 sysfs directory.

Controlling a DC Motor Using C++

A C++ class that you can use to control a DC motor is available in the GitHub repository. The constructor expects a PWM input, for which the overlay has already been loaded, and a GPIO object or GPIO number. If a GPIO number is passed, then the pin is automatically exported and un-exported. Listing 9-1 displays the C++ header file for the DCMotor class.

LISTING 9-1: library/motor/DCMotor.h

```cpp
class DCMotor {
public:
    enum DIRECTION{ CLOCKWISE, ANTICLOCKWISE };
private:
    ...
public:
    DCMotor(PWM *pwm, GPIO *gpio);
    DCMotor(PWM *pwm, int gpioNumber);
    DCMotor(PWM *pwm, GPIO *gpio, DCMotor::DIRECTION direction);
    DCMotor(PWM *pwm, int gpioNumber, DCMotor::DIRECTION direction);
    DCMotor(PWM *pwm, GPIO *gpio, DCMotor::DIRECTION direction,
            float speedPercent);
    DCMotor(PWM *pwm, int gpioNumber, DCMotor::DIRECTION direction,
            float speedPercent);
    virtual void go();
    virtual void setSpeedPercent(float speedPercent);
    virtual float getSpeedPercent() { return this->speedPercent; }
    virtual void setDirection(DIRECTION direction);
    virtual DIRECTION getDirection() { return this->direction; }
    virtual void reverseDirection();
    virtual void stop();
    virtual void setDutyCyclePeriod(unsigned int period_ns);
    virtual ~DCMotor();
};
```

An example application that uses the DCMotor class is provided in Listing 9-2. Notice that the header file is in the motor subdirectory.

LISTING 9-2: /chp09/dcmotor/DCMotorApp.cpp

```cpp
#include <iostream>
#include "motor/DCMotor.h"
using namespace std;
using namespace exploringBB;

int main(){
    cout << "Starting EBB DC Motor Example" << endl;
    DCMotor dcm(new PWM("pwm_test_P9_42.12"), 116); // exports GPIO116
    dcm.setDirection(DCMotor::ANTICLOCKWISE);
    dcm.setSpeedPercent(50.0f);    //make it clear that a float is passed
    dcm.go();
    cout << "Rotating Anti-clockwise at 50% speed" << endl;
    usleep(5000000);    //sleep for 5 seconds
    dcm.reverseDirection();
    cout << "Rotating clockwise at 50% speed" << endl;
    usleep(5000000);
    dcm.setSpeedPercent(100.0f);
    cout << "Rotating clockwise at 100% speed" << endl;
```

```
    usleep(5000000);
    dcm.stop();
    cout << "End of EBB DC Motor Example" << endl;
}
```

The build script assumes that the example application source is in /exporingbb/chp09/dcmotor/ and that the shared library and header files are in the directory /exploringbb/library. This conforms to the directory structure of the GitHub repository. The code can be built using the build script that is in the dcmotor directory and executed using the following:

```
molloyd@beaglebone:~/exploringbb/chp09/dcmotor$ more build
#!/bin/bash
g++ DCMotorApp.cpp ../../library/libEBBLibrary.so -o DCApp -I "../../
library"
molloyd@beaglebone:~/exploringbb/chp09/dcmotor$ ./build
molloyd@beaglebone:~/exploringbb/chp09/dcmotor$ ls
DCApp  DCMotorApp.cpp  build
molloyd@beaglebone:~/exploringbb/chp09/dcmotor$ sudo ./DCApp
Starting EBB DC Motor Example
Rotating Anti-clockwise at 50% speed
Rotating clockwise at 50% speed
Rotating clockwise at 100% speed
End of EBB DC Motor Example
```

At the end of this chapter a description is provided that shows how to build code into dynamic libraries, such as libEBBLibrary.so, using the Eclipse IDE. This enables you to alter the library to suit your requirements.

Stepper Motors

Unlike DC motors, which rotate continuously when a DC voltage is applied, *stepper motors* normally rotate in discrete fixed-angle steps. For example, the stepper motor that is used in this chapter rotates with 200 *steps per revolution*, and therefore has a *step angle* of 1.8°. The motor steps each time a pulse is applied to its input, so the speed of rotation is proportional to the rate at which pulses are applied.

Stepper motors can be positioned very accurately, as they typically have a positioning error of less than 5% of a step (i.e. typically ±0.1°). The error does not accumulate over multiple steps, so stepper motors can be controlled in an open-loop form, without the need for feedback. Unlike servo motors, but like DC motors, the absolute position of the shaft is not known without the addition of devices like rotary encoders, which often include an absolute position reference that can be located by performing a single shaft rotation.

> **NOTE** You can find a comprehensive video on interfacing to stepper motors using the BBW, describing the operation of stepper motors in detail, at the web page for this chapter, www.exploringbeaglebone.com/chapter9/, and directly at the link tiny.cc/ebb902. The code described in the video has been updated for this book and is available in the GitHub repository.

Stepper motors, as illustrated in Figure 9-4(a), have toothed permanent magnets that are fixed to a rotating shaft, called *the rotor*. The rotor is surrounded by coils (grouped into *phases*) that are fixed to the stationary body of the motor (*the stator*). The coils are electromagnets that, when energized, attract the toothed shaft teeth in a clockwise or counterclockwise direction, depending on the order in which the coils are activated, as illustrated in Figure 9-4(b) for full-step drive:

- **Full step:** Two phases always on (max torque).
- **Half step:** Double the step resolution. Alternates between two phases on and a single phase on (torque at about 3/4 max).
- **Microstep:** Uses sine and cosine waveforms for the phase currents to step the motor rather than the on/off currents illustrated in Figure 9-4 (b) and thus allows for higher step resolutions (though the torque is significantly reduced).

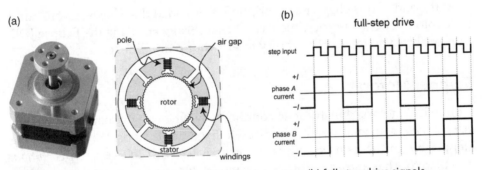

Figure 9-4: (a) Stepper motor external and internal structure; (b) full-step drive signals

The EasyDriver Stepper Motor Driver

An easy way to generate the stepper motor pulse signals is to use a stepper-motor driver board. The EasyDriver board (illustrated in Figure 9-5) is a low-cost (~$15) open-hardware stepper motor driver board that is widely available. It can be used to drive four-, six- and eight-wire stepper motors, as illustrated in Figure 9-6. The board has an output drive capability of between 7V and 30V at ±750mA per phase. The board uses the Allegro A3967 Microstepping Driver with Translator, which allows for full, half, quarter, and one-eighth step microstepping modes.

In addition, the board can be driven with 5V or 3.3V logic levels, which makes it an ideal board for the BBB. For 3.3V logic control levels, there is a jumper (SJ2) that has to be solder bridged.

MS1	MS2	Step
0	0	full
0	1	half
1	0	quarter
1	1	eight

Figure 9-5: Driving a stepper motor using the open-hardware EasyDriver board

WARNING   Do not disconnect a motor from the EasyDriver board while it is powered, as it may destroy the board.

The merit in examining this board is that many boards can be used for higher-powered stepper motors that have a very similar design.

NOTE   If you don't have access to a datasheet for a stepper motor (e.g., you rescued it from an old printer), you can determine the connections to the coils by shorting pairs of wires and rotating the motor. If there is noticeable resistance to rotation for a particular shorted pairing, then you have identified the connections to a coil. You cannot determine the coils using the colors of the wires alone, as there is no standard format.

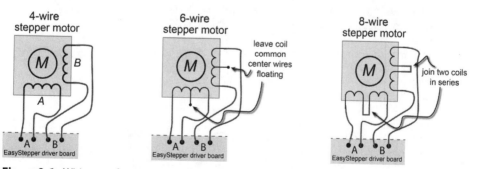

Figure 9-6: Wiring configuration for different stepper motor types

A BBB Stepper Motor Driver Circuit

The EasyDriver board can be connected to the BBB as illustrated in Figure 9-7, using GPIOs for each of the control signals. The pins are described in Figure 9-5, and a table is provided in the figure for the MS1/MS2 inputs. A C++ class called `StepperMotor` is available that accepts alternative GPIO numbers.

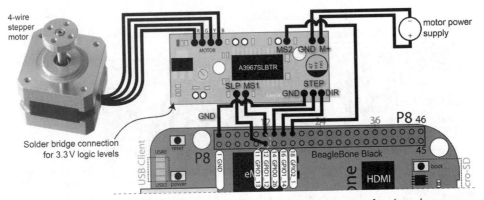

Figure 9-7: Driving a stepper motor using the BBB and the EasyDriver interface board

Controlling a Stepper Motor Using C++

Listing 9-3 presents the description of a class that can be used to control the EasyDriver driver board using five BBB GPIO pins. This code can be adapted to drive most types of stepper driver boards.

LISTING 9-3: /library/motor/StepperMotor.cpp (Segment)

```
class StepperMotor {
public:
    enum STEP_MODE { STEP_FULL, STEP_HALF, STEP_QUARTER, STEP_EIGHT };
    enum DIRECTION { CLOCKWISE, ANTICLOCKWISE };
private:
    // The GPIO pins MS1, MS2 (Microstepping options), STEP (The low->high step)
    // SLP (Sleep - active low) and DIR (Direction)
    GPIO *gpio_MS1, *gpio_MS2, *gpio_STEP, *gpio_SLP, *gpio_DIR;
    ...
public:
    StepperMotor(GPIO *gpio_MS1, GPIO *gpio_MS2, GPIO *gpio_STEP, GPIO *gpio_SLP,
            GPIO *gpio_DIR, int speedRPM = 60, int stepsPerRevolution = 200);
    StepperMotor(int gpio_MS1, int gpio_MS2, int gpio_STEP, int gpio_SLP,
            int gpio_DIR, int speedRPM = 60, int stepsPerRevolution = 200);
    virtual void  step();
    virtual void  step(int numberOfSteps);
    virtual int   threadedStepForDuration(int numberOfSteps, int duration_ms);
    virtual void  threadedStepCancel() { this->threadRunning = false; }
    virtual void  rotate(float degrees);
```

```
   virtual void   setDirection(DIRECTION direction);
   virtual DIRECTION getDirection() { return this->direction; }
   virtual void   reverseDirection();
   virtual void   setStepMode(STEP_MODE mode);
   virtual STEP_MODE getStepMode() { return stepMode; }
   virtual void   setSpeed(float rpm);
   virtual float  getSpeed() { return speed; }
   virtual void   setStepsPerRevolution(int steps) { stepsPerRevolution = steps; }
   virtual int    getStepsPerRevolution() { return stepsPerRevolution; }
   virtual void   sleep();
   virtual void   wake();
   virtual bool   isAsleep() { return asleep; }
   virtual ~StepperMotor();
   ...   //Full code available in /library/motor/StepperMotor.h
};
```

The library code is used in Listing 9-4 to create a `StepperMotor` object, and rotate the motor counterclockwise 10 times at full-step resolution. It then uses a threaded step function to microstep the stepper motor clockwise for one full revolution over five seconds at one-eighth step resolution.

LISTING 9-4: /chp09/stepper/StepperMotorApp.cpp

```cpp
#include <iostream>
#include "motor/StepperMotor.h"
using namespace std;
using namespace exploringBB;

int main(){
   cout << "Starting EBB Stepper Motor Example:" << endl;
   //Using 5 GPIOs, RPM=60 and 200 steps per revolution
   StepperMotor m(44,65,26,45,46,60,200);
   m.setDirection(StepperMotor::ANTICLOCKWISE);
   m.setStepMode(StepperMotor::STEP_FULL);
   m.setSpeed(100);  //rpm
   cout << "Rotating 10 times at 100 rpm anti-clockwise, full step..." << endl;
   m.rotate(3600.0f);   //in degrees
   cout << "Finished regular (non-threaded) rotation)" << endl;
   m.setDirection(StepperMotor::CLOCKWISE);
   cout << "Performing 1 threaded revolution in 5 seconds using micro-stepping:"
        << endl;
   m.setStepMode(StepperMotor::STEP_EIGHT);
   if(m.threadedStepForDuration(1600, 5000)<0){
      cout << "Failed to start the Stepper Thread" << endl;
   }
   cout << "Thread should now be running..." << endl;
      for(int i=0; i<10; i++){ // sleep for 10 seconds.
      usleep(1000000);
      cout << i+1 << " seconds has passed..." << endl;
```

continues

LISTING 9-4: *(continued)*

```
    }
    m.sleep();   // cut power to the stepper motor
    cout << "End of Stepper Motor Example" << endl;
}
```

After calling the associated build script, the program can be executed and should result in the following output:

```
molloyd@beaglebone:~/exploringbb/chp09/stepper$ ./StepperApp
Starting EBB Stepper Motor Example:
Rotating 10 times at 100 rpm anti-clockwise, full step...
Finished regular (non-threaded) rotation)
Performing 1 threaded revolution in 5 seconds using micro-stepping:
Thread should now be running...
1 seconds has passed...
2 seconds has passed...
...
10 seconds has passed...
End of Stepper Motor Example
```

It is important to note that the threaded revolution completes the revolution after five seconds. The counter continues for a further five seconds, during which time a holding torque is applied. The final call to m.sleep() removes power from the stepper motor coils, thus removing holding torque.

It is possible to further reduce the number of pins that are used in this motor controller example by using 74HC595 ICs and the SPI bus. That topic is discussed in the section "Interfacing to Display Modules," later in this chapter.

Relays

Traditional relays are electromechanical switches that are typically used to control a high-voltage/high-current signal using a low-voltage/low-current signal. They are constructed to enable a low-powered circuit to apply a magnetic force to an internal movable switch. The internal switch can turn on or turn off a second circuit that often contains a high-powered DC or AC load. The relay itself is chosen according to the power requirements; whether the circuit is designed so that the high-powered circuit is normally powered or normally disabled; and the number of circuits being switched in parallel.

Electromechanical relays (EMRs) are prone to switch bounce and mechanical fatigue, so they have a limited life span, particularly if they are switched constantly at frequencies of more than a few times per minute. Rapid switching of EMRs can also cause them to overheat. More recent, solid-state relays (SSRs) are electronic switches that consist of FETs, thyristors, and opto-couplers. They have no moving parts and therefore have longer life spans and higher maximum switching frequencies (about 1kHz). The downside is that SSRs are more expensive, and they are prone to failure (often in the switched "on" state) due to overloading or improper wiring. They are typically installed with heat sinks and fast-blow fuses on the load circuit.

EMRs and SSRs are available that can switch very high currents and voltages. That makes them particularly useful for applications like smart home installations, the control of mains-powered devices, motor vehicle applications for switching high-current DC loads, and powering high-current inductive loads in robotic applications. **Importantly, wiring mains applications are for expert users only, as even low currents coupled with high voltages can be fatal. Please seek local professional advice if dealing in any way with high currents or high voltages, including, but not limited to, AC mains voltages.**

WARNING The circuit in Figure 9-8 is intended for connection to low-voltage supplies only (e.g., 12V supplies). High voltages can be extremely dangerous to human health, and only suitably trained individuals with appropriate safety equipment and taking professional precautions should wire mains-powered devices. Suitable insulation, protective enclosures, or additional protective devices such as fuses or circuit breakers (possibly including both current-limiting circuit breakers and earth-leakage circuit breakers) may be required to prevent creating either a shock or a fire hazard. Seek advice from a qualified electrician before installing mains-powered home automation circuitry.

Figure 9-8(a) illustrates the type of circuit that can be used to interface the BBB to a relay. It is important that the relay chosen is capable of being switched at 5V and that, like the motor circuit in Figure 9-2, a flyback diode is placed in parallel to the relay's inductive load in order to protect the FET from damage. Pololu (www.pololu.com) sells a small SPDT relay kit (~$4), as illustrated in Figure 9-8(b), that can be used to switch 8A currents at 30V DC using an Omron G5LE power relay. The breakout board contains a BSS138 FET, the flyback diode, and LEDs that indicate when the relay is switched to enable—that is, close the circuit connected to the normally open (NO) output.

The relay can be connected to a regular GPIO for control. For example, if the relay were connected as shown in Figure 9-8(a), to P8_17 (GPIO0_27), then it can be switched using the following:

```
molloyd@beaglebone:/sys/class/gpio$ echo 27 > export
molloyd@beaglebone:/sys/class/gpio$ cd gpio27
```

```
molloyd@beaglebone:/sys/class/gpio/gpio27$ echo out > direction
molloyd@beaglebone:/sys/class/gpio/gpio27$ echo 1 > value
molloyd@beaglebone:/sys/class/gpio/gpio27$ echo 0 > value
```

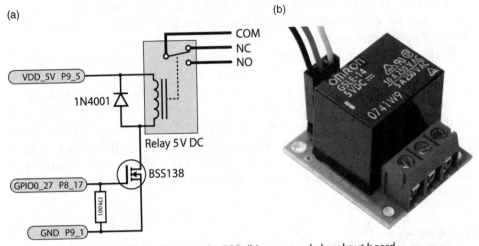

Figure 9-8: (a) Controlling a relay using the BBB; (b) an example breakout board

Interfacing to Analog Sensors

A *transducer* is a device that converts variations in one form of energy into proportional variations in another form of energy. For example, a microphone is an acoustic transducer that converts variations in sound waves into proportional variations in an electrical signal. In fact, actuators are also transducers, as they convert electrical energy into mechanical energy.

Transducers, the main role of which is to convert information about the physical environment into electrical signals (voltages or currents) are called *sensors*. Sensors may contain additional circuitry to further condition the electrical signal (e.g., by filtering out noise or averaging values over time), and this combination is often referred to as an *instrument*. The terms *sensor, transducer,* and *instrument* are in fact often used interchangeably, so too much should not be read into the distinctions between them. Interfacing to sensors enables you to build an incredibly versatile range of project types using the BBB, some of which are described in Table 9-2.

The ADXL345 I²C/SPI digital accelerometer is discussed in Chapter 8, and Table 9-2 identifies another accelerometer, the ADXL335, which is an analog accelerometer. Essentially, the ADXL345 digital accelerometer is an analog sensor that also contains filtering circuitry, analog-to-digital conversion, and input/output circuitry. It is quite often the case that both analog and digital sensors are available that can perform similar tasks. Table 9-3 provides a summary comparison of digital versus analog sensors.

Table 9-2: Example Analog Sensor Types and Applications

MEASURE	APPLICATIONS	EXAMPLE SENSORS
Temperature	Smart home, weather monitoring	TMP36 temperature sensor. MAX6605 low-power temperature sensor
Light Level	Home automation, display contrast adjustment	Mini photocell/photodetector (PDV-P8001)
Distance	Robotic navigation, reversing sensing	Sharp infrared proximity sensors (e.g., GP2D12)
Touch	User interfaces, proximity detection	Capacitive touch. The BBB's ADC has touch screen functionality
Acceleration	Determine orientation, impact detection	Accelerometer (ADXL335). Gyroscope (LPR530) detects change in orientation.
Sound	Speech recording and recognition, UV meters	Electret microphone (MAX9814), MEMS microphone (ADMP401)
Magnetic Fields	Noncontact current measurement, home security, noncontact switches	100A non-invasive current sensor (SCT-013-000). Hall effect and reed switches. Linear magnetic field sensor (AD22151)
Motion Detection	Home security, wildlife photography	PIR Motion Sensor (SE-10)

Table 9-3: Comparison of Typical Digital and Analog Sensor Devices

DIGITAL SENSORS	ANALOG SENSORS
ADC is handled by the sensor, freeing up limited microcontroller ADC inputs.	Provide continuous voltage output and capability for very fast sampling rates.
The real-time issues surrounding embedded Linux, such as variable sampling periods, are not as significant.	Typically less expensive, but may require external components to configure the sensor parameters.
Often contain advanced filters that can be configured and controlled via registers.	Output is generally easy to understand without the need for complex datasheets.
Bus interfaces allow for the connection of many sensor devices.	Relatively easy to interface.
Less susceptible to noise.	

Digital sensors typically have more advanced features (e.g., the ADXL345 has double-tap and free-fall detection), but at a greater cost and level of complexity. Many sensors are not available in a digital package, so it is very important to understand how to connect analog sensors to the BBB. Ideally, the analog sensor that you connect should not have to be sampled at a rate of thousands of times per second, or it will add significant CPU overhead.

> **WARNING**   You have to be particularly careful when connecting powered sensors to the BBB ADC inputs, as the ADC contains very sensitive circuitry that can be easily damaged by going outside its 0V to 1.8V limits. You should not sink current to or source current from the ADC inputs or voltage reference pins.

Protecting the BBB ADC Inputs

The BBB's ADC is easily damaged. In addition, many of the analog sensors that are described in Table 9-2 require 3.3V or 5V supplies. This is a particular concern when prototyping a new sensor interface circuit, as one connection mistake could physically damage the BBB. The BBB's ADC inputs do have some internal circuitry to protect the inputs, but it is not designed to carry even a modest current for more than very short periods of time. The internal circuitry is mainly present for electrostatic discharge (ESD) protection, rather than to be relied on for clamping input signals. Therefore, external circuit protection is very useful in preventing damage.

Diode Clamping

Figure 9-9(a) illustrates a simple *diode clamping* circuit that is typically used to limit voltage levels applied to ADCs. The circuit consists of two diodes and a current-limiting resistor. The diodes are reverse-biased when the voltage level is within the range 0V to V_{ref}. Current flows to the notional AIN0 input, and the circuit behaves correctly as illustrated in Figure 9-9(b) when a sine wave is applied (V_{IN}) that oscillates within the 0V to V_{ref} range. However, if V_{IN} exceeds the V_{ref} level (plus the forward voltage drop of the diode), then the upper diode is forward-biased and current would flow to the V_{ref} rail. If V_{ref} is 1.8V and silicon diodes are used (~0.7V forward voltage), then this signal will be clamped at 2.5V. For the lower diode, if V_{IN} falls below 0V to 0.7V then the diode will be forward-biased and AGND will source current. The resistor R can be used to limit the upper current level. The resulting clamped output is illustrated in Figure 9-9(c) when a sine wave is applied to the input that exceeds the permitted range.

The clamping circuit in Figure 9-9(a) is not recommended for use with the BBB for two reasons. First, the forward voltage drop of a typical silicon diode extends the nonclamped range to approximately −0.7V to 2.5V, which is well outside acceptable levels. More expensive Schottky diodes can be used that have a forward voltage drop of about 0.25V at 2mA and 25°C (e.g., the 1N5817G). These would bring the effective output range to about −0.25V to 2.05V, which is better but still not ideal. The second reason is that when clamping occurs, the current would have to be sourced from or sinked to the BBB's AGND or V_{ref} rails. Sinking current to the V_{ref} rail could damage the V_{ref} input and/or affect the reference voltage level. However, diode clamping is preferable to no protection whatsoever.

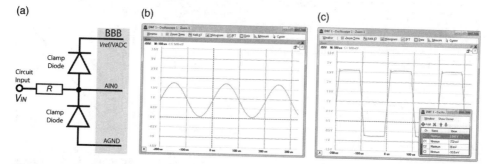

Figure 9-9: (a) A typical diode clamping circuit (not recommended); (b) the signal response of the circuit to an input signal that is in range; (c) the clipped signal response of the circuit to an input signal that is out of range

Op-Amp Clamping

A recommended circuit to protect the BBB ADC circuitry is presented in Figure 9-10(a). While it appears complex, it is reasonably easy to connect, as it requires only three ICs and seven resistors to protect all seven AINs. This voltage follower circuit uses a 5V powered single op-amp package to provide a 1.8V voltage reference source to an array of low-voltage op-amps. The Microchip MCP6001/2 or LM358 can be used for this voltage supply task.

An array of modern op-amps, supplied at 1.8V (i.e., V_{CC+} = 1.8V), are configured in voltage follower configuration and placed in front of each of the BBB ADC inputs (AIN0 to AIN6). These op-amps are supplied with $V_{DD} = V_{CC+}$ = 1.8V and $V_{SS} = V_{CC-}$ = GND, so it is not possible for their output voltage level to exceed the range 0V to 1.8V. The MCP600x is a low-cost DIP packaged op-amp that is suitable for this role. In particular, the MCP6004 has four op-amps within the one package, so only two MCP6004s (plus the 1.8V supply circuit op-amp) are required to protect all seven ADC inputs.

Figure 9-10(b) illustrates the behavior of this circuit when a 0.9V amplitude sine wave (biased at +0.9V) is applied to the Analog0 circuit input. The output signal overlays precisely on the input signal. Older op-amps (including the LM358) would have difficulty with this type of *rail-to-rail operation* (i.e., 0V to 1.8V) and would behave in a nonlinear way near the rail voltages. As shown in the plot of the Analog0 input versus the AIN0 output in Figure 9-10(b), there is a very strong linear relationship, even at the supply rail voltage levels. Figure 9-10(c) and (d) illustrate the consequence of the input signal (accidentally) exceeding the allowable range. In both cases the output is clamped to the 0V to 1.8V range and the BBB ADC is protected, though of course the signal input to the ADC is distorted.

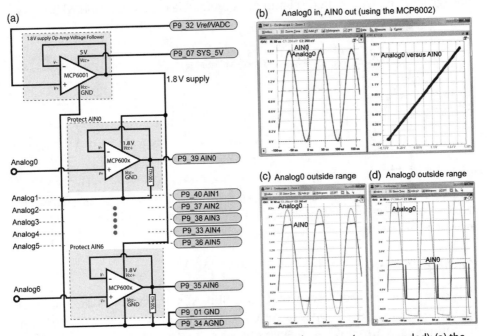

Figure 9-10: Protecting the ADC inputs using 1.8V powered op-amps (recommended); (a) the circuit to protect all BBB analog inputs; (b) linear response characteristic; (c) clipped response to an out-of-range input; (d) clipped response to a significantly out-of-range input

The circuit can be connected to the BBB as illustrated in Figure 9-10, and its impact can be evaluated in a terminal using the following steps:

```
molloyd@beaglebone:~$ sudo sh -c "echo BB-ADC > $SLOTS"
molloyd@beaglebone:~$ cat $SLOTS|grep ADC
 7: ff:P-O-L Override Board Name,00A0,Override Manuf,BB-ADC
molloyd@beaglebone:~$ cd /sys/bus/iio/devices/iio:device0
```

Setting the DC voltage levels at Analog0 to be 0V, 0.9V, 1.8V, and 2.1V results in the respective raw input values from the 12-bit ADC (0-4095) as follows:

```
molloyd@beaglebone:/sys/bus/iio/devices/iio:device0$ cat in_voltage0_raw
94
molloyd@beaglebone:/sys/bus/iio/devices/iio:device0$ cat in_voltage0_raw
2140
```

```
molloyd@beaglebone:/sys/bus/iio/devices/iio:device0$ cat in_voltage0_raw
4092
molloyd@beaglebone:/sys/bus/iio/devices/iio:device0$ cat in_voltage0_raw
4093
```

The 100kΩ resistor ensures that current flows to GND through the resistor rather than through the AINx input. (For your reference, the ADC functional block diagram is shown in Figure 12-2 of the *AM335x TRM*.) The AM335x datasheet at `tiny.cc/ebb903` provides further details about the limitations of the BBB ADC.

Analog Sensor Signal Conditioning

One of the problems with analog sensors is that they may have output signal voltage levels quite different from those required by the BBB. For example, the Sharp GP2D12 distance sensor that is used as an example in this section outputs a DC voltage of ~2.6V when it detects an object at a distance of 10cm, and ~0.4V when the object is detected at a distance of 80cm. If this sensor is connected to the clamping circuit in Figure 9-10, the BBB's ADC would not be damaged, but the sensing range would be reduced by clamping.

Signal conditioning is the term used to describe the manipulation of an analog signal so that it is suitable for the next stage of processing. In order to condition a sensor output as an input to the BBB, this often means ensuring that the signal's range is less than 1.8V, with a DC bias of +0.9V.

Scaling Using Voltage Division

The voltage divider circuit described at the beginning of Chapter 4 can be used to condition a sensor output. If the output voltage from the sensor is greater than 1.8V but not less than 0V, then a voltage divider circuit can be used to linearly reduce the voltage to remain within a 0V to 1.8V range.

Figure 9-11 illustrates a voltage division circuit and its integration with the 1.8V op-amp protection circuitry discussed in the last section. Voltage follower circuits also act as *buffer* circuits. The maximum input impedance of the AM335x ADC inputs ranges from about 76kΩ at the highest frequencies to many megaohms at low frequencies.[1] The voltage divider circuit will further load the sensor output impedance (perhaps requiring further unity-gain buffers before the voltage divider). However, the MCP6002 will act as a buffer that prevents the sensor circuit from exceeding the maximum input impedance of the ADC (remember that ideal voltage follower circuits have infinite input impedance and zero output impedance). There are some important points to note about this circuit:

- Resistors have a manufacturing tolerance (often 5%–10% of the resistance value), which will affect the scaling accuracy of the voltage division circuit. You may need to experiment with combinations or use a potentiometer to adjust the resistance ratio.

- A capacitor C_1 can be added across V_{OUT} to reduce noise if required. The value of C_1 can be chosen according to the value of R_1 and the desired cutoff frequency f_C, according to the equation: $R_1 C_1 = 1 / (2\pi \times f_c)$. There is an example in the next section.

- With multi-op-amp packages, unused inputs should be connected as shown in Figure 9-11 (in light gray) to avoid random switching noise.

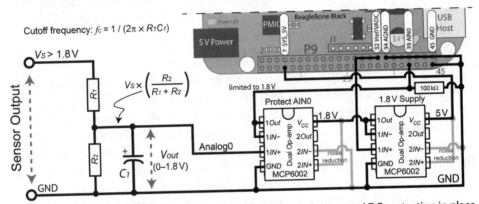

Figure 9-11: Scaling an input signal using voltage division with op-amp ADC protection in place

This circuit works well for linearly scaling down an input signal, but it would not work for a zero-centered or negatively biased input signal. For that, a more general and slightly more complex op-amp circuit is required.

Signal Offsetting and Scaling

Figure 9-12(a) provides a general op-amp circuit that can be used to set the gain and offset of an input signal. Do not connect this circuit directly to the BBB—it is designed as an adjustable prototyping circuit to use in conjunction with an oscilloscope to design a fixed-signal conditioning circuit for your particular application. Some notes on this circuit:

- The $V_{cc}-$ input of the op-amp is tied to GND, which is representative of the type of circuit that is built using the BBB, as a −5V rail is not readily available.

- If an LM358 is used, then a load resistor is required to prevent the output from being clamped below 0.7V. According to the National Semiconductor Corporation (1994), "the LM358 output voltage needs to raise approximately one diode drop above ground to bias the on-chip vertical PNP transistor for output current sinking applications."[2]

- The 1.8V level can be provided by the analog voltage reference on the BBB, but do not connect it without the use of a voltage follower circuit as shown earlier. Alternatively, a voltage divider could be used with the 5V rail.

▪ A 100nF decoupling capacitor can be used on the V_{IN} input to remove the DC component of the incoming sensor signal. However, for many sensor circuits the DC component of the sensor signal is important and should not be removed.

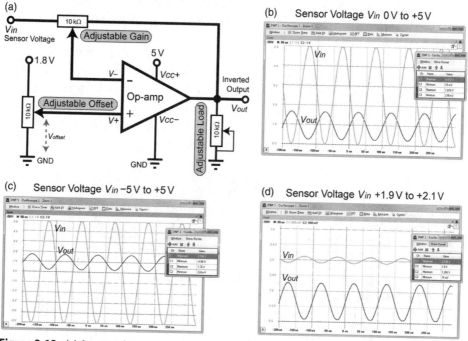

Figure 9-12: (a) A general op-amp signal conditioning circuit that inverts the input; (b) conditioned output when V_{in} is 0V to 5V; (c) output when V_{in} is −5V to +5V; (d) conditioned and amplified output when the input signal is 1.9V to 2.1V

The circuit in Figure 9-12(a) amplifies (or attenuates), offsets, and inverts the input signal according to the settings of the potentiometers:

▪ The gain is set using the adjustable gain potentiometer, where $V_- = G \times V_{IN}$.

▪ The offset is set using the adjustable offset potentiometer. This can be used to center the output signal at 0.9V.

▪ The output voltage is approximately $V_{OUT} = V_+ - V_- = offset - (G \times V_{IN})$. As such, the output is an inverted and scaled version of the input signal.

▪ The inversion of the signal (you can see that the output is at a maximum when the input is at a minimum) is a consequence of the circuit used. Noninverting circuits are possible, but they are more difficult to configure. The inversion can easily be corrected in software by subtracting the received ADC input value from 4,095.

In Figure 9-12(b), (c), and (d) the offset voltage is set to 0.9V and the gain is adjusted to maximize the output signal (between 0V and 1.8V) without clipping the signal. In Figure 9-12(b) the gain and offset are adjusted to map a 0V to +5V signal to a 1.8V to 0V inverted output signal. In Figure 9-12(c) a −5V to +5V signal is mapped to a 1.8V to 0V signal. Finally, in Figure 9-12 (d) a 1.9V to 2.1V input signal is mapped to a 1.3V to 0V output (this is the limit for the LM358 in this case). The last case is applied to an example application in the next section.

Figure 9-13 illustrates a full implementation of the op-amp signal conditioning circuit as it is attached to the BBB. In this example only two op-amps are required in total. This is because the MCP6002 on the left is used to both condition the signal and protect the ADC input. This is possible because it is powered using a V_{CC} = 1.8V supply, which is provided by the 1.8V voltage follower circuit on the right-hand side. The MCP6002 is a dual op-amp package, and it is used because the MCP6001 is not readily available in a DIP package. You could use the MCP6002 to condition two separate sensor signals.

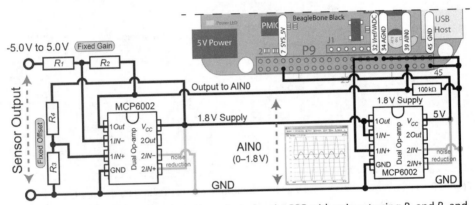

Figure 9-13: Signal conditioning circuit connected to the BBB with gain set using R_1 and R_2 and offset set using R_3 and R_4

The potentiometers in Figure 9-12 are replaced by fixed-value resistors in Figure 9-13 in order to demonstrate how a fixed offset and gain can be configured. In addition, the MCP6002 does not require a load resistor on the output, but a 100kΩ resistor is used to protect the ADC input.

If the input voltage is −5V to +5V, then this circuit will give an output of 0.048V to 1.626V with the resistor values R_1 = 9.1kΩ, R_2 = 1.5kΩ, R_3 = 4.7kΩ, and R_4 = 6.5kΩ. A general equation to describe the relationship between the input and output can be determined as follows:

$$V_{OUT} = 1.8 \times \left(\frac{R_3}{R_3 + R_4} \right) \left(\frac{R_1 + R_2}{R_1} \right) - V_{IN} \left(\frac{R_2}{R_1} \right)$$

At V_{IN} = 5V, V_{OUT} = −0.05V, and at V_{IN} = −5V, V_{OUT} = 1.71V.

Listing 9-5 displays a test program that can be used to read in 1,000 values from AIN0 at about 20Hz, with the output presented on a single line.

LISTING 9-5: /exploringbb/chp09/testADC/testADC.cpp (segment)

```
#define LDR_PATH "/sys/bus/iio/devices/iio:device0/in_voltage"

int readAnalog(int number){
    stringstream ss;
    ss << LDR_PATH << number << "_raw";
    fstream fs;
    fs.open(ss.str().c_str(), fstream::in);
    fs >> number;
    fs.close();
    return number;
}

int main(int argc, char* argv[]){
    cout << "The value on the ADC is:" << endl;
    for(int i=0; i<1000; i++){
        int value = readAnalog(0);
        cout << "  = " << readAnalog(0) << "/4095    " << '\r' << flush;
        usleep(50000);
    }
    return 0;
}
```

When built and executed, this code gives the following output:

```
molloyd@beaglebone:~/exploringbb/chp09/testADC$ ./build
molloyd@beaglebone:~/exploringbb/chp09/testADC$ ./testADC
The value on the ADC is: = 1940/4095
```

If a sine wave is inputted at a frequency of 0.1 Hz, then the output of the program will slowly increase and decrease between a value close to 0 and a value close to 4,095.

Analog Interfacing Examples

Now that the BBB's ADC inputs can be protected from damage using op-amp clamping, two analog interfacing examples are discussed in this section. The first example demonstrates how you can model the response of a sensor, and the second example employs signal offsetting and scaling.

Infrared Distance Sensing

Sharp infrared distance measurement sensors are very useful for robotic navigation applications (e.g., object detection and line following) and proximity switches (e.g., automatic faucets and energy-saving switches). These sensors can also be attached to servo motors and used to calculate range maps (e.g., on the front of a mobile platform). They work well in indoor environments but have limited use in direct sunlight. They have a response time of ~39ms, so at 25–26 readings per second they will not provide dense range images. Figure 9-14(a) shows two aspect views of a low-cost sensor, the Sharp GP2D12.

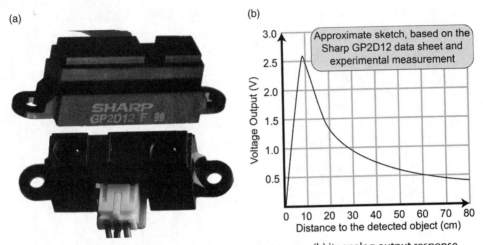

Figure 9-14: (a) Sharp infrared distance measurement sensor; (b) its analog output response

This is a good analog sensor integration example because four problems need to be resolved, which occur generally with other sensors:

1. The sensor response in Figure 9-14(b) is highly nonlinear, so that two different distances can give the same sensor output. Thus you need to find a way to disambiguate the sensor output. For example, if the sensor output is 1.5V, it could mean that the detected object is either 5cm or 17cm from the sensor. A common solution to this problem is to mount the sensor so that it is physically impossible for an object to be closer than 10cm from the sensor. This problem is not examined in further detail, and it is assumed here that the detected object cannot be closer than 10cm from the sensor.

2. The voltage value (0V to 2.6V) exceeds the ADC range. As shown, a signal conditioning circuit can be designed to solve this problem.

3. The output signal is prone to high-frequency noise. A low-pass RC filter can be designed to solve this problem.

4. Even for the assumed distances of 10cm or greater, the relationship between distance and voltage output is still nonlinear. A curve-fitting process can be employed to solve this problem if a linear relationship is required (e.g., threshold applications do not require a linear relationship—just a set value).

   To solve the second problem, a voltage divider configuration can be employed to map the output voltage range from 0V–2.6V to 0V–1.8V. A 10kΩ potentiometer can be used for this task as shown in Figure 9-15(a), where 69.2% (100 × 1.8V/2.6V) of the voltage needs to be dropped across the lower resistor. Therefore, if the total resistance is 10kΩ, then the lower resistor would be 6.92kΩ. If fixed-value resistors are to permanently replace the adjustable potentiometer, then 6.8kΩ and 3.3kΩ could be used. Accuracy is not vital, as the op-amp circuit protects the ADC input and the sensor is itself separately calibrated based on the actual resistor values used.

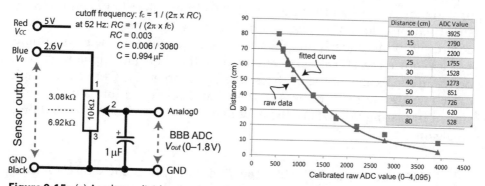

Figure 9-15: (a) A voltage divider circuit configured for the GP2D12 sensor; (b) the plot of the exponentially fitted data

   To solve the third problem, the circuit in Figure 9-15(a) includes a low-pass RC filter to remove high-frequency signal noise. The last step determined the series resistor to be approximately 3.3kΩ; therefore, a capacitor value must be chosen to suit the cutoff sampling frequency, which is about 52Hz (i.e., 2 × 26Hz) in this case (taking account of the Nyquist criterion). A capacitor value of 1μF provides an appropriate value, given the equation $RC = 1 / (2\pi \times f_c)$.

   To solve the final problem, a small test rig can be set up to calibrate the distance sensor. A measuring tape can be placed at the front of the sensor and a large object can be positioned at varying distances from the sensor, between 10cm and 80cm. In my case this provided the raw data for the table in Figure 9-15(b), which is plotted on the graph with the square markers.

   This raw data is not sufficiently fine to determine the distance value represented by an ADC measurement intermediate between the values corresponding to the squares. Therefore, curve fitting can be employed to provide an expression that can be implemented in program code. The data can be supplied to the curve fitting tools that are freely available on the Wolfram Alpha website at www.wolframalpha.com. Using the command string

```
exponential fit {3925,10}, {2790,15}, {2200,20}, {1755,25}, {1528,30},
{1273,40}, {851,50}, {726,60}, {620,70}, {528,80}
```

results in the expression $distance = 115.804e^{-0.000843107\,v}$ (see `tiny.cc/ebb904`). This curve is plotted in Figure 9-15(b) with the triangular markers. It could also be modeled with a quadratic using the following command string:

```
quadratic fit {3925,10}, {2790,15}, {2200,20}, {1755,25}, {1528,30},
{1273,40}, {851,50}, {726,60}, {620,70}, {528,80}
```

which results in the expression $distance = 8.93664 \times 10^{-6} x^2 - 0.0572854x + 99.7321$ (see `tiny.cc/ebb905`).

Note that this process can be used for many analog sensor types to provide an expression that can be used to interpolate between the measured sensor values. What type of fitting curve best fits the data will vary according to the underlying physical process of the sensor. For example, you could use the `linear fit` command on the Wolfram Alpha website to derive an expression for the LDR described in Chapter 6. A C++ code example can be written to read in the ADC value and convert it into a distance as shown in Listing 9-6, where the exponential fix expression is coded on a single line.

LISTING 9-6: /exploringbb/chp09/IRdistance/IRdistance.cpp (Segment)

```
...
int main(int argc, char* argv[]){
    cout << "Starting the IR distance sensor program:" << endl;
    for(int i=0; i<1000; i++){
        int value = readAnalog(0);
        float distance = 115.804f * exp(-0.000843107f * (float)value);
        cout << "The distance is: " << distance << " cm" << '\r' << flush;
        usleep(100000);
    }
    return 0;
}
```

When the code example is executed, it continues to output the distance of a detected object in centimeters, for about 100 seconds:

```
molloyd@beaglebone:~/exploringbb/chp09/IRdistance$ ./build
molloyd@beaglebone:~/exploringbb/chp09/IRdistance$ ./IRdistance
Starting the IR distance sensor program:
The distance is: 17.7579 cm
```

If the speed of execution of such code is vital in the application then, it is preferable to populate a lookup table (LUT) with the converted values. This means that each value is calculated once, either at the initialization stage of the program, or perhaps during code development, rather than every time a reading is made and has to be converted. When the program is in use, the subsequent memory accesses (for reading the LUT) are much more efficient than the corresponding floating-point calculations. This is possible because a 12-bit ADC can only output 4,096 unique values, and it is not unreasonable to store an array of the 4,096 possible outcomes in the memory associated with the program.

ADXL335 Conditioning Example

The ADXL335 is a small three-axis accelerometer that outputs an analog signal that has undergone conditioning. It behaves just like the ADXL345 except that the output is from three analog pins, one for each axis.

When measuring in a range of ±1g, the x-axis outputs ~1.30V at 0°, ~1.64V at 90°, and ~1.98V at 180°. This means that the output signal of the breakout board is centered on 1.64V and has a variation of ±0.34V. A circuit can be designed as shown in Figure 9-16 to map the center point to 0.9V and to extend the variation over the full 1.8V range.

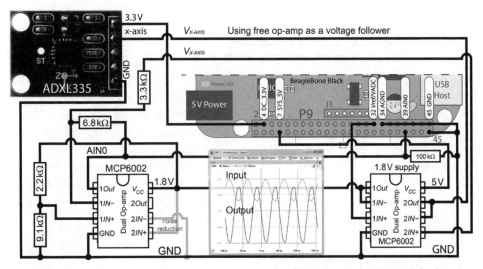

Figure 9-16: The ADXL335 analog accelerometer and its connection to the BBB with further signal conditioning

Unfortunately, there are output impedance problems with this particular ADXL335 breakout board, and the voltage divider circuit in the conditioning circuit will not function correctly. A buffer circuit is therefore required, and an op-amp in voltage follower configuration can be used. The 1.8V powered op-amp could not be used for this task, as the upper sensor output (at 1.98V) exceeds the 1.8V output limit of that op-amp and would thus have been clamped. The 1.8V supply op-amp IC on the right-hand side has a limit of 5V, so it is used for this task.

This circuit is a little complex and it may be overkill, as the amplification of a signal does not necessarily improve the information content of that signal—noise is amplified along with the signal. It is quite possible that the 12-bit ADC performs just as well over a linearly scaled 1.3V to 1.98V range as it does over the full 0V to 1.8V range for this particular sensor. However, it is important that you are exposed to the process of offsetting and scaling a signal using op-amps, as it is required for many sensor types, particularly those that are centered on 0V, such as microphone audio signals.

The `testADC` program that was used previously can be used to print out the digitized AIN value from the accelerometer. In this case, the program prints out

```
molloyd@beaglebone:~/exploringbb/chp09/testADC$ ./testADC
The value on the ADC is:  = 2174/4095
```

at rest (90°), 250 at 0°, and 4,083 at +180°. A simple linear interpolation can be used to approximate the intermediate values.

Interfacing to Display Modules

The BBB can be attached to computer monitors and digital televisions using the HDMI output connector. In addition, LCD touch screen capes can be attached to the P8 and P9 headers as discussed in Chapter 11. The downsides of such displays are that they may not be practical or they may be overly expensive for certain applications. When a small amount of information needs to be relayed to a user, a simple LED can be used—for example, the BBB on-board heartbeat LED is a very useful indicator that the board continues to function. For more complex information, two possibilities are to interface to low-cost seven-segment displays and low-cost character LCD modules.

Seven-Segment Displays

Seven-segment displays typically consist of eight LEDs that can be used to display decimal or hexadecimal numerals with a "decimal" point. They are available in a range of sizes and colors, with a typical example displayed in Figure 9-17(a). The segments are typically labeled as in Figure 9-17(b).

Seven-segment displays are described as being either *common cathode* or *common anode* displays. This means that the cathodes or anodes of the array of LEDs that make up the display are connected together as in Figure 9-17(c). You should not limit the current passing through the display by placing a single resistor on the common anode or the common cathode connection, as the limited current will be shared among the segments that are lighting. This results in an uneven light level, the intensity of which depends on the number of segments that are lit. Therefore, eight current-limiting resistors are required for each seven-segment display. Resistor networks are available that can be used to simplify such wiring configurations (see Figure 8-5).

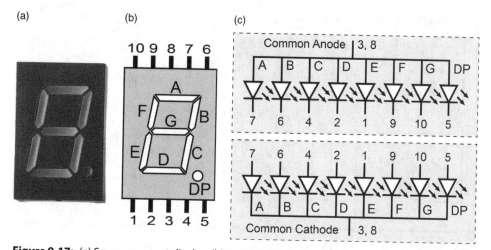

Figure 9-17: (a) Seven-segment display; (b) typical pin ordering; (c) typical common anode and cathode display configurations

It is possible to drive these displays using eight GPIO pins per seven-segment module, but it is also possible to use serial shift registers and the SPI interface, which provides the following advantages:

- Only three SPI pins are required, no matter how many seven-segment display modules are used. Using GPIOs would require a further eight outputs for each additional seven-segment display module.

- Seven-segment displays are available in a vast range of sizes and colors. For example, there are even large 6.5″ seven-segment displays available from SparkFun.

- There is no requirement to add FETs or BJTs to switch the individual segments, as most 74HC595s can deliver 70mA per pin.

Figure 9-18 illustrates a wiring configuration that can be used to connect an array of common cathode seven-segment displays to the BBB using its SPI interface. This is similar to the circuit in Figure 8-5, with the exception that the 74HC595 ICs are *daisy-chained* (i.e., the serial output of one stage is applied as the serial input to the next stage) by connecting the serial output $Q_{H'}$ from one stage to the SER input of the next stage. If there are three seven-segment displays in this configuration, then it is necessary to shift 24 bits (3 × 8 bits) to the BBB SPI0_D1 output before latching the 74HC595s using the BBB's SPI0_CS0 line.

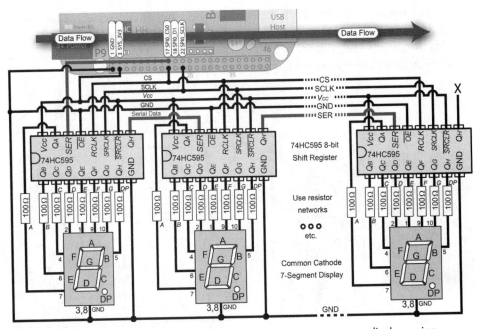

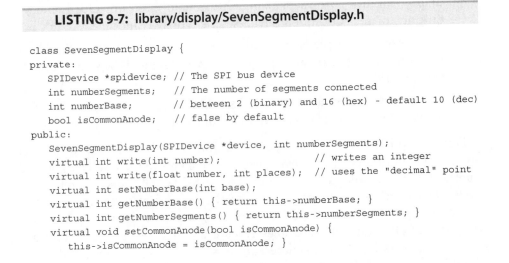

Figure 9-18: SPI interfacing to arrays of common cathode seven-segment displays using daisy-chained 74HC595 8-bit serial shift registers

A C++ class called SevenSegmentDisplay is available that uses the SPIDevice class from Chapter 8 to send data to the segments. The class definition is presented in Listing 9-7 and the implementation file is in /library/display/ SevenSegmentDisplay.cpp.

LISTING 9-7: library/display/SevenSegmentDisplay.h

```
class SevenSegmentDisplay {
private:
    SPIDevice *spidevice;  // The SPI bus device
    int numberSegments;    // The number of segments connected
    int numberBase;        // between 2 (binary) and 16 (hex) - default 10 (dec)
    bool isCommonAnode;    // false by default
public:
    SevenSegmentDisplay(SPIDevice *device, int numberSegments);
    virtual int write(int number);                  // writes an integer
    virtual int write(float number, int places);   // uses the "decimal" point
    virtual int setNumberBase(int base);
    virtual int getNumberBase() { return this->numberBase; }
    virtual int getNumberSegments() { return this->numberSegments; }
    virtual void setCommonAnode(bool isCommonAnode) {
        this->isCommonAnode = isCommonAnode; }
```

```
    virtual ~SevenSegmentDisplay();       // closes the SPI device
private:
    const static unsigned char symbols[];
};
```

This class can display the ciphers/symbols 0 to 9, and A to F using a static constant character array, called `symbols`. The symbols are defined in the `SevenSegmentDisplay.cpp` file as follows:

```
// The binary data that describes the LED state for each symbol
// A(top) B(top right) C(bottom right) D(bottom)
// E(bottom left) F(top left) G(middle)  H(dot)    (msb) HGFEDCBA (lsb)
const unsigned char SevenSegmentDisplay::symbols[16] = {
      0b00111111, 0b00000110, 0b01011011, 0b01001111,    //0123
      0b01100110, 0b01101101, 0b01111101, 0b00000111,    //4567
      0b01111111, 0b01100111, 0b01110111, 0b01111100,    //89Ab
      0b00111001, 0b01011110, 0b01111001, 0b01110001     //CdEF
};
```

For example, `0b00111111` displays the zero symbol, as all segments are on, except for the "decimal" point (DP) and the center segment (G)—see Figure 9-17(b). The code in Listing 9-8 provides an example of how to use an array of common cathode seven-segment displays, as shown in Figure 9-18. The constructor of the `SevenSegmentDisplay` class requires an `SPIDevice` object and the number of segments that are present in the display circuit.

LISTING 9-8: chp09/sevensegment/SevenSegmentApp.cpp

```cpp
#include <iostream>
#include "display/SevenSegmentDisplay.h"
using namespace std;
using namespace exploringBB;

int main(){
   cout << "Starting EBB Seven Segment Display Example" << endl;
   SevenSegmentDisplay display(new SPIDevice(1,0), 2);
   //counting in hexadecimal
   //display.setCommonAnode(true); //For a common anode display setup
   cout << "Counting in hexadecimal 0x00 to 0xFF" << endl;
   display.setNumberBase(16); //count in hexadecimal
   for(int i=0; i<=0xFF; i++){
      display.write(i);
      usleep(50000);
   }
   cout << "Counting 0.0 to 9.9 decimal in steps of 0.1..." << endl;
   display.setNumberBase(10); //count in decimal
```

continues

LISTING 9-8: *(continued)*

```
for(float f=0.0f; f<10; f+=0.1f){
    display.write(f,1);
    usleep(100000);
}
cout << "End of EBB Seven Segment Display Example" << endl;
}
```

If the circuit is built as in Figure 9-18 (but with two segments) and attached to the SPI0 bus, then the code in Listing 9-8 counts in hexadecimal in steps of 1 until it reaches 0xFF, whereupon it counts in decimal from 0.0 to 9.9 in steps of 0.1. This demonstrates the range of functionality that is available in the class. The DP segment lights as required—it can act as a "decimal point" for any base used. To build and execute this code, you must first ensure that the SPIDEV0 virtual cape is loaded:

```
~/exploringbb/chp09/sevensegment$ sudo sh -c "echo BB-SPIDEV0 > $SLOTS"
~/exploringbb/chp09/sevensegment$ cat $SLOTS|grep SPI
13: ff:P-O-L Override Board Name,00A0,Override Manuf,BB-SPIDEV0
molloyd@beaglebone:~/exploringbb/chp09/sevensegment$ ./build
molloyd@beaglebone:~/exploringbb/chp09/sevensegment$ ./SevenSegmentApp
Starting EBB Seven Segment Display Example
Counting in hexadecimal 0x00 to 0xFF
Counting 0.0 to 9.9 decimal in steps of 0.1 ...
End of EBB Seven Segment Display Example
```

The class can also be used with common anode display modules. The modules would be wired exactly as in Figure 9-18; however, pin 3 or 8 would be connected to the +5V line—see Figure 9-17(c). The role of the 74HC595 would then be to sink current in order to light one of the LED segments. For example, if the output of Q_H on the 74HC595 is logic high, then the DP will not be lit, as both the cathode and anode of the LED will be at a 5V level and the LED will not be forward-biased. However, if Q_H is logic low, then the anode of the DP will be at +5V and the cathode will be at 0V. The DP segment will then be forward-biased and will light. Therefore, the code to drive a common anode seven-segment display simply inverts the bits in the number that is sent to the 74HC595. For example, the number 0 is 0b00111111 for a common cathode display and 0b11000000 for a common anode display.

> **NOTE** In C/C++ the bit inversion operator is ~ and the logical inversion operator is !. Be careful not to confuse these operators, as inverting the unsigned char value x=0b01010101 using x=~x; results in x=0b10101010, but using x=!x; results in x=0b00000000. The logical inversion of any nonzero value is zero and the logical inversion of zero is one (i.e., 0b00000001). Using ! instead of ~ for bit operations does

not result in a compiler error, but the clue to finding your mistake is that your bit data is often unexpectedly zero.

An alternative to individual seven-segment displays is to use a low-cost character LCD display module (typically priced around $10).

Character LCD Modules

Character LCD modules are LCD dot matrix displays that feature pre-programmed font tables so that they can be used to display simple text messages without the need for complex display software. They are available in a range of character rows and columns (commonly 2×8, 2×16, 2×20, and 4×20) and usually contain an LED backlight, which is available in a range of colors. Recently, *OLED* (organic LED) versions and *E-paper* (e-ink) versions have been released that provide for greater levels of display contrast.

To understand the use of a character LCD module, you should study its datasheet. While most character LCD modules have common interfaces (often using a Hitachi HD44780 controller—see Further Reading), the display modules from Newhaven have some of the best datasheets. The datasheet for a typical Newhaven display module is available at `tiny.cc/ebb906`. It is recommended that the datasheet be read in conjunction with this discussion.

There are character LCD modules available with integrated I²C and SPI interfaces, but the majority of modules are available with an eight-bit and four-bit parallel interface. By adding a 74HC595 to the circuit it is possible to develop a custom SPI interface, which provides greater flexibility in the choice of modules. A generic character LCD module can be attached to the BBB using the wiring configuration illustrated in Figure 9-19.

You can interface to character LCD modules using either an eight-bit or a four-bit mode, but there is no difference in the functionality available with either mode. The four-bit interface requires fewer interface connections, but each eight-bit value has to be written in two steps—the lower four bits (*nibble*) followed by the higher four bits (nibble).

To write to the character LCD module two lines are required, the RS line (register select signal) and the E line (operational enable signal). The circuit in Figure 9-19 is designed to use a four-bit interface, as it requires only six lines, rather than the 10 lines that would be required with the eight-bit interface. This means that a single eight-bit 74HC595 can be used to interface to the module when it is in four-bit mode. The downside is that the software is slightly more complex to write, as each byte must be written in two nibbles. The four-bit interface uses the inputs DB4–DB7, whereas the eight-bit interface requires the use of DB0–DB7.

It is possible to read data values from the display, but it is not required in this application; therefore, the R/W (read/write select signal) is tied to GND in order to place the display in write mode. The power is supplied using VCC (5V) and

VSS (GND). VEE sets the display contrast level and must be at a level between VSS and VCC. A 10kΩ multi-turn potentiometer can be used to provide precise control over the display contrast. Finally, the LED+ and LED− connections supply the LED backlight power.

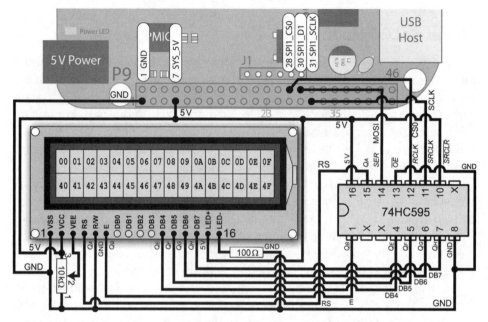

Figure 9-19: SPI interfacing to character LCD modules using a 74HC595 8-bit serial shift register

The display character address codes are illustrated on the module in Figure 9-19. Using *commands* (on pg. 6 of the datasheet), *data* values can be sent to these addresses. For example, to display the letter A in the top left corner, the following procedure can be used with the four-bit interface:

- Clear the display by sending the value 00000001 to D4–D7. This value should be sent in two parts: the lower nibble (0001), followed by the higher nibble (0000). The E line is set high then low after each nibble is sent. A delay of 1.52ms (datasheet pg. 6) is required. The module expects a *command* to be sent when the RS line is low. After sending this command, the cursor is placed in the top left corner.

- Write data 01000001 = 65_{10} = "A" (datasheet pg. 9) with the lower nibble sent first, followed by the upper nibble. The E line is set high followed by low after each nibble is sent. The module expects *data* to be sent when the RS line is set high.

A C++ class is available for you to use in interfacing the BBB to display modules using SPI. The class assumes that the 74HC595 lines are connected as shown in Figure 9-19 and the data is represented as in Table 9-4. The code does not use bits 2 (Q_D) and 3 (Q_C) on the 74HC595, so it is possible for you to repurpose these for your own application. For example, one pin could be connected to the gate of a FET and used to switch the backlight on and off. The class definition is provided in Listing 9-9 and the implementation is in the associated LCDCharacterDisplay.cpp file.

Table 9-4: Mapping of the 74HC595 Data Bits to the Character LCD Module Inputs, as Required for the C++ LCDCharacterDisplay Class

	BIT 7 MSB	BIT 6	BIT 5	BIT 4	BIT 3	BIT 2	BIT 1	BIT 0 LSB
Character LCD module	D7	D6	D5	D4	Not used	Not used	E	RS
74HC595 pins	Q_H	Q_G	Q_F	Q_E	Q_D	Q_C	Q_B	Q_A

LISTING 9-9: library/display/LCDCharacterDisplay.h

```
class LCDCharacterDisplay {
private:
    SPIDevice *device;
    int width, height;
    ...
public:
    LCDCharacterDisplay(SPIDevice *device, int width, int height);
    virtual void write(char c);
    virtual void print(std::string message);
    virtual void clear();
    virtual void home();
    virtual int  setCursorPosition(int row, int column);
    virtual void setDisplayOff(bool displayOff);
    virtual void setCursorOff(bool cursorOff);
    virtual void setCursorBlink(bool isBlink);
    virtual void setCursorMoveOff(bool cursorMoveOff);
    virtual void setCursorMoveLeft(bool cursorMoveLeft);
    virtual void setAutoscroll(bool isAutoscroll);
    virtual void setScrollDisplayLeft(bool scrollLeft);
    virtual ~LCDCharacterDisplay();
};
```

The constructor requires an SPIDevice object and details about the width and height of the character display module (in characters). The constructor provides functionality to position the cursor on the display and to describe how the cursor should behave (e.g., blinking or moving to the left/right). This class can be used as shown in Listing 9-10 to create an `LCDCharacterDisplay` object, display a string, and display a count from 0 to 10,000 on the module.

LISTING 9-10: chp09/LCDcharacter/LCDApp.cpp

```
#include <iostream>
#include <sstream>
#include "display/LCDCharacterDisplay.h"
using namespace std;
using namespace exploringBB;

int main(){
   cout << "Starting EBB LCD Character Display Example" << endl;
   SPIDevice *busDevice = new SPIDevice(2,0); //Using second SPI bus
   busDevice->setSpeed(1000000);        // Have access to SPI Device object
   ostringstream s;                     // Using this to combine text and int data
   LCDCharacterDisplay display(busDevice, 16, 2); // Construct 16x2 LCD Display
   display.clear();                     // Clear the character LCD module
   display.home();                      // Move the cursor to the (0,0) position
   display.print("EBB by D. Molloy");   // String to display on the first row
   for(int x=0; x<=10000; x++){         // Do this 10,000 times
      s.str("");                        // clear the ostringstream object s
      display.setCursorPosition(1,3);   // move the cursor to second row
      s << "X=" << x;                   // construct a string that has an int value
      display.print(s.str());           // print the string X=*** on the module
   }
   cout << "End of EBB LCD Character Display Example" << endl;
}
```

The code example in Listing 9-10 can be built and executed using the following steps:

```
~/exploringbb/chp09/LCDcharacter$ sudo sh -c "echo BB-SPIDEV1 > $SLOTS"
~/exploringbb/chp09/LCDcharacter$ cat $SLOTS|grep SPI
14: ff:P-O-L Override Board Name,00A0,Override Manuf,BB-SPIDEV1
~/exploringbb/chp09/LCDcharacter$ ./build
~/exploringbb/chp09/LCDcharacter$ ./LCDApp
```

The count incrementally updates on the display and finishes with the output illustrated in Figure 9-20.

It takes 26 seconds to display a count that runs from 0 to 10,000, which is approximately 385 localized screen updates per second. This means that you could potentially connect many display modules to a single SPI bus and still achieve reasonable screen refresh rates. You would require the type of multiple SPI slave circuitry that is discussed in Chapter 8, which would require $\lceil \log_2 x \rceil$

GPIOs for x modules. At its maximum refresh rate, the top command gives the following output:

```
  PID USER      PR  NI  VIRT  RES  SHR S  %CPU %MEM    TIME+   COMMAND
18227 root      20   0     0    0    0 S  34.6  0.0 25:02.50 spi2
20967 molloyd   20   0  2708  988  856 S  33.9  0.2  0:04.15 LCDApp
```

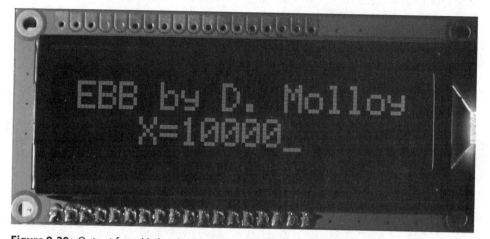

Figure 9-20: Output from Listing 9-10 on a Newhaven display module.

This indicates that the LCDApp program and its associated spi2 platform device are utilizing 68.5% of the available CPU time at this extreme module display refresh rate of 385 updates per second. To be clear, the display maintains its current display state without any BBB overhead, and refresh is only required to change the display contents.

Remote Control BeagleBone

The final section in Chapter 8 describes a framework that can be used to enable the BBB to take control of a microcontroller (like the Arduino) and issue commands to it using a serial data connection. As described in this chapter, the BBB itself is very useful for actuation, sensing, and information display applications. Just like the Arduino, the BBB itself can be configured to be a serial server device, enabling it to execute commands that are sent from another "master" device, such as a desktop computer, a server machine, or another BBB. For example, the BBB could be used as the central processor for a remote-controlled robot that receives commands over a wired serial link or a wireless Bluetooth connection.

The next chapter describes how a similar framework can be developed using Internet sockets, with either fixed-line or wireless Ethernet. However, depending on the application, Ethernet or Wi-Fi may not be viable options due to infrastructure requirements and/or power limitations. Therefore, remote control using wired and wireless serial connections is discussed in this section.

Before a serial server is established on the BBB, it is necessary to discuss the system management daemon, *systemd*, which is used to start and stop services under Linux. *Daemons* are background processes (usually ending in the letter d), and understanding systemd is particularly important if you are going to reconfigure the current serial interfaces or design an application that you wish to have start automatically when the BBB boots.

Managing Services with Systemd

Systemd was developed to replace the `init` system discussed in Chapter 3. It is a controversial Linux development, but it is likely that over time, `init` will be fully replaced by systemd on the BBB. Systemd is the first daemon process to execute on the BBB, and it is the last process to terminate when the BBB is shutting down. Its primary role is to manage many of the services that are available on the BBB. It provides for faster boot times, as it is designed to execute fewer scripts and to execute them in parallel. However, it does not present the same type of support for scripts that is available with `init`. Typing `systemctl` provides a full list of the services that are running on the BBB (use the spacebar to page, and q to quit):

```
molloyd@beaglebone:~$ systemctl list-units -t service
UNIT                    LOAD    ACTIVE  SUB      JOB DESCRIPTION
acpid.service           loaded  active  running  ACPI event daemon ...
```

For example, use the following to find the terminal services that are running on the BBB:

```
molloyd@beaglebone:~$ systemctl list-units -t service |grep tty
getty@tty1.service            loaded active running Getty on tty1
serial-getty@ttyGS0.service loaded active running Serial Getty on ttyGS0
serial-getty@ttyO0.service  loaded active running Serial Getty on ttyO0
```

The second service in the list is called *gadget serial*. It is the BBB end of the Serial-over-USB connection, which is discussed in Chapter 2 (see Figure 2-4). The Windows end of the connection appears in Device Manager as a port— "Gadget Serial (COM20)" in my case. You can get the status of this service as follows:

```
molloyd@beaglebone:~$ systemctl status serial-getty@ttyGS0.service
serial-getty@ttyGS0.service - Serial Getty on ttyGS0
```

```
Loaded:loaded(/etc/systemd/system/serial-getty@ttyGS0.service;enabled)
Active:active(running) since Sun, 01 Jun 2014 20:45:42 +0000; 8m ago
Main PID: 21142 (agetty)
CGroup: name=systemd:/system/serial-getty@.service/ttyGS0
 └ 21142 /sbin/agetty -s ttyGS0 115200 38400 9600
```

The gadget serial *agetty*, often just called *getty* ("get teletype"—hence the name PuTTY!), is a Linux program that manages terminal connections. The systemd service runs as a process, visible using the following:

```
molloyd@beaglebone:~$ ps -ef|grep GS0
root 918 1 0 13:46 ttyGS0 00:00:00 /sbin/agetty -s ttyGS0 115200 38400
```

Using either method you can see that the service is running. Several commands can be executed on such services, for example:

- `systemctl start [name]`: Start a service.
- `systemctl stop [name]`: Stop a service that is running.
- `systemctl restart [name]`: Restart a running service.
- `systemctl enable [name]`: Enable a service to start on boot.
- `systemctl disable [name]`: Disable a service from starting on boot.

One method of providing for remote control of the BBB is to replace a serial service with a custom application service. To replace the gadget serial service with a custom control service, it must be first shut down and disabled from starting on boot, using the following steps:

```
molloyd@beaglebone:~$ sudo systemctl stop serial-getty@ttyGS0.service
molloyd@beaglebone:~$ ps -ef|grep ttyGS
molloyd@beaglebone:~$ ls /dev/ttyGS*
/dev/ttyGS0
```

After this step, there should not be a ttyGS0 process running, but the device is still present. Systemctl should also indicate that it is inactive:

```
molloyd@beaglebone:~$ systemctl status serial-getty@ttyGS0.service
serial-getty@ttyGS0.service - Serial Getty on ttyGS0
 Loaded: loaded(/etc/systemd/system/serial-getty@ttyGS0.service;enabled)
 Active: inactive (dead) since Sun, 29 Jun 2014 ...
```

It can then be disabled from starting on boot as follows:

```
molloyd@beaglebone:~$ sudo systemctl disable serial-getty@ttyGS0.service
rm '/etc/systemd/system/getty.target.wants/serial-getty@ttyGS0.service'
```

A service of your own design can now be deployed that binds to /dev/ttyGS0.

BBB Serial Connection to Desktop

A bespoke serial server is presented in Listing 9-11 that can be used to remotely control the BBB. For this example there are several self-explanatory commands: "LED on," "LED off," and "quit." These commands could be linked to the actuator and sensor examples in this chapter. Essentially, this enables you to create a custom serial terminal connection to the BBB, where such commands are the only permitted interaction with the BBB. The same code example can be modified slightly and used on a desktop machine to form the client end of the connection (communicating with COM20 on my desktop machine).

LISTING 9-11: exploringbb/chp09/serialserver/BBBSerialServer.c

```c
#include<stdio.h>
#include<fcntl.h>
#include<unistd.h>
#include<termios.h>
#include<string.h>
#include<stdlib.h>

// Sends a message to the client and displays the message on the console
int message(int client, char *message){
   int size = strlen(message);
   printf(message);
   if (write(client, message, size)<0){
      perror("Failed to write to the client\n");
      return -1;
   }
   return 0;
}

// Checks to see if the command is one that is understood by the server
int processBBBCommand(int client, char *command){
   int return_val = -1;
   if (strcmp(command, "LED on")==0){
      return_val = message(client, "*** Turning the LED on  ***\n");
      //Add code to light the LED
   }
   else if(strcmp(command, "LED off")==0){
      return_val = message(client, "*** Turning the LED off ***\n");
      //Add code to turn off the LED
   }
   else if(strcmp(command, "quit")==0){
      return_val = message(client, "*** Killing the BBB Serial Server
                        ***\n");
   }
   else {
```

```
          return_val = message(client, "*** Unknown command! ***\n");
      }
      return return_val;
}


// The main application. Must be run as root and must pass the terminal name.
int main(int argc, char *argv[]){
    int client, count=0;
    unsigned char c;
    char *command = malloc(255);
    if(getuid()!=0){    // Is the user root?
        perror("You must run this program as root on the BBB. Exiting!\n");
        return -1;
    }
    if(argc!=2){        // Was the device passed?
        perror("You must provide the device name: e.g., /dev/ttyO0.
                Exiting!\n");
        return -1;
    }
    // Set up the connection
    if ((client = open(argv[1], O_RDWR | O_NOCTTY | O_NDELAY))<0){
        perror("UART: Failed to open the file.\n");
        return -1;
    }
    struct termios options;
    tcgetattr(client, &options);
    options.c_cflag = B115200 | CS8 | CREAD | CLOCAL;
    options.c_iflag = IGNPAR | ICRNL;
    tcflush(client, TCIFLUSH);
    fcntl(STDIN_FILENO, F_SETFL, O_NONBLOCK);   // make the reads non-blocking
    tcsetattr(client, TCSANOW, &options);
    if (message(client, "BBB Serial Server has started running.\n")<0){
        return -1;
    }
    do {    // Loop forever until the quit command is sent or Ctrl-C is typed
        if(read(client,&c,1)>0){
            write(STDOUT_FILENO,&c,1);
            command[count++]=c;
            if(c=='\n'){
                command[count-1]='\0';   //replace /n with /0
                processBBBCommand(client, command);
                count=0;          //reset the command string for the next command
            }
        }
        if(read(STDIN_FILENO,&c,1)>0){   //can send text from stdin to client
            write(client,&c,1);
        }
    }
    while(strcmp(command,"quit")!=0);
```

continues

LISTING 9-11 *(continued)*

```
    close(client);
    return 0;
}
```

Start the COM20 serial terminal session in PuTTY before you execute this program (in a regular SSH session) in order to see the full output. The output appears simultaneously in the desktop PuTTY terminal (115,200 baud), as captured in Figure 9-21 and the Linux SSH session that follows. Enable "Implicit LF in every CR" in the PuTTY settings to get the same output. This code can be built and executed as shown here, where it is attached to the gadget serial device:

```
~/.../chp09/serialserver$ gcc BBBSerialServer.c -o BBBSerialServer
~/.../chp09/serialserver$ sudo ./BBBSerialServer /dev/ttyGS0
BBB Serial Server has started running.
Test command from the PC
*** Unknown command! ***
LED on
*** Turning the LED on  ***
LED off
*** Turning the LED off ***
Typing a message on the PC
*** Unknown command! ***
Typing a message on the BBB
quit
*** Killing the BBB Serial Server ***
~/exploringbb/chp09/serialserver$
```

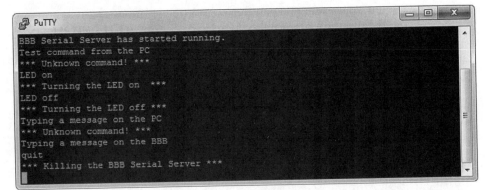

Figure 9-21: The COM20 serial console on the desktop machine as connected to the custom service

Starting a Custom Service on Boot

The service in the last section will halt when the BBB is restarted (or the quit command is sent). To set up a service to start automatically on boot, you should first place the executable service in a general directory. This will help prevent it from being accidentally deleted from a user account home directory:

```
/exploringbb/chp09/serialserver$ sudo cp BBBSerialServer /usr/bin
```

The BBB services configuration files (`.service` files) are stored in the `/lib/systemd/system` directory. For example:

```
/exploringbb/chp09/serialserver$ sudo su -
root@beaglebone:~# cd /lib/systemd/system
root@beaglebone:/lib/systemd/system# ls |less
bluetooth.service
bonescript-autorun.service
bonescript.service ...
```

The `.service` files themselves describe the order in which each service should be started. For example, a new service can be created that starts the `BBBSerialServer` when the BBB boots, as follows:

```
root@beaglebone:/lib/systemd/system# nano bbb-serial-server.service
root@beaglebone:/lib/systemd/system# more bbb-serial-server.service
[Unit]
Description=BBB Serial Server (from EBB)
Before=getty.target

[Service]
ExecStart=/usr/bin/BBBSerialServer /dev/ttyGS0
SyslogIdentifier=BBBSerialServer
Restart=on-failure
RestartSec=10

[Install]
WantedBy=multi-user.target
```

The setting `Multi-user.target` relates to the `init` "run-level 3" that is discussed in Chapter 3. The service can be enabled by using a `systemctl` call, as follows:

```
/lib/systemd/system# systemctl enable bbb-serial-server.service
ln -s '/lib/systemd/system/bbb-serial-server.service' ...
/lib/systemd/system# systemctl start bbb-serial-server.service
/lib/systemd/system# systemctl status bbb-serial-server.service
bbb-serial-server.service - BBB Serial Server (from EBB)
   Loaded: loaded(/lib/systemd/system/bbb-serial-server.service;enabled)
   Active: active(running) since Sun, 29 Jun 2014 19:40:43 +0000;6s ago
 Main PID: 3268 (BBBSerialServer)
    CGroup: name=systemd:/system/bbb-serial-server.service ...
```

The serial server is now running on the BBB, which can be accessed as before using a connection to COM20 on the desktop machine. The quit command is poorly designed, as it terminates the service—it should probably be removed if you use this code as a template. If the commands are entered as shown in Figure 9-22, then the service responds with the following status after a call to quit:

```
/lib/systemd/system# systemctl status bbb-serial-server.service
bbb-serial-server.service - BBB Serial Server (from EBB)
   Loaded: loaded(/lib/systemd/system/bbb-serial-server.service;enabled)
   Active: inactive(dead) since ...
Jun 29 19:42:45 beaglebone BBBSerialServer[3268]: Led on
Jun 29 19:42:47 beaglebone BBBSerialServer[3268]: LED on
Jun 29 19:43:37 beaglebone BBBSerialServer[3268]: quit
```

Figure 9-22: The COM20 serial console on the desktop machine as connected to the custom service

Bluetooth

Bluetooth is a popular wireless communication system that was created by Ericsson and is now managed by the Bluetooth Special Interest Group (SIG). Bluetooth was designed as an open standard to enable very different device types to communicate wirelessly over short distances. It is often used for the digital transfer of data for audio headsets, keyboards, computer mice, medical devices, and many more applications. The BBB does not have on-board support for Bluetooth, but support can be added using a low-cost USB Bluetooth adapter.

Installing an Adapter

The choice of Bluetooth adapter is very important—not every adapter has Linux driver support. Ideally, you should determine in advance of purchase if there is Linux support and it works with the BBB. Unfortunately, that is not always possible; furthermore, as Linux device driver support is usually chipset-dependent, it may even be the case that two devices with the same model number and ostensibly the same functionality have different chipsets, leaving one supported by Linux and the other not. The Bluetooth adapter used in this section is the Kinivo BTD-400 Bluetooth 4.0 USB adapter (~$15), shown in Figure 9-23. It is commonly available, and the current version uses a Broadcom chipset that has good Linux support.

The first step is to install the packages that are required for Bluetooth connectivity on the BBB. Check that you have sufficient free space on the BBB, as the installation requires about 200MB of storage:

```
molloyd@beaglebone:~$ sudo apt-get update
molloyd@beaglebone:~$ sudo apt-get install bluetooth bluez-utils
```

After installation, the BBB should be shut down and the adapter plugged into the BBB USB socket. Once the board is booted, you can list the USB modules that are currently connected to the BBB using the following, where the Broadcom Corp. listing indicates that the device has been detected:

```
root@beaglebone:~# lsusb
Bus 001 Device 002: ID 0a5c:21e8 Broadcom Corp. ...
```

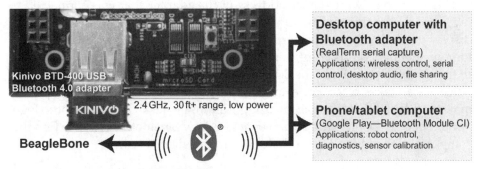

Figure 9-23: Bluetooth-connected BeagleBone

Loadable Kernel Modules

A Linux *loadable kernel module* (LKM) is a mechanism for adding code to the Linux kernel at run time. They are ideal for device drivers, enabling the kernel to communicate with the hardware without it having to know how the hardware works. The alternative to LKMs would be to build the code for each and every driver into the Linux kernel, which would lead to an impractical kernel size and constant kernel recompilations. LKMs are loaded at run time, but they do not exist in user space—they are essentially part of the kernel. When the Bluetooth adapter is plugged into the BBB, you can use the lsmod command to find out which modules are currently loaded. For example

```
molloyd@beaglebone:~$ lsmod
Module                    Size   Used by
```

```
btusb                      9835   0
bluetooth                150504   24 bnep,btusb,rfcomm
rfkill                    16656   2 bluetooth
```

The `modprobe` command enables you to add or remove an LKM to or from the Linux kernel at run time. However, if everything has worked correctly, the module should have loaded automatically. You can check `dmesg` for errors that may have arisen when the BBB was booting. Using `cat /proc/modules` provides similar information about the modules that are loaded, but it is in a less readable form.

Configuring a Bluetooth Adapter

The *hcitool* command is used to configure Bluetooth connections, and if the `dev` argument is passed it provides information about the local Bluetooth device:

```
molloyd@beaglebone:~$ hcitool dev
Devices:     hci0    00:02:72:C8:2F:FF
```

This is the hardware device address of the adapter that was connected to my board. Using this command you can scan for devices, display connections, display power levels, and perform many more functions—check `man hcitool` for more details. At this point, you should be able to scan for Bluetooth devices in the vicinity. Ensure that the devices are *discoverable*—that they can be found when a scan takes place. For example, under Windows you have to explicitly make an adapter discoverable, by using Window ➢ taskbar ➢ (Bluetooth logo) ➢ right-click ➢ Open Settings, and enable "Allow Bluetooth devices to find this computer." To scan for Bluetooth devices in the vicinity, use:

```
molloyd@beaglebone:$ hcitool scan
Scanning     00:26:83:32:CF:0D     DEREKMOLLOY-PC
```

This means that the adapter on the BBB has discovered my desktop computer, DEREKMOLLOY-PC (the `hcitool scan` command may activate Bluetooth devices in the nearby rooms that use Bluetooth remote controls—e.g., smart televisions!). The BBB can interrogate the available services using:

```
root@beaglebone:$ sdptool browse 00:26:83:32:CF:0D
Browsing 00:26:83:32:CF:0D ...
Service Name: Service Discovery
Service Provider: Microsoft...
```

This output is followed by a long list of available services, such as an audio source, audio sink, ftp server, printing service, and so on, each having its own unique channel number. Chapter 11 examines how you can pair an interface device to the BBB. However, the current chapter describes how you can send commands to the BBB from a desktop machine, tablet computer, or mobile phone.

Making the BBB Discoverable

If the BBB is to act as a wireless server, it is vital that the BBB is discoverable by the client machines. The `hciconfig` command can configure the Bluetooth device (`hci0`) to enable page and inquiry scans, as follows:

```
molloyd@beaglebone:$ sudo hciconfig hci0 piscan
```

A Serial Port Profile (SPP) is required on the BBB to define how virtual serial ports are connected via Bluetooth connections. The `sdptool` can be used to configure a profile for a serial port (SP) on channel 22 and find details about available services using:

```
molloyd@beaglebone:$ sudo sdptool add --channel=22 SP
molloyd@beaglebone:$ sdptool browse local
```

At this point, the desktop computer can be used to scan for devices. The BBB should be detected as `beaglebone-0`. The Windows OS installs several device drivers, as illustrated in Figure 9-24. These Bluetooth services are advertised by default on the BBB, but they are not necessarily available. However, in order to allow for communication between the BBB and the desktop PC, a serial connection needs to be established to channel 22. When `sdptool` is used to add channel 22, a "Serial port (SPP)" option should appear in the list of available services on the desktop computer—in my case it is COM22.

Figure 9-24: Windows connecting to the BeagleBone using an on-board Bluetooth interface

The BBB needs to run a service that can listen for incoming connections on channel 22. The `rfcomm` configuration utility can be used to listen for connections on a specific Bluetooth channel, as follows in the SSH session:

```
molloyd@beaglebone:$ sudo rfcomm listen /dev/rfcomm0 22
Waiting for connection on channel 22
```

A serial terminal can then be opened from the desktop machine to the BBB using PuTTY, by opening a connection to the associated COM port. In my case it is COM22 and the baud rate is 115,200 by default. When a connection is formed to the BBB, the SSH window displays:

```
molloyd@beaglebone:$ sudo rfcomm listen /dev/rfcomm0 22
Waiting for connection on channel 22
Connection from 00:26:83:32:CF:0D to /dev/rfcomm0
Press CTRL-C for hangup
```

Do *not* stop this service. While the service is listening, open a second SSH terminal to the BBB. In the second SSH terminal you can `cat` and `echo` to the device associated with the Bluetooth serial connection `rfcomm0`:

```
molloyd@beaglebone:/dev$ cat rfcomm0
Hello BeagleBone Black! from the desktop computer
^C
molloyd@beaglebone:/dev$ echo "Hello Desktop PC! from the BBB">>rfcomm0
```

Figure 9-25 captures the RealTerm application (`realterm.sourceforge.net/`) when it is connected to the BBB via Bluetooth.

Figure 9-25: RealTerm connected to the BBB using the Bluetooth Port 22

At this point it is clear that the device is working, and you can connect a `minicom` terminal to the RealTerm application as follows:

```
molloyd@beaglebone:/dev$ minicom -b 115200 -o -D /dev/rfcomm0
```

You can also use a tablet or phone device that has Bluetooth capability to communicate with the BBB directly. The "Bluetooth Module CI" Android application works perfectly for direct connection to the BBB, and so should many others.

Android Application Development with Bluetooth

There are substantial resources available for Bluetooth mobile application development with both Android and iOS. A great place to start is with the MIT App Inventor (`appinventor.mit.edu`). It consists of a very innovative web-based graphical programming language (like MIT Scratch) for mobile application development. You can pair an Android tablet or phone with the App Inventor environment and view your code developments live on your mobile device. The App Inventor API has Bluetooth client and server libraries that can be integrated with your program code. Figure 9-26 illustrates a full Bluetooth application running on my mobile phone that was built with App Inventor 2. It is communicating to a `minicom` session that is executing on the BBB, while the `rfcomm` service is started in a second terminal window. The (real) phone can communicate directly with the BBB via Bluetooth using the custom-developed mobile application. This could be altered to form any type of mobile GUI display that sends commands to the BBB or displays data in a rich user interface.

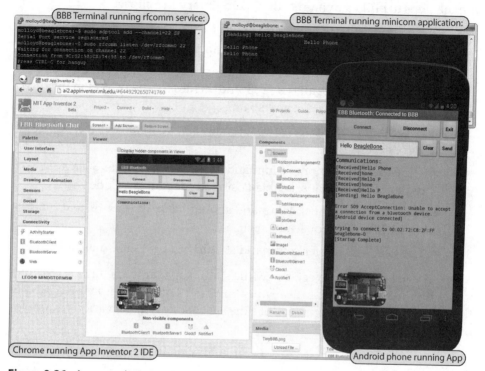

Figure 9-26: An example App Inventor Android application that uses the Bluetooth code library

This application was based on the *Pura Vida Apps* code example, which is available at: `tiny.cc/ebb907`. The code for the example in Figure 9-26 has not been made available in the GitHub repository, as it is strongly based on the linked code. Such a code example can be useful as the basis of an Android application that is capable of sending commands and receiving data from the BBB using Bluetooth communication. Notice that the receive function is on a 2.5-second timer, so if the timer triggers halfway through a string being entered, then the string is received in two parts. Applications that are developed with App Inventor 2 can be distributed like regular applications (e.g., using .apk files) to be side-loaded on Android devices. The `EBB_Bluetooth_Chat` `.apk` example application is available in the `/exploringbb/chp09/Android/` directory.

Building Dynamic Linked Libraries

The examples in this chapter are all linked to a dynamic library file in the directory /library with the name libEBBLibrary.so. This is very useful because it means that you do not have to compile the entire library of code each time you build an example. If you wish to modify the source code of this library, here are the steps to build a dynamically linked library in Eclipse:

1. Select File ≻ New Project ≻ C++ Project. Choose Shared Library ≻ Empty Project. Give it a suitable name, for example, "EBBLibrary."

2. Place all your library project files in the project directory. In this example case you would place all the .cpp and .h files for the project in the directories bus, display, gpio, and so on.

3. In Project ≻ Properties go to C/C++ Build ≻ Settings and set the following properties:

    ▪ The GCC C++ Compiler command should be arm-linux-gnueabihf-g++; under Miscellaneous, enable Position Independent Code (-fPIC).

    ▪ The GCC C++ Linker command should be arm-linux-gnueabihf-g++; under Miscellaneous, add –pthread.

    ▪ The GCC Assembler command should be arm-linux-gnueabihf-as.

When you build the project, a new file should appear in the Binaries directory with the name libEBBLibrary.so-[arm/le]. This can simply be copied to the BBB and used within a project. See the build scripts in the various examples of this chapter.

Summary

After completing this chapter, you should be able to do the following:

▪ Interface to actuators, such as DC motors, stepper motors, and relays.

▪ Protect the BBB ADC from damage using op-amp clamping.

▪ Condition a sensor signal so that it can be interfaced to the BBB ADCs, regardless of the output voltage levels.

▪ Interface analog sensors such as distance sensors and accelerometers to the BBB.

▪ Interface to low-cost display modules such as seven-segment displays and character LCD displays.

▪ Use systemd to control services and create custom services that start when the BBB boots.

- Use the BBB as a serial server, so that it can be remotely controlled.
- Use Bluetooth to communicate with the BBB and have exposure to the steps involved in desktop application or mobile application control.
- Build C/C++ code as a dynamic library to be used on the BBB.

Further Reading

The following additional links provide further information on the topics in this chapter:

- The Hitachi HD44780 datasheet: `tiny.cc/ebb908`
- There is an excellent guide on using Bluetooth with Linux at `tiny.cc/ebb909`

Notes

1. The input impedance varies according to the function: Impedance (ω) = 1/(65.97 $\times$ $10^{-12} \times f$). Texas Instruments. (March 26, 2013). AM335x Data Sheet. Dallas: Texas Instruments Incorporated. `http://www.ti.com/lit/ds/symlink/am3358.pdf`.
2. National Semiconductor Corporation. (1994). LM158/LM258/LM358/LM2904 Low Power Dual Operational Amplifiers. USA.: National Semiconductor Corporation.

Advanced BeagleBone Systems

In This Part

The Internet of Things

In this chapter you are introduced to the concept of the Internet of Things (IoT). Two new sensors are discussed—a simple temperature sensor and a more complex Bluetooth low-energy sensor. Using the BBB, these sensors are the example *things* that are connected to the Internet. Several different IoT communications architectures are described: The first architecture configures the BBB to be a web server that uses server-side scripting to display sensor data. Next, custom C/C++ code is described that can push sensor data to the Internet and to platform as a service (PaaS) offerings, such as ThingSpeak and Xively. Finally, a client/server pair for high-speed Transmission Control Protocol (TCP) socket communication is described. The latter part of the chapter introduces some techniques for managing distributed BBB sensors, and physical networking topics, including connecting the BBB to the Internet using Wi-Fi; setting the BBB to have a static IP address; and using Power over Ethernet (PoE) with the BBB. By the end of this chapter you should appreciate the power of the BBB to leverage Linux software in order to build complex network-attached devices, and you should be able to build your own IoT devices.

Equipment Required for This Chapter:

- BeagleBone Black
- Analog Devices TMP36 temperature sensor

- Texas Instruments SensorTag with Bluetooth adapter (optional)
- Linux-compatible USB Wi-Fi adapter

Further details on this chapter are available at `www.exploringbeaglebone` `.com/chapter10/`.

The Internet of Things (IoT)

The terms *Internet of Things* (IoT) and *cyber-physical systems* (CPS) are broadly used to describe the extension of the web and the Internet into the physical realm, by the connection of distributed embedded devices. Presently, the Internet is largely an internet of people—the IoT concept envisions that if physical sensors and actuators can be linked to the Internet, then a whole new range of applications and services are possible. For example, if sensors in a home environment could communicate with each other and the Internet, then they could be "smart" about how they function—a home heating system that could retrieve the weather forecast may be more efficient and could provide a more comfortable environment. Within smart homes, IoT devices should be able to automate laborious tasks; manage security; and improve energy efficiency, accessibility, and convenience. However, the IoT also has broad application to many large-scale industries, such as energy management, healthcare, transport, and logistics.

In Chapter 9, interaction with the physical environment is discussed in detail. When the physical world can be acted upon by devices that are attached to the Internet, such as actuators, then the devices are often called CPS. The terms IoT and CPS are often used interchangeably, with certain industries such as smart manufacturing favoring the term CPS. However, it is not unreasonable to consider a CPS to be a constituent building block that when combined with web sensors and large-scale communications frameworks forms the IoT.

In this chapter the implementation of several software communication architectures that can be used to realize IoT or CPS is described. Figure 10-1 illustrates a summary of the different communication architectures that are implemented in this chapter.

Each of the architectures in Figure 10-1 has a different structure, and each can be applied to different communications applications:

1. **The BBB Web Server**: A BBB that is connected to a sensor and running a web server can be used to present information to the web when it is requested to do so by a web browser. Communications take place using the Hypertext Transfer Protocol (HTTP).

2. **The BBB Web Client**: A BBB can initiate contact with a web server using HTTP requests to send and receive data. A C/C++ program is written

that uses the TCP and TCP sockets to build a basic web browser, which can communicate over HTTP, or if necessary, securely over HTTPS.

3. **The BBB TCP Client/Server**: A custom C++ client and server are presented that can intercommunicate at high speeds with a user-defined communications protocol.

4. **The BBB Web Sensor using a PaaS**: Code is written to enable the BBB to use HTTP and custom APIs to send data to, and receive data from, web services such as ThingSpeak and Xively. This code enables you to build large arrays of sensors that can intercommunicate and store data on remote servers. In addition, these web services can be used to visualize the data that is stored.

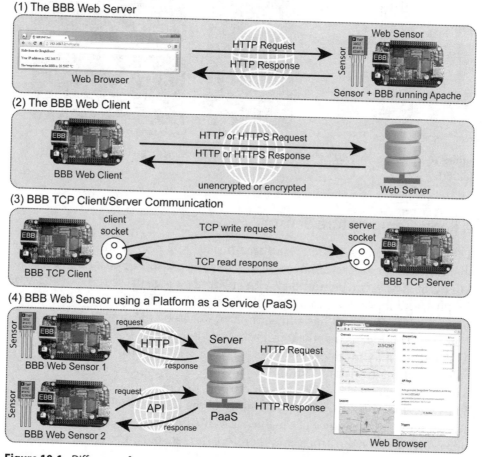

Figure 10-1: Different software communication architectures implemented in this chapter

Before examining these communication architectures, you need a *thing* to connect to the Internet, for which two new sensors are discussed.

More Sensors (Things!)

Two new sensors are illustrated in Figure 10-2, the *Analog Devices TMP36* temperature sensor and the *Texas Instruments SensorTag*. The TMP36 is used throughout this chapter, as it has a low cost ($1–$2) and is widely available. The SensorTag (~$25) is also introduced because it demonstrates the capability of Bluetooth 4.0/LE—a low-energy Bluetooth protocol that is ideal for connecting *things* to your BBB.

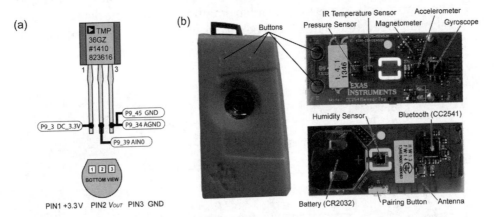

Figure 10-2: (a) The Analog Device TMP36 Temperature Sensor; (b) the Texas Instruments SensorTag

A Room Temperature Sensor

The Analog Devices TMP36 is a three-pin (TO-92 packaged) analog sensor that measures temperature over the range of –40°C to +125°C and is accurate to ±1°C at 25°C. It can be supplied with an input voltage using the BBB's 3.3V or 5V pins, and it provides an output of 750mV at 25°C. Unlike the distance sensor in the last chapter, it has a linear output, whereby the output scale factor is 10mV/°C. This means that the minimum output voltage is $0.75V – (65 \times 0.01V) = 0.1V$ and the maximum output voltage is $0.75V + (100 \times 0.01V) = 1.75V$. These voltage output levels are within the safe levels for the BBB ADC—the room temperature range is not! The sensor output current will be between 0μA and 50μA, depending on the input impedance of the device to which it is attached. The high input impedance of the BBB ADC means that current supplied to the BBB is only a few nano amps, and therefore the sensor can be safely connected directly to the BBB AIN pins.

A wiring configuration for the sensor to the BBB is identified in Figure 10-2(a). To set up and build the example code, follow these steps:

```
~/exploringBB/chp10/tmp36$ sudo sh -c "echo BB-ADC > $SLOTS"
~/exploringBB/chp10/tmp36$ cat $SLOTS|grep ADC
```

```
  7: ff:P-O-L Override Board Name,00A0,Override Manuf,BB-ADC
~/exploringBB/chp10/tmp36$ g++ tmp36.cpp -o tmp36
```

The temperature can be calculated using AIN0 by passing 0 to the program:

```
~/exploringBB/chp10/tmp36$ ./tmp36 0
Starting the TMP36 temperature sensor program
The ADC value is: 1775
The temperature is: 28.0029 degrees Celsius.
```

The C/C++ code required to convert the ADC value (e.g., 1775 in this case) to a temperature in degrees Celsius is expressed in C code as follows:

```
float getTemperature(int adc_value){
   float cur_voltage = adc_value * (1.80f/4096.0f);
   float diff_degreesC = (cur_voltage-0.75f)/0.01f;
   return (25.0f + diff_degreesC);
}
```

The TMP36 datasheet provides details on how the sensor can be wired using twisted pair cables to be physically distant from the BBB itself. Such a configuration would enable the sensor to be used for external temperature-monitoring applications. The datasheet for the TMP35/36/37 is available at tiny.cc/ebb1001.

Texas Instruments SensorTag

Bluetooth Low Energy (LE) (aka *Bluetooth Smart*) is a technology for wireless personal area network applications, such as home automation, healthcare, and home entertainment. Bluetooth Smart is focused on low-energy applications, while still maintaining the same communications range as regular Bluetooth. The SensorTag, which is illustrated in Figure 10-2(b), has a quiescent current consumption of 8µA, potentially enabling it to operate on a small CR2032 battery for many months. The SensorTag is a *Bluetooth Smart development kit* that is targeted in particular at smartphone application developers. However, it can also be used by the BBB as a sensor node that can collect data from its environment.

Connecting to Bluetooth Smart Devices

To use the SensorTag, first install the Bluetooth package:

```
molloyd@beaglebone:~$ sudo apt-get install bluetooth
```

This package contains the tools that are discussed in Chapter 9, such as the host controller interface tool (hcitool) that is used to configure Bluetooth connections. The hcitool executable also has low-energy device commands, such as scan (lescan), whitelist add (lewladd), create connection (lecc), disconnect (ledc), and connection update (lecup).

To connect to the SensorTag, press the button on the side of the SensorTag, scan for its Bluetooth ID, and connect to it as follows:

```
molloyd@beaglebone:~$ sudo hcitool lescan
LE Scan ...   BC:6A:29:AE:D1:27 SensorTag
molloyd@beaglebone:~$ sudo hcitool lewladd BC:6A:29:AE:D1:27
molloyd@beaglebone:~$ sudo hcitool lewlsz
White list size: 32
molloyd@beaglebone:~$ sudo /etc/init.d/bluetooth restart
[ ok ] Restarting bluetooth (via systemctl): bluetooth.service.
molloyd@beaglebone:~$ sudo hcitool lecc BC:6A:29:AE:D1:27
Connection handle 64
```

Before you start to control the SensorTag, it needs the latest version of the *Bluez* Bluetooth stack for Linux, which you may need to build yourself.

Building a Linux Package

It is often the case in Linux that the latest versions of software packages are not part of the current distribution—they may require further rigorous testing. One great thing about open-source software is that you yourself can build and add such packages to your Linux installation. Unfortunately, this task is not always straightforward—there may be interdependency requirements that need to be met, or the software may simply not yet be ready for rollout.

The version of the Bluez Bluetooth stack that is distributed with Debian (v5.18 at the time of writing) needs to be updated in order to communicate success-fully with the SensorTag. You can use a web browser to find the latest version of Bluez at www.kernel.org/pub/linux/bluetooth/. Download it and install any dependencies (which will otherwise be identified when you attempt to build the code) as follows on the BBB:[1]

```
~$ wget http://www.kernel.org/pub/linux/bluetooth/bluez-5.18.tar.xz
~$ tar xvf bluez-5.18.tar.xz
~$ sudo apt-get install libusb-dev libudev-dev libdbus-1-dev
~$ sudo apt-get install libical-dev libreadline-dev
~$ cd bluez-5.18
```

Then build the package using the following steps. The enable-library flag for this build allows C/C++ code to be written that interfaces directly to the Bluez library:

```
molloyd@beaglebone:~/bluez-5.18$ ./configure --enable-library
molloyd@beaglebone:~/bluez-5.18$ make
molloyd@beaglebone:~/bluez-5.18$ sudo make install
```

---

[1] For your convenience the built executable is available in the GitHub repository (chp10/gatttool/).

The *gatttool* is used to access the services on a Bluetooth device and the make install script does not install it by default. Therefore, you need to find and replace the current version of the tool:

```
molloyd@beaglebone:~/bluez-5.18$ whereis gatttool
gatttool: /usr/bin/gatttool /usr/bin/X11/gatttool
molloyd@beaglebone:~/bluez-5.18$ sudo cp attrib/gatttool /usr/bin
```

Controlling a Bluetooth Smart Device

The latest version of gatttool is now installed and can be used to access the SensorTag services, which may require pressing the button on the side of the SensorTag. You can then connect to the sensor and read from, and write to, handles (such as registers), where the full set of attributes are described at tiny.cc/ebb1002. For example, the following connects and reads the manufacturer name string from the SensorTag at the handle 0x1D:

```
molloyd@beaglebone:~$ gatttool -b BC:6A:29:AE:D1:27 --interactive
[BC:6A:29:AE:D1:27][LE]> connect
Attempting to connect to BC:6A:29:AE:D1:27 ... Connection successful
[BC:6A:29:AE:D1:27][LE]> char-read-hnd 0x1D
Characteristic value/descriptor: 02 1e 00 29 2a
```

Or, to read the infrared (IR) temperature sensor at 0x25, which is inactive until it is turned on by writing 01 to handle 0x29:

```
[BC:6A:29:AE:D1:27][LE]> char-read-hnd 0x25
Characteristic value/descriptor: 00 00 00 00
[BC:6A:29:AE:D1:27][LE]> char-write-cmd 0x29 01
[BC:6A:29:AE:D1:27][LE]> char-read-hnd 0x25
Characteristic value/descriptor: e8 fe 24 0d
```

It is also possible to use the gatttool command to read a value on a single line. For example, the following reads the manufacturer string on a single line:

```
~$ gatttool -b BC:6A:29:AE:D1:27 --char-read --handle=0x1D
Characteristic value/descriptor: 02 1e 00 29 2a
```

The next example reads the temperature sensor (it has to be performed in quick succession, e.g., within a script):

```
~$ gatttool -b BC:6A:29:AE:D1:27 --char-write --handle=0x29 --value=01
~$ gatttool -b BC:6A:29:AE:D1:27 --char-read --handle=0x25
Characteristic value/descriptor: ce fe c4 0c
```

The IR sensor returns two 16-bit values—the object temperature (die temperature) and the ambient temperature (target temperature). The formulae for converting these values into °C are at `tiny.cc/ebb1003`.

An excellent Python code example by Mike Saunby (`mike.saunby.net`) can be used to parse the data from the SensorTag:

```
~$ git clone git://github.com/msaunby/ble-sensor-pi.git
~$ cd ble-sensor-pi/sensortag/
~/ble-sensor-pi/sensortag$ python sensortag.py BC:6A:29:AE:D1:27
ACCL [-0.03125, -0.96875, 0.0625]
TO06 23.1
MAGN [-10.894775390625, 25.32958984375, -55.419921875]
GYRO [31L, 253L, 240L, 255L, 92L, 0L]
HUMD 37.8
BARO 26.19 995.21
```

Given the low-energy nature of the SensorTag, it is unlikely that any application developed using it would focus on high-frequency data capture, so interfacing to a Python script is acceptable. Because of the TMP36 temperature sensor's wide availability and low cost, it is chosen over the SensorTag as a proof-of-concept example for the remainder of this chapter. However, any developed code could be easily adapted to also interface to the SensorTag.

The BeagleBone as a Web Server

One significant advantage of an embedded Linux device over more traditional embedded systems is the vast amount of open-source software that is available. In this section, a web server is installed and configured on the BBB. It is a straightforward process compared to the steps involved for a typical non-Linux embedded platform. In fact, one of the more difficult challenges is choosing which Linux web server to use! There are low-overhead servers available such as lighttpd, Boa, Monkey and Nginx, but Apache is a good web server to use for getting started—in fact, it is currently installed in the BBB Debian image. Once you are familiar with Apache, you could then investigate web server solutions that are designed specifically for embedded Linux devices.

Running a web server on the BBB provides you with a number of application possibilities, including the following:

- Present general web content to the world.
- Integrate sensors and display their values to the world.
- Integrate sensors and use it to intercommunicate between devices.
- Provide web-based interfaces to tools that are running on the BBB.

Installing a Web Server

The Apache server is currently present in the BBB Debian distribution. You can use the following commands to install or upgrade it:

```
molloyd@beaglebone:~$ dpkg --get-selections|grep apache
apache2                                    install
molloyd@beaglebone:~$ sudo apt-get update
molloyd@beaglebone:~$ sudo apt-get install apache2
```

On the BBB Debian image the Apache web server is running on port number 8080 by default. A *port number* is an identifier that can be combined with an IP address to provide an endpoint for a communications session. It is effectively used to identify the software service that is required by a client. For example, you can find out the list of services that are listening to ports on the BBB by using the network statistics (netstat) command:

```
molloyd@beaglebone:~$ sudo netstat -tlpn
Active Internet connections (only servers)
Proto Local Address    Foreign Address    State      PID/Program name
tcp6  :::22             :::*               LISTEN     936/sshd
tcp6  :::8080           :::*               LISTEN     1055/apache2
tcp6  :::80             :::*               LISTEN     1/systemd  ...
```

Therefore, when a network request is received for port 8080 it is directed to the Apache2 web server application. The usual port number for unsecured web traffic is 80—this is assumed when you enter an URL in your web browser. You can see in the preceding list that port 80 is currently directed to systemd, which in turn uses bonescript.service to provide the Bone101 web pages.

Configuring an Apache Web Server

Apache can be configured using the files in /etc/apache2/

```
molloyd@beaglebone:/etc/apache2$ ls
apache2.conf  envvars  mods-available  ports.conf       sites-enabled
conf.d        magic    mods-enabled    sites-available
```

where the core configuration files are as follows:

- apache2.conf is the main configuration file for the server.
- ports.conf is for configuring virtual server port numbers (set to port 8080 by default on the BBB Debian image).
- The sites-available directory contains the configuration files for any virtual sites, and the sites-enabled directory should contain a symbolic link to a configuration file in the sites-available directory, in order to

activate a site. The a2ensite and a2dissite commands should be used to enable and disable sites. There is an example configuration file present, in which you should set the ServerAdmin e-mail address and the document root (the default is /var/www).

In addition to the configuration files, the functionality of Apache can be further extended (e.g., to provide Python support) with the use of modules (see tiny.cc/ebb1004 for a full list). You can identify the current modules that have been compiled into Apache using the following:

```
molloyd@beaglebone:/etc/apache2$ apache2 -l
Compiled in modules: core.c    mod_log_config.c    mod_logio.c
mod_version.c  worker.c   http_core.c   mod_so.c
```

Creating Web Pages and Web Scripts

To create a simple web page for the BBB web server you can use the nano editor and some basic HTML syntax as follows:

```
molloyd@beaglebone:/var/www$ nano index.html
molloyd@beaglebone:/var/www$ more index.html
<HTML><TITLE>BBB First Web Page</TITLE>
<BODY><H1>BBB First Page</H1>
The BeagleBoneBlack test web page.
</BODY></HTML>
```

Now when you connect to the web server on the BBB using a web browser, you will see the output displayed in Figure 10-3.

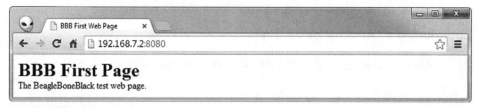

Figure 10-3: A first web page on the BBB

Web pages are ideal for the presentation of *static web content*, and by using an editor like KompoZer, CoffeeCup, or Notepad++ you can quickly build HTML content for a personal web server. You could then use the port forwarding functionality of your home router, and a dynamic DNS service, to share your static web content with the world.

More advanced *dynamic web content* can also be developed for the BBB that interfaces to the physical environment for such tasks as reading sensor data or actuating motors. One relatively straightforward method of doing this is to use

Common Gateway Interface (CGI) scripts. The configuration file in (or linked to in) the `sites-enabled` directory specifies a directory location in which scripts can be placed, so that they can be executed via a web browser request. The default location is the `/usr/lib/cgi-bin/` directory, where a simple script can be created as follows (see `/chp10/cgi-bin/test.cgi` in the GitHub repository):

```
molloyd@beaglebone:~$ cd /usr/lib/cgi-bin/
molloyd@beaglebone:/usr/lib/cgi-bin$ sudo nano test.cgi
molloyd@beaglebone:/usr/lib/cgi-bin$ more test.cgi
#!/bin/bash
echo "Content-type: text/html"
echo '<html><head>'
echo '<meta charset="UTF-8">'
echo '<title>Hello BeagleBone</title></head>'
echo '<body><h1>Hello BeagleBone</h1><para>'
hostname
echo ' has been up '
uptime
echo '</para></html>'
```

The script must then be made executable, and it can be tested as follows:

```
molloyd@beaglebone:/usr/lib/cgi-bin$ sudo chmod a+x test.cgi
molloyd@beaglebone:/usr/lib/cgi-bin$ ./test.cgi
Content-type: text/html
<html><head>
<meta http-equiv="Content-Type" content="text/html"; charset=UTF-8">
<title>Hello BeagleBone</title></head>
<body><h1>Hello BeagleBone</h1><para>
beaglebone
 has been up
 23:24:44 up  4:28,  2 users,  load average: 0.00, 0.01, 0.05
</para></html>
```

The script is quite verbose, but you can see that it is very easy to call system commands (e.g., `hostname` and `uptime`) directly from within it. When the script is tested in the terminal window, its output displays HTML source code. However, when this output is viewed using a web browser, as in Figure 10-4, the HTML is rendered correctly.

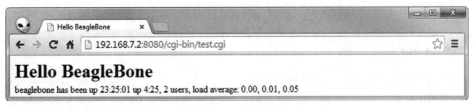

Figure 10-4: A simple CGI script example

As well as calling Linux system commands, you can also execute programs that have been written in C/C++. To demonstrate this capability, the `tmp36.cpp` program used earlier in this chapter can be modified so that it only outputs the raw temperature in degrees Celsius when it is executed. This new binary executable, called `tmp36raw`, can then be copied to the `/usr/local/bin` directory so that it is "permanently" installed on the BBB:

```
~/exploringBB/chp10/tmp36$ ./tmp36raw
28.8818
~/exploringBB/chp10/tmp36$ sudo cp tmp36raw /usr/local/bin
```

The CGI script can then be modified to output the temperature value directly from the TMP36 sensor as follows:

```
molloyd@beaglebone:~/exploringBB/chp10/cgi-bin$ more temperature.cgi
...
echo '<body><h1>Hello BeagleBone</h1><para>'
echo 'The temperature in the room is '
/usr/local/bin/tmp36raw
echo ' degress Celsius </para></html>'
```

This results in the output displayed in Figure 10-5. This code could easily be adapted to display the sensor data from the TI SensorTag. If you are experiencing difficulties with your scripts, the Apache log files are stored in `/var/log/apache2/`, which can be viewed with superuser access.

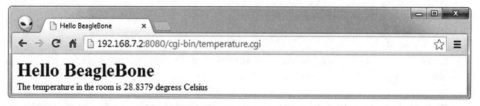

Figure 10-5: Temperature sensor web page

WARNING   CGI scripts can be structured to accept data from the web by using form fields. To do so, you must filter the input to avoid potentially damaging cross-site scripting. In particular, you should filter out the characters <>&*?./ from form field entry.

PHP on the BeagleBone

CGI scripts work very well for the short scripts used in the last section—they are lightweight and easy to edit. However, as well as security concerns (e.g., attacks via URL manipulations), they do not scale very well (e.g., for interfacing with databases). An alternative is to use the PHP server-side scripting language. PHP is a reasonably lightweight open-source scripting language with a C-like syntax that can be written directly within HTML pages. It can be installed within Apache as follows:

```
~$ sudo apt-get install apache2 apache2-utils
~$ sudo apt-get install php5 curl php5-curl php5-json
~$ sudo service apache2 restart
```

A PHP program can then be written as shown in Listing 10-1 and placed in the /var/www directory. Like the CGI script, it interfaces to the TMP36 by executing the tmp36raw program, resulting in the output shown in Figure 10-6.

LISTING 10-1: var/www/hello.php

```
<?php $temperature = shell_exec('/usr/local/bin/tmp36raw'); ?>
<html><head><title>BBB PHP Test</title></head>
 <body>
 Hello from the BeagleBone!
 <p>Your IP address is: <?php echo $_SERVER['REMOTE_ADDR']; ?></p>
 <p>The temperature at the BBB is: <?php echo $temperature ?> &#186C</p>
 </body>
</html>
```

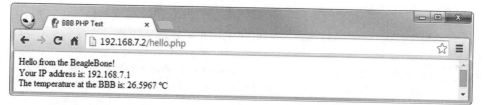

Figure 10-6: A PHP temperature sensor

NOTE In addition, it is possible to install a database such as MySQL onto the BBB, forming a LAMP (Linux, Apache, MySQL, PHP) server. This allows you to fur-ther install content management systems (CMSs) such as WordPress or Drupal, allowing you to create advanced web content that can even include hardware interaction.

Replacing Bone101 with the Custom Web Server

The Bone101 web server provides very valuable information about getting started with the BBB; however, it occupies the default web port (port 80). If you wish to replace Bone101 with your custom web server, you can shut down the `bonescript` service and configure the custom server to use port 80. To shut down the `bonescript` service you can use the following steps. First call

```
~$ systemctl list-units -t service |grep bonescript
```

to confirm that `bonescript.service` is running. To stop the service you need to stop `bonescript.socket` first and then the service, as follows:

```
~$ sudo systemctl stop bonescript.socket
~$ sudo systemctl stop bonescript.service
~$ sudo systemctl disable bonescript.socket
~$ sudo systemctl disable bonescript.service
```

You can then configure the Apache2 server to use port 80 by modifying the `ports.conf` file to listen to port 80 as follows:

```
/etc/apache2$ sudo nano ports.conf
/etc/apache2$ more ports.conf|grep 80
NameVirtualHost *:80
Listen 80
```

Then modify the file in (or file linked to in) the `/sites-enabled` directory so that the `VirtualHost` port is set to be 80, and restart the Apache2 server as follows:

```
/etc/apache2/sites-enabled$ more 000-default |grep 80
<VirtualHost *:80>
/etc/apache2$ sudo systemctl restart apache2.service
```

NOTE Google Dart is a very interesting platform for building web applications. The Dart platform can be installed on the BBB to create advanced interactive web applications. See `www.dartlang.org` and a guide at `tiny.cc/ebb1015` for further details.

A C/C++ Web Client

Installing a web server on a BBB provides it with a simple, intuitive way to present information to a client web browser application. It is important to understand that the distinction between a *client* and a *server* is nothing to do with the hardware capability of the interconnected devices; rather, it relates to the role of each device at that particular point in time. For example, when retrieving a web page from the BBB using its Apache web server, a desktop computer's web browser is a client of the BBB's web server. Table 10-1 provides a summary of the characteristics of the two types of application, which when used together is termed the *client-server model*.

Table 10-1: Characteristics of Server versus Client Applications

SERVER APPLICATIONS	CLIENT APPLICATIONS
Special-purpose applications that are typically dedicated to one service	Typically become a client temporarily, but perform other computation locally
Typically invoked on system startup and they attempt to run forever	Typically invoked by a user for a single session
Wait passively, and potentially forever, for contact from client applications	Actively initiate contact with the server. The client must know the address of the server.
Accept contact from client applications	Can access several servers simultaneously
Typically run on a shared machine	Typically run on a local machine

When the BBB acts as a server, it waits passively for a connection from a client machine, but there are many cases when the BBB might need to actively contact a server on another machine. In such cases, the BBB must act as a client of that server. At this point in the book you have already used many such client network applications on the BBB, such as `ping`, `wget`, `ssh`, `sftp`, and so on, and these applications can be used within shell scripts. However, it would also be useful if you could generate client requests from within C/C++ code, and for this you can use network sockets.

Network Communications Primer

A *socket* is a network endpoint that is defined using an IP address and a port number. An *IP address* (version 4) is simply a 32-bit number, which is represented as four eight-bit values (e.g., 192.168.7.2), and a *port number* is a 16-bit unsigned integer (0-65,535) that can be used to enable multiple simultaneous communications to a single IP address. Ports under 1,024 are generally restricted to root access in order to prevent users from hijacking core services (e.g., 80 for HTTP, 20/21 for FTP, 22 for SSH, 443 for HTTPS).

The description of a socket must also define the *socket type*, indicating whether it is a *stream socket* or a *datagram socket*. Stream sockets use the *transmission control protocol (TCP)*, which provides for reliable transfer of data where the time of transmission is not a critical factor. Its reliability means that it is used for services such as HTTP, e-mail (SMTP), and FTP, where data must be reliably and correctly transferred. The second type of socket is a datagram socket that uses the *user datagram protocol (UDP)*, which is less reliable but much faster than TCP, as there is no error-checking for packets. Time-critical applications such as voice over IP (VoIP) use UDP, as errors in the data will be presented in the output as noise, but the conversation will not be paused awaiting lost data to be resent.

When communication is established between two network sockets it is called a *connection*. Data can then be sent and received on this connection using write and read functions. It is important to note that a connection could also be created between two processes (programs) that are running on a single machine and thus used for *inter-process communication*.

A C/C++ Web Client

Full C/C++ support for socket communication can be added to your program by including the sys/socket.h header file. In addition, the sys/types.h header file contains the data types that are used in system calls, and the netint/in.h header file contains the structures needed for working with Internet domain addresses.

Listing 10-2 is the C source code for a basic web browser application that can be used to connect to a HTTP web server, retrieve a web page, and display it in raw HTML form—like a regular web browser, but without the pretty rendering. The code performs the following steps:

1. The server name is passed to the program as a string argument. The program converts this string into an IP address (stored in the hostent structure) using the gethostbyname() function.

2. The client creates a TCP socket using the socket() system call.

3. The hostent structure and a port number (80) are used to create a sockaddr_in structure that specifies the endpoint address to which to connect the socket. This structure also sets the address family to be IP-based (AF_INET) and the network byte order.

4. The TCP socket is connected to the server using the connect() system call—the communications channel is now open.

5. An HTTP request is sent to the server using the write() system call and a fixed-length response is read from the server using the read() system call. The HTML response is displayed.

6. The client disconnects and the socket is closed using close().

LISTING 10-2: /exploringBB/chp10/WebClient/WebClient.c

```
#include <stdio.h>
#include <sys/socket.h>
#include <sys/types.h>
#include <netinet/in.h>
#include <netdb.h>              //for the hostent stucture
#include <strings.h>

int main(int argc, char *argv[]){
    int    socketfd, portNumber, length;
```

```c
char    readBuffer[2000], message[255];
struct sockaddr_in serverAddress; //describes endpoint to connect a socket
struct hostent *server;           //stores information about a host name

// The command string for a HTTP request to get / (often index.html)
sprintf(message, "GET / HTTP/1.1\r\nHost: %s\r\n\r\n", argv[1]);
printf("Starting EBB Web Browser C Example\n");
printf("Sending the message: %s", message);
if (argc<=1){  // must pass the hostname
   printf("Incorrect usage, use: ./webBrowser hostname\n");
   return 2;
}
// gethostbyname accepts a string name and returns a host name structure
server = gethostbyname(argv[1]);
if (server == NULL) {
   perror("Socket Client: error - unable to resolve host name.\n");
   return 1;
}
// Create socket of IP address type, SOCK_STREAM is for TCP connections
socketfd = socket(AF_INET, SOCK_STREAM, 0);
if (socketfd < 0){
   perror("Socket Client: error opening TCP IP-based socket.\n");
   return 1;
}
// clear the data in the serverAddress sockaddr_in struct
bzero((char *) &serverAddress, sizeof(serverAddress));
portNumber = 80;
serverAddress.sin_family = AF_INET; //set the address family to be IP
serverAddress.sin_port = htons(portNumber);   //set port number to 80
bcopy((char *)server->h_addr,(char *)&serverAddress.sin_addr.s_addr,
      server->h_length);  //set address to resolved hostname address

// try to connect to the server
if (connect(socketfd, (struct sockaddr *) &serverAddress,
            sizeof(serverAddress)) < 0){
   perror("Socket Client: error connecting to the server.\n");
   return 1;
}
// send the HTTP request string
if (write(socketfd, message, sizeof(message)) < 0){
   perror("Socket Client: error writing to socket");
   return 1;
}
// read the HTTP response to a maximum of 2000 characters
if (read(socketfd, readBuffer, sizeof(readBuffer)) < 0){
   perror("Socket Client: error reading from socket");
   return 1;
}
printf("**START**\n%s\n**END**\n", readBuffer); //display the response
close(socketfd);                                //close the socket
printf("End of EBB Socket Example\n");
return 0;
}
```

This code can be built and executed as follows. In this example, the simple web page from the local BBB Apache web server is requested, by using *localhost,* which essentially means "this device," and it uses the Linux *loopback virtual network interface* (lo), which has the IP address 127.0.0.1:

```
~/exploringBB/chp10/webBrowser$ gcc webBrowser.c -o webBrowser
~/exploringBB/chp10/webBrowser$ ./webBrowser localhost
Starting EBB Web Browser C Example
Sending the message: GET / HTTP/1.1
Host: localhost
**START**
HTTP/1.1 200 OK
Date: Fri, 11 Jul 2014 00:13:02 GMT
Server: Apache/2.2.22 (Debian) ...
Content-Type: text/html
<HTML><TITLE>BBB First Web Page</TITLE>
<BODY><H1>BBB First Page</H1>
The BeagleBoneBlack test web page.
</BODY></HTML>
**END**
End of EBB Socket Example
```

The example works correctly, returning the index.html file from /var/www. It can also connect to other web servers (e.g., type **./webBrowser www.google.com**).

Secure Communication Using OpenSSL

One of the limitations of the TCP socket application in the previous section is that all communications are sent "in the clear" across IP networks. This may not be of concern for home networks, but if your client and server are on different physical networks, then the data that is transferred can be easily viewed on intermediary networks. Sometimes it is necessary to communicate securely between a client and a server—for example, if you are sending a username and password to an online service. In addition, particular care should be taken in applications where the BBB can actuate motors or relays—a malicious attack could cause physical destruction. One way to implement secure communications is to use the OpenSSL toolkit.

OpenSSL (www.openssl.org) is a toolkit that implements the *Secure Sockets Layer* (SSL) and *Transport Layer Security* (TLS) protocols and a cryptography library. This library can be installed using the following:

```
molloyd@beaglebone:~/$ sudo apt-get install openssl
```

OpenSSL is a complex and comprehensive toolkit that can be used to encrypt all types of communications. This section presents one example application to illustrate its use. For this example, the C/C++ web client code is modified to support SSL communications as shown in Listing 10-3. The code involved in this example is the same as in Listing 10-2, except for the following:

1. The TCP socket connection is formed to the *HTTP secure* (i.e., *HTTPS*) port, which is port 443 by default.

2. The *SSL library* is initialized using the `SSL_Library_init()` function.

3. A *SSL context object* is used to establish the TLS/SSL connection. The security and certificate options can be set in this object.

4. The network connection is assigned to an SSL object and a handshake is performed using the `SSL_connect()` function.

5. The `SSL_read()` and `SSL_write()` functions are used.

6. The `SSL_free()` function is used to shut down the TLS/SSL connection, freeing the socket and SSL context objects.

LISTING 10-3: /chp10/webBrowserSSL/webBrowserSSL.c (segment)

```
/*** After the connection to the server is formed:  ***/
// Register the SSL/TLS ciphers and digests
SSL_library_init();
// Create an SSL context object to establish TLS/SSL enabled connections
SSL_CTX *ssl_ctx = SSL_CTX_new(SSLv23_client_method());
// Attach an SSL connection to the socket
SSL *conn = SSL_new(ssl_ctx); // create an SSL structure for an SSL session
SSL_set_fd(conn, socketfd);    // Assign a socket to an SSL structure
SSL_connect(conn);             // Start an SSL session with a remote server
// send data across an SSL session
if (SSL_write(conn, message, sizeof(message)) < 0){ ... }
// read data scross an SSL session
if (SSL_read(conn, readBuffer, sizeof(readBuffer)) < 0){ ... }
printf("**START**\n%s\n**END**\n", readBuffer);  //display response
SSL_free(conn);                            //free the connection
close(socketfd);                           //close the socket
SSL_CTX_free(ssl_ctx);                     //free the SSL context
```

The full source code is in the /chp10/webClientSSL/ directory. It can be compiled and tested using the following commands:

```
.../chp10/webBrowserSSL$ gcc webBrowserSSL.c -o browserSSL -lcrypto -lssl
.../chp10/webBrowserSSL$ ./browserSSL www.google.com
```

The application can successfully communicate with the SSL port (443) on secured web servers (e.g., www.google.com). The current code does not verify the authenticity of the server owner, but it does encrypt communications.

The BeagleBone as a Web Sensor

Earlier in this chapter a web server is configured on the BBB so that it can present temperature sensing information to the Internet. This mechanism is very useful, as it provides a snapshot in time of sensor outputs. In order to provide trend data, it would be possible to store the data in flat files or to install a lightweight database on the BBB. PHP charting tools such as *phpChart* and *pChart* could be used to visually represent the data.

An alternative way of performing the collection and visualization of web sensor information is to connect the BBB to online data aggregation services, which enable you to push sensor data to the cloud, directly from the BBB. In this section, two such online services are utilized directly from within C/C++ programs that are executing on the BBB. This enables you to develop very lightweight operations that can leverage Internet services in order to intercommunicate between BBBs on different networks. It also enables the collection of sensor data from many BBB "web sensors" at the same time on different physical networks.

ThingSpeak

ThingSpeak is an open-source IoT application and API that can be used to store data from web sensors (*things*). Using HTTP, the sensors can push numeric or alphanumeric data to the server, where it can be processed and visualized. The ThingSpeak application can be installed on a server that is running the *Ruby on Rails* web application framework and an SQL database.

In this example, the BBB pushes temperature sensor data to a hosted free service at www.thingspeak.com, where data can also be visualized as shown in Figure 10-7. Once you set up an account, you can then create a new *channel*, which provides you with read and write API keys for the channel. These are used in the C++ code example in Listing 10-5.

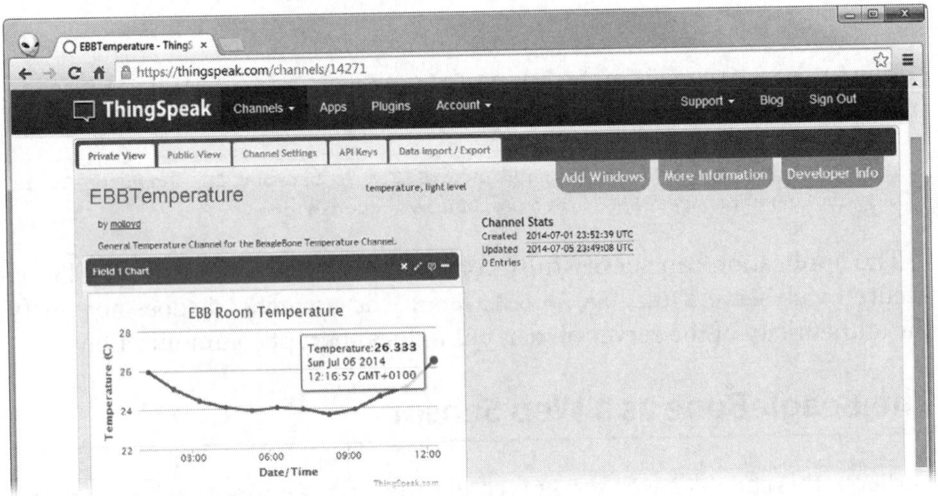

Figure 10-7: A ThingSpeak web sensor example

A C++ `SocketClient` is available for this example. This class simply wraps the C code that is used for the C/C++ web client application in Listing 10-2. The class interface definition is provided in Listing 10-4.

LISTING 10-4: */exploringBB/chp10/thingSpeak/network/SocketClient.h*

```
class SocketClient {
private:
    int         socketfd;
    struct      sockaddr_in   serverAddress;
    struct      hostent       *server;
    std::string serverName;
    int         portNumber;
    bool        isConnected;
public:
    SocketClient(std::string serverName, int portNumber);
    virtual int connectToServer();
    virtual int disconnectFromServer();
    virtual int send(std::string message);
    virtual std::string receive(int size);
    bool isClientConnected() { return this->isConnected; }
    virtual ~SocketClient();
};
```

The code example in Listing 10-5 uses this `SocketClient` class. The example reads the temperature sensor and pushes it to the hosted ThingSpeak server using an HTTP POST request.

LISTING 10-5: */exploringBB/chp10/thingSpeak/thingSpeak.cpp*

```
#include <iostream>
#include <sstream>
#include <fstream>
#include <stdlib.h>
#include "network/SocketClient.h"
using namespace std;
using namespace exploringBB;
#define LDR_PATH "/sys/bus/iio/devices/iio:device0/in_voltage"

int readAnalog(int number){ // returns the input as an int
    stringstream ss;
    ss << LDR_PATH << number << "_raw";
    fstream fs;
    fs.open(ss.str().c_str(), fstream::in);
    fs >> number;
    fs.close();
    return number;
}
```

LISTING 10-5: *(continued)*

```
float getTemperature(int adc_value){
    float cur_voltage = adc_value * (1.80f/4096.0f);
    float diff_degreesC = (cur_voltage-0.75f)/0.01f;
    return (25.0f + diff_degreesC);
}

int main(){
    ostringstream head, data;
    cout << "Starting EBB Thing Speak Example" << endl;
    SocketClient sc("thingspeak.com",80);
    data << "field1=" << getTemperature(readAnalog(0)) << endl;
    sc.connectToServer();
    head << "POST /update HTTP/1.1\n"
         << "Host: api.thingspeak.com\n"
         << "Connection: close\n"
         // This key is available from the API keys tab in Figure 10-7
         << "X-THINGSPEAKAPIKEY: G7MTQ21IVBFGYJG7\n"  // channel API key
         << "Content-Type: application/x-www-form-urlencoded\n"
         << "Content-Length:" << string(data.str()).length() << "\n\n";
    sc.send(string(head.str()));
    sc.send(string(data.str()));
    string rec = sc.receive(1024);
    cout << "[" << rec << "]" << endl;
    cout << "End of EBB Thing Speak Example" << endl;
}
```

To send data to the server at regular time intervals, POSIX threads and `sleep()` calls can be added to the code in Listing 10-5. However, an easier alternative is to use the Linux cron time-based job scheduler.

The Linux Cron Scheduler

The Linux *cron* daemon (named after Chronos, the Greek god of time) is a highly configurable utility for scheduling tasks to be performed at specific times and dates. It is typically used for system administration tasks, such as backing up data, clearing temporary files, rotating log files, updating package repositories, or building software packages during off-peak times.

When sensors or actuators are interfaced to the BBB, cron can also be very useful for applications such as logging data from these sensors at fixed intervals over long periods of time. On the BBB, you could use the scheduler for tasks such as collecting sensor data, building a stepper-motor clock, time-lapse photography, setting security alarms, and so on.

System crontab

Cron wakes once every minute and checks its configuration files, called *crontabs*, to see if any commands are scheduled to be executed. It can be used to schedule tasks to run with a maximum frequency of once per minute down to a minimum frequency of once per year. Configuration files for cron can be found in the /etc directory:

```
molloyd@beaglebone:~$ cd /etc/cron<Tab><Tab>
cron.d/ cron.daily/ cron.hourly/ cron.monthly/ cron.weekly/ crontab
```

The crontab file contains scheduling instructions for the cron daemon, according to the crontab fields that are listed in Table 10-2. Each line of the crontab file specifies the time at which the command field should execute. A wildcard value (*) is available—for example, if it is placed in the hour field, then the command should execute at each and every hour of the day.

Ranges are permitted (e.g., 1-5 for Monday to Friday) and so are lists of times (e.g., 1, 3, 5). In addition, strings can be used in place of the first five fields: @reboot, @yearly, @annually, @monthly, @weekly, @daily, @midnight, and @hourly. The following custom crontab file in Listing 10-6 provides some examples. There are comments in the file to explain the functionality of the entries.

Table 10-2:   Crontab Fields

FIELD	RANGE	DESCRIPTION
m	0–59	The minute field
h	0–23	The hour field
dom	1–31	Day of the month field
mon	1–12 (or name)	Month of the year (first three letters can be used)
dow	0–7 (or name)	0 or 7 is Sunday (first three letters can be used)
user		Can specify the user that executes the command
command		The command to be executed at this point in time

LISTING 10-6: /etc/crontab

```
# /etc/crontab: system-wide crontab
SHELL=/bin/sh
PATH=/usr/local/sbin:/usr/local/bin:/sbin:/bin:/usr/sbin:/usr/bin
# m h dom mon dow user          command
# Go to bed message, every night at 1am, sent to all users using wall
0  1    * * *    root    echo Go to bed! | wall
# Extra reminder, every work day night (i.e. 1:05am Monday-Friday)
5  1    * * 1-5 root    echo You have work in the morning! | wall
# Perform a task each day (same as 0 0  * * *). Clear /tmp directory
@daily          root    rm -r /tmp/*
# The following are present in the default Debian crontab file:
17 *    * * *    root    cd / && run-parts --report /etc/cron.hourly
25 6    * * *    root    test -x /usr/sbin/anacron || ( cd / && run-parts
--report /etc/cron.daily ) ...
```

Examples are added to the `crontab` file to send messages and to clear the `/tmp` directory (see the comments). You can also specify that a command should be executed every 10 minutes by using `*/10` in the minutes field.

You may have also noticed other entries in the `crontab` file that refer to an `anacron` command. *Anacron* (anachronistic cron) is a specialized cron utility for devices, such as laptop computers, that are not expected to be running 24/7. If regular cron were configured to back up files every week but the BBB happened to be powered off at that exact moment, then the backup would never be performed. However, with anacron the backup will be performed when the BBB next boots (i.e., jobs are queued). You can install anacron using the following:

```
molloyd@beaglebone:~$ sudo apt-get install anacron
```

Now there will be a new `/etc/anacrontab` file that performs the same role as `crontab` does for cron. The configuration file for anacron can be found in `/etc/init/anacron.conf`.

One problem with having both cron and anacron installed on one system is that it is possible for cron to run a job that anacron has already run, or vice versa. That is the reason for the `crontab` entries at the end of Listing 10-6. These entries ensure that `run-parts` is executed only if anacron is not installed on the BBB. This is tested by the call to `test -x /usr/sbin/anacron`, which returns 0 if the anacron command is present, and 1 if it is not. Calling `echo $?` displays the output value.

An alternative to adding an entry directly to the `crontab` file is to add a script to one of the directories: `cron.daily`, `cron.hourly`, `cron.monthly`, or `cron.weekly` in the `/etc` directory. Any scripts in these directories are executed by cron. For example, you could create a script in the `cron.hourly` directory to update the temperature on ThingSpeak as follows:

```
~/exploringBB/chp10/thingSpeak$ sudo cp thingSpeak /usr/local/bin
/etc/cron.hourly$ sudo nano thingSpeakUpdate
/etc/cron.hourly$ more thingSpeakUpdate
#!/bin/bash
/usr/local/bin/thingSpeak
/etc/cron.hourly$ sudo chmod a+x thingSpeakUpdate
```

An alternative to this is to execute the binary directly within the user account using *user crontab*, which is described in the next section.

User crontab

Each user account can have its own `crontab`. These files are placed in the `/var/spool/cron/crontabs` directory, but they should not be edited in this location. The following creates a `crontab` for the user `molloyd`:

```
molloyd@beaglebone:~$ crontab -e
no crontab for molloyd - using an empty one
crontab: installing new crontab
```

You can edit your user `crontab` file to upload the room temperature to ThingSpeak every 30 minutes by adding the following line:

```
# m  h dom mon dow command
*/30 *  *   *   * ~/exploringBB/chp10/thingSpeak/thingSpeak > /dev/null 2>&1
```

The end of this command redirects the standard output to `/dev/null`. The call `2>&1` redirects the standard error to the standard output, and therefore also to `/dev/null`. If this were not present, then by default the output of the `thingSpeak` command would be e-mailed to the system administrator (if mail is configured on the BBB). You can back up your crontab file as follows:

```
molloyd@beaglebone:~$ crontab -l > crontab-backup
```

To reinstate this backup file with crontab use the following:

```
molloyd@beaglebone:~$ crontab crontab-backup
```

The administrator account can control which users have access to cron by placing either a `cron.allow` or a `cron.deny` file in the `/etc` directory. Under Debian all users can have their own crontab by default. Use the following to remove this capability:

```
molloyd@beaglebone:/etc$ more cron.deny
molloyd
molloyd@beaglebone:/etc$ crontab -e
You (molloyd) are not allowed to use this program (crontab)
```

To use this cron configuration with the `thingSpeak` program, you must ensure that the ADC cape (described in Chapter 6) is set to load on a system reboot (i.e., by modifying the `uEnv.txt` file); otherwise, the program will fail after reboot.

Xively

Xively (by LogMeIn) provides a very powerful IoT PaaS that enables the interconnection of IoT devices. Xively's PaaS can be used to build applications similar to the ThingSpeak temperature sensor application. However, Xively's PaaS also provides advanced functionality that can be used to build enterprise-level solutions, such as the following:

- **Directory services:** Enables applications to search a directory of objects and permissions associated with devices

- **Data services:** For time-series data archival and retrieval
- **Business services:** For the provisioning, activation, and management of devices

> **NOTE** Xively's PaaS is a full cloud computing service, in that it provides the software libraries, data storage, and hardware that is necessary for its customers to build commercial-scale offerings. ThingSpeak also offers a hosted service through `www.thingspeak.com`, and it is also an open-source application that you can install on your own server machine.

Devices such as the BBB, backend data services, and applications can interface to these services using the Xively API, which supports real-time message management and routing. Such a PaaS is very useful if you have many BBB sensor nodes that must intercommunicate. You can also store vast quantities of time-series data. While the architecture is more complex than ThingSpeak, Xively's PaaS provides scalability and a C library for interfacing to its services.

Getting Started with Xively's PaaS

You can create an account on `www.xively.com` by signing up for a free developer account. Then under the Develop tab, you can select +Add a Device. After providing a brief description, you will see a page that you can use to create a channel with the +Add Channel option. In the following example, which is illustrated in Figure 10-8, the device is called `BeagleBone Temperature` and the channel is called `tempSensor`. The auto-generated *device key* and *feed ID* values are very important for the following examples, which utilize the Xively C library.

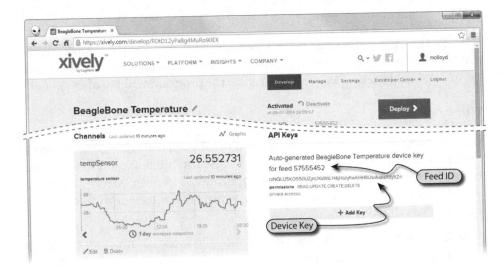

Figure 10-8: Xively channel with API keys

The Xively C Library

Xively has developed a low-overhead C library, called *libxively*, which provides an interface for Xively applications so that they can execute on an embedded platform like the BBB. The library is structured with three layers:

1. A communications layer to open socket connections and send data

2. A transport layer that encodes/decodes HTTP/WebSocket requests

3. A data layer that encodes/decodes Xively data formats

The library can be downloaded and built on the BBB using the following steps (use a temporary directory), where the `--recursive` flag instructs git to fetch any required sub modules:

```
~/temp$ git clone --recursive https://github.com/xively/libxively.git
Cloning into 'libxively'...
~/temp$ cd libxively/
~/temp/libxively$ make all
```

When the library is built, the following binary examples appear:

```
molloyd@beaglebone:~/temp/libxively/bin$ ls
asynch_feed_get    datastream_delete        feed_update  asynch_feed_update
datastream_get     looped_asynch_feed_get   datapoint_delete
datastream_update  looped_feed_update       datapoint_delete_range
feed_get           datastream_create        feed_get_all
```

These applications can be used on the BBB as the basis of scripts that interact with the Xively device. For example, the following pushes a fixed data value:

```
molloyd@beaglebone:~/temp/libxively/bin$ ./feed_update
rzNQLU5KOS5OUZjnUXsWsLH4jHozyhwKHH8UwAxeaXdy1EBB 57555452 tempSensor 26
[io/posix/posix_io_layer.c:182 (posix_io_layer_init)]...
```

The preceding pushes the fixed value 26 to the `tempSensor` channel. To retrieve a value from the same channel, the following application can be used:

```
molloyd@beaglebone:~/temp/libxively/bin$ ./feed_get_all
rzNQLU5KOS5OUZjnUXsWsLH4jHozyhwKHH8UwAxeaXdy1EBB 57555452
...   datasream_id: tempSensor  value: 26@1404848579
```

Writing scripts is useful, but for more dynamic applications the Xively C library can be used directly within C/C++ programs. The current version of libxively (at the time of writing) along with its associated header files are present in the `libxively/` subdirectory of the `/chp10/xively/` directory. The first example, in Listing 10-7, reads the TMP36 sensor value and sends its data to the Xively "tempSensor" channel.

LISTING 10-7: /chp10/xively/xivelySensor.c

```c
#include <xively.h>
#include <xi_helpers.h>
#include <stdio.h>
#include <stdlib.h>
#define ADC_PATH "/sys/bus/iio/devices/iio:device0/in_voltage"
#define DEVICE_KEY "rzNQLU5KOS50UZjnUXsWsLH4jHozyhwKHH8UwAxeaXdy1EBB"
#define FEED_ID 57555452
int readAnalog(int number){ // C version of the code in Listing 10-5
    int value;
    FILE* fp;
    char fullFileName[100];
    sprintf(fullFileName, ADC_PATH "%d_raw", number);
    fp = fopen(fullFileName, "r");
    fscanf(fp, "%d", &value);
    fclose(fp);
    return value;
}
float getTemperature(int adc_value){ ... } // Same as Listing 10-5
int main()
{
    // Create the Xively context
    xi_context_t* xi_context = xi_create_context(XI_HTTP, DEVICE_KEY, FEED_ID);
    if(xi_context==NULL){
        perror("XIVELY: Problem in creating the context");
        return 1;
    }
    // Create the feed and clear its contents
    xi_feed_t feed;
    memset(&feed, 0, sizeof(xi_feed_t));
    // Set the properties of the feed (id, number of streams and datstream)
    feed.feed_id          = FEED_ID;
    feed.datastream_count = 1;  //sending a single stream, datastream 0
    // Get a reference to the datastream
    xi_datastream_t* data = &feed.datastreams[0];
    // Only going to send a single data point in the stream
    data->datapoint_count = 1;
    // Set up the data stream identifier "tempSensor"
    int size = sizeof(data->datastream_id);
    xi_str_copy_untiln(data->datastream_id, size, "tempSensor", '\0' );
    // Set up the data point and set a floating-point value
    xi_datapoint_t* point = &data->datapoints[0];
    xi_set_value_f32(point, getTemperature(readAnalog(0)));
    // Update the feed
    xi_feed_update(xi_context, &feed);
    xi_delete_context(xi_context);
    return 0;
}
```

This code can be built and executed using the following call:

```
~/exploringBB/chp10/xively$ gcc -Wall -std=c99 xivelySensor.c libxively/
libxively.a -o xivelySensor -Ilibxively/include/
```

```
~/exploringBB/chp10/xively$ ./xivelySensor
... tempSensor,26.552731 ...
```

This program sends the value `26.552731` to the `tempSensor` channel. A cron job can be used to repeatedly call this program, which results in a visual display similar to that in Figure 10-8.

A second program is also available in this directory, called `readXively` (see Listing 10-8 for a segment of this code) that retrieves the current `tempSensor` channel value directly from the Xively PaaS. Such read and write functionality can be used to enable many BBBs to intercommunicate.

LISTING 10-8: /chp10/xively/readXively.c (segment)

```c
int main()
{  ...        // Get the feed and then the datapoint
   xi_feed_get(xi_context, &feed);
   xi_datapoint_t* point = &data->datapoints[0];
   printf("The current data point is: %f\n", point->value.f32_value);
   xi_delete_context(xi_context);
   return 0;
}
```

This code can be built in the same way and when executed gives the following output:

```
molloyd@beaglebone:~/exploringBB/chp10/xively$ ./readXively
The current data point is: 26.552731
```

This code example sends and receives floating-point data. By changing the code in Listing 10-7 to send data using the functions `xi_set_value_ i32()` and `xi_ set_value_str()`, integer and string data, respectively, can be written to the service. Also, Listing 10-8 can be modified to receive data using `i32_value` or `str_value`, for integer and string data, respectively.

Sending E-mail from the BBB

It can be very useful to send e-mail directly from the BBB so that detected system problems are relayed to a potentially remote administrator. In addition, it is useful for an e-mail to be sent when a sensor event occurs—for example, an e-mail could be sent if the room temperature exceeds 30°C. There are many mail client applications, but if you are using a secure *simple mail transfer protocol* (SMTP) server, like Gmail, then the `ssmtp` program works well. Install `ssmtp` using the following command:

```
molloyd@beaglebone:~$ sudo apt-get install ssmtp mailutils
```

Configure the e-mail settings in the file /etc/ssmtp/ssmtp.conf. For example, to configure your BBB to send e-mail through a Gmail account, replace the account name and password fields in the following:

```
molloyd@beaglebone:/etc/ssmtp$ more ssmtp.conf
# Config file for sSMTP sendmail
root=myaccountname@gmail.com
mailhub=smtp.gmail.com:587
AuthUser=myaccountname@gmail.com
AuthPass=mysecretpassword
UseTLS=YES
UseSTARTTLS=YES
rewriteDomain=gmail.com
hostname= myaccountname@gmail.com
```

The settings can be tested by sending an e-mail from the terminal:

```
molloyd@beaglebone:~$ ssmtp toname@destination.com
To: toname@destination.com
From: myaccountname@gmail.com
Subject: Testing 123
Hello World!^d
```

Typing Ctrl+D at the end of the message sends the e-mail. An alternative to this is to place the message text, which is the same as that just shown (including the To/From/Subject lines), in a file (e.g., ~/.message) and then send it using the following call:

```
~$ ssmtp toname@destination.com < ~/.message
```

Or, you can use the mail tool directly (from the mailutils package):

```
~$ echo "Test Body" | mail -s "Test Subject" toname@destination.com
```

All messages are sent using the user Gmail account. This command can be added to scripts or encapsulated within a C++ program that uses a system() call, as in Listing 10-9. C or C++ could be used for this example, but C++ strings make this task more straightforward.

LISTING 10-9: /chp10/cppMail/cppMail.cpp

```cpp
#include <iostream>
#include <sstream>
#include <stdlib.h>
using namespace std;

int main(){
    string to("toname@destination.com");
    string subject("Hello Derek");
```

```
    string body("Test Message body...");
    stringstream command;
    command << "echo \""<< body <<"\" | mail -s \""<< subject <<"\" "<< to;
    int result = system(command.str().c_str());
    cout << "Command: " << command.str() << endl;
    cout << "The return value was " << result << endl;
    return result;
}
```

When executed, the program in Listing 10-9 outputs the following:

```
molloyd@beaglebone:~/exploringBB/chp10/cppMail$ ./cppMail
Command: echo "Test Message body..." | mail -s "Hello Derek" toname@dest
ination.com
The return value was 0
```

Here the value 0 indicates success. As well as sending notification messages, e-mail can be used to trigger other types of events using web services such as www.ifttt.com, which is discussed in the next section.

If This Then That (IFTTT)

If This Then That (IFTTT) is a web service that enables you to create connections between online channels, such as Twitter, LinkedIn, Google Calendar, iPhone/Android Integration, YouTube, and many more. It works by connecting *triggers* and *actions* using the simple statement: "If *this* then *that*," where the trigger is the *this*, and the action is the *that*. For example, "If *it is night time* then *mute my phone ringer*," or "If *the weather forecast is for rain tomorrow* then *send me an Android or iOS notification*." These statements are called *recipes* and they can be activated in an IFTTT account and even shared with other users.

IFTTT has many triggers, but it does not have web triggers; however, it can be triggered using an e-mail message that is sent to trigger@recipe.ifttt.com from a linked Gmail account. Hashtags (e.g., #EBB) can be used to differentiate events, and the subject and body of the e-mail message can be used as *ingredients* for the recipe. For example, the recipe in Figure 10-9 states that: "If *a message is sent to trigger@recipe.ifttt.com from XXXX@gmail.com with #EBB in the subject* then *send me an SMS message*." The body of the e-mail can be passed as an ingredient to the SMS message, which enables personalized messages to be sent from the BBB via SMS messaging (in many cases at no cost).

IFTTT enables you to construct quite sophisticated interactions by simply sending e-mails from the BBB when certain events occur. For example, if a motion sensor is triggered, then you can message someone. Certain physical devices can also be triggered using IFTTT, such as Nest devices, WeMo switches, SmartThings devices, and the Aros smart air conditioner.

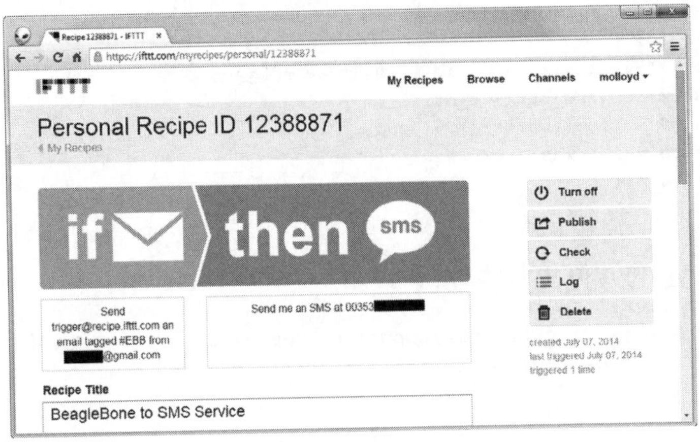

Figure 10-9: Example IFTTT recipe

The C++ Client/Server

The C/C++ client application described earlier in this chapter uses HTTP and HTTPS to connect to a web server and retrieve a web page. In this section a TCP server is described, to which a TCP client can connect in order to exchange information, which does not have to be in HTTP form. The same SocketClient class that is used earlier in the chapter is reused in this section, and a new class called SocketServer is described. Figure 10-10 illustrates the steps that take place during communication in this client/server example:

1. In Step 1, a TCP server that is running on the BBB at IP address 192.168.7.2 begins listening to a user-defined TCP port (54321). It will listen to this port forever, awaiting contact from a client.

2. In Step 2, a TCP client application is executed. The client application must know the IP address and port number of the server to which it is to connect. The client application opens a client socket, using the next available Linux port allocation. The server, which can be running on a different BBB, accepts a connection request from the client. It then retrieves a reference to the client IP address and port number. A connection is formed, and the client writes a message to this connection, which is "Hello from the client."

3. In Step 3, the server reads the message from the connection and sends back a new message to the client, which is "The Server says thanks!" The client reads the response message and displays it to the terminal. Then the client and server both close the network sockets. The programs run asynchronously—in this case running to completion.

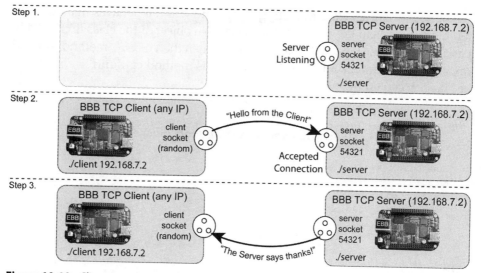

Figure 10-10: Client/server example

The full example is provided in the /chp10/clientserver/ directory. The client.cpp program in Listing 10-10 uses the SocketClient class from the network subdirectory (see Listing 10-4).

LISTING 10-10: /chp10/clientserver/client.cpp

```cpp
#include <iostream>
#include "network/SocketClient.h"
using namespace std;
using namespace exploringBB;

int main(int argc, char *argv[]){
   if(argc!=2){
      cout << "Incorrect usage: " << endl;
      cout << "   client server_name" << endl;
      return 2;
   }
   cout << "Starting EBB Client Example" << endl;
   SocketClient sc(argv[1], 54321);
   sc.connectToServer();
   string message("Hello from the Client");
   cout << "Sending [" << message << "]" << endl;
   sc.send(message);
   string rec = sc.receive(1024);
   cout << "Received [" << rec << "]" << endl;
   cout << "End of EBB Client Example" << endl;
}
```

The `SocketServer` class in Listing 10-11 is new, and it behaves in a quite different manner than the `SocketClient` class. An object of the class is created by passing the port number to the constructor. When the `listen()` method is called, the program counter will not return from this method call until a connection has been accepted by the server.

LISTING 10-11: /chp10/clientserver/network/SocketServer.h

```
class SocketServer {
private:
    int      portNumber;
    int      socketfd, clientSocketfd;
    struct   sockaddr_in    serverAddress;
    struct   sockaddr_in    clientAddress;
    bool     clientConnected;
public:
    SocketServer(int portNumber);
    virtual int listen();
    virtual int send(std::string message);
    virtual std::string receive(int size);
    virtual ~SocketServer();
};
```

The `server.cpp` code example in Listing 10-12 creates an object of the `ServerSocket` class and awaits a client connection.

LISTING 10-12: /chp10/clientserver/server.cpp

```
#include <iostream>
#include "network/SocketServer.h"
using namespace std;
using namespace exploringBB;

int main(int argc, char *argv[]){
    cout << "Starting EBB Server Example" << endl;
    SocketServer server(54321);
    cout << "Listening for a connection..." << endl;
    server.listen();
    string rec = server.receive(1024);
    cout << "Received from the client [" << rec << "]" << endl;
    string message("The Server says thanks!");
    cout << "Sending back [" << message << "]" << endl;
    server.send(message);
    cout << "End of EBB Server Example" << endl;
}
```

The code for this example can be built using the `build` script in the `chp10/clientserver` directory. The server can then be executed:

```
~/exploringBB/chp10/clientserver$ ./server
Starting EBB Server Example
Listening for a connection...
```

The server will wait at this point until a client request has been received. In order to execute the client application, a separate terminal session on the same BBB, another BBB, or a Linux desktop machine can be used. The client application can be executed by passing the IP address of the server. The port number (54321) is defined within the client program code:

```
~/exploringBB/chp10/clientserver$ ./client 192.168.7.2
Starting EBB Client Example
Sending [Hello from the Client]
Received [The Server says thanks!]
End of EBB Client Example
```

When the client connects to the server, both the client and server execute simultaneously, resulting in the preceding and following output:

```
~/exploringBB/chp10/clientserver$ ./server
Starting EBB Server Example
Listening for a connection...
Received from the client [Hello from the Client]
Sending back [The Server says thanks!]
End of EBB Server Example
```

This code is further improved in the next chapter to add threading support, and to enable it to communicate with a better structure than simple strings. However, it should be clear that this code enables you to intercommunicate between Linux client/servers that are located anywhere in the world. The client/server pair communicates by sending and receiving bytes; therefore, communication can take place at very high data rates and is only limited by the physical network infrastructure.

Managing Remote IoT Devices

One of the difficulties with remote web sensors is that they may be in physically inaccessible and/or distant locations. In addition, a period of system downtime may lead to a considerable loss of sensing data. If the problem becomes apparent you can SSH into the BBB and restart the application or perform a system reboot. In this section two quite different management approaches are described—the first is manual web-based monitoring and the second is automatic, through the use of Linux watchdog timers.

BeagleBone Remote Monitoring

One of the advantages of choosing the Apache web server in this chapter is that it supports a number of additional open-source services. One such example is a remote monitoring service called *Linux-dash*. The Apache server is likely already installed from earlier steps in this chapter, but for completeness, the installation steps are summarized here:

```
~$ sudo apt-get install apache2 apache2-utils
~$ sudo apt-get install php5 curl php5-curl php5-json
~$ sudo service apache2 restart
~$ cd /var/www
/var/www$ sudo git clone https://github.com/afaqurk/linux-dash.git
```

These steps result in a service running on the BBB's Apache web server that can be accessed using the URL: /linux-dash/ at the BBB's IP address. You can then remotely connect to the BBB in order to view system information, as shown in Figure 10-11. This approach can help you quickly identify system problems, such as unusual loads, network traffic, and so on, but it still requires that you manually check the web page.

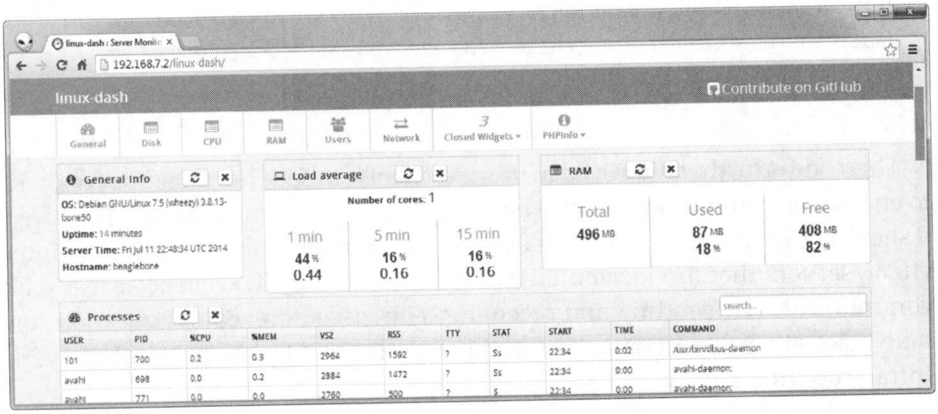

Figure 10-11: BBB remote monitoring

Linux Watchdog Timer

One solution to automatically determine if there has been a significant problem with your application is to use a watchdog timer. The Debian distribution has watchdog driver support enabled, and therefore there is a watchdog entry in /dev (/dev/watchdog). You can examine its functionality using the following:

```
root@beaglebone:/dev# ls -l watchdog
crw------- 1 root root 10, 130 Apr 25 00:07 watchdog
```

```
root@beaglebone:/dev# cat > watchdog
Testing but quitting now  ^C
```

The preceding steps will not cause the BBB to reboot. However, if you write anything to watchdog, do not close the file, and wait for 50 seconds after the last Return key is pressed; then the BBB will reboot!

```
root@beaglebone:/dev# cat > watchdog
This will reboot the BBB 50 seconds after I hit Return. Now!
Even if I type really slowly on this line but don't hit Return
```

This is because the watchdog has been activated, held open, and not "kicked" for 50 seconds, which is the default watchdog time on the BBB Debian distribution.

Watchdog timers can be integrated directly into program code. For example, Listing 10-13 is a watchdog timer example that opens the watchdog device and writes to it every time you "kick the dog" (or "feed the dog") by pressing "k." If you do not write to the device for more than 30 seconds (the user-defined interval), then the BBB will reboot.

LISTING 10-13: /chp10/watchdog/testWatchdog.c

```c
#include<stdio.h>
#include<fcntl.h>
#include<linux/watchdog.h>
#define WATCHDOG "/dev/watchdog"

int main(){
   int fd, interval=30, state;
   if ((fd = open(WATCHDOG, O_RDWR))<0){
     perror("Watchdog: Failed to open watchdog device\n");
     return 1;
   }                   // set the timing interval to 30 seconds
   if (ioctl(fd, WDIOC_SETTIMEOUT, &interval)!=0){
     perror("Watchdog: Failed to set the watchdog interval\n");
     return 1;
   }
   printf("Press k to kick the dog, h to say hello and q to quit:\n");
   do{
      state = getchar();
      switch(state){
      case 'k':
        printf("[kick!]");     // feeding the dog may be more PC
        ioctl(fd, WDIOC_KEEPALIVE, NULL);
        break;
      case 'h':
        printf("[hello]");
        break;
      }
```

```
    } while (state!='q');
    printf("Closing down the application\n");
    close(fd);
    return 0;
}
```

If you build the principles of this code into an application, then you should "kick the dog" each time an important block of code executes. For example, if a sensor value were read every 15 seconds in your code example, then you would also "kick the dog" each time you read the sensor value. That way, if the application locks up, then the BBB would reboot automatically. Having a watchdog timer can be very important in IoT applications if the BBB is inaccessible or performing an important role that should not be halted (e.g., a BBB intruder alarm).

IoT Physical Networking

It may be necessary in certain IoT applications for the BBB to be wirelessly connected to the Internet. Alternatively, a mains power supply may not be available in the desired sensor location. This section describes how you can use USB Wi-Fi adapters with the BBB and how you can use power over Ethernet (PoE) to deliver power to the BBB.

The BeagleBone and Wi-Fi

The BBB can communicate wirelessly with other devices using various different standards, each of which has its own advantages and disadvantages, as summarized in Table 10-3.

Table 10-3: Summary Comparison of Different Wireless Standards

	BLUETOOTH	**ZIGBEE**	**WI-FI**	**CUSTOM**
Standard	IEEE 802.15.1	IEEE 802.15.4	IEEE 802.11	2.4 GHz Custom
Range	10m to 100m	~100m	10m to 100m	10 to 100m
Power	Low	Very Low	High	Very Low
Data Rate	<2.1 Mb/s	<250kb/s	10 to 300Mb/s	250kb/s
Topology	Star	Mesh/Star	Star	Star
Organization	Bluetooth SIG	ZigBee Alliance	Wi-Fi Alliance	None

Bluetooth communication is discussed in Chapter 9 and Wi-Fi is discussed in this section. ZigBee communication can also be implemented by the BBB, usually through the use of XBee modules. The XBee modules can be controlled and can communicate via a UART device on the BBB. Low-cost, low-power custom 2.4GHz transceiver modules are also available, but they require a time investment in order to develop appropriate software interfaces.

Wireless Network Adapters

Various popular low-profile USB *Wi-Fi adapters* are tested in this section, with the adapters and summary results illustrated in Figure 10-12. These results are only indicative and may not be repeatable, as product revisions and Linux updates may affect the outcomes.

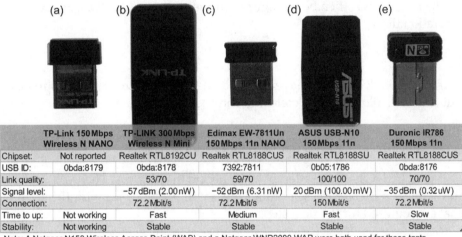

	TP-Link 150 Mbps Wireless N NANO	TP-LINK 300 Mbps Wireless N Mini	Edimax EW-7811Un 150 Mbps 11n NANO	ASUS USB-N10 150 Mbps 11n	Duronic IR786 150 Mbps 11n
Chipset:	Not reported	Realtek RTL8192CU	Realtek RTL8188CUS	Realtek RTL8188SU	Realtek RTL8188CUS
USB ID:	0bda:8179	0bda:8178	7392:7811	0b05:1786	0bda:8176
Link quality:		53/70	59/70	100/100	70/70
Signal level:		−57 dBm (2.00 nW)	−52 dBm (6.31 nW)	20 dBm (100.00 mW)	−35 dBm (0.32 uW)
Connection:		72.2 Mbit/s	72.2 Mbit/s	150 Mbit/s	72.2 Mbit/s
Time to up:	Not working	Fast	Medium	Fast	Slow
Stability:	Not working	Stable	Stable	Stable	Stable

Note: A Netgear N150 Wireless Access Point (WAP) and a Netgear WNR2000 WAP were both used for these tests. The adapter was placed 5.5 m (18.5 ft) from the WAPs. The BBB was running Debian Linux beaglebone 3.8.13-bone50.

Figure 10-12: A selection of Wi-Fi adapters and test results when they are connected to the BBB

After a USB adapter is inserted and the BBB booted, you can confirm that the network adapter is being detected using the lsusb command, which should result in an output of the following form:

```
root@beaglebone:~# lsusb
Bus 001 Device 002: ID 0bda:8178 Realtek Semiconductor Corp.
  RTL8192CU 802.11n WLAN Adapter  ...
```

The adapter should be detected by the BBB and its chipset identified (RTL8192CU in this case). You can search for the latest firmware that is available for your adapter:

```
root@beaglebone:~# sudo apt-get update
root@beaglebone:~# apt-cache search RTL8192
firmware-realtek - Binary firmware for Realtek network adapters
root@beaglebone:~# sudo apt-get install firmware-realtek
```

NOTE Many Wi-Fi adapter problems (including "wpasupplicant daemon failed to start" errors) are related to an insufficient power supply. You should use a 2A PSU that is connected to the 5V DC jack (before the USB client is connected).

If all goes well, the adapter should appear as wlanX in a call to ifconfig:

```
root@beaglebone:~# ifconfig -a
wlan0     Link encap:Ethernet  HWaddr 80:1f:02:4b:6d:7a
          BROADCAST MULTICAST  MTU:1500  Metric:1 ...
          RX bytes:0 (0.0 B)   TX bytes:0 (0.0 B)
```

The adapter can then be configured in the /etc/network/interfaces configuration file, as follows:

```
iface wlan0 inet dhcp
```

If the network connection is encrypted, then these settings are not sufficient, but they will allow you to determine your network settings:

```
root@beaglebone:/etc/network# ifup wlan0
Internet Systems Consortium DHCP Client 4.2.2 ... ^C
```

Typing Ctrl+C halts the attempt to connect to the network. Then you can scan for wireless network access points, which will provide you with the settings that are required for the next step:

```
root@beaglebone:~# iwlist wlan0 scan
wlan0     Scan completed :
          Cell 01 - Address: 20:4E:7F:66:AD:0A
                Channel:1            Frequency:2.412 GHz (Channel 1)
                Quality=70/70       Signal level=-35 dBm
                Encryption key:on   ESSID:"dereksSSID"
                Bit Rates:24 Mb/s; 36 Mb/s; 48 Mb/s; 54 Mb/s
                IE: IEEE 802.11i/WPA2 Version 1
                    Group Cipher : TKIP
                    Pairwise Ciphers (2) : CCMP TKIP
                    Authentication Suites (1) : PSK
```

You can then generate a *WPA passphrase* using your wireless access point name (*SSID*) and network password, as follows:

```
~# sudo wpa_passphrase dereksSSID myPassword > /etc/wpa.conf
network={
```

```
    ssid="dereksSSID"
    #psk="myPassword"
    psk=db23f50e71b7de4fc1234acef72f9e04a4a8c060131cdf2234ceef427f355805
}
```

You can then add other settings to the generated text. For example:

```
root@beaglebone:~# more /etc/wpa.conf
network = {
    ssid="dereksSSID"
    key_mgmt=WPA-PSK
    pairwise=CCMP TKIP
    group=CCMP TKIP
    psk=db23f50e71b7de4fc1234acef72f9e04a4a8c060131cdf2234ceef427f355805
}
```

This configuration file can then be linked to from the configuration file in /etc/network/interfaces to include the following entry:

```
root@beaglebone:~# more /etc/network/interfaces
# WiFi Example
iface wlan0 inet dhcp
  wpa-conf /etc/wpa.conf
```

If you are testing multiple Wi-Fi adapters (e.g., wlan0, wlan1), then they can all be directed at the same wpa.conf file. The network adapter interface can be restarted, the configuration checked, and then you can activate the wireless network adapter (wlan0) using the ifup (interface up) command, as follows:

```
root@beaglebone:~# sudo /etc/init.d/networking restart
root@beaglebone:~# ifconfig -a
root@beaglebone:~# ifup wlan0
...     DHCPREQUEST on wlan1 to 255.255.255.255 port 67
DHCPOFFER from 192.168.1.1  DHCPACK from 192.168.1.1
bound to 192.168.1.24 -- renewal in 42771 seconds.
```

The wireless adapter should now have been allocated an IP address via the wireless access point:

```
root@beaglebone:/etc/network# ifconfig -a
wlan0    Link encap:Ethernet  HWaddr c0:4a:00:10:ca:92
         inet addr:192.168.1.24  Bcast:192.168.1.255  Mask:255.255.255.0
         inet6 addr: fe80::c24a:ff:fe10:ca92/64 Scope:Link ...
         RX bytes:3645 (3.5 KiB)  TX bytes:8516 (8.3 KiB)
```

If you uncomment the auto wlan0 line in the /etc/network/interfaces file, then the wireless interface will start on boot. You should not make this change until the adapter is fully working.

If these commands fail then you should use dmesg to check for messages (e.g., sudo dmesg|grep wlan0|more). If you receive the message "wpasupplicant dae-mon failed to start," then check the file /etc/wpa.conf for any errors and check the power supply. If the adapter still fails to function correctly, then you may need to build drivers for the board. For example, for Realtek adapters you can download custom driver source code from www.realtek.com.tw/downloads/ and build them on the BBB.

> **NOTE** A video at tiny.cc/ebb1005 provides an example of the steps required to build custom network drivers.

You can bring the adapter down using ifdown wlan0 and get more informa-tion about your adapter configuration using iwconfig:

```
root@beaglebone:/etc/network# iwconfig wlan0
wlan0      IEEE 802.11bgn  ESSID:"dereksSSID"
     Mode:Managed  Frequency:2.437 GHz  Access Point: 20:4E:7F:66:AD:0A
     Bit Rate=72.2 Mb/s   Tx-Power=20 dBm ...
```

You use the following command to present a display of the signal strength properties, which updates the display every second:

```
root@beaglebone:/etc/network# watch -n 1 cat /proc/net/wireless
Inter-| sta-|  Quality        |Discarded packets            |Missed| WE
 face | tus |link level noise |nwid crypt  frag retry misc|beacon| 22
 wlan0: 0000  53.  -57.  -256  0      0      0    0    330    0
```

Alternatively, you can use the wavemon application (sudo apt-get install wavemon) to format that data appropriately for a Linux terminal.

Static IP Addresses

The BBB is configured by default to use the *dynamic host configuration protocol* (*DHCP*) for the allocation of its wired and wireless IP address. Network rout-ers typically run a DHCP server that allocates a pool of addresses to devices attached to the network. While DHCP works well for most devices on a local network, it can cause difficulties if you wish to make the BBB visible outside a home firewall via port forwarding. This is because DHCP devices may receive a different IP address each time they boot (depending on the router's lease time). *Port forwarding* (aka *port mapping*) means that a particular port on the BBB (e.g., port 80) can be mapped to a port that is visible outside your firewall, thus making a service on the BBB visible to the world. Many router/firewalls require the BBB to have a static IP address in order to set up a port forward to it.

To allocate a static IP address to the wireless adapter, you can alter the /etc/network/interfaces configuration file to manually specify the address (e.g., 192.168.1.80), the network mask, and the network gateway, with the following format:

```
molloyd@beaglebone:/etc/network$ more interfaces
# The primary network interface
auto eth0
iface eth0 inet static
    address 192.168.1.80
    netmask 255.255.255.0
    gateway 192.168.1.1
```

The BBB then has a static IP address after reboot. The same procedure applies to other adapter entries, such as the wlan0 wireless Ethernet adapter. Do not pick an address that is within the DHCP pool or assigned to another device, or it will result in IP conflicts on the network.

Power over Ethernet (PoE)

One common difficulty in using the BBB as a web sensor is related to the provision of power. It is possible to power the BBB using batteries, and there are many *USB battery pack* solutions available that can perform this role. For example, the *IntoCircuit Power Castle 11.2Ah* (~$40) is a popular choice that could in theory power the BBB for ~50hrs at an average load (this duration will fall dramatically if Wi-Fi is used). For example, such a battery configuration could be used for a BBB mobile robot platform.

When a fixed installation is required in a remote location (e.g., in a garden, gate/entrance) where power sockets are not readily available, then *power over Ethernet (PoE)* is a good option. Regular Ethernet cables (Cat 5e or Cat 6) contain four pairs of wires that are twisted together in order to cancel out electromagnetic interference from external power sources. Low-cost *unshielded twisted pair (UTP)* cables can therefore transmit data (and power) over long distances of up to 100m/328ft.

For standard Ethernet (100Base-T), only two of the twisted pair wires are actually used for data transfer; therefore, the other two pairs are available to carry power. However, it is also possible to inject a *common-mode voltage* onto the pair of wires that carry the data signals. This is possible because Ethernet over twisted pair (similar to CAN bus, USB, and HDMI) uses *differential signaling*, which means that the receiver reads the difference between the two signals, rather than their voltage level with respect to ground. External interference affects both of the paired wires in the same way, so its impact is effectively canceled out by the differential signaling. PoE can therefore use the network cable to deliver power to attached devices. This structure is commonly used by VoIP phones and IP cameras.

The BBB does not support PoE internally, so two main external options are available:

- **Use a *pseudo*-PoE cabling structure:** Adafruit sell a *Passive PoE Injector Cable Set* (~$6), illustrated in Figure 10-13, for which you can use a regular 5V mains supply to inject power into the unused twisted pair wires, and then draw that power at the other end of the cable. **Under no circumstance should such cables be connected to a true-PoE switch!**

- **Use a true PoE (IEEE 802.3af) switch:** In order to send power over long distances, PoE switches provide a 48V DC supply. Therefore, a *PoE power extraction module* is required to *step down* this voltage to a level that is acceptable by the BBB.

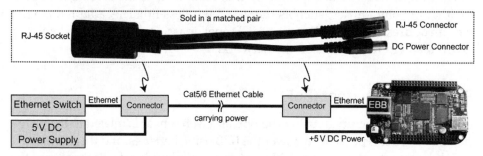

Figure 10-13: AdaFruit *pseudo*-PoE cable

PoE Power Extraction Modules (PEMs) (Advanced Topic)

Recently, low-cost network switches have become available that offer PoE functionality. *Power extraction modules* (PEMs) can be purchased to step down the 48V DC voltage that is supplied by these switches to lower, fixed DC levels (e.g., 3.3V, 5V, 12V). The low-cost ($10–$15) PEM that is used in this section is the PEM1305 (tiny.cc/ebb1006), which can be used to supply 5V to the BBB. PoE (802.3af) switches can provide up to 15.4W of power per attached device. The IEEE 802.3af standard (IEEE Standards Association, 2012) requires that true-PoE devices support two types of PoE:[1]

- **Type-B PoE:** Uses the spare pair of wires to carry power. The data pairs are untouched.

- **Type-A PoE:** Uses a 48V common-mode DC voltage on the data wires to carry power. The spare pairs are unused.

Gigabit Ethernet uses all four pairs of wires to transmit data, so it is likely that Type-A PoE will be dominant in future PoE network switches.

Figure 10-14 illustrates a circuit that can be used to power the BBB using a PoE (IEEE 802.3af) supply. The PEM1305 can extract power from type-A and type-B PoE configurations. However, you must connect the module to DC isolation transformers in order to extract the power from the data wires. To do this you can use a *MagJack* (a jack with integrated magnetics) with center-tapped outputs (e.g., the Belfuse 0826-1X1T-GJ-F). The MagJack contains the isolation transformers that are required to provide the 48V supply to the PoE PEM, and to deliver the data pair safely to the BBB Ethernet jack at Ethernet signal voltage levels.

The resistor that is placed on the input side of the PEM1305 is used to select the power output level of the PoE switch—accurately selecting the power output level results in a more power-efficient implementation. The output voltage adjustment resistor can further refine the PEM output voltage level. The PEM pin outputs can be connected directly to 5V DC jack or to the P9_01 (GND) and the P9_05 (VDD_5V) pins on the BBB P9 header.

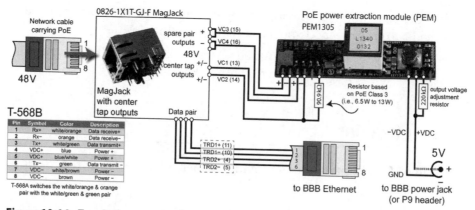

Figure 10-14: True PoE connection for the T-568B wiring scheme

NOTE Be careful in your choice of PoE power extraction module and MagJack. For example, the PEM1205 module appears to be very similar to the PEM1305, but it does not have rectifier bridges on the input, so you would need to add them yourself (otherwise, the circuit could not handle Ethernet cross-over cables). Also, many Ethernet MagJacks do not have center-tap outputs from the isolation transformers and so are unsuitable for use with PoE PEMs.

Summary

After completing this chapter, you should be able to do the following:

■ Interface to the Analog Devices TMP36 temperature sensor and to the Texas Instruments SensorTag using Bluetooth Smart.

- Install and configure a web server on the BBB and use it to display static HTML content.
- Enhance the web server to send dynamic web content that uses CGI scripts and PHP scripts to interface to BBB sensors.
- Write the code for a C/C++ client application that can communicate using either HTTP or HTTPS.
- Interface to platform as a service (PaaS) offerings, such as ThingSpeak and Xively, using HTTP and custom APIs.
- Use the Linux cron scheduler to structure workflow on the BBB.
- Send e-mail messages directly from the BBB and utilize them as a trigger for web services such as IFTTT.
- Build a C++ client/server application that can communicate at a high speed and a low overhead between any two TCP devices.
- Manage remote BBB devices, using monitoring software and watchdog code, to ensure that deployed services are robust.
- Configure the BBB to use Wi-Fi adapters and static IP addresses, and wire the BBB to utilize Power over Ethernet (PoE).

Further Reading

The following additional links provide further information on the topics in this chapter:

- TI SensorTag User Guide: `tiny.cc/ebb1003`
- Linux socket programming: `tiny.cc/ebb1007`
- Apache for Debian: `tiny.cc/ebb1008`
- Debian network configuration: `tiny.cc/ebb109`
- Xively REST API: `tiny.cc/ebb1010`
- The ABCs of PoE: `tiny.cc/ebb1011`
- TI SensorTag YouTube Video: `tiny.cc/ebb1012`

Note

1. IEEE Standards Association. (2012). IEEE 802.3-2012 Standard for Ethernet. IEEE Standards Association.

# CHAPTER 11

BeagleBone with a Rich User Interface

In this chapter you are introduced to rich user interface (UI) architectures and application development on the BeagleBone. Rich UIs allow for a depth of interaction with an application that is not possible with command-line interfaces (CLIs)—in particular, the addition of graphical display elements can result in easier-to-use applications. Also introduced are different BBB architectures that can support rich UIs, such as general-purpose computing, touch screen display modules, and virtual network computing (VNC). Different software application frameworks are examined for rich UI development, such as GTK+ and Qt. The Qt framework is the focus of the discussion, largely due to its comprehensive libraries of code. An example rich UI application is developed for the BBB that uses the TMP36 temperature sensor. Finally, a feature-rich remote fat-client application framework is developed, and two example applications are described—one that uses the TMP36 sensor and a second that uses the ADXL345 accelerometer.

Equipment Required for This Chapter:

- BeagleBone Black
- Analog Devices TMP36 temperature sensor
- USB/HDMI accessories from Chapter 1 (optional)
- ADXL345 accelerometer (optional)

Further resources for this chapter are available at `www.exploringbeaglebone`
`.com/chapter11/`.

Rich UI BBB Architectures

In Chapter 9, low-cost LED displays and character LCD displays are introduced.
They can be coupled with sensors, switches, or keyboard modules to form simple
low-cost UI architectures that are sufficient for many applications, such as for
configuration or interaction with hardware devices (e.g., vending machines,
printer control interfaces, etc.). However, the BBB has a powerful processor,
which when coupled with the Linux OS is capable of providing very sophisticated user interfaces—similar to those to which you are accustomed on your
desktop machine and/or mobile devices.

The BBB's LCD controller and HDMI framer enable it to be connected directly
to a physical display (e.g., monitor, television, or LCD touch screen) to create a
sophisticated self-contained physical UI device. This is one application of the
BBB that demonstrates the strength of embedded Linux in particular, as it supports open-source UI development frameworks such as GTK+ and Qt. These
frameworks provide libraries of visual components (aka *widgets*) that you can
combine to create applications with considerable depth of interaction.

Before examining software development frameworks, this section first introduces four different BBB UI hardware architectures:

- **General-purpose computing**: By connecting the BBB to a monitor/
  television by HDMI, and a keyboard and mouse by USB, it can be used
  as a general-purpose computer.
- **LCD touch screen display**: By attaching an LCD touch screen cape to the
  BBB P8/P9 headers, it can be used as a stand-alone UI device.
- **Virtual network computing (VNC)**: By using remote access and control
  software on a network-attached BBB, it can control UIs on a virtual display.
- **Remote fat-client applications**: By using custom client/server programming with a network-attached BBB, it can interact with remote UIs by
  sending and receiving messages.

These architectures are described in detail in this section, but to give the discussion some context, Table 11-1 summarizes the strengths and weaknesses of
each approach when used with the BBB.

The BBB as a General-Purpose Computer

The BBB is a very capable embedded device, largely due to its 1GHz ARM-A8
processor and 512MB of DDR3 RAM. The HDMI video output capability on the
BBB means that it can be directly connected to a monitor/television, enabling it to

be configured as a general-purpose desktop computer. For example, Figure 11-1(a) illustrates the use of a micro-HDMI adapter (described in Chapter 1) alongside the Kinivo Bluetooth adapter, together providing support for video output and keyboard/mouse input. Figure 11-1(b) displays a low-cost Bluetooth keyboard/touchpad that is used for this example—it is a compact device that is displayed to scale with the BBB.

Table 11-1: Strengths and Weaknesses of Different BBB UI Architectures

APPROACH	STRENGTHS	WEAKNESSES
BBB as a general-purpose computer	Low-cost computing platform with low power consumption. Ideal for a network-attached information display point application, by connecting it to a TV/monitor. Can interact with it using a USB keyboard and mouse.	Requires a dedicated monitor/TV. BBB lacks the processing power to replace a modern desktop computer. BBB HDMI has a limited resolution and uses a large number of the P8/P9 header pins.
BBB with an LCD touch screen	Very portable interactive display that can be battery powered. Ideal for custom UI process controls. A range of display sizes are available.	Expensive. Occupies many of the header pins (remainder not carried forward). Typically resistive touch, rather than capacitive touch.
VNC	No display required on the BBB (frees header pins). BBB could be battery powered and wireless.	Requires a desktop computer/tablet device and network connection. Display update over the network connection can be sluggish.
Fat-client applications	No display is required on the BBB. BBB could be battery powered and wireless. Very low BBB processor overhead, as the display is updated by the desktop computer. Many simultaneous displays possible.	Requires custom application development (e.g., using TCP socket programming). Requires network connection and a device on which to run the fat-client applications.

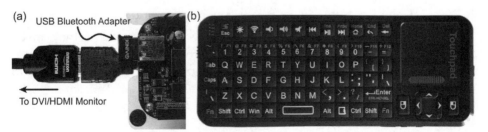

Figure 11-1: (a) Connection to an HDMI and a Bluetooth adapter (b) a Bluetooth keyboard/touchpad

The Ethernet connector can be used to provide network support, and a powered USB hub can be connected to the BBB in order to provide support for more devices, such as Wi-Fi adapters or separate keyboard and mouse peripherals. Figure 11-2 displays a screen capture of the BBB display output when connected directly to a computer monitor using the HDMI interface.

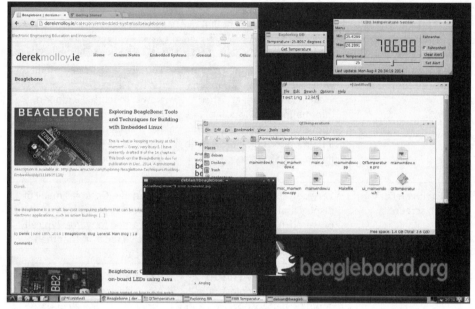

Figure 11-2: Screen capture of the BBB monitor display

To be clear, this display is running on a stand-alone monitor at a screen resolution of 1680 × 1050 pixels and the screen was captured on the BBB using a Linux tool called *scrot* that can be installed and executed from the CLI using the following:

```
molloyd@beaglebone:~$ sudo apt-get install scrot
molloyd@beaglebone:~$ scrot screenshot.png
```

Connecting a Bluetooth Input Peripheral

A regular USB keyboard and mouse can be directly connected to the BBB for this architecture. Bluetooth keyboard/touchpads are also useful, as they can be reused in other applications, such as wireless robotic control and home automation. The Kinivo Bluetooth adapter (see Chapter 9) can directly interface to devices such as the handheld *iPazzPort Bluetooth keyboard and touchpad* (~$20). Devices can be configured using the following steps:

```
molloyd@beaglebone:~$ sudo apt-get install bluez
molloyd@beaglebone:~$ hcitool scan
```

```
Scanning . . .
        00:26:83:32:CF:0D        DEREKMOLLOY-PC
        54:46:6B:01:E2:13        bluetooth iPazzport
molloyd@beaglebone:~$ sudo bluez-simple-agent hci0 54:46:6B:01:E2:13
RequestPinCode (/org/bluez/2130/hci0/dev_54_46_6B_01_E2_13)
Enter PIN Code: 0000
```

In order to pair the device, a pin code of 0000 is entered in the preceding instructions, so 0000 must also be keyed on the Bluetooth device (followed by Enter), which results in the following:

```
Release
New device (/org/bluez/2130/hci0/dev_54_46_6B_01_E2_13)
```

The device is now available to the BBB, but it is not trusted or configured as an input device. The final steps are as follows:

```
~$ sudo bluez-test-device trusted 54:46:6B:01:E2:13 yes
~$ sudo bluez-test-input connect 54:46:6B:01:E2:13 yes
```

The Bluetooth keyboard/touchpad is now attached to the BBB and it will automatically connect from then on. It can control the general-purpose computing environment that is displayed in Figure 11-2.

> **NOTE** Linux allows *virtual consoles* (aka *virtual terminals*) to be opened while an *X Window System* (windowing display) is executing. Use Ctrl+Alt+F1 to open a virtual console—there are six virtual text-based consoles (F1 to F6). Use Ctrl+Alt+F7 to return to the X Window System. Using Alt+Left arrow and Alt+Right arrow switches in order between the consoles.
>   Also, you can kill a frozen SSH session by typing **Enter ~ .** in sequence (i.e., the Return key followed by the tilde followed by a period). Use **Enter ~ ?** to display a list of the *escape sequences* that are available within an SSH session.

BBB with a LCD Touch Screen Cape

The BBB's AM335x system on a chip (SoC) includes an *LCD controller* (*LCDC*) that is capable of driving LCD modules (up to 2,048 × 2,048 with a 24-bits-per-pixel active TFT configuration) using TI Linux LCDC and backlight drivers. An LCD touch screen display, such as the LCD4 cape discussed in Chapter 1 (Figure 1-9), can be attached to the BBB as illustrated in Figure 11-3. The LCD4's 4.3" TFT display has a resolution of 480 × 272 pixels, which limits the desktop space for general-purpose computing applications. The cape also occupies many of the P8/P9 header pins, including the ADC inputs, which are used for the touch interface and the control buttons. Despite these limitations, it can be used to build sophisticated UI applications.

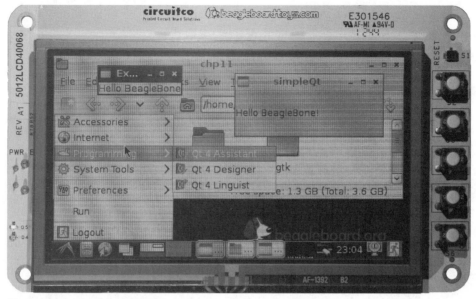

Figure 11-3: The CircuitCo LCD4 cape

> **NOTE** A full video example of the type of rich UI applications that are possible when using this cape is available at the chapter web page: www.exploringbeaglebone .com/chapter11/.

The LCD capes from CircuitCo are fully compatible with the BBB, and the BBB Debian image does not require specific software configuration in order to use them. The touch screen interface must be calibrated on its first use—for this task, and for general usage, a nylon-tipped stylus is a useful accessory, as pressure must be applied to resistive touch screens that can result in scratches. The Bluetooth keyboard/touchpad from the last section can also be used to control the BBB when it is attached to an LCD display, which is useful because entering text using onscreen touch keyboards can be frustrating.

Virtual Network Computing (VNC)

Virtual network computing (*VNC*) enables desktop applications on one computer (the server) to be shared and remotely controlled from another computer (the client). Keystrokes and mouse interactions on the VNC client are transmitted to the VNC server over the network. The VNC server determines the impact of these interactions and then updates the remote *frame buffer* (RAM containing bitmap image data) on the VNC client machine. VNC uses the *remote frame buffer protocol*, which is similar to the *remote desktop protocol* (*RDP*) that is tightly coupled to the Windows OS, but because VNC works at the frame buffer level, it is available for many OSs.

The BBB does not require a physical display in order to act as a VNC server, which means that the P8/P9 header pins that are allocated to HDMI output can be retasked. Importantly, with VNC the Linux applications are executing on the BBB using its processor, but the frame buffer display is being updated on the remote machine.

VNC Using VNC Viewer

Many VNC client applications are available, but VNC Viewer is described here because it is available for Windows, Mac OS X, and Linux platforms. It can be downloaded and installed free from www.realvnc.com. Once it is executed, a login screen appears that requests the VNC server address. However, for this configuration you must ensure that your BBB is running a VNC server before you can log in. The BBB Debian distribution has the *tightvncserver* installed by default. The first time you execute the server you will be prompted to define a password for remote access, as follows:

```
molloyd@beaglebone:~$ tightvncserver
You will require a password to access your desktops.
Password:
New 'X' desktop is beaglebone:1 ...
```

Once the server is running, you can check the process description to determine the port number—here it is running on port 5901:

```
molloyd@beaglebone:~$ ps aux|grep vnc
molloyd  24463  1.0  1.7  11364  8916 pts/2 S 16:15 0:00 Xtightvnc :1
-desktop X -auth /home/molloyd/.Xauthority -geometry 1024x768 -depth
24 -rfbwait 120000 -rfbauth /home/molloyd/.vnc/passwd -rfbport 5901 ...
```

The VNC Viewer session can then be started on your desktop machine using the server address and its port number (e.g., 192.168.7.2:5901). The BBB desktop is contained within a window frame, as displayed in Figure 11-4.

VNC with Xming and PuTTY

The Xming X Server (tiny.cc/ebb1101) for Windows, in combination with PuTTY, is a different approach to the same task; however, it does not require that a VNC server is running on the BBB. Once Xming is installed and executed, it appears only in the Windows taskbar with an "X" icon. The PuTTY BBB session can be configured using Connection ➢ SSH ➢ X11 to "Enable SSH X11 forwarding" to the local X display location and to set the X display location to be :0.0.

When an SSH session is opened to the BBB you can simply perform the following instructions, which result in the display of an xterm and xeyes display. The *xterm* window is the standard terminal emulator for the X Window System and the "magical" *xeyes* follow your mouse cursor around the desktop computer. Remember that the xeyes display is being updated by the BBB, not the desktop computer:

```
molloyd@beaglebone:~$ sudo apt-get install x11-apps
molloyd@beaglebone:~$ xterm &
molloyd@beaglebone:~$ xeyes &
```

Figure 11-4: VNC Viewer on Windows

One advantage of this approach is that you can seamlessly integrate BBB applications and Windows applications on the display. You can also start the BBB's *LXDE (Lightweight X11 Desktop Environment) standard panel* by calling `lxpanel` or `lxsession`, which results in the bottom-bar menu display (refer to Figure 11-4).

VNC with a Linux Desktop Computer

If you are running Linux as your desktop OS (e.g., Debian x64 on a VM), then you can usually start a VNC session using the following steps, where -X enables X11 forwarding and -C requests that compression is used in the transmission of frame buffer data:

```
molloyd@debian:~$ ssh -XC molloyd@192.168.7.2
BeagleBoard.org BeagleBone Debian Image 2014-05-14
molloyd@192.168.7.2's password:
molloyd@beaglebone:~$ xeyes &
molloyd@beaglebone:~$ xterm &
```

Fat-Client Applications

At the beginning of the previous chapter, the BBB is configured as a web server—essentially, the BBB is serving data to a *thin-client* web browser that is executing on a client machine. The temperature sensor application executes on the BBB and the data is served to the client's web browser using the Apache web server and CGI/PHP scripts. With thin-client applications, most of the processing takes place on the server machine (*server-side*). In contrast, *fat-client* (aka *thick-client*) applications execute on the client machine (*client-side*), and send and receive data messages to and from the server.

Recent computing architecture design trends have moved away from fat-client architectures and toward thin-client (and cloud) browser-based frameworks. However, the latter frameworks are usually implemented on a powerful cluster of server machines and are unsuitable for deployment on embedded devices. When working with the BBB, it is likely that the client desktop machine is the more computationally powerful device.

A fat-client application is typically more complex to develop and deploy than a thin-client application, but it reduces the demands on the server while allowing for advanced functionality and user interaction on the client machine. Later in this chapter, fat-client UI applications are developed that execute on a desktop computer and communicate to the BBB via TCP sockets. In turn, the BBB interfaces to the TMP36 temperature sensor and the ADXL345 accelerometer and serves their sensor data to the remote UI applications. Importantly, the fat-client applications use the resources of the desktop computer for graphical display, and therefore there is a minimal computational cost on the BBB. As such, it is possible for many fat-client applications on different desktop computers to simultaneously communicate with a single BBB.

Rich UI Application Development

Once a display framework is available to the BBB, a likely next step is to write rich UI applications that can utilize its benefits. Such applications are termed *graphical user interface* (*GUI*) applications; if you have used desktop computers, tablet computers, or smartphones, then you are familiar with their use. There are many different ways to implement GUI applications on the BBB—for example, Java has comprehensive built-in support for GUI development with its *abstract windowing toolkit* (*AWT*) libraries, and Python has libraries such as pyGTK, wxPython, and Tkinter.

To develop GUI applications under C/C++ for the BBB there are two clear options: the *GIMP Toolkit* (*GTK+*) and the *Qt* cross-platform development framework. This section describes how you can get started with both of these options. It is important to note that the applications in this section will function regardless of whether they are used directly on the BBB (i.e., general-purpose computer or touch screen form) or through VNC. GTK+ and Qt can also be used as the basis for building fat-client applications, which is covered later in this chapter.

Introduction to GTK+ on the BBB

GTK+ (www.gtk.org) is a cross-platform toolkit for creating GUI applications. It is most well known for its use in the *Linux GNOME desktop* and the *GNU Image Manipulation Program* (*GIMP*). Figure 11-5 illustrates a sample GTK+ application running on the BBB using VNC. The same application also works perfectly if the application is running on the BBB directly (e.g., refer to Figure 11-3).

Figure 11.5: The GTKsimple application

The "Hello World" GTK+ Application

The code for the application shown in Figure 11-5 is provided in Listing 11-1. The application consists of a single label, which contains the text "Hello BeagleBone" that has been added to a GTK+ window. Each line of the code has been commented in the listing in order to explain the important steps.

LISTING 11-1: /exploringBB/chp11/gtk/GTKsimple.cpp

```
#include<gtk/gtk.h>    // the GTK+ library header file

int main(int argc, char *argv[]){
        // This application will have a window and a single label
    GtkWidget *window, *label;
        // Initialize the GTK+ toolkit, pass command-line arguments
    gtk_init(&argc, &argv);
        // Create the top-level window (not yet visible)
    window = gtk_window_new(GTK_WINDOW_TOPLEVEL);
        // Set the title of the window to "Exploring BB"
    gtk_window_set_title ( GTK_WINDOW (window), "Exploring BB");
        // Create a label
    label = gtk_label_new ("Hello BeagleBone");
        // Add the label to the window
    gtk_container_add(GTK_CONTAINER (window), label);
        // Make the label visible (must be performed for every widget)
```

```
gtk_widget_show(label);
            // Make the window visible on the display
gtk_widget_show(window);
            // Runs the main loop until gtk_main_quit() is called
gtk_main(); // for example, if Ctrl C is typed
return 0;
}
```

The application can be compiled using the following call, which is also captured in the Git repository build script (use the grave accent `, not the single opening quotation mark character '):

```
molloyd@beaglebone:~/exploringBB/chp11/gtk$ g++ `pkg-config --libs
--cflags glib-2.0 gtk+-2.0` GTKsimple.cpp -o gtksimple
```

This call uses *pkg-config*, a tool that is useful when building applications and libraries under Linux, as it inserts the correct system-dependent options. It does this by collecting metadata about the libraries that are installed on the Linux system. For example, to get information about the current GTK+ library, you can use the following:

```
molloyd@beaglebone:~$ pkg-config --modversion gtk+-2.0
2.24.10
```

The application in Figure 11-5 does not quit when the X button (top right-hand corner) is clicked—the window itself disappears but the program continues to execute. This is because the preceding code has not defined that something should happen when the X button is clicked—you need to associate a "close" function with the signal that is generated when the button is clicked.

The Event-Driven Programming Model

GUI applications typically use an *event-driven programming model*. Under this model, the application waits in its main loop until an event (e.g., the user action of clicking a button) is detected, which triggers a callback function to be performed. In GTK+, a user action causes the main loop to deliver an event to GTK+, which is initialized by the call to gtk_init(). GTK+ then delivers this event to the graphical widgets, which in turn emit signals. These signals can be attached to callback functions of your own design or to windowing functions. For example, the following GTK+ code quits the application if the window X button is clicked:

```
g_signal_connect(window, "destroy", G_CALLBACK (gtk_main_quit), NULL);
```

The signal is attached to the window handle, so that when a signal named destroy is received, the gtk_main_quit() function is called, which causes the application to exit. The last argument is NULL because no data is required to be passed to the gtk_main_quit() function.

The GTK+ Temperature Application

Listing 11-2 provides the full source code for a more complete GTK+ application, which executes on the BBB as shown in Figure 11-6. It uses the same TMP36 temperature sensor and ADC configuration used in Chapter 10 (e.g., in Listing 10-5). This example is a GUI application that reads the BBB ADC when a button is clicked, and then displays the temperature in a label. In this example, a signal is connected to the button object, so when it is clicked the callback function getTemperature() is called.

Figure 11-6: The GTKtemperature application

LISTING 11-2: /exploringBB/chp11/gtk/GTKtemperature.cpp (segment)

```cpp
#include<gtk/gtk.h>
...
#define LDR_PATH "/sys/bus/iio/devices/iio:device0/in_voltage"

// Same function as in Chp. 10 to read the ADC value (Listing 10-5)
int readAnalog(int number){ ... }

// The callback function associated with the button. A pointer to the
// label is passed, so that the label can display the temperature
static void getTemperature(GtkWidget *widget, gpointer temp_label){
    // cast the generic gpointer into a GtkWidget * label
    GtkWidget *temperature_label = (GtkWidget *) temp_label;
    int adc_value = readAnalog(0);
    float cur_voltage = adc_value * (1.80f/4096.0f);
    float diff_degreesC = (cur_voltage-0.75f)/0.01f;
    float temperature = 25.0f + diff_degreesC;
    stringstream ss;
    ss << "Temperature: " << temperature << " degrees C";
    // set the text in the label
    gtk_label_set_text( GTK_LABEL(temp_label), ss.str().c_str());
    ss << endl;  // add a \n to the string for the standard output
    g_print(ss.str().c_str());  // output to the terminal (std out)
}
```

```c
int main(int argc, char *argv[]){
  GtkWidget *window, *temp_label, *button, *button_label;
  gtk_init(&argc, &argv);
  window = gtk_window_new(GTK_WINDOW_TOPLEVEL);
  gtk_window_set_title(GTK_WINDOW (window), "Exploring BB");

  // Fix the size of the window so that it cannot be resized
  gtk_widget_set_size_request(window, 220, 50);
  gtk_window_set_resizable(GTK_WINDOW(window), FALSE);
  // Place a border of 5 pixels around the inner window edge
  gtk_container_set_border_width (GTK_CONTAINER (window), 5);

  // Quit application if X button is pressed
  g_signal_connect(window, "destroy", G_CALLBACK (gtk_main_quit), NULL);

  // Set window to contain two stacked widgets using a vbox
  GtkWidget *vbox = gtk_vbox_new(FALSE, 5);   // spacing of 5
  gtk_container_add (GTK_CONTAINER (window), vbox); // add vbox
  gtk_widget_show (vbox);                       // set the vbox visible

  // This is the label in which to display the temperature
  temp_label = gtk_label_new ("Temperature is Undefined");
  gtk_widget_show(temp_label);                  // make it visible
  gtk_label_set_justify( GTK_LABEL(temp_label), GTK_JUSTIFY_LEFT);
  // Add the label to the vbox
  gtk_box_pack_start (GTK_BOX (vbox), temp_label, FALSE, FALSE, 0);

  // Create a button and connect it to the getTemperature() callback
  button = gtk_button_new();
  button_label = gtk_label_new("Get Temperature"); // button text label
  gtk_widget_show(button_label);                 // show label
  gtk_widget_show(button);                       // show button
  gtk_container_add(GTK_CONTAINER (button), button_label);
  // Connect the callback function getTemperature() to the button
  g_signal_connect(button, "clicked",
                   G_CALLBACK (getTemperature), (gpointer) temp_label);

  // Add the button to the vbox
  gtk_box_pack_start (GTK_BOX (vbox), button, FALSE, FALSE, 0);
  gtk_widget_show(window);
  gtk_main();
  return 0;
}
```

MAKEFILES

As the complexity of your C/C++ projects grows, an IDE such as Eclipse can be used to manage compiler options and program code interdependencies. However, there are occasions when command-line compilation is required, and when projects are complex, a structured approach to managing the build process is necessary. A good solution is to use the *make* program and *makefiles*. To compile the GTKsimple.cpp program in this project the build script is as follows:

```
#!/bin/bash
g++ 'pkg-config --libs --cflags glib-2.0 gtk+-2.0' GTKsimple.cpp -o
gtksimple
g++ 'pkg-config --libs --cflags glib-2.0 gtk+-2.0' GTKtemperature.cpp -o
gtktemperature
```

The script works perfectly fine in this case; however, if the project's complexity necessitated separate compilation, then this approach lacks structure. Following is a simple Makefile that could be used instead (it is very important to use the Tab key to indent the lines with the <Tab> marker below):

```
molloyd@beaglebone:~/exploringBB/chp11/gtk$ more Makefile
all: GTKsimple GTKtemperature

GTKsimple:
<Tab> g++ 'pkg-config --libs --cflags glib-2.0 gtk+-2.0' GTKsimple.cpp
-o GTKsimple

GTKtemperature:
<Tab> g++ 'pkg-config --libs --cflags glib-2.0 gtk+-2.0' GTKtemperature.
cpp-o GTKtemperature
```

If the make command is issued in this directory, then the Makefile file is detected and a call to "make all" will automatically be invoked. That will execute the commands under the GTKsimple: and GTKtemperature: labels, which builds the two programs. However, this makefile does not add much in the way of structure, so a more complete version is required, such as this:

```
molloyd@beaglebone:~/exploringBB/chp11/gtk$ more Makefile
CC      = g++
CFLAGS  = -c -Wall $(shell pkg-config --cflags glib-2.0 gtk+-2.0)
LDFLAGS = $(shell pkg-config --libs glib-2.0 gtk+-2.0)

all: GTKsimple GTKtemperature

GTKsimple: GTKsimple.o
<Tab>    $(CC) $(LDFLAGS) $< -o $@

GTKsimple.o: GTKsimple.cpp
<Tab>    $(CC) $(CFLAGS) $< -o $@

GTKtemperature: GTKtemperature.o
```

```
<Tab>    $(CC) $(LDFLAGS) $< -o $@


GTKtemperature.o: GTKtemperature.cpp
<Tab>    $(CC) $(CFLAGS) $< -o $@

clean:
<Tab>    rm -rf *.o GTKsimple GTKtemperature
```

In this version the compiler choice, compiler options, and linker options are defined at the top of the makefile. This enables the options to be easily altered for all files in the project. In addition, the objective files (.o files) are retained, which dramatically reduces repeated compilation times when there are many source files in the project. There is some shortcut syntax in this makefile—for example, $< is the name of the first prerequisite (GTKsimple.o in its first use) and $@ is the name of the target (GTKsimple in its first use). The project can now be built using the following steps:

```
molloyd@beaglebone:~/exploringBB/chp11/gtk$ ls
GTKsimple.cpp  GTKtemperature.cpp  Makefile
molloyd@beaglebone:~/exploringBB/chp11/gtk$ make
g++ -c -Wall -pthread ... GTKsimple.cpp -o GTKsimple.o ...
molloyd@beaglebone:~/exploringBB/chp11/gtk$ ls
GTKsimple  GTKsimple.cpp  GTKsimple.o  GTKtemperature.cpp  Makefile
molloyd@beaglebone:~/exploringBB/chp11/gtk$ make clean
molloyd@beaglebone:~/exploringBB/chp11/gtk$ ls
GTKsimple.cpp  GTKtemperature.cpp  Makefile
```

This description only scratches the surface of the capability of make and makefiles—a full GNU guide is available at tiny.cc/ebb1102.

Introduction to Qt on the BBB

Qt (pronounced "cute") is a powerful cross-platform development framework that uses standard C++. It provides libraries of C++ code for GUI application development and for database access, thread management, networking, and more. Importantly, code developed under this framework can be executed under Windows, Linux, Mac OS X, Android, iOS, and on embedded platforms, such as the BBB. Qt can be used under open-source or commercial terms and it is supported by freely available development tools, such as qmake and Qt Creator. The capability and flexibility of this framework make it an ideal candidate for GUI applications that are to run directly on the BBB, or on devices that control the BBB.

Qt is described in greater detail in the next section, but it is useful to get started using a simple "hello world" example, as illustrated in Figure 11-7, which can be compiled and executed on the BBB either directly or using VNC.

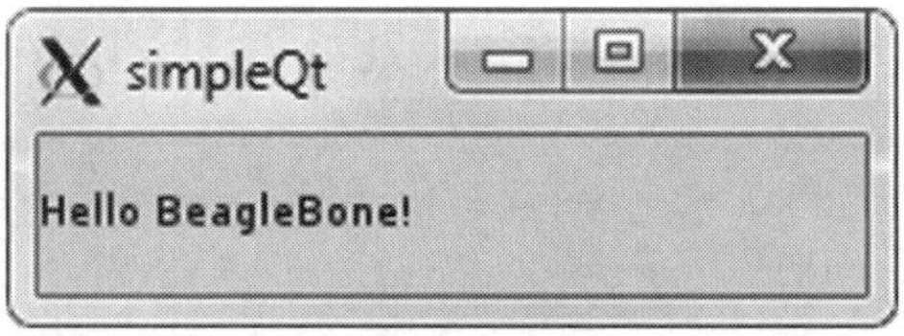

Figure 11-7: Qt "hello world" BBB example executing using VNC

Installing Qt Development Tools on the BBB

The first step is to install the Qt development tools on the BBB. The last command in the following code snippet installs a full suite of tools (~200MB of storage required). The middle command identifies the constituent components of the suite:

```
molloyd@beaglebone:~$ sudo apt-get update
molloyd@beaglebone:~$ apt-cache search qt4
molloyd@beaglebone:~$ sudo apt-get install qt4-dev-tools
```

You can then test the version of the installation using the following:

```
molloyd@beaglebone:~$ qmake -version
QMake version 2.01a
Using Qt version 4.8.2 in /usr/lib/arm-linux-gnueabihf
```

The "Hello World" Qt Application

Listing 11-3 is a very concise Qt application that can be used as a test—it does not represent good Qt programming practice! It uses an object of the QLabel class, which is a subclass of the QWidget class, to display a message in the application. A *widget* is the primary UI element that is used for creating GUIs with Qt. The parent QWidget class provides the code required to render (draw) the subclass object on the screen display.

LISTING 11-3:   /exploringBB/chp11/simpleQt/simpleQt.cpp

```cpp
#include <QApplication>
#include <QLabel>
int main(int argc, char *argv[ ]){
    QApplication app(argc, argv);
    QLabel label("Hello BeagleBone!");
    label.resize(200, 100);
    label.show();
    return app.exec();
}
```

The `simpleQt.cpp` file in Listing 11-3 is the only file required in a directory before the following steps take place. The *qmake* cross-platform makefile generator can then be used to create a default project:

```
molloyd@beaglebone:~/exploringBB/chp11/simpleQt$ ls
simpleQt.cpp
molloyd@beaglebone:~/exploringBB/chp11/simpleQt$ qmake -project
molloyd@beaglebone:~/exploringBB/chp11/simpleQt$ ls
simpleQt.cpp  simpleQt.pro
molloyd@beaglebone:~/exploringBB/chp11/simpleQt$ more simpleQt.pro
######################################################################
# Automatically generated by qmake (2.01a) Thu May 15 03:07:20 2014
######################################################################
TEMPLATE = app
TARGET =
DEPENDPATH += .
INCLUDEPATH += .
SOURCES += simpleQt.cpp
```

This project `.pro` file describes the project settings and, if required, it can be edited manually to add additional dependencies. The qmake makefile generator can then be executed again, this time with no `-project` argument:

```
molloyd@beaglebone:~/exploringBB/chp11/simpleQt$ qmake
molloyd@beaglebone:~/exploringBB/chp11/simpleQt$ ls
Makefile  simpleQt.cpp  simpleQt.pro
```

This step results in a `Makefile` file being created in the current directory that allows the executable to be built using a call to `make`, which in turn uses g++ to build the final application:

```
molloyd@beaglebone:~/exploringBB/chp11/simpleQt$ make
g++ -c -pipe -O2 -Wall -W ... -o simpleQt.o simpleQt.cpp ...
```

The executable is now present in the directory and can be executed as follows, which results in the visual display shown earlier in Figure 11-7:

```
molloyd@beaglebone:~/exploringBB/chp11/simpleQt$ ls
Makefile  simpleQt  simpleQt.cpp  simpleQt.o  simpleQt.pro
molloyd@beaglebone:~/exploringBB/chp11/simpleQt$ ./simpleQt
```

Clearly, there are additional steps involved in using qmake to build a Qt application, but these are necessary to take advantage of the cross-platform nature of Qt. For example, you can perform similar steps on your desktop machine to build the same application, regardless of its OS.

Qt Primer

Qt is a full cross-platform development framework that is written in C/C++. It is used in the preceding section for UI programming, but it also provides support for databases, threads, timers, networking, multimedia, XML processing, and more. Qt extends C++ by adding macros and *introspection,* code that examines the type and properties of an object at run time, which is not natively available in C++. It is important to note that *all the code is still just plain C++*!

Qt Concepts

Qt is built in modules, each of which can be added to your project by including the requisite header files in your C++ program and by identifying that the module is used in the project .pro file. For example, to include the classes in the QtNetwork module, you add #include<QtNetwork> to your program code and link against the module by adding QT += network to the qmake .pro file. A list of important Qt modules is provided in Table 11-2.

Table 11-2: Summary of the Important Qt Modules

NAME	DESCRIPTION
QtCore	Contains the core non-GUI classes, such as QString, QChar, QDate, QTimer, and QVector. It is included by default in Qt projects, as all other Qt modules rely on this module.
QtGui	Core module that adds GUI support to the QtCore module, with classes such as QDialog, QWidget, QToolbar, QLabel, QTextEdit, and QFont. This module is included by default—if your application has no GUI, then you can add Qt -= gui to your .pro file.
QtMultimedia	Contains classes for low-level multimedia functionality, such as QVideoFrame, QAudioInput, and QAudioOutput. To use this module, add #include <QtMultimedia> to your source file and QT += multimedia to your .pro file.
QtNetwork	Contains classes for network communication over TCP and UDP, including SSL communications, with classes such as QTcpSocket, QFtp, QLocalServer, QSslSocket, and QUdpSocket. As above, use #include <QtNetwork> and QT += network.
QtOpenGL	The *Open Graphics Library* (*OpenGL*) is a cross-platform application programming interface (API) for 3-D computer graphics, which is widely used in industrial visualization and computer gaming applications. This module makes it straightforward to contain OpenGL in your application with classes such as QGLBuffer, QGLWidget, QGLContext, and QGLShader. As above, use #include <QtOpenGL> and QT += opengl. The AM335x has OpenGL hardware acceleration capability, but it is currently difficult to utilize.

NAME	DESCRIPTION
QtScript	Enables you to make your Qt application *scriptable*. *Scripts* are used in applications such as Microsoft Excel and Adobe Photoshop to enable users to automate repetitive tasks. QtScript includes a JavaScript engine, which you can use within the core application to interlink functionality in scripts. It can also be used to expose the internal functionality of your application to users, enabling them to add new functionality without the need for C++ compilation. As above, use `#include <QtScript>` and `QT += script`.
QtSql	Contains classes for interfacing to databases using the SQL programming language, such as `QSqlDriver`, `QSqlQuery`, and `QSqlResult`. As above, use `#include <QtSql>` and `QT += sql`.
QtSvg	Contains classes for creating and displaying scalar vector graphics (SVG) files, such as `QSvgWidget`, `QSvgGenerator`, and `QSvgRenderer`. As above, use `#include <QtSvg>` and `QT += svg`.
QtTest	Contains classes for unit testing Qt applications using the QTestLib tool, such as `QSignalSpy` and `QTestEventList`. As above, use `#include <QtTest>` and `QT += testlib`.
QtWebKit	Provides a web browser engine and classes for rendering and interacting with web content, such as `QWebView`, `QWebPage`, and `QWebHistory`. As above, use `#include <QtWebKit>` and `QT += webkit`.
QtXml	Extensible markup language (XML) is a human-readable document format that can be used to transport and store data. The QtXml module provides a stream reader and writer for XML data, with classes such as `QXmlReader`, `QDomDocument`, and `QXmlAttributes`. As above, use `#include <QtXml>` and `QT += xml`.

The QObject Class

The `QObject` class is the base class of almost all the Qt classes and all the widgets.[1] This means that most Qt classes share common functionality for handling memory management, properties, and event-driven programming.

Qt implements introspection by storing information about every class that is derived from `QObject` using a `QMetaObject` object within its *Meta-Object System*. When you build projects using Qt you will see that new `.cpp` files appear in the build directory—these are created by the *Meta-Object Compiler (moc)*.[2] The C++

---

[1] Java programmers will notice that this is similar to the `Object` class in Java; however, in Qt, classes requiring object instances that can be copied do not subclass `QObject` (e.g., `QString`, `QChar`).

[2] At compile time, the `moc` uses information from the class header files (e.g., if the class is a descendent of `QObject`) to generate a "marked-up" version of the `.cpp` file. For example, if you have a class X that is defined in the files `X.h` and `X.cpp`, the `moc` will generate a new file called `moc-X.cpp`, which contains the meta-object code for the class X.

compiler will then compile these files into a regular C/C++ objective file (.o), which is ultimately linked to create an executable application.

Signals and Slots

Similar to GTK+, Qt has an event-driven programming model that enables events and state changes to be interconnected with reactions using a mechanism termed *signals and slots*. For example, a Qt button widget can be configured so that when it is clicked, it generates a *signal*, which has been connected to a *slot*. The slot, which is somewhat like a callback function, performs a user-defined function when it receives a signal. Importantly, the signals and slots mechanism can be applied to non-GUI objects—it can be used for intercommunication between any object that is in any way derived from the QObject class. Signals and slots provide a powerful mechanism that is possibly the most unique feature of the Qt framework.

A full-featured Qt temperature sensor application is developed shortly that makes extensive use of signals and slots. For example, the application updates the temperature display every five seconds by reading the ADC value; Figure 11-8 illustrates how this takes place. In this example, the QTimer class has a signal called timeout() that is emitted whenever an object called timer "times out" (which it does after five seconds). This signal is connected to the on_updateTemperature() slot on an object of the QMainWindow class called mainWindow. The connection is made by a call of the form

```
QObject::connect(source,SIGNAL(signature),destination,SLOT(signature));
```

where source and destination are objects of classes that are derived from the QObject class. The signature is the function name and argument types (without the variable names).

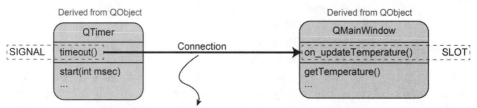

Figure 11-8: QTimer signals and slots example

The website qt-project.org provides an excellent detailed description of the behavior of signals and slots, but here are some further summary points on signals, slots, and connections that will get you started:

- Signals can be connected to any number of slots.
- Signals are defined in the signals section of the code (under a signals: label, which is usually in the class header file).

- Signal "methods" must return void and may not have any implementation.

- A signal can be explicitly emitted using the emit keyword.

- Slots can be connected to any number of signals.

- Slots are defined in the slots section of the code (under a slots: label that can be public, private, or protected).

- Slots are regular methods with a full implementation.

- Connections can be explicitly formed (as in the timer example shown earlier) or automatically created when using the Qt graphical design tools in the next section.

Qt Development Tools

The Qt framework also has associated development tools. As well as the qmake tool, there is a full-featured IDE called *Qt Creator*, which is similar in nature to Eclipse, except that it is specifically tailored for Qt development. The IDE, which is illustrated in Figure 11-9, is available for Linux, Windows, and Mac OS X, and its *Qt Designer* tool can even execute on the BBB directly. Qt Creator can be used to build native applications, or it can be used to cross-compile applications for the BBB, by installing a cross-platform toolchain (similar to Eclipse).

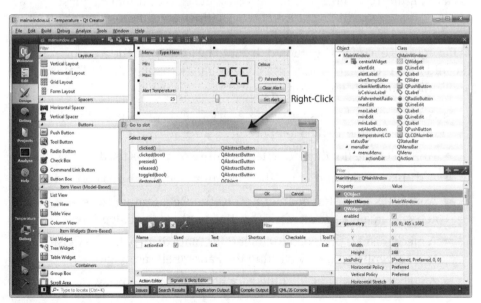

Figure 11-9: Qt Creator IDE visual design editor

One of the key features that Qt Creator provides is its *visual design editor*, which enables you to interactively drag-and-drop widgets onto window designs, called *forms*. The interface enables the properties of the widgets to be configured easily, and it provides a straightforward way of enabling signals and associating slots against the UI components. For example, to write code that executes when the "Set Alert" button is clicked (refer to Figure 11-9), you can simply right-click the button and choose "Go to slot," which provides a dialog with a list of available signals (such as `clicked()`, `pressed()`, and `released()`).[3] Once a signal is chosen, the IDE will automatically enable the signal, provide a slot code template, and associate the signal with the slot. The form UI's properties are stored in an XML file and associated with the project (e.g., `mainwindow.ui`).

> **NOTE**   When using Qt Creator, unusual problems can arise (e.g., changes to the code not appearing in the application build), particularly when switching projects—in such cases, go to the Build menu and choose Clean All.
>
> In addition, "unresolved external" link errors (e.g., when adding new classes) can often be resolved by selecting "Run qmake" from the Build menu.

A Qt Temperature Sensor GUI Application

In this section, the Qt Creator IDE is used to build a full-featured GUI temperature sensor application, as illustrated in Figure 11-10. This application executes directly on the BBB, regardless of the UI architecture used—in fact, if you look back at Figure 11-2 and Figure 11-4, you will see that it makes guest appearances in two of the different frameworks illustrated there. This application demonstrates some of the capabilities of Qt on the BBB, while being cognizant of the volume of code to be studied. It could be greatly extended—for example, it could also provide historical charting or fancy display dials. This example application supports the following features:

- A timer thread takes a reading every five seconds from the BBB ADC input using the TMP36 temperature sensor.
- An LCD-style floating-point temperature display is used.
- A display of the minimum and maximum temperature is provided.
- A slider is used that enables you to choose a temperature at which to activate an alert. An alert triggers the display of a dialog box.
- A mechanism is provided to convert the main display from a Celsius scale to a Fahrenheit scale by clicking the Fahrenheit radio widget.
- A status display is used at the very bottom of the window.

The full source code and executable for this application are available in the Git repository `/exploringBB/chp11/QtTemperature` directory.

---

[3] A click is a press and a release—code can be associated with the complete click action and/or the constituent actions.

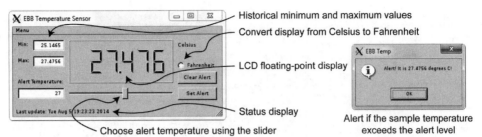

Figure 11-10: The Qt EBB Temperature Sensor GUI application

There are three important source files to describe for this application, the first of which is in Listing 11-4. It provides the `main()` starting point for the application in which an instance of the `QApplication` and `MainWindow` classes are created. The `QApplication` class manages the GUI application control flow (the main loop). The `MainWindow` class is defined in Listings 11-5 and 11-6.

LISTING 11-4: /exploringBB/chp11/QtTemperature/main.cpp

```
#include "mainwindow.h"
#include <QApplication>

int main(int argc, char *argv[]){
   QApplication a(argc, argv); // manages GUI application control flow
   MainWindow w;               // the user-defined class
   w.show();                   // shows the user-defined class UI
   return a.exec();            // without a.exec() the program would end here
}                              // it is the main loop that processes events
```

The `MainWindow` class is a child of the `QMainWindow` class (which is a child of `QWidget` and ultimately `QObject`). That means that any methods that are available in the parent classes are also available in the `MainWindow` class itself.

Figure 11-11 illustrates the relationship between the UI components and the slots that are declared in Listing 11-5 and defined in Listing 11-6. The timer code is also summarized—it is not a GUI component but it does generate a `timeout()` signal, which is connected to the `on_updateTemperature()` slot. The exact nature of the code in Listings 11-5 and 11-6 is described by the comments. However, the clearest way to fully understand the code is to edit it and see what impact your edits have. You do not require the temperature sensor to execute the code, but the temperature display will remain fixed at 25°C in its absence.

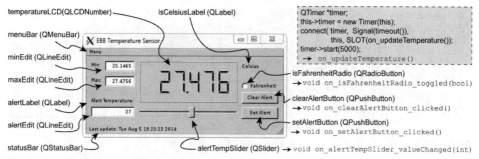

Figure 11-11: The UI components and associated slots

LISTING 11-5: /exploringBB/chp11/QtTemperature/mainwindow.h

```cpp
#include <QMainWindow>      // for the main GUI interface
#include <QTimer>           // for a timer that periodically reads temperature
#include <QDateTime>        // to find out the date/time of the sample
#include <QMessageBox>      // for pop-up message boxes - e.g., alert!

namespace Ui {
    class MainWindow;       // Places class MainWindow in UI namespace
}

class MainWindow : public QMainWindow   // a child of the QMainWindow class
{
    // This macro must appear in the private section of a class that
    // declares its own signals and slots
    Q_OBJECT
public:
    explicit MainWindow(QWidget *parent = 0);    // constructor
    ~MainWindow();                               // destructor
private slots:
    void on_setAlertButton_clicked();
    void on_isFahrenheitRadio_toggled(bool checked);
    void on_clearAlertButton_clicked();
    void on_alertTempSlider_valueChanged(int value);  // if alert slider moved
    void on_updateTemperature();  // this slot is triggered by the timer
private:
    Ui::MainWindow *ui;         // the main user interface
    QTimer *timer;              // timer thread that triggers after a delay
    bool   isFahrenheit;        // is the main display deg C or deg F
    int    alertTemperature;    // the alert temperature value
    bool   isAlertSet;          // is the alert set?
    float minTemperature, maxTemperature;        // min and max temp values
    float celsiusToFahrenheit(float valueCelsius); // function for conversion
    float getTemperature();       // get the temperature from the sensor
    int    readAnalog(int number); // used by getTemperature to read the ADC
};
```

LISTING 11-6: /exploringBB/chp11/QtTemperature/mainwindow.cpp

```cpp
#include "mainwindow.h"
#include "ui_mainwindow.h"
#include <fstream>
#include <sstream>
using namespace std;
#define LDR_PATH  "/sys/bus/iio/devices/iio:device0/in_voltage"

// Constructor used to set up the default values for the created object
MainWindow::MainWindow(QWidget *parent) :
    QMainWindow(parent), ui(new Ui::MainWindow)  {
    ui->setupUi(this);
    this->isFahrenheit = false;                // default to Celsius
    this->isAlertSet = false;                  // no alert set
    statusBar()->showMessage("No alert set");  // status at bottom of window
    this->timer = new QTimer(this);            // create a new timer
      // when the timer times out, call the slot on_updateTemperature()
    connect(timer, SIGNAL(timeout()), this, SLOT(on_updateTemperature ()));
    this->maxTemperature = -100.0f;            // pick an impossible min
    this->minTemperature = 200.0f;             // pick an impossible max
    this->on_updateTemperature();              // explicitly update the display
    timer->start(5000);                        // set the time out to be 5 sec
}

MainWindow::~MainWindow() { delete ui; }       // destructor, destroys UI

void MainWindow::on_setAlertButton_clicked() { // set the alert temperature
    int sliderValue = ui->alertTempSlider->value();  // get the slider value
    if(sliderValue < getTemperature()){       // lower than current temp?
       QMessageBox::warning(this, "EBB Temperature",
                  "Alert setting too low!", QMessageBox::Discard);
    }
    else{                                      // alert value fine
       QString tempStr("Alert is set for: ");  // form a message
       tempStr.append(QString::number(sliderValue)); // with the alert temp
       statusBar()->showMessage(tempStr);      // display the message
       this->isAlertSet = true;                // alert is set
       this->alertTemperature = sliderValue;   // alert temp set
    }
}

void MainWindow::on_isFahrenheitRadio_toggled(bool checked){
    this->isFahrenheit = checked;              // pressed the toggle button
    if(checked){
       ui->isCelsiusLabel->setText("Fahrenheit"); // display F on top-right
    }
    if(!checked){
       ui->isCelsiusLabel->setText("Celsius");  // display C on top-right
    }
```

continues

LISTING 11-6: *(continued)*

```
   this->on_updateTemperature();                      // update the temperature value
}

void MainWindow::on_clearAlertButton_clicked(){// remove the alert
   this->isAlertSet = false;
   statusBar()->showMessage("No alert set");
}

void MainWindow::on_alertTempSlider_valueChanged(int value) {
   ui->alertEdit->setText(QString::number(value)); // update alert text field
}

float MainWindow::getTemperature(){ ... }        // same as Chp.10 code (10-5)

int MainWindow::readAnalog(int number){ ... }    // same as Chp.10 code (10-5)

float MainWindow::celsiusToFahrenheit(float valueCelsius){
   return ((valueCelsius * (9.0f/5.0f)) + 32.0f);
}

// slot for the timer, called every 5 sec, and also explicitly in the code.
void MainWindow::on_updateTemperature() {      // called whenever temp updated
   float temperature = this->getTemperature();
   QDateTime local(QDateTime::currentDateTime()); // display sample time
   statusBar()->showMessage(QString("Last update: ").append(local.toString()));
   if(temperature >= this->maxTemperature){   // is this the max temperature?
      this->maxTemperature = temperature;
      ui->maxEdit->setText(QString::number(temperature));
   }
   if(temperature <= this->minTemperature){   // is this the min temperature?
      this->minTemperature = temperature;
      ui->minEdit->setText(QString::number(temperature));
   }
   if(this->isFahrenheit){                     // is the display in Fahrenheit?
      ui->temperatureLCD->display((double)this->celsiusToFahrenheit(temperature));
   }
   else{                                       // must be Celsius
      ui->temperatureLCD->display((double)temperature);
   }
   if(this->isAlertSet){                       // is the alert enabled?
      if(temperature>=this->alertTemperature){ // does it exceed alert temp?
         QString message("Alert! It is ");
         message.append(QString::number(temperature)).append(" degrees C!");
         QMessageBox::information(this, "EBB Temp", message,
                              QMessageBox::Ok);
      }
   }
}
```

Simple Qt Cross-Platform Development

The Qt temperature sensor application GUI can be edited using Qt Designer directly on the BBB (in general-purpose computer form, or by using VNC). Qt Designer is available directly from the BBB Launch Bar (under Programming ➤ Qt 4 Designer) or by typing `designer` at the shell prompt. Qt Designer is installed due to the following earlier call:

```
molloyd@beaglebone:~$ sudo apt-get install qt4-dev-tools
```

If you find that using Qt Designer and qmake on the BBB is too sluggish or onerous, you can develop and debug your application on your desktop computer and then transfer it to the BBB. For example, in this project you should copy the following files to the BBB from your desktop machine by using sftp, scp, or rsync (see the following feature on scp and rsync):

```
molloyd@beaglebone:~/tmp$ ls
Temperature.pro  main.cpp  mainwindow.cpp  mainwindow.h  mainwindow.ui
molloyd@beaglebone:~/tmp$ qmake
molloyd@beaglebone:~/tmp$ ls
Makefile         main.cpp         mainwindow.h
Temperature.pro  mainwindow.cpp   mainwindow.ui
molloyd@beaglebone:~/tmp$ make
/usr/bin/uic-qt4 mainwindow.ui -o ui_mainwindow.h ...
molloyd@beaglebone:~/tmp$ ls
Makefile         main.cpp         mainwindow.h    moc_mainwindow.cpp
Temperature      main.o           mainwindow.o    moc_mainwindow.o
Temperature.pro  mainwindow.cpp   mainwindow.ui   ui_mainwindow.h
molloyd@beaglebone:~/tmp$ ./Temperature &
```

The output will appear as shown in Figure 11-10 (when VNC is used).

Unfortunately, this approach does not allow you to test the software with BBB connected hardware until it has been built using the preceding steps. A more comprehensive approach, described at the end of this chapter, is required for full cross-platform Qt development.

SECURE COPY (SCP) AND RSYNC

The *secure copy* program, *scp*, provides a mechanism for transferring files between two hosts using the secure shell (SSH) protocol. For example, to transfer a file `test.txt` from a Linux desktop machine to the BBB you can use the following (all commands are executed on the desktop machine):

```
molloyd@debian:~/Temp$ echo "Testing SCP" >> test1.txt
molloyd@debian:~/Temp$ scp test1.txt molloyd@192.168.7.2:tmp/
```

```
molloyd@192.168.7.2's password:
test1.txt                        100%   12    0.0KB/s   00:00
```

To copy a file from the BBB back to the Linux desktop machine you can use the following:

```
molloyd@debian:~/Temp$ scp molloyd@192.168.7.2:tmp/test1.txt test2.txt
molloyd@192.168.7.2's password:
test1.txt                        100%   12    0.0KB/s   00:00
molloyd@debian:~/Temp$ more test2.txt
Testing SCP
```

Use -v to see full, *v*erbose output of the transfer. Using -C will automatically compress and decompress the files to speed up the data transfer. Using -r allows for the *r*ecursive copy of a directory, including all of its files and subdirectories. Using -p will *p*reserve the modification times, access times, and modes of the original files. Therefore, to copy the entire desktop Temp directory to the BBB tmp directory, you could use the following:

```
molloyd@debian:~$ scp -Cvrp Temp molloyd@192.168.7.2:tmp/
...Transferred: sent 8828328, received 74112 bytes, in 16.1 seconds...
```

Just like scp, the *rsync* utility can copy files; however, it can also be used to synchronize files and directories across multiple locations, where only the differences are transferred (*delta encoding*). For example, to perform the same operation using rsync, you can use the following:

```
molloyd@debian:~$ rsync -avze ssh Temp molloyd@192.168.7.2:tmp/Temp
molloyd@192.168.7.2's password:
sent 8941887 bytes  received 9719 bytes  577522.97 bytes/sec...
```

Using -a requests *a*rchive mode (like -p for scp), -v requests *v*erbose output, -z requests the compression of data (like -C for scp), and -e ssh requests rsync to use the SSH protocol. To test rsync, create an additional file in the Temp directory and perform the same command again using:

```
molloyd@debian:~$ touch Temp/test3.txt
molloyd@debian:~$ rsync -avze ssh Temp molloyd@192.168.7.2:tmp/Temp
molloyd@192.168.7.2's password:
sending incremental file list
Temp/    Temp/test3.txt
sent 16186 bytes  received 211 bytes  1561.62 bytes/sec...
```

Importantly, you can see that only one file has been transferred in this case. The rsync utility can delete files after transfer (using --delete), which you should only use after performing a dry run (using --dry-run).

Remote UI Application Development

In Chapter 10, a C++ Client/Server application is introduced that can be used for direct intercommunication between two processes that are running on two different machines (or the same machine) using TCP sockets. The machines could be situated on the same physical/wireless network, or could even be on different continents. Direct socket communication requires programmers to frame their own intercommunication protocol—that results in programming overhead, but it also leads to very efficient communication, which is only really limited by the speed of the network.

As a first application, the functionality of the Qt Temperature Sensor GUI application and the C++ Client/Server application (from Chapter 10) are combined. This enables the creation of a fat-client GUI Temperature application that can intercommunicate with a Temperature Service, which is running on the BBB. The Temperature Service server code is enhanced from that presented in Chapter 10, by making it multi-threaded. This change enables many client applications to attach to the server at the same time. The architecture is illustrated in Figure 11-12.

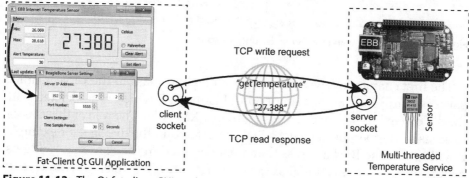

Figure 11-12: The Qt fat-client GUI application client/server architecture

The full source code for the Qt GUI application is available in the `chp11/QtSocketsTemperature` directory, and the server source code is available in the `chp11/threadedTemperatureServer` directory.

Fat-Client Qt GUI Application

In this section, the Qt Temperature Sensor GUI application from earlier in this chapter is modified so that it becomes "Internet enabled." This change means that the application does not have to execute on the BBB; rather, the GUI application can run on a desktop machine and communicate to the BBB sensor using

TCP sockets. To achieve this outcome, the following changes are made to the GUI application code:

1. A new dialog window is added to the application that can be used to enter the server IP address, the service port number, and the reading refresh frequency. This dialog is illustrated in Figure 11-13.

2. Rather than read from the BBB ADC, the GUI application must open a TCP socket and communicate to the BBB server application. The client application sends the string "getTemperature" to the server. The server is programmed to respond with the temperature, which it reads from the TMP36 sensor that is attached to an ADC input.

3. A menu is enabled on the application UI that can be used to open the Server Settings dialog or to quit the application. The respective key sequences Ctrl+S or Ctrl+X can also be used.

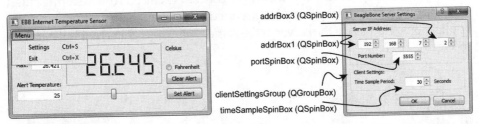

Figure 11-13: The Menu and the Server Settings dialog

The first change involves the addition of a new class to the project called ServerSettingsDialog, as described in Listing 11-7, which is associated with the dialog (and its serversettingsdialog.ui XML file). The role of this class is to act as a wrapper for the values that are entered in the dialog—for example, it will return the IPv4 address that a user entered in the QSpinBox widgets, by returning a single 32-bit unsigned int (quint32) when its getIPAddress() method is called.

LISTING 11-7: /chp11/QtSocketsTemperature/serversettingsdialog.h

```
class ServerSettingsDialog : public QDialog
{
    Q_OBJECT                          // the Qt macro required
public:
    explicit ServerSettingsDialog(QWidget *parent = 0); // ref to main window
    ~ServerSettingsDialog();
    quint32 virtual getIPAddress(); // return IP address as 32-bit int
    int virtual getTimeDelay()  { return timeDelay; }  // the sample time
    int virtual getServerPort() { return serverPortNumber; } // the port number
```

```
private slots:
    void on_buttonBox_accepted();    // OK button is pressed
    void on_buttonBox_rejected();    // Cancel button is pressed
private:
    Ui::ServerSettingsDialog *ui;    // pointer to the UI components
    int serverPortNumber;            // port number (default 5555)
    int timeDelay;                   // time delay sec (default 30)
    int address[4];                  // IP address (default 192.168.7.2)
};
```

The second change involves the addition of socket code to the getSensorTemperature() method, as provided in Listing 11-8. This code uses the QtNetwork module, which requires that you add

```
QT       += core gui network
```

to the SocketsTemperature.pro project file so that the project links to that module. The QTcpSocket class is used to create a client connection to the BBB TCP Temperature server. Regular TCP sockets are used on the BBB, which does not cause any difficulty in the transaction of string data. Interestingly, you could equivalently use Java socket code on either end of a connection—just be careful to ensure that the byte order is preserved.

> **LISTING 11-8: /chp11/QtSocketsTemperature/serversettingsdialog.cpp (segment)**

```
int MainWindow::getSensorTemperature(){
    // Get the server address and port number from the settings dialog box
    int serverPort = this->dialog->getServerPort();  // get from dialog box
    quint32 serverAddr = this->dialog->getIPAddress();  // from dialog box
    QTcpSocket *tcpSocket = new QTcpSocket(this);     // create socket
    tcpSocket->connectToHost(QHostAddress(serverAddr), serverPort); // connect
    if(!tcpSocket->waitForConnected(1000)){   // wait up to 1s for connection
        statusBar()->showMessage("Failed to connect to server...");
        return 1;
    }
    // Send the message "getTemperature" to the server
    tcpSocket->write("getTemperature");
    if(!tcpSocket->waitForReadyRead(1000)){   // wait up to 1s for server
        statusBar()->showMessage("Server did not respond...");
        return 1;
    }
    // If the server has sent bytes back to the client
    if(tcpSocket->bytesAvailable()>0){
        int size = tcpSocket->bytesAvailable(); // how many bytes are ready?
        char data[20];                           // upper limit of 20 chars
        tcpSocket->read(&data[0],(qint64)size); // read the number of bytes rec.
        data[size]='\0';                         // terminate the string
        this->curTemperature = atof(data);      // string -> float conversion
```

continues

LISTING 11-8: *(continued)*

```
        cout << "Received the data [" << this->curTemperature << "]" << endl;
    }
    else{ statusBar()->showMessage("No data available..."); }
    return 0;    // the on_updateTemperature() slot will update the display
}

void MainWindow::createActions(){
    QAction *exit = new QAction("&Exit", this);
    exit->setShortcut(QKeySequence(tr("Ctrl+X")));
    QAction *settings = new QAction("&Settings", this);
    settings->setShortcut(QKeySequence(tr("Ctrl+S")));
    QMenu *menu = menuBar()->addMenu("&Menu");
    menu->addAction(settings);
    menu->addAction(exit);
    connect(exit, SIGNAL(triggered()), qApp, SLOT(quit())); // quit application
    connect(settings, SIGNAL(triggered()), this, SLOT(on_openSettings()));
}

void MainWindow::on_openSettings(){   // the slot for the menu signal above
    this->dialog->exec();              // display the Server Settings dialog
    this->timer->start(1000*this->dialog->getTimeDelay()); // update delay
}
```

The third change is implemented by the `createActions()` method in Listing 11-8, which creates the GUI menu when it is called by the class constructor. It adds two actions to the menu: the Exit item quits the application, and the Settings item triggers the execution of the `on_openSettings()` slot, which opens the Server Settings dialog.

The BBB does not have to update the client-side GUI of the application in this architecture—rather, it manages TCP socket connections, processes strings, and reads values from an ADC input. Such operations have a very low overhead on the BBB, and therefore it is capable of simultaneously handling many client requests. Unfortunately, the server code that is presented in Chapter 10 is not capable of handling multiple *simultaneous* requests; rather, it processes requests in sequence, and would reject a connection if it is presently occupied.

Multi-Threaded Server Applications

For many server applications it is important that the server can handle multiple simultaneous requests—for example, if the Google search engine web page could only handle requests sequentially, then there might be a long queue and/or many rejected connections! Figure 11-14 illustrates the steps that must take place for a multi-threaded server application to communicate simultaneously with two individual client applications. The steps are as follows:

1. TCP Client 1 requests a connection to the BBB TCP Server. It must know the server's IP address (or name) and the port number.

2. The BBB TCP Server creates a new thread (Connection Handler 1) and passes the TCP Client's IP address and port number to it. The BBB TCP Server immediately begins listening for new connections (on port 5555). The Connection Handler 1 thread then forms a connection to the TCP Client 1 and begins communicating.

3. TCP Client 2 requests a connection to the BBB TCP Server. The Connection Handler 1 thread is currently communicating to TCP Client 1, but the BBB TCP Server is also listening for connections.

4. The BBB TCP Server creates a new thread (Connection Handler 2) and passes the second TCP Client's IP address and port number to it. The BBB TCP Server immediately begins listening for new connections. The Connection Handler 2 thread then forms a connection to the TCP Client 2 and begins communication.

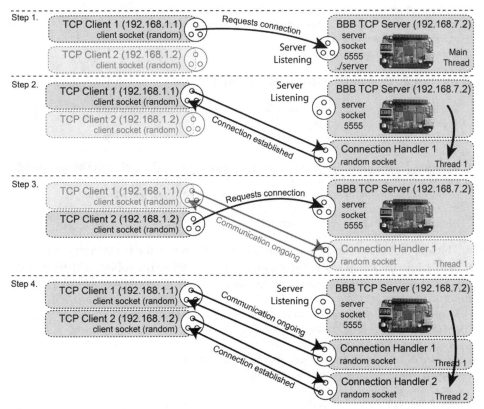

Figure 11-14: A multi-threaded server

At this point, communication is simultaneously taking place between both client/connection handler pairs, and the server main thread is listening for new connections. The client/connection handler communication session could persist for a long time—for example, for video streaming Internet services such as YouTube or Netflix.

If the connection handler objects were not implemented as threads, then the server would have to wait until the client/connection handler communication is complete before it could listen again for new connections. With the structure described, the server is only unavailable while it is constructing a new connection handler threaded object. Once the object is created, the server returns to a listening state. Client socket connections have a configurable time-out limit (typically of the order of seconds), so a short processing delay by the server should not result in rejected connections.

A C++ multi-threaded client/server example is available in the chp11/threadedclientserver directory. An artificial five-second delay is present in the ConnectionHandler class to prove conclusively that simultaneous communication is taking place. For example, you can open three terminal sessions on the BBB and start the server:

```
~/exploringBB/chp11/threadedclientserver$ ls
build  client  client.cpp  network  server  server.cpp
~/exploringBB/chp11/threadedclientserver$ ./server
Starting EBB Server Example
Listening for a connection...
```

Then start TCP Client 1 in the next terminal:

```
~/exploringBB/chp11/threadedclientserver$ ./client localhost
Starting EBB Client Example
Sending [Hello from the Client]
```

Then start TCP Client 2 in the last terminal (quickly—the delay is five seconds!):

```
~/exploringBB/chp11/threadedclientserver$ ./client localhost
Starting EBB Client Example
Sending [Hello from the Client]
```

The fact that the second client is able to connect while the first client is awaiting a (artificially delayed) response means that the server must be multi-threaded. The final output of the server is as follows:

```
~/exploringBB/chp11/threadedclientserver$ ./server
Starting EBB Server Example
Listening for a connection...
Received from the client [Hello from the Client]
Sending back [The Server says thanks!]
   but going asleep for 5 seconds first....
Received from the client [Hello from the Client]
Sending back [The Server says thanks!]
   but going asleep for 5 seconds first....
```

Both clients will display the same final output:

```
~/exploringBB/chp11/threadedclientserver$ ./client localhost
```

```
Starting EBB Client Example
Sending [Hello from the Client]
Received [The Server says thanks!]
End of EBB Client Example
```

The class definition for the ConnectionHandler class is provided in Listing 11-9. This class has a slightly complex structure so that a thread is created and started when an object of the class is created. This code can be used as a template—just rewrite the threadLoop() implementation.

LISTING 11-9: chp11/threadedclientserver/network/ConnectionHandler.h

```cpp
class SocketServer;   // class declaration, due to circular reference problem
                      // and C/C++ single definition rule.
class ConnectionHandler {
public:
   // Constructor expects a reference to the server that called it and
   // the incoming socket and file descriptor
   ConnectionHandler(SocketServer *server, sockaddr_in *in, int fd);
   virtual ~ConnectionHandler();
   int  start();
   void wait();
   void stop() { this->running = false; }  // stop the thread loop
   virtual int send(std::string message);  // send a message to the client
   virtual std::string receive(int size);  // receive a message
protected:
   virtual void threadLoop();      // the user-defined thread loop
private:
   sockaddr_in  *client;          // a handle to the client socket
   int          clientSocketfd;   // the client socket file desc.
   pthread_t    thread;           // the thread
   SocketServer *parent;          // a handle to the server object
   bool         running;          // is the thread running (default true)

   // static method to set the thread running when an object is created
   static void * threadHelper(void * handler){
         ((ConnectionHandler *)handler)->threadLoop();
         return NULL;
   }
};
```

A Multi-Threaded Temperature Service

The code in the previous section is modified in this section to create the Multi-threaded Temperature Service in Listing 11-10, which is available in the chp11/threadedTemperatureServer directory. In this example, the network request and response string lengths are short (e.g., "getTemperature" and "25.5555"). Also, it is unlikely that you will need to check the room temperature every fraction of a second. Therefore, a multi-threaded approach is overkill in this example. However, this structure is very important for applications that stream data, so it is useful to be exposed to it.

LISTING 11-10: chp11/threadedTemperatureServer/network/ ConnectionHandler.cpp

```
int ConnectionHandler::readAnalog(int number){ ... // same as before }

float ConnectionHandler::getTemperature(int adc_value){ ... // same as before }

void ConnectionHandler::threadLoop(){
    cout << "*** Created a Handler threaded Function" << endl;
    string rec = this->receive(1024);
    if (rec == "getTemperature"){
        cout << "Received from the client [" << rec << "]" << endl;
        stringstream ss;
        ss << this->getTemperature(this->readAnalog(0));
        this->send(ss.str());
        cout << "Sent [" << ss.str() << "]" << endl;
    }
    else {
        cout << "Received from the client [" << rec << "]" << endl;
        this->send(string("Unknown Command"));
    }
    cout << "*** End of the Connection Handler Function" << endl;
    this->parent->notifyHandlerDeath(this);
}
```

The Temperature Server code can be tested by using the `temperatureClientTest` CLI test application, which is in the same directory as the server, by using the following:

```
~/exploringBB/chp11/threadedTemperatureServer$ ./temperatureServer
Starting EBB Server Example
Listening for a connection...
```

Then execute the test client in a different terminal:

```
~/.../threadedTemperatureServer$ ./temperatureClientTest localhost
Starting EBB Temperature Client Test
Sending [getTemperature]
Received [25.498]
End of EBB Temperature Client Test
```

The `localhost` host name is resolved to the loopback address 127.0.0.1, which enables the BBB to communicate with itself. If the client application outputs a temperature (e.g., 25.498°C), then this test is successful and the Qt fat-client GUI application should also connect to the server, as illustrated in Figure 11-14.

The Fat-Client as a Server

In the last example, the Qt fat-client GUI application initiates contact with the BBB Temperature Service using the IP address (or host name) of the server and the port number of the service. It is possible to reverse this relationship by programming the GUI application to be the server and the BBB to be a client. Clearly, such a change would mean that the BBB is responsible for establishing communication with the GUI application, so it would therefore need to know the desktop computer's IP address and service port number.

For a single-client to single-server arrangement, the choice of which device is to be the server is not that important. The choice is likely resolved by deciding which party is most likely to initiate contact and then choosing it as the client. In fact, it would be possible to build client and server functionality into both parties, but that would add significant complexity to the program design. However, for single-party to multiple-party relationships, the decision is clearer. For example, the Temperature Service application is designed so that many client applications can make contact with a single server. It would be extremely difficult to reverse the client/server relationship in that case, as the BBB temperature sensor would have to somehow identify and push the temperature reading to each and every GUI application.

There are applications for which it is appropriate for the GUI application to be the server and for the BBB to act as the client. This is especially the case if one GUI application is responsible for aggregating sensor readings from many services and/or BBB devices. Figure 11-15 illustrates one such example. In this example the BBB is attached to the ADXL345 accelerometer using the I^2C bus. The BBB streams accelerometer data to the GUI application, which provides a "live" graphical display of the ADXL345's pitch and roll values. For brevity, this example uses one BBB client, but it could easily be adapted to use multiple clients and either display multiple GUI interfaces or average the sample data.

In this example, the controls on the Qt GUI Server application are *not used for input*; rather, they dynamically change according to the ADXL345's pitch and roll values—the only input controls on the GUI application are the Exit button and the menu. The current pitch and roll values are each described by three Qt widgets: a QDoubleSpinBox at the top, which displays the value as a double; a QDial, which rotates as the value changes from −90° to +90° (0° is when the dial indicator is at the very top); and a graduated QSlider which slides from −90° to +90° (0° is the center value). This application differs from the previous Qt GUI application in a number of ways:

- The BBB is the client and the GUI application is the server.
- The BBB sends a continuous stream of one thousand readings, each sent every 50ms. The GUI display is updated instantly without latency problems (geographical distance would have an impact).

■ The GUI application is threaded so that it can be "lively." A thread object is created to handle communication with the client so that the main loop can continue its role. If a thread were not used, then you would not be able to exit by clicking the Exit button.

■ The messaging protocol is much more sophisticated, as it uses XML data to communicate. This issue is discussed shortly.

The Qt GUI Server application is available in the Git repository directory /chp11/ QtSocketsAccelerometer and the BBB client application is available in the directory /chp11/ADXL345Client. Listing 11-11 provides the core thread loop that is used to communicate with the ADXL345 sensor client. Using threads in this way means that the code structure could be easily adapted for simultaneous communication with many client devices.

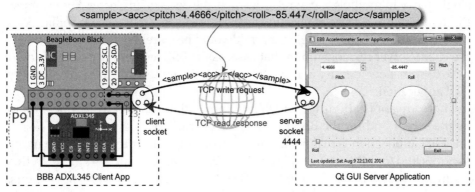

Figure 11-15: The Qt Accelerometer Client/Server application

LISTING 11-11: /chp11/QtSocketsAccelerometer/serverthread.cpp (segment)

```
void ServerThread::run(){                    // the main thread loop
   QTcpSocket clientSocket;                   // the clientSocket object
   this->running = true;                      // the main thread loop bool flag
   if (!clientSocket.setSocketDescriptor(socketDescriptor)){ //set up socket
      qDebug() << "Failed to setup the Socket";  // debug output
   }
   while(running){                            // loop forever until flag changes
      if(!clientSocket.waitForReadyRead(1000)){ // wait for up to 1 sec.
         this->running = false;               // failed - exit the loop
      }
      while(clientSocket.bytesAvailable()>0)   // are bytes available?
      {
         int x = clientSocket.bytesAvailable();  // how many?
         qDebug() << "There are " << x << " bytes available"; // debug
         char data[2000];                     // capacity for up to 2000 bytes
         x = (qint64) clientSocket.read(&data[0], (qint64) x);
```

```
                data[x] = '\0';                      // add null in case of print output
                this->parse(&data[0]);               // parse the XML string
        }
    }
    clientSocket.close();                            // if loop finished, close socket
    qDebug() << "The client just disconnected";      // debug output
}
```

The Qt GUI Server application has a number of classes, as illustrated in Figure 11-16. The `QMainWindow` object is created when the application is executed. Its primary role is to update the UI, which it performs using a slot called `sample-Consume()` that receives an object of the `SensorSample` class when data is sent to the server. The `SensorSample` object contains a pitch value and a roll value, which are used to update the UI components.

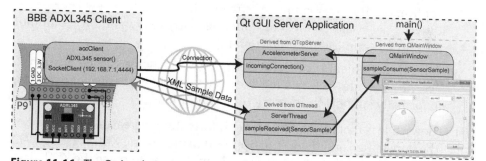

Figure 11-16: The Qt Accelerometer Client/Server application program structure

When the `QMainWindow` object is created, it instantiates an object of the `AccelerometerServer` class (child of `QTcpServer`). This server object awaits an incoming connection; when it receives one, it creates an object of the `ServerThread` class (child of `QThread`). The `ServerThread` object then forms a read/write connection with the BBB ADXL345 Client application. The client application sends the accelerometer data in XML form, which the `ServerThread` object parses to create a `SensorSample` object. If the data is parsed successfully, a signal is triggered that passes the `SensorSample` object to the `sampleConsume()` slot.

NOTE Both GUI client/server applications could be executed on a single BBB by using the loopback address (127.0.0.1) as the server IP address.

Parsing Stream Data

One criticism of the earlier approach of sending string data back and forth between the client and the server is that it is prone to parsing errors, particularly as the complexity of communication increases. One solution to this problem is to use an XML format to communicate between the client and the server. This example uses a simple XML format to pass the messages:

```
<sample><acc><pitch>4.4666</pitch><roll>-85.447</roll></acc></sample>
```

The Qt framework has full support for XML parsing in the `QtXml` module by using the `QXmlStreamReader` class. It can be used to efficiently convert such an XML string into a data structure, which offers the following advantages:

- It is possible to recover from communication errors should the data stream be corrupted—for example, by searching for the next valid tag in the stream.

- Having a human-readable format can greatly help in debugging code.

- Additional tags can be added to the stream and it will not affect legacy applications that are reading the stream—for example, a new `<gyro>` ... `</gyro>` tag could be introduced to the `<sample>` tag and it would not prevent this application from running.

- A DTD (document type definition) or XML Schema can be written to describe the rules (e.g., nesting and occurrence of elements) for the XML, to formally support third-party communication.

The downside is that the additional tag information increases the amount of data to be transmitted and there is an overhead in processing XML. Listing 11-12 provides the source code that is used in this application to parse the XML data that is sent from the BBB ADXL345 Client application.

LISTING 11-12: /chp11/QtSocketsAccelerometer/serverthread.cpp (segment)

```cpp
int ServerThread::parse(char *data){
  QXmlStreamReader xml(data);
  while(!xml.atEnd() && !xml.hasError()){
    if((xml.tokenType()==QXmlStreamReader::StartElement) &&     // found <sample>
       (xml.name()=="sample")){
      // this is a data sample <sample> - need to loop until </sample>
      float pitch = 0.0f, roll = 0.0f;
      xml.readNext();                                           // read next token
      while(!((xml.tokenType()==QXmlStreamReader::EndElement)&&  // </sample>
              (xml.name()=="sample"))){
        qDebug() << "Found a sample";
        if((xml.tokenType()==QXmlStreamReader::StartElement)       // <acc>
              &&(xml.name()=="acc")){
          xml.readNext();
          qDebug() << "-- it has an acceleration element";
          while(!((xml.tokenType()==QXmlStreamReader::EndElement)  // </acc>
                  &&(xml.name()=="acc"))){
            if(xml.tokenType() == QXmlStreamReader::StartElement){ // <pitch>
              if(xml.name() == "pitch") {
                QString temp = xml.readElementText();  // read the value
```

```
            pitch = (temp).toFloat();                    // convert to float
          }
          if(xml.name() == "roll") {               // <roll>
            QString temp = xml.readElementText();
            roll = (temp).toFloat();
          }
        }
      }
      xml.readNext();
    }
  }
  xml.readNext();
}
SensorSample sample(pitch, roll);    // create a sample object and
emit sampleReceived(sample);         // emit it as a signal – caught
}                                    // by a slot in mainWindow, which
xml.readNext();                      // updates the display widgets
}
return 0;
}
```

An alternative solution is to use *JavaScript object notation* (*JSON*), which is also human-readable and is commonly used to transmit data between server and web applications. The C++ Boost library, which is discussed in the next chapter, has full support for parsing JSON code. The same accelerometer data could be transmitted in the JSON format as follows:

```
{
    "acc": {
        "pitch": 32.55,
        "roll": 65.55
    }
}
```

The BBB Client Application

In this application example, the more complex programming is in the Qt GUI server application and not in the BBB client. In fact, the code for the BBB client application (provided in Listing 11-13) is quite straightforward. It uses the library of code that is developed throughout this book, and simple string processing to structure the XML messages that are transmitted.

LISTING 11-13: /exploringBB/chp11/ADXL345Client/accClient.cpp

```
#include <iostream>
#include "network/SocketClient.h"      // using the EBB library
#include "bus/I2CDevice.h"             // I2CDevice class see CHP8
#include "sensor/ADXL345.h"            // ADXL345 see CHP8
#include "sstream"                     // to format the string
```

continues

LISTING 11-13: *(continued)*

```
#include <unistd.h>                          // for the usleep()
using namespace std;
using namespace exploringBB;

int main(int argc, char *argv[]){
   if(argc!=2){
      cout << "Usage:  accClient server_name" << endl;
      return 2;
   }
   cout << "Starting EBB ADXL345 Client Example" << endl;
   I2CDevice i2c(1,0x53);                    // the I2C device P9_19 P9_20
   ADXL345 sensor(&i2c);                     // pass device to ADXL const.
   sensor.setResolution(ADXL345::NORMAL);    // regular resolution
   sensor.setRange(ADXL345::PLUSMINUS_4_G);  // regular +/- 2G
   SocketClient sc(argv[1], 4444);           // server addr and port number
   sc.connectToServer();                     // connect to the server
   for(int i=0; i<1000; i++){                // going to send 1000 samples
      stringstream ss;                       // use a stringstream for msg.
      sensor.readSensorState();              // update the sensor state
      float pitch = sensor.getPitch();       // get pitch and roll
      float roll = sensor.getRoll();         // structure as XML string
      ss << "<sample><acc><pitch>" << pitch << "</pitch>";
      ss << "<roll>" << roll << "</roll></acc></sample>";
      cout << ss.str() << '\xd';             // print to output on one line
      cout.flush();                          // flush to update the display
      sc.send(ss.str());                     // send the same str to server
      usleep(50000);                         // 50ms between samples
   }
   cout << "End of EBB Client Example" << endl;
}
```

The code can be built using the build script and can be executed by providing the address of the server machine, which is 192.168.7.1 in this case:

```
molloyd@beaglebone:~/.../ADXL345Client$ ./accClient 192.168.7.1
Starting EBB ADXL345 Client Example
<sample><acc><pitch>0.493899</pitch><roll>0.493899</roll></acc></sample>
```

The display continually updates on the same line while sending data to the server application. The use of XML messages and server threads means that the client application can be stopped and restarted without requiring the server application to be restarted.

Cross-Compiling Qt Applications

In Chapter 7, the Eclipse IDE is configured to cross-compile C/C++ applications for the BBB using desktop Linux. The Qt Creator IDE can also be configured on a desktop machine to cross-compile, remotely deploy, and remotely debug applications for the BBB. As with Eclipse, cross-development when using Qt Creator is best performed on a Linux desktop machine.

The first step is to configure a "BeagleBone Kit" in the IDE options. This step requires that you have installed a cross-development toolchain (see the first section in Chapter 7). Figure 11-17 displays the settings required for the "BeagleBone Kit."

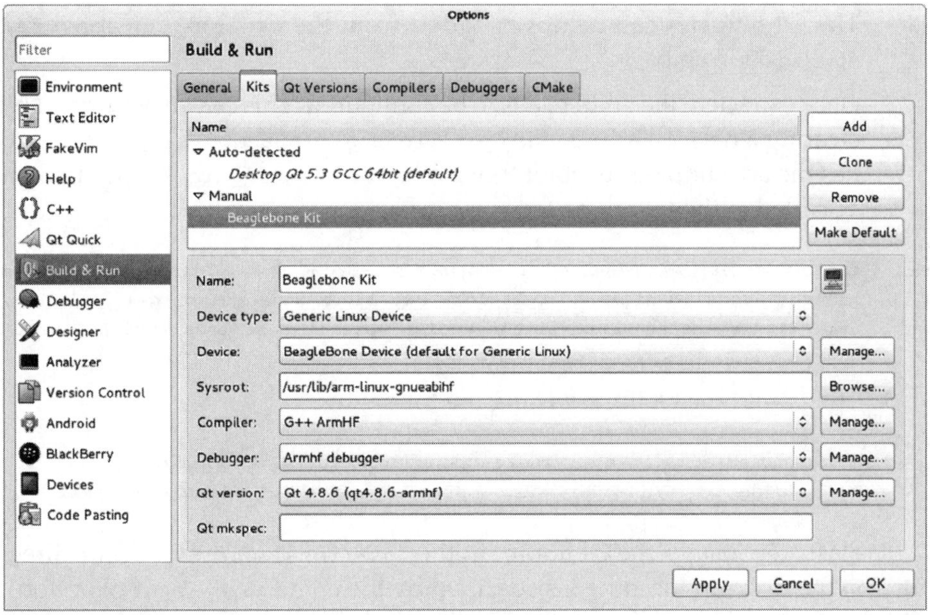

Figure 11-17: Qt Creator "BeagleBone Kit" configuration

To the right of each key setting is a Manage button. The settings required for each of these configuration options are as follows:

- The Device setting should be a "Generic Linux" device that is authenticated by password. Enter your username and password, and the BBB IP address. The connection should use SSH (port 22).

- The Compiler setting can be added manually by providing the compiler path (e.g., `/usr/bin/arm-linux-gnueabihf-g++`). Qt Creator will automatically detect the ABI.

- The Debugger setting can be added manually by providing the compiler path (e.g., `/usr/bin/gdb-multiarch`).

- The Qt version setting can be added manually by browsing and locating an appropriate qmake version. In this kit the path is `/usr/local/`

`qt4.8.6-armhf/bin/qmake`, which is consistent with the version of Qt that is installed on the BBB. Unfortunately, this version of the Qt libraries had to be built manually from source.

Building the Qt Libraries from Source

The exact steps for building the Qt libraries from source are available on the chapter web page, but here is a summary of the steps involved:

1. The Qt libraries can be downloaded from the `www.qt-project.org/ downloads` web page.

2. Once extracted, the build needs to be configured. This can be performed by creating a new `makespecs` file (`qws/linux-arm-gnueabi-g++`) that identifies the arm-linux-gnueabihf toolchain. The `./configure` script can then be called in the following form:

```
molloyd@debian:~/qt-everywhere-opensource-src-4.8.6$ ./configure -v -ope
nsource -confirm-license -xplatform qws/linux-arm-gnueabi-g++ -embedded
arm -little-endian -host-little-endian -prefix /usr/local/qt4.8.6-armhf
```

3. Then build the Qt library using the following:

```
molloyd@debian:~/qt-everywhere-opensource-src-4.8.6$ make
molloyd@debian:~/qt-everywhere-opensource-src-4.8.6$ make install
```

The last step installs the Qt library in the `/usr/local/qt4.8.6-armhf` directory on the desktop machine (as specified by the `configure -prefix` option). This is important, as otherwise the install step may overwrite your desktop Qt libraries with libraries that contain ARM machine instructions.

It is possible that this library is not compatible with the Qt library that is installed on the BBB itself. If that is the case, the library files in the `/usr/local/ qt4.8.6-armhf` directory can be copied (using scp) to the BBB, replacing the existing library files. The instructions for this step and how to enable the touch screen interface are available on the chapter web page.

Remote Deploying a Test Application

To test the final installation you can remotely deploy a simple console application to the BBB, such as the following:

```
#include <QCoreApplication>
#include <iostream>
```

```
using namespace std;
int main(int argc, char *argv[]){
    QCoreApplication a(argc, argv);
    cout << "Hello BeagleBone from a console application" << endl;
    return a.exec();
}
```

Choose BeagleBone Kit and then modify the project .pro file so that the target destination on the BBB is defined. Here is an example:

```
TARGET = BBBConsoleApp
    target.files = BBBConsoleApp
    target.path = /home/molloyd/temp
INSTALLS +=target
```

Choosing the menu options Project ➤ Build and Project ➤ Run should result in the application executing directly on the BBB.

Summary

After completing this chapter, you should be able to do the following:

- Configure the BBB as a general-purpose computing device and use Bluetooth peripherals to control it.
- Acquire hardware for LCD touch screen display applications.
- Use virtual network computing (VNC) to remotely execute graphical user interface (GUI) applications on the BBB.
- Build rich user interface (UI) applications that execute directly on the BBB using the GTK+ and Qt frameworks.
- Build Qt applications with advanced interfaces that interface to hardware sensors on the BBB.
- Build fat-client remote Qt applications that communicate using TCP sockets to a server that is executing on the BBB.
- Enhance TCP server code to be multi-threaded, in order to allow multiple simultaneous connections from TCP client applications.
- Build remote Qt GUI server applications that communicate, using TCP sockets and XML, to a client application on the BBB.
- Install a Qt Creator cross-development platform under desktop Linux for cross-building Qt applications and remotely deploying them to the BBB.

Further Reading

The following additional links provide further information on the topics in this chapter:

- Chapter web page: `www.exploringbeaglebone.com/chapter11`
- Core documentation on GTK+2.0: `tiny.cc/ebb1103`
- Qt Signals and Slots: `tiny.cc/ebb1104`

# CHAPTER 12

Images, Video, and Audio

In this chapter, USB peripherals are attached to the BBB so that it can be used for capturing image, video, and audio data using low-level Linux drivers and APIs. It describes Linux applications and tools that can be used to stream captured video and audio data to the Internet. Open Source Computer Vision (OpenCV) image processing and computer vision approaches are investigated that enable the BBB to draw inferences from the information content of the captured image data. Capture and playback of audio streams is described, along with the use of Bluetooth audio. The chapter also covers some applications of audio on the BBB, including streaming audio, Internet radio, and text-to-speech. The chapter finishes by describing how you can build a simple Bluetooth talking clock and thermometer.

Equipment Required for This Chapter:

- BeagleBone Black
- Linux USB webcam (ideally the Logitech HD Pro C920)
- USB audio and/or Bluetooth adapter

Further resources for this chapter are available at www.exploringbeaglebone .com/chapter12/.

Capturing Images and Video

In this section, the BBB is used as a platform for capturing image and video data from USB webcams and saving the data on the BBB file system. This is useful for BBB applications such as robotics, home security, home automation, and aeronautics, when networked image streaming is not an available option—for example, if the application is untethered and distant from a wireless network. With suitable peripherals, the BBB can be used to capture very high-quality video streams, which can be viewed asynchronously. The durations of the video streams are limited only by the available storage on the BBB—remember that Chapter 3 describes an approach for mounting a high-capacity micro-SD card on the BBB file system. Alternatively, the video can be streamed to the network, which is discussed in the next section of this chapter.

> **NOTE**   A full video on video capture and image processing on the BBB is available at `tiny.cc/ebb1201`. This video enables you to personally evaluate the quality of the video data described in this chapter.

USB Webcams

There are camera capes available for the BBB, such as the QuickLogic CAM I/F CSSP that is illustrated in Chapter 1, Figure 1-10(c). It uses the BBB's general-purpose memory interface (GPMC), which conflicts with the eMMC and therefore requires system boot from the SD card. It supports a five-megapixel camera at 10 frames per second, and it consumes less power than a USB webcam. More information is available at `tiny.cc/ebb1202`.

The main focus in this section is USB webcams, as they are widely available and can be reused as a general-purpose desktop peripheral. The Logitech HD C270 ($26), HD C310 ($30), and HD Pro C920 ($70), shown in Figure 12-1, are chosen, as they are commonly available HD cameras that are known to function under Linux. In fact, for the following tests the three cameras are connected simultaneously to the BBB using the USB hub displayed in Figure 1-8(c). It is not a powered USB hub, but the BBB is connected to a 5V, 2A supply in this case.

Figure 12-1: Logitech USB HD webcams (a) C270, (b) C310, and (c) C920

WARNING   Similarly to Wi-Fi adapters, many problems with USB webcams are caused by low power. The camera LED may indicate that the camera is working, but the lack of power may result in data transmission problems. You should use a powered USB hub or power the BBB using an external 5V power supply.

When the three USB cameras are connected to the BBB at the same time using a USB hub, the "list USB devices" utility provides the following output:

```
molloyd@beaglebone:~$ lsusb
Bus 001 Device 002: ID 1a40:0201 Terminus Technology Inc. FE 2.1 7-port Hub
Bus 001 Device 001: ID 1d6b:0002 Linux Foundation 2.0 root hub
Bus 002 Device 001: ID 1d6b:0002 Linux Foundation 2.0 root hub
Bus 001 Device 003: ID 046d:082d Logitech, Inc.
Bus 001 Device 004: ID 041e:30d3 Creative Technology, Sound Blaster Play!
Bus 001 Device 005: ID 0a5c:21e8 Broadcom Corp.
Bus 001 Device 006: ID 0d8c:013c C-Media Electronics,Inc.CM108 Audio
Bus 001 Device 007: ID 046d:0825 Logitech, Inc. Webcam C270
Bus 001 Device 009: ID 046d:081b Logitech, Inc. Webcam C310
```

The output lists the device IDs for the cameras, two USB sound adapters, and a Bluetooth adapter. The fact that "Logitech" is listed against the device IDs indicates that some level of Linux support is already present on the BBB for these devices. If this is not the case, then you will have to source proprietary Linux drivers from the webcam manufacturer. Typically, such drivers would have to be built and deployed on the BBB before the webcam could be used.

Full information about the modes that are available on the USB cameras can be displayed using the following:

```
molloyd@beaglebone:~$ lsusb -v|less
```

This command results in detailed and verbose output. In addition, the loadable kernel modules (LKMs) that are currently loaded can be listed using the following command:

```
molloyd@beaglebone:~$ lsmod
Module               Size    Used by
libcomposite        15028    1 g_multi
bluetooth          159258    24 bnep,btusb,rfcomm
uvcvideo            57013    0
snd_hwdep            4885    1 snd_usb_audio
videobuf2_vmalloc    2490    1 uvcvideo     ...
```

The uvcvideo LKM supports UVC (USB video class) compliant devices, such as the three webcams that are attached. The videobuf2_vmalloc LKM is the memory allocator for the Video4Linux video buffer. If everything is working as expected, there should be new video and audio devices available, which can be listed using the following:

```
molloyd@beaglebone:~$ ls /dev/{vid,aud}*
/dev/audio    /dev/audio2   /dev/audio4   /dev/video0   /dev/video2
/dev/audio1   /dev/audio3   /dev/audio5   /dev/video1
```

The device /dev/audio is mapped to the HDMI audio device, which will only appear if the HDMI cape is enabled. The other audio devices are mapped to the two USB audio adapters and the three USB webcams.

Video4Linux2 (V4L2)

Video4Linux2 (V4L2) is a video capture driver framework that is tightly integrated with the Linux kernel and is supported by the uvcvideo LKM. It provides drivers for video devices, such as webcams, PCI video capture cards, and TV (DVB-T/S) tuner cards/peripherals. V4L2 primarily supports video (and audio) devices through the following types of interfaces:

- **Video capture interface:** Used to capture video from capture devices, such as webcams, TV tuners, or video capture devices
- **Video output interface:** For video output devices, e.g., video transmission devices or video streaming devices
- **Video overlay interface:** Enables the direct display of the video data without requiring the data to be processed by the CPU
- **Video blanking interval (VBI) interface:** Provides access to legacy data that is transmitted during the VBI of an analog video signal (e.g., teletext)
- **Radio interface:** Provides access to AM/FM tuner audio streams

V4L2 provides support for many types of devices, and simply put: it is complex! In addition to supporting video input/output, the V4L2 API also has stubs for codec and video effect devices, which enable manipulation of the video stream data. The focus in this section is on the capture of video data from webcam devices using V4L2 by performing the following steps (not necessarily in this order):

- Opening the V4L2 device
- Changing the device properties (e.g., camera brightness)
- Agreeing on a data format and input/output method
- Performing the transfer of data
- Closing the V4L2 device

The main source of documentation on V4L2 is available from `www.kernel.org` at `tiny.cc/ebb1203`, and the V4L2 API specification is available at `tiny.cc/ebb1204`.

> **NOTE** The examples that follow in this chapter are written with the assumption that you have configured a display for your BBB, as described in Chapter 11. For example, a VNC client/server (e.g., Xming or VNC Viewer) allows the output images to be displayed on your desktop machine. An alternative approach is to `sftp` image files back and forth between the desktop machine and the BBB.

Image Capture Utility

The first step is to install the V4L2 development libraries, abstraction layer, utilities, and a simple webcam application for V4L2-compatible devices. Always update the package lists, to get information about the newest packages and their dependencies, before installing a system library:

```
molloyd@beaglebone:~$ sudo apt-get update
molloyd@beaglebone:~$ apt-cache search v4l2
fswebcam - Tiny and flexible webcam program
libv4l-dev - Collection of video4linux support libraries ...
```

Then, install the packages that are required for this section:

```
molloyd@beaglebone:~$ sudo apt-get install libv4l-dev v4l-utils fswebcam
 gpicview libav-tools
```

The fswebcam application can then be used to test that the attached web camera is working correctly. It is a surprisingly powerful and easy-to-use application that is best used by writing a configuration file, as shown in Listing 12-1, which contains settings for choosing the device, capture resolution, output file type, and the addition of a title banner. It can even be used on a continuous loop by adding a `loop` entry that specifies the time in seconds between frame captures.

LISTING 12-1: /exploringBB/chp12/fswebcam/fswebcam.conf

```
device /dev/video0
input 0
resolution 1280x720
bottom-banner
font /usr/share/fonts/truetype/ttf-dejavu/DejaVuSans.ttf
title "Exploring BeagleBone"
timestamp "%H:%M:%S %d/%m/%Y (%Z)"
png 0
save exploringBB.png
```

The fswebcam application can be configured with these settings by passing it the configuration filename on execution:

```
.../chp12/fswebcam$ ls
fswebcam.conf
.../chp12/fswebcam$ fswebcam -c fswebcam.conf
--- Opening /dev/video0... Trying source module v412...
/dev/video0 opened. --- Capturing frame...  ...
```

The image can then be viewed using gpicview, which requires that you have attached a display to the BBB, such as a VNC connection:

```
.../chp12/fswebcam$ gpicview exploringBB.png
```

This will result in output like that in Figure 12-2. The image data has been modified to include a formatted bottom text banner, which contains a title, and the date and time of image capture. Sample full-resolution capture images are available on the chapter web page.

Figure 12-2: The fswebcam webcam capture (640x360) displayed using gpicview via Xming

Interestingly, the fswebcam application could be executed on a loop and combined with the Apache web server (as described in Chapter 10) to create a simple web camera, which uses a web page that links to the captured image file present on the BBB file system.

Video4Linux2 Utilities

V4L2 provides a set of user-space utilities that can be used for obtaining information about connected V4L2-compatible devices. It is also possible to use the user-space utilities to change camera settings; however, it is possible that executed applications will be programmed to override such changes. The most important role of these tools is to verify that connected V4L2 devices are functioning correctly. You can list the available V4L2 devices using the following:

```
molloyd@beaglebone:~$ v4l2-ctl --list-devices
HD Pro Webcam C920 (usb-musb-hdrc.1.auto-1.1): /dev/video0
UVC Camera (046d:081b) (usb-musb-hdrc.1.auto-1.6): /dev/video1
UVC Camera (046d:0825) (usb-musb-hdrc.1.auto-1.7): /dev/video2
```

The devices appear in the order in which they are attached to the USB hub. You can get information about a particular device by listing its modes (where -d 0 refers to the HD Pro C920 in this instance):

```
molloyd@beaglebone:~$ v4l2-ctl --all -d 0
Driver Info (not using libv4l2):
        Driver name   : uvcvideo
        Card type     : HD Pro Webcam C920
        Bus info      : usb-musb-hdrc.1.auto-1.1
        Driver version: 3.8.13
        Capabilities  : 0x84000001  Video Capture  Streaming
```

Certain controls can be used to configure a camera, which can be accessed using the –list-ctrls option, as follows:

```
molloyd@beaglebone:~$ v4l2-ctl --list-ctrls -d 0
    brightness (int) : min=0 max=255 step=1 default=128 value=128
      contrast (int) : min=0 max=255 step=1 default=128 value=128
    saturation (int) : min=0 max=255 step=1 default=128 value=128
          gain (int) : min=0 max=255 step=1 default=0 value=0  ...
```

For the C920, other controls include white balance, color temperature, sharpness, backlight compensation, exposure (auto or absolute), focus, zoom, and support for pan/tilt. For example, to change the brightness on device 0 to 100 (currently 128 as shown in the preceding snippet), you can use the following:

```
molloyd@beaglebone:~$ v4l2-ctl --set-ctrl=brightness=100 -d 0
molloyd@beaglebone:~$ v4l2-ctl --list-ctrls -d 0 |grep brightness
    brightness (int) : min=0 max=255 step=1 default=128 value=100
```

You can also list the modes of the cameras. In this case there are three different video capture pixel formats, with *fourcc* color space video codes: 'YUYV'(a common broadcast format with one luminance and two chrominance channels), 'H264'(a common modern interframe video compression format), and 'MJPG'(a common, but older, intraframe-only motion JPEG video compression format). The listing is obtained using the following:

```
molloyd@beaglebone:~$ v4l2-ctl --list-formats -d 0
ioctl: VIDIOC_ENUM_FMT
        Index       : 0                  Type    : Video Capture
        Pixel Format: 'YUYV'            Name    : YUV 4:2:2 (YUYV)
        Index       : 1                  Type    : Video Capture
        Pixel Format: 'H264' (compressed)  Name    : H.264
        Index       : 2                  Type    : Video Capture
        Pixel Format: 'MJPG' (compressed)  Name    : MJPEG
```

The C270 and C310 cameras do not have a H.264 mode, but they both have 'YUYV' and 'MJPG' compressed pixel formats at indices 0 and 1 respectively. It is possible to explicitly set the resolution and pixel format of a camera as follows:

```
~$ v4l2-ctl --set-fmt-video=width=1920,height=1080,pixelformat=1 -d 0
~$ v4l2-ctl --all -d 0
Driver Info (not using libv4l2):
        Driver name   : uvcvideo
        Card type     : HD Pro Webcam C920 . . .
        Capabilities  : 0x84000001      Video Capture      Streaming
Format Video Capture:
        Width/Height  : 1920/1080       Pixel Format      : 'H264'
        Field         : None            Bytes per Line    : 3840
        Size Image    : 4147200         Colorspace        : SRGB
Crop Capability Video Capture:
        Bounds        : Left 0, Top 0, Width 1920, Height 1080
        Default       : Left 0, Top 0, Width 1920, Height 1080
        Pixel Aspect  : 1/1
Video input : 0 (Camera 1: ok)
Streaming Parameters Video Capture:
        Capabilities  : timeperframe    Frames per second: 30.000 (30/1)
        Read buffers  : 0               Priority: 2
```

This output provides very useful state information, such as the resolution, video frame image size, frame rate, and so on.

Writing Video4Linux2 Programs

As with other devices in Linux (e.g., SPI in Chapter 8), it is possible to send data to and receive data from a video device by opening its /dev/videoX file system entry by using a call to open(). Unfortunately, such an approach would not provide the level of control or the performance level that is required for video devices. Instead, low-level input/output control (ioctl()) calls are required to configure the settings of the device, and memory map (mmap()) calls are used to perform image frame memory copy, rather than using a byte-by-byte serial transfer.

The Git repository contains programs in the /chp12/v4l2/ directory that use V4L2 and its low-level ioctl() calls to perform video frame capture and video capture tasks:

- `grabber.c`: Grabs raw image frame data from a webcam into memory using libv4l2. The images can be written to the file system.

- `capture.c`: Grabs raw video data to a stream or file. It does this quickly enough to be used for real-time video capture.

These code examples are almost entirely based on the examples that are provided by the V4L2 project team. The code is too long to display here, but you can view it in the Git repository. To build and execute the code examples, use the following steps:

```
.../chp12/v4l2$ ls *.c
capture.c  grabber.c
.../chp12/v4l2$ gcc -O2 -Wall `pkg-config --cflags --libs libv4l2`
  grabber.c -o grabber
.../chp12/v4l2$ gcc -O2 -Wall `pkg-config --cflags --libs libv4l2`
  capture.c -o capture
.../chp12/v4l2$ ./grabber
.../chp12/v4l2$ ls *.ppm
grabber000.ppm  grabber005.ppm  grabber010.ppm  grabber015.ppm ...
.../chp12/v4l2$ gpicview grabber000.ppm
```

The .ppm file format describes an uncompressed color image format, which gpicview will display. You can use the "forward" button on gpicview to step through the 20 image frames. To capture data using the `capture.c` program, use a selection of the following options:

```
molloyd@beaglebone:~/exploringBB/chp12/v4l2$ ./capture -h
Usage: ./capture [options]
Version 1.3    Options:
-d | --device name   Video device name [/dev/video0] ...
-f | --format        Force format to 640x480 YUYV
-F | --formatH264    Force format to 1920x1080 H264
-c | --count         Number of frames to grab [100] - use 0 for infinite
Example usage: capture -F -o -c 300 > output.raw
Captures 300 frames of H264 at 1920x1080. Use raw2mpg4 script to convert
to mpg4
```

If you have the C920 camera, you can capture 100 frames of H.264 data using the first of the following commands. A second command then converts the .raw file to a .mp4 file format, which can be played on a desktop machine:

```
.../chp12/v4l2$ ./capture -d /dev/video0 -F -o -c 100 > output.raw
Force Format 2
.................................................................
.../chp12/v4l2$ avconv -f h264 -i output.raw -vcodec copy output.mp4
.../chp12/v4l2$ ls -l output*
-rw-r--r-- 1 molloyd molloyd 2065429 Sep  8 01:23 output.mp4
-rw-r--r-- 1 molloyd molloyd 2063177 Sep  8 01:22 output.raw
```

The file sizes are almost identical because the video data is actually captured in a raw H.264 format. The conversion is performed using the `avconv` (Libav) utility, which is a fork of the FFmpeg project that is better supported by the Debian Linux distribution. The `-vcodec copy` option enables the video to be copied without transcoding the video data format.

The `capture.c` program can also be used with cameras such as the C270 and C310, which do not have hardware H.264 functionality; however, the capabilities are more limited:

```
...$ v4l2-ctl --set-fmt-video=width=1280,height=720,pixelformat=1 -d 1
...$ v4l2-ctl --all -d 1
Format Video Capture: Width/Height:1280/720   Pixel Format:'MJPG'
.../chp12/v4l2$ ./capture -d /dev/video1 -o -c 100 > output.raw
Force Format 0 .........................................
.../chp12/v4l2$ ls -l output.raw
-rw-r--r-- 1 molloyd molloyd 4476448 Sep  8 01:58 output.raw
.../chp12/v4l2$ avconv -f mjpeg -i output.raw output.mp4
.../chp12/v4l2$ ls -l output.mp4
-rw-r--r-- 1 molloyd molloyd 1456040 Sep  8 02:06 output.mp4
```

The video conversion using avconv can take quite some time on the BBB! In this example you can see that the H.264 video file requires significantly less space than the MJPEG file, as it is a more efficient interframe video encoding format.

> **NOTE** A common problem arises when using the `capture.c` program: The camera returns a "select timeout" error. If this arises, then you need to change the time-out properties of the uvcvideo LKM as follows:

```
molloyd@beaglebone:~$ sudo rmmod uvcvideo
molloyd@beaglebone:~$ sudo modprobe uvcvideo nodrop=1 timeout=5000
molloyd@beaglebone:~$ lsmod |grep uvcvideo
uvcvideo              57013  0
videobuf2_vmalloc      2490  1 uvcvideo
```

Streaming Video

It is possible to use the BBB to capture and stream live video. The Logitech C920 is particularly useful for this purpose, as it has a built-in H.264 hardware encoder. The raw 1080p H.264 data can be passed directly from the camera stream to the network stream without transcoding, which means that the computational load on the BBB is low. Streaming scripts are available in the `/chp12/v4l2/` repository directory. For example, Listing 12-2 provides a script for sending H.264 video data over UDP to a desktop PC at 192.168.7.1.

```
#!/bin/bash
echo "Video Streaming for the Beaglebone - Exploring BeagleBone"
v4l2-ctl --set-fmt-video=width=1920,height=1080,pixelformat=1
./capture -F -o -c0|avconv -re -i - -vcodec copy -f mpegts udp://192.168.7.1:123
```

This script pipes the raw video output from the capture program to the avconv application, which "copies" the raw data to the network stream using UDP. There is an additional script to multicast the video stream to multiple network points (streamVideoMulti) using the broadcast network address 226.0.0.1 and to stream the video using the Real-Time Transport Protocol (RTP) (streamVideoRTP). A full video on my YouTube channel describes the steps involved in detail: tiny.cc/ebb1205.

It is possible to build a custom Qt application that can receive the video stream on a desktop computer. This can be combined with the Qt client/server applications in Chapter 11 to provide network control and support for video streaming. Further details are available at tiny.cc/ebb1206.

A second BBB can be used to receive the network video stream; however, it does not have sufficient capability to render the HD video stream to a display. Interestingly, it is possible to use a Raspberry Pi B/B+ to capture the UDP stream and display it using a video player that takes advantage of the Raspberry Pi's H.264 hardware decoder. For example, the OMXplayer supports hardware decoding, and it can be used to open the network broadcast stream using the following:

```
molloyd@raspberryPI$ omxplayer -o hdmi udp://226.0.0.1:123
```

The Raspberry PI can decode the C920 video stream and display it live on a monitor, albeit with a varying degree of latency.

Image Processing and Computer Vision

Once a USB camera or camera cape is attached to the BBB, it is possible to capture images and process them using a comprehensive high-level library called Open Source Computer Vision (OpenCV). OpenCV (www.opencv.org) provides a cross-platform library of functions for computer vision, such as gesture recognition, motion understanding, motion tracking, augmented reality, and structure-from-motion. It also provides supporting libraries for applications such as artificial neural networks, support vector machines, classification, and decision tree learning. OpenCV is written in C/C++ and is optimized for real-time applications, including support for multi-core programming. The OpenCV libraries are installed by default on the BBB Debian image.

Image Processing with OpenCV

OpenCV supports V4L2 and provides a high-level interface for capturing image data, which can be used instead of the `grabber.c` program. Listing 12-3 is an OpenCV application that captures data from a webcam and filters it using some simple image processing techniques. The steps that it performs are as follows:

1. Capture of the image from the webcam

2. Conversion of the image into grayscale form

3. Blurring of the image to remove high-frequency noise

4. Detecting regions in the image where the image brightness changes sharply. This is achieved using an image processing operator known as an edge detector—the Canny edge detector in this example

5. Storage of the image files to the BBB file system

OpenCV uses a file-naming convention whereby an `.hpp` file extension is used for header files that contain C++ code. This convention enables a C version of a header file (e.g., `opencv.h`) to coexist alongside a C++ header file (e.g., `opencv .hpp`). Because OpenCV mixes both C and C++ code, this is an appropriate way to distinguish one form from the other.

LISTING 12-3: /exploringBB/chp12/openCV/boneCV.cpp

```cpp
#include<iostream>
#include<opencv2/opencv.hpp>    // C++ OpenCV include file
using namespace std;
using namespace cv;             // using the cv namespace too

int main()
{
    VideoCapture capture(0);    // capturing from /dev/video0
    cout << "Started Processing - Capturing Image" << endl;
    // set any  properties in the VideoCapture object
    capture.set(CV_CAP_PROP_FRAME_WIDTH,1280);   // width in pixels
    capture.set(CV_CAP_PROP_FRAME_HEIGHT,720);   // height in pixels
    capture.set(CV_CAP_PROP_GAIN, 0);            // enable auto gain
    if(!capture.isOpened()){    // connect to the camera
       cout << "Failed to connect to the camera." << endl;
    }
    Mat frame, gray, edges;    // original, grayscale, and edge images
    capture >> frame;          // capture the image to the frame
    if(frame.empty()){         // did the capture succeed?
       cout << "Failed to capture an image" << endl;
       return -1;
    }
    cout << "Processing - Performing Image Processing" << endl;
    cvtColor(frame, gray, CV_BGR2GRAY);    // convert to grayscale
```

```
blur(gray, edges, Size(3,3));           // blur image using a 3x3 kernel
// use Canny edge detector that outputs to the same image
// low threshold = 10, high threshold = 30, kernel size = 3
Canny(edges, edges, 10, 30, 3);         // run Canny edge detector
cout << "Finished Processing - Saving images" << endl;

imwrite("capture.png", frame);          // store the original image
imwrite("grayscale.png", gray);         // store the grayscale image
imwrite("edges.png", edges);            // store the processed edge image
return 0;
}
```

This example can be built and executed as follows, which results in the output displayed in Figure 12-3:

```
.../chp12/openCV$ g++ -O2 `pkg-config --cflags --libs opencv` boneCV.cpp
  -o boneCV
.../chp12/openCV$ ./boneCV
Started Processing - Capturing Image
Processing - Performing Image Processing
Finished Processing - Saving images
.../chp12/openCV$ ls *.png
capture.png   edges.png   grayscale.png
.../chp12/openCV$ gpicview capture.png
```

(a)   (b)

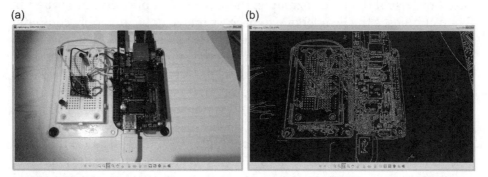

Figure 12-3: The OpenCV image processing example: (a) the webcam image; (b) the edge-processed image

A second example application in the same directory can be used to test the performance of using OpenCV for image processing. In each iteration, it performs an image capture at a 640×480 resolution, converts the image to grayscale form, and performs an edge detection operation. The program performs 100 iterations, after which the execution time is measured:

```
.../chp12/openCV$ ./boneCVtiming
It took 21.2737 seconds to process 100 frames
Capturing and processing 4.70065 frames per second
```

During this test the application uses 95% of CPU and 6% of memory capacity.

> **NOTE** The BBB's AM335x has a NEON SIMD (single instruction multiple data) engine that allows you to perform certain instructions in parallel on multiple data values. The engine is capable of greatly accelerating image processing operations; however, utilizing the engine may require that inline assembly language code is written in your C/C++ programs. Details of the NEON SIMD engine are available at `tiny.cc/ebb1212` and `tiny.cc/ebb1213`.

Computer Vision with OpenCV

Image processing involves manipulating images by filters (e.g., smoothing, contrast enhancement) or transformations (e.g., scaling, rotation, stretching) for purposes such as enhancing or even reducing the information content of digital images. Image processing is one tool that is used in *computer vision*, which often has the goal of "understanding" the information content within digital images.

Computer vision applications often try to replicate the capabilities of human vision by drawing inferences, making decisions, and taking actions based on visual data. For example, the OpenCV application described in this section uses the BeagleBone to process image data and apply computer vision techniques to determine whether a human face is present in a webcam image frame or an image file. Importantly, the approach is designed for face detection, not face recognition. Face detection can be used for applications such as security and photography; however, the processing required has a significant computational overhead and is not suitable for high frame rates on the BBB.

Listing 12-4 provides an example computer vision application that uses OpenCV for face detection. It uses a Harr feature-based cascade classifier, which uses a characterization of adjacent rectangular image regions to identify regions of interest—for example, in human faces the region near the eyes has a darker intensity than the region containing the cheeks. Human faces can be detected using such observations. Usefully, OpenCV provides some codified rules for detecting human faces, which have been used in this example.

Computer vision is an entire research domain, and it requires a significant time investment before you will be able to perform some of its more complex operations. The "Further Reading" section provides links to resources to get you started.

LISTING 12-4: /exploringBB/chp12/openCV/face.cpp

```cpp
#include <iostream>
#include <opencv2/highgui/highgui.hpp>
#include <opencv2/objdetect/objdetect.hpp>
#include <opencv2/imgproc/imgproc.hpp>
using namespace std;
using namespace cv;

int main(int argc, char *args[])
{
   Mat frame;
   VideoCapture *capture;    // capture needs full scope of main(), using ptr
   cout << "Starting face detection application" << endl;
   if(argc==2){  // loading image from a file
      cout << "Loading the image " << args[1] << endl;
      frame = imread(args[1], CV_LOAD_IMAGE_COLOR);
   }
   else {
      cout << "Capturing from the webcam" << endl;
      capture = new VideoCapture(0);
      // set any  properties in the VideoCapture object
      capture->set(CV_CAP_PROP_FRAME_WIDTH,1280);    // width pixels
      capture->set(CV_CAP_PROP_FRAME_HEIGHT,720);    // height pixels
      if(!capture->isOpened()){   // connect to the camera
         cout << "Failed to connect to the camera." << endl;
         return 1;
      }
      *capture >> frame;          // populate the frame with captured image
      cout << "Successfully captured a frame." << endl;
   }
   if (!frame.data){
      cout << "Invalid image data... exiting!" << endl;
      return 1;
   }
// loading the face classifier from a file (standard OpenCV example)
CascadeClassifier faceCascade;
faceCascade.load("haarcascade_frontalface.xml");

// faces is a STL vector of faces - will store the detected faces
std::vector<Rect> faces;
// detect objects in the scene using the classifier above
// (frame, faces, scale factor, min neighbors, flags, min size, max size)
faceCascade.detectMultiScale(frame, faces, 1.1, 3,
                         0 | CV_HAAR_SCALE_IMAGE, Size(50,50));
   if(faces.size()==0){
      cout << "No faces detected!" << endl;     // display the image anyway
   }
// draw oval around the detected faces in the faces vector
for(int i=0; i<faces.size(); i++)
{
   // Using the center point and a rectangle to create an ellipse
```

continues

LISTING 12-4: *(continued)*

```
   Point cent(faces[i].x+faces[i].width*0.5, faces[i].y+faces[i].height*0.5);
   RotatedRect rect(cent, Size(faces[i].width,faces[i].width),0);
   // image, rectangle, color=green, thickness=3, linetype=8
   ellipse(frame, rect, Scalar(0,255,0), 3, 8);
   cout << "Face at: (" << faces[i].x << "," <<faces[i].y << ")" << endl;
   }
   imshow("EBB OpenCV face detection", frame);   // display image results
   imwrite("faceOutput.png", frame);              // save image too
   waitKey(0);                                    // display until key press
   return 0;
   }
```

The face detection example can be built and executed using the following commands:

```
.../chp12/openCV$ g++ -O2 `pkg-config --cflags --libs opencv` face.cpp
-o face
.../chp12/openCV$ ./face
Starting face detection application
Capturing from the webcam
Successfully captured a frame.
Face at: (697,470)  Face at: (470,152)  Face at: (82,192) Face at:
(966,296)
.../chp12/openCV$ ./face Lena.png
Starting face detection application
Loading the image Lena.png
Face at: (217,201)
```

When executed it results in displaying the images in Figure 12-4 (if an X Window session is configured), with ellipses identifying any faces that are detected in the image.

(a)   (b)

Figure 12-4: OpenCV face detection on the BBB: (a) grabbed live using the C270 webcam; (b) loaded from the Lena image file

Boost

Similar to OpenCV, Boost (www.boost.org) provides a comprehensive free library of C++ source code that can be used for many applications on the BBB. There are libraries for multithreading, data structures, algorithms, regular expressions, memory management, mathematics, and more. The range of libraries available is too exhaustive to detail here, but a full listing is available at www.boost.org/doc/libs/. Boost can be installed on the BBB using the following:

```
molloyd@beaglebone:~$ sudo apt-get install libboost-dev
Setting up libboost-dev (1.49.0.1) ...
```

Listing 12-5 provides an example of usage of the Boost library for calculating the geometric distance between two 2-D points.

LISTING 12-5: /exploringBB/chp12/boost/testBoost.cpp

```
#include <boost/geometry.hpp>
#include <boost/geometry/geometries/point_xy.hpp>
using namespace boost::geometry::model::d2;
#include <iostream>

int main(){
    point_xy<float> p1(1.0,2.0), p2(3.0,4.0);
    float distance = boost::geometry::distance(p1,p2);
    std::cout << "The distance between points is: " << distance << std::endl;
    return 0;
}
```

Similarly to OpenCV, it utilizes an .hpp extension form. It also makes extensive use of C++ namespaces. The preceding code can be built and executed using the following:

```
~/exploringBB/chp12/boost$ g++ testBoost.cpp -o testBoost
~/exploringBB/chp12/boost$ ./testBoost
The distance between points is: 2.82843
```

BeagleBone Audio

There are several approaches to utilizing audio inputs and outputs with the BBB, including the following:

- **HDMI audio:** This output is enabled by default on the BBB and allows audio signals to be sent to a television via HDMI (not DVI).

- **USB audio:** Low-cost USB adapters can be attached to the BBB that have Linux driver support for the input/output of audio. In addition, USB webcams can be used as audio input devices.

- **Bluetooth audio:** A Linux-compatible Bluetooth adapter can be used to input from, or output to, external Bluetooth recorder/speaker devices.

- **Multichannel audio serial port (McASP):** The BBB has header pins for McASP that can be used to interface to McASP-capable audio codecs (e.g., the TI TLV320AIC series). This is a complex task that requires proprietary (typically SMT) components.

It is also possible to use the built-in ADC inputs to capture audio events at low sample rates. For example, the SparkFun electret microphone breakout board (BOB-09964) can be connected via an op-amp circuit to the BBB ADC (with a 10kΩ potentiometer on the GND line) and used for tasks such as impact detection (e.g., a door knock). The sample rate of such a microphone circuit could be improved by using an external ADC that has an SPI interface, such as the low-cost ($3) MCP3008, which has eight 10-bit ADCs. In addition, the TI ADS8326 16-bit 250kS/s SPI out could be interfaced to the PRU-ICSS, which is described in Chapter 13.

In this section, the most common approaches are examined, as is software that enables you to perform basic audio input/output tasks.

Core Audio Software Tools

The following tools are used in this section of the book:

- **MPlayer:** A movie player for Linux that has optimized built-in support for audio devices. It works very well as an MP3 audio stream player on the BBB.

- **ALSA utilities:** Contains tools for configuring and using ALSA (advanced Linux sound architecture) devices. It includes the `aplay`/`arecord` utilities for the playback and recording of audio streams; the `amixer` tool for controlling volume levels; and the `speaker-test` utility.

- **Libav:** Contains libraries and programs for handling multimedia data. In particular, `avconv` is a fast video and audio conversion tool that can also be used to capture audio data from devices or to stream data to the network (see `libav.org/avconv.html`).

To install these tools, ensure that your packages lists are up-to-date and install the tools as follows:

```
~$ sudo apt-get update
~$ sudo apt-get install mplayer alsa-utils libav-tools
```

Audio Devices for the BBB

After you have the core software installed, the next step is to utilize an audio device that is connected to the BBB. In this section, an example is used in which six audio devices are attached simultaneously to the BBB—the HDMI audio interface, three webcams, and two USB audio adapters. Remember that the HDMI cape must be enabled in order to utilize the HDMI audio output.

HDMI and USB Audio Playback Devices

Figure 12-5(a) illustrates the USB hub with three USB devices attached—the two USB audio adapters and the Bluetooth adapter. When the three webcams are also attached to the Velleman USB hub, then a call to lsusb results in the following:

```
molloyd@beaglebone:~$ lsusb
. . .
Bus 001 Device 003: ID 046d:082d Logitech, Inc.
Bus 001 Device 004: ID 041e:30d3 Creative Technology, Sound Blaster Play!
Bus 001 Device 006: ID 0d8c:013c C-Media Electronics,Inc.CM108 Audio
Bus 001 Device 007: ID 046d:0825 Logitech, Inc. Webcam C270
Bus 001 Device 009: ID 046d:081b Logitech, Inc. Webcam C310
```

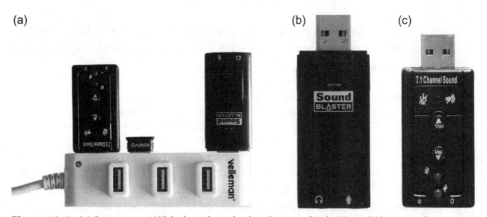

(a)   (b)   (c)

Figure 12-5: (a) Seven-port USB hub with multiple adapters; (b) the Sound Blaster audio adapter; (c) the Dynamode USB audio adapter

The USB hub in Figure 12-5(a) is not a powered hub; however, the BBB is powered via the BBB 5V connector using a 2A power supply, which provides sufficient power to use all of these devices simultaneously. The Sound Blaster ($20) and Dynamode ($5) USB adapters are illustrated in Figure 12-5(b) and (c), respectively. These adapters can be hot-plugged into the BBB, where their LKMs can be dynamically loaded and unloaded during Linux execution.

When the various adapters are connected to the BBB, you can obtain information about them as follows:

```
molloyd@beaglebone:~/exploringBB/chp12/audio$ cat /proc/asound/pcm
00-00: HDMI nxp-hdmi-hifi-0 :  : playback 1
01-00: USB Audio : USB Audio : capture 1
02-00: USB Audio : USB Audio : playback 1 : capture 1
03-00: USB Audio : USB Audio : capture 1
04-00: USB Audio : USB Audio : capture 1
05-00: USB Audio : USB Audio : playback 1 : capture 1
```

In this case, the HDMI adapter is capable of playback only, the two USB adapters are capable of playback and capture, and the USB webcams are only capable of capture. An alternative approach is to use the aplay utility to list the available playback devices:

```
molloyd@beaglebone:~/exploringBB/chp12/audio$ aplay -l
**** List of PLAYBACK Hardware Devices ****
card 0: Black [TI BeagleBone Black], device 0: HDMI nxp-hdmi-hifi-0 []
  Subdevices: 1/1 Subdevice #0: subdevice #0
card 2: Device [USB PnP Sound Device], device 0: USB Audio [USB Audio]
  Subdevices: 1/1 Subdevice #0: subdevice #0
card 5: U0x41e0x30d3 [USB Device 0x41e:0x30d3], device 0:  [USB Audio]
  Subdevices: 1/1 Subdevice #0: subdevice #0
```

Once you have identified the devices, you can play back an audio file on the Dynamode and Creative Sound Blaster USB adapters, respectively, using the mplayer and aplay utilities, as follows:

```
.../chp12/audio$ mplayer -ao alsa:device=hw=2 320sample.mp3
.../chp12/audio$ mplayer -ao alsa:device=hw=5 320sample.mp3
.../chp12/audio$ aplay -D plughw:2,0 cheering.wav
.../chp12/audio$ aplay -D plughw:5,0 cheering.wav
```

The sound quality is audibly richer on the Sound Blaster adapter (card 5) than the Dynamode adapter (card 2). However, the quality of the Dynamode adapter is good for its price and its manual volume control feature is useful.

The HDMI device adapter can also be used, either by connecting the BBB directly to an HDMI receiver or HDMI television (or a monitor with built-in speakers), or by using the VGA adapter shown in Figure 1-6(b) to extract the HDMI audio channel to a 3.5mm stereo audio jack. The quality of the audio that is extracted from the latter devices can be quite variable and can suffer from auto-gain line noise when no audio stream is being played back.

To test an output device, you can use the speaker-test utility (where -c2 indicates two channels are to be tested):

```
.../chp12/audio$ speaker-test -D plughw:2,0 -c2
```

The ALSA utilities also provide you with detailed information about the capabilities of a USB device. For example, `amixer` can be used to get and set an adapter's available properties. Using `amixer` on the Sound Blaster device provides its current state information:

```
.../chp12/audio$ amixer -c 5
Simple mixer control 'Speaker',0
  Capabilities: pvolume pswitch pswitch-joined penum
  Playback channels: Front Left - Front Right
  Limits: Playback 0 - 151
  Mono: Front Left: Playback 44 [29%] [-20.13dB] [on]
  Front Right: Playback 44 [29%] [-20.13dB] [on]
Simple mixer control 'Mic',0
  Capabilities: pvolume pvolume-joined cvolume cvolume-joined pswitch
    pswitch-joined cswitch cswitch-joined penum
  Playback channels: Mono     Capture channels: Mono
  Limits: Playback 0 - 32 Capture 0 - 16
  Mono: Playback 23 [72%] [34.36dB] [off] Capture 0 [0%] [0.00dB] [on]
Simple mixer control 'Auto Gain Control',0
  Capabilities: pswitch pswitch-joined penum
  Playback channels: Mono     Mono: Playback [on]
```

To get its available control settings, use the following:

```
.../chp12/audio$ amixer -c 5 controls
numid=2,iface=MIXER,name='Mic Playback Switch'
numid=3,iface=MIXER,name='Mic Playback Volume'
numid=6,iface=MIXER,name='Mic Capture Switch'
numid=7,iface=MIXER,name='Mic Capture Volume'
numid=8,iface=MIXER,name='Auto Gain Control'
numid=4,iface=MIXER,name='Speaker Playback Switch'
numid=5,iface=MIXER,name='Speaker Playback Volume'
numid=1,iface=PCM,name='Playback Channel Map'
```

Therefore, to control the Speaker Playback Volume setting you can use this:

```
~$ amixer -c 5 cset iface=MIXER,name='Speaker Playback Volume' 10,10
numid=5,iface=MIXER,name='Speaker Playback Volume'
  ; type=INTEGER,access=rw---R--,values=2,min=0,max=151,step=0
  : values=10,10 | dBminmax-min=-28.37dB,max=0.06dB
```

This adjusts the volume on the speaker output of the Sound Blaster USB card—the `10,10` values are the left and right volume percentage settings, so `0,30` would turn off the left channel and set the volume level at 30% for the right channel.

Internet Radio Playback

You can play Internet radio channels using the same `mplayer` application. For example, by using www.xatworld.com/radio-search/ you can search for a radio station of your preference to determine its IP address. You can then stream the audio to your USB adapter using the following:

```
.../chp12/audio$ mplayer -ao alsa:device=hw=5 http://178.18.137.246:80
MPlayer svn r34540 (Debian), built with gcc-4.6 (C)
Connecting to server 178.18.137.246[178.18.137.246]: 80...
Name    : Pinguin Radio
Genre   : Alternative
Website: http://www.pinguinradio.nl
Public : yes
Bitrate: 320kbit/s ...
AO: [alsa] 44100Hz 2ch s16le (2 bytes per sample)
Video: no video Starting playback...
A: 533.8 (08:53.7) of -0.0 (unknown) 35.0% 45%
ICY Info: StreamTitle='Sun Kil Moon  - Ben's My Friend ';
A: 842.9 (14:02.8) of -0.0 (unknown) 35.4% 45%
ICY Info: StreamTitle='Cage the Elephant  - Shake Me Down ';
```

This stream runs at 34% CPU and 1.7% memory usage on the BBB with good sound quality (regardless of what you might think of the music itself!). In fact, with multiple sound output devices, there is no difficulty in configuring the BBB to connect to multiple Internet radio streams simultaneously and streaming audio to separate audio adapters.

Recording Audio

The USB adapters and the USB webcams can be used to capture audio directly to the BBB file system. You can use the `arecord` utility to provide a list of the available devices—for example, with one webcam and the two USB audio adapters connected:

```
molloyd@beaglebone:~$ arecord -l
**** List of CAPTURE Hardware Devices ****
card 1: Device [USB PnP Sound Device], device 0: USB Audio [USB Audio]
    Subdevices: 1/1    Subdevice #0: subdevice #0
card 2: U0x46d0x825 [USB Device 0x46d:0x825], device 0: ... [USB Audio]
    Subdevices: 1/1    Subdevice #0: subdevice #0
card 3: U0x41e0x30d3 [USB Device 0x41e:0x30d3], device 0:... [USB Audio]
    Subdevices: 1/1    Subdevice #0: subdevice #0
```

These devices are also indexed at the following /proc location:

```
molloyd@beaglebone:~/tmp$ cat /proc/asound/cards
 0 [Black  ]: TI_BeagleBone_B - TI BeagleBone Black
    TI BeagleBone Black
 1 [Device ]: USB-Audio - USB PnP Sound Device
    USB PnP Sound Device at usb-musb-hdrc.1.auto-1.2, full speed  ...
```

You can record audio from each of the audio capture devices using the `arecord` utility and the device's address. Interestingly, the LED does not light on the webcams described when they are recording only audio!

```
molloyd@beaglebone:~/tmp$ arecord -f cd -D plughw:3,0 -d 20 test3.wav
Recording WAVE 'test3.wav' : Signed 16 bit Little Endian, Rate 44100 Hz
molloyd@beaglebone:~/tmp$ arecord -f cd -D plughw:2,0 -d 20 test2.wav
Recording WAVE 'test2.wav' : Signed 16 bit Little Endian, Rate 44100 Hz
```

The waveform audio file format (WAV) stores uncompressed audio data, which will quickly consume your BBB file storage free space. In order to avoid this you can compress WAV files into the popular MP3 compressed format using the LAME MP3 encoder, as follows:

```
molloyd@beaglebone:~/tmp$ sudo apt-get install lame
molloyd@beaglebone:~/tmp$ lame test2.wav output.mp3
LAME 3.99.5 32bits (http://lame.sf.net)
Using polyphase lowpass filter, transition band: 16538 Hz - 17071 Hz
Encoding test2.wav to output.mp3
Encoding as 44.1 kHz j-stereo MPEG-1 Layer III (11x) 128 kbps qval=3
    Frame     | CPU time/estim | REAL time/estim | play/CPU | ETA
    767/767   (100%)|   0:09/   0:09|   0:09/   0:09|  2.0980x|0:00 ...
```

A recording test was performed on the BBB that uses each of the two USB adapters. A Zoom H1 Handy Recorder (www.zoom.co.jp/products/h1) was used to capture my voice (and an action that was often necessary to get this book written!). The analog stereo line output of the Zoom H1 was connected to the analog stereo line in of each adapter and the following steps were used to record the audio for each adapter:

```
.../audio/testMicrophone$ arecord -f cd -D plughw:2,0 -d 45 testX.wav
.../chp12/audio/testMicrophone$ lame -b 128 testX.wav testX.mp3
```

A digital copy of the audio (i.e., digitally copied off the Zoom H1) is also provided in the Git repository for comparison. All three files are encoded at a sampling rate of 44.1kS/sec with a bit rate of 128Kb/sec. You can play these files directly on your desktop computer using the address tiny.cc/ebb1208:

```
.../chp12/audio/testMicrophone$ ls
ZoomH1DigitalSource.mp3   testCreative.mp3   testDynamode.mp3
```

Line noise is audible in both versions when compared to the original digital audio data, but there is not a very significant difference in the quality of the audio recording from each USB audio adapter.

Audio Network Streaming

Earlier in this chapter, a description is provided of video streaming to the network using `avconv`. It is also possible to use the same application to stream audio as it is captured by an audio device, live to the network. For example, here is the command required to stream audio from a device attached to the address 2,0 using UDP to a desktop computer (at 192.168.7.1):

```
molloyd@beaglebone:~/tmp$ avconv -ac 1 -f alsa -i hw:2,0 -acodec
    libmp3lame -ab 32k -ac 1 -re -f mp3 udp://192.168.7.1:1234
avconv version 0.8.15-6:0.8.15-1, (c) 2000-2014 Libav developers
    built on Aug  9 2014 23:45:32 with gcc 4.6.3
[alsa @ 0x40b60] Estimating duration from bitrate, may be inaccurate
Input #0, alsa, from 'hw:2,0': ...
Output #0, mp3, to 'udp://192.168.7.1:1234': ...
size=     547kB time=139.99 bitrate=  32.0kbits/s
```

A desktop player such as VLC can be used to open the network UDP stream. For example, in VLC use Media ➢ Open Network Stream . . . and set the network URL to be: "udp://@:1234". Streaming audio from the BBB in this form has a 52% CPU load in this instance.

> **NOTE**   Wireshark (www.wireshark.org) is a great tool for debugging network connection and communications problems that might occur in audio/video streaming and network socket programming (as in Chapters 10 and 11).

Bluetooth A2DP Audio

The use of a Bluetooth adapter is first introduced in Chapter 9 for general-purpose serial communication. It is used again in Chapter 10 to connect to the TI SensorTag, and in Chapter 11 to attach peripherals to the BBB. Here again, Bluetooth can be used with the BBB—this time to communicate with audio devices.

One of the most common uses of the Bluetooth wireless communication system is for the connection of smartphones to in-car audio systems, or to home entertainment centers. For this purpose, the Bluetooth *Advanced Audio Distribution Profile* (*A2DP*) can be used to stream high-quality stereo audio from a media source to a media sink. The *source device* (*SRC*) acts as the source of a digital audio stream (e.g., Bluetooth headset, smartphone media player), which is sent in a compressed format to a *sink device* (*SNK*) (e.g., Bluetooth headphones, stereo receiver, in-car receiver).

When connected to a USB Bluetooth adapter, the BBB can be configured to act as an A2DP SRC or SNK. In this example, the BBB is configured as a SRC that is connected to a Hi-Fi system and Windows PC SNK. There are many low-cost A2DP audio receivers available that provide audio output on a 3.5mm stereo jack, which can be used to retrospectively add A2DP capability to Hi-Fi systems. However, the Sony Hi-Fi system that is used as the test platform has built-in A2DP support.

> **NOTE** It is recommended that you go through the process of connecting a smartphone to a Bluetooth A2DP SNK before attempting to connect the BBB. This will help you to verify that a connection is possible and help you to become familiar with the steps that are required to pair A2DP devices.

After a Bluetooth adapter is attached to the BBB, the first step is to install the necessary packages, configure the BBB to support A2DP, and test that the Bluetooth audio SNKs are visible:

```
molloyd@beaglebone:~$ sudo apt-get update
molloyd@beaglebone:~$ sudo apt-get install bluez-utils bluez-alsa
molloyd@beaglebone:~$ hcitool scan
Scanning ...   00:26:83:32:CF:0D      DEREKMOLLOY-PC
               00:1D:BA:2E:BC:36      CMT-HX90BTR
```

The BBB has detected the desktop PC and the Sony Hi-Fi system. The BBB must then be configured to have the following Bluetooth profiles enabled:

```
molloyd@beaglebone:~$ cd /etc/bluetooth/
molloyd@beaglebone:/etc/bluetooth$ sudo nano audio.conf
molloyd@beaglebone:/etc/bluetooth$ more audio.conf
# Configuration file for the audio service
[General]
Enable=Source,Sink,Media,Socket         ...
```

You can then connect to the SNKs using the following commands (you will likely have to enter a code (e.g., 0000) on both devices in order to pair the devices in the first step):

```
molloyd@beaglebone:~$ sudo bluez-simple-agent hci0 00:1D:BA:2E:BC:36
molloyd@beaglebone:~$ sudo bluez-test-device trusted 00:1D:BA:2E:BC:36 yes
```

Finally, a new file /etc/asound.conf must be created in order for ALSA to work correctly (for the Hi-Fi system in this example):

```
molloyd@beaglebone:/etc$ sudo nano asound.conf
molloyd@beaglebone:/etc$ more asound.conf
pcm.bluetooth {
        type bluetooth
        device "00:1D:BA:2E:BC:36"
        profile "auto"
}
```

Restart the Bluetooth service using `systemctl`:

```
molloyd@beaglebone:/etc$ systemctl list-units|grep bluetooth
bluetooth.service          loaded active running       Bluetooth service
bluetooth.target           loaded active active        Bluetooth
molloyd@beaglebone:/etc$ sudo systemctl restart bluetooth.service
```

You can then play a MP3 file to the Bluetooth SNK using the MPlayer utility and the ALSA device that is configured in `/etc/asound.conf`. There are some creative-commons MP3 files in the Git repository that you can use:

```
~/chp12/audio$ mplayer -ao alsa:device=bluetooth 320sample.mp3
MPlayer svn r34540 (Debian)(C) 2000-2012 MPlayer Team ...
Playing 320sample.mp3.    libavformat version 53.21.1 (external)
Audio only file format detected ...
AUDIO: 44100 Hz, 2 ch, floatle, 320.1 kbit/11.34% ...
Starting playback... A: 103.0 (01:43.0) of 103.0 (01:43.0) 33.4%
```

The audio plays correctly on the Sony Hi-Fi, displaying the message shown in Figure 12-6(a). Playing audio in this way has a manageable load on the BBB of 41% CPU and 1.7% of memory for the 44.1kS/sec, 320Kb/sec MP3 audio file.

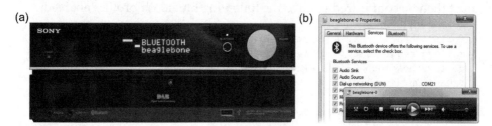

Figure 12-6: Bluetooth A2DP connections: (a) Sony Hi-Fi; (b) Windows machine via motherboard Bluetooth

The same steps can be used to connect the BBB to a Windows computer Bluetooth audio SNK. Be sure to enable the Audio Sink option on the Bluetooth device by right-clicking on the "beaglebone-0" device and choosing Advanced Operation ➤ Connect to stereo audio source device, which results in the dialog settings shown in Figure 12-6(b).

You can play Internet radio stations using the same MPlayer tools described earlier. For example, to stream the same Internet radio station to your Bluetooth Hi-Fi system, use the following:

```
~$ mplayer -ao alsa:device=bluetooth http://178.18.137.246:80
MPlayer svn r34540 (Debian), 2000-2012 MPlayer Team
Playing http://178.18.137.246:80.    ... Bitrate: 320kbit/s
ICY Info: StreamTitle='Radiohead  - Weird Fishes';
A: 654.2 (10:54.2) of -0.0 (unknown) 32.8% 46%
```

This stream runs at 34% CPU and 1.7% memory usage on the BBB with excellent sound quality.

NOTE Deserving mention is an additional Linux service called PulseAudio, a background process that reroutes all audio streams. It aims to support legacy devices, as well as to provide support for network audio (e.g., for VNC). PulseAudio is complex and should be avoided unless you have a specific need to use it on the BBB. It does provide useful user-interface tools, such as pavucontrol, and can be installed using the following:

```
.../chp12/audio$ sudo apt-get install pavucontrol
```

PulseAudio can be configured as follows:

```
molloyd@beaglebone:/etc/pulse$ sudo nano default.pa
```

The service can be started and stopped using the following (note: no sudo**):**

```
.../chp12/audio$ pulseaudio –kill
.../chp12/audio$ pulseaudio –start
```

PulseAudio provides support for Bluetooth devices, but the connections can intermittently fail, requiring the Bluetooth service to be restarted:

```
.../chp12/audio$ hcitool con
Connections:< ACL 00:1D:BA:2E:BC:36 handle 12 state 1 lm ...
.../chp12/audio$ sudo apt-get install pulseaudio-module-bluetooth
.../chp12/audio$ sudo pactl load-module module-bluetooth-discover
.../chp12/audio$ pactl load-module module-alsa-sink device=bluetooth
```

Text-to-Speech

Once you have a working playback adapter connected to the BBB, you can then utilize Linux tools and online services to perform some interesting audio applications. One such application is text-to-speech—it is possible to generate very high-quality speech output on the BBB using online and offline tools. Two examples are described in this section: The first "takes advantage" of the features of Google's online translator, and the second uses the Android text-to-speech (TTS) engine.

Online Text-to-Speech

Google's translation service provides very good quality text-to-speech output. It can be called directly from a browser—for example, to generate an MP3 audio sample for the string "Hello from the BeagleBone Black," you can construct an URL of the following form (the space character is encoded as %20):

```
http://translate.google.com/translate_tts?tl=en&q=Hello%20from%20the%20
BeagleBone%20Black
```

You can listen to the output at `tiny.cc/ebb1209`. The audio can be adapted to have a strong French accent (not translation) by changing the `tl` value—to `fr`, for example (listen at `tiny.cc/ebb1210`): https://translate.google.com/translate_tts?tl=fr&q=Hello%20from%20the%20BeagleBone%20Black

It is possible to pass the output audio file to the MPlayer application using the following command (which is present in `chp12/speech/onlineSpeechTest.sh`):

```
.../chp12/speech$ mplayer -ao alsa:device=hw=5 "https://translate.google
.com/translate_tts?tl=en&q=Hello%20from%20the%20BeagleBone%20Black"
```

The script can be adapted to accept command-line arguments, as follows:

```
.../chp12/speech$ ./speech.sh testing 1 2 3
.../chp12/speech$ more speech.sh
#!/bin/bash
mplayer -ao alsa:device=hw=5
"https://translate.google.com/translate_tts?tl=en&q=$*"
```

Unfortunately, your BBB has to be continuously online for this script to work correctly—it is also possible that Google could alter the online service interface or its availability in the future.

Offline Text-to-Speech

You can use the Pico Android TTS engine for offline applications. The engine can be installed and used offline as follows:

```
~/$ sudo apt-get install libttspico-utils
.../chp12/speech$ pico2wave -w picoTest.wav "Test of using the text to
   speech Android engine on the BeagleBone Black"
.../chp12/speech$ ls
picoTest.wav
.../chp12/speech$ mplayer -ao alsa:device=hw=5 picoTest.wav
```

Or, on a single line:

```
$ pico2wave -w test.wav "test" | mplayer -ao alsa:device=hw=5 test.wav
```

The quality of the output is not as good as the online service, but it is still quite impressive.

A Bluetooth Speaking Clock and Temperature Sensor

You can integrate the TTS engines into your own applications. For example, Listings 12-6 and 12-7 demonstrate how it is possible to develop a speaking clock that uses the online and offline TTS engines, respectively. In this example, the scripts use the Bluetooth adapter to stream the output to the Bluetooth Hi-Fi system, but you can alter them to suit your specific configuration.

LISTING 12-6: /exploringBB/chp12/speech/clock.sh

```
#!/bin/bash
NOW=$(date +"It is %M minutes past %l %p")
echo $NOW
mplayer -ao alsa:device=bluetooth "http://translate.google.com/
translate_tts?tl=en&q=$NOW"
```

LISTING 12-7: /exploringBB/chp12/speech/offlineClock.sh

```
#!/bin/bash
NOW=$(date +"It is %M minutes past %l %p")
echo $NOW
pico2wave -w temporaryTime.wav "$NOW"
lame temporaryTime.wav temporaryTime.mp3
mplayer -ao alsa:device=bluetooth temporaryTime.mp3
rm temporaryTime.*
```

This code can be adapted to use the TMP36 temperature sensor that is described at the beginning of Chapter 10. The `tmp36raw` binary executable in the `/chp10/tmp36/` directory can be called from the scripts in Listing 12-6 and 12-7 to create a speaking clock temperature service, as shown in Listing 12-8 (remember to load the BBB-ADC cape!).

LISTING 12-8: /EXPLORINGBB/CHP12/SPEECH/CLOCKANDTEMP.SH

```
#!/bin/bash
TEMP=$(./tmp36raw)
NOW=$(date +" It is %M minutes past %l %p and it is $TEMP degrees
Celsius")
echo $NOW
mplayer -ao alsa:device=bluetooth "http://translate.google.com/
translate_tts?tl=en&q=$NOW"
```

Finally, it is also possible to install the CMU Sphinx Speech Recognition Toolkit on the BBB. Open-source speech recognition tools are notoriously difficult to train when compared to commercial offerings such as Nuance's Dragon NaturallySpeaking. However, with some time investment, PocketSphinx can be trained to provide good results. To install it on the BBB, you must manually download and build two repositories: `sphinxbase` and `pocketsphinx`. You can use SourceForge (`sourceforge.net`) to find the latest versions of both repositories. Build them directly on the BBB using steps such as `./configure -enable-fixed`, followed by `make`, and `sudo make install`.

Summary

After completing this chapter, you should be able to do the following:

- Capture image and video data on the BBB using USB webcams combined with Linux Video4Linux2 drivers and APIs.
- Use Video4Linux2 utilities to get information from and adjust the properties of video capture devices.
- Stream video data to the Internet using Linux applications and UDP, multicast, and RTP streams.
- Use OpenCV to perform basic image processing on the BBB.
- Use OpenCV to perform a computer vision face-detection task.
- Utilize the Boost C++ libraries on the BBB.
- Play audio data on the BBB using HDMI audio and USB audio adapters. The audio data can be raw waveform data or compressed MP3 data from the BBB file system or from Internet radio streams.
- Record audio data using USB audio adapters or webcams.
- Stream audio data to the Internet using UDP.
- Play audio to Bluetooth A2DP audio devices, such as Hi-Fi systems.
- Use text-to-speech (TTS) approaches to verbalize the text output of commands that are executed on the BBB.

Further Reading

There are many links to websites and documents provided throughout this chapter. Additional links and further information on the topics are provided at `www.exploringbeaglebone.com/chapter12/` and the following:

- Video4Linux2 core documentation: `tiny.cc/ebb1203`
- V4L2 API Specification: `tiny.cc/ebb1204`
- Computer Vision Cascaded Classification: `tiny.cc/ebb1207`
- CVonline: The Evolving, Distributed, Non-Proprietary, On-Line Compendium of Computer Vision, at `tiny.cc/ebb1211`
- The Boost C++ Libraries, Boris Schäling: `tiny.cc/ebb1214`

# CHAPTER 13

Real-Time BeagleBone Interfacing

In this chapter you are introduced to real-time interfacing with the BeagleBone. Linux is by default a nonpreemptive OS, which means that it has difficulty performing certain real-time interfacing tasks, such as generating or sampling bit patterns on GPIOs at high speeds. The BBB has two programmable real-time units (PRUs) that can be used for certain real-time operations, and these are the focus of this chapter, which describes input and output examples that help explain the operation of the PRUs and their encompassing industrial communication subsystem (PRU-ICSS). Finally, the real-time capabilities of the BBB are demonstrated using two applications—the first generates a custom waveform on a GPIO, and the second uses a low-cost ultrasonic distance sensor that requires precise timing in order to communicate the distance to an obstacle.

Equipment Required for This Chapter:

- BeagleBone Black
- LED, FET (e.g., BS270), push button, capacitors, and resistors
- Oscilloscope (optional, but useful)
- HC-SR04 ultrasonic sensor and logic-level translator board

Further resources for this chapter are available at www.exploringbeaglebone .com/chapter13/.

Real-Time BeagleBone

The advantages of integrating the Linux OS with an embedded system are described throughout this book. The quantity and quality of device drivers, software packages, programming languages, and software APIs available for the Linux platform is immense. However, certain features that you may take for granted, on even low-cost microcontrollers, may be absent—the most notable of which is the capability to perform input/output operations in a time-critical manner. Systems are described as being *real-time* if they can guarantee a valid response within a specified time frame (often of the order of ms/µs), regardless of their system load.

Real-time systems are often used for mission-critical applications. *Hard real-time systems* are used in applications for which a total systems failure could result from missing a deadline (e.g., power steering, self-balancing robots). *Soft real-time systems* are used in applications that require meeting deadlines. In such applications, missing a deadline might result in a reduced quality of service, but certainly not systems failure (e.g., live video transmission, mobile phone communication). The mainline Linux kernel can typically meet soft real-time requirements (e.g., playing desktop audio), but it is not designed to meet hard real-time requirements.

Real-Time Kernels

The use of the BBB GPIOs is described in detail in Chapter 6, as are the switching frequency limitations that are present when using sysfs. In particular, Figure 6-3 illustrates the result of a shell script that is switching a GPIO output at approximately 2.2kHz, in which it is clear that the output signal suffers from *jitter* (i.e., a deviation from true periodicity of a periodic signal). When a more sophisticated C/C++ program is used in Chapter 6 to increase the switching frequency, the same jitter issue arises. This is largely because mainline Linux is a *nonpreemptive* OS. For example, it could be time for a GPIO to be toggled in a time-critical manner, but the Linux process scheduler may already have determined that the Apache web server should execute. Because Linux is a nonpreemptive OS, Apache cannot be interrupted until it finishes its kernel service time. Therefore, the toggling of the GPIO will be delayed and signal jitter arises.

Preemptive scheduling means that kernel scheduling is based on the priority of the tasks to be executed. Therefore, if the GPIO toggle task is designated to be of a higher priority than the Apache web server, then the Apache task will be interrupted, even though its kernel service time has not expired. For hard real-time systems, the *preemption period* is typically on the order of microseconds or lower. The *latency* of a task is the key measurement of the real-time performance of the system, and it is largely dependent on the tasks that are running at equal or higher priorities on the same machine.

One way to implement preemptive scheduling on the BBB is to apply the RT-Preempt patch (aka `PREEMPT_RT`) to a Linux kernel build. This patch converts the mainline Linux kernel into a preemptive system (with the exception of interrupt handling and certain regions that are guarded by spinlocks). To apply the patch, you must rebuild the Linux kernel (see Chapter 7) and add `CONFIG_PREEMPT_RT_FULL=y` to the build configuration (see `tiny.cc/ebb1301` for further details). When applied to the BBB, the RT-Preempt patch typically results in worst-case latency times of single-digit milliseconds when executing C/C++ real-time applications.

Xenomai (`www.xenomai.org`) provides a different type of solution. It supplements mainline Linux with a real-time co-kernel, called Cobalt, which is responsible for performing all time-critical activities. The co-kernel has higher priority than Linux—it processes hardware interrupts and passes virtual interrupts to the underlying Linux kernel. The Machinekit (`tiny.cc/ebb1302`) distribution is a good way to get started with Xenomai on the BBB, as it is based on the official Debian release for the BBB. The distribution is targeted specifically at computer numerical control (CNC) and 3D printing applications.

Note also that the BBB can be used without mainline Linux. For example, the following platforms can be downloaded without cost:

- **StarterWare for ARM-based TI Sitara processors:** This is a *no-OS* platform for devices such as the BBB. It provides a device abstraction layer (e.g., for UART, SPI, I²C, LCD, Ethernet) that can be programmed using open-source tools and C-based library APIs to build applications that can perform peripheral configuration and I/O. See `tiny.cc/ebb1303` for further details.

- **QNX Neutrino RTOS on OMAP and Sitara:** This is a full-featured real-time OS (RTOS) that is available with BBB reference designs for in-car, digital instrument, and smart home displays. See `tiny.cc/ebb1304` and `tiny.cc/ebb1305`.

While suitable for hard real-time applications, both of these commercial offerings are not general-purpose OSs and require significant expertise.

Real-Time Hardware Solutions

In Chapter 8, a communications framework is described that can be used to offload real-time processing to low-cost microcontrollers, such as the Arduino, Atmel AVR, and TI Stellaris platforms. The framework uses a UART device for communication, but the SPI or I²C buses could also be used. Using this framework, a set of microcontrollers could be connected to the BBB and used to take responsibility for hard real-time processing and interfacing. The BBB could then be used for centralized high-level tasks, such as GUI display, network communication, data aggregation/storage, and algorithmic tuning.

Sophisticated capes are available for the BBB that can be used for real-time processing, the most notable being the *Valent F(x) LOGi-Bone FPGA development board*,[1] which is illustrated in Chapter 1 (see Figure 1-10). Hardware description languages (HDLs), such as Verilog or VHDL, can be used in programming *field-programmable gate arrays (FPGAs)* to create high-speed logic circuits. FPGAs are particularly useful for parallel processing, as they can perform many thousands of operations in a single clock cycle. Unfortunately, not all tasks are suitable for a parallel implementation and there is a steep learning curve in developing FPGA software. The LOGi-Bone cape provides a good introduction to FPGA development, as the associated applications are open source and a growing community of users is working on this platform. The guide at `tiny.cc/ebb1306` provides a detailed overview of the steps required to interface the cape to the BBB.

The BBB's AM335x processor has two programmable real-time units (PRUs) that can be used for certain real-time interfacing operations, and these are the focus of this chapter. This is an advanced topic, and it is not possible to cover all the functionality available on the PRUs within a single chapter. Therefore, the aim of this chapter is to impart an understanding of the core principles, enabling you to get started by presenting some practical examples that you can use as the basis of your own implementations. In addition, the underlying technology and software is undergoing constant development, so please check the chapter web page for updates.

> **NOTE** The PRU-ICSS is not currently supported by Texas Instruments; rather, it is a "community supported" initiative.

The PRU-ICSS Architecture

The Programmable Real-Time Unit and Industrial Communication Subsystem (PRU-ICSS) on the BBB's AM335x processor contains two 32-bit 200MHz RISC cores, called PRUs. These PRUs have their own local memory allocation, but they can also use the BBB P8/P9 header pins and trigger interrupts and share memory with the Linux host device.

The PRU-ICSS is a valuable addition to a general embedded Linux platform, as it can provide support for interfacing applications that have hard real-time constraints. It is important to note that the PRU-ICSS is not a hardware accelerator—it cannot be used to improve the general performance of code that is executing on the Linux host device. Rather, it can be used to manipulate inputs, outputs, and memory-mapped data structures to implement custom communication interfaces (e.g., simple I/O manipulation, bit-banging, SPI, UARTs).

---

[1] Uses a Xilinx Spartan 6 LX9 TQFP-144 FPGA with 9,152 logic cells, 11,440 CLB flip-flops, 16 DSP48A1 slices, and 576Kb RAM. The board also contains a 256Mb SDRAM and Arduino compatible headers, and is accessed using GPMC, SPI, or I²C from the BBB.

For example, in this chapter the PRU-ICSS is used to interface to an ultrasonic distance sensor, by measuring PWM signal properties.

The PRU-ICSS architecture is outlined in Figure 13-1. There are two independent 32-bit RISC PRU cores (PRU0 and PRU1), each with 8KB of program memory and 8KB of data memory. The program memory stores the instructions to be executed by each PRU, and the data memory is typically used to store individual data values or data arrays that are manipulated by the program instructions. The PRU0 uses Data RAM0 and the PRU1 uses Data RAM1; however, each PRU can access the data memory of the other PRU, along with a separate 12KB of general-purpose shared memory.

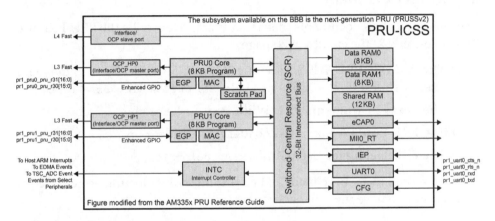

Figure 13-1: The PRU-ICSS architecture

Customized for the BBB from an image that is courtesy of Texas Instruments

The PRU-ICSS subsystem that is available on the BBB is the second-generation PRUSSv2, but not all of its features are available on the BBB platform. In addition to the PRU cores and memory blocks, the most important blocks are illustrated in Figure 13-1, including the following:

- **Enhanced GPIO (EGP):** The PRU subsystem has a specific set of fast GPIOs, many of which are accessible via the P8/P9 headers.

- **OCP master port:** Facilitates access to external Linux host memory. For example, this block also allows the PRUs to manipulate the state of GPIOs that are used in Chapter 6.

- **Multiplier with optional accumulation (MAC):** This block can be used to multiply two 32-bit operands and provide a 64-bit result.

- **Interrupt controller (INTC):** An interrupt controller can be used to notify each PRU that an event has occurred or to notify the host device of events (e.g., that the PRU program has run to completion).

- **Scratch pad (SPAD):** This provides three banks of 30 × 32-bit registers that are shared between the two PRU cores.

■ **UART0:** A UART device with a dedicated 192MHz clock is available on the P8/P9 headers.

The Switched Central Resource (SCR) connects the PRUs to the other resources inside the PRU-ICSS. PRUs have access to all the resources on the AM335x (e.g., regular GPIOs) using the Interface/OCP master port. Linux host memory can also be used by the PRUs; however, its use is several times slower than using PRU memory, as memory access needs to be routed external to the PRU-ICSS, and back in via the PRU-ICSS Interface/OCP slave port.

Important Documents

The most important documents that are available to describe the PRU-ICSS are linked here and at the chapter web page:

■ **The AM335x PRU-ICSS Reference Guide:** This document is the main reference for the PRU-ICSS hardware (289 pages): `tiny.cc/ebb1307`.

■ **The Texas Instruments PRU Wiki:** `tiny.cc/ebb1308`

■ **The PRU Linux Application Loader API Guide:** `tiny.cc/ebb1309`

■ **The PRU Debugger User Guide:** `tiny.cc/ebb1310`

The descriptions in this chapter refer to the preceding documents repeatedly, so it is useful to have them to hand.

Getting Started with the PRU-ICSS

A "hello world" LED flashing application is developed in this section, so that you can quickly get started with the PRU-ICSS. The subsequent sections provide more detailed instruction. Several steps are required, so it is useful to map them as shown in Figure 13-2. As illustrated, once a custom device tree overlay is created, a Linux host program (.c) and a PRU program (.p) must be written. The role of the Linux host program is to transfer the PRU program binary (.bin) to the PRU-ICSS and then to act as the communications bridge between the PRU and the Linux host machine. These steps are employed in this section to deploy the "hello world" example.

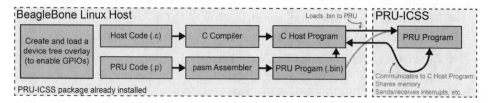

Figure 13-2: Summary of the steps involved in deploying a PRU-ICSS program

PRU-ICSS Enhanced GPIOs

Each PRU has a set of GPIOs that have enhanced functionality, such as parallel-to-serial conversion. Their internal signal names have the following naming convention: pr1_pru**x**_pru_r3**y**_**z**, where **x** is the PRU number (0 or 1), **y** defines whether the pin is an input (1) or an output (0), and **z** is the pin number (0–16). For example, pr1_pru0_pru_r30_5 is output 5 for PRU0, and pr1_pru0_pru_r31_3 is input 3 for PRU0.

In Chapter 6, Figures 6-6 and 6-7 list the enhanced GPIO pins that are available on the P8 and P9 headers. It is clear from these figures that the pin mux must be configured in Mode5 or Mode6 using device tree overlays in order to utilize these inputs/outputs. Not all of the pins are exported to the P8/P9 headers—for example, no PRU0 8–13 or PRU1 14–15 (inclusive) pins are available, and PRU0/1 16 is only an input.

A circuit is illustrated in Figure 13-3 that uses two enhanced PRU pins. This circuit is used for many of the examples in this chapter. To use the enhanced GPIOs, a device tree overlay must be created and loaded.

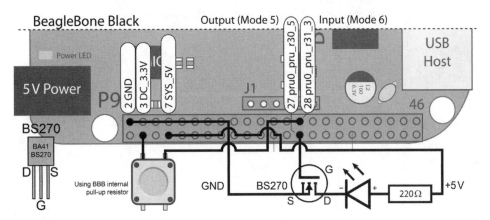

Figure 13-3: An example BBB PRU circuit

PRU-ICSS Device Tree Overlay

A device tree overlay is provided in Listing 13-1 that can be used for all of the examples in this chapter. It enables two regular GPIOs and two enhanced PRU GPIOs, as follows:

- P9_11: **gpio0[30]** output ($PINS 28, mode 7, pull-down) **0x07**
- P9_13: **gpio0[31]** input ($PINS 29, mode 7, pull-down) **0x27**
- P9_27: **pr1_pru0_pru_r30_5** output ($PINS 105, mode 5, pull-down) **0x05**
- P9_28: **pr1_pru0_pru_r31_3** input ($PINS 103, mode 6, pull-down) **0x26**

HDMI must be disabled for this overlay to load correctly, as it conflicts with the enhanced GPIO pins above (see Chapter 6). You can verify the address settings and pin mux settings in this overlay using Figure 6-7.

LISTING 13-1: /exploringBB/chp13/overlay/EBB-PRU-Example.dts

```
/dts-v1/;
/plugin/;
/ {
    compatible = "ti,beaglebone", "ti,beaglebone-black";

    part-number = "EBB-PRU-Example";
    version = "00A0";

    /* This overlay uses the following resources */
    exclusive-use = "P9.11", "P9.13", "P9.27", "P9.28", "pru0";

        gpio_pins: pinmux_gpio_pins {        // The GPIO pins
            pinctrl-single,pins = <
                0x070 0x07  // P9_11 MODE7 GPIO output pull-down
                0x074 0x27  // P9_13 MODE7 GPIO input pull-down
            >;
        };
        pru_pru_pins: pinmux_pru_pru_pins {    // The PRU pin modes
            pinctrl-single,pins = <
                0x1a4 0x05  // P9_27 pr1_pru0_pru_r30_5, Mode5 output pull-down
                0x19c 0x26  // P9_28 pr1_pru0_pru_r31_3, Mode6 input pull-down
            >;
        };
    };
};
fragment@1 {            // Enable the PRUSS
    target = <&pruss>;
    __overlay__ {
        status = "okay";
        pinctrl-names = "default";
        pinctrl-0 = <&pru_pru_pins>;
    };
};
fragment@2 {            // Enable the GPIOs
    target = <&ocp>;
    __overlay__ {
        gpio_helper {
            compatible = "gpio-of-helper";
            status = "okay";
            pinctrl-names = "default";
            pinctrl-0 = <&gpio_pins>;
        };
    };
};
};
```

This overlay can then be built and deployed using the following steps:

```
molloyd@beaglebone:~/exploringBB/chp13/overlay$ ls
EBB-PRU-Example.dts  build
.../chp13/overlay$ ./build
Compiling the overlay from .dts to .dtbo
.../chp13/overlay$ ls
EBB-PRU-Example-00A0.dtbo  EBB-PRU-Example.dts  build
.../chp13/overlay$ sudo cp EBB-PRU-Example-00A0.dtbo /lib/firmware
.../chp13/overlay$ sudo sh -c "echo EBB-PRU-Example > $SLOTS"
.../chp13/overlay$ cat $SLOTS
 8: ff:P-O-L Override Board Name,00A0,Override Manuf,EBB-PRU-Example
```

The overlay must be loaded before any of the following examples can be
executed. You can use dmesg to check for load issues, and you can catenate
$PINS to verify the PRU GPIO pin settings—for example:

```
molloyd@beaglebone:/$ sudo cat $PINS|grep '103\|105'
pin 103 (44e1099c) 00000026 pinctrl-single
pin 105 (44e109a4) 00000005 pinctrl-single
```

Importantly, if you type **lsmod** you should now see that the uio_pruss module
has loaded (if not, use **modprobe uio_pruss**):

```
~/exploringBB/chp13/overlay$ lsmod
Module                Size  Used by
uio_pruss             4066  0
```

The PRU-ICSS Package

The BBB Debian image has pre-installed support for using the PRU-ICSS. If
you are using a different distribution or need to upgrade the installation, then
please see the note on manually building the PRU Package.

The *PRU-ICSS Package* includes the *PRU Linux Application Loader API*, which
is used in this example to load a PRU program into the PRU-ICSS. It can also
be used to communicate between the PRUs and the Linux user space. You can
check whether the PRU Linux Application Loader API is installed using the
following:

```
molloyd@beaglebone:/usr/include$ ls pru*
pruss_intc_mapping.h  prussdrv.h
molloyd@beaglebone:/usr/lib$ ls libpru*
libprussdrv.a  libprussdrv.so  libprussdrvd.a  libprussdrvd.so
```

The PRU-ICSS Package includes the CLI *PRU Assembler*, which is used to build
binary images that can be executed by the PRUs. The source file programs (.p)
are written in assembly language and must be compiled to *little-endian binary*

files to be executed on the PRUs. The PRU Assembler is also installed by default on the BBB Debian distribution:

```
molloyd@beaglebone:~$ pasm
PRU Assembler Version 0.84
Copyright (C) 2005-2013 by Texas Instruments Inc.
Usage:pasm[-V#EBbcmLldz][-Idir][-Dname=value][-Cname]InFile[OutFile]...
```

MANUAL AM335X PRU-ICSS PACKAGE BUILD INSTRUCTIONS

To install or upgrade the AM335x PRU-ICSS Package on your BBB you can use the following steps:

```
~$ git clone https://github.com/beagleboard/am335x_pru_package
Cloning into 'am335x_pru_package'... ...
molloyd@beaglebone:~$ cd am335x_pru_package/
~/am335x_pru_package$ ls
Documentation  README.txt    am335xPruReferenceGuide.pdf
Makefile       am335xPruPackage_1_2_Manifest.pdf  pru_sw
~/am335x_pru_package$ cd pru_sw/app_loader/interface/
~/am335x_pru_package/pru_sw/app_loader/interface$ make CROSS_COMPILE=""
```

This will create the PRU libraries. The header files are already present in the include directory:

```
molloyd@beaglebone:~/am335x_pru_package/pru_sw/app_loader/lib$ ls
libprussdrv.a  libprussdrv.so  libprussdrvd.a  libprussdrvd.so
molloyd@beaglebone:~/am335x_pru_package/pru_sw/app_loader/include$ ls
pruss_intc_mapping.h  prussdrv.h
```

Finally, the PRU Assembler must be built using the following steps:

```
~/am335x_pru_package/pru_sw/utils/pasm_source$ ./linuxbuild
~/am335x_pru_package/pru_sw/utils/pasm_source$ cd ..
~/am335x_pru_package/pru_sw/utils$ ls
LICENCE.txt  pasm  pasm_source
~/am335x_pru_package/pru_sw/utils$ ./pasm
PRU Assembler Version 0.86
Copyright (C) 2005-2013 by Texas Instruments Inc.
```

The libraries, include files, and assembler can be copied to their respective BBB directories: /usr/lib, /usr/include, and /usr/bin.

A First PRU Program

The first PRU program is designed to flash the LED that is connected to pr1_pru0_pru_r30_5 until a button that is connected to pr1_ pru0_pru_r31_3 is

pressed (refer to Figure 13-3). The code for the PRU program is provided in
Listing 13-2.

LISTING 13-2: /exploringBB/chp13/ledButton/ledButton.p

```
// PRU-ICSS program to flash a LED on P9_27 (pru0_pru_r30_5) until a button
// that is connected to P9_28 (pru0_pru_r31_3 is pressed.

.origin 0                          // start of program in PRU memory
.entrypoint START                  // program entry point (for a debugger)

#define INS_PER_US    200          // 5ns per instruction
#define INS_PER_DELAY_LOOP 2       // two instructions per delay loop
                                   // set up a 50ms delay
#define DELAY  50 * 1000 * (INS_PER_US / INS_PER_DELAY_LOOP)
#define PRU0_R31_VEC_VALID 32      // allows notification of program completion
#define PRU_EVTOUT_0     3         // the event number that is sent back

START:
        SET    r30.t5              // turn on the output pin (LED on)
        MOV    r0, DELAY           // store the length of the delay in REG0
DELAYON:
        SUB    r0, r0, 1           // Decrement REG0 by 1
        QBNE   DELAYON, r0, 0      // Loop to DELAYON, unless REG0=0
LEDOFF:
        CLR    r30.t5              // clear the output bin (LED off)
        MOV    r0, DELAY           // Reset REG0 to the length of the delay
DELAYOFF:
        SUB    r0, r0, 1           // decrement REG0 by 1
        QBNE   DELAYOFF, r0, 0     // Loop to DELAYOFF, unless REG0=0
        QBBC   START, r31.t3       // is the button pressed? If not, loop
END:                              // notify the calling app that finished
        MOV    r31.b0, PRU0_R31_VEC_VALID | PRU_EVTOUT_0
        HALT                       // halt the pru program
```

Details about the available assembly language instructions are provided later
in this chapter, but the important instructions that are used in Listing 13-2 are
as follows:

- SET r30.t5: Sets bit 5 on register 30 to be high. REG30 is used to set the
  PRU0 GPIO pins high. Bit 5 specifically controls the pr1_pru0_pru_r30_5
  pin output.

- MOV r0, DELAY: Stores the delay value (i.e., 5,000,000) in the register REG0.
  Registers are used here, just as variables are used in C. Assembly operations are performed on registers.

- DELAYON: A user-defined label to which the code can branch

- SUB r0, r0, 1: Subtracts 1 from REG0 and stores the result in REG0. It
  is essentially the same as the code REG0 = REG0 - 1.

- `QBNE DELAYON, r0, 0`: Performs a quick branch if REG0 is not equal to 0. This creates a loop that loops these two instructions 5,000,000 times (taking exactly 50ms!).

- `CLR r30.t5`: Clears bit 5 on register 30, setting the output low and turning the LED off

- `QBBC START, r31.t3`: Does a quick branch to START if the r31.t3 bit is clear (i.e., 0). REG31 is the input register that is used to read the state of the input—t3 is bit 3, which is connected to the pr1_pru0_pru_r31_3 pin. As the button input pin is configured in the overlay to have a pull-down resistor enabled, it will return 0 when it is not pressed and 1 when it is pressed. If the button is not pressed, then the program loops forever, continually flashing the LED. When the button is first found to be in the pressed state at this point during program execution, then the program continues to the next line.

- The next instruction is discussed shortly. The instruction generates an interrupt that is sent to the host program, notifying it that the PRU program is ending. The program then ends with the call to HALT.

This program can then be assembled using a call to the pasm assembler, which will identify syntactical errors. It should be called with the -b option, which results in the generation of a little-endian binary file:

```
molloyd@beaglebone:~/exploringBB/chp13/ledButton$ pasm -b ledButton.p
PRU Assembler Version 0.84
Copyright (C) 2005-2013 by Texas Instruments Inc.
Pass 2 : 0 Error(s), 0 Warning(s)
Writing Code Image of 13 word(s)
```

This results in a file ledButton.bin in the same directory. The file is 52 bytes in size (13 words), which will easily fit within the 8KB PRU program memory. The next step is to write a Linux host program that is used to place the little-endian binary program into PRU instruction memory.

> **NOTE** Remember that using nano -c ledButton.p displays line numbers, which is helpful in locating errors, as pasm identifies errors by line number.

Listing 13-3 provides the source code for a C host program that executes in Linux user space and uses the PRU Linux Application Loader API. It transfers the PRU program binary (ledButton.bin) to the PRU, executes it, and awaits a response (i.e., when the button is pressed). The code is described in the comments, and further details about the functions used are provided in the *PRU Linux Application Loader API Guide.*

LISTING 13-3: /exploringBB/chp13/ledButton/ledButton.c

```c
#include <stdio.h>
#include <prussdrv.h>
#include <pruss_intc_mapping.h>
#define PRU_NUM 0   // using PRU0 for these examples

void main (void){
   // Initialize structure used by prussdrv_pruintc_intc
   // PRUSS_INTC_INITDATA is found in pruss_intc_mapping.h
   tpruss_intc_initdata pruss_intc_initdata = PRUSS_INTC_INITDATA;
   // Allocate and initialize memory
   prussdrv_init ();
   prussdrv_open (PRU_EVTOUT_0);
   // Map PRU's interrupts
   prussdrv_pruintc_init(&pruss_intc_initdata);
   // Load and execute the PRU program on the PRU
   prussdrv_exec_program (PRU_NUM, "./ledButton.bin");
   // Wait for event completion from PRU, returns PRU_EVTOUT_0 number
   int n = prussdrv_pru_wait_event (PRU_EVTOUT_0);
   printf("EBB PRU program completed, event number %d.\n", n);
   // Disable PRU and close memory mappings
   prussdrv_pru_disable(PRU_NUM);
   prussdrv_exit ();
}
```

This program can be built and executed using the following commands:

```
.../chp13/ledButton$ gcc ledButton.c -o ledButton -lpthread -lprussdrv
.../chp13/ledButton$ sudo ./ledButton
EBB PRU program completed, event number 1.
.../chp13/ledButton$ sudo ./ledButton
EBB PRU program completed, event number 2.
```

Each time that the program is executed, the LED will flash at 10 Hz until the button is pressed. When the button is pressed, the event number will be displayed—then the event number will increment by one each time the program is run, until power is cycled, whereupon it will reset to 0. This program must be executed with superuser permissions, or it will cause a segmentation fault.

One very impressive feature of this application is the regularity of the output signal, which can be observed when the circuit is connected to an oscilloscope. Figure 13-4 illustrates the output and the frequency measurements, and it is clear from the measurements that the signal does not suffer from the jitter issues that affect a similar circuit in Chapter 6. Also, the program is running with negligible overhead (0.2% CPU, 0.3% MEM):

```
~/exploringBB/chp13/ledButton$ ps aux|grep ledButton
root 9966 0.2 0.3 3512 1548 pts/1 S+ 14:30 0:00 sudo ./ledButton
```

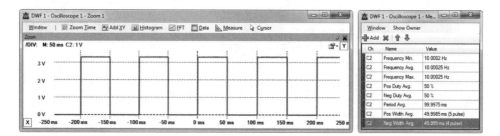

Figure 13-4: The PRU example output

The PRU-ICSS in Detail

It is useful to have a working example in place, but some features of the PRU-ICSS must be covered in more detail, to ensure that you can write your own applications that build on the preceding example.

Registers

In the last example, one register (REG0) is used as the memory location in which to store and decrement the time delay. *Registers* provide the fastest way to access data—assembly instructions are applied to registers and they complete in a single clock cycle. However, each PRU core has 32 registers (0–31). Registers REG1 to REG29 are general-purpose registers, whereas REG30 and REG31 are special-purpose registers, and REG0 is used for indexing (or as a general-purpose register). It should be noted that 30 general-purpose registers is a generous number for a microcontroller, as they can be reused repeatedly. For example, in the previous PRU program, both delays are performed using a single register.

Register values are 32-bit values that can be accessed using a suffix notation, which is illustrated in Figure 13-5. In Listing 13-2, shown earlier, bit 5 of REG30 is accessed using r30.t5. There are three suffixes:

- word .wn (where n is 0 . . . 2)
- byte .bn (where n is 0 . . . 3)
- bit .tn (where n is 0 . . . 31)

It is important to note that there are three word indices—w1 is offset by eight bits and therefore overlaps half the contents of w0 and w2. Figure 13-5 also provides some usages—for example, `r2.w1.b1` requests byte 1 of word 1, which is eight bits in length (i.e., bits 16 to 23 of `r2`). This is equivalent to a request for `r2.b2` (eight bits), but it is *not* equivalent to `r2.w2`, which has the same starting address but is 16 bits in length. Examples of illegal register calls include `r2.w2.b2`, `r2.t4.b1`, `r2.w1.t16`, and `r2.b0.b0`.

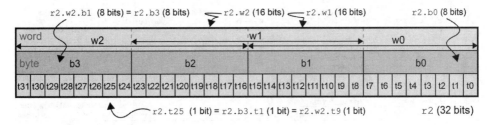

Figure 13-5: PRU register bit field notation

REG31 is called the *PRU Event/Status Register* (r31). It is a particularly complex register, which behaves differently depending on whether you are writing to it or reading from it. When writing to REG31, it provides a mechanism for sending output events to the Interrupt Controller (INTC). By writing an event number (0 to 31) to the five LSBs (`PRU_VEC[4:0]`) and setting bit 5 (`PRU_VEC_VALID`) high, an output event can be sent to the Linux host. The second-last line of Listing 13-2 does exactly that. The line is written as follows:

```
MOV     R31.b0, PRU0_R31_VEC_VALID | PRU_EVTOUT_0
```

It can be rewritten as `MOV R31.b0, 32|3`, or `MOV b31.b0, 35`. Essentially, it means "store the number 35_{10} in the least-significant byte of REG31." This sets bit 5 high (i.e., 32_{10}) and passes the value of 3_{10}, which is used to identify `PRU_EVTOUT_0` to the Linux host C program. This notifies the Linux host program that the PRU program has almost run to completion.

When reading from REG31, it provides the state of the enhanced GPIO inputs. For example, in Listing 13-2, the line `QBBC START, r31.t3` reads bit 3 from REG31 to determine whether the button is in a pressed state. Essentially, it reads the state of the GPIO that is connected to bit 3.

REG30 is used by the PRU to set enhanced GPIO outputs. For example, in Listing 13-2, the line `SET r30.t5` is used to set bit 5 of REG30 high. In turn, this results in the associated GPIO output switching the LED on.

Local and Global Memory

The PRUs have general-purpose local memory that can be used by PRU programs to store and retrieve data. Because this local PRU memory is mapped to a global address space on the Linux host, it can also be used to share data between PRU programs and programs running on the Linux host. Figure 13-6 illustrates the memory mappings.

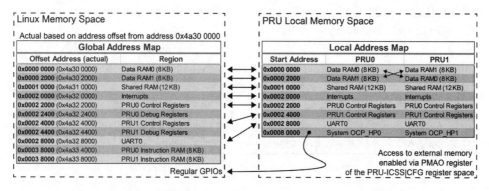

Figure 13-6: The PRU-ICSS memory address maps

Image created from data that is courtesy of Texas Instruments

It is important to note that there is a slight difference between the PRU memory spaces. PRU0 accesses its primary memory (Data RAM0) at address 0x00000000, and PRU1 also accesses its primary memory (Data RAM1) at address 0x00000000. However, each PRU can also access the data RAM of the other PRU at address 0x00002000. In addition, 12KB of shared memory can be used by both PRUs at the local address 0x00010000. The PRU cores can also use the global memory map, but there is latency as access is routed through the OCP slave port (refer to Figure 13-1).

You can find the actual address to which the offset applies using sysfs. For example, the PRU memory is mapped to the following locations on the current BBB Debian image:

```
molloyd@beaglebone:~$ cd /sys/class/uio/uio0/maps/map0/
molloyd@beaglebone:/sys/class/uio/uio0/maps/map0$ cat addr
0x4a300000
```

Here is a segment of code that sends values to different PRU memory spaces from Linux user space using the PRU Application Loader API (the full example is in chp13/memExample/memExample.c):

```
// Write a single word into PRU0 Data RAM0 (i.e., 4 bytes, offset 0)
unsigned int pru0 = 0xFEEDBBB0;
prussdrv_pru_write_memory(PRUSS0_PRU0_DATARAM, 0, &pru0, 4);
unsigned int pru1 = 0xFEEDBBB1;
prussdrv_pru_write_memory(PRUSS0_PRU1_DATARAM, 0, &pru1, 4);
unsigned int pruins0 = 0xFEEDBBB2;
prussdrv_pru_write_memory(PRUSS0_PRU0_IRAM, 0, &pruins0, 4);
unsigned int pruins1 = 0xFEEDBBB3;
```

```
prussdrv_pru_write_memory(PRUSS0_PRU1_IRAM, 0, &pruins1, 4);
// Load and execute the PRU program on the PRU
prussdrv_exec_program (PRU_NUM, "./memExample.bin");
```

Once this code is executed, you can access the memory addresses from Linux user space using the devmem2 tool and the address map in Figure 13-6, which results in the following:

```
~/exploringBB/chp13/devmem2$ sudo ./devmem2 0x4a300000
Memory mapped at address 0xb6ff7000.
Value at address 0x4A300000 (0xb6ff7000): 0xFEEDBBB0
~/exploringBB/chp13/devmem2$ sudo ./devmem2 0x4a302000
Value at address 0x4A302000 (0xb6f15000): 0xFEEDBBB1
~/exploringBB/chp13/devmem2$ sudo ./devmem2 0x4a334000
Value at address 0x4A334000 (0xb6fad000): 0x0
~/exploringBB/chp13/devmem2$ sudo ./devmem2 0x4a338000
Value at address 0x4A338000 (0xb6fc1000): 0xFEEDBBB3
```

The preceding values confirm that the mappings are correct and that devmem2 is very useful for verifying that the values in memory are as expected (remember that it can also write to memory). The value at the third address (PRU0 instruction RAM) is 0x0, rather than 0xFEEDBBB2. This is because the last line of the preceding segment of C code writes the PRU program (memExample.bin) to the PRU0 Instruction RAM. As expected, this overwrites the 0xFEEDBBB2 value that was previously set.

The PRUs also have a *constants table*, which contains a list of commonly used addresses that are often used in memory load and store operations. This reduces the time required to load memory pointers into registers. Most of the constants are fixed, but some are programmable by using PRU control registers. The constants table is utilized later, so that the PRU can access regular GPIOs that are outside the PRU-ICSS.

PRU Assembly Instruction Set

The PRU-ICSS has a relatively small RISC *instruction set architecture* (*ISA*), with approximately 45 instructions that can be categorized as arithmetic operations, logical operations, register load and store, and program flow control. A summary description of each of the instructions is provided in Figure 13-7. The full description of each instruction is available in the *AM335x PRU-ICSS Reference Guide*.

Instructions consist of an *operation code* (*opcode*) and a variable number of operands, where the third operand can often be a register or an *immediate value* (a simple number or an expression that evaluates to a constant value). For example:

```
ADD REG1, REG2, OP(255)
```

Arithmetic Operations

	Short Description:	Definition:	Full Description:
ADD	Unsigned integer add	ADD REG1, REG2, OP(255)	Performs 32-bit add on two 32-bit zero extended source values
ADC	Unsigned integer add (carry)	ADC REG1, REG2, OP(255)	Performs 32-bit add on two 32-bit zero extended source values, plus a stored carry bit
SUB	Unsigned integer subtract	SUB REG1, REG2, OP(255)	Performs 32-bit subtract on two 32-bit zero extended source values
SUC	Unsigned integer subtract (carry)	SUC REG1, REG2, OP(255)	Performs 32-bit subtract on two 32-bit zero extended source values with carry (borrow)
RSB	Reverse unsigned int subtract	RSB REG1, REG2, OP(255)	Performs 32-bit subtract on two 32-bit zero extended source values. Source values reversed
RSC	Reverse unsigned integer subtract (carry)	RSC REG1, REG2, OP(255)	Performs 32-bit subtract on two 32-bit zero extended source values with carry (borrow). Source values reversed

Logical Operations

	Short Description:	Definition:	Full Description:
LSL	Logical shift left	LSL REG1, REG2, OP(31)	Performs 32-bit shift left of the zero extended source value
LSR	Logical shift right	LSR REG1, REG2, OP(31)	Performs 32-bit shift right of the zero extended source value
AND	Bitwise AND	AND REG1, REG2, OP(255)	Performs 32-bit logical AND on two 32-bit zero extended source values
OR	Bitwise OR	OR REG1, REG2, OP(255)	Performs 32-bit logical OR on two 32-bit zero extended source values
XOR	Bitwise XOR	XOR REG1, REG2, OP(255)	Performs 32-bit logical XOR on two 32-bit zero extended source values
NOT	Bitwise NOT	NOT REG1, REG2	Performs 32-bit logical NOT on the 32-bit zero extended source value
MIN	Copy minimum	MIN REG1, REG2, OP(255)	Compares two 32-bit zero extended source values and copies the smaller to REG1
MAX	Copy maximum	MAX REG1, REG2, OP(255)	Compares two 32-bit zero extended source values and copies the larger to REG1
CLR	Clear bit	CLR REG1, REG2, OP(31)	Clears the specified bit in the source and copies the result to the destination Also: **CLR REG1, OP(31) CLR REG1, Rn.tx CLR Rn.tx**
SET	Set bit	SET REG1, REG2, OP(31)	Sets the specified bit in the source and copies the result to the destination Also: **SET REG1, OP(31) SET REG1, Rn.tx SET Rn.tx**
SCAN	Register field scan	SCAN Rn, OP(255)	The SCAN instruction scans the register file for a particular value. It includes a configurable field width and stride. The width of the field to match can be set to 1, 2, or 4 bytes.
LMBD	Left-most bit detect	LMBD REG1, REG2, OP(255)	Scans REG2 from its left-most bit for a bit value matching bit 0 of OP(255), and writes the bit number in REG1 (writes 32 to REG1 if the bit is not found)

Register Load and Store

	Short Description:	Definition:	Full Description:
MOV	Copy value	MOV REG1, OP(65535)	Moves the value from OP(65535), zero extends it, and stores it into REG1
LDI	Load immediate	LDI REG1, IM(65535)	The LDI instruction moves value from IM(65535), zero extends it, and stores it into REG1
MVIB	Move register file indirect (8)	MVIB [*&]REG1, [*&]REG2	The MVIx instruction family moves a value from the source to the destination. The source,
MVIW	Move register file indirect (16)	MVIW [*&]REG1, [*&]REG2	destination, or both can be register pointers.
MVID	Move register file indirect (32)	VID [*&]REG1, [*&]REG2	
LBBO	Load byte burst	LBBO REG1, Rn2, OP(255), IM(124) LBBO REG1, Rn2, OP(255), bn	The LBBO instruction is used to read a block of data from memory into the register file. The memory address to read from is specified by a 32-bit register, using an optional offset
SBBO	Store byte burst	SBBO REG1, Rn2, OP(255), IM(124) SBBO REG1, Rn2, OP(255), bn	The SBBO instruction is used to write a block of data from the register file into memory. The memory address to which to write is specified by a 32-bit register, using an optional offset
LBCO	Load byte burst with constant table offset	LBCO REG1, Cn2, OP(255), IM(124) LBCO REG1, Cn2, OP(255), bn	The LBCO instruction is used to read a block of data from memory into the register file. The memory address from which to read is specified by a 32-bit constant register (Cn2), using an optional offset from an immediate or register value
SBCO	Store byte burst with constant table offset	SBCO REG1, Cn2, OP(255), IM(124) SBCO REG1, Cn2, OP(255), bn	The SBCO instruction is used to write a block of data from the register file into memory. The memory address to write to is specified by a 32-bit constant register (Cn2), using an optional offset from an immediate or register value
ZERO	Clear register space	ZERO IM(123), IM(124)	This pseudo-op is used to clear space in the register file. Also: **ZERO &REG1, IM(124)**

Program Flow Control

	Short Description:	Definition:	Full Description:
JMP	Unconditional jump	JMP OP(65535)	Unconditional jump to a 16-bit instruction address, specified by register or immediate value
JAL	Unconditional jump and link	JAL REG1, OP(65535)	Unconditional jump to a 16-bit instruction address, specified by register or immediate value. Address following the JAL instruction is stored into REG1, so that REG1 can later be used as a "return" address
CALL	Call procedure	CALL OP(65535)	The CALL instruction is designed to emulate a subroutine call on a stack-based processor
RET	Return from procedure	RET	The RET instruction is designed to emulate a subroutine return on a stack-based processor
QBGT	Quick branch if >	QBGT LABEL, REG1, OP(255)	Jumps if the value of OP(255) is greater than REG1
QBGE	Quick branch if ≥	QBGE LABEL, REG1, OP(255)	Jumps if the value of OP(255) is greater than or equal to REG1
QBLT	Quick branch if <	QBLT LABEL, REG1, OP(255)	Jumps if the value of OP(255) is less than REG1
QBLE	Quick branch if ≤	QBLE LABEL, REG1, OP(255)	Jumps if the value of OP(255) is less than or equal to REG1
QBEQ	Quick branch if =	QBEQ LABEL, REG1, OP(255)	Jumps if the value of OP(255) is equal to REG1
QBNE	Quick branch if ≠	QBNE LABEL, REG1, OP(255)	Jumps if the value of OP(255) is NOT equal to REG1
QBA	Quick branch always	QBA LABEL	Jump always. This is similar to the JMP instruction, only QBA uses an address offset and thus can be relocated in memory
QBBS	Quick branch if bit is set	QBBS LABEL, REG1, OP(31)	Jumps if the bit OP(31) is set in REG1. Also: **QBBS LABEL, Rn.tx**
QBBC	Quick branch if bit is clear	QBBC LABEL, REG1, OP(31)	Jumps if the bit OP(31) is clear in REG1. Also: **QBBC LABEL, Rn.tx**
WBS	Wait until bit set	WBS REG1, OP(31) WBS Rn.tx	The WBS instruction is a pseudo op that uses the QBBC instruction. It is used to poll on a status bit, spinning until the bit is set
WBC	Wait until bit clear	WBC REG1, OP(31) WBC Rn.tx	The WBC instruction is a pseudo op that uses the QBBS instruction. It is used to poll on a status bit, spinning until the bit is clear
HALT	Halt operation	HALT	The HALT instruction disables the PRU. This instruction is used to implement software breakpoints in a debugger
SLP	Sleep operation	SLP IM(1)	The SLP instruction will sleep the PRU, causing it to disable its clock. This instruction can specify either a permanent sleep or a "wake on event"

See: http://processors.wiki.ti.com/index.php/PRU_Assembly_Instructions for further information.

REG, REG1, REG2, ...	A register field from 8 to 32 bits	bn	A field that must be b0 to b3
Rn, Rn1, Rn2, ...	A 32-bit register field (r0 to r31)	LABEL	A valid label
Rn.tx	A 1-bit register field	IM(n)	An immediate value from 0 to n
Cn, Cn1, Cn2, ...	A 32-bit constant constant register (c0 to c31)	OP(n)	Operand - either a REG or IM(n)

Figure 13-7: Summary of the PRU instruction set

Image created from information that is courtesy of Texas Instruments where ADD is a mnemonic that evaluates to an opcode (e.g., 0x01 for ADD),[2] REG1 is the target register, REG2 is a source register, and OP(255) can be another register field or an immediate value—it must be, or evaluate to, the range of 0_{10} to 255_{10} for the ADD operation. Here are some example usages:

```
MOV   r1, 0x25        // set r1 = 0x25 = 37 (dec)
MOV   r2, 0b100       // set r2 = 100 (binary) = 4 (dec)
ADD   r1, r1, 5       // set r1 = r1 + 5 = 42 (dec)
ADD   r2, r2, 1<<4    // set r2 = r2 + 10000 (bin) = 20 (dec)
ADD   r1, r2, r1.w0   // set r1 = r2 + r1.w0 = 20 + 42 = 62 (dec)
MOV   r0, 0x00002000  // place PRU1 data RAM1 base address in r0
SBBO  r1, r0, 4, 4    // write r1 to the address that is stored in r0
                      // offset = 4 bytes, size of data = 4 bytes
```

If this example is run on PRU0, the value of r1 ($62_{10} = $ 0x3e) is written to the PRU1 Data RAM1, which is at address 0x0000 2000 in the PRU1 memory space, and is at 0x4A30 2000 in Linux host memory space. The value is written at an offset of four bytes, so it appears at the address 0x4A30 2004 in the Linux host memory space. This code segment is at the end of the memExample.p code example, so it does not overwrite the 0xFEEDBBB1 value when this offset of four bytes is used:

```
.../chp13/memExample$ sudo ../devmem2/devmem2 0x4a302000
Value at address 0x4A302000 (0xb6f15000): 0xFEEDBBB1
.../chp13/memExample$ sudo ../devmem2/devmem2 0x4A302004
Value at address 0x4A302004 (0xb6f46004): 0x3E
```

It is useful to note that instructions can be grouped together using macros. For example, a macro is of the following form:

```
.macro LED_ON
    ... // place instructions here
.endm
```

The macro can then be called using LED_ON in place of a mnemonic.

Applications of the PRU-ICSS

In this section, several example applications are developed to test the performance of the PRU-ICSS and to illustrate how you can build Linux host applications that interact with it. Each application introduces additional features of the PRU-ICSS, so it is important that you read each one, even if you do not intend to build a particular type of application.

---

[2] You can use pasm -l -b memExample.p to see the listing file for the source code, which contains the generated opcodes (see /chp13/memExample/memExample.lst).

PRU-ICSS Performance Tests

In Chapter 6, a test is described that evaluates the performance of a Linux user space C/C++ application that lights an LED when a button is pressed. A similar test is presented here that uses the PRU-ICSS. The project is available in the /chp13/buttonTest directory, and the PRU code is provided in Listing 13-4. A second test is also presented here that flashes the LED at an approximate frequency of 10MHz (see /chp13/signalTest), which is based on the code shown earlier in Listing 13-2.

Both of the tests stretch the capabilities of the Analog Discovery (5MHz, 50MSPS). The sample values are represented by "x" markers in Figure 13-8, which are spaced at 10ns intervals (curve fitting is used to display the outputs). Despite the shortcomings of the Analog Discovery, the graphs are indicative of the capability of the PRU-ICSS. In the first test, the LED lights approximately 30ns after the button is pressed—see Figure 13-8(a). To put this number in context, in this time a light pulse would have traveled nine meters through free space (at 3×10^8m/s) and sound would have traveled one-hundredth of a millimeter in air (340m/s at sea level). The latter means that this time resolution, coupled with suitable acoustic sensor(s), makes accurate distance measurements very feasible.

Figure 13-8(b) illustrates the outcome of the second test, which indicates that each PRU can be used to output user-configurable signals at very high frequencies (note that the PRU-ICSS also has dedicated clock outputs—e.g., a 192MHz UART clock). Importantly, neither of these tests have significant CPU or memory load on the Linux host.

LISTING 13-4:   /exploringBB/chp13/buttonTest/buttonTest.p

```
.origin 0
.entrypoint START
START:
        CLR     r30.t5      // turn off the LED
        WBS     r31.t3      // wait bit set - i.e., button press
        SET     r30.t5      // set the output bit - turn on the LED
        MOV     r31.b0, 35
        HALT
```

Utilizing Regular Linux GPIOs

Each PRU is attached to an OCP master port, as illustrated in Figure 13-1, which permits access to memory addresses on the Linux host device. This functionality allows the PRUs to manipulate the state of the regular GPIOs that are used in Chapter 6. The first step is to enable the OCP master port using the following instructions (with reference to Table 205 and Table 207 in the *AM335x PRU Reference Guide*):

```
LBCO    r0, c4, 4, 4  // load SYSCFG register to r0(use c4 const addr)
CLR     r0, r0, 4     // clear bit 4 (STANDBY_INIT)
SBCO    r0, c4, 4, 4  // store the modified r0 back at the load addr
```

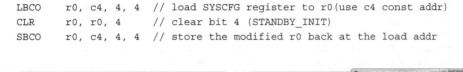
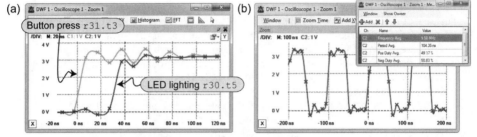

Figure 13-8: (a) Button press test; (b) high-frequency switching test output

Here, c4 refers to entry 4 in the constants table, which is the PRU_ICSS CFG (local) address. Therefore, offset 4 refers to the SYSCFG register. The CLR instruction sets bit 4 (STANDBY_INIT) to be 0, thus enabling the OCP master ports when r0 is written back to the SYSCFG register using the SBCO (store byte burst with constant table offset) instruction.

The next step is to determine the explicit Linux host memory addresses for the GPIOs—this is described in the section "Memory-Based GPIO Switching" in Chapter 6. The GPIO bank addresses and states can be defined using the following addresses and offsets:

```
#define GPIO0 0x44e07000              // GPIO Bank 0, See the AM335x TRM
#define GPIO1 0x4804c000              // GPIO Bank 1, Tab.2.2 Peripheral Map
#define GPIO2 0x481ac000              // GPIO Bank 2,
#define GPIO3 0x481ae000              // GPIO Bank 3,
#define GPIO_CLEARDATAOUT 0x190       // for clearing the GPIO registers
#define GPIO_SETDATAOUT   0x194       // for setting the GPIO registers
#define GPIO_DATAOUT      0x138       // for reading the GPIO registers
#define GPIO0_30 1<<30                // P9_11 gpio0[30] Output - bit 30
#define GPIO0_31 1<<31                // P9_13 gpio0[31] Input - bit 31
```

The PRU code is provided in Listing 13-5. It is similar to Listing 13-2, with the exception that the GPIO addresses must be loaded into registers and manipulated at the bit level. The C code is not listed here, as it is very similar to Listing 13-3. However, the full project is available in the /chp13/gpioLEDButton/ repository directory.

LISTING 13-5: /exploringBB/chp13/gpioLEDButton/ledButton.p

```
.origin 0                        // start of program in PRU memory
.entrypoint START                // program entry point (for a debugger)

#define GPIO0 0x44e07000         // GPIO Bank 0, See the AM335x TRM
#define GPIO1 0x4804c000         // GPIO Bank 1, Table 2-2 Peripheral Map
#define GPIO2 0x481ac000         // GPIO Bank 2,
#define GPIO3 0x481ae000         // GPIO Bank 3,
#define GPIO_CLEARDATAOUT 0x190  // for clearing the GPIO registers
#define GPIO_SETDATAOUT   0x194  // for setting the GPIO registers
#define GPIO_DATAOUT      0x138  // for reading the GPIO registers
#define GPIO0_30 1<<30           // P9_11 gpio0[30] Output - bit 30
#define GPIO0_31 1<<31           // P9_13 gpio0[31] Input - bit 31
#define INS_PER_US   200         // 5ns per instruction
#define INS_PER_DELAY_LOOP 2     // two instructions per delay loop
                                 // set up a 50ms delay
#define DELAY  50 * 1000 * (INS_PER_US / INS_PER_DELAY_LOOP)
#define PRU0_R31_VEC_VALID 32    // allows notification of program completion
#define PRU_EVTOUT_0    3        // the event number that is sent back

START:
        // Enable the OCP master port
        LBCO    r0, C4, 4, 4     // load SYSCFG reg into r0 (use c4 const addr)
        CLR     r0, r0, 4        // clear bit 4 (STANDBY_INIT)
        SBCO    r0, C4, 4, 4     // store the modified r0 back at the load addr
MAINLOOP:
        MOV     r1, GPIO0 | GPIO_SETDATAOUT  // load addr for GPIO Set data  r1
        MOV     r2, GPIO0_30     // write GPIO0_30 to r2
        SBBO    r2, r1, 0, 4     // write r2 to the r1 address value - LED ON
        MOV     r0, DELAY        // store the length of the delay in REG0
DELAYON:
        SUB     r0, r0, 1        // Decrement REG0 by 1
        QBNE    DELAYON, r0, 0   // Loop to DELAYON, unless REG0=0
LEDOFF:
        MOV     r1, GPIO0 | GPIO_CLEARDATAOUT // load addr for GPIO Clear data
        MOV     r2, GPIO0_30     // write GPIO_30 to r2
        SBBO    r2, r1, 0, 4     // write r2 to the r1 address - LED OFF
        MOV     r0, DELAY        // Reset REG0 to the length of the delay
DELAYOFF:
        SUB     r0, r0, 1        // decrement REG0 by 1
        QBNE    DELAYOFF, r0, 0  // Loop to DELAYOFF, unless REG0=0

        MOV     r5, GPIO0 | GPIO_DATAOUT     // load read addr for DATAOUT
        LBBO    r6, r5, 0, 4     // Load the value at r5 into r6
        QBBC    MAINLOOP, r6.t31 // is the button pressed? If not, loop
END:                             // notify the calling app that finished
        MOV     R31.b0, PRU0_R31_VEC_VALID | PRU_EVTOUT_0
        HALT                     // halt the pru program
```

The device tree overlay in Listing 13-1 configures two regular GPIO pins, P9_11 (output) and P9_13 (input). P9_11 should be connected to the FET gate input and P9_13 should be connected to the button, as described in Figure 13-3. Ensure that the overlay is loaded and that the GPIOs are exported, as follows, before the application is executed:

```
/lib/firmware$ sudo sh -c "echo EBB-PRU-Example > $SLOTS"
/lib/firmware$ cat $SLOTS
8: ff:P-O-L Override Board Name,00A0,Override Manuf,EBB-PRU-Example
/sys/class/gpio$ sudo sh -c "echo 30 > export"
/sys/class/gpio$ sudo sh -c "echo 31 > export"
```

When executed, the code will provide output similar to that shown in Figure 13-4:

```
~/exploringBB/chp13/gpioLEDButton$ sudo ./ledButton
EBB PRU program completed, event number 1.
```

A PRU PWM Generator

As described in Chapter 6, PWM has many applications, such as motor and lighting control, and there is hardware PWM support available on the BBB that can be accessed directly from Linux user space. However, sysfs is slow at adjusting the duty cycle, and it is prone to the same type of nonpreemptive latency issues as regular GPIOs. In the next section, PWM is used to output a sine wave signal, by rapidly changing the duty cycle of a high-frequency switched digital output cyclically as a function of time. In this section, we prepare for this by setting up a square waveform with a constant duty cycle.

Listing 13-6 is the Linux host code that loads the PRU program. It also uses the prussdev_pru_write_memory() function to transfer the PWM duty cycle percentage and the delay factor (i.e., how many instructions × 5ns there should be for each of the 100 samples per period). The values passed by the code in Listing 13-6 result in a PWM signal with a duty cycle of 75% and a period of approximately 11 μs (i.e., 100 samples per period × 10 delay steps per sample × 2 instructions per delay × 5ns per instruction + looping overhead).

> **LISTING 13-6:** /exploringBB/chp13/pwm/pwm.c

```
#include <stdio.h>
#include <prussdrv.h>
#include <pruss_intc_mapping.h>
```

continues

LISTING 13-6: *(continued)*

```
#define PRU_NUM    0

void main (void){
    // Initialize structure used by prussdrv_pruintc_intc
    tpruss_intc_initdata pruss_intc_initdata = PRUSS_INTC_INITDATA;
    // Allocate and initialize memory
    prussdrv_init ();
    prussdrv_open (PRU_EVTOUT_0);
    // Map PRU interrupts
    prussdrv_pruintc_init(&pruss_intc_initdata);
    // Copy the PWM percentage and delay factor into PRU memory
    unsigned int percent = 75;   // (0-100)
    prussdrv_pru_write_memory(PRUSS0_PRU0_DATARAM, 0, &percent, 4);
    unsigned int sampletimestep = 10;   // delay factor
    // write it into the next word location in memory (i.e.,4-bytes later)
    prussdrv_pru_write_memory(PRUSS0_PRU0_DATARAM, 1, &sampletimestep, 4);

    // Load and execute binary on PRU
    prussdrv_exec_program (PRU_NUM, "./pwm.bin");
    // Wait for event completion from PRU
    int n = prussdrv_pru_wait_event (PRU_EVTOUT_0);
    printf("PRU program completed, event number %d.\n", n);
    // Disable PRU and close memory mappings
    prussdrv_pru_disable(PRU_NUM);
    prussdrv_exit ();
}
```

The PRU code is provided in Listing 13-7. It consists of a main loop that loops once for each signal period, until a button that is attached to r31.t3 is pressed. Within the main loop are two nested loops. One iterates for the number of samples that the signal is high and the second iterates for the number of samples that the signal is low. The total number of nested iterations is 100, where each iteration has a user-configurable delay.

LISTING 13-7: /exploringBB/chp13/pwm/pwm.p

```
.origin 0              // offset of start of program in PRU memory
.entrypoint START      // program entry point used by the debugger
#define PRU0_R31_VEC_VALID 32
#define EVENTOUT0 3

START:
        // Reading the memory that was set by the C program into registers
        // r1 - Read the PWM percent high (0-100)
        MOV    r0, 0x00000000    // load the memory location
        LBBO   r1, r0, 0, 4      // load the percent value into r1
        // r2 - Load the sample time delay
```

```
          MOV     r0, 0x00000004      // load the memory location
          LBBO    r2, r0, 0, 4        // load the step delay value into r2
          // r3 - The PWM percentage that the signal is low (100-r1)
          MOV     r3, 100             // load 100 into r3
          SUB     r3, r3, r1          // subtract r1 (high) away from 100
MAINLOOP:
          MOV     r4, r1              // start counter at number of steps high
          SET     r30.t5              // set the output P9_27 high
SIGNAL_HIGH:
          MOV     r0, r2              // the delay step length - load r2 above
DELAY_HIGH:
          SUB     r0, r0, 1           // decrement delay loop counter
          QBNE    DELAY_HIGH, r0, 0   // repeat until step delay is done
          SUB     r4, r4, 1           // the signal was high for a step
          QBNE    SIGNAL_HIGH, r4, 0  // repeat until signal high steps are done

          // Now the signal is going to go low for 100%-r1% - i.e., r3
          MOV     r4, r3              // number of steps low loaded
          CLR     r30.t5              // set the output P9_27 low
SIGNAL_LOW:
          MOV     r0, r2              // the delay step lenght - load r2 above
DELAY_LOW:
          SUB     r0, r0, 1           // decrement loop counter
          QBNE    DELAY_LOW, r0, 0    // repeat until step delay is done
          SUB     r4, r4, 1           // the signal was low for a step
          QBNE    SIGNAL_LOW, r4, 0   // repeat until signal low % is done

          QBBS    END, r31.t3         // quit if button on P9_28 is pressed
          QBA     MAINLOOP            // otherwise loop forever
END:                                  // end of program, send back interrupt
          MOV     r31.b0, PRU0_R31_VEC_VALID | EVENTOUT0
          HALT
```

The circuit is wired as shown in Figure 13-3, and the same device tree overlay is used for this example. The output of the circuit is displayed in Figure 13-9. A simple low-pass filter is added to the P9_27 output pins and results in the "Low-pass filtered output" signal in Figure 13-3. In this example, the RC filter consists of a 4.7kΩ resistor that is connected to P9_27 and a 0.1μF capacitor connected from the output side of the resistor to GND (i.e., *not* between P9_27 directly and GND). The RC filter results in a time-averaged output, which is representative of the duty cycle. For example, if the PWM duty cycle is 75%, then the output voltage of the RC filter is approximately $0.75 \times 3.3V = 2.625V$, as illustrated in Figure 13-9.

A PRU Sine Wave Generator

The PRU PWM generator code can be adapted to generate user-defined waveforms on a GPIO pin. This is achieved by altering the PWM signal duty cycle rapidly over time, and passing the output through a low-pass filter. Figure 13-10(b) illustrates the output of such as circuit, where a 4.7kΩ resistor and a 4.7nF capacitor are used to form the requisite low-pass filter. The smoothing is effectively of shorter duration than the previous RC component values. Figure 13-10(a) displays the PWM signal with a duty cycle that changes over time. The low-pass filtered output is displayed in Figure 13-10(b), where it is clearly a good approximation to a sine waveform signal. The full project is available in the chp13/sineWave directory.

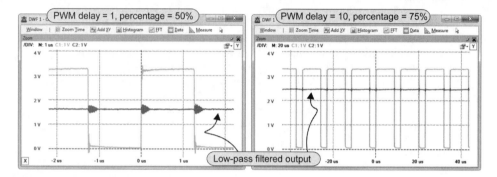

Figure 13-9: The PWM generator output

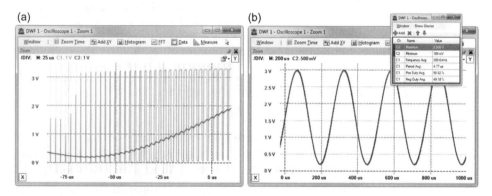

Figure 13-10: User-defined waveform output

A segment of the Linux host C code is provided in Listing 13-8. The main novelty in this code is the generation of a set of 100 values representing a single cycle of a sine waveform. The values of the sine wave cycle are designed to have an amplitude of 50 and an offset of +50, so that the output can be directly used as the duty cycle percentage values for the PWM generator code described in the previous section.

In this example, the memory is mapped to the PRU in a slightly different way. The prussdrv_map_prumem() function is used, which identifies the address of the PRU memory map using a pointer. Pointer operations can then be (carefully) used to read from or write to PRU memory directly.

LISTING 13-8: /exploringBB/chp13/sineWave/pwm.c (segment)

```c
static void *pru0DataMemory;              // need a void pointer memory map
static unsigned int *pru0DataMemory_int; // will cast void pointer to this

void main (void){ ...
   // Generate a periodic sine wave in an int array of 100 values
   unsigned int waveform[100];
   float gain = 50.0f;                    // want the full range 0-99
   float phase = 0.0f;                    // phase can be changed
   float bias = 50.0f;                    // center on 1.65V, for full range
   float freq = 2.0f * 3.14159f / 100.0f;
   for (i=0; i<100; i++){                 // general sine wave equation
      waveform[i] = (unsigned int)(bias + (gain * sin((i * freq) + phase)));
   }
   // set up the pointer to PRU memory
   prussdrv_map_prumem(PRUSS0_PRU0_DATARAM, &pru0DataMemory);
   pru0DataMemory_int = (unsigned int *) pru0DataMemory;
   unsigned int sampletimestep = 1;  //delay factor
   *(pru0DataMemory_int) = sampletimestep;
   unsigned int numbersamples = 100;  //number of samples
   *(pru0DataMemory_int+1) = numbersamples;
   // copy the waveform data into PRU memory - could be any waveform
   for (i=0; i<numbersamples; i++){
      *(pru0DataMemory_int+2+i) = waveform[i];
   }
   prussdrv_exec_program (PRU_NUM, "./pwm.bin");
   ...
}
```

The PRU code in Listing 13-9 builds on the PWM code in Listing 13-7. The main difference is an additional loop that loads a PWM duty cycle for each data array value that is passed to PRU memory by the Linux host C program. The code will output any periodic waveform that is passed to it, with a maximum periodic sample length of just under 8KB (PRU0 RAM0) in this example. The code could be improved to extend this limit, or to iterate with fewer instructions. However, the code demonstrates the principle that a PRU can be used to generate custom analog waveforms using its digital GPIO outputs.

LISTING 13-9: /exploringBB/chp13/sineWave/pwm.p (segment)

```
...
START:
        MOV     r0, 0x00000000    // load the time delay
        LBBO    r2, r0, 0, 4      // load the step delay value into r2
        MOV     r0, 0x00000004    // load the number of samples
        LBBO    r5, r0, 0, 4      // load the number of samples into r5
```

continues

LISTING 13-9: *(continued)*

```
        MOV     r6, 0               // r6 is the counter 0 to r5
        MOV     r7, 0x00000008      // base memory location for the array
SAMPLELOOP:
        // is the counter r6  >= the number of samples r5, if so go back to 0
        QBLT    CONTINUE, r5, r6    // otherwise continue to next line
        MOV     r7, 0x00000008      // reset the base memory location again
        MOV     r6, 0               // and loop all over again
CONTINUE:
        ADD     r7, r7, 4           // r1 - Read the PWM percent high (1-99)
        LBBO    r1, r7, 0, 4        // load the percent value into r1
        QBLT    GREATERTHANZERO, r1, 0  // test that the value is >0
        MOV     r1, 1               // if less than 1 set the value to 1
GREATERTHANZERO:
        QBGT    LESSTHAN100, r1, 100    // test value is <100
        MOV     r1, 99              // if greater, then set value to 99
LESSTHAN100:
...         // At this point generate a single PWM period output (Listing 13-7)
        QBBS    END, r31.t3         // quit if button on P9_28 is pressed
        ADD     r6, r6, 1           // increment the counter by 1
        QBA     SAMPLELOOP          // otherwise loop forever
END:                                // end of program, send back interrupt
        MOV     R31.b0, PRU0_R31_VEC_VALID | EVENTOUT0
        HALT
```

An Ultrasonic Sensor Application

The HC-SR04 is a low-cost (~$5) ultrasonic sensor that can be used to determine the distance to an obstacle using the speed of sound. The sensor has a range of approximately 1″ (2.5cm) to 13′ (4m). Unlike the IR distance sensor that is used in Chapter 9, it is not affected by sunlight, but it does not perform well with soft materials that do not reflect sound well (e.g., clothing and soft furnishings). It is a 5V sensor, so logic-level translation circuitry is required (as described at the end of Chapter 8). The final circuit is illustrated in Figure 13-11. It uses the same device tree overlay that is described earlier in this chapter.

Figure 13-12 illustrates how interaction takes place with this sensor. A 10µs trigger pulse is sent to the "Trig" input of the sensor; the sensor then responds on its "Echo" output with a pulse that has a width that corresponds to the distance of an obstacle (approximately 150µs to 25ms, or 38ms if no obstacle is in range).

The nonpreemptive nature of Linux means that it would be difficult to use this sensor directly from Linux user space using regular GPIOs. There are UART versions of this sensor that contain a microcontroller, but they are much more expensive. In fact, the solution that is presented here is fast enough to enable you to connect ten or more such sensors to a single PRU—a single trigger signal could be sent to many sensors simultaneously, and different enhanced GPIOs could be used to measure the response signals from each sensor. Assembly language code is developed with the following structure:

1. Initialization takes place to set up shared memory.
2. The main loop begins.
3. A pulse is sent to the output pin. The output pin (P9_27) is set high and the code delays for exactly 10 μs before switching low.
4. The input pin (P9_28) is then polled until it goes high. At that point a "width" timer counts until the input pin goes low.
5. The width timer value is written into shared memory. The code generates an interrupt, and the main loop begins again.

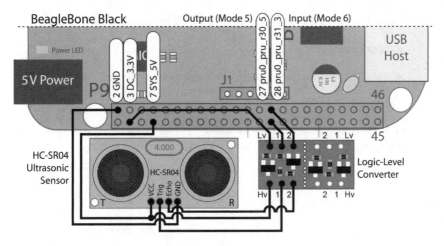

Figure 13-11: The HC-SR04 ultrasonic distance sensor circuit

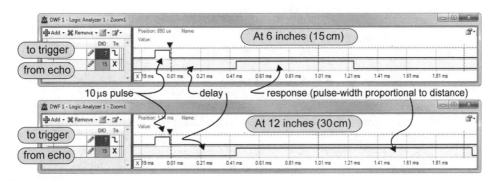

Figure 13-12: Signal response of the HC-SR04

The project code is available in the directory /chp13/ultrasonic/. Listing 13-10 contains a threaded function that is designed to wait for an interrupt to be sent. It waits for a different interrupt (PRU_EVTOUT_1) than the one that is used to notify the application of imminent termination (PRU_EVTOUT_0). This interrupt notifies the Linux host application that a new measurement has been placed in memory by the PRU program.

LISTING 13-10: /exploringBB/chp13/ultrasonic/ultrasonic.c

```c
#include <stdio.h>
#include <prussdrv.h>
#include <pruss_intc_mapping.h>
#include <pthread.h>
#include <unistd.h>
#define PRU_NUM 0

static void *pru0DataMemory;
static unsigned int *pru0DataMemory_int;

void *threadFunction(void *value){
   do {
      int notimes = prussdrv_pru_wait_event (PRU_EVTOUT_1);
      unsigned int raw_distance = *(pru0DataMemory_int+2);
      float distin = ((float)raw_distance / (100 * 148));
      float distcm = ((float)raw_distance / (100 * 58));
      printf("Distance is %f inches (%f cm)            \r", distin, distcm);
      prussdrv_pru_clear_event (PRU_EVTOUT_1, PRU0_ARM_INTERRUPT);
   } while (1);
}

void main (void){
   pthread_t thread;
   tpruss_intc_initdata pruss_intc_initdata = PRUSS_INTC_INITDATA;

   // Allocate and initialize memory
   prussdrv_init ();
   prussdrv_open (PRU_EVTOUT_0);
   prussdrv_open (PRU_EVTOUT_1);

   // Map PRU's INTC
   prussdrv_pruintc_init(&pruss_intc_initdata);

   // Copy data to PRU memory - different way
   prussdrv_map_prumem(PRUSS0_PRU0_DATARAM, &pru0DataMemory);
   pru0DataMemory_int = (unsigned int *) pru0DataMemory;
   // Use the first 4 bytes for the number of samples
   *pru0DataMemory_int = 500;
   // Use the second 4 bytes for the sample delay in ms
   *(pru0DataMemory_int+1) = 100;   // 2 milli seconds between samples

   // Load and execute binary on PRU
```

```
prussdrv_exec_program (PRU_NUM, "./ultrasonic.bin");
if(pthread_create(&thread, NULL, &threadFunction, NULL)){
    printf("Failed to create thread!");
}
int n = prussdrv_pru_wait_event (PRU_EVTOUT_0);
printf("PRU program completed, event number %d.\n", n);
printf("The data that is in memory is:\n");
printf("- the number of samples used is %d.\n", *pru0DataMemory_int);
printf("- the time delay used is %d.\n", *(pru0DataMemory_int+1));
unsigned int raw_distance = *(pru0DataMemory_int+2);
printf("- the last distance sample is %d.\n", raw_distance);

// raw_distance is in 10ns samples
// distance in inches = time (ms) / 148 according to datasheet
float distin = ((float)raw_distance / (100 * 148));
float distcm = ((float)raw_distance / (100 * 58));
printf("-- A distance of %f inches (%f cm).\n", distin, distcm);

/* Disable PRU and close memory mappings */
prussdrv_pru_disable(PRU_NUM);
prussdrv_exit ();
}
```

The PRU code is provided in Listing 13-11. The program loops as described and generates an interrupt using the line of code MOV R31.b0, PRU0_R31_VEC_ VALID | PRU_EVTOUT_1 whenever a new sample is ready. This is the interrupt for which the threaded function in Listing 13-10 is waiting.

LISTING 13-11: /exploringBB/chp13/ultrasonic/ultrasonic.p

```
.origin 0                  // offset of start of program in PRU memory
.entrypoint START          // program entry point used by the debugger

#define TRIGGER_PULSE_US      10
#define INS_PER_US            200
#define INS_PER_LOOP          2
#define TRIGGER_COUNT         (TRIGGER_PULSE_US * INS_PER_US) / INS_PER_LOOP
#define SAMPLE_DELAY_1MS      (1000 * INS_PER_US) / INS_PER_LOOP
#define PRU0_R31_VEC_VALID    32;
#define PRU_EVTOUT_0          3
#define PRU_EVTOUT_1          4

// Using register 0 for all temporary storage (reused multiple times)
START:
   // Read number of samples to read and inter-sample delay
   MOV    r0, 0x00000000      // load the memory location, number of samples
   LBBO   r1, r0, 0, 4        // load the value into memory - keep r1
   // Read the sample delay
   MOV    r0, 0x00000004      // the sample delay is in the second 32-bits
```

continues

LISTING 13-11: *(continued)*

```
    LBBO   r2, r0, 0, 4              //the sample delay is stored in r2

MAINLOOP:
    MOV    r0, TRIGGER_COUNT     // store length of the trigger pulse delay
    SET    r30.t5                // set the trigger high

TRIGGERING:                      // delay for 10us
    SUB    r0, r0, 1             // decrement loop counter
    QBNE   TRIGGERING, r0, 0     // repeat loop unless zero
    CLR    r30.t5                // 10us over, set the trigger low - pulse sent
    // clear the counter and wait until the echo goes high
    MOV    r3, 0                 // r3 will store the echo pulse width
    WBS    r31.t3                // wait until the echo goes high

    // start counting (measuring echo pulse width)  until the echo goes low
COUNTING:
    ADD    r3, r3, 1             // increment the counter by 1
    QBBS   COUNTING, r31.t3      // loop if the echo is still high
    // at this point the echo is now low - write the value to shared memory
    MOV    r0, 0x00000008        // going to write the result to this address
    SBBO   r3, r0, 0, 4          // store the count at this address
    // one more sample iteration has taken place
    SUB    r1, r1, 1             // take 1 away from the number of iterations
    MOV    r0, r2                // need a delay between samples

SAMPLEDELAY:                     // do this loop r2 times (1ms delay each time)
    SUB    r0, r0, 1             // decrement counter by 1
    MOV    r4, SAMPLE_DELAY_1MS  // load 1ms delay into r4

DELAY1MS:
    SUB    r4, r4, 1
    QBNE   DELAY1MS, r4, 0       // keep going until 1ms has elapsed
    QBNE   SAMPLEDELAY, r0, 0    // repeat loop unless zero
    // generate an interrupt to update the display on the host computer
    MOV R31.b0, PRU0_R31_VEC_VALID | PRU_EVTOUT_1
    QBNE   MAINLOOP, r1, 0       // loop if the no of iterations has not passed
END:
    MOV R31.b0, PRU0_R31_VEC_VALID | PRU_EVTOUT_0
    HALT
```

The code example can be built using the build script, and results in the following output when executed:

```
~/exploringBB/chp13/ultrasonic$ sudo ./ultrasonic
Distance is 6.965540 inches (17.774137 cm)
PRU program completed, event number 169.
The data that is in memory is:
- the number of samples used is 5.
- the time delay used is 2.
```

```
 - the last distance sample is 103090.
 -- A distance of 6.965540 inches (17.774137 cm).
```

The program output updates on a single shell console line whenever an interrupt is received by the Linux host code. This continues until the user-defined maximum number of samples is reached. The signal output is displayed in Figure 13-13. The sampling rate is variable in this example, partly to demonstrate the use of interrupts. It could be altered to a fixed sample period if required; however, a fixed sampling rate would have to account for the 38ms pulse that the sensor returns when no obstacle is detected.

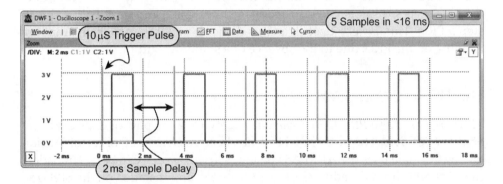

Figure 13-13: Signal response of the HC-SR04

Additional PRU-ICSS Tools

Two additional tools can aid with development for the PRU-ICSS. The first is a PRU debugger and the second is a TI C compiler that can be used to write PRU programs, in place of writing assembly code.

The PRU Debugger

The PRU Debugger, prudebug (tiny.cc/ebb1310), is a useful tool for identifying problems with your PRU program code. It can be executed in a separate terminal and used to view the registers when the PRU program is halted. For example, it can display the registers as shown here:

```
PRU0> R
Register info for PRU0
    Control register: 0x00000001
        Reset PC:0x0000  STOPPED, FREE_RUN, COUNTER_DISABLED, NOT_SLEEPING
```

```
Program counter: 0x0012
  Current instruction: HALT
R00: 0x0000000a     R08: 0xd626828a     R16: 0xced9df71     R24: 0x0e492713
R01: 0x00000000     R09: 0xf4847bf7     R17: 0xdc1d5f3e     R25: 0x73ac4b40
R02: 0x4804c194     R10: 0xbb7ff666     R18: 0xe44e9ecd     R26: 0x3a00158f
R03: 0x00020000     R11: 0x531ad382     R19: 0xc9087283     R27: 0xaa7a1ae9
R04: 0x00000005     R12: 0x4011dcbf     R20: 0xfdf1003c     R28: 0x0f5fe4dd
R05: 0x00000000     R13: 0xe2259f2e     R21: 0xc763fc2c     R29: 0xe6b71da6
R06: 0x00000000     R14: 0x92f9ba70     R22: 0xe6516729     R30: 0x3024130e
R07: 0xabcd1234     R15: 0xe6c171fc     R23: 0xf0990d24     R31: 0x00000000
PRU0>
```

It can also be used to load binaries into the PRUs, display instruction/data memory spaces, disassemble instruction memory space, and start/halt or single-step a PRU. This is very useful, as it is difficult to debug programs that are running on the PRU, due to the absence of a standard output.

The TI PRU C Compiler

TI has released the *PRU Code Generation Tools (CGT)* as part of *Code Composer Studio v6 (CCSv6)*. The PRU CGT have also been released in CLI form. The following example uses the ARM A8 version (~40MB), which can be downloaded, free of charge, from the address `tiny.cc/ebb1311` and installed on the BBB. You will have to register to download the installer, which should then be transferred to the BBB. The following steps install the CGT on the BBB:

```
molloyd@beaglebone:~/ $ ls
ti_cgt_pru_2.0.0B2_armlinuxa8hf_installer.sh
~/$ chmod ugo+x ti_cgt_pru_2.0.0B2_armlinuxa8hf_installer.sh
~/$ ./ti_cgt_pru_2.0.0B2_armlinuxa8hf_installer.sh
~/$ cd pru_2.0.0B2/
~/pru_2.0.0B2$ ls
LICENSE.txt  PRU_Compiler_2_0_manifest.html  bin       example  lib
License.txt  README.txt                      bin.cmd   include
molloyd@beaglebone:~/pru_2.0.0B2/bin$ ls
abspru     asmpru     clpru     embedpru  libinfopru  ofdpru    xrefpru
acpiapru   cgpru      dempru    hexpru    lnkpru      optpru
arpru      clistpru   dispru    ilkpru    nmpru       strippru
```

The binary directory includes the C compiler (clpru), the assembler (asmpru), the linker (lnkpru), and the output file generation tool (hexpru). For example, the compiler can be used as follows:

```
.../prussC$ ~/pru_2.0.0B2/bin/clpru -i~/pru_2.0.0B2/include testPRU.c
```

A PRU C program is provided in Listing 13-12. The code example performs a similar function to the code in Listing 13-2, which is wired as shown in Figure 13-3. The code segment in Listing 13-13 loads the binary into the PRU that results from the build script in Listing 13-14.

The process is slightly more complex than using the pasm assembler, as you have to provide linker command files (AM3359_PRU.cmd), and the binary output has to be converted into a hexadecimal file that can be loaded onto the PRU. A full project example with a build script is provided in the /chp13/prussC/ directory—it can be used as a template for your own applications.

LISTING 13-12: /exploringBB/chp13/prussC/testPRU.c

```
/** Basic PRU C program to flash an LED that is attached to P9_27 at a
*    frequency of 10 Hz, until a button that is attached to P9_28 is pressed */
// the registers for I/O and interrupts
volatile register unsigned int __R31, __R30;

int main(){
    unsigned int i;                    // the counter in the time delay
    unsigned int delay = 588260;       // the delay (manually determined)

    // Just a test to show how you can use assembly instructions directly
    // subtract 1 from REG1
    __asm__ __volatile__
    (
       " SUB r1, r1, 1 \n"
    );
    // while the button r31.3 has not been pressed, keep looping
    while(!(__R31 & 1<<3)){
       __R30 = __R30 | 1<<5;           // turn on the LED r30.5
       for(i=0; i<delay; i++) {}       // loop delay - don't optimize!
       __R30 = __R30 & 0<<5;           // turn off the LED r30.5
       for(i=0; i<delay; i++) {}       // loop delay - don't optimize!
    }
    // Exiting the application - send the interrupt
    __R31 = 35;                        // PRUEVENT_0 on PRU0_R31_VEC_VALID
    __halt();                          // halt the PRU
}
```

LISTING 13-13: /exploringBB/chp13/prussC/testBBB.c (segment)

```
...
    /* Load and execute binary on PRU */
    prussdrv_exec_program (PRU_NUM, "./text.bin");
    /* Wait for event completion from PRU */
    n = prussdrv_pru_wait_event (PRU_EVTOUT_0);  ...
```

> **LISTING 13-14:** /exploringBB/chp13/prussC/build

```sh
#!/bin/sh
export PRU_SDK=/home/molloyd/pru_2.0.0B2/
echo "Compiling the testPRU.c application"
$PRU_SDK/bin/clpru --silicon_version=3 testPRU.c -i$PRU_SDK/include \
    -i$PRU_SDK/lib -z AM3359_PRU.cmd -o testPRU.out -m testPRU.map
echo "Converting the executable to a ARM object file"
$PRU_SDK/bin/hexpru $PRU_SDK/bin.cmd testPRU.out
echo "Compiling the testBBB.c application"
gcc testBBB.c -o test -lpthread -lprussdrv
```

Make sure that you change the PRU_SDK path to the location of the PRU compiler binary that you installed on your BBB. Do not add optimization to the clpru compilation call (e.g., the command-line parameter -o3); otherwise, the time delay, which is a loop that seems to do nothing, will be "optimized out" and the LED will not flash in this case!

Summary

After completing this chapter, you should be able to do the following:

- Describe real-time kernel and hardware solutions that can be used on the BBB.

- Write a PRU program that can flash an LED and transfer it to the PRU-ICSS using a Linux host application.

- Describe the important features of the PRU-ICSS, such as its structure, registers, memory addressing, and assembly language instructions.

- Write a PRU program that shares memory with a Linux host application.

- Write a PRU program that interfaces to regular GPIOs that are in Linux host space.

- Write a PRU program that generates PWM signals and adapt it to output user-defined analog waveforms on BBB GPIO pins.

- Apply the PRU to sensor interfacing applications for which time measurement is important, such as interfacing to ultrasonic distance sensors.

- Use interrupts to notify a Linux host when key events have occurred, such as the availability of new sensor data.

- Use tools such as the PRU Debugger and Texas Instruments' PRU Code Generation Tools to aid with PRU-ICSS application development, including compiling and loading C programs to run on the PRUs.

Further Reading

There are many links to websites and documents provided throughout this chapter. Additional links and further information on the topics in this chapter are provided at `www.exploringbeaglebone.com/chapter13/`.

Index